THE STUDENT EDITION OF
MINITAB® FOR WINDOWS
Statistical software... adapted for education

THE STUDENT EDITION OF
MINITAB® FOR WINDOWS

Statistical software... adapted for education

John McKenzie
Babson College

Robert L. Schaefer
Miami University of Ohio

Elizabeth Farber
Bucks County Community College

Addison-Wesley Publishing Company, Inc.

Reading, Massachusetts • Menlo Park, California • New York
Don Mills, Ontario • Wokingham, England • Amsterdam • Bonn
Sydney • Singapore • Tokyo • Madrid • San Juan • Milan • Paris

Julia G. Berrisford, Senior Sponsoring Editor
Maureen Lawson, Project Coordinator
Craig Bleyer, Marketing Manager
Joan Carey, Development Editor
Patsy DuMoulin, Production Supervisor
Sarah Couch, Manufacturing Coordinator
Lisa Delgado, Text Designer
Trudi Gershenor, Package Design and Illustration
Polly Kornblith, Editorial Services of New England, Inc., Copy Editor
Editorial Services of New England, Inc., Compositor

Photo, Minitab at Work, and data set credits appear on p. I-21, which constitutes an extension of the copyright page.

Library of Congress Cataloging-in-Publication Data
The Student edition of Minitab for Windows [computer file]. — Release 9.
3 computer disks : 3 1/2 in. + 1 manual.
"Copyright...Minitab Inc." — Disk labels.
Manual by John McKenzie, Robert L. Schaefer, and Elizabeth Farber.
System requirements: IBM PC (386 and above); 4MB RAM (6MB recommended); DOS 3.3 or later; Windows 3.1; 1 high density disk drive; hard disk with 10MB available space; VGA or SVGA monitor; math coprocessor recommended; mouse recommended.
Title from title screen.
Title on disk labels: Minitab student edition for Windows.
Audience: College and business students.
Summary: A student version of a professional statistical software package that imports and exports data, processes it, and describes, analyzes, and displays it in a graphic format.
ISBN 0-201-59157-X
1. Statistics — Software. I. Minitab Inc. II. Title: Minitab student edition for Windows. III. Title: Minitab.
QA276.4 <MRCRR>   94-8128
519.5 — dc 12   CIP

ISBN 0-201-59157-X (User's Manual/Software Package)
0-201-59886-8 (User's Manual)

7 8 9 10 — CRW— 97

PREFACE

Welcome to *The Student Edition of MINITAB for Windows*.

The Student Edition of MINITAB for Windows is an educational version of Minitab statistical software. It is designed to provide students with an easy-to-learn software package to be used in describing, analyzing, and displaying the data that is so integral a part of statistical education today. It is well-suited for use in a wide variety of statistics, business, and engineering courses.

Minitab is a powerful tool originally developed at The Pennsylvania State University as a teaching aid for introductory statistics courses. It is now one of the most widely accepted statistical analysis packages for college instruction, as evidenced by the fact that it is currently used at over 2000 schools worldwide. Minitab has also proven itself as an established research tool and is installed on mainframe, mini-, and microcomputers at over 5000 sites in 51 countries, and is used by three-quarters of the companies listed in *Fortune* magazine's listing of the top 50 companies.

The Student Edition of MINITAB for Windows includes the following:

- comprehensive statistical capabilities, including descriptive statistics, simulations and distributions, elementary inferential statistics, analysis of variance, regression, analysis of categorical data, nonparametrics, control charts, and time series analysis

- a menu-driven interface providing easy access to Minitab statistical, graphical, and data management capabilities

- a Data window permitting data entry, editing, and browsing in a spreadsheet-like display

- an on-line Help window using the Microsoft Windows Help system to provide context-specific help at the click of a button

- the ability to import and export data, including data from Excel

- Lotus 1-2-3 compatibility

- quality management tools

- professional graphics, which enable users to produce a comprehensive array of presentation-quality graphs

- similar interface, commands, and output across DOS and Macintosh platforms

Objectives

The Student Edition of MINITAB for Windows is designed to introduce students to a powerful statistical analysis program that they can use to describe, analyze, and display data. The primary objectives of the package are

- to provide a complete educational environment for learning Minitab for Windows

- to provide students with a powerful and versatile tool that will enhance their learning experience

- to teach students the basics of Minitab for Windows in the context of case studies and **real** data drawn from business, psychology, education, engineering, health care, and the life and physical sciences

- to provide teachers with a flexible means of integrating technology into their classrooms

What's in This Edition

The Student Edition of MINITAB for Windows includes the standard features professors have come to expect, but it includes more functionality than ever before, particularly those that would be useful in business courses. There are more quality tools to assist management. Additional capabilities for analysis include advanced regression options and classical time series analysis. There is also the capability to produce a wide variety of high-resolution graphs suitable for use in presentation.

Software Features

- worksheets that allow up to 3500 data points and 1000 columns

- complete Windows interface with menus and dialog boxes, making full use of copying, cutting, and pasting commands, data, and graphs between Minitab for Windows and other applications

- easy access to the Minitab command language

- a Data window that allows data entry, editing, and browsing in a spreadsheet-like format

- Lotus 1-2-3 compatibility

- comprehensive statistics capabilities, including additional distributions, regression subcommands, time series commands, and quality management tools

- professional graphics, offering a wide array of customization tools

- context-specific help for all Minitab commands

- improved printing capabilities

- Minitab Exec macros

Manual Features

- 16 hands-on, self-paced tutorials, including two new tutorials on high-resolution graphics and regression analysis

- many new examples, case studies, Minitab at Work essays, problems, and exercises, all carefully checked for accuracy

- over 60 real data sets chosen for their interest level as well as their applicability to the techniques under discussion

- a comprehensive Reference section, organized by menu, which documents every feature of *The Student Edition of MINITAB for Windows*

Networks

The Student Edition of MINITAB for Windows is designed to be used by a single user on a single computer. It will not run as a shared application installed on a network server. If more than one user tries to run *The Student Edition of MINITAB for Windows* at the same time, *The Student Edition of MINITAB for Windows* will terminate.

Organization of This Manual

This manual is organized into four sections. Part I, Getting Started, begins with an overview in Chapter 1 of what is needed to successfully use *The Student Edition of MINITAB for Windows*. It includes a concise explanation of the conventions used throughout the manual, the systems requirements needed to run the software, and information regarding technical support. Chapter 2 provides thorough instruction on Windows basics. Chapters 3 and 4 follow with complete and easy-to-use instructions for installing, starting, and exiting Minitab. Chapter 5, then, takes the reader through a sample session designed to give students an introduction to the program and to interest them in its capabilities and the features of the manual.

Part II, Tutorials, is the heart of the manual. It contains 16 interactive tutorials that expose students to the full power of the software through careful, step-by-step explanation of the necessary procedures to follow—as well as in many tutorials—through case studies from business, psychology, education, engineering, and the life and physical sciences. These case studies give students the opportunity to immediately apply their knowledge of the software within an interesting and real-life context, using real data provided for this purpose.

Each tutorial begins with a list of objectives, and most contain case studies that introduce students to the necessary Minitab for Windows procedures. As students perform steps in the tutorial, screen views are shown in the manual to teach and illustrate Minitab concepts and features with as little additional outside instruction as possible. Each tutorial requires approximately 45 to 60 minutes to complete (not including end-of-chapter material).

Each tutorial ends with a summary and review section that includes a Minitab command summary, followed by a section testing the students' mastery of the material through matching and true/false exercises, and practice problems using the data sets from the tutorial as well as new data sets incorporated especially for this portion of the tutorial. In selected tutorials, a "Minitab at

Work" feature illustrates how Minitab is used in organizations of the type students may find themselves working for upon graduation.

Students unfamiliar with Minitab should complete the sample session in Getting Started and the first two tutorials, dealing with data entry and manipulation, before moving on to the other tutorials. Most students will complete Tutorials 3 through 7—which cover graphics, descriptive statistics, basic probability, and elementary statistical inference — in order. The remaining tutorials can be completed in any sequence. An experienced Minitab user could proceed with any tutorial. Students should notice that some tutorials, however, contain case studies that are continued from earlier tutorials.

Part III, Exploring Data, contains descriptions of all the real data sets used in the tutorials and practice problems. It also contains descriptions of other data sets students may want to use for additional practice.

Part IV, Reference, describes all Minitab for Windows features. It contains comprehensive descriptions of the Minitab commands and dialog boxes, organized by menu. It also contains discussions of special topics, such as the Data window, file types, Session commands, importing and exporting data, and macros. Menu commands are cross-referenced to their corresponding Session window commands and the tutorials.

Differences Between the Student Edition and the Professional Version of Minitab for Windows

The Student Edition of MINITAB for Windows is compatible with the professional version, but with the following differences:

- the worksheet size is limited to 3500 data points and 1000 columns
- selected advanced commands and subcommands have not been included (see Appendix B for a complete listing)
- matrix functions are not included
- the new macro capability (%Macros) is not included

Acknowledgments

The completion of this manual took a great deal of concentrated effort not possible without the full support and cooperation of a diverse team. Everyone on the team, both within Addison-Wesley and Minitab Inc., was crucial to our success. In particular, we would like to recognize those individuals with whom we worked on a regular basis and without whom we could not have accomplished our ambitious goals.

At Addison-Wesley, we would like to thank Julia Berrisford, Senior Sponsoring Editor, and Maureen Lawson, Project Coordinator, for undertaking the daunting and often seemingly thankless work associated with coordinating the team's efforts and ensuring that a high-quality, competitive product was produced under an extremely tight schedule. Also of particular note are the efforts of Patsy DuMoulin, Production Supervisor, for her mastery of the production dimensions of the project, and Peter Blaiwas, Cover Design Supervisor, for his direction of cover and packaging aspects, which resulted in a new, dynamic look for the product.

Of special note was the dedication of our Development Editor, Joan Carey, whose work was critical to our success. Her consummate professionalism and her skills as both writer and editor are seen literally in every paragraph. The suggestions she made and the improvements she implemented are too numerous to mention here. For these, as well as her steady good humor throughout, we owe her an enormous debt of gratitude.

Our thanks also to the staff and programmers of Minitab Inc., especially Dave Yancey, Bob Reitman, Terry Ziemer, Denny Huber, Dean Lapp, and Cheryl Maki, who provided us with their technical expertise and created the software for this version of The Student Edition.

We thank Michael Andrzejewski, Patrick Carey, Bernard Gillett, Robert Gillett, Siu Lok, and Sarah McKenzie, without whose assistance we never could have finished this work.

Finally, we are grateful to the reviewers and beta-testers whose diligent reading of the manual and verification of the manual against the software strengthened the work immeasurably.

Reviewers

Lloyd Jaisingh, Morehead State University, Kentucky
Henry Reynolds, University of Delaware, Delaware
Dan Toy, California State University — Chico, California
Calvin Williams, Carnegie Mellon University, Pennsylvania
Wayne Winston, Indiana University, Indiana
Mustafa R. Yilmaz, Northeastern University, Massachusetts
Jack Yurkiewicz, Pace University, New York
Peter Zehna, Naval Postgraduate School, California

J. M.
R. L. S.
E. F.

CONTENTS

ABOUT THE AUTHORS

John McKenzie has been teaching applied statistics courses to business students at Babson College since 1978. He also provides statistical advice to the school's faculty and staff. He has used statistical software in his teaching and consulting for over 25 years, and he has been a co-editor of the Minitab User's Group Newsletter. McKenzie has also been a member of the Planning Committee of the Making Statistics More Effective in Schools of Business conferences. He has an A.B. in mathematics from Amherst College, and a master's degree in mathematics, a master's degree in statistics, and a Ph.D. in statistics from the University of Michigan.

Bob Schaefer has been teaching a wide variety of statistics courses over the past 15 years at Miami University, Oxford, including introductory courses in statistics; advanced undergraduate courses on regression, design of experiments, and time series; and advanced graduate courses on quality control and survival data analysis. He has authored or coauthored numerous journal articles on statistics, and he has worked on a number of consulting projects and grants. Schaefer has a master's degree in mathematics from Michigan Technological University, and a master's degree and Ph.D. in biostatistics from the University of Michigan.

Betsy Farber has been teaching mathematics and statistics for 29 years and has spent the last 18 of those years in the mathematics department at Bucks County Community College. She uses Minitab in her elementary statistics classroom and is dedicated to integrating technology into the classroom. Farber has a master's degree in mathematics from Trenton State University.

PART I

GETTING STARTED

CHAPTER
I

Before You Begin

Checking Your Package

You can purchase *The Student Edition of MINITAB for Windows* in either of two ways.

Without the Minitab software: If you are using a school computer with the Minitab software already loaded, you probably want to purchase just this book. You also need to buy a high-density disk on which you will store the data sets used in the tutorials and the files you save during the exercises. The section entitled "Your Student Disk" in Chapter 3 of Getting Started provides instructions for formatting your personal Student disk and copying the data files from your school computer to it.

With the Minitab software: If you plan to run Minitab on your own computer, you need to buy the entire package, which includes the Minitab software. You can save the files you create during the exercises on your personal computer's hard disk or you can buy a separate high-density disk to store them.

The entire package of *The Student Edition of MINITAB for Windows* contains these items:

- The User's Manual for *The Student Edition of MINITAB for Windows* (this book).

- Three 3½-inch program disks that contain the Minitab program and the data files you need to complete the tutorials in this book.

- A Warranty Registration Card, which registers you as a licensee of this package and makes you eligible to receive the latest product information. Complete this card and mail it to the Addison-Wesley Publishing Company right away.

- A Special Offer Upgrade Card. If you want to upgrade from the student edition to the full commercial Minitab version, return this card to Minitab Inc.

- A Quick Reference Card. This card summarizes all the menu and Session commands in *The Student Edition of MINITAB for Windows.* You will find this reference handy when you work on your own after completing the tutorials. Instead of searching through the tutorials to find a command, you can consult the Quick Reference Card.

Note: In this manual, "Minitab" refers only to the version of the software you received in *The Student Edition of MINITAB for Windows* package.

What's in This Book?

Part I, Getting Started, contains five chapters. Chapter 1, "Before You Begin," familiarizes you with this book and explains its typographical conventions. Chapter 2, "Windows Basics," introduces you to Microsoft Windows, version 3.1.

Chapter 3, "Installing Minitab," shows you how to install the Minitab software. Chapter 4, "Using Minitab," describes how to start and stop Minitab; it also explains some of its basic features. Chapter 5, "Sample Session," guides you through an actual Minitab session so you can try out Minitab's capabilities before you begin the tutorials. If you have Windows experience and Minitab is already installed, you can skip directly to Chapter 5.

Part II, Tutorials, is the heart of this book. Beginning with the simplest features of Minitab, the sixteen tutorials introduce the major features of the software in a step-by-step, hands-on format. The exercises and practice problems at the end of each tutorial reinforce the concepts you've learned. Most of the tutorials and practice problems use the data sets that come with the Minitab program. You should start with Tutorials 1 and 2, but proceed from there in the order most useful to you. Some of the later tutorials continue case studies introduced in earlier ones, but you can still do most of these problems independently.

Part III, Exploring Data, describes the data sets installed with the Minitab program. These data sets cover a variety of fields, including business, psychology, education, engineering, health care, and the life and physical sciences.

Part IV, Reference, describes all the Minitab menu commands and provides information on special topics. As you work through the tutorials and exercises, use the Reference section to look up commands by menu. The Reference section also includes chapters on Minitab's features, the Minitab command language, importing and exporting data, and Minitab macros. This section will be especially helpful after you have completed the tutorials and begin to use Minitab to analyze your own data.

Required Computer System

You need the following computer equipment to run Minitab:

- An IBM or compatible microcomputer with the Intel 80386 processor or higher

- Windows version 3.1, or later

- A hard disk drive with at least eight megabytes (8 MB) of available space and one floppy disk drive

- At least four megabytes (4 MB) of random access memory (RAM)

- A math coprocessor (optional, but strongly recommended)

Note: The hard disk on which you install *The Student Edition of MINITAB for Windows* cannot be a network server, as this product does not run on a network.

Typographical Conventions

Typographical conventions and symbols are used throughout this manual to make the material easier to use.

Any action that you should perform appears on a line by itself, indented, and preceded by a square bullet (■). For example:

- Type **GRADES** and press ⏎Enter

Boldface type indicates letters, numbers, or symbols you enter using the keyboard. Elements, including commands, that you see on the screen are also in boldface.

Italics introduce a new term or concept.

Choose tells you to make a menu selection by using either the keyboard or the mouse. Specific mouse techniques are described in Chapter 2, "Windows Basics" (see "Using the Mouse").

Type instructs you to enter text using the keyboard. It is important to type this information *exactly* as shown, including any punctuation or spaces.

Press indicates that you should either press the specified key on the keyboard, such as Tab or ⏎Enter, or hold down the mouse button.

This book assumes you are using a mouse, although it indicates keyboard shortcuts when appropriate.

In later tutorials, as you become more familiar with Minitab, this book displays instructions in an abbreviated form using the greater than symbol (>).

For example, instructions to open the **Stat** menu, choose **Basic Statistics**, and then choose **Descriptive Statistics** are shortened to:

- Choose **Stat** > **Basic Statistics** > **Descriptive Statistics**

Technical Support

Neither Addison-Wesley Publishing Company, Inc., nor Minitab Inc. provides telephone assistance to users of *The Student Edition of MINITAB for Windows*. However, registered instructors who have adopted this product for their students are entitled to telephone support. You should report any problems you encounter with the Minitab software to your professor. Be sure to note exactly what action you are performing when the problem occurs, as well as the exact error message.

Instructors can register by completing the Warranty Registration Card included with the package.

If you would like to receive newsletters and product announcements from Minitab Inc., send your name, address, and telephone number to Minitab and ask to be added to its mailing list. Mail your request to Minitab Inc., 3081 Enterprise Drive, State College, PA 16801-3008.

CHAPTER
2

Windows Basics

This chapter introduces you to Microsoft Windows, version 3.1. If you're an experienced Windows user, proceed to Chapter 3, "Installing Minitab," for installation instructions. If you are new to Windows, you should read this chapter. You also might want to consult the Microsoft Windows *User's Guide*, especially Part I, Windows Fundamentals.

Welcome to Windows

It's easy to get up and running in Windows. Once you become familiar with the standard screen elements and learn how to use the mouse, you'll be ready to run Minitab and other Windows applications. The consistency of the interface makes most Windows applications seem familiar right from the start.

Starting Your System

Windows is an *operating system* that helps you and your computer manage files and applications. To start Windows:

■ Make sure your computer, monitor, and printer are plugged in and then turn them on

Depending on how your system is set up, Windows might display automatically, in which case you see a *window*, or rectangular box, entitled

Program Manager. If the DOS prompt (usually C:\) appears, you start Windows as follows:

■ Type **win** and press ⏎Enter

The Windows logo appears and then, after a brief pause, Windows opens.

The Desktop

When you start Windows, you see the *desktop*. Like a regular desk, the Windows desktop is a place on which you store your tools and your work. Each tool, or *application*, is represented by a small graphic symbol called a *program-item icon*. These icons appear on the screen in rectangular areas with borders called *windows*. When you open an application, you display your work — documents, spreadsheets, and so on — in other windows. This section explains how to navigate through the Windows environment.

Program Manager

When you first open Windows, the *Program Manager* window appears on the desktop. Other windows might also be open within it. Figure GS-1 at the top of the next page shows Program Manager with the Main window open within it.

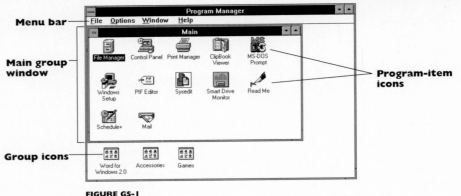

Menu bar

Main group window

Program-item icons

Group icons

FIGURE GS-1

The Program Manager window

Note: If a previous user exited the Windows program with other windows open, your opening screen might not look exactly like Figure GS-1. You can ask either your instructor or your technical resource person to restore the opening screen to this configuration, or you can continue reading this chapter until you learn how to open and close windows. Your system may not have all the icons shown in Figure GS-1; it may also have additional ones.

The Windows Program Manager is like "home base." From it, you start applications, manage files, organize the contents of the desktop, and so on. Its main elements include the Program Manager menu, group icons, and group windows that contain program-item icons.

Program Manager Menu Bar

The Program Manager *menu bar* is the horizontal bar at the top of the Program Manager window that contains the four main menus: File, Options, Window, and Help. A *menu* is a list of *commands*, or instructions, you can use to tell Minitab to perform actions. The commands are grouped together logically. For example, you will find all the commands that help you organize files on the File menu.

Icons

The Main group window shown in Figure GS-1 displays program-item icons for File Manager, Control Panel, and so on. You select a program-item icon to start the associated Windows application. The next section, "Using the Mouse," describes the techniques you use to select icons and start programs. The *group icons* at the bottom of the Program Manager window represent other windows that contain additional program-item icons.

Using the Mouse

The mouse simplifies many common tasks, such as selecting icons, choosing menu commands, and moving from window to window.

Use the left mouse button to perform the mouse tasks in this book, unless the right button is specified.

Moving the Mouse

Whenever you move your mouse, the small pointer arrow ⌖ on the screen moves in the same direction. For example, if you move your mouse to the right, the pointer arrow moves to the right on your screen. For practice, look at the screen as you:

■ Move the mouse to the right and then to the left on your desk

Note: If you are using a trackball, roll the ball instead of moving the mouse.

The pointer arrow on the screen mirrors your actions.

Note: The pointer's appearance changes depending on the action you are performing, as you will see when you start working with Minitab.

Mouse Techniques

There are four basic mouse techniques: *pointing, clicking, dragging,* and *double-clicking.*

The table shown here describes the mouse terminology used in this manual.

Term	Technique
Point	Position the mouse pointer in a particular location.
Click	Point to the desired item and then quickly press and release the left mouse button one time. Do not hold the mouse button down for longer than a fraction of a second.
Drag	Point to the desired item, press and hold down the mouse button, move the mouse with the button still pressed to a new location, and then release the mouse button to reposition or accept the item.
Double-click	Point to the desired item and then click the mouse button twice in quick succession.

■ Move the mouse away from you and to the right until the pointer reaches the upper right corner of the screen

Although you may be able to physically move the mouse further on your desk, the pointer reaches the upper boundary and then disappears off the right side of the screen.

■ Pick up the mouse, circle it in the air, and then put it down

Nothing happens — the mouse's rolling mechanism must be in contact with a surface (preferably a mouse pad) to work. If you don't have enough room to move the mouse or it runs into an object on your desk, simply lift it, put it down where there is space, and then continue.

Pointing and Clicking

To select an object you want to work with, you point at it on the screen and then click the left mouse button (that is, press it quickly and release it). Try pointing at and clicking an item in the Program Manager window to select it:

■ Move the mouse until the tip of the pointer arrow touches the word **File** at the left end of the Program Manager menu bar

■ Without moving the mouse, quickly press and then release the left button

When you click File, the color of the letters and the background changes to indicate that it's selected. Exactly how this *highlight* appears depends on your monitor. Also, a list of the File commands appears, as shown in Figure GS-2.

- Continue holding down the mouse button and move the mouse away from you about an inch

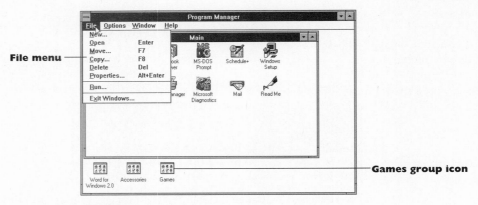

FIGURE GS-2

Program Manager with File menu open

Most actions in Windows are reversible. This makes it easy to experiment, change your mind, and correct mistakes. Try closing the File menu:

- Move the pointer off the menu and click anywhere else on the desktop

  The menu and the highlight disappear.

Dragging

You can also use the mouse to move items around on the desktop. Try dragging one of the group icons:

- Move the mouse so the pointer is over the **Games** group icon (or any other icon if you can't see Games)

- Press and hold down the left mouse button

  This action highlights the word Games, indicating that you have selected the Games group icon.

Note: The Games group icon is automatically installed with Windows. If it doesn't appear on your computer, you can reinstall Windows or ask your technical resource person to do so.

As you move the mouse, the pointer and the word Games disappear. The icon moves in the direction you move the mouse.

- Release the mouse button

  The icon "snaps" into its new position, and the word Games reappears. Because the group icon is the last item you selected, it is still highlighted.

  It is important to hold down the mouse button until you have completed your action — in this case, until the icon is where you want it. If you accidentally let go of the mouse button, just drag the icon again until it is in the desired location.

  To return the Games icon to its original location:

- Point at the **Games** icon with the pointer

- Press and hold down the left mouse button

- Drag the icon back to its original position

  You will use the dragging technique often in Minitab (and other Windows applications) to move and copy objects, select blocks of figures or text, and change the size of objects.

Double-Clicking

To open a group window, you click twice in rapid succession, or *double-click*, the corresponding group icon. Try using this technique to open the Games group window:

■ Double-click the **Games** group icon

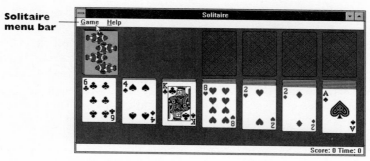

Solitaire menu bar

FIGURE GS-3

The Solitaire window

The Games group window opens, displaying icons for the games stored on your computer.

Note: If you only clicked once, or didn't double-click quickly enough, the Games Control menu pops up. Each group icon has its own Control menu; you will learn more about this menu in the next section, "Working with Windows." For now, click in a blank area on the desktop to close the menu; then double-click the Games group icon again.

You perform a variety of functions in the Windows environment by double-clicking. For example, in addition to opening windows, you can double-click to start an application. Try opening one of the most entertaining Windows applications — Solitaire:

■ Double-click the **Solitaire** program-item icon

The Solitaire application deals you a hand, and you're ready to play.

Choosing Menu Commands

Just as in the Program Manager, you choose commands from menus to perform actions in Window applications. The menu bar at the top of the Solitaire window, shown in Figure GS-3, displays the two main menus for this application: Game and Help.

Note: The designs on your cards may differ from the one shown in the figure. You can select a different deck design with the Deck command on the Game menu. Windows uses this new design until you choose another.

Each of the menus in the menu bar contains a group of commands. You have already opened the File menu on the Program Manager menu bar. Now open the Game menu on the Solitaire menu bar in the same manner:

■ Click **Game**

There are five commands listed on the Game menu, shown in Figure GS-4.

FIGURE GS-4

The Game menu on Solitaire game

Notice that Undo is dimmed, while Deck and Options have ellipses (...) after them. These conventions give you more information about the commands.

Dimmed Menu Commands

Some of the items on a menu may appear *dimmed*, or gray. Dimmed commands are commands that are not available at the moment. For example, the Undo command on the Game menu is unavailable because you haven't started to play the game yet; there is nothing to undo. If you had moved any card, Undo would appear in black, and you could choose it to reverse the previous action.

Underlined Letters

An underlined letter in a command's name indicates the key you can press to choose the command from the keyboard. For example, to choose the Options command, you can simply type **O** (instead of clicking the word Options with the mouse).

Checkmarks

A checkmark √ next to a command tells you the command is currently in force. You can clear the selection by clicking the command. None of the commands in Solitaire have checkmarks, but you will see them in other applications.

Commands with Keyboard Shortcuts

If a keyboard shortcut exists for a command, it appears next to it on the menu. A shortcut is either a single key or a key combination, as indicted by two keys joined with a plus sign (+) that you press to select the command without first opening the menu. For example, in Windows applications, you can press the [Ctrl]+**C** combination to copy data. None of the commands in Solitaire have keyboard shortcuts for menu items, but you will see them in other applications.

Commands with Ellipses

When an ellipsis (...) displays next to a command, it indicates that you need to supply additional information.

For example, the Deck and Options commands have ellipses after them. When you choose a command with an ellipsis, a *dialog box* appears, prompting you for the information needed to carry out the command. The "Dialog Boxes" section in this chapter describes how you select options and input data in a dialog box.

You can cancel almost any operation by pressing the [Esc] key. To close the Game menu:

- Press [Esc]

Practice working in a Windows application by playing the Solitaire game:

- Click an unexposed card to turn it over
- Double-click any card you want to move up to the suit stacks
- Drag a card to move it (similarly, you can move a group by dragging the first card in the stack)

Playing Solitaire gives you the opportunity to practice mouse techniques.

Working with Windows

When you win or have no more moves left in the game, take a moment to examine the Solitaire window. It shares a number of features common to all Windows applications.

Most windows contain the basic elements shown in Figure GS-5.

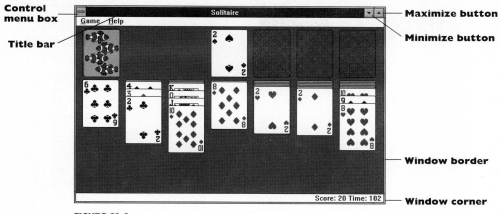

Control menu box

Title bar

Maximize button

Minimize button

Window border

Window corner

FIGURE GS-5
Solitaire game

Title Bar

The *title bar* displays the name of the application or document, in this case, Solitaire. If more than one window is open, the title bar of the *active* window (the one in which you are working) appears in a different color or intensity than the others.

Control Menu Box

The *Control menu box* is the small box with a dash in it that is located in the upper left corner of the window. You click the Control menu box to display the commands on the Control menu, which let you resize, move, or close the window. Switch To lets you move to another window and make it active. You can also close a window by double-clicking its Control menu box.

Maximizing and Minimizing Windows

Every window has two buttons in its upper right corner that you can use to change the window's size. The *minimize* ▾ button shrinks the active window to an icon. The *maximize* ▴ button enlarges the active window so it fills the entire screen. Try resizing the Solitaire window to make it as big as your screen allows:

■ Click the maximize button ▴

Note: You can also click the Control menu box and then choose the Maximize command to enlarge the window.

The Solitaire game now fills the entire screen. Notice that the maximize button changes to a *restore* ▴▾ button when you maximize a window.

■ Click the restore button ▴▾ to return the window to its previous size

To reduce the window to an icon:

■ Click the minimize button ▾

You now see Program Manager, with the Games window open.

Using Icons

You should now be able to see two Solitaire icons: one in the Games window and one at the bottom of your screen. If not, the Program Manager window is probably covering it. In this case, redisplay the Solitaire icon:

■ Minimize the Program Manager window (and any other window that is hiding the Solitaire icon)

Minimizing an application temporarily closes the window but leaves the program running. Windows lets you have multiple applications open at one time. For example, you might be in the middle of a Solitaire game and want to work in Minitab. Minimize the Solitaire window so you can work in Minitab, finish your analyses, and then pick up the game where you left off. You can jump from application to application by activating minimized icons. Each icon at the bottom of your screen represents a program that is running.

- Double-click the **Solitaire** icon at the bottom of the screen to reopen the window

The Solitaire window reappears in its original size.

Resizing Windows

You can change the size of a window by dragging any corner or side of its thin gray outer edge, or *border*.

- Point to the upper-right corner of the window border so that the pointer becomes a diagonal, two-headed arrow

- Drag the double-headed arrow toward the lower-left corner of the window and then release the mouse button

The window size changes to fit within the new border. The border's sides lengthen or shorten simultaneously, depending on the direction you choose. You can resize any group, application, or document window in this manner.

- Drag the borders back to their original position to reveal the entire Solitaire game

Moving Windows

You can also use the mouse to move the entire window.

- Drag the title bar toward the lower edge of the screen

The Solitaire window moves in the same direction as the pointer.

- Drag the window back to its original location

Getting Online Help

Whenever you need help with a particular action or procedure, you can consult *online Help*. Because Help is online, you can display this information on the screen while you're running a program. For example, examine the Help Solitaire offers:

- Click **Help** on the Solitaire menu bar

- Click **Contents**

The available Solitaire Help topics appear in a separate window, as shown in Figure GS-6.

FIGURE GS-6
Solitaire Help

To review the rules of the game:

- Click the maximize button ▲ to enlarge the Solitaire Help window

- Move the pointer to **Rules of the Game**

The pointer arrow turns into a pointing finger.

- Click **Rules of the Game**

The Help window displays the rules of Solitaire. When you are finished reading:

- Click **File** on the Solitaire Help menu bar

- Click **Exit**

You see the regular Solitaire window again.

Dialog Boxes

Windows often prompts you for more information in order to execute a command. It usually does so by displaying a dialog box. Dialog boxes request information, help you keep track of the selections you make, and show you the current settings for the options associated with a task. There are several dialog box components:

- *Text boxes*, in which you type information

- *List boxes*, which display all the options you can select

- *Drop-down list boxes*, which may display a default and list all the options when you click an arrow

- *Option buttons*, which present mutually exclusive choices

- *Check boxes*, which you can either select or clear

- *Command buttons*, which execute actions (such as OK or Cancel)

Open the Options dialog box to see some examples of these components:

- Click **Game** on the Solitaire menu bar

- Click **Options**

The Options dialog box appears, shown in Figure GS-7.

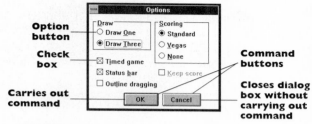

FIGURE GS-7
The Options dialog box

Control Menu

All Windows dialog boxes have a *Control menu* with commands similar to those on an application control menu, as previously described in the "Working With Windows" section.

Command Buttons

All dialog boxes have at least two *command buttons* that initiate immediate actions: OK and Cancel. When you have finished entering information in the dialog box, you click OK to confirm and implement your selections. If, on the other hand, you decide you don't want to proceed with the command, click Cancel to close the dialog box.

Option Buttons

Option buttons give you a choice between two or more possibilities. You can select only one option button in each category. In the Options dialog box, for example, you can choose to draw one card or three cards, but not both, when you play Solitaire. To select an option, click the small circle, or button, in front of it; a dark dot appears in the circle.

Check Boxes

Check boxes provide "either/or" choices. For example, the Solitaire Options dialog box includes four check boxes; you can select or clear as many as you want. (Your Options dialog box may look different from that shown in Figure GS-7.) One of

Windows redisplays the desktop; both the Program Manager and Main windows are open.

Scrolling

Most windows display *scroll bars* and *scroll arrows* like the ones shown in Figure GS-8. You

FIGURE GS-8
Generic scroll bar

these, **Keep Score**, is dimmed because it's unavailable; it becomes available only if you choose the **Vegas** scoring option. The X in the **Timed Game** check box tells the Solitaire application to track and display the time during the current game. You simply click a check box to select or clear it.

To see the effects of selecting options in this dialog box:

- Change the current selections to suit your preferences

- Click **OK** or press ⏎Enter to implement your selections

- Click **Game** on the Solitaire menu bar

- Click **Deal** to play a hand with the new settings (enlarge the window if you can't see all the stacks)

After you finish playing:

- Double-click the Solitaire Control menu box to close the Solitaire window

If your Program Manager is minimized, double-click its icon to open it.

- Double-click the Games Control menu box to close the Games window

use the scroll bars and arrows to move, or *scroll*, through the entire window to see any additional information it contains.

There are three ways to scroll through the contents of a window:

- Click the scroll arrows that appear at either end of the scroll bar.

- Click the gray area in the scroll bar.

- Drag the scroll box in the scroll bar.

To practice working with scroll bars:

- Click **Help** on the Program Manager menu and then click **Contents**

- Click **Arrange Windows and Icons**

A scroll bar appears on the right side of the window, indicating that the active window does not display its entire contents. (If you don't see a scroll bar, drag the top border of the window downward so that some of the text is hidden.)

Windows can have a vertical scroll bar along the right side of the window, a horizontal scroll bar at the bottom, or both. For example, the Help window shown in Figure GS-9 displays only the vertical scroll bar.

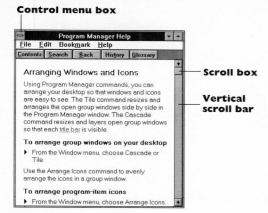

Control menu box

Scroll box

Vertical scroll bar

FIGURE GS-9
Program Manager Help

To move through the Help window line-by-line, click the scroll arrow at the bottom of the vertical scroll bar:

■ Click the bottom scroll arrow repeatedly to scroll through the contents of the window

Whenever a scroll bar appears, you can click a scroll arrow to display information just above, below, to the right, or to the left of what currently appears on the screen. There are two other ways to scroll:

■ To scroll a greater distance all at once, drag the scroll box within the scroll bar.

■ To quickly move an entire screen in one direction or another, click the shaded gray area in the scroll bar on either side of the scroll box.

Dragging the scroll box to the top or bottom of the scroll bar is the quickest way to move to the beginning or end of an open document.

■ Close the Help window by double-clicking its Control menu box

Multiple Windows

Often you'll have several windows open at once on your desktop or even within a single application. Currently, both the Main group window and the Program Manager window are open. Now try opening several more windows:

■ Double-click the **Accessories** group icon (you may need to move other windows to see it)

The Accessories window opens.

■ Double-click the **Calculator** program-item icon in the Accessories window

A facsimile of a calculator appears. You can use this electronic calculator in the same way as you would a handheld one. You click the mouse or use the numeric keypad (with the [Num Lock] key on) to enter numbers and symbols.

■ Move the Calculator window to the bottom of the screen

You now have the Program Manager, Main, Accessories, and Calculator windows open. To open yet another window:

■ Double-click the **Notepad** icon in the Accessories window

The Notepad window opens. (The Notepad is a text editor that comes with Windows.) Because you opened the Notepad last, its title bar is highlighted to indicate it is the current or active window.

Moving Among Windows

You can easily switch between Windows applications. For example, if you want to enter arithmetic computations in a Notepad document, you can switch to the Calculator, perform the calculation, and copy the results to the Notepad. As long as one window does not cover the other completely, you simply click anywhere on the other window to move it to the front and make it active. Otherwise:

■ Click the Notepad Control menu box

■ Click **Switch To**

The *Task List*, which is a list of all open groups and applications, appears.

■ Double-click **Calculator**

■ Click the Notepad Control menu box

■ Click **Switch To**

■ Click the **Cascade** button in the Task List window

The Cascade command neatly arranges all the open application windows one in front of the other, with the title bars showing, as shown in Figure GS-10.

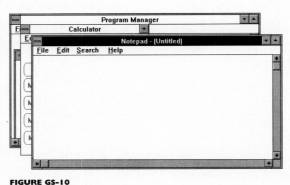

FIGURE GS-10
Cascading windows

The Calculator becomes the active window and appears in front of the other open windows on the desktop. To return to the Notepad:

■ Click anywhere in the Notepad window

Note: You can open the Task List by double-clicking on the desktop outside of any window's borders or by pressing Ctrl+Esc.

Arranging Windows

When windows cover each other up, you can use two features to rearrange them on the screen. To stack windows so that all the title bars display:

You can move any window to the front by simply clicking its title bar.

■ Click the Calculator title bar

The Calculator window moves to the foreground.

The Tile command resizes and rearranges the open windows on the screen so you see them all at once and they don't overlap.

■ Choose **Switch To** from the Calculator's Control menu

■ Click the **Tile** button

Now you can see the contents of each window, as shown in Figure GS-11.

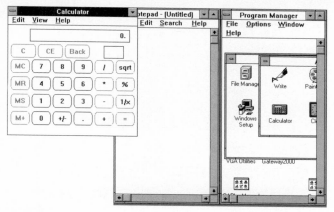

FIGURE GS-11

Tiled windows

Closing Windows

The quickest way to close a window is by double-clicking its Control menu box. Alternatively, you can choose Close from the Control menu.

    To "clean up" your desktop:

- Close all the windows, except the Program Manager (click **No** if the Notepad window asks you if you want to save your changes)

    To restore the Program Manager to its original size:

- Resize the Program Manager window by dragging its border so you can see all the group icons again

Windows 3.1 Online Tutorial

You can practice the skills covered in this section by completing the online Windows 3.1 tutorial. To start the tutorial:

- Click **Help** on the Program Manager menu bar

- Click **Windows Tutorial**

    Follow the instructions that appear on the screen. You can exit at any time by pressing the [Esc] key.

CHAPTER 3

Installing Minitab

If you are using your own computer, you need to install *The Student Edition of MINITAB for Windows* software on your hard disk by following the instructions in the next two sections. If you are using a school computer, you can skip to the section entitled "Your Student Disk," because Minitab should already be installed. If it's not, contact your instructor or technical resource person.

Note: The hard disk on which you install *The Student Edition of MINITAB for Windows* cannot be on a network server, as this product does not run on a network.

Before Installation

Before installing Minitab on your hard disk, you should:

- Refer to the "Checking Your Package" section in Chapter 1 for a list of the contents of your Minitab package.

- Make sure you have the current version of Windows (3.1 or later) and that your system satisfies the requirements outlined in the section "Required Computer System" in Chapter 1.

Note: Because the disks contain compressed files, you must use the installation program that comes with Minitab to load the files on your hard disk. You will not be able to use these files if you copy them directly from the original disks to your hard disk.

Installing Minitab

The Minitab installation program automatically installs Minitab in a directory named MTBSEW on your hard disk. A *directory* is like a file folder in which you store pieces of related information. Usually when you install a program it creates its own directory.

To install *The Student Edition of MINITAB for Windows*:

- Turn on the computer, if necessary

- Be sure Windows is running and Program Manager is open

- Insert the first Minitab disk in your computer's floppy drive (referred to in this section as drive A; substitute the appropriate letter if you are using a different drive)

- Click **File** from the Program Manager menu bar

- Click **Run**

- Type **A:\SETUP** in the Command Line text box and then press ⎵Enter⎵ to begin the installation (if your Minitab disk isn't in drive A, substitute the appropriate letter)

A series of MINITAB Setup dialog boxes appear, giving you the opportunity to customize your installation. The instructions that follow show you how to proceed through a normal installation.

- Click **Continue** in the first MINITAB Setup dialog box

- Click **OK** to acknowledge the disk caching message (normally you won't have to worry about this, but see your Windows documentation if you want more information)

Note: If this is the first time you have installed Minitab, you next personalize your Minitab disks. If Minitab has already been installed from your disks, a MINITAB Setup dialog box warns you about unauthorized reproduction.

- If this is the first time you have installed Minitab, personalize your Minitab program by entering your name, academic site (school), and the serial number on MINITAB Disk 2 (press ⎵Tab⎵ to move to the next text box), then click **Continue**. If you have already installed Minitab from the disks you are using, click **Continue** to acknowledge the copyright law information.

- Click **Install** in the MINITAB Setup dialog box that gives you installation options

- Click **Continue** to verify the installation directory

The installation program copies the files to your hard drive.

- Insert Disk 2 when requested, then click **OK** to continue installation, and repeat with Disk 3

- Click **OK** when the next MINITAB Setup dialog box tells you that the Setup is completed

The installation takes about five minutes, depending on your computer's speed. When it's complete, the MINITAB Student group window opens with all the Minitab icons displayed.

- Minimize the MINITAB Student group window

Your Student Disk

The Student Edition of MINITAB for Windows includes disks that contain the Minitab program and data sets. If you are working on your own computer, you can open the data sets on the hard drive and save your work in the same place. However, if you are working on a school computer, you need a Student disk on which to store your work. (You shouldn't count on saving your work on the school's computer.)

You need to buy one high-density 3½-inch blank disk and *format* it. When you format a disk, you set it up so that Minitab (or any other application) can store and read information on it. Windows provides a special application called File Manager to help you manage files and disks. The Format Disk command is available in the File Manager.

To format your Student disk:

- Make sure your Student disk is not *write-protected* (the tab in a 3½-inch disk's corner should be closed)

- Double-click the **Main** group icon to open it, if necessary (if you don't see this icon, it's probably hidden behind other open windows; close those windows using the techniques described in "Closing Windows" in Chapter 2)

- Insert your blank Student disk into drive A (or the appropriate drive)

- Double-click the **File Manager** icon in the Main group window, as shown in Figure GS-12 (your windows may show different icons)

FIGURE GS-12

Program Manager with Main group window open

- Click **Disk** on the File Manager menu
- Click **Format Disk** on the Disk menu

    The Format Disk dialog box opens, as shown in Figure GS-13 (yours may look slightly different).

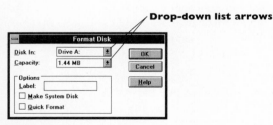

FIGURE GS-13

The Format Disk dialog box

- Be sure the appropriate drive letter is displayed in the **Disk In** text box (if it isn't, click the drop-down list arrow and then select the correct drive)
- Be sure the information in the **Capacity** box is correct (refer to the disk packaging or label to verify the capacity; if it's different, click the drop-down list arrow and then click the appropriate size)

- Click **OK**; if File Manager warns you that formatting will erase existing files, either click **OK** to continue, or click **Cancel** if you want to check your disk contents.

    File Manager formats the disk. It notifies you when the format is complete and asks if you want to format another.

- Click **No** and then click **Cancel**
- Double-click the File Manager Control menu box to close File Manager
- Double-click the Main window Control menu box to close the Main window
- Remove the formatted disk from the disk drive
- Write your name and **Minitab Student disk on the disk label**

    Your Student disk is now ready to store information. The instructions in this book assume that you will save all the files you work with during the tutorials on this disk. If you're using your own computer, you can store your work directly on your hard drive by substituting your file path for those specified in this book.

CHAPTER 4

Using Minitab

If you have not installed *The Student Edition of MINITAB for Windows* on your computer's hard disk, you should do so now. Refer to Getting Started Chapter 3, "Installing Minitab," for instructions on how to do so.

- Start Windows and display the Program Manager window

- Double-click the **MINITAB Student** group icon to open the Minitab group window (Figure GS-14)

MINITAB Student Edition program-item icon —

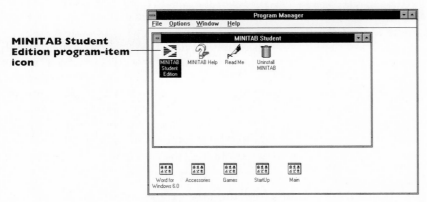

FIGURE GS-14
The Minitab group window

Starting Minitab

To start *The Student Edition of MINITAB for Windows*:

- Turn on your computer, if necessary

Note: If you are running Minitab on a school computer, you may need to ask your technical resource person where the Minitab window is located.

- Double-click the **MINITAB Student Edition** program-item icon

The Student Edition of MINITAB for Windows welcome screen appears for a moment and then clears automatically. The main Minitab window opens, as shown in Figure GS-15.

but this name changes depending on the data with which you are working.

When you first start Minitab, it creates a temporary storage area in your computer's memory called the *worksheet.* Minitab stores all the data you work with during a session in the current

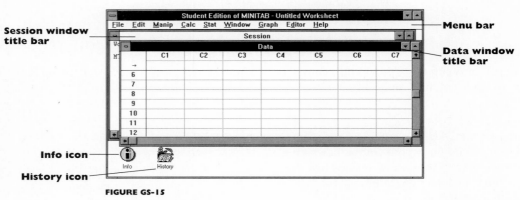

FIGURE GS-15

The Minitab window

The Minitab menu bar appears at the top of the window. Each menu lists groups of related commands you use to operate the program. You can also see some of Minitab's open windows: the Data window and the Session window. The Data title bar is highlighted, which tells you that it is the active window. Two other windows, Info and History, are minimized to icons at the bottom of the Minitab window.

Minitab Windows

The main Minitab window opens when you first start Minitab. Initially, the window title is "Student Edition of MINITAB - Untitled Worksheet,"

worksheet. You can have only one worksheet open at a time.

Minitab provides six window types to facilitate your work with the worksheet: Data, Session, History, Info, Graph, and Help. Each window is briefly described in this section. These summaries are provided for reference only—at this point, don't try to duplicate what you see in the figures. You will learn more about these windows as you proceed through the tutorials.

Data Window

The *Data window* (Figure GS-16) is active when you first start Minitab. It presents a view of the

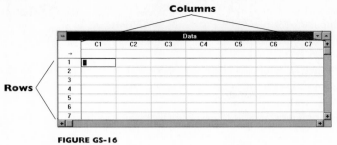

FIGURE GS-16

The Data window

worksheet columns and rows, providing a convenient way to name columns and enter, browse, and edit data.

Like a spreadsheet, a worksheet has *columns* and *rows*. However, unlike electronic spreadsheets such as Lotus 1-2-3 and Microsoft Excel, Minitab worksheets contain only numbers, not formulas. Minitab worksheets can also store single-number constants, but you can't see them in the Data window.

Generally, each column lists data for one variable and each row displays a set of observations for an individual case. The worksheet has 1000 columns and as many rows as your computer's available memory allows. However, the total number of rows times the number of columns must be

shown in Figure GS-16 are unnamed.) Rows are referred to by number: 1, 2, and so on.

A *cell* is the intersection of a column and a row. Notice that the cell in column C1, row 1, is highlighted, which indicates that it's the *current*, or *active* cell. You can activate any cell in the worksheet by clicking it. Minitab updates the Data window automatically whenever you make any changes to the worksheet.

Session Window

The *Session window* contains a record of your entire session. It logs the commands you use and the statistical output, except high-resolution graphs. Figure GS-17 shows a Session window with some

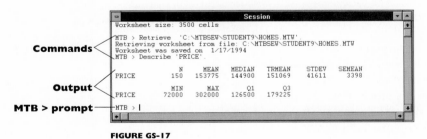

FIGURE GS-17

The Session window

less than 3500. Columns are referred to by column numbers (C1, C2, ..., C1000) or by names. Assigning names to the columns makes it easier to remember what they contain. (The columns in the worksheet

sample commands in it. (You'll learn how to produce these commands later.) Minitab also displays notes or error messages in the Session window. You can refer to the Session window to view numerical summaries, statistical analyses, and certain types of Minitab graphs.

Whenever you issue a command from a menu, its corresponding Session command appears in the Session window. You can also type Session commands directly into the Session window at the MTB > prompt (see Tutorial 2, "Summarizing, Transforming, and Manipulating Data").

History Window

The *History window* lists all the commands issued during a given session. Figure GS-18 depicts a History window with some sample commands. You can copy commands from the History window and paste them into the Session window to execute them again. Similarly, you can paste commands from the History window into a Windows word processor, such as Microsoft Word or Word-Perfect, to create a Minitab Exec macro.

FIGURE GS-18
The History window

Info Window

The *Info window* contains a summary of the columns and stored constants in the current active worksheet. It lists the names of all the columns that contain data, the number of present and missing values in each column, as well as the names, values, and locations of all stored constants. It also displays an A next to each alpha column. Figure GS-19 shows the Info window for a sample data set.

FIGURE GS-19
The Info window

The Info window is a convenient way to see the contents of your worksheet when you are performing a lengthy analysis on many columns. You'll find the information particularly meaningful if you name your columns. The Info window is automatically updated as you work in Minitab.

Graph Window

Graph windows display high-resolution graphs created with Minitab's Professional graph commands. Figure GS-20 shows a sample graph in the Graph window. Each graph you create displays in its own Graph window; up to 15 Graph windows can be open simultaneously. You can use standard Windows techniques to move among and resize these windows. You can also click the name of a Graph window at the bottom of the Window menu (discussed in the next section) to display it.

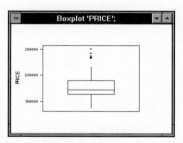

FIGURE GS-20
The Graph window

Help Window

The *Help window* (Figure GS-21) displays information about how to use Minitab. You can copy, paste, annotate, and print Help text using commands on the File and Edit menus.

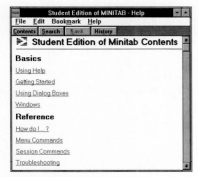

FIGURE GS-21

The Help window

Minitab Menus

This section itemizes the basic functions of each Minitab main menu. As you read about each menu, use the procedures described in Chapter 2, "Choosing Menu Commands," to open each menu and see the commands. Do not select any commands at this time. You'll learn more about the individual commands in the tutorials.

File Menu

The commands on the File menu let you:

- create, open, save, and revert to previous worksheets
- import and export text
- start or stop recording the contents of the Session window
- work with macro files
- save the contents of a window to a separate file

- set printer options
- print the contents of windows and text files
- display worksheet information and data
- restart or quit Minitab

Edit Menu

The commands on the Edit menu let you:

- undo the previous operation (you can undo most, but not all, operations)
- delete, copy, cut, paste, and select cells in a window
- return to the last dialog box that you edited
- save your preferences for window size, location, visibility, and operation

Manip Menu

The commands on the Manip menu let you:

- manipulate data
- sort and rank rows
- delete rows
- erase variables
- copy columns
- code data values
- stack, unstack, convert, and concatenate columns

Calc Menu

The commands on the Calc menu let you:

- generate and work with random numbers
- apply various functions to data
- obtain basic column and row statistics
- place repetitive data in a column

- create indicator, or dummy, variables

- standardize data

Stat Menu

The commands on the Stat menu let you:

- obtain basic descriptive and inferential statistics, linear regression, and ANOVA

- display control charts, Pareto charts, and cause-and-effect diagrams

- perform time series analyses, cross-tabulation, chi-square analysis, and various nonparametric tests

- fit with and without an intercept

Window Menu

The commands on the Window menu let you:

- rearrange the Minitab windows and icons

- work with Graph windows

- move among windows

Graph Menu

The commands on the Graph menu let you:

- display various graphs, including plots, charts, histograms, boxplots, and time series plots in high-resolution, customized form or as Character graphs

Editor Menu

The commands on the Editor menu let you:

- move around the Data window

- format columns and set column widths

- compress the display

- change the data entry direction

- insert cells and rows

- switch to cell edit mode

- change the Clipboard settings

Help Menu

The commands on the Help menu let you:

- access Minitab's online Help system by displaying the Contents, Getting Started, a list of common "How do I" questions, the Index, or the How to Use Help window

- see basic information about your version of Minitab

Exiting Minitab

To exit from Minitab:

- Click **File** on the Minitab menu bar

- Click **Exit**

    Minitab returns you to Program Manager.

CHAPTER
5

Sample Session

Objectives

In this sample session, you:

- open and explore an existing worksheet

- create a new variable by using basic arithmetic functions that operate on existing variables within a worksheet

- describe the characteristics of a variable by using basic statistics

- create two high-resolution graphs based on data in the worksheet

- correlate two variables in the worksheet

    Before beginning this session, make sure you:

- install Minitab on your computer's hard disk (refer to Chapter 3, "Installing Minitab," for instructions)

- format a Student disk for storing your work (refer to "Your Student Disk" in Chapter 3 for instructions)

CASE STUDY: EDUCATION—FACULTY SURVEY

As president of the student government at your school, you have just received the results of a faculty survey conducted by the student government. You want to prepare an article for the student government newsletter that describes some high points of the survey results. You decide to use Minitab to perform your preliminary analysis. (The data set used in this case study reflects the actual results of a recent survey at a U.S. university.)

Exploring an Existing Worksheet

Now you'll explore an existing worksheet named PROF.MTW. To open the file that contains the survey data:

- Be sure your computer is on, Windows is started, and Program Manager is displayed

- Double-click the **MINITAB Student** group icon to open the MINITAB Student group window

- Double-click the **MINITAB Student Edition** program-item icon in the MINITAB Student group window

    After a moment, the Minitab welcome screen appears. Click it to immediately open the

Student Edition of MINITAB window or wait until Minitab does so automatically (Figure GS-22).

■ Once the Data window appears, click **File** on the Minitab menu bar

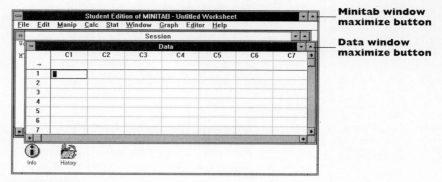

Minitab window maximize button

Data window maximize button

FIGURE GS-22
The Minitab window

■ Click the maximize button ▲ in the upper right corner of the Student Edition of MINITAB window so it fills the screen

Note: From now on, we will refer to the Student Edition of MINITAB simply as Minitab.

■ Click the maximize button ▲ in the upper right corner of the Data window so it fills the Minitab window

■ Click **Open Worksheet**

The Open Worksheet dialog box appears.

■ Click the **Select File** button

■ Scroll through the **Files** list box on the left-hand side of the dialog box to find PROF.MTW

■ Double-click **PROF.MTW**

The Data window should now look like Figure GS-23. Minitab displays the survey data in

FIGURE GS-23
PROF.MTW worksheet

the Data window; the name in the title bar is PROF.MTW.

The student government randomly distributed surveys to students in 146 class sections in a variety of disciplines. The survey asked students to evaluate both the course and the instructor. Each participating section received 15 surveys. Some sections returned all 15 surveys while others returned fewer. The results for each section were averaged for use in this worksheet. The worksheet consists of 9 columns and 146 rows. Each row summarizes the answers on the 1 to 15 surveys returned from a particular class.

The nine columns in the PROF.MTW worksheet present the following information:

Number	Name	Description
C1-A	DEPT	The academic department of the course to which the 15 surveys were distributed. The A following the column number C1 denotes a column that contains *alpha* (meaning alphabetic, as opposed to numeric) data.
C2	NUMBER	The course number.
C3	INTEREST	The section average of the surveyed students' responses to the statement: *The course stimulated your interest in this area.* The scale for this statement is: 0 = strongly disagree; 1 = disagree; 2 = neutral; 3 = agree; and 4 = strongly agree.
C4	MANNER	The section average of the surveyed students' responses to the statement: *The instructor presented course material in an effective manner.* The scale for this statement is: 0 = strongly disagree; 1 = disagree; 2 = neutral; 3 = agree; and 4 = strongly agree.
C5	COURSE	The section average of the surveyed students' responses to the statement: *Overall, I would rate this course as....* The scale for this statement is: 0 = poor; 1 = below average; 2 = average; 3 = above average; and 4 = excellent.
C6	INSTRUCR	The section average of the surveyed students' responses to the statement: *Overall, I would rate this instructor as....* The scale for this statement is: 0 = poor; 1 = below average; 2 = average; 3 = above average; and 4 = excellent
C7	RESPONDS	The number of completed surveys returned out of the 15 surveys distributed to the section.
C8	SIZE	The number of students in the section.
C9	YEAR	The level of the course: 1 = first year; 2 = sophomore; 3 = junior; and 4 = senior.

To display the Info window:

- Click **Window** on the Minitab menu bar

- Click **Info**

The Info window (Figure GS-24) is displayed in front of the Data window.

In your article, you want to report the percentage of students within a given class that completed the survey. To find this percentage, use the equation:

% of responses in the section = (number of responses in the section/number of students in the section) × 100

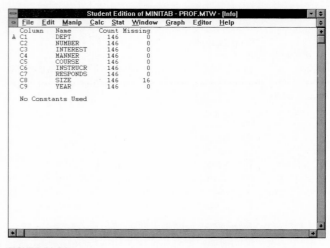

FIGURE GS-24

The Info window

The Info window summarizes the worksheet contents; Minitab updates it automatically as the worksheet changes. The Info window for this worksheet lists the nine variables in the worksheet, the name of each variable, the number of cells in each column (146), and the number of missing cells in each column. The number that appears in the Missing column for variable C8, for example, indicates that the size of 16 of the classes surveyed was unavailable or missing.

Minimize the Info window:

- Click the Info window Control menu box (the bottom of the two)

- Click **Minimize**

Minitab returns you to the Data window.

- Click the Data window maximize button ▲

The numerator in the fraction corresponds to variable C7 (RESPONDS) in the worksheet, and the denominator to variable C8 (SIZE). You store the results in C10 (PERCENT). Using the variables in the worksheet the equation becomes:

C10 = (C7/C8) × 100 (or C7/C8 * 100, in Minitab's language)

To perform these calculations using the menu:

- Click **Calc** on the Minitab menu bar

- Click **Mathematical Expressions**

The Mathematical Expressions dialog box (Figure GS-25) appears.

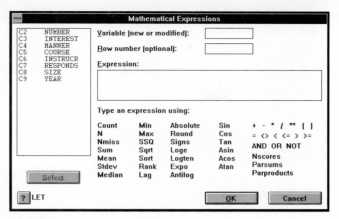

FIGURE GS-25

The Mathematical Expressions dialog box

The blinking I-bar in the Variable (new or modified) text box indicates that it's active.

■ Type **PERCENT**

■ Press Tab twice

The I-bar moves to the **Expression** text box.

■ Type **C7/C8*100**

■ Press ←Enter

The dialog box closes and the Data window becomes visible again. The tenth column in the worksheet (you may have to scroll to see it) now shows the percent of students in each section who completed surveys, and is properly labeled (Figure GS-26).

	C4	C5	C6	C7	C8	C9	C10	C1
→	MANNER	COURSE	INSTRUCR	RESPONDS	SIZE	YEAR	PERCENT	
1	2.67	2.27	2.73	15	41	2	36.585	
2	3.07	2.75	3.38	15	41	2	36.585	
3	3.36	3.00	3.45	11	31	3	35.484	
4	3.67	3.42	3.67	12	36	3	33.333	
5	3.50	3.13	3.13	8	52	1	15.385	
6	3.12	3.35	3.41	15	15	4	100.000	
7	1.73	2.33	2.00	15	22	1	68.182	
8	3.42	3.08	3.17	12	21	1	57.143	
9	2.00	2.67	2.33	6	15	2	40.000	
10	3.90	3.50	3.70	10	15	4	66.667	
11	2.64	2.79	3.00	14	49	1	28.571	
12	3.09	2.83	3.17	12	46	2	26.087	
13	2.78	2.00	2.78	9	68	1	13.235	
14	3.42	2.75	3.17	12	114	1	10.526	
15	0.92	1.46	1.46	13	64	1	20.313	
16	3.64	3.36	3.64	14	44	1	31.818	
17	3.83	3.83	3.83	6	16	2	37.500	
18	3.73	3.20	3.67	15	27	2	55.556	
19	3.00	3.00	3.20	10	29	3	34.483	

FIGURE GS-26

The Data window with C10 labeled PERCENT

If you scroll through the data in C10, you see that 100.00% of two classes was surveyed, but the percent surveyed in others was as low as 6.429%. Is this the maximum and minimum? What is the average percent surveyed? Can you summarize the results? Investigate the percent variable further to learn more about its characteristics.

Describing a Variable Using Basic Statistics

To find out more about the average percentage of the section that filled out questionnaires, you decide to obtain some basic statistics for the C10 variable you just created.

- Click **Stat** on the menu bar

- Click **Basic Statistics** to display the Basic Statistics submenu

- Click **Descriptive Statistics**

The Descriptive Statistics dialog box (Figure GS-27) appears.

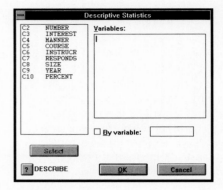

FIGURE GS-27

The Descriptive Statistics dialog box

- Double-click **C10 PERCENT** in the list box on the left

    The variable name now appears in the **Variables** box.

- Click the **OK** button

    The Session window (Figure GS-28) moves to the forefront.

```
Worksheet size: 3500 cells
MTB > Retrieve   'C:\MTBSEW\STUDENT9\PROF.MTW'.
Retrieving worksheet from file: C:\MTBSEW\STUDENT9\PROF.MTW
Worksheet was saved on 10/20/1991
MTB > Name c10 = 'PERCENT'
MTB > Let 'PERCENT' = C7/C8*100
MTB > Describe 'PERCENT'.

                 N       N*      MEAN    MEDIAN    TRMEAN    STDEV    SEMEAN
PERCENT        130       16     42.06     39.21     41.23    19.15      1.68

               MIN      MAX        Q1        Q3
PERCENT       6.43   100.00     28.50     54.66

MTB >
```

FIGURE GS-28

The Session window

The upper part of the Session window displays the commands you've used and the results of your actions. The lower part contains 11 statistics related to the C10 variable, including the mean, median, and standard deviation.

The output shown in the Session window tells you that an average of approximately 42% (MEAN = 42.06) of the students were surveyed in each class. There was a fair amount of variability, as indicated by a standard deviation of 19.15% (STDEV = 19.15). For example, in some classes, only 6.4% (MIN = 6.43) of the class was surveyed—probably a large class—while in others, 100% (MAX = 100.00) of the class provided information. You will learn more about these and other statistics in the tutorials.

Creating Graphs

As a senior looking back over your college career, it seems like your classes this year are much more interesting than the ones you took during your first year. You wonder if this holds true for other students. To find out, you decide to see if there's any relationship between the level of a course and the students' interest in it. You create a boxplot display to examine this information:

■ Choose **Graph > Boxplot**

The Boxplot dialog box (Figure GS-29) appears.

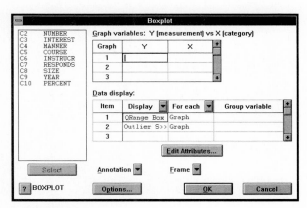

FIGURE GS-29

The Boxplot dialog box

■ Double-click **C3 INTEREST** in the list box on the left

The variable name, INTEREST, appears in the Y box, and the I-bar moves to the X box.

■ Double-click **C9 YEAR**

■ Click **OK**

Minitab displays four boxplots (Figure GS-30) that portray the trend in students' interest as they progress through college.

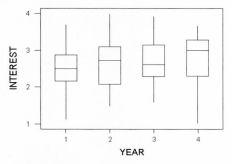

FIGURE GS-30

Boxplots, showing student interest by class

The horizontal line that breaks each box in two represents the median interest level for each rating. The graph indicates that senior and sophomore classes are more interesting than freshman and junior classes. The ends of the "whiskers" that extend up and down from the boxes represent the largest and smallest values. Note the extensive range of interest ratings for each level. Due to the large variability in student interest, you wouldn't want to claim that seniors are more interested than first year students in their classes.

You also wonder whether students who dislike the subject matter of a course rate their instructors lower. You use a scatter plot to show the relationship between course and instructor ratings.

■ Choose **Graph Plot**

The Plot dialog box (Figure GS-31) appears.

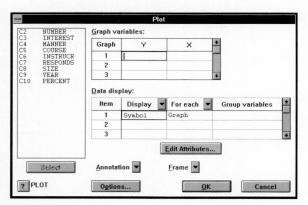

FIGURE GS-31

The Plot dialog box

■ Double-click **C6 INSTRUCR**

The variable name, INSTRUCR, appears in the Y text box.

■ Double-click **C5 COURSE**

That variable name appears in the X text box.

■ Click **OK**

Minitab displays a scatter plot (Figure GS-32) that depicts the relationship between course and instructor ratings. The boxplot you created still exists in its own window, which is hidden behind the Plot window.

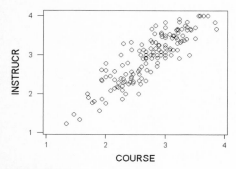

FIGURE GS-32

Scatter plot

Your suspicions are confirmed. In general, students rate instructors relatively lower in courses they don't like than in those they do. However, regardless of course rating, there is quite a bit of variation in professor ratings. For example, students who rated the course 3.00 (a high rating) rated the instructor from approximately 2.8 to 3.8. Again, the data are highly variable.

Correlating Two Variables

To verify the apparent linear relationship between course and instructor ratings, you decide to correlate the variables you used to create the scatter plot.

■ Choose **Stat > Basic Statistics > Correlation**

The Correlation dialog box (Figure GS-33) appears.

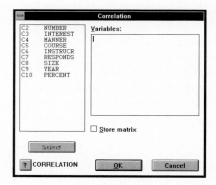

FIGURE GS-33

The Correlation dialog box

■ Double-click **C5 COURSE**

■ Double-click **C6 INSTRUCR**

■ Click **OK**

The Session window (Figure GS-34) moves to the front and displays the correlation between the COURSE and INSTRUCR variables.

```
MTB > Boxplot 'INTEREST'*'YEAR';
SUBC>    Box;
SUBC>    Symbol;
SUBC>      Outlier.
MTB > Plot 'INSTRUCR'*'COURSE';
SUBC>    Symbol.
MTB > Correlation 'COURSE' 'INSTRUCR'.

Correlation of COURSE and INSTRUCR = 0.873
```

FIGURE GS-34

The Session window

The correlation value of 0.873 indicates that there is indeed a strong positive and linear relationship between course and instructor ratings.

Printing a Graph

You want to use the scatter plot in your article, so you need to print it. You can use the Window menu, which lists the names of all the open windows in an application, to redisplay the scatter plot graph:

■ Make sure your printer is turned on

■ Choose **Window > Plot 'INSTRUCR'*'COURSE';**

The Graph window that contains the scatter plot becomes active.

■ Choose **File > Print Window**

The Microsoft Windows Print dialog box appears.

■ Click **OK** to print the plot on the printer shown at the top of the dialog box.

Note: If you are using a school computer and the printer isn't directly attached to it, ask your instructor or technical resource person for the location of the printer.

You now have a copy of the graph that you can include in your article to show the relationship between course and instructor ratings. You could use the Windows Copy and Paste commands to insert the graph directly into your word processor.

Exiting Minitab

Exit Minitab:

■ Choose **File > Exit**

A dialog box (Figure GS-35) appears, asking if you want to save the changes made to this worksheet.

FIGURE GS-35

There is no need to save this file.

■ Click **No**

You have seen some of Minitab's potential. Now proceed to the tutorials, where you'll get hands-on experience using Minitab to create your own worksheets and graphs. You may also refer to Part IV of this book, Reference, which documents all of Minitab's capabilities.

PART II
TUTORIALS

TUTORIAL 1

Working with Data

In each of the sixteen tutorials in *The Student Edition of MINITAB for Windows*, you solve typical statistical problems from such diverse fields as business, psychology, education, engineering, health care, and science. Tutorial 1 introduces the fundamentals of working with Minitab, including various ways of collecting and organizing data — the initial step in solving any statistical problem. You learn how to work with data and navigate through Minitab by exploring three different scenarios.

Objectives

In this tutorial, you learn how to:

- enter and manipulate data in the Data window

- save and open Minitab data files

- use Minitab's Help system to find online information about a topic

CASE STUDY: HEALTH MANAGEMENT — NUTRITION ANALYSIS

You have just been hired as a nutritionist for a major hospital. You are responsible for planning healthy, economical meals. The first day, your supervisor, Patricia Johnson, assigns you the task of planning a meal that includes yogurt. She furnishes you with data collected by a research company that tested 14 brands of plain yogurt. The tests evaluated overall nutritional quality, cost per ounce, and the number of calories per serving. In the past, there have been many complaints about the hospital's food. By statistically analyzing the various brands, you hope to improve the caliber of the food service while staying within a tight budget.

In this tutorial, you begin the statistical analysis by entering the data shown in Figure 1-1 into Minitab. You then compute other factors using the cost and calorie variables. In a later tutorial, when you are more familiar with Minitab, you perform more sophisticated analyses to help determine which brand of yogurt to recommend to Ms. Johnson.

FIGURE 1-1

Yogurt data

Row (brand)	Rating	Cost per ounce (cents)	Calories per 8 oz. serving
1	EXCELLENT	11	120
2	EXCELLENT	11	120
3	VERY GOOD	9	100
4	GOOD	9	90
5	POOR	12	253
6	GOOD	8	250
7	VERY GOOD	9	100
8	EXCELLENT	7	100
9	GOOD	11	240
10	FAIR	11	240
11	FAIR	9	190
12	FAIR	7	190
13	POOR	7	240
14	GOOD	10	160

Starting Minitab

You will perform most of your work in Minitab in two windows: the Data window, which provides for easy data entry, and the Session window, in which you conduct statistical analysis.

To start Minitab:

■ Start Windows and open the Program Manager window, if necessary

■ Double-click the **MINITAB Student** group icon to open the Minitab group window

■ Double-click the **MINITAB Student Edition** program-item icon

When you start Minitab, the Minitab window opens, with the Data window open within it. The Session window appears behind the Data window, as shown in Figure 1-2. The other available windows (Info and History) are reduced to icons at the bottom of the Minitab window.

FIGURE 1-2

The Minitab window

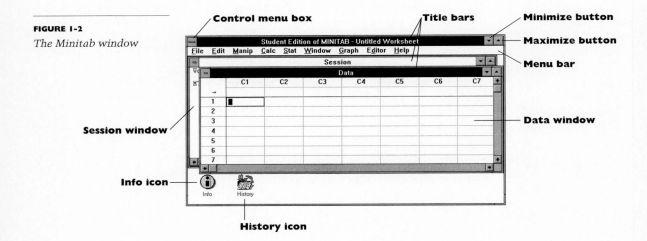

Note: See Chapter 4 of Getting Started for information about starting Minitab and the different Minitab windows.

The title bar of each window displays its name. The *Control menu box*, which you learned about in Chapter 2 of Getting Started, appears to the left of each window's title bar. The Control menu lets you manage window size and placement. To the right of each title bar is the *minimize button* , which you use to reduce the window to an icon on the desktop. The *maximize button* , which you use to enlarge the window to its maximum size, is next to the minimize button.

Generally, you'll find it helpful to maximize the Minitab window to view as much data as possible on the screen.

To maximize the Minitab window:

■ Click the Student Edition of MINITAB window's maximize button

The Minitab window now fills your screen. The maximize button turns into a *restore button*  with a double-headed arrow. You click the restore button to return the window to its previous size.

The horizontal bar across the top of the screen is the *menu bar*. It contains the names of Minitab's nine *menus*: File, Edit, Manip, Calc, Stat, Window, Graph, Editor, and Help. These menus list groups of Minitab *commands*, which are the actions you perform to accomplish a task in Minitab. The menus organize the Minitab commands by function; each menu's name reflects the type of commands it includes. The Window menu, for example, contains commands you use to manipulate and move among windows.

You will enter the yogurt data in the Data window. If the Data window isn't already in the foreground (it is possible to change the settings so that it doesn't open automatically), you can activate it by using one of the commands on the Window menu:

■ Click **Window** on the menu bar to open the Window menu (Figure 1-3)

FIGURE 1-3

The Window menu with Data selected

■ Click **Data** on the Window menu

The Data window is open and in front, if it wasn't already.

Viewing the Data Window

Notice that each open window has its own minimize and maximize buttons, just like the main Minitab window: You use these buttons to size windows within windows. Maximize the Data window so you can see as many rows and columns as possible:

■ Click the maximize button on the Data window

The Data window fills the Minitab window, as shown in Figure 1-4.

FIGURE 1-4

The Data window

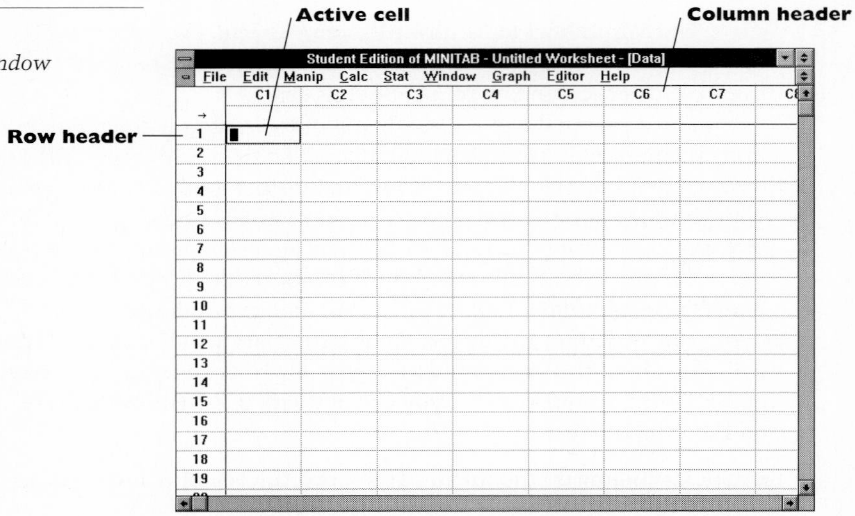

Active cell   **Column header**

Row header

Note: Your screen may show fewer or more rows and columns, depending on your monitor.

The grid, or *worksheet,* you see consists of rows and columns. The intersection of a row and a column is called a *cell.* Each cell is identified by its column (C1, C2, C3...) and its row (1, 2, 3...). For example, the cell in the upper-left corner of the worksheet corresponds to column 1, row 1; its *cell address* is C1, row 1.

Only one cell in the Data window is active at a given time. When you first start Minitab and open the Data window, the *active* cell is C1 row 1. The active cell appears *highlighted* — that is, shaded or with a thick border, depending on your monitor. Minitab enters the information you type at the keyboard in the active cell.

If C1 row 1 is not the active cell:

■ Click C1 row 1 to make it active

▼

Moving Around
the Data
Worksheet

▲

You can easily make a different cell active in the worksheet by using either the keyboard or the mouse.

■ Press ⏎Enter

This action highlights C2 row 1. Now change the active cell:

■ Press and hold ⬇ until you reach row 10

The active cell is now C2 row 10. You can also click a cell to make it active.

In Minitab, you can see only a certain number of columns and rows at a time. The number you see depends on the size of your screen. The Data window in *The Student Edition of MINITAB for Windows* actually has 1000 columns. To see additional columns:

■ Click the right scroll arrow and hold down the mouse button

The window scrolls horizontally to reveal more columns; it continues until you release the mouse button. To scroll downwards in the worksheet:

■ Click the down scroll arrow and hold down the mouse button

The window scrolls down to show additional rows. To return to the beginning of the worksheet:

■ Press Ctrl+Home (press both keys at once)

You move directly to C1 row 1; Minitab highlights the cell.

Using the Go To Command

You can also move around the Data window using the commands on the Editor menu.

■ Click **Editor** to open the Editor menu

The first command, Next Row, moves you to the next row in the worksheet. The Go To command moves you to any cell you specify. Try using Go To to make C30 row 40 the active cell:

■ Click **Go To**

Whenever Minitab requires additional information from you, it displays a *dialog box*. You provide information by filling in text boxes, clicking option buttons, and selecting or clearing check boxes (see Chapter 2 of Getting Started for more information about using dialog boxes).

The Go To dialog box, shown in Figure 1-5, displays the column and row numbers of the active cell, in this case C1 row 1.

FIGURE 1-5

The Go To dialog box

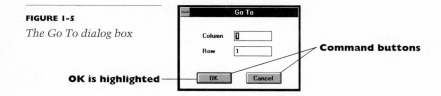

The 1 in the Column text box is highlighted; whatever you type will be entered in this box.

■ Type **30**

In the tutorials, any text you should type appears in boldface, like **30**. Highlight the Row text box and enter data in it:

■ Press [Tab]

■ Type **40** in the **Row** text box

Now that you've entered the desired cell location, you're ready to tell Minitab to carry out the command. Notice that there are two command buttons in this dialog box: OK and Cancel. Clicking OK tells Minitab to carry out the command; clicking Cancel closes the dialog box without performing the action.

The OK button has a thick border to indicate that it's highlighted. Whenever a command button is highlighted, pressing [←Enter] has the same effect as clicking the button with the mouse.

■ Press [←Enter] to accept the information in the dialog box

Minitab moves to C30 row 40.

The tutorial directions may tell you to press [←Enter] or to click OK to carry out a command, depending on which is more convenient. If you're using the keyboard to complete the dialog box, the directions tell you to press [←Enter]; if you're using the mouse to select options, the directions tell you to click OK.

▼ Pressing Key Combinations ▲

You can also use a keyboard shortcut to activate a different cell:

■ Click **Editor** to open the Editor menu

Next to certain commands, you see a *key combination* you can use to execute the command without opening a menu. You simply press both keys at the same time to bypass the menu and choose the command. As shown in Figure 1-6, the key combination for the Go To command is [Ctrl]+**G**.

FIGURE 1-6
The Editor menu

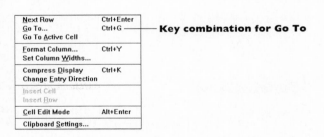

Key combination for Go To

Use this key combination to return to C1 row 1:

■ Press [Esc] twice, first to close the Editor menu and then to return to the Data window

■ Press and hold down the [Ctrl] button, and then press **G**

Minitab displays the Go To dialog box.

- Type **1** (for C1) in the **Column** text box

- Press [Tab] to move to the **Row** text box

- Type **1** (for row 1)

- Press [←Enter] to move to C1 row 1

  You return to the first cell in the worksheet.

Entering Data

You are now ready to enter the yogurt data from Figure 1-1 into the Data window. Each row will contain data from one individual case — in this example, a certain brand of yogurt. Each column will record a different variable: you enter the yogurt's nutritional rating in C1, the cost per ounce of yogurt in C2, and the calories per serving in C3.

- Type the first rating, **EXCELLENT**, in C1 row 1

  If you make a mistake, press the Backspace key to delete a character.
  In a moment, you press [Tab] to accept the data you just entered. When you do so, the cursor moves one cell either to the right or down, depending on the direction of the *data-entry arrow* in the upper left corner of the Data window. To change the direction of the data-entry arrow:

- Click the data-entry arrow

  The direction of the data-entry arrow changes. Change it back so that it's horizontal:

- Click the data-entry arrow again

  Enter the yogurt data row-by-row:

- Make sure the data-entry arrow is pointing to the right; if not, click it

- Press [Tab] to accept the entry you already typed and activate the cell to the right

  Notice that column C1 widens automatically to accommodate the entire entry. Enter the rest of the data for the first yogurt brand, as it appears in Figure 1-1.

- Type **11** and press [Tab]

Note: If you are using the numeric keypad to enter numbers, be sure to press the [Num Lock] key (the NUM LOCK light is lit on your keyboard) so that the keys enter numbers instead of moving the active cell.

- Type **120**

  Now you are ready to enter the second-row data. You can move to the beginning of the next row by pressing a key combination. You already know that you can press ⌨Tab (or ⌨←Enter) to move to the next cell; similarly, you move to the beginning of the next row or column (depending on the direction of the data-entry arrow) by pressing ⌨Ctrl and ⌨←Enter at the same time.

- Hold down ⌨Ctrl while you press ⌨←Enter to move to the beginning of the second row

    From now on, directions in this manual will indicate key combinations as two keys joined by a plus (+) sign, such as ⌨Ctrl+⌨←Enter.

    Enter the next row of data.

- Type **EXCELLENT** and then press ⌨Tab

- Continue in this manner until you have entered all 14 rows of data shown in Figure 1-1 into the Data window

- When you are ready to enter the last value, 160, into C3 row 14, deliberately make a mistake so you can see how to correct it: type **660**, and then press ⌨←Enter to accept it

▼
Correcting Mistakes
▲

If you discover a typographical error after you enter data in a cell, you can easily fix it. Because you just typed 660, instead of 160, in C3 row 14, you need to correct this entry.

- Click cell C3 row 14 to make it active

    Notice that when you click the cell, Minitab highlights the entire entry. If you type a new value and then press ⌨←Enter, it replaces the original entry. You can also edit individual characters in the cell without retyping the entire entry.

- Double-click the active cell (quickly click the mouse button two times)

    When you double-click the cell, the highlight disappears and a vertical bar, or *insertion point*, appears. If you type new characters, Minitab inserts them at the location of the insertion point; any characters to the right of the insertion point move further to the right. To delete characters:

- Press ⌨Alt+⌨← (the arrow key, not the backspace key) to move the insertion point to the right of the mistake, press Backspace, and then type the correct entry

- Press ⌨←Enter to accept the corrected entry

    You can also use the Delete key to delete characters to the right of the cursor.

▼
Identifying Alpha Data
▲

Notice that C1 contains words, called *alpha data*, whereas C2 and C3 contain numbers. When you start typing in a column, Minitab classifies a column as alpha if it detects alphabetic characters. Minitab also marks the column with an A suffix. The first column heading in the Data window is now C1-A, not C1.

Note: Once a column is designated as numeric, you cannot enter alpha data in it unless you erase the variable. This technique is discussed later in this tutorial.

Naming Columns

You'll find it easier to work with data if you assign a meaningful name to each column in your worksheet. Column or variable names may contain up to eight characters. When you name a column, avoid using an apostrophe or a pound sign (' or #). Also, for now, do not include spaces in variable names. Minitab displays column names in the *name row* below the column labels (C1, C2, C3, and so on). To name C1:

- Click the first cell in the name row (the cell between the C1-A label and the first entry in the column) to highlight it

- Type **RATING** as the name for C1

- Press ⏎Enter to accept the entry and move to the name cell for C2

- Type **CENTS** as the name for C2, press ⏎Enter, and then type **CALS** as the name for C3

- Press ⏎Enter

Note: This book presents data you should type in upper case. However, you can enter it in any mixture of upper- and lower-case letters.

Your Data window should now look like Figure 1-7.

FIGURE 1-7

Yogurt data with columns named

	C1-A	C2	C3	C4	C5	C6	C7	
→	RATING	CENTS	CALS					
1	EXCELLENT	11	120					
2	EXCELLENT	11	120					
3	VERY GOOD	9	100					
4	GOOD	9	90					
5	POOR	12	253					
6	GOOD	8	250					
7	VERY GOOD	9	100					
8	EXCELLENT	7	100					
9	GOOD	11	240					
10	FAIR	11	240					
11	FAIR	9	190					
12	FAIR	7	190					
13	POOR	7	240					
14	GOOD	10	160					
15								
16								
17								
18								
19								

Student Edition of MINITAB - Untitled Worksheet - [Data]

File Edit Manip Calc Stat Window Graph Editor Help

Saving Data

Unsaved work exists only temporarily in the computer's memory until you save it to disk. It is good practice to save your work frequently to guard against losing it in the event of a power failure.

The instructions in this manual presume you save your files to a Student disk, which you created in Chapter 3 of Getting Started. If your disk is in a drive other than A or you are saving your work to a different location, substitute the correct specifications when you save your work. If you are using your own computer, you can save your work to your hard disk.

This manual also uses a file-naming convention to help you remember which version of your work you are using at any given time. Each file you save on your Student disk has a prefix to indicate the tutorial number. For example, you will save the yogurt data you just entered as 1YOGURT. When you use this file again in Tutorial 5, you will save it with a new name, 5YOGURT, so you can easily distinguish which file you used in which tutorial.

To save your data:

■ Click **File** on the menu bar to open the File menu

■ Click **Save Worksheet As**

The Save Worksheet As dialog box gives you the option to save the worksheet in any one of several formats. To save the yogurt data as a Minitab worksheet:

■ Click the **Select File** button

A second Save Worksheet As dialog box appears, as shown in Figure 1-8.

FIGURE 1-8

Save Worksheet As dialog box

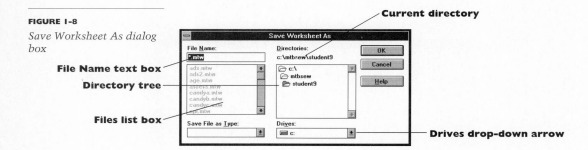

You specify a file name and location in the File Name text box and the Drives drop-down list box, respectively. (The Directories list box lets you specify a directory in which to save your file; because you are saving your work to your Student disk, you don't need to select a directory.)

Save the yogurt data to your Student disk:

■ Insert your Student disk into drive A (if that's the drive you plan to use)

■ Click the **Drives** drop-down arrow

■ Click **a:** in the list of drives that appears (if necessary, scroll to find **a:**)

Note: If your disk is in a different drive, click that drive instead.

- Double-click the **File Name** text box

- Type **1YOGURT**

    The Save Worksheet As dialog box should now look like Figure 1-9.

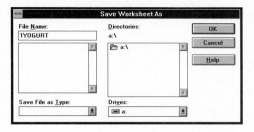

- Press ⏎Enter

Note: If an error message indicates that your disk is "write-protected," click OK to acknowledge the message and then remove the disk. On a 3½-inch disk, move the small tab in the disk's upper right corner so you can no longer see through the square hole. This unlocks the disk and lets you copy data to it. Then try saving your yogurt data once more.

Once you save your data, the Minitab window title bar changes from Untitled Worksheet to 1YOGURT.MTW, and tells you which window is currently open (in this case, the Data window).

When you save the 1YOGURT file, Minitab automatically adds an MTW *file extension.* This three-letter suffix indicates the file type, which makes it easier to find files.

As you will see in later tutorials, you can create and use files of various types for different purposes in Minitab. Not all applications use the same file types. For example, Minitab can read files with an MTW extension, but other software programs, such as text editors, cannot.

Note: When you work with your own data, you should always save your data before you restart or exit from Minitab, and before you open a new worksheet. To help you remember, Minitab prompts you to save your work when you perform these actions.

To exit from Minitab:

- Click **File** on the menu bar

- Click **Exit**

This is a good time to take a break. Your data are secure on your Student disk.

▼

Retrieving Data

▲

Your yogurt data are stored on your Student disk. To retrieve your data:

- Restart Minitab

- Maximize the Minitab window and the Data window

- Make sure your Student disk is in the disk drive

To select the Open Worksheet command from the File menu, you can use either the mouse or a keyboard shortcut. Notice that one letter in each menu name is underlined. By combining the Alt key with the underlined letter, such as Alt+**F** for File, you can open the corresponding menu.

To open your yogurt worksheet using the keyboard shortcut:

- Press Alt+**F**

- Press **O** for Open Worksheet (the underlined letter)

  The first Open Worksheet dialog box appears.

- Press ←Enter to confirm that you want to open a Minitab worksheet.

  The second Open Worksheet dialog box appears.

- Click the **Drives** drop-down arrow and then click **a:** (or the drive containing your Student disk)

- Double-click **1YOGURT.MTW** in the **File** list box just below the File Name text box.

  The Data window now displays the yogurt data you saved.

▼

Manipulating Data with the Mathematical Expressions Command

▲

In developing your yogurt budget, you must compute the total cost of feeding 200 patients. The Mathematical Expressions command lets you perform many mathematical operations on columns. Minitab uses the symbols +, =, *, /, and ** to add, subtract, multiply, divide, and raise to a power, respectively.

Note: In later tutorials, you use the Mathematical Expressions command to perform various algebraic and statistical operations.

The following steps show you how to multiply the cost per ounce by 200 using Minitab.

- Press Alt+**C** to open the Calc menu.

- Press **E** to choose the Mathematical Expressions command.

Note: For the remainder of this book, instructions to choose a command are abbreviated in the format *Choose **Calc** > **Mathematical Expressions***. Use whichever method you prefer to choose the command.

The Mathematical Expressions dialog box appears, similar to the one shown in Figure 1-10.

FIGURE 1-10

The Mathematical Expressions dialog box

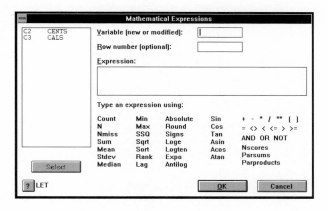

You want to compute the daily cost per ounce of serving each brand of yogurt to 200 patients and store the results in C4. First, name the new variable in the Variable text box:

■ Type **COST200** in the **Variable** text box

When you type in a name for a new variable, Minitab automatically assigns the entry you type as the name of the next available column (C4, in this example). If you include spaces or other special characters in a name, you must enter single quotes around the column name. For example, if you wanted to name the variable *COST 200* (with a space) you would type 'COST 200'. (Remember, you cannot use the characters ' or # in a variable name.)

To move the cursor to the Expression text box:

■ Press Tab twice

Note: Tab moves the cursor from one item to another in a dialog box. If you want to return to an item that appears above your present location, either press Tab until you return to it or press Shift + Tab to move the cursor backwards. If you are using a mouse, you can quickly move the cursor to any item by clicking it (depending on the item, this action may also select it).

Enter the formula in the Expression text box:

■ Type **C2*200** (remember, the asterisk is Minitab's symbol for multiplication)

■ Press ←Enter to create the new variable

This formula tells Minitab to multiply each of the values in C2 by 200.

The worksheet displays the results of the calculation in C4. Your original cost per ounce was in cents, so the cost to feed 200 patients also appears in cents. To convert this amount to dollars, divide each entry in C4 by 100:

- Choose **Calc > Mathematical Expressions**

- Type **DOL200** in the **Variable** text box

- Press $\boxed{\text{Tab}}$ twice

- Type **C4/100** in the **Expression** text box and then press $\boxed{\leftarrow\text{Enter}}$

The Data window now contains a new column that shows the cost in dollars of providing yogurt to 200 patients.

Getting Help

Next, you want to compute the cost of feeding yogurt to 250 patients and 300 patients. You may wonder if there's a way to calculate the cost and convert it into dollars in the same step. You can find an answer to this question using Minitab's online Help system, which you can access easily from almost any dialog box. Look at the Help topic associated with the Mathematical Expressions command:

- Choose **Calc > Mathematical Expressions**

- Click the question mark (?) in the lower left-hand corner of the dialog box

The Minitab Help window opens with an explanation of the Mathematical Expressions command displayed (Figure 1-11). (Your Help window may be a different size than the one shown; Chapter 2 of Getting Started describes how you can easily resize a window.)

FIGURE 1-11

The Mathematical Expressions Help window

Control menu box

Rules

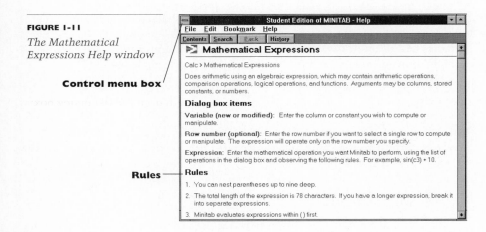

You can use the scroll bar or $\boxed{\downarrow}$ and $\boxed{\uparrow}$ on your keyboard to scroll through the information in the Help window. The information next to the heading

Expression says you can use a list of operations in the dialog box by observing the following rules.

■ Scroll down to the Rules section

Rule 2 indicates you can enter an expression of up to 78 characters; Rule 4 tells you that you can perform a combination of operations. You now have the answer to your question: you can multiply the cost by 250 and divide by 100 at the same time.

When you are done reading the information:

■ Double-click the Help window Control menu box to close the Help window

There are other ways to access online Help in Minitab. Instead of clicking the ? in the dialog box you can press F1 to display either a Help topic for the action you are currently performing or the Student Edition of MINITAB Contents screen (a table of contents for the Help window).

▼ Creating New Variables by Combining Operations ▲

Now you'll practice creating new variables by calculating the cost (in dollars) of feeding 250 patients and 300 patients in C6 and C7, respectively. But this time, you multiply the quantity and convert the amount to dollars in a single step. When you close Help, you should still be in the Mathematical Expressions dialog box.

■ Click the **Variable (new or modified)** text box, type **DOL250**, and then press Tab twice

■ Type **C2*250/100** in the **Expression** text box and then press ←Enter

To calculate the cost of feeding 300 patients, you need to change the 250 in the formula to 300. You can do this without retyping the entire expression:

■ Click **Edit** to open the Edit menu.

Notice the second-to-last command on the Edit menu, Edit Last Command Dialog. This command redisplays whichever dialog box you had open most recently. You can press the Ctrl+**E** key combination, which appears to the right, to issue this command without using the menu.

Close the Edit menu, and then use this shortcut to open the last dialog box:

■ Press Esc twice to close the Edit menu and return to the Data window

■ Press Ctrl+**E**

Minitab displays the last dialog box you opened, with your most recent entries.

To change DOL250 to DOL300, you can simply replace the last three characters:

■ Click to the right of the 0 in the current entry in the **Variable (new or modified)** text box

The arrow ⇞ turns into an *I-bar* I , indicating that you can enter text.

- Drag the I-bar to the left to highlight 250 and then release the mouse button

- Type **300**

    The entry in the Variable text box now reads DOL300. Now change the entry in the Expression text box to 300:

- Highlight 250 in the **Expression** text box in the same manner as before

- Type **300**

    The Expression now reads C2*300/100.

- Press [←Enter] to create the new variable, DOL300

    Your worksheet displays the costs of providing each brand of yogurt to 200, 250, and 300 patients.

    Many of the patients are on an 1800-calorie-per-day diet. For each brand, calculate how many calories remain for the day presuming a patient on such a diet consumes one serving of yogurt for breakfast.

- Press [Ctrl]+**E** to redisplay the Mathematical Expressions dialog box

- Type **CALLEFT** in the **Variable** text box and then press [Tab] twice

- Type **1800-C3** in the **Expression** text box and then press [←Enter]

Note: If your Data window isn't visible, you can choose Data from the Window menu.

C8 now lists the daily calories remaining after a patient has eaten an eight-ounce serving of each brand of plain yogurt. (You may have to scroll to see all the values in this column.) You can use this information to determine which brand gives you the most flexibility for planning patients' diets.

Copying Columns

Although you initially recorded the rating for each brand in C1, you'd like to repeat this information in C9 so it's still visible when you use columns farther to the right in the worksheet. You can use Minitab's online Help system to find out how to copy a column:

- Click **Help** on the menu bar to open the Help menu

- Click **Search for Help on**

    The Search window opens with the insertion point blinking in the first text box. The Search window is like an index: you can look up a keyword to help you locate the information you need. For example, you might try entering the word *Copy* as a keyword to find out more about duplicating a column.

- Type **COPY** in the text box

    As you type, the list box below the text box scrolls to show entries that begin with the letters you type. By the time you've typed the entire word, *Copy* appears highlighted in the list box, as shown in Figure 1-12.

FIGURE 1-12

The Search window

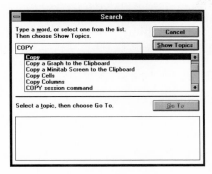

    There may be one or several topics associated with the keyword *Copy*. To see any associated topics:

- Click the **Show Topics** button

    The lower list box shows the topics associated with the word *copy*. Copy Columns seems like the topic you need:

- Click **Copy Columns** in the lower list box

- Click **Go To** to move to the appropriate Help topic

    The Minitab Help window opens to the Copy command (Figure 1-13).

FIGURE 1-13

Copy in the Minitab Help window

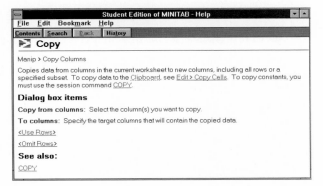

The Help topic describes the Copy Columns command on the Manip menu. Close the Help window when you finish reading the information:

- Double-click the Help window Control menu box to close the window and return to the Data Window.

Use Minitab's Copy Columns command to copy the data from C1 RATING to C9:

- Choose **Manip > Copy Columns** to open the Copy dialog box (Figure 1-14)

FIGURE 1-14

The Copy dialog box

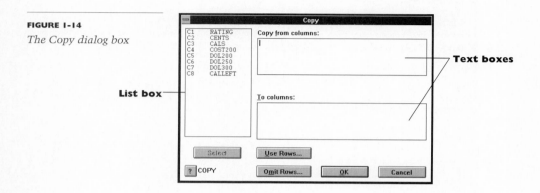

Like the Mathematical Expressions dialog box, the Copy dialog box indicates the available columns (variables) in the Data window in a list box on the left-hand side.

- Be sure the cursor is blinking in the Copy from columns text box; if not, click the text box.
- Double-click **C1 RATING** to enter it in the **Copy from columns** text box
- Press [Tab] to move to the **To columns** text box
- Type **COPY** as the column to which you want to copy and then press [←Enter]

Minitab copies the ratings into C9; the ratings now appear in both C1 and C9 (you may have to scroll to see both columns). This is a good time to save your work again.

▼

Updating an Existing File

▲

You already saved your data once by using the Save Worksheet As command. Now you want to replace that file with this updated one. You use the Save Worksheet command, not the Save Worksheet As command, to save a new version of an existing file. Unlike the Save Worksheet As command that lets you specify a filename and location, Save Worksheet automatically saves the file to the previous location under the same name. Save Worksheet provides the quickest way to update a file that already has a name.

- Choose **File > Save Worksheet** (or press the keyboard shortcut, Ctrl+**S**)

    Minitab saves the updated 1YOGURT.MTW file to your Student disk.
    Now that you've edited and manipulated some sample data, as well as used online Help, you may want to take a break before starting another case study. If so, exit Minitab:

- Choose **File > Exit**

    If, on the other hand, you want to begin the next case study right away:

- Choose **File > Restart Minitab** to clear the worksheet

CASE STUDY: MANAGEMENT — SALARY STRUCTURE

Technitron, a midsize corporation, recently hired you as a managerial consultant. Your task is to analyze the salary structure of the Sales Department and then eliminate any inequities. Brett Reid, one of your coworkers, has already gathered data on the Sales Department personnel and entered it in a Minitab file named PAY.MTW. (This file comes with *The Student Edition of MINITAB for Windows.*) Brett informs you that some employees have left Technitron since he entered the data; there are also some new employees whose records must be added.

Start by updating the information in the file:

Note: You'll work more with these data in Tutorial 3.

- Start Minitab and maximize both the Minitab and Data windows, if necessary
- Choose **File > Open Worksheet**
- Press ←Enter to open a Minitab worksheet

    The Open Worksheet dialog box usually opens by default with drive C selected. All the data sets that you need in the tutorials should be installed on this drive, so you should see a list of files similar to the one shown in Figure 1-15.

FIGURE 1-15

The Open Worksheet dialog box

Files list box →

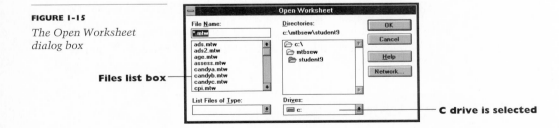

C drive is selected

Note: If you do not see these files in the list box, ask your instructor or technical resource person where on the computer the tutorial files are located.

- Scroll through the **Files** list box until you see **PAY.MTW**, and then double-click it

The worksheet shown in Figure 1-16 appears on your screen.

FIGURE 1-16

The sales department Data worksheet

	C1	C2	C3	C4	C5	C6	C7-A	C8
→	SALARY	YRS EM	PRIOR YR	EDUC	AGE	ID	GENDER	GENDE
1	38985	18	7	9	52	412	M	
2	28938	12	5	4	39	517	F	
3	32920	15	3	9	45	458	F	
4	29548	5	6	1	30	604	M	
5	31138	11	11	6	46	562	F	
6	24749	6	2	0	26	598	F	
7	41889	22	16	7	63	351	M	
8	31528	3	11	3	35	674	M	
9	38791	21	4	5	48	356	M	
10	39828	18	6	5	47	415	F	
11								

Student Edition of MINITAB - PAY.MTW - [Data]
File Edit Manip Calc Stat Window Graph Editor Help

Brett measured seven variables for each employee:

C1	Individual's annual salary
C2	Number of years at Technitron
C3	Years of experience prior to hiring by Technitron
C4	Years of post-secondary (after high school) education
C5	Age at last birthday
C6	Employee identification number
C7	Gender (because this is an alpha variable, it is left-justified)
C8	Gender in numeric format (1 for female; 0 for male)

▼

Deleting and Inserting Rows

▲

Start updating Brett's data by removing employee 562 (row 5), who has left Technitron:

- Click the row header for row 5 to highlight the entire row, as shown in Figure 1-17

FIGURE 1-17

*PAY.MTW with row 5
highlighted*

Row header ──

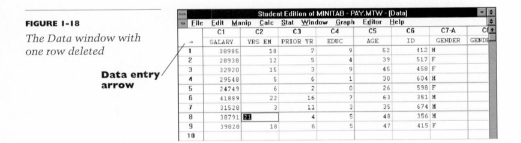

	C1	C2	C3	C4	C5	C6	C7-A	C8
→	SALARY	YRS EM	PRIOR YR	EDUC	AGE	ID	GENDER	GENDE
1	38985	18	7	9	52	412	M	
2	28938	12	5	4	39	517	F	
3	32920	15	3	9	45	458	F	
4	29548	5	6	1	30	604	M	
5	31138	11	11	6	46	562	F	
6	24749	6	2	0	26	598	F	
7	41889	22	16	7	63	351	M	
8	31528	3	11	3	35	674	M	
9	38791	21	4	5	48	356	M	
10	39828	18	6	5	47	415	F	
11								

■ Choose **Edit > Delete Cells** (or press the Del key)

Minitab moves rows 6 and beyond up one to fill in the gap left by the deleted row 5. There are now only nine employees in the worksheet.

If you were to hire a replacement, you might want to insert the new employee's data into the worksheet at a particular location. Try inserting a row above the current row, row 8.

■ Click any cell in row 8

■ Choose **Editor > Insert Row**

Minitab inserts a blank row in this position and moves all the rows below it down one. Minitab displays an asterisk (*) in each cell in row 8 to indicate that the information is missing. Delete the empty row:

■ Click the row header for row 8 and then choose **Edit > Delete Cells** (or press Del)

Your worksheet should now look like the one shown in Figure 1-18.

FIGURE 1-18

*The Data window with
one row deleted*

**Data entry
arrow**

	C1	C2	C3	C4	C5	C6	C7-A	C8
→	SALARY	YRS EM	PRIOR YR	EDUC	AGE	ID	GENDER	GENDE
1	38985	18	7	9	52	412	M	
2	28938	12	5	4	39	517	F	
3	32920	15	3	9	45	458	F	
4	29548	5	6	1	30	604	M	
5	24749	6	2	0	26	598	F	
6	41889	22	16	7	63	351	M	
7	31528	3	11	3	35	674	M	
8	38791	21	4	5	48	356	M	
9	39828	18	6	5	47	415	F	
10								

Brett tells you that the department is hiring two new employees. You want to enter the data for these employees in rows 10 and 11. When you enter the new data, remember that pressing ←Enter moves the cursor across the row if the data-entry arrow (in the upper left corner of the screen) points to the right.

■ Click the data-entry arrow so that it points to the right if necessary

The new employee in row 10, a 23-year-old female, earns a salary of $28,985. She has one year of prior experience and four years of post-secondary education. Her employee number is 693. As a new employee, she has 0 years at Technitron (the entry in C2 'YRS EM').

- Click C1 row 10 (the cell address for the first cell in row 10)

- Type the data in row 10, starting in C1 (press Tab between each value): **28985 0 1 4 23 693 F 1**

- Press Ctrl + ←Enter to accept the final value and move to the beginning of row 11

Note: If you notice a mistake after you press ←Enter, correct the cell entry using the techniques discussed in the section "Creating New Variables by Combining Operations."

You have much less information about the second new employee. He is male, his employee number is 694, and his salary is $32,782. Place an asterisk in each cell for which you're missing information.

- Type the second employee's data in row 11: **32782 0 * * * 694 M 0**

- Press Ctrl + ←Enter to move to the beginning of row 12

The Data window should now resemble Figure 1-19. Notice that an entry of 0 (zero) is different than the entry *, which indicates a missing value. Also note that you didn't — and shouldn't — enter commas or dollar signs.

FIGURE 1-19

The Data window with new employee information

	C1 SALARY	C2 YRS EM	C3 PRIOR YR	C4 EDUC	C5 AGE	C6 ID	C7-A GENDER	C8 GENDE
1	38985	18	7	9	52	412	M	
2	28938	12	5	4	39	517	F	
3	32920	15	3	9	45	458	F	
4	29548	5	6	1	30	604	M	
5	24749	6	2	0	26	598	F	
6	41889	22	16	7	63	351	M	
7	31528	3	11	3	35	674	M	
8	38791	21	4	5	48	356	M	
9	39828	18	6	5	47	415	F	
10	28985	0	1	4	23	693	F	
11	32782	0	*	*	*	694	M	
12								
13								

Student Edition of MINITAB - PAY.MTW - [Data]

File   Edit   Manip   Calc   Stat   Window   Graph   Editor   Help

Deleting Columns

Technitron recently enacted a new policy against recording age, so you need to delete the age variable.

- Choose **Manip > Erase Variables**

- Double-click **C5 AGE** in the list box to place it in the **Columns and constants** text box

- Click **OK**

C5 is now blank. Check to see that your Data window contains only the information shown in Figure 1-20.

FIGURE 1-20

The Data window without the AGE variable

	C1	C2	C3	C4	C5	C6	C7-A	C
	SALARY	YRS EM	PRIOR YR	EDUC		ID	GENDER	GENDE
1	38985	18	7	9		412	M	
2	28938	12	5	4		517	F	
3	32920	15	3	9		458	F	
4	29548	5	6	1		604	M	
5	24749	6	2	0		598	F	
6	41889	22	16	7		351	M	
7	31528	3	11	3		674	M	
8	38791	21	4	5		356	M	
9	39828	18	6	5		415	F	
10	28985	0	1	4		693	F	
11	32782	0	*	*		694	M	
12								
13								

Student Edition of MINITAB - PAY.MTW - [Data]
File Edit Manip Calc Stat Window Graph Editor Help

Copying Parts of a Column

Earlier in this tutorial, you copied a column in the yogurt worksheet. Now you learn to copy only *part* of a column.

One aspect of your salary structure investigation is examining the relationship between different variables, such as gender, and salary. To do this, you need to list the male and female salaries in separate columns. First, copy only the male employees' salaries from C1 into C9.

- Choose **Manip > Copy Columns**

Indicate the column from which you want to copy:

- Double-click **C1 SALARY** to enter it in the **Copy from columns** text box

- Click the **To columns** text box

- Type **'SAL MALE'** (you must include the quotes because you're including a space in the column name)

To select only the salaries of the male employees for this column:

- Click the **Use Rows** button

The Copy-Use Rows dialog box appears (Figure 1-21).

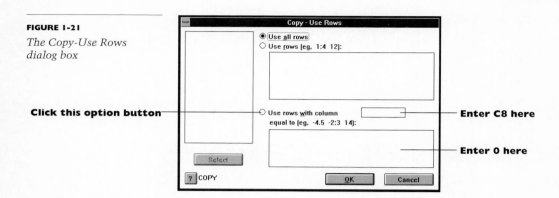

FIGURE 1-21

The Copy-Use Rows dialog box

Click this option button

Enter C8 here

Enter 0 here

- Click the **Use rows with column__ equal to** option button
- Click the text box to the right of the option button

   The list box on the left lists the column names of all the numeric variables. C7 GENDER doesn't appear because you can't use alpha data to designate which rows to use.

- Double-click **C8 GENDER N** as the column to use

   Now tell Minitab to copy only the salaries of male employees from C1. (Remember that a value of 0 corresponds to a male.) In the lower, unmarked text box:

- Type **0**

- Press ⬅Enter to return to the Copy dialog box, and then click **OK** to carry out the command

   The Data window now includes a list of male salaries in C9 (scroll to see it, if necessary).
   Repeat this procedure to place the salaries of female employees in C10. Name the column 'SAL FEM' and enter 1 in the text box in which you specify the values to use:

- Choose **Manip** > **Copy Columns**

   The Copy dialog box reflects your most recent selections.

- Double-click **MALE** in the **To columns** text box

- Type **FEM'** so that the **To column** reads 'SAL FEM' (be sure to include the quotation mark)

- Click **Use Rows** to open the Copy-Use Rows dialog box

- Double-click **0** in the unmarked text box on the lower right

- Type **1**

- Click **OK** twice to create the new variable

- Scroll to the right to view columns C9 and C10

You can now see the two subsets of the salary variable side by side (Figure 1-22).

		Student Edition of MINITAB - PAY.MTW - [Data]								
File	Edit	Manip	Calc	Stat	Window	Graph	Editor	Help		
	C7-A	C8	C9	C10	C11	C12	C13	C1		
→	GENDER	GENDER N	SAL MALE	SAL FEM						
1	M	0	38985	28938						
2	F	1	29548	32920						
3	F	1	41889	24749						
4	M	0	31528	39828						
5	F	1	38791	28985						
6	M	0	32782							
7	M	0								

It appears that salaries of males and females are similar. In a later tutorial, you will examine the salary structure in more depth, so save your data now.

Save your file on your Student disk:

- Choose **File > Save Worksheet As**

- Press (←Enter) to confirm that you want to save a Minitab worksheet

- Insert your Student disk in drive A (or a different drive, if appropriate)

- Click the **Drives** drop-down list arrow and then click **a:**

- Double-click the **File Name** text box and type **1PAY**

- Press (←Enter)

- Choose **File > Exit**

Congratulations. You have finished the first tutorial. Now that you have learned some of the skills you need to prepare data for analysis, you are ready to take a closer look at how Minitab operates. In the next tutorial you learn more ways to manipulate your data.

Minitab Command Summary

This section describes the menu commands and Session commands introduced in or related to this tutorial. For a complete explanation of all menus and commands, refer to the Reference section of this manual.

Minitab Menu Commands

Menu	Command	Description
File		
	Open Worksheet	Retrieves a previously saved worksheet
	Save Worksheet	Saves a copy of the current worksheet to a previously saved file
	Save Worksheet As	Saves a copy of the current worksheet to a file whose name you specify
	Exit	Exits from the Minitab application
Edit		
	Delete Cells	Deletes the selected cells and moves all the cells in each column up
	Edit Last Command Dialog	Recalls the last command dialog box that was open, retaining the previous information
Manip		
	Delete Rows	Deletes the specified row(s) in the worksheet in the specified columns
	Erase Variables	Erases or deletes a column(s) in the worksheet
	Copy Columns	Creates a duplicate of a column(s) or part(s) of a column(s)
Calc		
	Mathematical Expressions	Performs arithmetic using algebraic expressions, which may contain arithmetic operators, comparison operators, logical operators, and functions; arguments may be columns, constants, or numbers
	Functions	Performs various mathematical functions row-by-row on a column, constant, or number
	Column Statistics	Calculates various statistics for the selected column, displaying the results and, optionally, storing each result in a constant

Menu	Command	Description
	Row Statistics	Computes a value for each row in a set of columns
Window		
	Data	Displays the worksheet in a spreadsheet format
Editor		
	Go To	Activates a given cell in a worksheet
	Insert Cell	Inserts a cell in the position of the active cell and moves down all cells below it
	Insert Row	Inserts a row in the worksheet above the current one and moves down all the rows below it
Help		
	Contents	Displays contents of Help system
	Getting Started	Displays Getting Started screen, giving you access to Help on basic Minitab procedures
	How do I	Displays How do I screen, giving you access to a list of common questions and answers about using Minitab
	Search for Help on	Displays Search screen, which lets you search for help on a single word, like an index
	How to Use Help	Opens the Microsoft Windows How to Use Help system, which describes the basics of using Windows Help systems
	About Minitab	Displays basic information about the current release of Minitab

Minitab Session Command

NAME   Assigns names to columns and stored constants

Matching

Match the following terms to their definitions by placing the correct letter next to the term it describes.

_____ Session window

_____ Alpha data

_____ *

_____ 1000

_____ Data worksheet

_____ MTW

_____ Open Worksheet

_____ Variable

_____ Cell

_____ F1

a. A series of rows and columns in which Minitab displays data and information

b. The maximum number of columns in *The Student Edition of Minitab*

c. Minitab commands and output are displayed in this location

d. Minitab's default designation for a missing numeric value

e. The intersection of a row and column in a worksheet

f. The Minitab command to retrieve a previously saved worksheet

g. A file extension added to Minitab files you create with the Save Worksheet As command

h. A data type that contain characters other than numbers

i. Another name Minitab uses for a column of information or data in a worksheet

j. The key you press to open the Help window for the current dialog box

True/False

Mark the following statements with a *T* or an *F*.

_____ 1. You can assign a name to a column by typing the name in the Data worksheet.

_____ 2. The Insert Row command inserts an empty row immediately below the current one.

_____ 3. The Minitab symbol for multiplication is *x*.

_____ 4. You use the Copy command to copy any part of a row to another row.

_____ 5. You can edit Minitab worksheet files saved with the MTW extension with any popular word processor.

_____ 6. To save a worksheet to a floppy disk, select drive C.

_____ 7. You choose the Stop command on the File menu to exit Minitab.

_____ 8. The Minitab Help command is available on the File menu.

_____ 9. Column or variable names must be eight characters or less.

_____ 10. When entering data into the worksheet, pressing ⏎Enter always moves you to the next cell to the right in the same row.

Practice Problems

The practice problems instruct you to save your worksheets with a filename that begins with P followed by the tutorial number. In this tutorial, for example, you use P1 as the prefix.

1. The following data represent the total snowfall (in inches) for a large city on the East Coast for the 32 years between 1962 and 1993:

   38.6 42.4 57.5 40.5 51.7 67.1 33.4 60.9 64.1 40.1 40.7 6.4 42.5 41.4 45.4 46.2 89.2 19.5 18.7 31.9 49.7 29.8 44.1 27.2 20.7 52.1 39.8 22.5 29.7 23.6 26.5 85.2

   a. Enter the 32 years into C1 and name the column YEAR.

   b. Enter the snowfall data in C2 and name that column SNOW.

   c. Create a new column named RAINFALL that represents the equivalent rainfall (1" of rain equals approximately 10" of snow).

   d. Save your worksheet as P1SNOW on your Student disk.

2. The following table represents the TV viewing times (in hours) of ten married couples who volunteered to monitor their habits for several months:

Household	Husband	Wife
1	21	24
2	56	55
3	34	34
4	30	34
5	38	45
6	27	29
7	30	41
8	36	35
9	20	34
10	43	32

   a. Enter the data into C1 and C2 in a new worksheet; name the two columns HUSBAND and WIFE.

b. Compute the total viewing times for husbands and wives combined for the ten households and store these values in C3; name this column TOTAL.

c. Compute the difference in viewing times (C1-C2) for husbands and wives, store your results in C4, and name the column DIFF.

d. Save your worksheet as P1TVVIEW on your Student disk.

3. The following table summarizes the campus newspaper ratings for 13 pizza shops for two fall semesters:

Pizza shop	Current fall rating	Last fall rating
A	6.7	6.73
B	5.4	7.29
C	4.9	5.77
D	4.8	6.69
E	3.9	4.33
F	3.2	*
G	3.2	*
H	3.1	5.01
I	2.8	2.58
J	2.8	6.88
K	2.6	5.08
L	2.2	7.50
M	1.5	*

a. Enter these data into C1, C4, and C5 in a new worksheet, and name the columns PIZZERIA, FALLSCOR, and LFALL, respectively. The asterisks represent missing values.

b. Compute the sum of the two ratings for the 13 pizza shops and store these values in C7. What shop has the highest combined rating?

c. Compute the difference between the two ratings for each of the 13 pizza shops and store these values in C8. Which shop has the greatest difference in ratings?

d. How did the missing values affect your sum and difference computations?

e. Erase C7 and C8.

f. Save your worksheet as P1PIZZA on your Student disk.

4. Open the NOTE.MTW data set, which contains information about a selection of notebook (portable) computers on the market.

   a. Scroll through the worksheet to review the information about the notebook computers.

   b. Use the Go To command to activate the last cell in the last named column.

   c. Add the following information about a Zenith notebook computer to the worksheet in C1 through C8:

      SL 25 124 20 MONO TRACKBALL YES 2499

   d. Save the worksheet as P1NOTE.MTW on your Student disk.

TUTORIAL
2

Summarizing, Transforming, and Manipulating Data

Now that you know how to enter data in Minitab, you are ready to organize and manipulate it to perform various statistical analyses. In this tutorial, imagine that you are a new teacher using Minitab to summarize and study your class's grades.

Objectives

In this tutorial, you learn how to:

- work with data in the Session window
- summarize rows (individual cases) and columns (variables)
- combine and breakdown columns of data
- code, rank, and sort data
- standardize data from different variables in order to compare them
- view and print data

CASE STUDY: EDUCATION — CLASS EVALUATION

You have just completed your first marking period as a social studies teacher. You entered your students' grades for the first three tests into a Minitab worksheet. Your principal, Ms. Taylor, would like you to prepare a report about your students' progress.

Start Minitab and open the MARKS data:

- Start Minitab

- Maximize the Minitab window and the Data window

- Choose **File > Open Worksheet**

- Press (←Enter) to select a file

- Double-click **MARKS.MTW** in the **Files** list box (you may have to scroll to see it)

▼
**Computing the
Mean, Median,
and Round**
▲

You want to compute each student's average grade for the three exams. You could, of course, add each student's test grades in the third, fourth, and fifth columns of the appropriate row, divide by three using a calculator, and then enter the results in a column. Instead, you can use a single Minitab command to compute each student's average test score:

- Choose **Calc > Mathematical Expressions**

    The Mathematical Expressions dialog box appears.

- Type **AVERG** in the **Variable** text box and then press (Tab) twice

    Minitab assigns the name to the next available column, which in this case is C6. Tell Minitab to average the three test scores:

- Type **(C3+C4+C5)/3** in the **Expression** text box and press (←Enter) (be sure to include parentheses in this expression; otherwise, you'll get the wrong result)

    Minitab stores the results in C6.
    The Row Statistics command on the Calc menu provides an even easier way to calculate the mean (or other statistic) of some or all of the data in a particular row, and then save the results in a column. This command does it all for you—you don't even enter a formula. Try using the Row Statistics command:

- Choose **Calc > Row Statistics**

The Row Statistics dialog box appears (Figure 2-1).

Mean option button

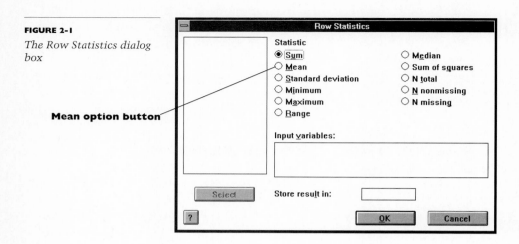

The Row Statistics dialog box provides options that compute common statistics for each row. To compute the mean of the three grades recorded for each student in C3, C4, and C5:

■ Click the **Mean** option button

■ Press Tab to move the cursor to the **Input variables** text box

You could type C3-C5 in this text box (a hyphen between columns designates a series of consecutive columns), or you could double-click each column individually in the list box on the left. On the other hand, you can use a shortcut to enter the three columns in the Input variables text box:

■ Click **C3 TEST1** in the list box on the left and hold down the mouse button while you drag the highlight through **C4 TEST2** and **C5 TEST3**

■ Click the **Select** button

The three columns now appear in the Input variables text box.

Dragging the highlight is usually the quickest way to select consecutive variables in a list box. Alternatively, you can click the first variable, hold down Shift, and then click the last variable to highlight all the variables in between. To select several nonconsecutive variables, hold down the Ctrl key while you click each one.

Tell Minitab where to display the resulting means:

- Press $\boxed{\text{Tab}}$ to move to the **Store result in** text box

- Type **RMEAN** (for row mean) and then press $\boxed{\leftarrow\text{Enter}}$

If you compare the entries in C6 and C7 (Figure 2-2), you can see that the two methods produce the same results. You now have a test average and mean for each student. Several students are performing extremely well (Jonathan Goldberg and Kathleen Sheppard, for example) while others (such as Jason Douglas and Mark McClure) may not be studying enough.

FIGURE 2-2

The Data window, showing the mean calculated two ways

	C1-A	C2-A	C3	C4	C5	C6	C7
→	LAST NAM	FIRST	TEST1	TEST2	TEST3	AVERG	RMEAN
1	ADAMS,	JAMES	72	93	93	86.0000	86.0000
2	BENSON,	MELISSA	99	86	83	89.3333	89.3333
3	BROWN,	LAMAR	59	59	90	69.3333	69.3333
4	DOUGHERTY,	MEGAN	79	69	60	69.3333	69.3333
5	DOUGLAS,	JASON	48	77	25	50.0000	50.0000
6	GIGLIOTTI,	ANDREW	78	94	50	74.0000	74.0000
7	GOLDBERG,	JONATHAN	98	98	94	96.6667	96.6667
8	GREEN,	JENNIFER	92	91	99	94.0000	94.0000
9	KENNEDY,	KEVIN	71	78	62	70.3333	70.3333
10	LEE,	SANG	64	68	97	76.3333	76.3333
11	MCCLURE,	MARK	49	79	43	57.0000	57.0000
12	MESSINA,	STEVEN	94	93	95	94.0000	94.0000
13	NORMAN,	BARBARA	99	95	84	92.6667	92.6667
14	NOWICKI,	AMY	91	81	79	83.6667	83.6667
15	PATEL,	HIMA	90	100	62	84.0000	84.0000
16	PIERSON,	RICHARD	100	77	100	92.3333	92.3333
17	ROJAS,	LUIS	73	79	83	78.3333	78.3333
18	RYAN,	MATT	77	79	85	80.3333	80.3333
19	SCHMIDT,	NANCY	83	79	52	71.3333	71.3333

For additional practice, use the Row Statistics command to compute the median of each row:

- Press $\boxed{\text{Ctrl}}$+**E** to issue the Edit Last Command Dialog command and reopen the Row Statistics dialog box (you learned this keyboard shortcut in Tutorial 1)

- Click the **Median** option button

    You want to use the same input variables.

- Press $\boxed{\text{Tab}}$ twice to move to the **Store result in** text box

- Type **RMEDIAN** in the **Store result in** text box and then press $\boxed{\leftarrow\text{Enter}}$

C8 RMEDIAN, shown in Figure 2-3, now contains the median of each student's test score (you may have to scroll to see this column).

FIGURE 2-3

The Data worksheet with median test scores

	C2-A	C3	C4	C5	C6	C7	C8
	FIRST	TEST1	TEST2	TEST3	AVERG	RMEAN	RMEDIAN
1	JAMES	72	93	93	86.0000	86.0000	93
2	MELISSA	99	86	83	89.3333	89.3333	86
3	LAMAR	59	59	90	69.3333	69.3333	59
4	MEGAN	79	69	60	69.3333	69.3333	69
5	JASON	48	77	25	50.0000	50.0000	48
6	ANDREW	78	94	50	74.0000	74.0000	78
7	JONATHAN	98	98	94	96.6667	96.6667	98
8	JENNIFER	92	91	99	94.0000	94.0000	92
9	KEVIN	71	78	62	70.3333	70.3333	71
10	SANG	64	68	97	76.3333	76.3333	68
11	MARK	49	79	43	57.0000	57.0000	49
12	STEVEN	94	93	95	94.0000	94.0000	94
13	BARBARA	99	95	84	92.6667	92.6667	95
14	AMY	91	81	79	83.6667	83.6667	81
15	HIMA	90	100	62	84.0000	84.0000	90
16	RICHARD	100	77	100	92.3333	92.3333	100
17	LUIS	73	79	83	78.3333	78.3333	79
18	MATT	77	79	85	80.3333	80.3333	79
19	NANCY	83	79	52	71.3333	71.3333	79

In your final grade report, you want each student's average grade to appear as an integer. Minitab can round the scores for you:

- Choose **Calc > Functions**

    To tell Minitab which column to round:

- Click the **Input column** text box

- Double-click **C7 RMEAN** to enter it in the **Input column** text box

- Type **AVERAGE** in the **Result in** text box (Minitab moves to this text box automatically)

- Select the **Round** option button and then click **OK**

    Each student's average score, rounded to the nearest integer, appears in C9.

Summarizing Columns

Each row in a Minitab worksheet represents an individual case, such as one particular student's test scores. When you perform *row operations*, you calculate a statistic (for example, the mean for each case) and display the results in a designated column in the Data window.

Minitab's columns contain values of the same variable; for example, C3 contains all scores for Test 1. When you want to compute statistics for a particular variable, or column, you use *column operations*. Column operations produce single numbers that appear in the Session window, not in the Data window. Minitab can store such values in specific constant locations that you assign, such as K1, K2, K3, and so on. You can also assign names to constants. If you plan to use a result again later, it's useful to store it as a constant.

Explore how Minitab operates on columns (variables) by finding the mean score of Test 1. Remember, this is not the mean of a single student's performance — it is the mean the whole class' performance on the first test.

- Choose **Calc > Column Statistics**

    The Column Statistics dialog box appears (Figure 2-4).

FIGURE 2-4

*The Column Statistics
dialog box*

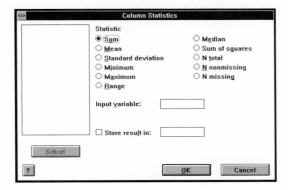

- Click the **Mean** option button
- Click the **Input variable** text box
- Double-click **C3 TEST1** in the list box on the left to enter it in the **Input variable** text box
- Click the **Store result in** check box and then click the text box to its right
- Type **MEANC3** as the constant name in the **Store result in** text box and press (←Enter)

    To see the column statistics in the Session window:

- Choose **Window > Session** (or press (Ctrl)+**M**, the keyboard shortcut for moving to the Session window)

The Session window appears (Figure 2-5).

FIGURE 2-5

*The Session window,
showing the mean of Test 1*

Commands ⎯

Mean of TEST 1 ⎯

MTB > prompt ⎯

```
MTB > Retrieve 'C:\MTBSEW\STUDENT9\MARKS.MTW'.
Retrieving worksheet from file: C:\MTBSEW\STUDENT9\MARKS.MTW
Worksheet was saved on  1/18/1994
MTB > Name c6 = 'AVERG'
MTB > Let 'AVERG' = (C3+C4+C5)/3
MTB > Name c7 = 'RMEAN'
MTB > RMean 'TEST1'-'TEST3' 'RMEAN'.
MTB > Name c8 = 'RMEDIAN'
MTB > RMedian 'TEST1'-'TEST3' 'RMEDIAN'.
MTB > Name c9 = 'AVERAGE'
MTB > Round 'RMEAN' 'AVERAGE'.
MTB > Name k1 = 'MEANC3'
MTB > Mean 'TEST1' 'MEANC3'.
  MEAN    =       80.000
MTB >
```

You can see the mean you requested — 80.000 — near the bottom of the Session window. Your students performed relatively well on the first test.

▼

Using the Session Window

▲

Until now, you have primarily worked in the Data window and issued commands by choosing them from the Minitab menu bar. Every command you issue from the menu has a corresponding Session command that appears in the Session window in a special *Session command language.*

As you see in Figure 2-5, Minitab entered Mean 'TEST1' 'MEANC3' in the line just above MEAN = 80.000 when you requested a column mean. You could have typed this command directly in the Session window just as Minitab did and avoided the menu altogether.

Note the MTB > prompt at the bottom of the Session window. This prompt is Minitab's way of telling you that it is ready for you to type a command. To enter commands in this way, you need to know the correct words to type in Minitab's special command language.

Each line preceded by MTB > is a command. You can see that the command language is fairly straightforward. The first MTB > prompt is followed by Retrieve 'C:\MTBSEW\STUDENT9\MARKS.MTW'. This command corresponds to your choosing File > Open Worksheet and then selecting MARKS.MTW. The next command, Name C6 = 'AVERG' , indicates that you used the Mathematical Expressions command to create a new column called AVERG to contain the test averages. Minitab computes the averages in the third command, Let 'AVERG' = (C3+C4+C5)/3, which is exactly what you typed in the dialog box.

As long as you're in the Session window, try typing a simple command. Although you can view data in the Data window, sometimes it's quicker to look at it in the Session window. The PRINT command displays whatever values you specify in the Session window. In other words, it "prints" to the screen, not to paper. To see the names of your students followed by their test averages, enter the PRINT command and specify columns C1, C2, and C9 after the MTB > prompt at the bottom of the Session window (where the cursor is blinking):

- Type **PRINT C1 C2 C9**

Note: The tutorials show all typing in uppercase, but you can use either upper or lowercase. Minitab displays commands in the Session window in both cases.

- Press ⏎Enter to tell Minitab to print the three columns containing the last name, first name, and test average in the Session window

Minitab lists the data in row and column format, along with the corresponding row numbers (Figure 2-6).

FIGURE 2-6

The Session window with test grades

```
MTB > PRINT C1 C2 C9

ROW      LAST NAM      FIRST    AVERAGE
 1    ADAMS,          JAMES        86
 2    BENSON,         MELISSA      89
 3    BROWN,          LAMAR        69
 4    DOUGHERTY,      MEGAN        69
 5    DOUGLAS,        JASON        50
 6    GIGLIOTTI,      ANDREW       74
 7    GOLDBERG,       JONATHAN     97
 8    GREEN           JENNIFER     94
 9    KENNEDY,        KEVIN        70
10    LEE,            SANG         76
11    MCCLURE         MARK         57
12    MESSINA,        STEPHEN      94
13    NORMAN,         BARBARA      93
14    NOWICKI,        AMY          84
15    PATEL,          HIMA         84
16    PIERSON,        RICHARD      92
17    ROJAS,          LUIS         78
18    RYAN,           MATT         80
19    SCHMIDT,        NANCY        71
20    SCOTT,          MICHAEL      85
21    SHEPPARD,       KATHLEEN     97
22    SMITH,          HOLLY        53
23    THOMPSON,       SUSAN        68
24    WATSON,         KEISHA       74

MTB >
```

The Session window automatically scrolls to keep the last line of output and the current MTB > prompt visible. If you want to see other areas of the window, you can scroll up and down or right and left using the scroll bars, or you can use the directional keys to move quickly through one section at a time. To move around the Session window:

- Press Pg Up to move up one screen
- Press Pg Dn to move down one screen
- Press Ctrl+Home to move to the beginning of the Session window
- Press Ctrl+End to move to the end of the Session window

These key combinations also work in the Data window.

Note: Users develop preferences on how to issue commands: using the menus or typing them at the Session window prompt. Usually, this book directs you to use the menus, except in certain cases in which it's easier to type directly in the Session window.

Now try printing the same three columns again, using the menu command that corresponds to the Session PRINT command:

- Choose **File > Display Data**

- Press and hold down the [Ctrl] key while you click **C1**, **C2**, and **C9** in the list box that appears in the Display Data dialog box

- Click the **Select** button

The three columns you selected appear in the Columns and constants to display text box.

- Click **OK**

Choosing the Display Data command from the menus produces the same results as typing PRINT in the Session window. Notice that Minitab issued the command a little differently in the Session window; it used Print 'LAST NAM' 'FIRST' 'AVERAGE'. You can specify columns by either number or name when you use Session commands.

▼
Combining Data
with the Stack
Command
▲

Your principal, Ms. Taylor, has asked you to include statistical information for all three tests in your report. Minitab lets you combine data from several columns into a single column by *stacking* them on top of each other. This method creates a new variable that consists of data from all the selected columns.

- Choose **Window > Data** to return to the Data window (or press [Ctrl]+**D**)

- Choose **Manip > Stack**

The Stack dialog box appears. To indicate the three columns you want to stack:

- Double-click **C3 TEST 1** to enter it in the first **Stack the following blocks** text box.

- Click the second **Stack the following blocks** text box

- Double-click **C4 TEST 2** and then click the third **Stack the following blocks** text box

- Double-click **C5 TEST 3** and then click the **Store results in** text box

- Type **TOTAL** in the **Store results in** text box

When you stack data, you can tell Minitab to store a subscript variable that indicates the column from which the data originated:

- Click the **Store subscripts in** check box and then click the text box to its right

- Type **TEST** in the **Store subscripts in** text box

  Your Stack dialog box should look like the one shown in Figure 2-7.

FIGURE 2-7

Stack dialog box

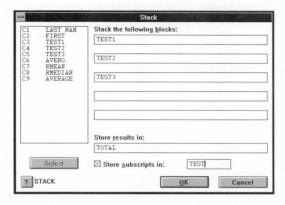

- Press (←Enter) to stack the three test variables in the same column

- Scroll to the right so you can see C10 and C11

- Scroll down to view all the data in C10

  Notice how all the grades are stacked on top of one another; in other words, all three columns are listed in a single vertical column). Note, too, that C11 (the subscript) identifies the test from which each grade originated.
  Calculate the mean of C10 and view it in the Session window:

- Choose **Calc > Column Statistics** to open the Column Statistics dialog box, which contains the selections you made the last time you issued this command

- Double-click the **Input variable** text box to highlight the variable you previously specified

- Double-click **C10 TOTAL** to enter it in the **Input variable** text box

- If necessary, click the **Store results in** check box to select it and then double-click the text box to its right

- Type **MEANTEST** in the **Store results in** text box and then press (←Enter)

- Choose **Window > Session** to view the results

  The last line of the Session window shows the mean for all the test scores you stacked in C10. You can report to Ms. Taylor that the average for all your tests is a respectable 78.569.

You moved to the Session window using a Window menu command. You can also use a keyboard shortcut to activate a different window:

■ Press [Ctrl]+[Tab]

The Data window is now the active window. Try activating the other Minitab windows this way:

■ Press [Ctrl]+[Tab] several times

The title bar changes as you move from one window to another, identifying which is the active one.

■ Continue to press [Ctrl]+[Tab] until the Session window is active again (the title bar displays **Session** on the right)

Coding Data

The school district where you work uses the letter grades A, B, C, D, and F, based on a four-point scale in which 4 = A and 0 = F. To compute the students' grades, you need to create a new variable based on grade intervals and translate the existing grades to the four-point scale. You want to code grades falling in the interval of 90 to 100 as a 4 (A), grades of 80 to 89 as a 3 (B), grades of 70 to 79 as a 2 (C), grades of 60 to 69 as a 1 (D), and grades 59 and below as a 0 (F).

To code the students' averages:

■ Choose **Manip > Code Data Values** to display the Code Data Values dialog box

■ Double-click **C9 AVERAGE** to enter it in the **Code data from columns** text box

■ Press [Tab] and then type **GRADE** in the **Into columns** text box

To specify the intervals, you can either list all the values in the interval (separated by commas) or specify the first and last value in the range (separated by a colon).

■ Press [Tab] to move to the first **Original Values** text box

■ Type **90:100** and then press [Tab] to move to the first **New** text box

Minitab interprets the entry 90:100 as all the grades between 90 and 100, inclusive. To indicate the new values that you want Minitab to assign:

■ Type **4** in the first **New** text box and then press [Tab]

■ Type **80:89**, press [Tab], type **3**, and then press [Tab] to enter data in the second **Original Values** and **New** text boxes, respectively

■ Type **70:79**, press [Tab], type **2**, and then press [Tab] to enter data in the third **Original Values** and **New** text boxes, respectively

■ Type **60:69**, press [Tab], type **1**, and then press [Tab] to enter data in the fourth **Original Values** and **New** text boxes, respectively

- Type **0:59**, press (Tab) and then type **0** to enter data in the fifth **Original Values** and **New** text boxes, respectively

    Your Code Data Values dialog box should look like the one shown in Figure 2-8.

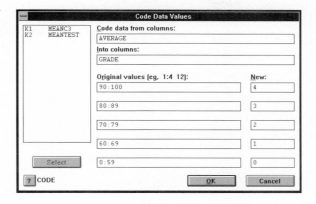

- Click **OK** to code the average grades with a number representing a letter grade

- Choose **Window > Data** to view the new column

- Scroll up and to the right to see C12 GRADE

    Compare columns C9 and C12. Notice that those students whose rounded mean falls between 90 and 100, inclusive, have a code of 4 assigned to them, those whose rounded mean falls between 80 and 89, inclusive, are coded as 3, and so on. By scanning this column, you can quickly determine which students are doing well and which ones need help.

Ranking Data

Ms. Taylor asked you to rank your students' average exam scores in numerical order so she can see how each student's performance compares to the rest of the class's. Minitab ranks the data listed in any column by assigning a value of 1 to the lowest score, 2 to the second lowest, and so on. The top student is ranked number 24 because this is the total number of students in the class. To rank the average exam scores:

- Choose **Manip > Rank**

- Double-click **C9 AVERAGE** to enter it in the **Rank data in** text box

- Type **RANK** in the **Store ranks in** text box

The completed Rank dialog box should look like the one shown in Figure 2-9.

FIGURE 2-9

The completed Rank dialog box

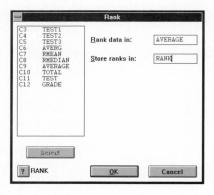

■ Press (←Enter) and scroll to view C13 RANK

If two or more scores are "tied," Minitab assigns them a rank equal to the average of the two separate ranks. For example, if you look at the scores that placed 21st and 22nd in C13, you can see that Minitab assigned them each the rank of 21.5 (rows 8 and 12, Steven Messina and Jennifer Green). Minitab averages the ranks whenever there is a tie. Verify that two students are tied for the top place in your class (remember that rank 1 is the lowest, not the highest). What are their names?

Sorting Data

Ms. Taylor also wants you to create and print a list of the students ordered by their mean score. In other words, the student who had the highest mean should appear first, the second highest should be listed next, and so on. Minitab can use up to four columns as sorting criteria.

If you simply sort C7 RMEAN, Minitab rearranges the entries in that particular column but leaves the others intact. Sorting in this way usually creates unexpected and confusing results, such as one student's grade appearing next to another name and vice versa. Usually when you sort, you want to "carry along" all of the columns in a worksheet that correspond to the data for an individual case. For example, here you want to keep all the data related to a given student in a single row.

Before you sort data, it's a good idea to save it just in case your data get mixed up. As usual, you'll save your data to your Student disk:

■ Choose **File > Save Worksheet As**

■ Press (←Enter) to confirm that you want to save a Minitab worksheet

■ Insert your Student disk in the drive A (or a different drive, if appropriate)

- Click the **Drives** drop-down list arrow and then click **a:**

- Double-click the **File Name** text box, type **2MARKS**, and then press ⏎Enter

  Now you're ready to sort your data by mean test score:

- Choose **Manip > Sort**

- Highlight all the columns in the list box except C10 TOTAL and C11 TEST (remember to press Ctrl while you click the individual column names)

  You don't want to sort C10 and C11 because they contain information about all of the exams for all the students, not a particular row or student.

- Click **Select** to display the columns in the **Sort column(s)** text box

  You need to specify where you want Minitab to store the sorted data. In this case, put them in the same location they currently occupy.

- Click the **Store sorted column(s) in** text box

- Select all the columns, except C10 and C11, to enter them in the **Store sorted column(s) in** text box (make sure that the column order is identical to that in the **Sort column(s)** text box)

  Now tell Minitab to use the student's average on the three exams, the C7 RMEAN variable, as the sort criterion:

- Click the first **Sort by column** text box

- Select **C7 RMEAN** to enter it in the first **Sort by column** text box

- Click **Descending** to sort the students' average grade in descending order

  Your Sort dialog box should look like the one shown in Figure 2-10.

FIGURE 2-10

The completed Sort dialog box

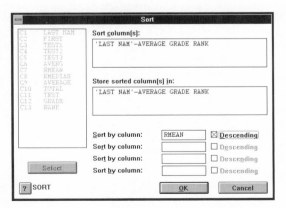

- Click **OK**

- Press ⌃Ctrl+⌂Home to move to the beginning of the Data window

    The students' data are ordered according to their mean scores (Figure 2-11). If you had forgotten to "carry along" a column, however, its contents would not have been included in the sort. The wrong grade would then appear next to the wrong student.

	C1-A	C2-A	C3	C4	C5	C6	C7
→	LAST NAM	FIRST	TEST1	TEST2	TEST3	AVERG	RMEAN
1	SHEPPARD,	KATHLEEN	94	97	100	97.0000	97.0000
2	GOLDBERG,	JONATHAN	98	98	94	96.6667	96.6667
3	GREEN,	JENNIFER	92	91	99	94.0000	94.0000
4	MESSINA,	STEVEN	94	93	95	94.0000	94.0000
5	NORMAN,	BARBARA	99	95	84	92.6667	92.6667
6	PIERSON,	RICHARD	100	77	100	92.3333	92.3333
7	BENSON,	MELISSA	99	86	83	89.3333	89.3333
8	ADAMS,	JAMES	72	93	93	86.0000	86.0000
9	SCOTT,	MICHAEL	81	75	100	85.3333	85.3333
10	PATEL,	HIMA	90	100	62	84.0000	84.0000
11	NOWICKI,	AMY	91	81	79	83.6667	83.6667
12	RYAN,	MATT	77	79	85	80.3333	80.3333
13	ROJAS,	LUIS	73	79	83	78.3333	78.3333
14	LEE,	SANG	64	68	97	76.3333	76.3333
15	GIGLIOTTI,	ANDREW	78	94	50	74.0000	74.0000
16	WATSON,	KEISHA	88	93	41	74.0000	74.0000
17	SCHMIDT,	NANCY	83	79	52	71.3333	71.3333
18	KENNEDY,	KEVIN	71	78	62	70.3333	70.3333
19	BROWN,	LAMAR	59	59	90	69.3333	69.3333

    You now have a summary of your class's performance. Since your worksheet is sorted, you can quickly see which students are not doing well (those at the bottom of the list) and help them improve their grades.

Separating Data with Unstack

Ms. Taylor would like a separate listing of all the grades that fall within each of the ranges you specified earlier with the Code Data Values command. Just as you were able to combine several columns into a single column with the Stack command, Minitab lets you take a single column and break it into several new columns, according to criteria you specify.

    In this section, you *unstack* C9 AVERAGE into five columns, C14 through C18. You put all the grades within the range 0 to 59 in the first column (C14), all grades from 60 to 69 in the second column (C15), and so on, using the grade data that appears in C12:

- Choose **Manip > Unstack**

- Double-click **C9 AVERAGE** to enter it as the variable to unstack in the Unstack text box

- Click the **Using subscripts in** text box and then double-click **C12 GRADE**, which contains the subscripts

  Starting with the lowest category, specify the blocks of data you want to unstack:

- Type **F**, press ⎡Tab⎤, type **D**, press ⎡Tab⎤, type **C**, press ⎡Tab⎤, type **B**, press ⎡Tab⎤, and then type **A** to complete the **Store results in blocks** text boxes

  The completed Unstack dialog box should look like the one shown in Figure 2-12.

FIGURE 2-12

The completed Unstack dialog box

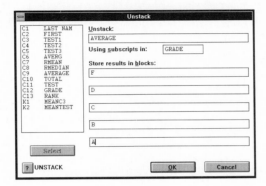

- Press ⎡←Enter⎤

- Scroll to the right to see the new columns, C14 through C18

  The Data window (Figure 2-13) shows the grades grouped by category.

FIGURE 2-13

The Data window, with grades unstacked into intervals

C14	C15	C16	C17	C18
F	D	C	B	A
57	69	78	89	97
53	69	76	86	97
50	68	74	85	94
		74	84	94
		71	84	93
		70	80	92

At this point, you have eighteen students earning grades of A, B, or C, with only six earning Ds and Fs. Also, your three students with Ds are almost getting Cs. All in all, it appears your class is doing fairly well.

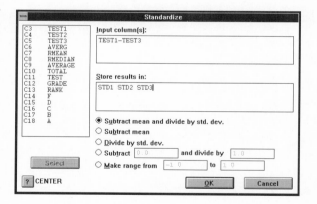

Standardizing Data

▼

▲

In addition to submitting the grades, you'd like to report each student's progress during the marking period by comparing the grades from the three tests. Each test reflects a score based on 100 possible points. However, an 87 on an easy test might actually reflect less knowledge than a 75 on a more difficult test. If two scores come from two different populations, each with its own mean and standard deviation, you cannot compare them unless you *standardize* them. To compute z-scores for the various test grades:

- Choose **Calc > Standardize** to open the Standardize dialog box

- Select **C3 TEST1**, **C4 TEST2**, and **C5 TEST3** to enter them in the **Input column(s)** text box

- Press ⌐Tab⌐

- Type **STD1 STD2 STD3** in the **Store results in** text box

The completed Standardize dialog box should look like the one in Figure 2-14. Notice that the first option, **Subtract mean and divide by std. dev.**, is already selected; it is the *default*, or preselected, option. This option computes z-scores.

FIGURE 2-14

The completed Standardize dialog box

- Press ⏎Enter to calculate the standardized scores
- Scroll to look at C19, C20, and C21, which contain the z-scores

The standardized scores, the first few of which are shown in Figure 2-15, allow you to easily determine how each student performed on each test, relative to the class.

FIGURE 2-15

The Data window, showing standardized grades

	C15	C16	C17	C18	C19	C20	C21	C2
→	D	C	B	A	STD1	STD2	STD3	
1	69	78	89	97	0.89626	1.18275	1.05442	
2	69	76	86	97	1.15233	1.25805	0.80713	
3	68	74	85	94	0.76822	0.73098	1.01321	
4		74	84	94	0.89626	0.88157	0.84835	
5		71	84	93	1.21635	1.03216	0.39498	
6		70	80	92	1.28037	-0.32314	1.05442	
7					1.21635	0.35451	0.35376	
8					-0.51215	0.88157	0.76592	
9					0.06402	-0.47373	1.05442	
10					0.64018	1.40864	-0.51176	
11					0.70420	-0.02196	0.18890	
12					-0.19206	-0.17255	0.43619	
13					-0.44813	-0.17255	0.35376	
14					-1.02429	-1.00079	0.93078	
15					-0.12804	0.95687	-1.00634	
16					0.51215	0.88157	-1.37727	
17					0.19206	-0.17255	-0.92391	
18					-0.57617	-0.24784	-0.51176	
19					-1.34439	-1.67844	0.64227	

You can quickly spot trends in a student's performance. For example, the performance of the student in row 5 dropped off on the last exam, while that of the student in row 19 improved.

Getting Worksheet Information

When you work with a data set over the course of several days, it's easy to forget what you have done so far, especially if you have used many variables and performed many manipulations. Minitab's Info window provides a record of the columns and their names in the worksheet. It also lists any constants you have used. To open the Info window:

- Choose **Window > Info**

The Info window opens (Figure 2-16), and the Minitab window title bar changes accordingly.

FIGURE 2-16

The Info window, showing worksheet information

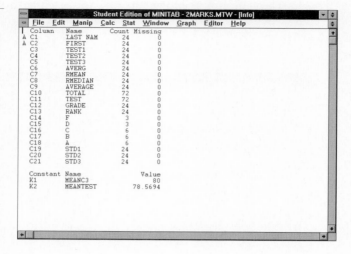

```
Student Edition of MINITAB - 2MARKS.MTW - [Info]
 File   Edit   Manip   Calc   Stat   Window   Graph   Editor   Help
   Column    Name        Count  Missing
 A C1        LAST NAM      24       0
 A C2        FIRST         24       0
   C3        TEST1         24       0
   C4        TEST2         24       0
   C5        TEST3         24       0
   C6        AVERG         24       0
   C7        RMEAN         24       0
   C8        RMEDIAN       24       0
   C9        AVERAGE       24       0
   C10       TOTAL         72       0
   C11       TEST          72       0
   C12       GRADE         24       0
   C13       RANK          24       0
   C14       F              3       0
   C15       D              3       0
   C16       C              6       0
   C17       B              6       0
   C18       A              6       0
   C19       STD1          24       0
   C20       STD2          24       0
   C21       STD3          24       0

   Constant  Name               Value
   K1        MEANC3                80
   K2        MEANTEST         78.5694
```

The Info window provides information about your worksheet in a compact form. It also shows you why it's important to give your columns meaningful names—they help you remember where you have stored information. The Info window lists the number, name, and amount of data (Count) in each column, along with the number of missing values (there are none in this data set). For example, you see that columns C10 and C11 are each 72 rows long. These are the two columns in which you stacked the results from Tests 1 through 3.

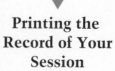

Printing the Record of Your Session

Now that you have summarized your class's performance, you want to print your worksheet on paper (or, in computer lingo, "hard copy") to submit to Ms. Taylor. First, save your data. Then resort your grades in alphabetical order (excluding the columns that you created with the Stack and Unstack commands).

- Choose **File > Save Worksheet** to save the updated 2MARKS.MTW to your Student disk before sorting

- Choose **Manip > Sort**

- Select **C1** through **C9**, **C12** through **C13**, and **C19** through **C21** (scroll down to highlight the last two columns) to enter them in the **Sort Column(s)** text box, and then press `Tab`

- Select **C1** through **C9**, **C12** through **C13**, and **C19** through **C21** again to enter them in the **Store sorted column(s) in** text box, and then press `Tab` (make sure the column order is identical to that in the **Sort column(s)** text box)

- Select **C1 LAST NAM** to enter it in the **Sort by column** text box

- Click the first **Descending** check box to deselect it and then press `Tab`

- Select **C2 FIRST** to enter it in the second **Sort by column** text box, in case you have two students with the same last name

- Click **OK**

- Choose **Window > Data** to see the results of your sort

- Press `Ctrl`+`Home` to move to the beginning of the worksheet

  Your worksheet is alphabetized again. Save the worksheet one last time:

- Choose **File > Save Worksheet**

  Now you are ready to print out your grades data. You could use the File > Print Window command to print the entire worksheet, but Ms. Taylor probably wants to see only your students' names, test averages, and grades. The easiest way to select only those columns that contain this data is by using the Session window.

- Choose **Window > Session**

  You've already seen how to send your data to the Session window by using File > Display Data. Now use the equivalent PRINT command to display the data you want (C1 LAST NAM, C2 FIRST, C9 AVERAGE, and C12 GRADE) in the Session window. Then highlight the data and print it:

- Type **PRINT C1 C2 C9 C12** after the MTB > prompt and then press `←Enter`

  Minitab displays the data you requested.

- Highlight the data by clicking the upper left corner (just to the left of the ROW heading) and dragging the pointer to the lower right corner (to the right of the final grade); don't include any of the commands or prompts

The Session window should look like Figure 2-17, with the data highlighted.

```
MTB > PRINT C1 C2 C9 C12
ROW     LAST NAM      FIRST   AVERAGE   GRADE
  1   ADAMS,          JAMES        86      3
  2   BENSON,         MELISSA      89      3
  3   BROWN,          LAMAR        69      1
  4   DOUGHERTY,      MEGAN        69      1
  5   DOUGLAS,        JASON        50      0
  6   GIGLIOTTI,      ANDREW       74      2
  7   GOLDBERG,       JONATHAN     97      4
  8   GREEN           JENNIFER     94      4
  9   KENNEDY,        KEVIN        70      2
 10   LEE,            SANG         76      2
 11   MCCLURE         MARK         57      0
 12   MESSINA,        STEVEN       94      4
 13   NORMAN          BARBARA      93      4
 14   NOWICKI,        AMY          84      3
 15   PATEL,          HIMA         84      3
 16   PIERSON,        RICHARD      92      4
 17   ROJAS,          LUIS         78      2
 18   RYAN,           MATT         80      3
 19   SCHMIDT,        NANCY        71      2
 20   SCOTT,          MICHAEL      85      3
 21   SHEPPARD,       KATHLEEN     97      4
 22   SMITH,          HOLLY        53      0
 23   THOMPSON,       SUSAN        68      1
 24   WATSON,         KEISHA       74      2

MTB >
```

- Choose **File > Print Window**

The Print dialog box lets you specify how much of the window to print. The Selection option button is chosen by default, indicating that Minitab will print only the highlighted data.

- Click **OK** to print the selection you highlighted

Figure 2-18 shows the printed grade list.

ROW	LAST NAM	FIRST	AVERAGE	GRADE
1	ADAMS,	JAMES	86	3
2	BENSON,	MELISSA	89	3
3	BROWN,	LAMAR	69	1
4	DOUGHERTY,	MEGAN	69	1
5	DOUGLAS,	JASON	50	0
6	GIGLIOTTI,	ANDREW	74	2
7	GOLDBERG,	JONATHAN	97	4
8	GREEN	JENNIFER	94	4
9	KENNEDY,	KEVIN	70	2
10	LEE,	SANG	76	2
11	MCCLURE	MARK	57	0
12	MESSINA,	STEPHEN	94	4
13	NORMAN,	BARBARA	93	4
14	NOWICKI,	AMY	84	3
15	PATEL,	HIMA	84	3
16	PIERSON,	RICHARD	92	4
17	ROJAS,	LUIS	78	2
18	RYAN,	MATT	80	3
19	SCHMIDT,	NANCY	71	2
20	SCOTT,	MICHAEL	85	3
21	SHEPPARD,	KATHLEEN	97	4
22	SMITH,	HOLLY	53	0
23	THOMPSON,	SUSAN	68	1
24	WATSON,	KEISHA	74	2

Creating a Text File

Minitab printed the grades data in the Windows default fonts without any formatting. Ultimately, you'd like to format the report with boldface, italics, and borders before you present it to Ms. Taylor. To do so, you must first save the grades data in the Session window as an *ASCII* (American Standard Code for Information Interchange) text file. You can then open this file in any text editor or word processor.

Save the highlighted data as an ASCII file called MARKS.TXT:

- Choose **File > Save Window As** to display the Save As dialog box (this command saves the selected text in the window)

- Insert your Student disk in drive A (or a different drive, if appropriate)

- Click the **Drives** drop-down list arrow and then click **a:** (or a different drive, if appropriate)

- Double-click the **File Name** text box and type **MARKS**

- Press ⎆Enter to save the text file

When you save a text file with **Save File As**, Minitab automatically adds the extension TXT, which is a common extension for text files that makes them easy to find. You can exit Minitab and take a look at your text file in Notepad. Notepad is a Windows accessory that lets you open and work with text files; it's like a miniature word processor. You open Notepad from the Program Manager:

- Press [Alt]+[Tab] until you see a box with Program Manager in it (this keyboard shortcut cycles through all the applications open on your desktop)

- Double-click the **Accessories** group icon in Program Manager to open the Accessories window (Figure 2-19)

Note: Move open windows out of the way as necessary to find the Accessories group icon.

FIGURE 2-19

The Accessories window

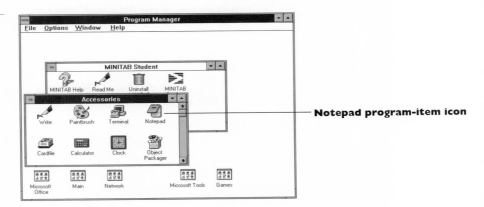

Notepad program-item icon

The Accessories window contains a number of Windows accessories, including a calculator, a calendar, a clock, Notepad, Write (a more sophisticated text editor), and similar applications.

- Double-click the **Notepad** program-item icon

- Choose **File > Open** from the Notepad menu bar

- Click the **Drives** drop-down list arrow and then click **a:**

- Double-click **MARKS.TXT** in the **File** list box

The Notepad window displays your grades data. Create a title for your grades listing:

- Press ⟨←Enter⟩ twice to create two blank lines above the grades list, and then press ⟨↑⟩ twice to move back to the top

- Type *Your Name:* **Grades Report for Ms. Taylor**

The Notepad window should look like the one in Figure 2-20.

FIGURE 2-20

MARKS.TXT in the Notepad

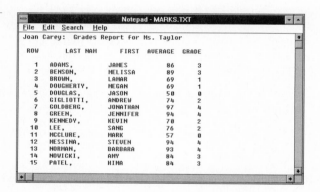

Although you can't do any formatting in Notepad, you could open this file in a more sophisticated text editor or word processor and work with it there. For now, print the file with your name on it:

- Choose **File > Print**

- Choose **File > Exit** to exit Notepad

- Click **Yes** to save the changes to MARKS.TXT

You return to Program Manager. You now have two hard copies of your grade report (one with a title) and a file that you can format in your word processor. At the end of the next marking period, it should be much easier for you to organize your grades.

- Press ⟨Alt⟩+⟨Tab⟩ until you see Minitab

The next two tutorials detail how you produce graphical displays of your data. You can restart Minitab to continue to the Review and Practice problems or you can exit Windows to take a break.

If you plan to continue directly to the next tutorial:

■ Choose **File > Restart Minitab**

If you want to take a longer break:

■ Choose **File > Exit**

<table>
<tr><td></td><td>This section describes the menu commands introduced in or related to this tutorial. To find a complete explanation of all menus and commands, refer to the Reference section of this manual.</td></tr>
</table>

▼
Minitab Command Summary
▲

This section describes the menu commands introduced in or related to this tutorial. To find a complete explanation of all menus and commands, refer to the Reference section of this manual.

Minitab Menu Commands

Menu	Command	Description
File		
	Save Window As	Saves the contents of the active Session, Info, Graph, or History window to a file
	Print Window	Prints the contents of the active Session, Data, Info, Graph, or History window
	Get Worksheet Info	Prints a record in the Session window of the columns and stored constants used in a worksheet
	Display Data	Prints one or more columns in the Session window
	Restart Minitab	Closes the current worksheet, erases all the output in the Session window, and opens a blank worksheet in the Data window
Manip		
	Sort	Sorts selected columns of the worksheet using up to four columns as the sorting criteria
	Rank	Ranks the data in a column and stores the ranks in another column

Menu	Command	Description
	Code Data Values	Changes the numeric values or ranges in a column to a specified coding scheme
	Stack	Stacks the contents of two or more columns and to form a new column; the number of cells in the stacked column equals the total number of cells in the columns selected for stacking
	Unstack	Creates several columns of data by splitting a given column
Calc		
	Mathematical Expressions	Performs arithmetic using algebraic expressions, which may contain arithmetic operators, comparison operators, logical operators, and functions; arguments may be columns, constants, or numbers
	Functions	Performs various mathematical functions row-by-row on a column, constant, or number
	Column Statistics	Calculates various statistics for the selected column, displaying the results and, optionally, storing each result in a constant
	Row Statistics	Computes a value for each row in a set of columns
	Standardize	Centers and scales columns of data
Window		
	Session	Moves to the Session window, which contains a record of all the commands issued in the current session and the resulting output; lets you enter Session commands
	Info	Moves to the Info window, which displays worksheet information such as the columns and stored constants

Review and Practice

Matching

Match the following terms to their definitions by placing the correct letter next to the term it describes.

_____ Display Data

_____ 1

_____ Functions

_____ Row operation

_____ Stack

_____ N missing

_____ TXT

_____ Subscripts

_____ Window > Info

_____ MTB >

a. Value assigned to the highest score by the Rank command

b. The Minitab command that creates a new column by placing several columns on top of each other

c. An optional indicator variable created when Minitab stacks several columns into one column

d. The Minitab command that displays nonempty column numbers and corresponding names in the worksheet

e. An arithmetic process performed on the entries in each row for a given set of columns in the worksheet

f. The file extension given to files created with the Save Window As command

g. The Minitab command that displays one or many columns in the Session window

h. A summary statistic that reflects the number of missing values in a row or column

i. Standard, preprogrammed numeric operations stored in Minitab

j. Minitab prompt

True/False

Mark the following statements with a *T* or an *F*.

_____ 1. You must always store row operation results in a column.

_____ 2. The results of column operations can either be stored in a column or not at all.

_____ 3. The Get Worksheet Info command displays all the columns that contain data in the current worksheet, the column names (if any), and the number of observations in the column.

_____ 4. The Sort command automatically sorts all the columns in the worksheet.

_____ 5. You can use the Display Data command to print on a piece of paper.

_____ 6. The interquartile range is one of the statistics available in the Row Statistics and Column Statistics dialog boxes.

_____ 7. The Standardize dialog box's default operation subtracts the mean and then divides by the standard deviation.

_____ 8. The Sort command sorts only numeric variables or columns.

_____ 9. Many of the statistics available in the Row Statistics dialog box are also available in the Column Statistics dialog box.

_____ 10. Code Data Values interprets 10:20 as the numbers between 10 and 20, inclusive.

Practice Problems

1. Print out a copy of the SNOW.MTW worksheet. You must first open the worksheet and then print the data.

2. Open TVVIEW.MTW, which contains the data you worked with in the Tutorial 1 Practice Problems.

   a. Compute the mean, median, and sample standard deviation of TV viewing time for husbands, wives, and households.

   b. Compute the mean, median, and sample standard deviation of the difference between husbands and wives, using the difference variable from Tutorial 1.

   c. Stack the times for both husbands and wives in C5 and save the subscripts in C6. Name these columns ADULTS and GENDER, respectively.

   d. Print the worksheet.

3. Open PIZZA.MTW, which contains the data you worked with in the Tutorial 1 Practice Problems.

   a. Compute the mean, median, and standard deviation of the FALLSCOR column.

   b. Rank the FALLSCOR column and place the results in C7. Name this variable FSRANK1.

   c. Note that one way the computed ranks are different from the given ranks is that 1 does not indicate the greatest value. Transform C7 to conform to the newspaper ranks by subtracting each number from 14. Place the results in C8. Name this variable FSRANK2.

   d. What is another difference between FALLRANK and FSRANK2? Which column is most informative? Explain your answer.

   e. Print the worksheet.

4. Open RADLEV.MTW.

   a. Use the Get Worksheet Info command to determine what information has been saved in this data set. Which columns are used? What names have been assigned to them? How many observations does the data set contain?

b. Code the age variable so that new homes are those that are less than 2 years old. Assign newer homes a code value of 0 and older homes a code of 1.

c. Save the worksheet as P2RADLEV on your Student disk.

d. Sort the data set using the coded age variable.

e. Delete the rows that correspond to older homes. You don't need to save your changes.

5. Open NOTE.MTW.

a. Use the Get Worksheet Info command to determine what information was saved in this data set. Which columns are used? What names have been assigned to these columns? How many observations does the data set contain?

b. Sort the complete worksheet using the chip, speed, and price columns as the sorting criteria.

c. Print the worksheet. Which notebook computer with an SL chip is the least expensive? Most expensive? Which 25-megahertz notebook computer with an SL chip is the least expensive? After how many minutes is a recharge needed for this notebook computer? Is there an 800 number for tech support?

TUTORIAL
3

Graphical Methods for Describing Data

Describing data graphically is an essential aspect of statistical analysis. In this tutorial, you return to your role as a managerial consultant at Technitron. You use Minitab's Character graphs to depict the data you worked with in Tutorial 1 and explore the relationship between salary and variables that might affect salary. When you have selected the graphs that best represent Technitron's salary structure, you will proceed to Tutorial 4, where you will produce and format Professional high-resolution graphs that you can print for your report.

Objectives

In this tutorial you learn how to:

- save your session in an outfile

- graphically display any worksheet variable using Character graphs

- graph single variables using histograms, dotplots, stem-and-leaf plots, and boxplots

- plot variables against each other using scatter plots and multiple scatter plots

- plot variables against time

CASE STUDY: MANAGEMENT — SALARY STRUCTURE (CONTINUED)

In Tutorial 1, you updated the Technitron employee worksheet. Senior management wants you to present a report of your preliminary findings about the Sales Department's salary structure at the next staff meeting. Management would also like you to investigate whether recent changes in the Consumer Price Index (CPI) may affect salary levels. You will use Minitab's Character graphs to summarize the data values and investigate the relationship between salary and the CPI.

Creating an Outfile

In Tutorial 2, you learned to highlight text (your alphabetized grades listing) in the Session window and save it to a text file. This method works well when you're saving small selections of output from a session. In many cases, however, you may want to keep a record of the entire session.

The Session window stores only as much output as your computer's memory can manage at a given time. If you use many commands and produce large quantities of output, the Session window saves only your most recent work. During a long session, you may scroll to the top of the Session window to find that the work you performed earlier no longer appears.

You can tell Minitab to store all the commands, output, and data listings from an entire session in an *outfile*. Because Minitab stores an outfile in text format, you can import it into a word processing program. You can then edit, format, and print the data to produce the reports you need.

You want to save a record of this session so you can examine the graphs you create to determine which display the information most effectively.

- Start Minitab

- Maximize both the Minitab window and the Data window

    To have Minitab create an outfile of your session:

- Choose **File > Other Files > Start Recording Session**

    The Start Recording Session dialog box opens (Figure 3-1).

FIGURE 3-1

Start Recording Session dialog box

By default, Minitab sends output to both an outfile and the Session window. In this book, you will use a simple file naming system for outfiles: the letter *T* followed by the number of the tutorial.

- Press ⬅Enter to confirm that you want to record the output in a file as well as display it in the Session window

- Insert your Student disk in drive A (or a different drive, if appropriate)

- Click the **Drives** drop-down list arrow and then click **a:**

- Double-click the **File Name** text box, type **T3**, and then press ⬅Enter

Until you issue the Stop Recording Session command, Minitab will store all the Minitab commands you execute and the output you generate in the T3.LIS file. Minitab automatically adds the file extension LIS to indicate an outfile. Because LIS files consist of ASCII text, you can open them in most text editors.

Note: If you want to transfer worksheet information to the Session window and then directly to an outfile, choose File > Get Worksheet Info instead of opening the Info window.

If you completed all the steps in Tutorial 1, you saved the data you need in a file called 1PAY.MTW on your Student disk. Whenever a file has been changed from an earlier tutorial, this book provides an updated file with a version suffix. Although you could use 1PAY.MTW for this tutorial, the instructions in this book tell you to use the updated version provided with *The Student Edition of MINITAB for Windows* (PAY2.MTW), primarily to ensure that your results will match the results in the book.

To open the PAY2.MTW file:

- Choose **File > Open Worksheet**

- Press ⬅Enter to confirm that you want to open a Minitab file

- Click the **Drives** drop-down list arrow and then click **c:**

- Double-click the **MTBSEW** directory folder in the Directory tree (you may have to scroll to see it)

- Double-click the **STUDENT9** directory folder that appears under MTBSEW

- Double-click **PAY2.MTW** in the **Files** list box (you may have to scroll to see it)

The worksheet opens, displaying information about eleven Technitron employees, including salary, work history, and gender.

▼
Introducing Graphics Modes
▲

Minitab displays graphics in two modes, Character and Professional. Character graphs consist of keyboard characters such as *, +, -, and letters. Professional graphs are high-resolution; they use more *pixels* (short for picture elements) per inch and produce clearer graphs. Although a Professional graph may look more impressive, a Character graph actually provides you the same kind of information. Figures 3-2 and 3-3 depict histograms of the same salary data in Character and Professional modes, respectively.

FIGURE 3-2

Character histogram

```
Histogram of SALARY    N = 11

Midpoint    Count
   24000      1    *
   26000      0
   28000      2    **
   30000      1    *
   32000      3    ***
   34000      0
   36000      0
   38000      2    **
   40000      1    *
   42000      1    *
```

FIGURE 3-3

Professional high-resolution histogram

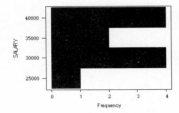

Minitab places Character graphs in the Session window, but it places each Professional graph in its own Graph window. You probably wouldn't use Character graphs in a presentation because they don't look as professional, but they offer several advantages over Professional graphs for classroom study:

• They are quicker to produce.

• They are easier to save and use in an outfile.

• The files are smaller and therefore use less disk space.

• You don't need a high-quality printer to print them.

This tutorial introduces you to Character graphs. In Tutorial 4, you produce some of the same graphs in Minitab's Professional mode, where you can compare the advantages and disadvantages of the two graph modes.

Note: Not all graph types are available in both modes. The default is professional.

▼
Graphing Single Variables
▲

Minitab offers four types of graphs that summarize information in a single column: histograms, dotplots, stem-and-leaf plots, and boxplots. To decide which graphs to include in your presentation, consider the benefits and limitations of each type:

• A *histogram* is a clean, easy-to-read graph that groups data into *classes* and uses bars to represent class frequencies. The distribution of data is easy to see from this type of graph, but when you have a limited amount of data it is not as useful a graph because it masks patterns.

- A *boxplot* (or *box-and-whisker plot*) lets you see distribution characteristics of data. Boxplots provide useful statistical information, such as quartiles and outliers. However, because there is no standard type of a boxplot, these graphs don't depict information in a uniform way.

- A *dotplot* displays each data value as a dot stacked above a horizontal axis so you can see exactly where each data point falls. Similar to the histogram, it displays distribution characteristics for the data it describes, but it does so by showing individual points or small groups of points rather than summarizing the data in bars. It is not available in Professional mode.

- A *stem-and-leaf plot* displays each data value and the distribution characteristics of the data. This graph type is more difficult to interpret, though, and therefore isn't as useful for presentation purposes. Also, if your data set is large, Minitab may truncate the display and, as a result, the graph won't illustrate the entire data set. The stem-and-leaf plot isn't available in Professional mode.

Creating a Histogram

For the Technitron staff presentation, you want to show the salary distribution among employees by describing the C1 SALARY data in a histogram.

- Choose **Graph > Character Graphs** to open the Character Graphs submenu (Figure 3-4)

FIGURE 3-4

Graph menu with Character Graphs submenu

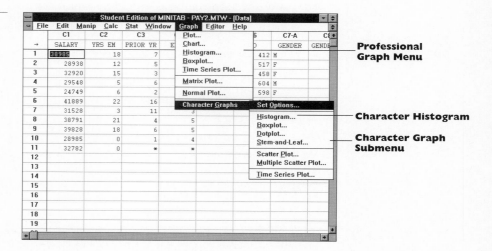

The main Graph menu lists a number of different graph types; these are all Professional graphics. At the bottom of the menu is the Character Graphs command, which opens the submenu you use to produce Character graphs.

■ Click **Histogram** on the **Character Graphs** submenu

The Histogram dialog box appears.

■ Double-click **C1 SALARY** to enter it in the **Variables** text box

Figure 3-5 shows the completed Histogram dialog box.

FIGURE 3-5

The Histogram dialog box

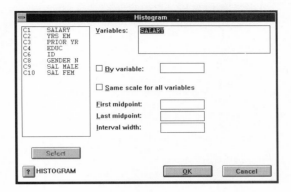

■ Click **OK**

Because this is not a high-resolution Professional graph, the Session window automatically becomes active, displaying the histogram shown in Figure 3-6. The GStd and GPro Session commands tell Minitab the type of graph you're creating. *GStd*, or Standard Graph, tells Minitab that the next graph is a Character graph; *GPro* enables Professional Graphics again.

FIGURE 3-6

Character-based salary histogram

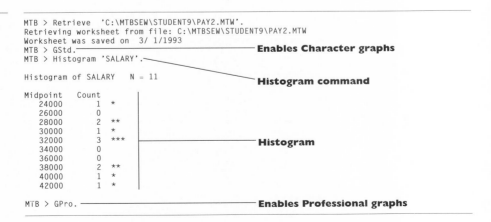

```
MTB > Retrieve 'C:\MTBSEW\STUDENT9\PAY2.MTW'.
Retrieving worksheet from file: C:\MTBSEW\STUDENT9\PAY2.MTW
Worksheet was saved on  3/ 1/1993
MTB > GStd.─────────────────────── Enables Character graphs
MTB > Histogram 'SALARY'.────────
                                       Histogram command
Histogram of SALARY    N = 11

Midpoint   Count
   24000       1   *
   26000       0
   28000       2   **
   30000       1   *
   32000       3   ***
   34000       0                      Histogram
   36000       0
   38000       2   **
   40000       1   *
   42000       1   *

MTB > GPro.──────────────────────── Enables Professional graphs
```

The histogram shows which classes contain the most data values in your sample. Minitab uses asterisks (*) to depict the extent of the data in each group. The vertical axis lists the midpoints of each salary class. The number of asterisks indicates the variable's frequency of occurrence within that particular class. For example, there were three employees with salaries greater than or equal to $31000 and up to, but not including, $33000.

Generally speaking, the more bars your histogram contains, the more finely it "chops up" your data. By default, Minitab divides these data into ten classes. After looking at the first histogram, you decide that having this many classes chops up the data *too* much. You think a histogram with five classes would make the data easier to understand at a glance.

You can determine the current class width by subtracting a midpoint from an adjacent one. In this case, you can subtract 24000 from 26000 to find a class width of 2000 (26000 – 24000 = 2000). To modify the histogram so it reflects approximately five classes, you can double the class width to 4000:

- Choose **Edit > Edit Last Command Dialog**

- Click the **Interval width** text box

- Type **4000** and then press ⏎Enter

The resulting histogram has five classes, each with a width of 4000 (Figure 3-7).

FIGURE 3-7

Salary histogram with five classes

```
MTB > GStd.
MTB > Histogram 'SALARY';
SUBC>   Increment 4000.

Histogram of SALARY   N = 11

Midpoint   Count
   24000      1   *
   28000      3   ***
   32000      3   ***
   36000      0
   40000      4   ****

MTB > GPro.
```

If, instead, you wanted more classes, you could reduce the interval width in the same manner.

The histogram reveals that there are more Sales Department employees in the highest salary class than in any of the lower ones. Perhaps the employees in the top category have worked at Technitron the longest. If so, it might be cost-effective to suggest a retirement incentive to reduce salary costs. The histogram also indicates a large gap between the highest salary level and lower ones — jumping from a midpoint of 40000 to one of 32000. Is this bad for employee morale?

You also want to compare male to female salaries to determine whether Technitron's pay structure is discriminatory. To do so, you must produce two histograms: one that displays male salaries, and another that depicts female salaries.

- Choose **Edit > Edit Last Command Dialog**

You can produce separate histograms for each value of this second factor, or *By variable*. For your report, use C8 GENDER N as your By variable:

- Click the **By variable** check box and then press ⌐Tab⌐ to move to the text box to the right

- Double-click **C8 GENDER N** to enter it in the **By variable** text box

- Click **OK**

Note: By variables can contain only integer values.

Minitab generates two separate histograms, one above the other (Figure 3-8). The top one reflects men's salaries (GENDER N = 0); the bottom one shows women's salaries (GENDER N = 1).

```
MTB > GStd.
MTB > Histogram 'SALARY';
SUBC>   By 'GENDER N';
SUBC>   Increment 4000.

Histogram of SALARY    GENDER N = 0    N = 6

Midpoint   Count
   24000      0
   28000      1    *
   32000      2    **
   36000      0
   40000      3    ***

Histogram of SALARY    GENDER N = 1    N = 5

Midpoint   Count
   24000      1    *
   28000      2    **
   32000      1    *
   36000      0
   40000      1    *

MTB > GPro.
```

The same salary classes are used in both histograms. When you compare the two histograms, you see that male salaries are concentrated toward the upper end of the range while female salaries are more equally distributed. It appears that Technitron's salary structure may be discriminatory; however, such a conclusion is premature since male employees might have been at the company longer. Further analysis should clarify this issue.

Creating a Dotplot

Next, you look at a dotplot representation of the data in C1 SALARY, which gives you an opportunity to compare the relative advantages of a dotplot versus a histogram. You will then be in a better position to decide which graph types you want to include in your presentation.

- Choose **Graph > Character Graphs > Dotplot**

The Dotplot dialog box appears.

■ Double-click **C1 SALARY** to enter it in the **Variables** text box

The completed Dotplot dialog box should look like the one in Figure 3-9.

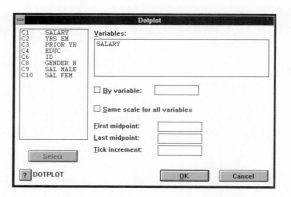

■ Click **OK**

The dotplot appears, as shown in Figure 3-10.

```
MTB > DotPlot 'SALARY'.

         .       :.    .  :              :  .   .
    ---+---------+---------+---------+---------+---------+---SALARY
    24500     28000     31500     35000     38500     42000
```

The dotplot of the salary data tells the same story as the histogram. Salaries range from approximately $24000 to $42000, with a fairly large gap in the middle. Change the dotplot scale so that it is comparable to the scale shown in the histogram in Figure 3-7:

■ Choose **Edit > Edit Last Command Dialog** and then press Tab three times

■ Type **20000** in the **First midpoint** text box and then press Tab twice

■ Type **4000** in the **Tick increment** text box and then press ←Enter

As usual, Minitab records all commands (and, in this case, the output) in the Session window, as shown in Figure 3-11.

```
MTB > DotPlot 'SALARY';
SUBC>   Start 20000;
SUBC>   Increment 4000.

             .       :    .  :              :  .   .
    +---------+---------+---------+---------+---------+------SALARY
    20000     24000     28000     32000     36000     40000
```

As you have already seen, each time you make a menu selection, Minitab displays the corresponding command in the Session window. Now look at the last three commands that appear above the dotplot in Figure 3-11. The display includes a *subcommand*, as indicated by *SUBC*, which provides additional information about the preceding command. Subcommands represent the options you select in dialog boxes. The following table describes each entry in the Session window:

Entry	Represents
MTB >	The Minitab prompt, which Minitab displays when it's ready for your next command.
DotPlot 'SALARY';	Your choice of Dotplot from the menu; the semicolon indicates that you made additional selections in the dialog box (if you hadn't, this command would be the only one that appeared in the Session window before the graph)
SUBC>	The Minitab prompt that indicates that a subcommand follows
Start 20000;	The First midpoint option you selected, which Minitab interprets as the Start subcommand; the semicolon indicates that another subcommand follows.
Increment 4000.	Your selection of 4000 as the tick increment; the period after 4000 indicates that this is the last subcommand issued for the main DotPlot 'SALARY'; command

Note: Minitab uses a mixture of upper and lower case when it records commands and dialog box choices.

Most users find that making choices from the Minitab menus and selections in dialog boxes is the most straightforward and error-free method of issuing commands. However, more advanced users who use Minitab frequently, especially those who are proficient typists, may find that typing the Minitab command language in the Session window is more efficient. (The Reference section contains more information about the Minitab command language.) These tutorials, however, primarily use the menu commands.

Creating a Stem-and-Leaf Diagram

A stem-and-leaf display is similar to a histogram, except that it shows each data value. An important part of your report concerns the length of time employees have been at Technitron. To construct a stem-and-leaf display for C2 YRS EM using Minitab's choice of scaling:

■ Choose **Graph > Character Graphs > Stem-and-Leaf**

■ Double-click **C2 YRS EM** to enter it in the **Variables** text box

The completed Stem-and-Leaf dialog box appears in Figure 3-12.

FIGURE 3-12

The Stem-and-Leaf dialog box

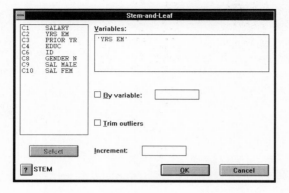

■ Click **OK**

Figure 3-13 shows the resulting stem-and-leaf display.

FIGURE 3-13

Stem-and-leaf display of years employed

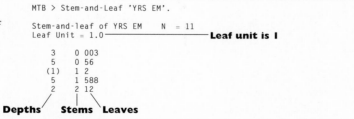

For now, ignore the numbers in the first column. The numbers in the column on the right contains the *leaves*, or rightmost digits, of the data values. The numbers in the center column represent the *stems*, or leftmost digits, of the data values. Because Minitab reports a leaf unit of 1 (Leaf Unit = 1.0), each leaf represents the one's digit of a data value and each stem represents the ten's digit of the data value. For example, the last line of the stem-and-leaf plot shown in Figure 3-13 indicates a stem of 2 followed by leaves of 1 and 2. You reconstruct these numbers into the data values 21 and 22.

Many stem-and-leaf displays use one line per stem, but in some cases, such as this one, Minitab uses two lines per stem. When two lines per stem are used, the first line contains leaves with the first five digits (0, 1, 2, 3, 4), and the second line contains leaves with the last five digits (5, 6, 7, 8, 9). To break up the data even more finely, you could use five lines per stem corresponding to the leaf digits (0,1), (2,3), (4,5), (6,7), and (8,9).

The first column in the stem-and-leaf display indicates the *depths*, which are used to show cumulative frequencies. Starting at the top, the depths indicate the number of leaves that lie in the given row (or stem) plus any previous rows. For example, the 5 in the first column of the second line in Figure 3-13 indicates that there are five leaves (0, 0, 3, 5, and 6) in the first two rows (or stems). If the line containing the median has any entries, the number in the left column represents the number of leaves on that line and appears in parentheses. The median for this data set is 12.

Change the increment from the default of 5 (which divides each stem value of 10 into two lines) to 10.

- Choose **Edit > Edit Last Command Dialog** and then press [Tab] three times

- Type **10** in the **Increment** text box and then press [←Enter]

Minitab records all values from the same stem on one line. Your new display should look like the one shown in Figure 3-14.

FIGURE 3-14

*Stem-and-leaf display
with an increment of 10*

```
MTB > Stem-and-Leaf 'YRS EM';
SUBC> Increment 10.

Stem-and-leaf of YRS EM    N  = 11
Leaf Unit = 1.0

     5     0 00356
    (4)    1 2588
     2     2 12
```

If you compare Figures 3-13 and 3-14, you can see that Minitab's default graph with two lines per stem breaks the data up more finely and therefore provides a more descriptive picture of it.

Now use Minitab's default settings to construct a stem-and-leaf display of the data values in C1 SALARY.

- Choose **Edit > Edit Last Command Dialog**

Because you want to examine a different variable, you want to clear the previous settings that appear in the Stem-and-Leaf dialog box. You can quickly restore the default settings by using the Control menu. To restore the default settings:

- Click the Control menu box of the Stem-and-Leaf dialog box to open its Control menu

- Click **Reset Defaults**

The Variables box is now empty and the Increment setting is cleared.

Create the SALARY stem-and-leaf plot:

- Double-click **C1 SALARY** to enter it in the **Variables** text box

- Click **OK**

The new plot appears in the Session window (Figure 3-15).

FIGURE 3-15

Stem-and-leaf display of SALARY

```
MTB > Stem-and-Leaf 'SALARY'.

Stem-and-leaf of SALARY    N  = 11
Leaf Unit = 1000

     1      2 5
     1      2
     3.     2 99
     4      3 0
    (3)     3 233
     4      3
     4      3
     4      3 99
     2      4 0

        HI  42.
```

Because Minitab reports a leaf unit of 1000 (Leaf Unit = 1000), each leaf represents the thousand's digit of the data value and each stem represents the ten thousand's digit. For example, the first entry of 2 5 translates to a data value of 25000 (20000 for the stem and 5000 for the leaf). This entry represents the actual salary value of 24749. (To simplify the stem-and-leaf plot, Minitab rounds to only the first two digits of a salary.)

There are five lines for each stem in this particular display. To condense the salary stem-and-leaf display to two lines per stem, tell Minitab to use an increment of 5000. (Recall that the leaf unit is 1000, so $10/2 \times 1000 = 5000$.)

- Choose **Edit > Edit Last Command Dialog**

- Click the **Increment** text box, type **5000,** and then press (←Enter)

Minitab consolidates the display to show only two lines per stem.

In deciding whether to use any of these stem-and-leaf displays, you should consider how much opportunity you will have to interpret them. As you can see, they require some careful explanation. If your audience is familiar with these plots, they could provide an excellent picture of your information.

Creating a Boxplot

Of the four ways to graphically display a single variable, boxplots contain the most statistical information.

- Choose **Graph > Character Graphs > Boxplot**

- Double-click **C1 SALARY** to enter it in the **Variables** text box

The completed Boxplot dialog box looks like the one shown in Figure 3-16.

FIGURE 3-16

The Boxplot dialog box

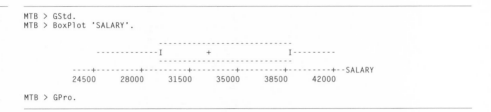

■ Click **OK**

The SALARY boxplot appears in the Session window (Figure 3-17).

FIGURE 3-17

Salary boxplot

```
MTB > GStd.
MTB > BoxPlot 'SALARY'.

                              ------------------------------
              -------------I         +                 I---------
                              ------------------------------
            ----+---------+---------+---------+---------+---------+--SALARY
              24500     28000     31500     35000     38500     42000

MTB > GPro.
```

A boxplot uses five numbers to describe a set of data:

● Maximum value

● Upper hinge (approximately equivalent to the 75th percentile)

● Median (the 50th percentile)

● Lower hinge (approximately equivalent to the 25th percentile)

● Minimum value

Minitab constructs a rectangle between the lower and upper hinges, and displays a plus (+) sign at the location of the median. A box encloses the middle half of the data. The *whiskers* that extend in either direction indicate the non-outlying data. If there are extreme values, Minitab identifies them with asterisks (*) or zeros (0), as you'll see in a moment.

In this case, the boxplot quickly shows that the middle half of the salaries in the Sales Department fall between about 29000 and 39000. The median indicates that half of all the salaries fall below 32000, and half above.

Minitab can display boxplots for different groups of data, one above the other. Earlier Minitab constructed two histograms for salary using

C8 GENDER N as the By variable. Now create two boxplots of the same data and compare them to the histograms in Figure 3-8.

- Choose **Edit > Edit Last Command Dialog**
- Click the **By variable** check box and then press ⸢Tab⸥ to move to the text box to the right
- Double-click **C8 GENDER N** to enter it in the **By Variable** text box
- Click **OK**

Figure 3-18 shows the two boxplots. The top one depicts male salaries (0 = male); the bottom displays female salaries (1 = female).

FIGURE 3-18

Boxplot of salary for males and females

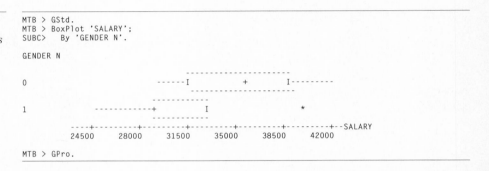

```
MTB > GStd.
MTB > BoxPlot 'SALARY';
SUBC>    By 'GENDER N'.

GENDER N

                         ----------------------
0                ------I         +      I---------
                         ----------------------
                    ------------
1           -----------+        I                *
                    ------------
        ----+---------+---------+---------+---------+---------+--SALARY
          24500     28000     31500     35000     38500     42000

MTB > GPro.
```

You can see that male salaries fall over a wider range and their median is higher than that of female salaries by about $7000. Referring back to Figure 3-8 you note the same conclusions: men earn more than women at Technitron.

The * in the boxplot for females represents an outlier. An *outlier* is a data value that is far removed from the rest of the data. The salary of this female is significantly higher than the other female salaries.

▼
Plotting One Variable Against Another
▲

While some types of graphics are appropriate for displaying single variables, scatter plots and multiple scatter plots illustrate the relationship between two variables.

Creating a Scatter Plot

Up to this point, each of the graphs you constructed described a single variable, such as C1 SALARY. Scatter plots show the relationship between two variables. Since your supervisor wanted you to concentrate on salary structure, you began with four single-variable salary graphs. To examine the possibility of sex discrimination, you produced two histograms and two boxplots: one of each type for male salaries and one each for female salaries. These graph pairs made it easy to compare salary levels.

The question arose as to whether higher male salaries might be the result of longer tenure with Technitron, not discrimination. You can create a scatter plot of the two variables, C1 SALARY and C2 YRS EM, to examine the relationship between the two variables:

■ Choose **Graph > Character Graphs > Scatter Plot**

■ Double-click **C1 SALARY** to enter it in the **Y variable** text box

■ Double-click **C2 YRS EM** to enter it in the **X variable** text box

The completed Scatter Plot dialog box looks like the one in Figure 3-19.

FIGURE 3-19

The Scatter Plot dialog box

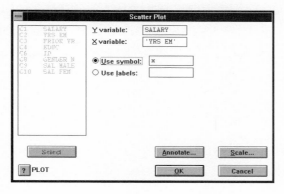

■ Click **OK**

Minitab displays the scatter plot in the Session window (Figure 3-20).

FIGURE 3-20

Scatter plot of salary versus years employed

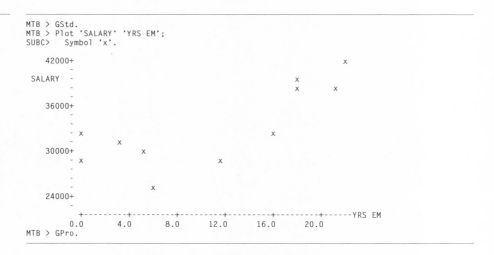

From this scatter plot, it appears that the people who have worked longer at Technitron tend to have higher salaries. However, some of the new personnel have salaries higher than those who have worked there for six years.

Using Tags in Scatter Plots

You can refine the scatter plot of C1 SALARY against C2 YRS EM by labeling the data points with a third, or *tag*, variable. To further investigate the possibility of sex discrimination, label the points on the scatter plot using the data in C8 GENDER N:

Note: Variables used as tags can contain only integer values.

■ Choose **Edit > Edit Last Command Dialog**

■ Click **Use labels** and then press ⌨Tab

■ Double-click **C8 GENDER N** as the label variable and then click **OK**

The scatter plot with the labeled values displays, as shown in Figure 3-21.

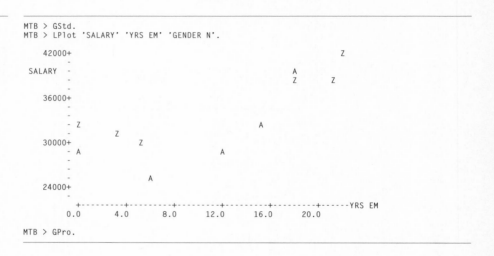

```
MTB > GStd.
MTB > LPlot 'SALARY' 'YRS EM' 'GENDER N'.

    42000+                                              Z
SALARY   -                                      A
         -                                      Z    Z
         -
    36000+
         -
         - Z
         -        Z                                 A
    30000+            Z
         - A                              A
         -
         -
         -              A
    24000+
         -
          +---------+---------+---------+---------+---------+------YRS EM
        0.0       4.0       8.0      12.0      16.0      20.0
MTB > GPro.
```

Minitab plots all female salaries with the letter A and all male salaries with the letter Z. (See the Reference section for details about why Minitab designates these two letters for the labels.)

The points in the upper right corner of the graph show that males with higher salaries also have the most experience with Technitron. However, one female with six years at Technitron has a lower salary than coworkers hired after her. Also, of the two most recently hired people, the female's salary is noticeably lower than the male's. Perhaps it would be wise to look into the reason for this.

Creating a Multiple Scatter Plot

Minitab lets you display several scatter plots on one set of axes. In this case, you want to compare the variable C1 SALARY with both C2 YRS EM and C4 EDUC at the same time to determine the effect of education on salary level:

- Choose **Graph** > **Character Graphs** > **Multiple Scatter Plot**
- Double-click **C1 SALARY** to enter it in the first **Y Variables** text box
- Double-click **C2 YRS EM** to enter it in the first **X Variables** text box
- Double-click **C1 SALARY** to enter it in the second **Y Variables** text box
- Double-click **C4 EDUC** to enter it in the second **X Variables** text box

Your completed Multiple Scatter Plot dialog box should look like the one shown in Figure 3-22.

FIGURE 3-22

The Multiple Scatter Plot dialog box

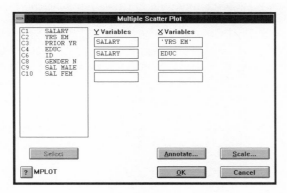

- Click **OK**

Minitab produces the multiple scatter plot shown in Figure 3-23.

FIGURE 3-23

Multiple scatter plot

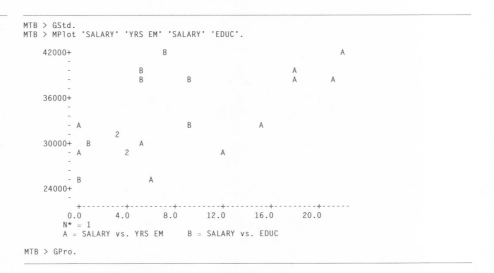

MINITAB AT WORK

FORESTRY: Foresters rely on easily obtained measurements to estimate how much timber a given forest contains. Researchers at Allegheny National Forest hoped to find a way to predict the volume of an individual tree by measuring only its base diameter.

The Allegheny team cut down 31 black cherry trees and measured the diameter and timber volume of each tree. They entered the resulting data into Minitab and created scatter plots of various combinations of the two variables. They found that plotting volume against the square of the diameter produced a strong linear relationship: if they wanted to estimate the volume of a tree with, say, a 1-foot diameter, they would mark 12^2, or 144 inches, on the x-axis, and find the corresponding volume on the y-axis — approximately 23 cubic feet of timber.

The foresters now had a tool that allowed them to estimate timber volume without having to cut down trees. Although they used other Minitab procedures that gave a more accurate estimate of volume, the plotting phase helped them single out the best variable transformation to use as a predictor.

Minitab displays the multiple scatter plot by using a different symbol for each set of paired values. Minitab uses the symbol A to plot salary versus years employed, and uses B to plot salary versus education. Both variables on the horizontal axis seem to have a positive relationship with salary.

Creating a Time Series Plot

Management also wants to know whether any recent changes in the Consumer Price Index (CPI) will necessitate bigger salary increases in the future than those given in the last few years. You can use a time series plot of the percent change in the CPI to determine if any significant variations have occurred in recent years.

A time series plot is a special type of scatter plot in which one or more variables are plotted on the vertical axis and integers representing observations made at equally spaced intervals of time are plotted on the horizontal axis. In addition to designating a time series variable to be plotted, it is often useful to enter the value of the initial time integer so you can tag each of the observations.

- Open **CPI.MTW**

- Choose **Window > Data** to see the worksheet.

C1 YEAR indicates the year and C2 CPICHNGE shows the corresponding percent change in the CPI.

- Choose **Graph > Character Graphs > Time Series Plot**

- Double-click **C2 CPICHNGE** to enter it in the first **Series** text box

■ Type **1960** in the corresponding **Origin** text box so that the horizontal axis shows the data for the years in C1

The dialog box should now look like the one shown in Figure 3-24.

FIGURE 3-24

The Time Series Plot dialog box

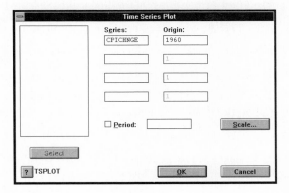

■ Press ⏎Enter

The Session window shows the time series plot (Figure 3-25).

FIGURE 3-25

Time series plot

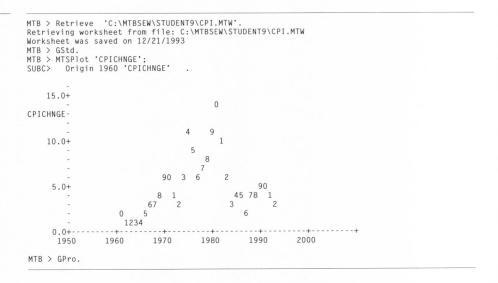

As you can see, the CPI didn't change much between 1983 and 1992. All of the values are at or around 4%. Because you typed 1960 in the Origin text box, Minitab uses each year's final digit to label its observation. Based on this plot, there doesn't appear to be a need to increase salaries beyond the percent increases of recent years.

Since your deadline is fast approaching, you need to decide which graphs to prepare for the staff meeting as a supplement to your report. First, stop recording the session, and then, in Notepad, open the LIS outfile you created to consider which graphs to keep.

- Choose **File > Other Files > Stop Recording Session**

    Open T3.LIS, which is stored on your Student disk:

- Press [Alt]+[Tab] until Program Manager appears

- Double-click the **Accessories** group icon to open the Accessories group window in Program Manager

- Double-click the **Notepad** program-item icon to open the Notepad

- Choose **File > Open** from the Notepad menu bar

- Click the **List files of Type** drop-down arrow and click **All Files** to list files of all types, not just TXT files

- Click the **Drives** drop-down list arrow and then click **a:**

- Double-click **T3.LIS** in the **Files** list box (you may have to scroll to see it)

    A record of your entire session appears.

- Maximize the Notepad window

- Scroll through the Notepad window to examine all the graphs you created

    Upon review, you decide to include the histogram with five classes (Figure 3-7) because it best shows the distribution of salaries at Technitron. You also want to use the scatter plot of salary versus years employed tagged by gender (Figure 3-21) in your presentation, because it suggests that management may need to explore whether salary discrimination occurs at Technitron.

    You could edit, print, and save the record of your session, T3.LIS, for further consideration, but there's no need to do so because you're confident about your decision.

    Exit Notepad and return to Minitab:

- Choose **File > Exit**

- Press [Alt]+[Tab] until Minitab appears

    In Tutorial 4, you create these two plots using Professional graphics. You also work with other Professional graph types to see if there are any others you might want to include in your presentation. You can restart Minitab to continue or you can exit Windows to take a break.

    If you plan to continue directly to the next tutorial:

- Choose **File > Restart Minitab**

If you want to take a longer break:

■ Choose **File > Exit**

▼

**Minitab
Command
Summary**

▲

This section describes the menu commands and Session commands introduced in or related to this tutorial. To find a complete explanation of all menus and commands, refer to the Reference section of this manual.

Minitab Menu Commands

Menu	Command	Description
File		
	Other Files	
	Start Recording Session	Writes all Minitab commands and output to an outfile
	Stop Recording Session	Stops writing to the outfile
Graph		
	Character Graphs	
	Set Options	Sets the height and width of all subsequent character graphs
	Histogram	Produces a character-based histogram for each column of data requested
	Boxplot	Produces a character-based boxplot display of a single column of data
	Dotplot	Produces a character-based dotplot for each column requested
	Stem-and-Leaf	Produces a character-based stem-and-leaf diagram for each column requested
	Scatter Plot	Displays a character-based plot of two variables
	Multiple Scatter Plot	Plots several pairs of variables on the same axes using characters
	Time Series Plot	Plots one or more variables against time on the same axes using characters

Minitab Session Commands

GPRO	Enables Professional graphics
GSTD	Enables Standard Character graphs
NEWPAGE	Starts the output of the next command on a new page when recording a session
NOTE	Displays messages in the Session window

▼
Review and Practice
▲

Matching

Match the following terms to their definitions by placing the correct letter next to the term it describes.

_____ multiple scatter plot

_____ stem-and-leaf plot

_____ outfile

_____ By variable

_____ +

_____ scatter plot

_____ Origin

_____ tag variable

_____ histogram

_____ dotplot

a. An integer variable used to define groups

b. A text file that optionally stores commands and output from a Minitab session

c. A plot in which several pairs of variables are depicted on one graph

d. An integer variable used to define plot characters

e. The text box in the Time Series dialog box in which you indicate the starting point for the horizontal axis

f. The symbol used by Minitab to represent the median in a boxplot

g. A plot with one variable on the vertical axis and another on the horizontal axis

h. A display that is similar to a histogram but has a horizontal axis that's divided into more classes

i. A graphical description of the frequency of a variable

j. A graphical description of the data in which some digits of the original data are evident

True/False

Mark the following statements with a *T* or an *F*.

_____ 1. All graphical displays in Minitab can be either character-based or high-resolution.

_____ 2. Character plots are displayed in the Session window.

_____ 3. For most displays (either Character or Professional), you can change the scale, starting points, and increment values.

_____ 4. All displays can be done separately for each value of a By variable.

_____ 5. In a scatter plot, the Y variable is plotted on the vertical axis and the X variable is plotted on the horizontal axis.

_____ 6. Minitab lets you annotate some graphical displays with titles and footnotes.

_____ 7. Boxplots, dotplots, histograms, and stem-and-leaf plots are different types of one-variable displays.

_____ 8. A time series plot displays integers that represent equally spaced observations on the vertical axis.

_____ 9. You can display multiple boxplots at the same time.

_____ 10. Minitab always assigns the LIS extension to files produced by the Start Recording Session menu command.

Practice Problems

1. Open MARKS.MTW.

   a. Create a histogram, dotplot, stem-and-leaf diagram, and boxplot of the first exam data. Compare the four displays. Do all three provide the same information about the class's performance on the first exam?

   b. Compare the four displays' ability to identify extreme scores. What were the minimum and maximum scores, based on each display?

   c. Compare the four displays' ability to identify individual scores. How many students scored more than 75% on the first exam? What were their scores?

   d. Compare the four displays' ability to identify median scores. What is the median score based on each display?

   e. Briefly explain why you might use more than one of these displays in a report.

2. Open ADS.MTW, which describes full-page ads in two magazines in 1989, 1991, and 1993.

   a. Compute the ratio of full-page ads to pages. Name the new column C5 ADRATIO.

   b. Save your worksheet as P3ADS.MTW.

   c. Produce a boxplot of the ads ratio data. Do the data appear symmetric? If not, in which direction is the ads ratio skewed?

   d. Produce a boxplot of the ads ratio data for each magazine. How does the type of magazine affect the ads ratio?

   e. Produce a boxplot of the ads ratio data for each year. (You will have to recode C3 because Minitab does not allow large integers.) How does year affect the ads ratio?

3. Open MARKS.MTW.

   a. Plot the second exam score against the first exam score. Does there appear to be a relationship between them?

   b. Plot the third exam score against the second exam score. Does there appear to be a relationship between them?

   c. Plot the third exam score against the first exam score. Does there appear to be a relationship between them?

   d. Which of the three plots displays the strongest relationship? Explain.

   e. Based on the information given in C2, enter a new variable named GENDER in C6. Let 1 represent males, 2 represent females, and * represent unknown entries.

   f. Produce the plot you selected in part d with GENDER as a tag variable. Does it display more information than the scatter plot without the tag variable? Briefly explain your answer.

4. Open MNWAGE.MTW.

   a. Create a scatter plot of minimum wage versus year.

   b. Create a time series plot of minimum wage.

   c. What are the similarities between the two plots? What are the differences? Which plot do you prefer? Briefly explain your answer.

TUTORIAL 4

Graphical Presentations

In this tutorial, you continue your work with the Technitron salary structure data from Tutorial 3. You use Minitab's Professional graph capabilities to annotate and format graphs that present the information most effectively. You also use Minitab's Chart command to produce a graph that depicts the relationship between salary and gender. Finally, you select and print the graphs to present at the staff meeting.

Objectives

In this tutorial you learn how to:

- produce high-resolution Professional graphs for presentation

- format and customize Professional graphs

- save Professional graph files and discard unwanted graphs

- print graph files

CASE STUDY: MANAGEMENT — SALARY STRUCTURE (CONTINUED)

In Tutorial 3, you created graphs that effectively described the salary structure at Technitron. At the end of the tutorial, you selected two graphs for your presentation. The first graph, a histogram, depicts the distribution of salaries. The second graph is a scatter plot that shows the relationship between salary and years at Technitron, and labels the values by gender. In this tutorial, you reproduce these graphs using Minitab's Professional graphics.

Professional Graphics

You can annotate and customize Minitab Professional graphics in almost an unlimited number of ways. Minitab displays each Professional graph you produce in its own Graph window. Although Minitab has only one Data window and one Session window, you can have up to 15 Graph windows open at once. You can save, print, or import graphics into other programs.

There are five basic Professional graph types: plot, chart, histogram, boxplot, and time series plot.

To get started:

- Start Minitab and maximize the Minitab window and the Data window

- Open **PAY2.MTW**

    The salary data from Tutorial 3 appear in the Data window.

Creating a Professional Histogram

In Tutorial 3, you decided to use the histogram of the five salary classes at Technitron as the first graph in your presentation on Technitron's salary structure. The histogram shows the distribution of C1 SALARY in the PAY2 data set. In Character graph mode, this histogram looks like the one shown in Figure 4-1.

FIGURE 4-1

Character histogram of salary at Technitron

```
MTB > GStd.
MTB > Histogram 'SALARY';
SUBC>   Increment 4000.
Histogram of SALARY    N = 11

Midpoint    Count
   24000       1    *
   28000       3    ***
   32000       3    ***
   36000       0
   40000       4    ****

MTB > GPro.
```

Try producing this graph using Professional graphics:

■ Choose **Graph > Histogram**

The Histogram dialog box opens, as shown in Figure 4-2. The dialog boxes for the five types of Professional graphics look similar to each other: there is a section for defining variables (Graph variables), a section for defining how the data values look on the graph (Data display grid), and a set of buttons you click to specify further formatting and display options.

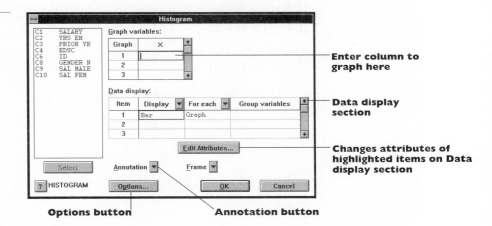

The Edit Attributes button lets you change the appearance (color, patterns, size, and so on) of the element indicated in the highlighted Display text box in the Data display section. There are two arrow buttons that display menus with further options: Annotation and Frame. The Annotation button lets you annotate graphs with titles, footnotes, text, and lines. You can format these annotations in any number of ways. The Frame button lets you customize the axes, the minimum and maximum values on the axes, and lets you control multiple graphs.

The Options button displays another dialog box that offers additional formatting choices specific to the type of graph with which you are currently working.

First, specify the variable you want to graph:

■ Double-click **C1 SALARY** to enter it in the first graph's **X** text box in the **Graph variables** section

When you created the Character histogram in Tutorial 3, you divided salary into five classes by specifying an interval width of 4000. You want to divide your Professional graphic in the same way.

- Click the **Options** button

  The Histogram Options dialog box opens, which lets you specify the type of histogram, the type of interval, and if you want to interchange the variables defining the vertical and horizontal axes. Just like the Character histogram, you want the interval to extend from one class midpoint to the next, so leave the MidPoint option selected.

  To specify 4000 as the interval width, you must tell Minitab the range of the data, divided by the interval width. In Tutorial 3, Minitab used a low value of 24000 and a high value of 42000. You can specify your five classes with the following expression: 24000:42000/4000. The colon (:) indicates the range; the slash (/) indicates division.

- Click the **Define intervals using values** text box, type **24000:42000/4000**, and press ⏎Enter

- Click **OK** to create the graph, as shown in Figure 4-3

FIGURE 4-3

Salary histogram with vertical bars

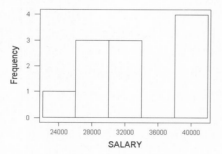

Interchanging Histogram Axes

Minitab uses vertical bars to construct histograms in Professional graphics. If you compare the new graph shown in Figure 4-3 to the Character histogram shown in Figure 4-1, you see that Minitab interchanged the variables on the axes. After considering the two layouts, you decide you prefer the axes setup of the first graph. It's easy to interchange axes in a Professional histogram:

- Choose **Edit > Edit Last Command Dialog**

- Click the **Options** button

- Click the **Transpose X and Y** check box

- Click **OK** twice

  The new histogram looks like the one shown in Figure 4-4.

FIGURE 4-4

Salary histogram with horizontal bars

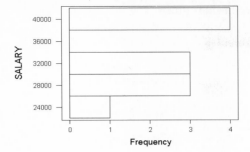

Notice that the Y axis in this histogram progresses from the minimum to the maximum value (24000 to 40000), which is the opposite order from the graph shown in Figure 4-1.

You can use the new histogram at the staff meeting to point out that four individuals have salaries in the upper interval while seven have salaries in the lower three intervals.

Annotating Your Histogram

To finalize your graph, add a descriptive title:

- Choose **Edit > Edit Last Command Dialog**

- Click the **Annotation** button to open the Annotation menu

  The Annotation menu lists four commands.

- Click **Title** to display the Title dialog box

- Type **Salary at Technitron** in the first Title text box and press ⏎Enter twice

  The histogram appears with a title (Figure 4-5).

FIGURE 4-5

Salary histogram with title

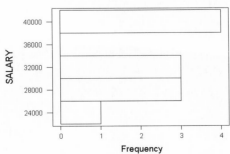

Formatting Histogram Bars

The bars that represent the data values in the histogram are difficult to distinguish from the graph's background. Add a colored pattern to make them stand out:

■ Choose **Edit > Edit Last Command Dialog**

The Edit Attributes button opens a list of options for whatever element you have chosen. The Data display section of the Histogram dialog box indicates *Bar* as the current item, so choosing Edit Attributes lets you format the bars in the graph.

■ Click the **Edit Attributes** button

The Bar dialog box opens, showing the available formatting options for your histogram bars. You want to add a green "criss-cross" pattern with a yellow background.

■ Click the **Fill Type** drop-down arrow

■ Click **Cross Slant**

■ Click the **Fore Color** drop-down arrow

■ Click **Green**

■ Click the **Back Color** drop-down arrow

■ Click **Yellow**

The Bar dialog box should look like Figure 4-6.

FIGURE 4-6

The Bar dialog box

Fill Type drop-down arrow

■ Click **OK** twice to produce the new histogram (Figure 4-7)

FIGURE 4-7

*Histogram with
cross-slanted bars*

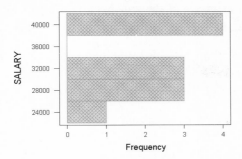

Salary at Technitron

The bars stand out now; the graph is ready for your presentation.

Saving Graphs

You are pleased with this graph, so save it to your Student disk:

- Choose **File > Save Window As**

- Insert your Student disk in drive A (or a different drive, if appropriate)

- Click the **Drives** drop-down list arrow and then click **a:**

- Double-click the **File Name** text box, type **HISTGRAM**, and then press ⏎Enter (remember you are limited to eight-character file names)

Minitab saves the graph with an MGF (Minitab Graphics Format) file extension. Once you save a graph, you can view it again by simply choosing File > Other Files > Open Graph.

Discarding Graphs

Minitab stores each Professional graph you create in its own window. A Graph window appears just like any other on the Window menu:

- Click **Window** on the menu bar

Below the names of the standard Minitab windows (Session, Data, History, and Info), Minitab lists the histograms you created in this tutorial. Because you have saved the one you want for your presentation on your Student disk, you can discard the others:

- Click **Discard Graph** to open a submenu

- Click **All Graphs**

Minitab removes the histograms you created.

Creating a Professional Scatter Plot

You now turn your attention to the other graph you wanted to use in your presentation: the scatter plot showing the relationship between salary and years at Technitron. In Tutorial 3, you labeled the data values by gender (reproduced in Figure 4-8).

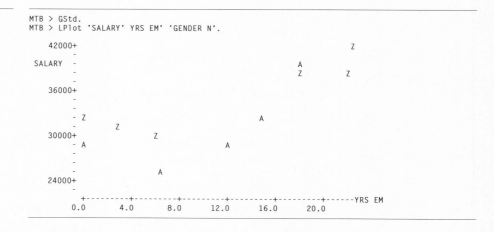

```
MTB > GStd.
MTB > LPlot 'SALARY' YRS EM' 'GENDER N'.

   42000+                                                   Z
        -
SALARY  -                                          A
        -                                          Z       Z
        -
   36000+
        -
        -
        - Z                                  A
        -        Z
   30000+             Z
        - A                          A
        -
        -
        -                 A
   24000+
        -
        +---------+---------+---------+---------+---------+------YRS EM
      0.0       4.0       8.0      12.0      16.0      20.0
```

The graph shows that some women who work at Technitron are paid less than men who were hired more recently. In addition, in the case of the two most recent hires, the woman's salary was substantially lower than the man's.

Produce this graph in Professional graphics, using some of the formatting techniques you've already learned:

- Choose **Graph > Plot**

- Double-click **C1 SALARY** to enter it in the first **Y** text box

- Double-click **C2 YEARS EM** to enter it in the first **X** text box

Defining Group Variables

To identify each data value by gender, you must define gender as a grouping variable. The first Display element in the Data display section is *Symbol*. You want to define a symbol for each group.

- Click the **For each** drop-down arrow in the **Data display** section

- Click **Group**

- Click the first **Group variables** text box in the Data display section

- Double-click **GENDER** to enter it as the Group variable

Assign colors to the data values. Then add a title and subtitle to your graph:

- Click the **Edit Attributes** button
- Click the first **Color** text box (for males), click the **Color** drop-down arrow, and then click **Magenta** for the males
- Click the second **Color** text box (for females), click the **Color** drop-down arrow again, and click **Green**
- Click **OK**
- Click the **Annotation** button and then click **Title** to add a title to your scatter plot
- Type **Salary vs. Years at Technitron** in the first **Title** text box
- Press ⬇ to move to the second **Title** text box
- Type **Tagged by Gender** as the subtitle

Formatting Text

You want the letters in the main title to be larger than those in the subtitle when the graph displays. In the lower half of the dialog box, there are a several options that let you customize the titles. The first Text Size text box indicates that the current height of the letters in the main title is 1.5 (see Figure 4-9).

FIGURE 4-9

Title dialog box

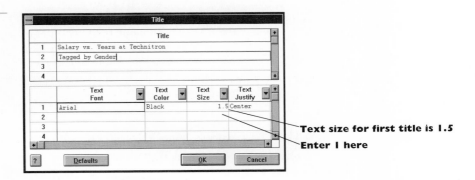

Reduce the height of the letters in the subtitle to 1.

- Click the second **Text Size** text box
- Type **1** and press ⏎Enter to return to the Plot dialog box
- Press ⏎Enter again to create the scatter plot (Figure 4-10)

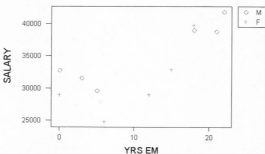

You want to save the scatter plot for your report and then discard the graph:

- Choose **File > Save Window As**

- Insert your Student disk in drive A (or a different drive, if appropriate)

- Click the **Drives** drop-down list arrow and then click **a:**, if necessary

- Double-click the **File Name** text box, type **PLOT**, and then press ⏎Enter

- Choose **Window > Discard Graph > This Graph** to discard the scatter plot

The two graphs you originally wanted for your presentation are stored on your Student disk.

You examined the relationship between salary and tenure at Technitron, but now you wonder whether years of education might have some bearing on the salary structure at Technitron. There are many different ways you could graph salary and years of education, but you decide to try a new Professional graph type: a Minitab chart.

Charting Variables

Before you "go public" with a finding that suggests gender discrimination at Technitron, you want to make sure that differences in education don't justify these differentials. As a managerial consultant, you certainly don't want to alarm your client only to discover that the male employees have more education than the females and therefore might deserve higher salaries.

Minitab's Chart command can help you find out if this is the case. It produces many kinds of charts, using a variety of summary statistics, such as sums, means, standard deviations, maximums, minimums, and so on. You want to chart the mean salary for males and females, grouped by educational background.

Creating a Grouping Variable

First, you need to create the grouping variable. C4 EDUC lists the number of years of post-secondary education completed by each employee. You create a new variable, EDLEVEL, to assign a code of 1 to those employees with up to four years of post-secondary education, and a code of 2 to those with 5 or more years. Most likely, an employee coded as a 1 has a bachelor's degree, whereas a 2 has completed some graduate work.

You learned how to code data values in Tutorial 2. To assign codes based on the number of years of education after high school:

- Choose **Manip > Code Data Values**

- Double-click **C4 EDUC** to enter it in the **Code data from columns** text box and press Tab

- Type **EDLEVEL** in the **Into columns** text box and press Tab

- Type **0:4** in the first **Original values** text box, press Tab, type **1** as the code in the first **New** text box, and then press Tab again

- Type **5:10** in the second **Original values** text box, press Tab, and then type **2** as the second **New** code

The completed Code Data Values dialog box should look like the one shown in Figure 4-11.

- Press ←Enter

In Tutorial 1, you added the data for a new employee in row 11. You have since learned that he didn't last long at Technitron — you need to delete his data from the Data window and then save the updated worksheet.

- Click the row header for row 11 to select it (not the first cell, but the row number)

- Choose **Edit > Delete Cells**

- Save your worksheet with the name 4PAY2 on your Student disk

Creating the Chart

Create the chart:

- Choose **Graph > Chart**

- Click the **Function** drop-down arrow and then click **Mean** so the chart displays the mean salary for each group

- Double-click **C1 SALARY** to enter it in the first **Y** text box

- Double-click **C11 EDLEVEL** to enter it in the first **X** text box

    You want to display two bars in each of the two education groupings: one for males, and one for females. You also want each bar to have its own distinctive pattern and color. To achieve this effect in Minitab, you define GENDER as a *cluster variable* that shows subgroups of data.

- Click the **For each** drop-down arrow and then click **Group**

- Click the first **Group variables** text box and then double-click **C7 GENDER**

- Click the **Options** button

- Click the **Cluster** check box, click the text box to its right, and then double-click **C7 GENDER** to enter it as the cluster variable

- Click **OK** in the Chart Options dialog box

    The Chart dialog box reappears (Figure 4-12).

FIGURE 4-12

The Chart dialog box

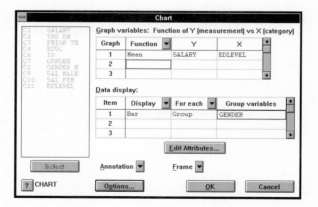

T-98   TUTORIAL 4: GRAPHICAL PRESENTATIONS

Add a title:

- Click the **Annotation** button and then click **Title**

- Type **Mean Salary by Amount of Education** in the first **Title** text box and **Grouped by Gender** in the second

- Type **1** in the second **Text Size** text box to change the size of the subtitle text

- Click **OK**

Editing Bar Attributes

Your chart uses bars to represent mean salary by gender for each of two education levels. Assign different patterns and colors to the bars for males and females:

- Click **Edit Attributes**

- Click the first **Fill Type** text box (for males), click the **Fill Type** drop-down arrow, and then click **Left Slant**

- Click the **Fore Color** drop-down arrow and then click **Yellow**

- Click the **Back Color** drop-down arrow and then click **Green**

- Click the second **Fill Type** text box (for females), click the **Fill Type** drop-down arrow, and then click **Right Slant**

- Click the **Fore Color** drop-down arrow and then click **Red**

- Click the **Back Color** drop-down arrow and then click **Blue**

Your Bar dialog box should look like Figure 4-13.

FIGURE 4-13

The Bar dialog box

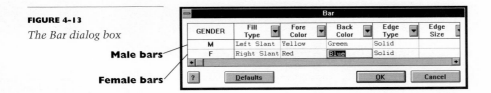

- Click **OK** twice

Minitab creates the Chart shown in Figure 4-14.

FIGURE 4-14

Chart showing mean salary versus level of education

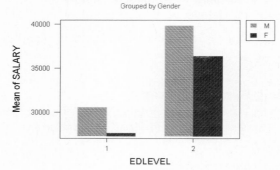

Mean Salary by Amount of Education
Grouped by Gender

The height of the bars represents the mean salary for each gender in each education level. The bars on the left show the mean salary for males and females who have a bachelor's degree or less. On the right, the chart shows the mean salary for males and females who have completed at least some graduate work.

The chart is disturbing — it appears that Technitron pays females less than males regardless of education level. With this chart and the scatter plot you created earlier in hand, you think you have enough proof to warrant further investigation into the question of gender discrimination at Technitron. Of course, these graphs alone aren't enough to make a case, but they do suggest that additional statistical analysis is in order to determine if there is a systematic difference between male and female salaries.

Save your chart before you print it:

- Choose **File > Save Window As**

- Insert your Student disk in drive A (or a different drive, if appropriate)

- Click the **Drives** drop-down list arrow and then click **a:**

- Double-click the **File Name** text box, type **CHART**, and then press ⏎Enter

Your Student disk now contains the three charts you want to use in your presentation at the staff meeting.

Opening and Printing a Graph

Print the first graph you saved, the histogram:

- Choose **File > Other Files > Open Graph**

- Click the **Drives** drop-down list arrow and then click **a:**

- Double-click **HISTGRAM.MGF** in the **Files** list box

Minitab displays the histogram.

- Choose **File > Print Window**

- Click **OK** in the Microsoft Windows Print dialog box

You now have a hard copy of the histogram you plan to use during your presentation. You probably had to print your color graph on a black-and-white printer. As a managerial consultant at Technitron, you might have access to a color printer, or, even better, hardware that you could use to print an overhead color transparency.

You can print color graphs on a black-and-white laser printer. The printer renders the colors in shades of black, gray, and white. You could experiment with Minitab's colors until you find the best combination for printing, but, for now, exit Minitab:

- Choose **File > Exit**

▼ Minitab Command Summary ▲

This section describes the Minitab menu commands introduced in or related to this tutorial. To find a complete explanation of all menus and commands, refer to the Reference section of this manual.

Minitab Menu Commands

Menu	Command	Description
File		
	Other Files	
	Open Graph	Opens a Minitab graph file
Window		
	Discard Graph	Removes one or more Professional Graph windows
Graph		
	Plot	Displays a Professional graph of two variables, or several pairs of variables on the same axes
	Chart	Produces many kinds of charts, including bar charts, line charts, symbol charts, and area charts
	Histogram	Produces a Professional histogram for each column of data requested

Menu	Command	Description
	Boxplot	Produces a Professional boxplot display of a single column of data
	Time Series Plot	Produces a Professional time series plot for one or more columns of data against time on the same axes

Review and Practice

Matching

Match the following terms to their definitions by placing the correct letter next to the term it describes.

_____ Annotation

_____ Plot

_____ Discard Graph

_____ Open Graph

_____ Professional Graphics

_____ Edit Attributes

_____ 15

_____ Print Window

_____ Save Window As

_____ Start Recording Session

a. A Minitab command located on the Window menu

b. A Minitab subcommand that activates a Professional graph

c. The maximum number of open Graph windows

d. A Minitab command that produces a Professional scatter diagram of two variables

e. The Minitab command you use to save a Professional graph

f. The Minitab command that prints a Professional graph

g. The Minitab subcommand that does not store Professional graphs in an outfile

h. The button used to change plot colors

i. High-resolution graphics

j. The button you use to add titles and footnotes to plots

True/False

Mark the following statements with a *T* or an *F*.

_____ 1. Professional graphics in Minitab are viewed in the Session window.

_____ 2. You can attach labels of your own choosing to the axes of Professional histograms.

_____ 3. The Professional graph Histogram dialog box contains a By variables button.

_____ 4. One way to print a Professional graph is to use the PAPER command.

_____ 5. Professional graphs are more appropriate for final reports.

_____ 6. Save Window As is a command on the Windows menu.

_____ 7. Minitab's Chart command produces many kinds of charts using a variety of summary statistics.

_____ 8. Minitab can interchange the variables on the axes of a Professional histogram.

_____ 9. The Plot command allows several pairs of variables on the same axes.

_____ 10. You can produce bar plots, line plots, symbol plots, and area plots with Minitab's Chart command.

Practice Problems

1. Open ADS2.MTW.

   a. Produce a Professional histogram of the ad ratio data. Do the data appear symmetric? If not, in which direction is the ads ratio skewed?

   b. Interchange the histogram axes. Which histogram do you prefer? Why?

   c. Annotate your preferred histogram by adding the title *Ratio of Full Page Ads and Total Number of Pages Histogram*.

   d. Format your histogram bars with a horizontal line.

   e. Print a hard copy of this histogram.

2. Open ADS2.MTW.

   a. Produce a Professional boxplot of the ad ratio data for each magazine. (Use Graph > Boxplot and set the Y Graph Variable equal to ADRATIO and the X Graph Variable equal to MAGAZINE.) How does the type of magazine affect the ads ratio?

   b. Add the title *Ads Ratio by Magazine Boxplot* to this display.

   c. Repeat step a for each year.

   d. Add the title *Ads Ratio by Year Boxplot* to this display.

3. Open ADS2.MTW.

   a. Produce a Professional bar chart of the Mean Ads Ratio by Magazine Grouped by Year. Be sure to add a title to your bar chart.

   b. Produce a Professional bar chart of the Mean Ads Ratio by Year Grouped by Magazine. Be sure to add a title to your bar chart.

4. Open HOMES.MTW.

   a. Open the Info window to see what information the file contains.

   b. Construct a Professional plot of PRICE versus AREA. Does a linear relationship exist among these data?

   c. Add the title *Plot of PRICE vs. AREA* and the footnote *Tutorial 4: Practice Problem 4 to your plot. (Remember that Edit > Edit Last Command Dialog is useful in situations like this.)*

5. Open MNWAGE.MTW.

   a. Create a Character graph time series plot of the minimum wage. Enter 50 as the Origin value.

   b. Create a Professional time series plot of minimum wage. Enter 50 as the Start Time Index after clicking the Options button.

   c. Compare the two time series plots. How are they similar? How are they different?

TUTORIAL
5

Numerical Methods for Describing Data

In this tutorial, you return to the yogurt data you worked with in Tutorial 1 to determine which brand to recommend in your report. You need to produce various descriptive statistics summarizing the data. Measures of central tendency and variation are the foundation of descriptive statistics but most of these formulas are quite tedious to compute, even with a calculator. Fortunately, Minitab lets you generate a number of commonly used descriptive statistics for as many columns as you designate, using just a single command.

Objectives

In this tutorial you learn how to:

- produce descriptive statistics

- convert alpha data to numeric data

- describe data separately for each value of a variable

- calculate frequencies for classes of data

- compute the covariance and correlation between variables

CASE STUDY: HEALTH MANAGEMENT — NUTRITION ANALYSIS (CONTINUED)

Your supervisor, Patricia Johnson, asks you to produce a report with Minitab that includes basic statistics describing the yogurt data. Your goal is to recommend a brand of yogurt for the hospital to vend.

▼
Describing Data
▲

Ms. Johnson will certainly want to know the steps involved in deciding which brand of yogurt to recommend, so you should create an outfile, as you did in Tutorial 3.

　　To get started:

- Start Minitab and maximize the Minitab window and the Data window

- Start an outfile named **T5** and save it on your Student disk (use the **File > Other Files > Start Recording Session** command)

　　You entered the data into Minitab in Tutorial 1 and stored it on your Student disk as 1YOGURT.MTW. In case you didn't complete that tutorial or you misplaced the file, you can use the YOGURT.MTW file, which comes with *The Student Edition of MINITAB for Windows*. You can open either file; they should contain the same data. If you think you made any mistakes, you may want to use YOGURT.MTW instead:

- Open **YOGURT.MTW**

　　YOGURT.MTW contains only the original data shown in Figure 1-1 in Tutorial 1: rating, cents per ounce, and calories per ounce. You need only these three columns of information in this tutorial.

　　First, you want to obtain descriptive statistics for the cost per ounce and number of calories per serving. These variables plus the nutrition rating will determine which brand of yogurt you ultimately recommend. To generate the basic descriptive statistics:

- Choose **Stat > Basic Statistics > Descriptive Statistics**

- Double-click **C2 CENTS** and **C3 CALS** to enter them in the **Variables** text box

　　The completed Descriptive Statistics dialog box looks like the one in Figure 5-1.

FIGURE 5-1

The Descriptive Statistics dialog box

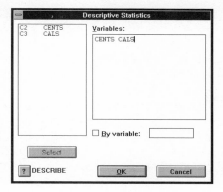

- Click **OK**

  Minitab automatically displays the Session window with the statistics you requested (Figure 5-2).

FIGURE 5-2

Basic statistics for cents and calories

```
MTB > Describe 'CENTS' 'CALS'.

               N     MEAN   MEDIAN   TRMEAN   STDEV   SEMEAN
CENTS         14    9.357    9.000    9.333   1.692    0.452
CALS          14    170.9    175.0    170.8    65.0     17.4

              MIN      MAX       Q1       Q3
CENTS       7.000   12.000    7.750   11.000
CALS         90.0    253.0    100.0    240.0

MTB >
```

For each variable you selected, Minitab produces a row containing the following statistics:

- N, the number of cases

- MEAN, the mean

- MEDIAN, the median

- TRMEAN, the trimmed mean

- STDEV, the sample standard deviation

- SEMEAN, the standard error of the mean

- MIN, the variable's lowest value

- MAX, the variable's highest value

- Q_1, the first quartile

- Q_3, the third quartile

You have probably studied most of these terms in class, but some may not be familiar to you. For example, the sample mean can be distorted by extreme values. In such cases, it is often desirable to obtain a *trimmed mean*, TRMEAN, which provides a more representative measure of central tendency. Minitab calculates the trimmed mean by discarding the top 5% and the bottom 5% of the data. It then computes the mean of the central 90%. When no extreme values are present, the mean and the trimmed mean are relatively close in value, as they are here for both CENTS and CALS.

You may find it helpful to look at a graph as you study descriptive statistics. As you saw in Tutorial 3, boxplots give you useful statistical information about single variables. Construct a Character boxplot for the cost data (Minitab automatically includes a Character graph in your outfile):

- Choose **Graph > Character Graphs > Boxplot**
- Double-click **C2 CENTS** to enter it in the **Variables** text box
- Click **OK**

The boxplot looks like Figure 5-3.

FIGURE 5-3

Boxplot of cents

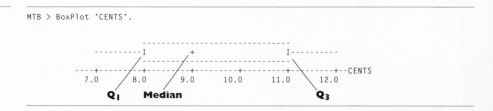

The plus sign (+) that appears in the box is the second quartile, Q2, which marks the median. The descriptive statistics in the Session window (Figure 5-2) indicate that the median is 9.0 cents. Q1 (7.75 cents) and Q3 (11.000 cents) represent the 25th and 75th percentiles, respectively, which approximate the vertical edges of the box.

▼
Measuring Other Descriptive Statistics
▲

A measure of dispersion commonly used in business is the *Mean Absolute Deviation (MAD)*. The MAD is the average of the absolute values of the deviations of the data from the mean. The MAD is not available in Minitab, but can be readily obtained using Minitab functions. You first store the mean as a constant, and then create a new variable representing the absolute values of the differences between the cents and the mean (9.357).

- Choose **Calc > Column Statistics**
- Click **Mean**
- Click the **Input variable** text box and then double-click **C2 CENTS**

- Click the **Store result in** check box and press `Tab`

- Type **MEANCENT** and press `←Enter`

- Choose **Calc > Mathematical Expressions**

- Type **'ABS DEVS'** in the **Variable (new or modified)** text box (be sure to include the single quotes) and then press `Tab` twice.

- Type **ABSOLUTE(**

- Double-click **C2**, and then type **-**

- Double-click **K1 MEANCENT**, and then type **)** so the Expression is ABSOLUTE ('CENTS'-'MEANCENT')

- Press `←Enter`

- Move to the Data window to see C4

Column C4 displays the absolute values of the difference between cost per ounce and the average cost per ounce. To obtain the mean of these absolute deviations:

- Choose **Calc > Column Statistics**

- Verify that **Mean** is selected

- Enter **C4 ABS DEVS** as the **Input variable**

- Deselect the **Store result in** check box

- Click **OK**

- Move to the Session window to see the MAD statistic

The Session window displays the value of the MAD statistic (Figure 5-4), 1.4082. This value indicates that, on average, the absolute difference of the cost from the mean is approximately 1.4 cents.

FIGURE 5-4

MAD statistic

```
MTB > Name k1 = 'MEANCENT'
MTB > Mean 'CENTS' 'MEANCENT'.
   MEAN     =       9.3571
MTB > Name c4 = 'ABS DEVS'
MTB > Let 'ABS DEVS' = ABSOLUTE( 'CENTS'- 'MEANCENT')
MTB > Mean 'ABS DEVS'.
   MEAN     =       1.4082
```

As a nutritionist, you want to provide healthy, delicious meals. But you also need to stay within your budget, and you probably want to select a brand of yogurt that is on or below average in cost. In this case, you want to use a brand that costs less than 9 cents per ounce.

Converting Alpha Data to Numeric Data

The statistics you have computed so far represent summaries of all the brands you are considering. Since nutritional value is an important concern, your supervisor asks you to analyze the information further to determine whether the brands rated highest in terms of nutritional value are also the most expensive with the fewest calories.

To investigate this matter, you need to examine the cost and calorie data for each rating value. However, you recall from Tutorial 3 that By variables must be integer values. Alpha variables cannot be used as By variables. Before you continue you must convert the alpha ratings variable to a numeric variable with corresponding integer values.

To convert alpha data to numeric variables, you must first enter a *conversion table* in the worksheet. A conversion table comprises a pair of columns: one contains the various alpha values; the other contains the corresponding numeric values.

In each row of the table, the alpha column entries show the possible alpha variable values, and the numeric column reflects the numbers to assign to these alpha values. You convert the alpha ratings data in C1 RATINGS using these values:

Alpha Rating Value	Numeric Rating Value
EXCELLENT	1
VERY GOOD	2
GOOD	3
FAIR	4
POOR	5

For convenience, enter the data in adjacent columns. Be sure to type the values *exactly* as they appear — data conversion is case-sensitive; that is, upper and lower case are treated as different letters.

- Choose **Window > Data**
- Click **C5 row 1**
- If necessary, click the data-entry arrow so that it is pointing downwards
- Type **EXCELLENT** and press (←Enter)
- Type **VERY GOOD** and press (←Enter)

- Type **GOOD** and press [↵Enter]
- Type **FAIR** and press [↵Enter]
- Type **POOR** and press [Ctrl]+[↵Enter]
- Type **1** and press [↵Enter]
- Type **2** and press [↵Enter]
- Type **3** and press [↵Enter]
- Type **4** and press [↵Enter]
- Type **5** and press [↵Enter]
- Click the column name cell for C5-A
- Type **CONV A** and press [Tab]
- Type **CONV N** and press [↵Enter]

The conversion columns in the Data window should resemble those in Figure 5-5.

FIGURE 5-5
Conversion table

C5-A	C6
CONV A	CONV N
EXCELLENT	1
VERY GOOD	2
GOOD	3
FAIR	4
POOR	5

To convert the alpha data in C1 RATING:

- Choose **Manip** > **Convert**
- Double-click **C1 RATING** to enter it in the **Input data** text box

Tell Minitab the name to assign to the column containing the converted data and the location of the conversion table:

- Type **'RATING N'** in the **Output** data text box and press [Tab]
- Double-click **C5 CONV A** to enter it in the **Original** Conversion Table text box
- Double-click **C6 CONV N** to enter it in the **Converted** Conversion Table text box

Figure 5-6 shows the completed Convert dialog box.

FIGURE 5-6

The Convert dialog box

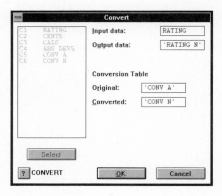

■ Click **OK**

Minitab converts the ratings using the conversion table in C5 and C6. Compare the alpha rating data in C1 RATING to the numeric rating data in C7 RATING N, as shown in Figure 5-7.

FIGURE 5-7

The Data window with converted data

Student Edition of MINITAB - YOGURT.MTW - [Data]

File Edit Manip Calc Stat Window Graph Editor Help

↓	C1-A	C2	C3	C4	C5-A	C6	C7
	RATING	CENTS	CALS	ABS DEVS	CONV A	CONV N	RATING N
1	EXCELLENT	11	120	1.64286	EXCELLENT	1	1
2	EXCELLENT	11	120	1.64286	VERY GOOD	2	1
3	VERY GOOD	9	100	0.35714	GOOD	3	2
4	GOOD	9	90	0.35714	FAIR	4	3
5	POOR	12	253	2.64286	POOR	5	5
6	GOOD	8	250	1.35714			3
7	VERY GOOD	9	100	0.35714			2
8	EXCELLENT	7	100	2.35714			1
9	GOOD	11	240	1.64286			3
10	FAIR	11	240	1.64286			4
11	FAIR	9	190	0.35714			4
12	FAIR	7	190	2.35714			4
13	POOR	7	240	2.35714			5
14	GOOD	10	160	0.64286			3
15							
16							
17							
18							
19							

Note: In this section you convert an alpha variable to a numeric variable. You can also convert a numeric variable to an alpha variable by reversing the original and converted entries.

Describing Data Separately for Each Value of a By Variable

Once you have converted the alpha ratings to numeric ratings, you can use this data to summarize the cost and calorie information for each rating level:

- Choose **Stat > Basic Statistics > Descriptive Statistics**
- If necessary, select **C2 CENTS** and **C3 CALS** to enter them in the **Variables** text box
- Click the **By variable** check box and enter **C7 RATING N** in the **By variable** text box
- Click **OK**

The Session window appears as in Figure 5-8.

FIGURE 5-8

Descriptive statistics of cents and calories, by rating

```
MTB > Name c7 = 'RATING N'
MTB > Convert 'CONV A' 'CONV N' 'RATING' 'RATING N'.
MTB > Describe 'CENTS' 'CALS';
SUBC>   By 'RATING N'.
```

	RATING N	N	MEAN	MEDIAN	TRMEAN	STDEV	SEMEAN
CENTS	1	3	9.67	11.00	9.67	2.31	1.33
	2	2	9.0000	9.0000	9.0000	0.0000	0.0000
	3	4	9.500	9.500	9.500	1.291	0.645
	4	3	9.00	9.00	9.00	2.00	1.15
	5	2	9.50	9.50	9.50	3.54	2.50
CALS	1	3	113.33	120.00	113.33	11.55	6.67
	2	2	100.00	100.00	100.00	0.00	0.00
	3	4	185.0	200.0	185.0	75.1	37.5
	4	3	206.7	190.0	206.7	28.9	16.7
	5	2	246.50	246.50	246.50	9.19	6.50

	RATING N	MIN	MAX	Q1	Q3
CENTS	1	7.00	11.00	7.00	11.00
	2	9.0000	9.0000	*	*
	3	8.000	11.000	8.250	10.750
	4	7.00	11.00	7.00	11.00
	5	7.00	12.00	*	*
CALS	1	100.00	120.00	100.00	120.00
	2	100.00	100.00	*	*
	3	90.0	250.0	107.5	247.5
	4	190.0	240.0	190.0	240.0
	5	240.00	253.00	*	*

Minitab summarizes each of the variables for each of the five ratings. It uses an asterisk (*) to indicate a missing value.

Examine the statistics to see how they might help you make your decision. The brands with poor nutritional ratings (RATING N = 5) have a mean cost of 9.5 cents, which is higher than you wanted to spend, so you can eliminate those from consideration. They also seem to be very high in calories, with a mean of 246.50 calories. Not surprisingly, the calorie count in general increases as the nutritional rate decreases (the higher RATING N is, the higher the mean calorie count is).

Calculating Frequencies

In your report, you would like to include information on how many brands you considered at each rating level. The Tally command computes a *frequency*, or count, for each category of a variable or column. To count how many brands are in each rating category:

■ Choose **Stat > Tables > Tally**

■ Double-click **C7 RATING N** to enter it in the **Variables** text box

You can display the frequency in four formats: Counts (an integer value), Percents (the number in each category divided by the total number), Cumulative counts, and Cumulative percents (the numbers and the percent of data values at or below the given value). To display the frequencies in all four formats:

■ Verify that **Counts**, the default, is selected.

■ Click the check boxes next to **Percents**, **Cumulative counts**, and **Cumulative percents**.

The completed Tally dialog box should look like the one shown in Figure 5-9.

FIGURE 5-9

The Tally dialog box

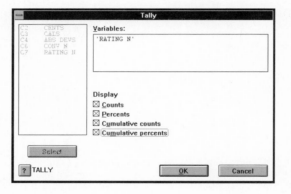

Note: Variables used in the Tally command must contain integer values only.

■ Click **OK**

Minitab produces a table containing the values for all the options you selected. Figure 5-10 shows the Session window with the tallied ratings.

FIGURE 5-10

Tally results for taste ratings

```
MTB > Tally 'RATING N';
SUBC>   Counts;
SUBC>   Percents;
SUBC>   CumCounts;
SUBC>   CumPercents.


RATING N   COUNT  PERCENT  CUMCNT   CUMPCT
      1        3    21.43       3    21.43
      2        2    14.29       5    35.71
      3        4    28.57       9    64.29
      4        3    21.43      12    85.71
      5        2    14.29      14   100.00
     N=       14
```

Minitab lists the numeric categories (1 for EXCELLENT, 2 for VERY GOOD, 3 for GOOD, and so on) in the first column, named RATING N. The next column reflects the default COUNT (or frequency) data for each category. The PERCENT column shows the percent of the total represented by each rating class. You can see that most of the brands available through your supplier (4, or 28.57%) are in the 3, or GOOD, category.

The CUMCNT column reveals that 9 of the 14 brands are rated GOOD or better, corresponding to a cumulative percent CUMPCT of 64.29. To highlight the fact that over 64% of the brands available are rated at least GOOD, collapse the rating data into two groups and then tally their statistics:

■ Choose **Manip > Code Data Values**

■ Double-click **C7 RATING N** to enter it in the **Code data from columns** text box and then press Tab

■ Type **TWORATE** in the **Into columns** text box and then press Tab

■ Type **1:3** in the first **Original values** text box, press Tab, type **1** in the first **New** text box, and then press Tab

■ Type **4:5** in the second **Original values** text box, press Tab, and type **2** in the second **New** text box

■ Press ←Enter

■ Choose **Window > Data**

C8 TWORATE now contains only 1s and 2s. The 1s represent brands rated GOOD or better, while the 2s represent brands rated only FAIR or POOR. Now tally this column:

■ Choose **Stat > Tables > Tally**

■ Double-click **C8 TWORATE** to enter it in the **Variables** text box

- Verify that the check boxes next to **Counts**, **Percents**, **Cumulative counts**, and **Cumulative percents** are selected

- Click **OK**

This new table tells you that 9 of the 14 brands, or 64.29%, are rated good or better (TWORATE = 1).

▼ Computing Covariance ▲

So far in this tutorial, you have characterized the behavior of individual variables such as the cost per ounce or the number of calories per serving. You now examine the relationship between cost and calories to find out whether more expensive brands have more or fewer calories than their less expensive counterparts. To produce a pictorial display, in the form of a scatter plot, of the relationship between these two variables:

- Choose **Graph > Character Graphs > Scatter Plot**

- Double-click **C2 CENTS** to enter it in the **Y variable** text box

- Double-click **C3 CALS** to enter it in the **X variable** text box

- Click **OK**

The scatter plot should look like Figure 5-11.

FIGURE 5-11

Scatter plot of calories and cost

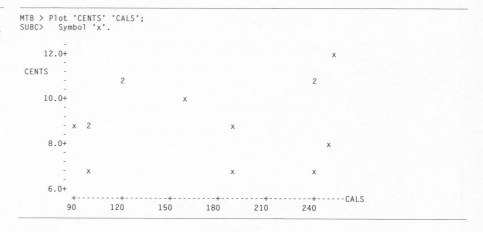

At first glance, the scatter plot doesn't seem to show much of a relationship between cost and calories. You decide to quantify this information by finding the *covariance*, a numerical summary of a relationship between two variables. In addition, you want to see the covariance of the numerical rating with cost per ounce and number of calories per serving.

- Choose **Stat > Basic Statistics > Covariance**

- Double-click **C2 CENTS**, **C3 CALS**, and **C7 RATING N** to enter them in the **Variables** text box

The completed Covariance dialog box should look like the one shown in Figure 5-12.

FIGURE 5-12

The Covariance dialog box

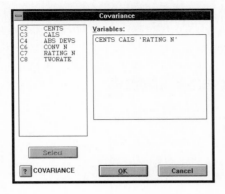

- Click **OK**

The Session window should resemble Figure 5-13.

FIGURE 5-13

Covariance matrix

```
MTB>  Covariance 'CENTS' 'CALS' 'RATING N'.

                  CENTS        CALS     RATING N
CENTS            2.8626
CALS            14.9505   4228.9946
RATING N        -0.1264     68.9945       1.9176
```

Entries along the diagonal of the covariance matrix represent the covariance of each variable with itself. This is the *variance* of the variable. The other three values in the matrix are the covariance between the variables identified in the row and column.

When the covariances are positive, it indicates that high values of one variable in the pair are generally associated with high values in the other. In this case, there is a positive covariance between calories and cents and between calories and rating, suggesting that brands with higher calories are more expensive, and that the higher the calorie count the worse the nutritional value. (Recall that RATING N has 1 = EXCELLENT and 5 = POOR.) You would like to understand this relationship better.

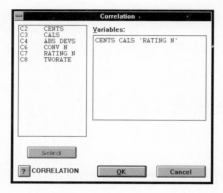

Determining Correlation

Determining the *correlation* provides you with information similar to the covariance, but it assesses the strength of the relationships on a scale of –1 to 1. This way you can assess the direction and strength of the pairwise linear relationship among the same three variables:

- Choose **Stat > Basic Statistics > Correlation**

- Double-click **C2 CENTS**, **C3 CALS**, and **C7 RATING N** to enter them in the **Variables** text box

   The completed Correlation dialog box should look like the one shown in Figure 5-14.

FIGURE 5-14

The Correlation dialog box

- Click **OK**

   The correlation matrix appears as in Figure 5-15.

FIGURE 5-15

Correlation matrix

```
MTB > Correlation 'CENTS' 'CALS' 'RATING N'.

            CENTS     CALS
CALS        0.136
RATING N   -0.054    0.766
```

The correlation between cost and calories is 0.136, which is only slightly positive. The correlation between cents and rating is slightly negative (–0.054), suggesting that the cheaper brands may be associated with lower nutritional value. But the calorie count and the rating are highly correlated with each other (0.766): yogurts that have high calorie counts have poor nutritional ratings.

Viewing the History Window

You have looked at the yogurt data from several different perspectives. Because it's easy to forget what you have already done with your data, Minitab includes a separate History window that lists all the commands you have used in a session. To view this window:

■ Choose **Window > History**

Figure 5-16 shows a portion of the History window (minimized).

FIGURE 5-16

The History window

Whereas the Session window contains Minitab commands, subcommands, and the resulting displays, the History window records only the commands and subcommands Minitab has processed, not the output. For example, the History window displays the last command you issued, Correlation 'CENTS' 'CALS' 'RATING N'. In contrast, the Session window displays not only the command but the resulting matrix as well.

You can use the History window to retrace your analysis of a data set. You can scroll upwards to view commands you issued earlier during the current session. In Tutorial 16, you learn how you can save the contents of the History window to a file and then execute the commands from the file itself.

After reviewing the History window, you think you have analyzed the data enough and are ready to make an informed decision. You want to look over the outfile you've been creating throughout the session and then make your recommendation. First, print the data in the Session window so that it appears in your outfile. Then, stop sending output to the outfile:

■ Choose **Window > Session**

■ Choose **File > Display Data**

■ Highlight **C1** through **C3** and then click **Select**

■ Click **OK** so the data appear in your outfile

■ Choose **File > Other Files > Stop Recording Session**

■ Save your worksheet with the name 5YOGURT.MTW on your Student disk

Now take a look at your session record in Notepad (the Windows text editor accessory you used in Tutorial 2) to help you make your final decision:

■ Press [Alt]+[Tab] until Program Manager appears

Note: If Alt + Tab does not move you through the open windows, you can also reach Program Manager by minimizing Minitab.

- Double-click the **Accessories** group icon (you may have to minimize or move other windows to see it)

- Double-click the **Notepad** program-item icon

- Open **T5.LIS** (click the **List Files of Type** arrow, then click **All Files** to see your file)

The record of your session appears in the Notepad window (Figure 5-17).

FIGURE 5-17

Notepad window showing T5 outfile

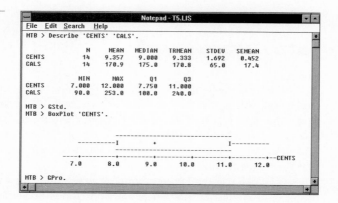

Scroll through the window to review your work.

You have taken the first steps toward the ultimate goal of providing a nutritious, low-cost snack. You found that the cost for an ounce of yogurt can range from 7 to 12 cents, but that the majority of the brands cost less than 9 cents per ounce. Over 64% of the brands were rated good or better in terms of nutritional value. There are three brands of yogurt with excellent ratings, but one appears better than the others. The yogurt brand in row 8 appears to be the best. It costs only 7 cents per ounce and its calorie count of 100 is below the mean of 170.9. After examining the printout of the data at the end of the outfile, you decide to recommend brand 8.

- Choose **File > Exit** from the Notepad menu bar

- Press Alt + Tab until Minitab reappears

You can restart Minitab to continue or you can exit Windows to take a break. If you plan to continue directly to the next tutorial:

- Choose **File > Restart Minitab**

If you want to take a longer break:

- Choose **File > Exit**

Minitab Command Summary

This section describes the menu commands introduced in or related to this tutorial. To find a complete explanation of all menus and commands, refer to the Reference section of this manual.

Minitab Menu Commands

Menu	Command	Description
File		
	Other Files	
	Start Recording History	Stores executed Minitab commands, which can then be used as an Exec macro, into a file
	Stop Recording History	Stops entering Minitab commands into the file
Manip		
	Convert	Converts alpha data to numeric data and vice versa
Stat		
	Basic Statistics	
	Descriptive Statistics	Provides a numeric summary of central tendency and variability for one or more columns; optionally, summarizes each level of a specified By variable
	Correlation	Computes the correlation between pairs of variables
	Covariance	Determines the covariance between pairs of variables
	Tables	
	Tally	Calculates a count (or frequency) of each value of an integer variable
Window		
	History	Displays a record of all the commands issued during a session

Matching

Match the following terms to their definitions by placing the correct letter next to the term it describes.

_____ SEMEAN

_____ Trimmed mean

_____ Correlation

_____ CUMPCT

_____ Convert

_____ Second quartile

_____ Tally

_____ STDEV

_____ By variable

_____ History window

a. A sample mean after deleting the top 5% and bottom 5% of the data

b. Another name for the median

c. Minitab notation for the sample standard deviation

d. Minitab notation for the standard error of a sample mean

e. Minitab notation for the cumulative percent less than or equal to a given category

f. The Minitab command to determine frequencies for discrete data

g. The Minitab command that converts alpha data to numeric data and vice versa

h. The Minitab command that summarizes the linear relationship between two variables

i. A record of commands issued during a session

j. A column for which each of its values is used to separate one or more other columns for describing data

True/False

Mark the following statements with a T or an F.

_____ 1. Conversion tables are created in the Data worksheet.

_____ 2. The Tally command can only be used with integer data.

_____ 3. The output from the Descriptive Statistics command is displayed in the Session window.

_____ 4. The Descriptive Statistics output includes the sample standard deviation.

_____ 5. The sample variance is part of the Descriptive Statistics output.

_____ 6. By variables must be integer values.

_____ 7. When Minitab prints an asterisk (*) for a summary statistic in the Descriptive Statistics output, it indicates that the number is too large to fit in the space provided.

_____ 8. You can perform both Tally and Correlation using a By variable.

_____ 9. Minitab designates the cumulative number of values greater than the given category with CUMCNT.

_____ 10. The Descriptive Statistics command's output doesn't include the maximum and minimum values of a column.

Practice Problems

1. Open CRIMES.MTW, which contains 1991 violent crime rates for the 50 states and the District of Columbia by U.S. Census division and region. See Exploring Data for a full description of these data.

   a. Summarize the rates for each division. Does there appear to be any difference among districts?

   b. Repeat part a for each region. Do you reach the same conclusions as you did before?

2. Open ADS2.MTW, which describes full-page ads in two magazines in 1989, 1991, and 1993.

   a. Describe the ratio data for these three years. Has the ratio increased over the years? If so, did it increase consistently?

   b. Unstack the ratio by YEAR. Place the data in C6 through C8. Name these columns 1989, 1991, and 1993.

   c. Compute the correlation matrix for the yearly ratio data. Are the ratios for each year correlated with one another? If so, to what extent are they correlated?

   d. Determine the covariances between each year's data. What value is on the diagonal of the resulting matrix? Verify your answer using the results from part a. Is the covariance matrix as informative as the correlation matrix in part b?

3. Open TVVIEW.MTW.

   a. Describe the TV-viewing habits of husbands, wives, and households. According to your figures, who watches more TV: husbands or wives?

   b. Describe the difference in the TV-viewing times of husbands and wives. Do your numbers indicate that this difference is different from zero?

4. Open PROF.MTW.

   a. Use the Tally command to summarize the frequency of the different levels or years of courses surveyed (C9).

   b. How many questionnaires were filled out, on average, in the surveyed courses? Is the median much different from the mean?

   c. Correlate the INSTRUCT and COURSE ratings. Are the two correlated? Interpret your findings.

5. Open MNWAGE.MTW.

   a. Summarize the minimum wage variable. What is the most appropriate measure of central tendency? What is the most appropriate measure of spread?

   b. Create a scatter plot of minimum wage versus year. Describe its shape.

   c. Would you prefer to use the output from part a, part b, or both in a report? Briefly explain your answer.

TUTORIAL
6

Distributions and Random Data

Probability distributions are the foundation of inferential statistics. In this tutorial, you examine several frequently used probability and probability density functions. You then generate random samples from these distributions. First, you act as a Red Cross volunteer trying to ascertain various probabilities of obtaining Type O blood donors from a given sample. Next, you produce a random sample for a term paper on the number of employees in businesses of various sizes. Finally, you assist a physiology professor in a study of the height of U.S. college students.

Objectives

In this tutorial you learn how to:

- compute probabilities, using both discrete probability functions and continuous probability density functions

- compute cumulative probabilities for various probability distribution functions

- generate random samples from populations with given probability distributions

- generate normal scores and produce normal probability plots

- use the inverse cumulative probability function to look up percentiles of various distributions

- sample from a column, with and without replacement

CASE STUDY: BIOLOGY — BLOOD TYPES

You have been a Red Cross volunteer for the last few years. The volunteer coordinator, Paul Van Vleck, hears that you are learning how to use Minitab. Eager to put your skills to work, he tells you that the Type O blood supply is running dangerously low and that he anticipates needing from 10 to 12 additional pints for surgeries scheduled in the upcoming week. Paul has already recruited 25 unrelated potential donors. He wants to know if it is likely that next week's need for Type O blood can be met using these donors or if he will have to recruit more.

▼
Calculating Discrete Probability Functions
▲

Your reference books tell you that 45 out of 100 people have Type O blood, so the probability of a randomly selected individual having Type O blood is 0.45. To help Paul, you need to compute P(X = K), the probability of K people having Type O blood, for the values of K = 0, 1, 2,..., 25. In this case P(X = K) is a binomial probability function with n = 25 trials and p = 0.45. You could compute these probabilities using a calculator, but it would be very tedious. You could also obtain these probabilities from a table, but not all sets of probability tables cover all values of K and P. Instead, you decide calculate the probabilities using Minitab.

To get started:

- Start Minitab and maximize the Minitab window and the Data window

- Start an outfile named **T6**

Create a column that contains the integers 0 to 25. Although you could enter these numbers directly into the Data window by typing, there is a much easier way to do so:

- Choose **Calc > Set Patterned Data**

- Type **K** in the **Store result in column** text box and then press [Tab] twice

- Type **0** (a zero) in the **Start at** text box and press [Tab]

- Type **25** in the **End at** text box

The completed Set Patterned Data dialog box looks like the one shown in Figure 6-1.

FIGURE 6-1

*The Set Patterned Data
dialog box*

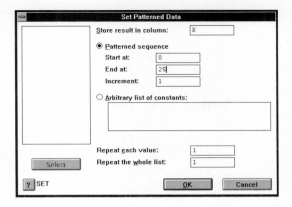

■ Click **OK**

Minitab enters the integers from 0 to 25 in the first column much more quickly than you could type them into the Data window.

Obtain the binomial probabilities for each value of K in C1:

■ Choose **Calc > Probability Distributions > Binomial**

■ Press ⌈Tab⌉

■ Type **25** in the **Number of trials** text box and press ⌈Tab⌉

■ Type **.45** in the **Probability of success** text box and press ⌈Tab⌉

■ Enter **C1 K** in the **Input column** text box

The completed Binomial Distribution dialog box looks like the one in Figure 6-2.

FIGURE 6-2

*The Binomial Distribution
dialog box*

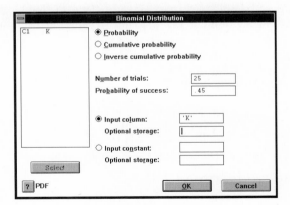

- Click **OK**

Minitab lists the complete binomial probability distribution for n = 25 and p = 0.45 in the Session window, as shown in Figure 6-3. Scroll the Session window to see the complete listing.

FIGURE 6-3

Binomial probability distribution in the Session window

```
MTB > PDF 'K';
SUBC>   Binomial 25 .45.
     K          P( X = K)
   0.00           0.0000
   1.00           0.0000
   2.00           0.0001
   3.00           0.0004
   4.00           0.0018
   5.00           0.0063
   6.00           0.0172
   7.00           0.0381
   8.00           0.0701
   9.00           0.1084
  10.00           0.1419
  11.00           0.1583
  12.00           0.1511
  13.00           0.1236
  14.00           0.0867
  15.00           0.0520
  16.00           0.0266
  17.00           0.0115
  18.00           0.0042
  19.00           0.0013
  20.00           0.0003
  21.00           0.0001
  22.00           0.0000
  23.00           0.0000
  24.00           0.0000
  25.00           0.0000
```

Minitab displays the probability distribution in two columns. The first column contains the values representing the possible number of successes (people with Type O blood); the second lists the corresponding probability of obtaining that number of successes. For example, the probability of having exactly 11 people in this sample with Type O blood is 0.1583.

The Session window probability values are rounded to the nearest ten-thousandth so probabilities less than 0.00005 are listed as 0.0000. In other words, the probability of obtaining 22 Type O individuals in your sample isn't really 0.0000 — it's less than 0.00005.

You can tell Minitab to save the probabilities in a column in the worksheet:

- Choose **Edit > Edit Last Command Dialog**
- Click the first **Optional storage** text box
- Type **'P(X=K)'** (be sure to type the single quotation marks) and press ⏎Enter
- Return to the Data window

Column C2, with the name P(X = K), lists the binomial probabilities, as shown in Figure 6-4.

FIGURE 6-4

Binomial probability distribution in the Data window

Student Edition of MINITAB - Untitled Worksheet - [Data]

File Edit Manip Calc Stat Window Graph Editor Help

	C1	C2	C3	C4	C5	C6	C7	C8
→	K	P(X=K)						
1	0	0.000000						
2	1	0.000007						
3	2	0.000065						
4	3	0.000407						
5	4	0.001830						
6	5	0.006290						
7	6	0.017155						
8	7	0.038097						
9	8	0.070133						
10	9	0.108387						
11	10	0.141889						
12	11	0.158306						
13	12	0.151110						
14	13	0.123636						
15	14	0.086705						
16	15	0.052023						
17	16	0.026603						
18	17	0.011523						
19	18	0.004190						

Minitab rounds probabilities to the nearest ten thousandth in the Session window. In the worksheet, by default, Minitab displays results to the nearest one millionth. As you can see, P(X = 11), which was rounded to 0.1583 in the Session window, displays the more accurate value 0.158306 in the worksheet.

According to the distribution data, you are most likely to obtain 10, 11, or 12 people with Type O blood in your sample of 25. However, these values will occur only 14.2%, 15.8%, and 15.1% of the time, respectively. Collectively, though, you have approximately a 50% chance that the 25 donors will yield 10, 11, or 12 people with Type O blood (14.2 + 15.8 + 15.1 = 45.1%).

In cases when you don't need all values of the probability distribution, you can compute the probability for only a single value:

■ Choose **Edit > Edit Last Command Dialog**

■ Click the **Input constant** option and then press ⌈Tab⌉

■ Type **10** in the **Input constant** text box and press ⌈←Enter⌉

The Session window shows that the probability that X = 10 is 0.1419. Verify that you obtained equivalent results in Figures 6-3 and 6-4.

To confirm that the most likely values (highest probabilities) are 10, 11, and 12, produce a scatter plot of this binomial distribution:

■ Choose **Graph > Character Graph > Scatter Plot**

■ Double-click **C2 P(X=K)** to enter it in the **Y variable** text box

■ Double-click **C1 K** to enter it in the **X variable** text box and then click **OK**

The scatter plot appears (Figure 6-5).

FIGURE 6-5

Scatter plot of probability versus number of successes

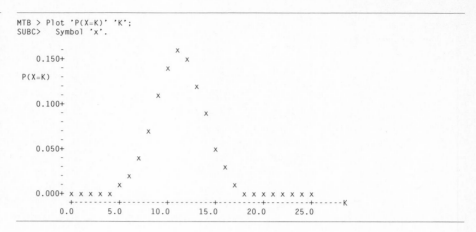

```
MTB > Plot 'P(X=K)' 'K';
SUBC>    Symbol 'x'.
            -
            -                                    x
   0.150+                                     x
            -                             x
P(X=K)   -
            -                                        x
   0.100+                              x
            -                                          x
            -
            -                         x
   0.050+                                                x
            -                       x
            -                                              x
            -                     x
   0.000+ x x x x x                                x x x x x x x x
          +---------+---------+---------+---------+---------+------K
          0.0       5.0      10.0      15.0      20.0      25.0
```

The probabilities appear as Xs on the plot centered over each value of K, which is the number of successes (K = 0, 1, 2, ..., 25). The position of each X corresponds to the probability that K Type O blood donors will be found in the sample of 25.

The peak of your plot occurs at K = 11 and the next highest points are at K = 10 and 12. Indeed, the most likely numbers of Type O donors are 10, 11, and 12. Also, note the shape of your plot; it is approximately bell-shaped. You will see another bell-shaped distribution later in this tutorial.

▼

Computing Cumulative Probability Distributions for Discrete Variables

▲

In addition to calculating individual probabilities, Minitab can compute cumulative probabilities for either an entire column or an individual value using the Cumulative probability option. After talking with the surgeons who will perform next week's surgery, Paul informs you that at least 13 pints of Type O blood will be needed; he needs to know the probability of getting 13 or more Type O donors in his sample of 25.

Find this figure by determining the probability of obtaining 12 or fewer individuals with Type O blood from the sample of 25:

- Choose **Calc > Probability Distributions > Binomial**

- Click **Cumulative probability**

- Verify that **Number of trials** is **25** and **Probability of success** is **.45**

- Type **12** in the **Input constant** text box, and press ⏎Enter

The Session window (Figure 6-6) appears.

FIGURE 6-6

Cumulative probability in the Session window

```
MTB > CDF 12;
SUBC>   Binomial 25 .45.
        K  P( X LESS OR = K)
    12.00          0.6937
```

You tell Paul that there is a probability of 69.37% that 12 or fewer people in this group of 25 will have Type O blood. Therefore the likelihood of getting the 13 pints he needs is less than one-third (30.63%).

Paul is concerned. The odds are pretty good that he won't be able to provide enough Type O blood with only the current donors. He asks you the fewest number of donors he must have to be reasonably certain (probability $\geq$ 75%) there will be at least 13 with Type O blood. You need to find the value of n so that $P(X \leq 12)$ is less than 25%.

You must repeat the actions above, substituting different values of n. To save you some time, start with a value of n = 33:

■ Choose **Edit > Edit Last Command Dialog**

■ Type **33** in the **Number of trials** text box and press ⏎Enter

In the Session window, Minitab reports that a pool of 33 donors gives Paul a 20.62% chance of getting 12 or fewer Type O donors (and hence a 79.38% chance of getting 13 or more). To determine if you can get by with fewer donors, try n = 32:

■ Choose **Edit > Edit Last Command Dialog**

■ Type **32** in the **Number of trials** text box and press ⏎Enter

Using 32 donors, the probability of 12 or fewer is 25.12% (which means only a 74.88% chance of getting 13 or more). This doesn't quite meet Paul's requirements. You tell Paul that he will need at least 33 donors to obtain 13 pints of Type O blood with a probability of 75% or more. Minitab saved you quite a bit of calculation time.

You have completed your volunteer research on blood type samples. Before you turn your attention to the next case study, in which you're completing a term paper for a course on business management, clear the current worksheet:

■ Choose **File > Other Files > Stop Recording Session**

■ Choose **File > Restart Minitab**

■ Save your worksheet with the name **6TYPEO** on your Student disk

CASE STUDY: MANAGEMENT — ENTREPRENEURIAL STUDIES

One of the references used in your Business Management course, *The Statistical Abstract of the United States 1993*, presents the approximate number of employees by five employment-class sizes for 1990.

Class	Size	Number of Employees
1	Under 20 employees	24,373,000
2	20 to 99 employees	27,414,000
3	100 to 499 employees	22,926,000
4	500 to 999 employees	6,551,000
5	1,000 or more employees	12,212,000

According to these data, the probability of a person working in an American firm with fewer than 20 employees is 0.2607. To derive this number, add up the number of employees in the United States, for a total of 93,476,000. Then divide the number of employees working in firms with fewer than 20 employees by the total: (24,373,000/93,476,000 = 0.2607). Similarly, the probability of a person working in a firm with 20 to 99 employees is 27,414,000/93,476,000, or 0.2933, and so on.

Your management professor, Dr. Michaels, assigns a term paper about the number of employees in different-sized establishments. He particularly asks you to focus your research on small-scale enterprises of the type usually started by entrepreneurs. As part of your project, you generate a random sample of employees and conduct various experiments of your own; this is called a *simulation*. You simulate the results of a hypothetical experiment.

▼

Generating Random Data from Discrete Distributions

▲

Minitab allows you to obtain a random sample of data and simulate an experiment right from your computer. This saves not only time but money.

In the worksheet, you enter two columns: one contains the five different employee-size classes, the other displays the theoretical probabilities of each employee-size class. Because the Minitab command you use to simulate the experiment requires you to describe the employee-size classes with numbers, you create the following numeric codes:

Class	Size	Probability
1	Under 20 employees	0.2607
2	20 to 99 employees	0.2933
3	100 to 499 employees	0.2453
4	500 to 999 employees	0.0701
5	1,000 or more employees	0.1306

Enter this information into the worksheet:

- Start the T6 outfile again; Minitab appends the subsequent session record to your previous outfile

- Maximize the Minitab window and the Data window

- Assign the names **CLASS** and **PROB** to columns C1 and C2, respectively

- Enter the values **1**, **2**, **3**, **4**, and **5** in C1 CLASS to represent the four classes

- Enter the values **.2607**, **.2933**, **.2453**, **.0701**, and **.1306** in C2 PROB to represent the corresponding probabilities

As part of your research, you will tell Minitab to produce a batch of random numbers. If you don't specify a *base*, or starting point, when generating random numbers, Minitab chooses its own. On the other hand, when you set a base, you can generate the same random data again simply by entering the same "seed" number. Specify 1993 as the base Minitab should use when generating the random numbers.

- Choose **Calc > Set Base**

- Type **1993** in the **Set base of random data generator to** text box

- Press ⏎Enter

Generate a random sample of 1000 employees using the theoretical probabilities provided by the U.S. Bureau of the Census that can be duplicated for future use:

- Choose **Calc > Random Data > Discrete**

- Type **1000** in the **Generate [ ] rows of data** text box and press Tab

- Type **SAMPLE** in the **Store in column(s)** text box and press `Tab`
- Enter **C1 CLASS** in the **Values in** text box
- Enter **C2 PROB** in the **Probabilities in** text box

The completed Discrete Distribution dialog box should look like the one shown in Figure 6-7.

FIGURE 6-7

The Discrete Distribution dialog box

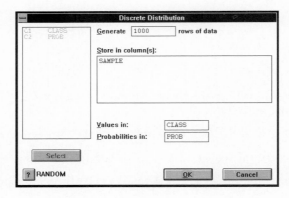

- Click **OK**

C3 SAMPLE now lists 1000 entries of the numbers 1, 2, 3, 4, and 5 in random order.

Note: If you want to regenerate these same data later, be sure to set the base to 1993.

Presume these 1000 values are the results of asking 1000 randomly selected people to specify the size of the company for which they work. Count the number of 1s, 2s, 3s, 4s, and 5s in your sample:

- Choose **Stat > Tables > Tally**
- Double-click **C3 SAMPLE** to enter it in the **Variables** text box
- Click the **Percents** check box
- Click **OK**

The frequency distribution for your sample appears in the Session window (Figure 6-8). (If you didn't use Set Base, your random sample COUNT and PERCENT values will be slightly different from those in Figure 6-8.)

FIGURE 6-8

Frequency distribution of firms in the sample

```
MTB > Base 1993.
MTB > Name c3 = 'SAMPLE'
MTB > Random 1000 'SAMPLE';
SUBC>    Discrete 'CLASS' 'PROB'.
MTB > Tally 'SAMPLE';
SUBC>    Counts;
SUBC>    Percents.

  SAMPLE  COUNT PERCENT
       1    274   27.40
       2    290   29.00
       3    243   24.30
       4     64    6.40
       5    129   12.90
      N=   1000
```

The percentage of each employee-size class in this simulation experiment is quite close to the probabilities presented by the Census Bureau. For example, your results predict that 27.4% of the people work at firms with fewer than 20 employees, versus the Census Bureau's statistic of 26.1%; your value is slightly high. The simulation shows 29% of the sample work at firms with between 20 and 99 people, which is just shy of the actual 29.3%. The figures for the other three employment-class sizes are slightly underestimated (24.3% vs. 24.5%, 6.4% vs. 7.0%, and 12.9% vs. 13.1%).

In a matter of minutes, you generated data similar to that presented by the U.S. government. You return to this case study and a similar data set in Tutorial 12.

■ Save your simulation with the name **6FIRM.MTW** on your Student disk

■ Choose **File > Other Files > Stop Recording Session**

■ Choose **File > Restart Minitab**

CASE STUDY: PHYSIOLOGY — HEIGHTS

Dr. Wei is a professor in the Physiology Department of the medical school on campus. She hopes that you can help her with a lecture she is preparing for her physiology class. She would like to show that many physiological variables in nature are approximately normally distributed. For example, the actual heights of college-age women are very close to a normal distribution, with a mean of 64 inches and a standard deviation of 3.1 inches. Dr. Wei would like to illustrate this fact using the height data for the 60 women in her class.

Dr. Wei's students filled out a questionnaire that asked about a number of physiological variables, including height. You suggest that the best way to demonstrate the normal distribution of physiological variables might be to compare the self-reported female heights to the known normal distribution.

Generating Random Data from a Continuous Distribution

You propose that you simulate a sample of heights from the college-age female population, using the values $\mu = 64$ and $\sigma = 3.1$. To generate a sample of 60 observations from a normal population with a mean of 64 and a standard deviation of 3.1:

- Start the T6 outfile again; Minitab appends the subsequent session record to your previous outfile

- Maximize the Minitab window and the Data window

- Choose **Calc > Set Base**

- Type **333** in the **Set base of random data generator to** text box to enter it as the base and press ⏎Enter

- Choose **Calc > Random Data > Normal**

- Type **60** in the **Generate [ ] rows of data** text box and press Tab

- Type **'RAN HGTS'** in the **Store in column(s)** text box and press Tab

- Type **64** in the **Mean** text box and press Tab

- Type **3.1** in the **Standard deviation** text box

The completed Normal Distribution dialog box should look like the one shown in Figure 6-9.

FIGURE 6-9

The Normal Distribution dialog box

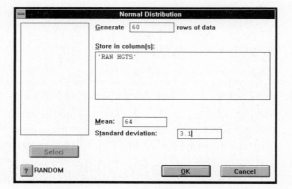

- Press ⏎Enter

The worksheet contains 60 random values from a normal ($\mu = 64$ and $\sigma = 3.1$) distribution. Dr. Wei can present this data to her class as a random sample of the heights of 60 college-age women.

Using this simulated sample, she can show the class how such a normal distribution appears in a graphical summary, and can compare the result to the class data she collected. In preparation, you decide to preview a histogram of the randomly generated heights:

- Choose **Graph > Character Graphs > Histogram**
- Double-click **C1 RAN HGTS** to enter it in the **Variables** text box
- Click **OK**

The histogram appears in the Session window (Figure 6-10).

FIGURE 6-10

Histogram of random heights

```
MTB > Base 333.
MTB > Name c1 = 'RAN HGTS'
MTB > Random 60 'RAN HGTS';
SUBC>    Normal 64 3.1.
MTB > GStd.
MTB > Histogram 'RAN HGTS'.

Histogram of RAN HGTS    N = 60

Midpoint    Count
      56        1   *
      58        3   ***
      60        7   *******
      62       11   ***********
      64        8   ********
      66       20   ********************
      68        7   *******
      70        2   **
      72        1   *
```

Check the mean and standard deviation of your random sample to see how close it is to 64 and 3.1:

- Choose **Stat > Basic Statistics > Descriptive Statistics**
- Double-click **C1 RAN HGTS** to enter it in the **Variables** text box
- Click **OK**

The results appear in the Session window (Figure 6-11).

FIGURE 6-11

Descriptive statistics

```
MTB > Describe 'RAN HGTS'.
```

	N	MEAN	MEDIAN	TRMEAN	STDEV	SEMEAN
RAN HGTS	60	64.247	65.052	64.290	3.226	0.417

	MIN	MAX	Q1	Q3
RAN HGTS	56.795	71.268	61.780	66.531

The mean is 64.247; the standard deviation is 3.226.

The histogram in Figure 6-10 is basically bell-shaped. While this graph might be sufficient to convince her class of the data's validity, you can use another Minitab feature to determine whether normality is a reasonable assumption.

Obtaining the Normal Probability Plot Using Normal Scores

A common graphical technique for checking whether a sample comes from a normal population is to create a *normal probability plot (NPP)*. You can easily generate an NPP in Minitab:

- Choose **Calc > Functions**
- Click the **Input column** text box and then double-click **C1 RAN HGTS**
- Type **NS** in the **Result in** text box
- Click the **Normal scores** option button
- Click **OK**

  Minitab computes the normal scores and stores them in column C2 NS. To obtain the NPP:

- Choose **Graph > Character Graphs > Scatter Plot**
- Double-click **C2 NS** to enter it in the **Y variable** text box
- Double-click **C1 RAN HGTS** to enter it in the **X variable** text box
- Click **OK**

  The NPP appears in the Session window (Figure 6-12).

FIGURE 6-12

Normal probability plot of randomly generated female heights

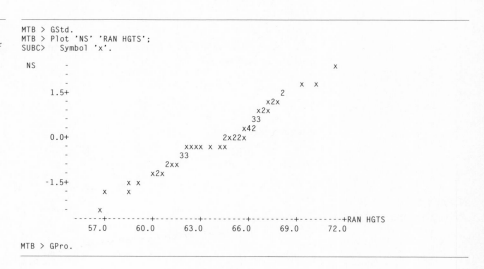

```
MTB > GStd.
MTB > Plot 'NS' 'RAN HGTS';
SUBC>   Symbol 'x'.

 NS    -                                                   x
       -
       -                                             x  x
   1.5+                                          2
       -                                       x2x
       -                                      x2x
       -                                      33
       -                                    x42
   0.0+                              2x22x
       -                         xxxx x xx
       -                        33
       -                     2xx
       -                   x2x
  -1.5+           x   x
       -       x    x
       -
       -     x
       ------+---------+---------+---------+---------+---------+RAN HGTS
           57.0      60.0      63.0      66.0      69.0      72.0

MTB > GPro.
```

If an NPP approximates a straight line, you may reasonably conclude that the sample comes from a population that is approximately normal. Since you generated the data from the normal distribution and it basically looks like a straight line, the scatter plot will make a good illustration for Dr. Wei's lecture on how to show that a variable is approximately normally distributed.

MINITAB AT WORK

PUBLIC SAFETY: Six years after a rural university in Pennsylvania installed a nuclear reactor for educational purposes, concerned residents of the surrounding town claimed that the presence of the reactor was increasing infant mortality in the area. To support their contention, they presented the following data, which compared infant mortality in their town to that in another town similar in size and character.

A statistician examined the data to help determine whether the infant mortality rate over the nine-year period was unusually high. The statistician focused on several aspects of the claim; one was whether the town's 1968 rate of 10 infant deaths was unusually high, given a community where the average mortality rate was 6 deaths per year.

The statistician decided to see if randomly generated samples of similar data would contain any values as high as the 1968 value. He had Minitab randomly generate 100 Poisson distributions of nine-year spreads. He found that 58% of those randomly generated spreads contained one or more years with an infant mortality rate of at least 10. Since a majority of the spreads included a value as high as the 1968 rate, the statistician decided that the peak of 10 in 1968 was not uncommon in a situation with 6 deaths in an average year.

In the end, no dangerous environmental effects were linked with the presence of the reactor and it was allowed to remain. The causes of infant mortality remain a vital concern, but it is important to recognize that peaks and valleys normally do occur in a nine-year period.

Dr. Wei can then produce a similar NPP for the self-reported heights she collected from her class. She stored the female students' heights and an ID variable in a Minitab file called HEIGHT.MTW. Again, you want to preview the results of plotting the data before Dr. Wei does so in class:

- Save your worksheet with the name **6RANHT** on your Student disk

- Choose **File > Other Files > Stop Recording Session**

- Choose **File > Restart Minitab**

- Start the T6 outfile again; Minitab appends the subsequent session record to your previous outfile

- Maximize the Minitab window and the Data window

- Open **HEIGHT.MTW**

To produce the NPP, you need to obtain the normal scores for the heights in C2 HEIGHTS and then create the scatter plot:

- Choose **Calc > Functions**

- Click the **Input column** text box and then double-click **C2 HEIGHTS**

- Type **NS** in the **Results in** text box

- Click the **Normal scores** option button

- Click **OK**

    After Minitab computes the normal scores:

- Choose **Graph > Character Graphs > Scatter Plot**

- Double-click **C3 NS** to enter it in the **Y variable** text box

- Double-click **C2 HEIGHTS** to enter it in the **X variable** text box

- Click **OK**

    The NPP for the self-reported female heights appears in the Session window (Figure 6-13).

FIGURE 6-13

Normal probability plot of self-reported female heights

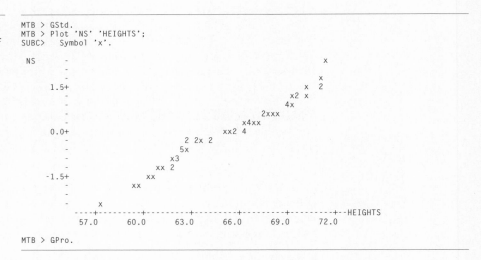

```
MTB > GStd.
MTB > Plot 'NS' 'HEIGHTS';
SUBC>   Symbol 'x'.

  NS     -                                               x
         -                                                     x
         -                                                x  2
    1.5+ -                                           x2 x
         -                                           4x
         -                                      2xxx
         -                                  x4xx
         -                             xx2  4
    0.0+ -                    2  2x  2
         -                   5x
         -                 x3
         -               xx  2
   -1.5+ -             xx
         -          xx
         -     x
         ----+---------+---------+---------+---------+---------+--HEIGHTS
            57.0      60.0      63.0      66.0      69.0      72.0

MTB > GPro.
```

Although the plot isn't quite as straight as your simulation NPP, it's close enough for Dr. Wei's purposes. You report to Dr. Wei that, based on the NPP, self-reported heights of college-age women seem to be approximately normally distributed. She is pleased with the idea of comparing the simulation scatter plot to the actual scatter plot. She plans to use both graphics for her lecture on the normal distribution of physiological variables.

Note: Normal probability plots are frequently used in regression and analysis of variance, which are covered in Tutorials 9–11.

Determining Inverse Cumulative Functions for Continuous Distributions

▼

▲

Impressed with your work, Dr. Wei returns a few weeks later to show you her follow-up work on self-reported heights. Using extensive information from her classes, she found that self-reported heights of college-age women appear to be approximately normally distributed with a mean of 64.25 and a standard deviation of 3.82.

Dr. Wei is planning another study to investigate the relationship between bone structure and height. She wants to compare the bone structure distribution in four height groups. The height groups will be based on the quartiles of the population height distribution. She asks you to find the first and third quartiles.

To find the first quartile, Q1 (the 25th percentile):

- Choose **Calc > Probability Distributions > Normal**

- Click **Inverse cumulative probability** and press ⌜Tab⌝

- Type **64** in the **Mean** text box and press ⌜Tab⌝

- Type **3.1** in the **Standard deviation** text box

- Click the **Input constant** option button and then press ⌜Tab⌝

- Type **.25** in the **Input constant** text box

The completed Normal Distribution dialog box should look like the one shown in Figure 6-14.

FIGURE 6-14

The Normal Distribution dialog box

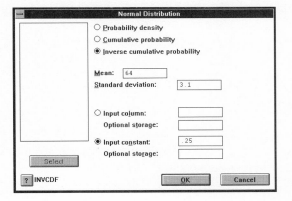

- Click **OK**

The Session window displays the results (Figure 6-15).

FIGURE 6-15

Session window, showing inverse cumulative values

```
MTB > InvCDF .25;
SUBC>   Normal 64 3.1.
   0.2500   61.9091
```

The results indicate that 25% of the female heights are less than 61.91 inches. The first study group, therefore, comprises women who are less than 61.91 inches tall. The second group consists of women whose height falls between 61.91 inches and the median of 64 inches.

To obtain the third quartile, Q3 (75th percentile):

■ Choose **Edit > Edit Last Command Dialog**

■ Press Tab four times

■ Type **.75** in the **Input constant** text box and press ←Enter

The third group consists of women with heights between 64 and 66.09 inches. The last group contains those women who are taller than 66.09 inches.

Note: Tutorial 7 introduces another use of the inverse cumulative probability function.

▼

**Sampling from
a Column**

▲

Dr. Wei will be presenting a paper at a convention in Chicago and would like to have eight students in the class accompany her, four men and four women. To be fair, she asks you to use Minitab to select four female students at random from those whose heights are reported in C2 HEIGHTS. (She will then select the male students in a similar manner.) Recall that Dr. Wei included a student ID number in C1 ID.

Note: You cannot obtain a random sample from a column containing alpha data.

To randomly select the four female students to travel to the Chicago convention:

■ Choose **Calc > Set Base**

■ Type **444** in the **Set base of random data generator to** text box to enter it as your base and then press ←Enter

■ Choose **Calc > Random Data > Sample From Columns**

■ Type **4** in the **Sample [ ] rows from column(s)** text box and press Tab

■ Double-click **C1 ID** to enter it as the column to sample and press Tab

■ Type **CHICAGO** in the **Store samples in** text box

The completed Sample From Columns dialog box resembles Figure 6-16.

FIGURE 6-16

*The Sample From
Columns dialog box*

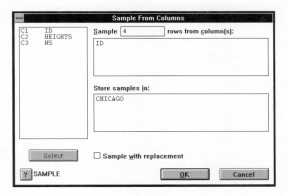

- Press ⌅Enter

- Return to the Data window

    Sort the column you just created:

- Choose **Manip > Sort**

- Double-click **C4 CHICAGO** to enter it in the **Sort column(s)** text box and press Tab

- Double-click **C4 CHICAGO** to enter it in the **Store sorted column(s) in** text box and press Tab

- Double-click **C4 CHICAGO** to enter it in the first **Sort by column** text box and press ⌅Enter

    The ID numbers of the four lucky students display in C4 CHICAGO (Figure 6-17). You can now inform Dr. Wei that the following students were selected: 2, 550, 552, and 939. (Because this sample is random, your selections would be different if you used a different base.)

FIGURE 6-17

*Data window, showing
four randomly selected ID
numbers*

C4
CHICAGO
2
550
552
939

To allow for a situation in which you would want to sample with replacement (the same population unit could be chosen more than one time), you could select the Sample with replacement option in the Sample From Columns dialog box.

Save your work and close your outfile:

- Save your worksheet with the name **6HEIGHT** on your Student disk

- Choose **File > Other Files > Stop Recording Session**

In this tutorial, you worked with several of the most commonly used distributions. In later tutorials, you use the Probability Distributions commands to help solve other statistical problems. In Tutorials 7 and 8, you use Minitab to perform some parametric hypothesis tests and confidence intervals.

If you plan to continue directly to the next tutorial:

- Choose **File > Restart Minitab**

If you want to take a longer break:

- Choose **File > Exit**

Minitab Command Summary

This section describes the Minitab menu commands introduced in or related to this tutorial. To find a complete explanation of all menus and commands, refer to the Reference section of this manual.

Minitab Menu Commands

Menu	Command	Description
Calc		
	Set Base	Allows the user to specify the "seed" number used to generate random data
	Random Data	Produces random samples from specified discrete and continuous distributions given below
	Sample From Columns	Takes random samples, with or without replacement, from a given column or columns

Menu	Command	Description

Chisquare
Normal
F
T
Uniform
Bernoulli
Binomial
Discrete
Integer
Poisson
Beta
Cauchy
Exponential
Gamma
Laplace
Logistic
Lognormal
Weibull

} Creates various discrete and continuous distributions from which random samples can be generated

Probability Distributions — Calculates probabilities, density function values, cumulative probabilities, and percentiles for the discrete and continuous random variables given below

Chisquare
Normal
F
T
Uniform
Binomial
Discrete
Integer
Poisson
Beta
Cauchy
Exponential
Gamma
Laplace
Logistic
Lognormal
Weibull

} Various discrete and continuous distributions on which probability distribution calculations are based

Menu	Command	Description
	Set Patterned Data	Generates sequences or repetitive patterns of numbers and stores the results in a column

Matching

Match the following terms to their definitions by placing the correct letter next to the term it describes.

_____ Start at

_____ Set Patterned Data

_____ 0

_____ Random Data

_____ Sample From Columns

_____ Sample with replacement

_____ Inverse cumulative probability

_____ Normal scores

_____ Base

_____ Repeat each value

a. A Minitab command that allows you to enter sequences and/or repetitive patterns of data in the worksheet

b. The Minitab option in the Sample From Columns dialog box that can eliminate without replacement sampling

c. The "seed" number used to generate random data

d. The Minitab option that can provide percentiles, quartiles, or deciles

e. The Minitab function used in normal probability plots

f. The text box in which you specify the beginning value for the Set Patterned Data command

g. The Minitab command that generates random data from a large number of discrete or continuous distributions

h. The Minitab command you use to sample values from a column, with or without replacement

i. An option available in the Set Patterned Data dialog box

j. The default value for a Normal distribution mean

True/False

Mark the following statements with a *T* or an *F*.

_____ 1. Minitab can compute probabilities for individual values and for whole columns of data, for both discrete and continuous random variables.

_____ 2. Minitab can compute probability density function values for individual values and for whole columns of data for continuous random variables.

_____ 3. Minitab can sample both with and without replacement from any column.

_____ 4. Minitab can generate random data from over 20 continuous and discrete distributions.

_____ 5. By default, the Set Patterned Data command uses an increment of one.

_____ 6. You use the Inverse cumulative probability option to determine percentiles for random variables.

_____ 7. The output of the Probability Distribution command is always displayed in the Session window.

_____ 8. The default percentile for the cumulative probability option is 95%.

_____ 9. The Random Data command allows you to simulate the outcome of experiments without actually performing them.

_____ 10. Minitab calculates probabilities for the Bernoulli random variable.

Practice Problems

1. Assume X is a Poisson random variable with parameter 6.

   a. Obtain the individual probabilities for X = K, with K = 0 to 20. Also obtain the cumulative probabilities for these values.

   b. What is the most likely value of X?

2. This problem explores the effect of degrees of freedom on the Chisquare distribution.

   a. Use the Set Patterned Data command to store the values between 0 and 20, in increments of 0.2; store your results in C1.

   b. Use the Probability Distributions command to store the Chisquare density values for a Chisquare distribution with 3 degrees of freedom in C2.

   c. Plot the density values versus C1. Does your plot look like a Chisquare density? In which direction is the distribution skewed?

   d. Repeat parts b and c using a Chisquare distribution with 10 degrees of freedom. Is your curve more symmetrical? What appears to happen to the Chisquare distribution as the degrees of freedom increase?

3. Use the patterned data you generated in part a of Problem 2 to display the following cumulative probabilities.

   a. Obtain the cumulative probabilities for the values in C1 using a Normal distribution with a mean of 10 and standard deviation of 2. Store your results in C4.

   b. Obtain the cumulative probabilities for the values in C1 using a Normal distribution with a mean of 10 and a standard deviation of 8. Store your results in C5.

   c. Obtain the cumulative probabilities for the values in C1 using a Normal distribution with a mean of 5 and a standard deviation of 2. Store your results in C6.

d. Plot these cumulative distributions against C1 on the same graph. What happens to the cumulative distribution function if the standard deviation increases? What happens to the cumulative distribution function if the mean changes? What is the percentile of the mean for each of the distributions?

4. Mr. Sims, the executive director of a professional organization, plans to contact 18 firms in the hopes of recruiting five as members. He estimates that the probability of recruiting any firm is 0.6.

   a. What is the probability that he will recruit 5 or more firms? What is the most likely number of firms that he will recruit?

   b. Based on your analysis, has the executive director over or underestimated his ability to recruit new members? Briefly explain your answer.

5. Open CANDYB.MTW.

   a. Scroll through the worksheet to see the information the file contains.

   b. Describe C6 NETWGT. What is its mean? What is its standard deviation?

   c. Generate 57 observations from a normal distribution with the same mean and standard deviation. Place these data in C7. Name the column RNDNET.

   d. Obtain normal probability plots for C5 and C6. Which variable is more normal? Briefly explain your answer.

6. Open CRIMES.MTW.

   a. Use the Sample From Columns command to obtain five 1991 violent crime rates.

   b. Which states (or districts) were selected? Explain how you determined the corresponding states.

   c. From which region(s) did your states come? Could they all come from one region? Briefly explain your answer.

TUTORIAL 7

Inference from One Sample

Normally, it is either impossible or impractical to conduct a study of an entire population to obtain the value of a parameter, such as a population mean. Statisticians have developed techniques that allow them to make inferences about parameters based on sample statistics. Two indispensable statistical decision-making tools for a single parameter are:

- *hypothesis tests* to investigate theories about parameters

- *confidence intervals* to estimate the value of a parameter

In this tutorial, you examine four case studies that illustrate how to use Minitab to make inferences about the value of a parameter of a single population. In the first case study, you analyze the age of death from a sociologist's point of view. In the second scenario, you are a Realtor investigating housing prices in a community. In the third example, you are a campaign worker who wants to determine your candidate's chances of winning the election. Finally, you estimate the proportion of times a spinning coin lands on "tails."

Objectives

In this tutorial you learn how to:

- test a population mean when σ is known

- compute a confidence interval for a population mean when σ is known

- test a population mean when σ is unknown

- compute a confidence interval for a population mean when σ is unknown

- test a population proportion

- compute a confidence interval for a population proportion

CASE STUDY: SOCIOLOGY — AGE AT DEATH

To determine the death age reported in a major metropolitan U.S. city, Dr. Ford, a professor of sociology, asks his class to randomly select 37 obituaries from the city's largest newspaper. The sample includes 18 males and 19 females. A student volunteer enters the death age for females in C1 and for males in C2 in a file called AGE.MTW.

Recent studies of this nature for the entire United States found that the mean age at death of both males and females was 75, with a standard deviation of 15. Dr. Ford asks your class to test, at the 0.05 level, the hypothesis that the mean death age of women in this city is less than 75.

▼

Testing μ When σ Is Known

▲

To perform a hypothesis test on the value of μ, *the population mean*, when the value of σ, *the population standard deviation*, is known, you use the Z-test. As you can imagine, the population standard deviation is available only on rare occasions.

To get started:

- Start Minitab and maximize the Minitab window and the Data window

- Start an outfile named **T7** on your Student disk

- Open **AGE.MTW**

The worksheet shows female data in C1 DAGEF and male data in C2 DAGEM.

Set up the following hypotheses to determine whether the mean age of death for women has decreased significantly from the mean of 75 reported in previous studies:

The null hypothesis, H_0: $\mu = 75$

The alternative hypothesis, H_1: $\mu < 75$, a decrease in death age for this metropolitan area

Perform the hypothesis test:

- Choose **Stat > Basic Statistics > 1-Sample Z**

- Double-click **C1 DAGEF** to enter it in the **Variables** text box

- Click the **Test mean** option button and press [Tab]

- Type **75** in the **Test mean** text box

- Click the **Alternative** drop-down arrow and select **less than** from the list box

- Press [Tab]

- Type **15** in the **Sigma** text box

The completed 1-Sample Z dialog box should look like the one shown in Figure 7-1.

FIGURE 7-1

The 1-Sample Z dialog box

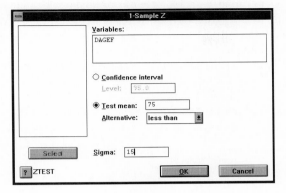

- Press ←Enter

  Determine the critical z-value:

- Choose **Calc > Probability Distributions > Normal**

- Click the **Inverse cumulative probability** option button

- Click the **Input constant** option button and press Tab

- Type **.05** in the **Input constant** text box and press ←Enter

  The Session window (Figure 7-2) displays Minitab's commands and output corresponding to your previous menu choices.

FIGURE 7-2

Results of Z-test for female death age

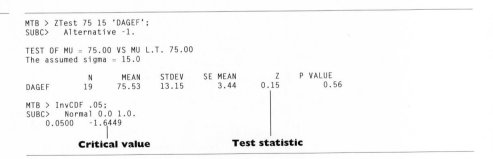

```
MTB > ZTest 75 15 'DAGEF';
SUBC>   Alternative -1.

TEST OF MU = 75.00 VS MU L.T. 75.00
The assumed sigma = 15.0

              N     MEAN    STDEV   SE MEAN      Z   P VALUE
DAGEF        19    75.53    13.15      3.44    0.15      0.56

MTB > InvCDF .05;
SUBC>   Normal 0.0 1.0.
     0.0500    -1.6449
```

      Critical value   **Test statistic**

The subcommand Alternative –1 designates the *left-tailed* (less-than or lower-tailed) alternative hypothesis. Correspondingly, +1 designates a *right-tailed* test and 0 indicates a *two-tailed* test.

Assuming the null hypothesis is true, the sample mean of 75.53 has a test statistic of 0.15. The critical z-value is –1.6449, so the test statistic of 0.15

does not fall in the rejection region. Fail to reject H_0. There is no significant evidence to conclude that the mean reported death age is less than 75 for women in the metropolitan area you are studying.

You can also decide to reject or fail to reject the null hypothesis using the p-value in the Z-test output. When the p-value is less than your chosen level of significance, reject H_0. In this case, the p-value of 0.56 is greater than 0.05, so your decision would be the same, as it should be: fail to reject H_0 at the 0.05 level.

Now test the same hypothesis for men:

- Choose **Stat > Basic Statistics > 1-Sample Z**

- Double-click **C2 DAGEM** to enter it in the **Variables** text box

- Verify that the **Test mean** option button is selected with a value of 75, that **Alternative** is set to **less than**, and that **Sigma** is **15**

- Click **OK**

The Session window should look like Figure 7-3.

FIGURE 7-3

Results of Z-test for male deaths

```
MTB > ZTest 75 15 'DAGEM';
SUBC>   Alternative -1.

TEST OF MU = 75.00 VS MU L.T. 75.00
The assumed sigma = 15.0

                N      MEAN     STDEV    SE MEAN      Z    P VALUE
DAGEM          18     74.22     13.19      3.54    -0.22    0.41
```

In this case, the test statistic is -0.22. Since the critical value at the 0.05 level of significance is -1.6449 (the same as that computed for the female test), again the test statistic does not fall in the critical region. So, at the 0.05 level, do not reject H_0. Apparently, the reported death age of neither men nor women is less than 75.

Note that the p-value for this test is 0.41. Since this value is greater than 0.05, you would not reject H_0 at the 0.05 level. Moreover, if you performed the test at any reasonable level, you would still reject H_0 because the p-value of 0.41 is greater than any such level. Many statisticians believe that reporting test results in terms of the p-value avoids confusion by letting readers use their own judgment as to whether the p-value is small enough.

▼

Computing a Confidence Interval for μ When σ Is Known

▲

As part of your sociology project, Dr. Ford asks you to estimate the mean death age for all adult men and women. Begin by forming two 90% confidence intervals:

- Choose **Stat > Basic Statistics > 1-Sample Z**

- Double-click **C1 DAGEF** and **C2 DAGEM** to enter them in the **Variables** text box

- Click the **Confidence interval** option button, press (Tab), and then enter **.90** in the **Level** text box

- Verify that the **Sigma** text box contains **15**

Note: You can enter a confidence interval as a whole number (90) or as a decimal number (.90) in the Level text box.

The completed 1-Sample Z dialog box should look like the one shown in Figure 7-4.

FIGURE 7-4

The 1-Sample Z dialog box

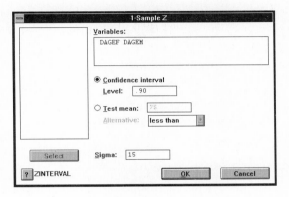

- Press (←Enter)

Figure 7-5 shows the results in the Session window.

FIGURE 7-5

90% confidence intervals

```
MTB > ZInterval .90 15  'DAGEF'  'DAGEM'.

THE ASSUMED SIGMA =15.0

            N     MEAN    STDEV   SE MEAN    90.0 PERCENT C.I.
DAGEF      19    75.53    13.15      3.44    ( 69.86,  81.19)
DAGEM      18    74.22    13.19      3.54    ( 68.40,  80.04)
```

Based on the results, you can be 90% confident that:

- Women have a mean death age between 69.86 and 81.19.

- Men have a mean death age between 68.40 and 80.04.

Note that the confidence intervals for both men and women include the age 75. This outcome is consistent with the results of the hypothesis tests performed in the section "Testing μ When σ Is Known."

Clear the worksheet in preparation for the next case study:

- Choose **File > Other Files > Stop Recording Session**

- Choose **File > Restart Minitab**

CASE STUDY: REAL ESTATE — HOUSING PRICES

As newly hired Realtor for Consolidated Properties, your want to investigate housing prices in a district. Previously, the mean housing price was $165,000; you want to see if this price is still current. You formulate two hypotheses to test using randomly selected 150 homes:

$$H_0: \mu = 165000$$

$$H_1: \mu \neq 165000$$

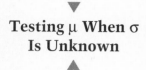

Testing μ When σ Is Unknown

The records for past home sales figures in this particular area show that the prices are nearly normally distributed (bell-shaped). Because you do not know the population standard deviation, you cannot use a Z-test. However, the population is approximately normally distributed, so you can use a t-test instead.

- Start the T7 outfile again on your Student disk; Minitab appends the subsequent session record to your previous outfile

- Open **HOMES.MTW**

- Choose **Stat > Basic Statistics > 1-Sample t**

- Double-click **C1 PRICE** to enter it in the **Variables** text box

- Click the **Test mean** option button and press Tab

- Type **165000** in the **Test mean** text box

- Click the **Alternative** drop-down arrow and select **not equal** from the list, if necessary

   The completed 1-Sample t dialog box should look like the one shown in Figure 7-6.

FIGURE 7-6

The 1-Sample t dialog box

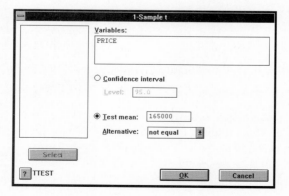

MINITAB AT WORK

RETAILING: Frozen foods are a common staple in many American households, especially frozen pizzas. Pizza producers must carefully monitor how bacteria respond to prolonged refrigeration temperatures. Microbiologists used Minitab to help determine how long pizza can be refrigerated without becoming a threat to public health.

In order to examine the effect of freezing on specific bacteria, researchers inoculated the pizzas with measured amounts of *Escherichia coli* and other potential contaminants. They stored the pizzas at various temperatures, retrieving samples every other day for microbiological analysis. They counted colonies of bacteria at each testing and entered that data into Minitab. When they compared each day's count with the initial count, using a 1-sample t-test, they found that the *E. coli* colonies increased significantly (p-value < 0.05) between days 8 and 10.

This result suggests *E. coli* will grow when acceptable refrigeration temperatures are not maintained. Pizza producers could best safeguard public health by carefully monitoring bacteria levels before beginning the freezing process, while the vendors must ensure adequate refrigeration and carefully monitor shelf dates.

■ Press ⏎Enter

The Session window (Figure 7-7) appears with the t-test results.

FIGURE 7-7

Results of t-test

```
MTB > TTest 165000 'PRICE';
SUBC>   Alternative 0.

TEST OF MU = 165000 VS MU N.E. 165000

                N      MEAN    STDEV   SE MEAN       T    P VALUE
PRICES        150    153775    41611      3398    -3.30    0.0012
```

The sample mean sales price of 153775 corresponds to the t-value of –3.30. The corresponding p-value is 0.0012. Since the p-value is less than 0.05, reject H_0 and conclude that there is apparently significant evidence of a change in home sales prices. This change probably reflects a broader trend in U.S. housing prices during recent years.

Computing a Confidence Interval for μ When σ Is Unknown

To compute a 95% confidence interval for the price of homes:

■ Choose **Edit > Edit Last Command Dialog**

■ Click **Confidence interval**

■ Click **OK**

The 95% confidence interval (the default confidence level) appears in the Session window, as shown in Figure 7-8.

FIGURE 7-8

95% confidence interval

```
MTB > TInterval 95.0 'PRICE'.
              N    MEAN   STDEV  SE MEAN   95.0 PERCENT C.I.
PRICES      150  153775   41611     3398   ( 147060, 160490)
```

You can report, with 95% confidence, that the mean sale price of the surveyed homes falls between $147,060 and $160,490.

Clear the worksheet before proceeding to the next case study:

■ Choose **File > Other Files > Stop Recording Session**

■ Choose **File > Restart Minitab**

CASE STUDY: POLITICAL SCIENCE — ELECTION POLL

You are a campaign volunteer for Ann Gomez, one of two candidates running for State Senator in your district. Election day is only five days away. Gomez believes she has 55% voter support and will therefore win the race. However, a random sample of registered voters conducted earlier today shows that only 86 of the 200 (43%) voters sampled favor Ms. Gomez. Ms. Gomez asks you to analyze the data to determine whether she does or doesn't have 55% of the voters behind her. If so, she's confident that she can win the election; otherwise, she needs to intensify her campaign efforts.

Testing a Population Proportion

Use a 5% level of significance to determine if the data indicate that the true proportion of favorable voters is less than 55%. First formulate the hypotheses:

H_0: p = 0.55

H_1: p < 0.55

Minitab has no direct command to perform hypothesis tests on and obtain a confidence interval for proportions. However, it can store a sequence of commands in a file called a *macro*. You can then use the macro to execute the commands in one easy step. The commands you need to perform this particular test are stored in PINF.MTB. This file is an example of a Minitab *Exec* macro. (You'll learn more about Execs in Tutorial 16.)

The test uses the normal approximation to the binomial and hence assumes np and n(1 − p) are both greater than 5. Because 200*0.55 = 102 > 5 and 200*(1 − 0.55) = 98 > 5, you proceed:

■ Start the T7 outfile again on your Student disk; Minitab appends the subsequent session record to your previous outfile

■ Choose **File > Other Files > Run an Exec**

■ Press [←Enter] to select the file and execute the Exec once

■ Double-click **PINF.MTB** in the STUDENT9 subdirectory of the MTBSEW directory

The Session window appears and prompts you to input values for p-naught (p_0, the hypothesized value of the population proportion), x (the observed number of successes), and n (the sample size).

At the DATA> prompt, enter the values on one line:

■ Type **0.55 86 200** (put at least one space between each value)

The Session window should look like Figure 7-9.

FIGURE 7-9

First DATA prompt for the PINF.MTB Exec

```
MTB > Execute 'C:\MTBSEW\STUDENT9\PINF.MTB' 1.
Executing from file: C:\MTBSEW\STUDENT9\PINF.MTB

  At the "DATA>" prompt below, enter the following values:
  1. p-naught, the hypothesized value of the population proportion;
  2. x, the observed number of successes; and
  3. n, the sample size.

DATA> 0.55 86 200
```

■ Press [←Enter]

Minitab then asks you to indicate the direction of your test: upper-tailed, two-tailed, or lower-tailed:

■ Type **-1** to perform a lower-tailed test

The Session window should look like Figure 7-10.

FIGURE 7-10

Second DATA prompt for the PINF.MTB Exec

```
Input:
  0.55  86.00  200.00

  At the "DATA" prompt below, enter a
      1 to perform an upper-tailed test, or
      0 to perform a two-tailed test, or
     -1 to perform a lower-tailed test.

DATA> -1
```

■ Press [←Enter]

After Minitab runs the test, the results appear in the Session window, as shown in Figure 7-11.

FIGURE 7-11

PINF.MTB results of the hypothesis test

```
Ho: p = 0.5500   vs.  Ha: p  <  0.5500

z = -3.41121      p-value = 0.00032

A confidence interval for the true population proportion will be
produced below. At the "DATA" prompt below, enter the confidence
level (95 for a 95% confidence interval) for the confidence interval.

DATA>
```

Minitab requests information about the confidence interval. In this case, you're not interested in obtaining a confidence interval so you enter 0:

■ Type **0** at the prompt and press ⌷←Enter⌷

Examine the results of the hypothesis test. Figure 7-11 displays the null and alternative hypotheses as well as the Z-test statistic and the p-value. The Z-test statistic is –3.41121, with a p-value of 0.00032. Reject H_0. As the campaign heads into the homestretch, it appears that Ms. Gomez has less than 55% of the voters' support, at a 5% level of significance. You advise her of your results so she can plan accordingly.

CASE STUDY: MATHEMATICS — PROBABILITY

In a probability class, the instructor asks a student to spin a coin 100 times and observe how many times it lands on "tails." It lands 62 times on "tails." Based on this experiment, what is the 95% confidence interval for the proportion of "tails" resulting from a spinning coin?

▼

Computing a Confidence Interval for a Population Proportion

▲

To obtain this confidence interval, you again use the Minitab Exec, PINF.MTB.

■ Choose **File > Other Files > Run an Exec**

■ Press ⌷←Enter⌷ to select the file and execute the Exec once

■ Double-click **PINF.MTB** in the STUDENT9 subdirectory of the MTBSEW directory

Minitab prompts you to enter values for p-naught, x, and n (you need to enter a value for p-naught even though you don't need to perform a hypothesis test).

■ Type **0.5 62 100** (0.5 is the value for p-naught) at the DATA> prompt, separating the values with at least one space

- Press [←Enter]

Minitab prompts you for the direction of your test; you may enter any value because you are interested only in a confidence interval:

- Type **0** and press [←Enter]

Minitab asks you to enter information about the confidence level at the DATA> prompt.

- Type **95** and press [←Enter]

The Session window should resemble Figure 7-12.

FIGURE 7-12

Results of PINF.MTB confidence interval computations

```
MTB > Execute 'C:\MTBSEW\STUDENT9\PINF.MTB' 1.
Executing from file: C:\MTBSEW\STUDENT9\PINF.MTB

   At the "DATA>" prompt below, enter the following values:
   1.  p-naught, the hypothesized value of the population proportion;
   2.  x, the observed number of successes; and
   3.  n, the sample size.

DATA> 0.5   62   100


Input:
    0.5     62.00     100.00

   At the "DATA>" prompt below, enter a
        1 to perform an upper-tailed test, or
        0 to perform a two-tailed test, or
       -1 to perform a lower-tailed test.

DATA> 0

                    Ho: p = 0.5000   vs.   Ha:  p not = 0.5000

                    z = 2.40000        p-value = 0.01640


   A confidence interval for the true population proportion will be
   produced below. At the "DATA" prompt below, enter the confidence
   level (95 for a 95% confidence interval) for the confidence interval.

DATA>  95

CI Level
   95

   The 95% confidence interval is ( 0.5249 to 0.7151)
MTB >
```

The lower confidence limit is 0.5249 and the upper confidence limit is 0.7151. You can be 95% confident that the proportion of tails resulting from a spinning coin is between 52.49% and 71.51%.

Note that this interval does not include 0.5. The instructor asks if this is due to the definition of a confidence interval or the physical properties of a spinning coin. He then tells each member of the class to repeat the experiment and construct a similar 95% confidence interval and bring it to the next class.

Stop your outfile:

- Choose **File > Other Files > Stop Recording Session**

In this tutorial you used Minitab to perform hypothesis tests and form confidence intervals about the parameter of a single population. In Tutorial 8, you compare the difference between the parameters of two populations.

If you plan to continue directly to the next tutorial:

- Choose **File > Restart Minitab** and then click **No** at the prompt

If you want to take a longer break:

- Choose **File > Exit**

▼

Minitab Command Summary

▲

This section describes the Minitab menu commands introduced in or related to this tutorial. To find a complete explanation of all menus and commands, refer to the Reference section of this manual.

Minitab Menu Commands

Menu	Command	Description
File		
	Other Files	
	Run an Exec	Executes the commands in an Exec file one or more times, as specified by the user
Stat		
	Basic Statistics	
	1-Sample Z	Performs inferences (tests and confidence intervals) on a population mean when σ is known
	1-Sample t	Performs inferences (tests and confidence intervals) on a population mean when σ is unknown

Review and Practice

Matching

Match the following terms to their definitions by placing the correct letter next to the term it describes.

_____ Do not reject H_0

_____ 1-Sample t

_____ PINF.MTB

_____ Alternative

_____ Sigma

_____ Level

_____ p-value

_____ 1-Sample Z

_____ σ

_____ Run an Exec

a. The probability for which a value of less than the chosen level of significance indicates rejection of the null hypothesis

b. The Minitab command used to perform a 1-sample inference about a mean, assuming σ is unknown

c. The name Minitab uses for the population standard deviation

d. One of two conclusions to a possible hypothesis test

e. The Minitab subcommand that carries out the commands in a macro file

f. The Minitab command you use to perform a 1-sample inference about a mean, assuming σ is known

g. The option that allows you to change the amount of confidence in an interval estimate

h. A set of commands stored by Minitab that test a population proportion and provide a confidence interval for the population proportion

i. The Minitab subcommand that allows you to specify the direction of the alternative hypothesis

j. The symbol used to represent the population standard deviation

True/False

Mark the following statements with a _T_ or an _F_.

_____ 1. Confidence intervals can be entered in Minitab as a percentage (99) or as a decimal (.99).

_____ 2. The population standard deviation must be known to perform a 1-sample test of a mean in Minitab.

_____ 3. Confidence intervals and 1-sample tests are performed using the same Minitab command on the Stat menu.

_____ 4. An upper-tailed test is the default alternative for a 1-sample test of a population mean.

_____ 5. The confidence level for population confidence intervals can be set to any value you specify.

_____ 6. Minitab allows you to specify a significance level for a hypothesis test.

_____ 7. An upper-tailed test is designated Alternative 0.

_____ 8. The PINF.MTB Exec performs only a two-tailed test.

_____ 9. In Minitab's 1-sample confidence intervals, the default confidence level is 90%.

_____ 10. Most of Minitab's 1-sample inference commands are found on the File menu.

Practice Problems

1. Open CANDYB.MTW. The mean net weight of a candy package is advertised as 20.89 grams. Use the CANDYB.MTW data to determine if the mean net weight is less than the advertised value at a significance level of 0.05. Why is this one-sided alternative appropriate?

2. Open PROF.MTW.

   a. Obtain confidence intervals for the mean Course and Prof ratings at the university.

   b. Unstack the Course ratings into four columns using the year variable. Obtain confidence intervals for the mean course rating for each of the four years. Describe the results.

   c. Code the professor ratings into two groups: a low group with ratings below 2, and a high group with ratings of 2 or above. Use the Tally command to determine the number of professors in each group. Using 90% confidence, estimate the percentage of professors that the students consider to be 2 or above.

3. Open WASTES.MTW.

   a. Examine the information in the file.

   b. Stack the eight districts and obtain a 95% confidence interval for the mean number of hazardous waste sites in the entire country.

   c. Obtain 95% confidence intervals for the mean number of hazardous waste sites in each of the eight districts. How do these confidence intervals compare to the interval computed in part b?

   d. Would you prefer to use the interval from part b or the intervals from part c in a report? Briefly explain your answer.

4. Open PAY.MTW. The industry average salary has been found to be approximately $35,000.00. Is this company's average salary comparable to the industry?

5. Open PROF. MTW. Determine if the proportion of surveyed courses with senior numbers (400's) is different from 0.25 at a significance level of 0.05.

TUTORIAL
8

Inferences on Means from Two Samples

In the first case study in this tutorial, you investigate whether there is a difference between the mean age at death of women and men. In the second case study, you determine whether the number of rooms or baths affects mean housing prices. Finally, you perform a before-and-after inference to determine whether time has an impact on mean mortgage interest rates for lenders.

Objectives

In this tutorial, you learn how to:

- test the difference between two population means when two independent samples are recorded in separate columns

- form a confidence interval for the difference between two population means when two independent samples are recorded in separate columns

- test the difference between two population means when two independent samples are stacked in a single column

- form a confidence interval for the difference between two population means when two independent samples are stacked in a single column

- test the difference between two population means when two dependent samples are paired

- form a confidence interval for the difference between two population means when two dependent samples are paired

CASE STUDY: SOCIOLOGY — AGE AT DEATH (CONTINUED)

In Tutorial 7, you performed hypothesis tests on the mean and the proportion of a single population. As you examined the ages at death of females and males, you may have wondered whether there was a *difference* between the means of these two distinct populations. Statisticians must often determine whether one group is inherently different from another because of a particular treatment or characteristic, such as gender, or whether any apparent differences should simply be attributed to sampling variation.

▼

Using Two-Independent-Sample Inferences for Unstacked Data

▲

Minitab offers several options for testing differences between two population means. Because the males and females were randomly and independently selected from the newspaper obituaries, use the test for independent samples. Pose the hypotheses to test for a difference between mean male and female age at death, using a significance level of 0.05:

$H_0: \mu_F = \mu_M$

$H_1: \mu_F \neq \mu_M$

To open the sample file and perform the t-test:

- Start Minitab and maximize the Minitab window and the Data window
- Start an outfile named **T8** on your Student disk
- Open **AGE.MTW**
- Choose **Stat > Basic Statistics > 2-Sample t**
- Click the **Samples in different columns** option button and then press `Tab`
- Double-click **C1 DAGEF** to enter it in the **First** text box
- Double-click **C2 DAGEM** to enter it in the **Second** text box
- Click the **Assume equal variances** check box

Note: In this case, the sample standard deviations of the two genders support an assumption of equal variances. In other cases, if there isn't a strong reason to make such an assumption, do not select the Assume equal variances check box.

The completed 2-Sample t dialog box should look like the one shown in Figure 8-1.

FIGURE 8-1

The 2-Sample t dialog box

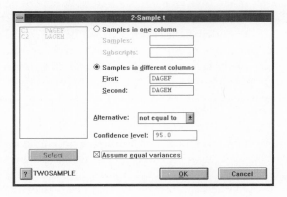

■ Click **OK**

The results appear in the Session window (Figure 8-2).

FIGURE 8-2

Results of 2-Sample t test comparing mean female and male death age

```
MTB > TwoSample 95.0 'DAGEF' 'DAGEM';
SUBC>    Alternative 0;
SUBC>    Pooled.

TWOSAMPLE T FOR DAGEF VS DAGEM
          N      MEAN     STDEV    SE MEAN
DAGEF    19      75.5      13.2      3.0
DAGEM    18      74.2      13.2      3.1

95 PCT CI FOR MU DAGEF - MU DAGEM: ( -7.5,  10.1)

TTEST MU DAGEF = MU DAGEM (VS NE): T= 0.30  P=0.77  DF=  35

POOLED STDEV =       13.2
```

Minitab presents summary information (sample size, mean, standard deviation, and standard error) for the females and males, and then displays the t-statistic (T = 0.30), p-value (P = 0.77), and degrees of freedom of the t-statistic (DF = 35). Since the p-value of 0.77 exceeds the level of significance of 0.05, fail to reject the null hypothesis and conclude that there is no significant evidence of a difference between the age at death of females and males. You can therefore attribute the differences in the sample means to sampling variation.

Note that Minitab also provides a confidence interval for the difference in the means. The 95% confidence interval is (–7.5, 10.1).

Clear the worksheet before proceeding to the next case study:

■ Choose **File > Restart Minitab**

CASE STUDY: REAL ESTATE — HOUSING PRICES (CONTINUED)

To continue the housing price study you started in Tutorial 7, you decide to test, at a significance level of .01, whether homes with 9 or fewer rooms have a different selling price than homes with 10 or more rooms.

You've collected data on selling prices (C1 PRICE), living areas (C2 AREA), lot sizes (C3 ACRES), rooms (C4 ROOMS), and number of baths (C5 BATHS) in a file called HOMES.MTW. (See the data set descriptions in Part III, Exploring Data, for a complete description of this data set.)

Using Two-Independent-Sample Inferences for Stacked Data

- Start the T8 outfile again; Minitab appends the subsequent session record to your previous outfile

- Open **HOMES.MTW**

   Create a column that codes houses with 9 or fewer rooms as a 1 and those with 10 or more rooms as a 2:

- Choose **Manip > Code Data Values**

- Double-click **C4 ROOMS** to enter it in the **Code data from columns** text box and press Tab

- Type **ROOMSIZE** in the **Into columns** text box and press Tab

- Type **1:9** in the first **Original Values** text box, press Tab, type **1** in the corresponding **New** text box, and then press Tab

- Type **10:100** in the second **Original Values** text box, press Tab, and type **2** in the corresponding **New** text box

   The Code Data Values dialog box should look like the one shown in Figure 8-3.

FIGURE 8-3

The Code Data Values dialog box

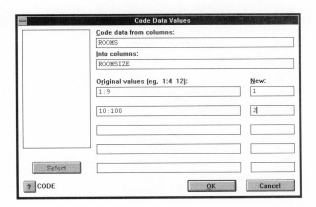

■ Press ⎡←Enter⎤

Now formulate the hypotheses:

$H_0: \mu_1 = \mu_2$

$H_1: \mu_1 \neq \mu_2$

C1 PRICE lists selling prices and the column you just created, C6 ROOMSIZE, indicates the size of the houses. Perform the hypothesis test and obtain a 99% confidence interval for the difference between selling prices of medium-sized and large-sized homes:

■ Choose **Stat > Basic Statistics > 2-Sample t**

The two samples are in one column:

■ Click the **Samples** text box, double-click **C1 PRICE**

■ Double-click **C6 ROOMSIZE** to enter it in the **Subscripts** text box and then press ⎡Tab⎤ twice

■ Type **99** in the **Confidence level** text box

Note: The Subscripts variable in a 2-Sample t must be an integer and have two distinct values. Your subscripts are 1 for medium-sized homes and 2 for large-sized homes

The completed 2-Sample t dialog box should look like the one shown in Figure 8-4.

FIGURE 8-4

The 2-Sample t dialog box

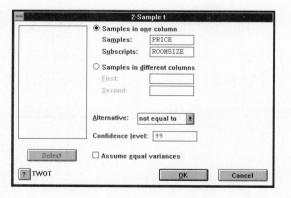

■ Click **OK**

The Session window should look like Figure 8-5.

FIGURE 8-5

Results of 2-sample t

```
MTB > TwoT 99 'PRICE' 'ROOMSIZE';
SUBC>   Alternative 0.

TWOSAMPLE T FOR PRICE
ROOMSIZE    N      MEAN     STDEV    SE MEAN
1          142    151635    40862       3429
2            8    191769    38477      13604

99 PCT CI FOR MU 1 - MU 2: ( -89238,   8969)

TTEST MU 1 = MU 2 (VS NE): T= -2.86  P=0.024  DF=  7
```
                      99% confidence interval

The difference in sample means, 151635 – 191769 = –40134, corresponds to a t-value with 7 degrees of freedom of –2.86. The p-value for this test is 0.024, which is greater than 0.01. Therefore, fail to reject H_0 and conclude that there is no significant evidence of a difference between the mean selling price of homes with 9 or fewer rooms and homes with 10 or more rooms. Once again, Minitab provides a confidence interval for the difference.

To pursue the investigation further, you examine whether the number of baths influences selling price. Do homes with one bath or less have lower selling prices than homes with more than one bath?

To assign identifying subscripts for the bath variable:

■ Choose **Manip > Code Data Values**

■ Double-click **C5 BATHS** to enter it in the **Code data from columns** text box and press Tab

■ Type **BATHSIZE** in the **Into columns** text box and press Tab

■ Type **0:1** in the first **Original values** text box, press Tab, type **1** in the first **New** text box, if necessary, and then press Tab

■ Type **1.5:100** in the second **Original values** text box, press Tab, and then type **2** in the corresponding **New** text box, if necessary

The completed Code Data Values dialog box should look like the one shown in Figure 8-6.

FIGURE 8-6

The Code Data Values dialog box

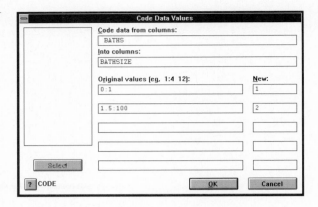

- Press ⏎Enter

Next, formulate hypotheses to test whether homes with one bath (BATHSIZE 1 = homes with 1 or less bath) have lower selling prices than those with more than one bath (BATHSIZE 2 = homes with more than 1 bath):

$$H_0: \mu_1 = \mu_2$$

$$H_1: \mu_1 < \mu_2$$

- Choose **Stat > Basic Statistics > 2-Sample t**

- Verify that the **Samples in one column** option button is selected and that **C1 PRICE** appears in the **Samples** text box

- Click the **Subscripts** text box and then double-click **C7 BATHSIZE**

- Click the **Alternative** drop-down arrow and then select **greater than** (because Minitab first prints the sample that appears first in the subscript column)

- Click **OK**

The Session window looks like Figure 8-7.

FIGURE 8-7

Results of t-test comparing mean selling price by bath size

```
MTB > TwoT 'PRICE' 'BATHSIZE';
SUBC>   Alternative 1.

TWOSAMPLE T FOR PRICE
BATHSIZE    N     MEAN    STDEV   SE MEAN
2          112   167056   38797    3666
1           38   114632   18698    3033

95 PCT CI FOR MU 2 - MU 1: ( 43009,  61840)

TTEST MU 2 = MU 1 (VS GT): T= 11.02  P=0.0000  DF=  130
```

MINITAB AT WORK

SCIENTIFIC RESEARCH: A supernova, the explosion of a star, is a rarely observed phenomenon, and researchers often study it by examining remnants it leaves behind. Astronomers have charted 29 supernova remnants (SNRs) in a nearby galaxy named the Large Magellanic Cloud. They predicted that SNRs produced by stars with relatively short lives would be close to areas of recent star formation, called H II regions. A physicist, a mathematician, and an undergraduate at a Colorado university teamed up to study the Large Magellanic Cloud supernovas by testing whether the remnants are indeed close to H II regions.

The team calculated the distance between each of the 29 known SNRs in the Large Magellanic Cloud and its nearest H II region and then found the mean distance. They used Minitab to simulate what the mean distance would have been had the SNRs been randomly distributed throughout the galaxy. A 2-sample t-test showed that the actual mean distance was significantly less than Minitab's randomly generated SNR locations had led them to expect.

They concluded that supernova remnants in the Large Magellanic Cloud are not randomly distributed; the SNRs cluster around areas of recent star formation and are likely to have resulted from the explosions of short-lived stars.

Because the p-value of 0.000 is less than 0.01, reject H_0 and conclude that there is statistical evidence for rejecting the equality of mean selling prices for homes with at least one bath and homes with more than one bath when the alternative is that the mean selling price of homes with at least one bath is less than that of homes with more than one bath. In other words, the number of baths appears to affect the selling price of the home.

Save the file on your Student disk and then clear the worksheet:

- Save your worksheet with the name **8HOMES** on your Student disk

- Choose **File > Other Files > Stop Recording Session**

- Choose **File > Restart Minitab**

CASE STUDY: FINANCE — MORTGAGE INTEREST RATES

In your finance class, Professor Ruiz asks you to investigate the perception that 30-year mortgage interest rates have decreased in the last year. You examine the mortgage interest rates of six lenders in December of 1992 and in December of 1993.

Using Two-Dependent-Sample Inferences

▼

▲

In the previous case studies in this tutorial, samples were drawn independently from each of two populations. Pairing subjects, like identical twins or before-and-after measurements of a subject, can eliminate the effect of extraneous variables. Such data are called *paired* or *dependent* data.

■ Start the T8 outfile again on your Student disk; Minitab appends the subsequent session record to your previous outfile

■ Open **MORT.MTW**

C1 30YR1992 and C2 30YR1993 contain the mortgage interest rates (in percentages) in 1992 and 1993, respectively, for each of the six lenders in the study. Assume that the difference between the mortgage interest rates follows a normal distribution. Compute the difference between the interest rates in the two years and place the result in C3:

■ Choose **Calc > Mathematical Expressions**

■ Type **'D=92-93'** in the **Variable (new or modified)** text box and then press Tab twice

■ Type **C1-C2** in the **Expression** text box

The completed dialog box should look like the one shown in Figure 8-8.

■ Press ↵Enter

Minitab stores the differences in C3. Next, form the hypotheses to test:

$H_0: \mu_D = 0$

$H_1: \mu_D > 0$

The hypothesis is upper-tailed, since your difference is the 1992 rates minus the 1993 rates. If mortgage interest rates decreased over time, the 1993 values will be less that the 1992 ones, and the mean difference will be greater than 0.

To perform a paired t-test, use the 1-sample t-test you used in Tutorial 7.

- Choose **Stat > Basic Statistics > 1-Sample t**
- Double-click **C3 D=92-93** to enter it in the **Variables** text box
- Click the **Test mean** option button

  Since you are testing a mean difference of 0, use the default of 0.0.

- Choose **greater than** in the **Alternative** drop-down list

  The completed 1-Sample t dialog box should look like the one shown in Figure 8-9.

FIGURE 8-9

The 1-Sample t dialog box

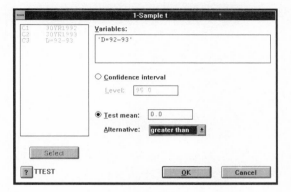

- Click **OK**

  The Session window resembles Figure 8-10.

FIGURE 8-10

Results of t-test investigating the effect of time on mortgage interest rates

```
MTB > TTest 0.0 'D=92-93';
SUBC>    Alternative 1.

TEST OF MU = 0.0000 VS MU G.T. 0.0000

              N     MEAN    STDEV   SE MEAN      T    P VALUE
D=92-93       6   1.0825   0.1068   0.0436   24.82    0.0000
```

The mean of the differences is 1.0825%, corresponding to a t-value of 24.82. Since the p-value for this test is 0.0000 (less than 0.01), fail to reject H_0 at the 1% level of significance. When you submit your study to Professor Ruiz, you are careful to state the alternative: that the mean 1992 interest rate is greater than the mean 1993 interest rate. You can report that this test provides significant evidence to reject the null hypothesis that the mean difference between the two interest rates is 0.

Use the difference to obtain a 98% confidence interval:

■ Choose **Edit > Edit Last Command Dialog**

■ Click the **Confidence interval** option button and then press `Tab`

■ Type **98** in the **Level** text box

The completed 1-Sample t dialog box should resemble the one shown in Figure 8-11.

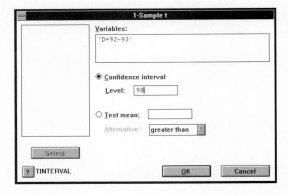

■ Click **OK**

The Session window contains the information shown in Figure 8-12.

```
MTB > TInterval 98 'D=92-93'.

              N     MEAN   STDEV  SE MEAN    98.0 PERCENT C.I.
D=92-93       6   1.0825  0.1068   0.0436  ( 0.9357,  1.2293)
```

According to the results, you can be 98% confident that the difference between mean mortgage interest rates in 1992 and 1993 for lenders is between 0.9357 and 1.2293%. Your previous conclusion, that the mean interest rate has been reduced, is reinforced.

In this tutorial, you performed hypothesis tests on and computed confidence intervals for the difference between the means of two populations. Minitab can test independent samples, as in the age at death and housing price investigations, or it can test dependent samples, as in the 1992–1993 mortgage interest rate study. In Tutorial 9, you compare the means of more than two populations.

Save the file on your Student disk and stop your outfile:

- Save your worksheet with the name **8MORT** on your Student disk

- Choose **File > Other Files > Stop Recording Session**

    If you plan to continue directly to the next tutorial:

- Choose **File > Restart Minitab**

    If you want to take a longer break:

- Choose **File > Exit**

Minitab Command Summary

This section describes the Minitab menu commands introduced in or related to this tutorial. To find a complete explanation of all menus and commands, refer to the Reference section of this manual.

Minitab Menu Commands

Menu	Command	Description
Stat		
	Basic Statistics	
	1-Sample t	Performs inferences (tests and confidence intervals) on the differences between two population means using paired data
	2-Sample t	Performs inferences (tests and confidence intervals) on the differences between two population means using independent samples

Matching

Match the following terms to their definitions by placing the correct letter next to the term it describes.

_____ Level

_____ Samples in
one column

_____ Assume equal
variances

_____ Samples in dif-
ferent columns

_____ The "not
equal to"
Alternative

_____ Alternative 1

_____ Basic Statistics

_____ 2-Sample t

_____ P

_____ Pairing

a. The default alternative hypothesis in Minitab commands

b. The Minitab option that lets you perform a 2-sample t-test assuming the standard deviations of the populations are equal

c. The Minitab submenu that includes all the parametric two-sample commands

d. The Minitab command that performs inference on the differences between two population means using independent samples

e. Minitab subcommand that specifies an upper-tailed test be performed

f. The Minitab option that specifies the degree of confidence for the interval estimate of the difference between means from two independent samples

g. The Minitab 2-sample test option that performs inference on means from two different populations using data in one column with a sample identifier in another column

h. The Minitab 2-sample test option that performs inference on means from two different populations using sample data stored in two different columns

i. Minitab's notation for a p-value in a 2-sample t-test

j. A technique that eliminates the effect of extraneous variables

True/False

Mark the following statements with a *T* or an *F*.

_____ 1. Minitab can perform a 2-sample t-test if the data from the populations are stored in either one column or two.

_____ 2. You use the Minitab menu command, Paired-T, to perform a paired t-test.

_____ 3. The 2-Sample t menu command performs a 2-sample t-test.

_____ 4. The output of the test of the two population means includes a confidence interval for the difference between two population means.

_____ 5. Minitab can perform independent, 2-sample t-tests assuming the population variances are equal or unequal.

_____ 6. You can perform only two-tailed 2-sample tests in Minitab.

_____ 7. The default confidence level for 2-sample confidence intervals is 95%.

_____ 8. In a 2-sample test, Minitab requires a subscripts column when the two sample data are stored in a single column.

_____ 9. The subscript column used in the 2-sample t-test must be numeric.

_____ 10. Minitab automatically computes the differences for the paired t-test.

Practice Problems

1. Open PROF.MTW.

   a. Test whether first-year courses have a different mean rating than fourth-year courses. (To do so, you can create a variable that is 1 for first-year courses, 2 for fourth-year courses, and missing for second-and third-year courses. Alternatively, you can unstack the course rating data into four columns and then use the appropriate columns.)

   b. Repeat part a using the Prof rating.

   c. Based on your results in parts a and b, do students' opinions about their instructors change over the course of their college careers?

2. Open ADS2.MTW.

   a. Test whether the news magazine has a higher mean ad ratio than the sports magazine. Use $\alpha = 0.05$.

   b. Obtain histograms of the ADRATIO variable for each magazine using the same scale.

   c. Repeat part b with boxplots.

   d. Repeat part b with dotplots.

   e. Repeat part b with stem-and-leaf diagrams.

   f. Which of the four plots best displays the results of your test in part a? Explain your choice.

3. Open RIVERS.MTW. Determine if the mean temperature of the river is different at site 2, directly upriver from the power plant, from site 3, directly downriver from the cooling towers' discharge. To do so, create a new column with the code 1 for site 2, 2 for site 3, and missing for all others. Use the Code Data Values command to code only the site 2 and 3 values.

4. Use the WASTES.MTW data set to determine whether the mean number of hazardous waste sites for the eight districts are different.

   a. You want to compare each district's mean number to every other district's mean number. How many 2-sample tests will you need to do?

   b. Suppose you use an alpha of 5% for each test. Is the probability of making a mistake in the total set of tests equal to, much less than, or much greater than 5%?

5. Open TVVIEW.MTW.

   a. What is the sample mean difference in the TV-viewing times of husbands and wives?

   b. Is the distribution of the difference normal? Use a normal probability plot. Why is it difficult to use a one-variable graph such as a histogram to answer this question?

   c. Estimate, using 99% confidence, the mean difference in the TV-viewing times of husbands and wives. Interpret this interval estimate.

TUTORIAL
9

Comparing Population Means: Analysis of Variance

In Tutorial 8, you used Minitab to perform hypothesis tests to compare the means of two populations. *Analysis of variance (ANOVA)* is a statistical tool that lets you extend this capability to compare the means of several populations. In the first case study, you're a journalism student who needs to determine whether the average size of nonprint displays (photographs and graphs) varies depending on the type of newspaper. Later in the tutorial, you take the place of a data analyst investigating which of the combination of two factors — advertising medium (news or sports magazine) and year — provides the highest or lowest ratio of full-page ads to total number of pages in the magazine.

In situations such as these, the ANOVA test requires three basic assumptions about the measurements in the study: (1) The observations must be randomly selected. (2) The populations from which the observations are taken must all be normally distributed. (3) The variables in each group must come from populations with equal variances.

Objectives

In this tutorial, you learn how to:

- compare the means of several populations when all the observations are in one column and all the subscripts are in another

- generate residual and fitted values

- perform a Tukey multiple comparison test to determine which specific means are different from one another

- compare the means of several populations when the samples from each population are placed in different columns

- assess the effects of two factors on a response

CASE STUDY: JOURNALISM — PAGE LAYOUT

You are a member of a journalism class taught by Professor Sarah Camden. The current topic of the course is the different ways that various types of newspapers present nonprint displays (photographs and graphs). Professor Camden asks each student to collect some data to verify the information covered in her lecture. You decide to examine the average number of nonprint displays on the "easily seen" pages of three different types of newspapers. The easily seen pages are the top half of a full-sized paper's sections, and the front and back page of a tabloid. (The section sizes are all the same.) You plan to examine three papers: (1) a regional newspaper, (2) a local tabloid, and (3) a national newspaper.

You randomly select a date, and then measure the size in square inches of nonprint displays in each section of each paper. In a Minitab worksheet, you record the average sizes in C1 AVESIZE and the paper in C2 PAPER. You save the worksheet in the file NONPRT.MTW.

To start Minitab and start an outfile:

- Start Minitab and maximize the Minitab window and the Data window

- Start an outfile named **T9**

- Open **NONPRT.MTW**

▼

Comparing the Means of Several Populations

▲

When performing an ANOVA test, there are two relevant hypotheses for the journalism experiment:

H_0: The average sizes of the nonprint displays from the three newspapers are equal.

H_1: The average sizes of the nonprint displays from the three newspapers are not equal.

To test the hypotheses using Minitab and the data you collected:

- Choose **Stat > ANOVA > Oneway**

- Double-click **C1 AVESIZE** to enter it in the **Response** text box

- Double-click **C2 PAPER** to enter it in the **Factor** text box

The completed dialog box should look like Figure 9-1.

FIGURE 9-1

The completed Oneway Analysis of Variance dialog box

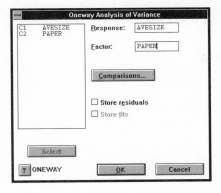

■ Click **OK**

The Session window resembles Figure 9-2.

FIGURE 9-2

Results of one-way ANOVA of mean average sizes

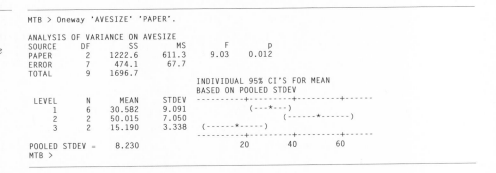

```
MTB > Oneway 'AVESIZE' 'PAPER'.

ANALYSIS OF VARIANCE ON AVESIZE
SOURCE     DF        SS        MS        F         p
PAPER       2    1222.6     611.3     9.03     0.012
ERROR       7     474.1      67.7
TOTAL       9    1696.7
                                    INDIVIDUAL 95% CI'S FOR MEAN
                                    BASED ON POOLED STDEV
 LEVEL      N      MEAN     STDEV  ----------+---------+---------+------
     1      6    30.582     9.091          (---*---)
     2      2    50.015     7.050                    (------*------)
     3      2    15.190     3.338  (------*-----)
                                    ----------+---------+---------+------
POOLED STDEV =    8.230             20        40        60
MTB >
```

The Session window display includes four components:

● An ANOVA table including the F test result, 9.03, and corresponding p-value, 0.012; you would reject the null hypothesis at the 0.05 level (but fail to reject it at the 0.01 level)

● A descriptive summary of the papers (treatment) including the sample size, the sample mean, and the sample standard deviation

● A diagram of the individual 95% confidence interval for the mean average size for each of the papers (treatments), based on the pooled standard deviation; the asterisk represents the sample mean and the parentheses indicate the 95% confidence limits

● The pooled standard deviation, in this case, 8.230

At this point in your analysis you notice some differences among the average size means for the three papers. The national newspaper (3) appears to have smaller-sized nonprint displays than tabloid (2), based on the way the confidence intervals don't overlap. You want to follow up this observation.

▼ Generating Fitted and Residual Values ▲

Before you proceed, check whether the assumptions of ANOVA are valid. If you click the Store residuals and Store fits check boxes in the Oneway Analysis of Variance dialog box, Minitab stores the fitted values and the residual values in the next available columns. Using the residuals and the fitted values, you can examine whether the results satisfy the ANOVA assumptions.

- Choose **Edit > Edit Last Command Dialog**
- Click the **Store residuals** and **Store fits** options
- Click **OK**
- Return to the Data window

The Data window displays columns containing the residuals and the fitted values. Compare the fitted values in C4 FITS1 to the sample means shown in Figure 9-2. Note that the fitted values (30.5817, 50.0150, and 15.1900) are the sample means of each paper. Minitab obtains the residuals, stored in C3 RESI1, by subtracting the corresponding fitted value (paper mean) from each average size. Next, use the residuals Minitab just computed to check the normality of the pooled samples.

▼ Obtaining NScores and a Check for Normality ▲

When performing an ANOVA test, you assume that all the observations come from normally distributed populations. To determine if it is reasonable to assume the average sizes of the displays are normally distributed, obtain the normal probability plot (NPP) for the combined (pooled) samples as introduced in Tutorial 6.

First, compute the normal score for each residual:

- Choose **Calc > Functions**
- Click the **Input column** text box
- Double-click **C3 RESI1** to enter it in the **Input column** text box
- Type **NSCORES** in the **Result in** text box
- Click **Normal scores** (in the lower right corner of the dialog box)

The completed Functions dialog box should resemble the one shown in Figure 9-3.

FIGURE 9-3

The completed Functions dialog box

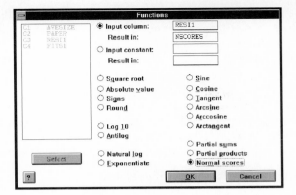

- Click **OK**

    Minitab computes the normal scores and stores them in C5 NSCORES.
    Use a scatter plot to plot these normal scores against the residuals. If the plot is linear, then the normality assumption is reasonable.

- Choose **Graph > Character Graphs > Scatter Plot**

- Double-click **C5 NSCORES** to enter it in the **Y variable** text box

- Double-click **C3 RESI1** to enter it the **X variable** text box

- Click **OK**

    The scatter plot appears in the Session window (Figure 9-4).

FIGURE 9-4

Scatter plot of normal scores versus residuals

```
MTB > Name c5 = 'NSCORES'
MTB > NScores 'RESI1' 'NSCORES'.
MTB > GStd.
MTB > Plot 'NSCORES' 'RESI1';
SUBC>   Symbol 'x'.

 NSCORES -                                              x
         -
         -
    1.0+                                          x
         -
         -                                     x
         -                                  x
         -                            x
    0.0+
         -                       x
         -                   x
         -              x
         -
   -1.0+      x
         -
         -    x
         +---------+---------+---------+---------+---------+------RESI1
        -12.0     -8.0      -4.0       0.0       4.0       8.0

MTB > GPro.
MTB >
```

Since the plot is approximately a straight line, it is reasonable to assume that the populations are approximately normally distributed. This result is not unexpected since you are working with averages. However, you should be careful about such conclusions because you are dealing with small sample sizes.

▼

Checking for Constant Variance

▲

To check for constant variance, use the graphical method of plotting the residuals versus the paper type. (Alternatively, you could use the fitted values instead of the paper type.) If the residuals have roughly the same range or vertical spread in each shift, then they satisfy the constant variance assumption.

- Choose **Edit > Edit Last Command Dialog**
- Double-click **C3 RESI1** to enter it in the **Y variable** text box
- Double-click **C2 PAPER** to enter it in the **X variable** text box
- Click **OK**

The resulting scatter plot appears in the Session window (Figure 9-5).

FIGURE 9-5

Scatter plot of residuals versus paper type

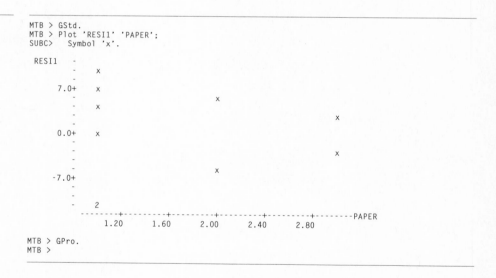

```
MTB > GStd.
MTB > Plot 'RESI1' 'PAPER';
SUBC>   Symbol 'x'.

 RESI1  -
        -        x
        -
   7.0+        x
        -                                      x
        -        x
        -                                              x
        -
   0.0+        x
        -
        -                                              x
        -
   -7.0+                                  x
        -
        -      2
        --------+---------+---------+---------+---------+--------PAPER
              1.20      1.60      2.00      2.40      2.80

MTB > GPro.
MTB >
```

For the three shifts, the residuals have slightly different ranges, but given the limited amount of data that you have, the constant variance assumption does not appear to be violated.

Performing a Tukey Multiple Comparison Test

Recall that you rejected the null hypothesis of equality of means at the 0.05 level. You can use Minitab's multiple comparison capabilities to determine which means differ from one another. Minitab provides four different multiple comparison procedures: Tukey, Fisher, Dunnett, and Hsu. You use the Tukey method in this tutorial. (Your professor can provide you with more information about the other procedures.)

For the Tukey multiple comparison test, you form three null hypotheses:

$H_0: \mu_1 = \mu_2$
$H_1: \mu_1 \neq \mu_2$

$H_0: \mu_1 = \mu_3$
$H_1: \mu_1 \neq \mu_3$

$H_0: \mu_2 = \mu_3$
$H_1: \mu_2 \neq \mu_3$

The Tukey test forms confidence intervals for the differences between the regional paper and the tabloid (1 and 2), the regional paper and the national paper (1 and 3), and the tabloid and the national paper (2 and 3). To perform the Tukey multiple comparison:

- Choose **Stat > ANOVA > Oneway**

- Verify that **C1 AVESIZE** appears in the **Response** text box and **C2 PAPER** displays in the **Factor** text box

- Click the **Store fits** and **Store residuals** options to deselect them

- Click **Comparisons**

- Click **Tukey's, family error rate**

- Click **OK** twice

Figure 9-6 shows the matrix of confidence intervals.

FIGURE 9-6

Results of Tukey multiple comparison

```
Tukey's pairwise comparisons

    Family error rate = 0.0500
Individual error rate = 0.0214

Critical value = 4.17

Intervals for (column level mean) - (row level mean)

                 1          2

    2       -39.25
              0.38

    3        -4.42      10.56
             35.21      59.09


MTB >
```

According to Tukey's procedure, you should reject the null hypothesis that the two means are equal whenever the confidence interval for the difference in the means does not contain 0.

A summary of the Tukey test follows:

Difference between	Confidence Interval 95% Family Confidence	Decision
Paper 1 and Paper 2	– 39.25 to 0.38	Fail to reject H_0: $\mu_1 = \mu_2$
Paper 1 and Paper 3	– 4.42 to 35.21	Fail to reject H_0: $\mu_1 = \mu_3$
Paper 2 and Paper 3	10.56 to 59.09	Reject H_0: $\mu_2 = \mu_3$

From the results of the Tukey test (with a default error rate of 5%), you determine that there is significant evidence of a difference between the mean average size of the nonprint displays between the tabloid and the national newspaper. You conclude your journalism assignment with this result.

■ Save your worksheet with the name **9NONPRT** on your Student disk

Comparing the Means of Several Populations with Responses in Separate Columns

In your journalism class, you observe that some students entered their data in separate columns and used a different Minitab command, Stat > ANOVA, Oneway [Unstacked]. You decide to restructure your data by placing the average sizes for the regional newspaper (1) in C6, the average sizes for the tabloid (2) in C7, and the average sizes for the national newspaper (3) in C8.

To unstack your data:

■ Choose **Manip > Unstack**

■ Double-click **C1 AVESIZE** to enter it in the **Unstack** text box

■ Click the **Using subscripts in** text box

■ Double-click **C2 PAPER** to enter it in the **Using subscripts in** text box

■ Type **AVESIZE1** in the first **Store results in blocks** text box and press ⁅Tab⁆

■ Type **AVESIZE2** in the second **Store results in blocks** text box and press ⁅Tab⁆

■ Type **AVESIZE3** in the third **Store results in blocks** text box and press ⁅←Enter⁆

■ Look at the Data window to see the unstacked data

Now repeat the ANOVA test. Use the Oneway (Unstacked) command that is appropriate when the sample data are in different columns. The statistical results are the same, but appear with slightly different labels.

■ Choose **Stat > ANOVA > Oneway [Unstacked]**

■ Select **C6 AVESIZE1**, **C7 AVESIZE2**, and **C8 AVESIZE3** to enter them in the **Responses (in separate columns)** text box

The completed dialog box should look like Figure 9-7.

FIGURE 9-7

The completed Oneway Analysis of Variance dialog box

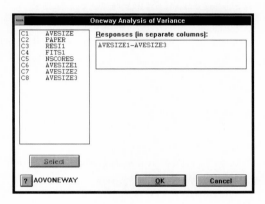

■ Click **OK**

The results, shown in Figure 9-8, appear in the Session window.

FIGURE 9-8

Results of one-way (unstacked) ANOVA of average sizes

```
MTB > Name c6 = 'AVESIZE1' c7 = 'AVESIZE2' c8 = 'AVESIZE3'
MTB > Unstack (C1) ('AVESIZE1') ('AVESIZE2') ('AVESIZE3');
SUBC>   Subscripts 'PAPER'.
MTB > AOVOneway 'AVESIZE1'-'AVESIZE3'.

ANALYSIS OF VARIANCE
SOURCE     DF       SS       MS       F       p
FACTOR      2   1222.6    611.3    9.03   0.012
ERROR       7    474.1     67.7
TOTAL       9   1696.7
                                  INDIVIDUAL 95% CI'S FOR MEAN
                                  BASED ON POOLED STDEV
 LEVEL      N     MEAN    STDEV  ----------+---------+---------+------
AVESIZE1    6   30.582    9.091             (---*---)
AVESIZE2    2   50.015    7.050                       (------*------)
AVESIZE3    2   15.190    3.338   (------*-----)
                                  ----------+---------+---------+------
POOLED STDEV =    8.230             20        40        60
MTB >
```

Minitab produces the same display for this test as it did for the one-way test in which all data were stacked in one column. There are only two differences in the labels: the analysis of variance table no longer identifies the response variable and the levels now have names. However, there are some disadvantages to storing your data in separate columns. The Minitab dialog box associated with this data structure doesn't let you store fitted values and residuals, nor make pairwise comparisons. In order to accomplish these tasks for one-way ANOVA data stored in separate columns, you must stack your data and create a subscript column.

There is no need to retain the unstacked variables. Save your work and clear the worksheet before you start the next case study.

- Save your worksheet with the name **9NONPRT** on your Student disk

- Choose **File > Other Files > Stop Recording Session**

- Choose **File > Restart Minitab** and maximize the Minitab window and the Data window

▼

Assessing the Effects of Two Factors on a Response

▲

You just analyzed the effect of a single factor with three levels (the three papers in which the nonprint displays appeared). However, many responses are affected by more than one factor. Statisticians must design experiments to take this fact into account.

CASE STUDY: MARKETING — AD CAMPAIGN

The marketing department for a company just hired you as data analyst. As part of a new campaign, manager Elaine Lasser plans to place a full-page ad in one of two media: a news magazine or a sports magazine. She wants you to determine which magazine has the lowest ratio of full-page ads to the number of pages in the magazine. She also wants you to determine whether there has been a change in this ratio in recent years.

▼

Performing a Two-Factor Analysis of Variance

▲

For your experiment, you decide to examine the ad ratio in 1989, 1991, and 1993. You randomly select issues from each magazine for each of these three years. You determine the number of full-page ads and the number of pages in each of the issues. Then you calculate the ad ratio by dividing the number of full-page ads by the number of pages in each of the issues. You record the results in a table (Figure 9-9).

FIGURE 9-9

Ad ratios for the two
magazine types

Year	News Magazine	Sports Magazine
1989	0.79	0.60
	0.80	0.46
	0.54	0.38
	0.72	0.42
1991	0.49	0.39
	0.85	0.56
	0.50	0.57
	0.67	0.46
1993	0.36	0.37
	0.65	0.64
	0.47	0.52
	0.68	0.41

Your coworker, Manuel Gonzales, has entered the ad ratio data in a Minitab worksheet. The data are in column C1 ADRATIO in the RATIO.MTW file. You can use an ANOVA test to see if year and/or magazine affect the ad ratio at a significance level of 0.05.

- Start the T9 outfile again; Minitab appends the subsequent session record to your previous outfile

- Open **RATIO.MTW**

- Go to the Data window if necessary

Notice how Manuel has stored the data (Figure 9-10).

FIGURE 9-10

*The RATIO.MTW
worksheet*

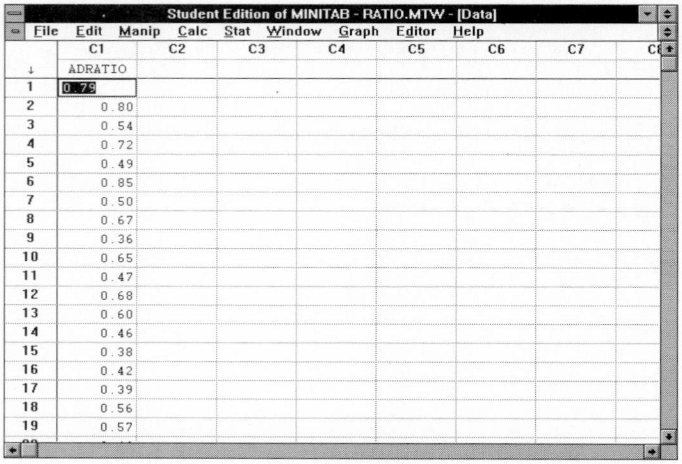

The first 12 values in C1 ADRATIO correspond to the news magazine; the last 12 relate to the sports magazine. Likewise, the first through fourth values and the thirteenth through sixteenth values correspond to 1989. The other values in C1 ADRATIO similarly correspond to the other years.

To perform the two-factor ANOVA, you need to add the two columns that identify the year and the magazine for each row of C1 ADRATIO. These two columns correspond to the *factors*. You use them to determine the effect of year and magazine on ad ratio.

Designate 1989, 1991, and 1993 as 1, 2, and 3, respectively. To identify the year category for each row in C1, you could enter the number sequence 1,1,1,1,2,2,2,2,3,3,3,3,1,1,1,1,2,2,2,2,3,3,3,3 in column C2 of the worksheet. For small data sets like this one, this might be the easiest method; however, for practice, use the Set Patterned Data command to enter this sequence of numbers:

- Choose **Calc > Set Patterned Data**

- Type **YEAR** in the **Store result in column** text box and press ⒯ab twice

Determine the data pattern you need to specify to achieve the desired result. Note that the sequence consists of the values 1, 2, and 3; the values start at 1, end at 3, and increment by 1. Each value repeats four times and the whole list repeats twice. To have Minitab enter this sequence:

- Type **1** in the **Start at** text box and press ⒯ab

- Type **3** in the **End at** text box and press ⒯ab twice

- Type **4** in the **Repeat each value** text box and press ⒯ab

- Type **2** in the **Repeat the whole list** text box and press ⏎Enter

Now store the values for the magazine. Since there are two magazines, identify them as 1 for the news magazine and 2 for the sports magazine. The news magazine values are the first 12 values in C1 ADRATIO. The next 12 values are for the sports magazines. Hence you need to enter this pattern of numbers in C3 MAGAZINE: 1,1,1,1,1,1,1,1,1,1,1,1,2,2,2,2,2,2,2,2,2,2,2,2. Use the Set Patterned Data command:

- Choose **Edit > Edit Last Command Dialog**

- Type **MAGAZINE** in the **Store result in column** text box and press Tab three times

Analyzing the data pattern for the magazines, you see that it is made up of the sequence 1,2; it starts at 1, ends at 2, and uses an increment of 1. Each value repeats 12 times and the whole list repeats once.

- Type **2** in the **End at** text box and press Tab twice

- Type **12** in the **Repeat each value** text box and press Tab

- Type **1** in the **Repeat the whole list** text box and press ←Enter

The Data window should look like Figure 9-11.

FIGURE 9-11

The Data window

	C1	C2	C3	C4	C5	C6	C7	C8
↓	ADRATIO	YEAR	MAGAZINE					
1	0.79	1	1					
2	0.80	1	1					
3	0.54	1	1					
4	0.72	1	1					
5	0.49	2	1					
6	0.85	2	1					
7	0.50	2	1					
8	0.67	2	1					
9	0.36	3	1					
10	0.65	3	1					
11	0.47	3	1					
12	0.68	3	1					
13	0.60	1	2					
14	0.46	1	2					
15	0.38	1	2					
16	0.42	1	2					
17	0.39	2	2					
18	0.56	2	2					
19	0.57	2	2					

Student Edition of MINITAB - RATIO.MTW - [Data]
File Edit Manip Calc Stat Window Graph Editor Help

If columns 2 and 3 do not look exactly like those shown in Figure 9-11, erase them and start over.

Note: It is very important that each of your columns have exactly the same number of entries. The ANOVA command requires that the response and factor columns contain an identical number of rows. You must also be sure to correctly identify the factor levels for each data point. If you fail to do so, your analysis will be inaccurate.

- Save your worksheet with the name **9RATIO** on your Student disk

Now you want to test three sets of hypotheses:

H_0: There is no interaction between year and magazine.
H_1: There is an interaction between year and magazine.

H_0: There is no difference in the average ad ratio for different years.
H_1: There is a difference in the average ad ratio for different years.

H_0: There is no difference in the average ad ratio when using different magazines.
H_1: There is a difference in the average ad ratio when using different magazines.

Two Minitab commands perform a multiway ANOVA: Twoway and Balanced ANOVA. Use the Twoway command when you have exactly two factors (as in the present example) and the Balanced ANOVA command when you have two or more factors. The Twoway command does not print the F-statistics and the p-values, but it does produce graphical displays of individual confidence intervals of each factor.

Note: Both the Twoway and Balanced ANOVA commands require that all combinations of factor levels have an equal number of observations. That is, the data must be balanced.

In your example, each combination of year and type of magazine has four values, so the data are balanced. You decide to use the Balanced ANOVA command to investigate the effects of year and magazine agency.

The Balanced ANOVA command accommodates many model types in which you can use crossed factors. (See your instructor for more information on the meaning and use of such factors.) In this case, you analyze the year factor, the magazine factor, and the interaction between the two. Many texts designate this model as follows:

$$y_{ijk} = \mu + a_i + b_j + ab_{ij} + \varepsilon_{k(ij)}.$$

Substituting the variable names for the factors a_i and b_j, the model is:

$$y_{ijk} = \mu + YEAR_i + MAGAZINE_j + YEAR * MAGAZINE_{ij} + \varepsilon_{k(ij)}.$$

Use Minitab to perform the analysis:

- Choose **Stat > ANOVA > Balanced ANOVA**

- Double-click **C1 ADRATIO** to enter it in the **Responses** text box and press Tab

- Type **YEAR   MAGAZINE   YEAR*MAGAZINE** in the **Model** text box (do not forget the *)

The completed dialog box should resemble Figure 9-12. Note the similarity between the model you enter in the Model text box and the second model described previously.

FIGURE 9-12

*The completed Balanced
Analysis of Variance
dialog box*

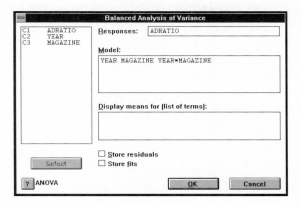

■ Click **OK**

The Session window contains the results shown in Figure 9-13.

FIGURE 9-13

*Results of ad ratios
ANOVA*

```
MTB > ANOVA 'ADRATIO' = YEAR MAGAZINE YEAR*MAGAZINE.

Factor     Type Levels Values
YEAR       fixed    3   1    2    3
MAGAZINE   fixed    2   1    2


Analysis of Variance for ADRATIO

Source          DF        SS        MS       F      P
YEAR             2   0.02386   0.01193    0.73  0.494
MAGAZINE         1   0.12615   0.12615    7.76  0.012
YEAR*MAGAZINE    2   0.03753   0.01876    1.15  0.338
Error           18   0.29265   0.01626
Total           23   0.48018


MTB >
```

The first column in the first table lists the factors, identifying them as fixed and not random. The next column tells you that the year variable has three levels (corresponding to 1989, 1991, and 1993) and the magazine variable has two (news magazine and sports magazine). The remaining columns simply list the values for each factor (1, 2, and 3 for year; 1 and 2 for magazine).

Note: The difference between fixed and random factors is a complex topic. See your instructor for more information.

The standard ANOVA table follows. It lists the sources of variation (year, magazine, interaction, and error), the F-ratios for each test, and the corresponding p-values.

The results of the tests are described in the following table.

Test	Effect	F-ratio	p-value	Decision
1	YEAR* MAGAZINE	1.15	0.338	Do not reject H_0; do not conclude that there is significant interaction between year and magazine
2	YEAR	0.73	0.494	Do not reject H_0; the mean ad ratios are probably the same for the three years
3	MAGAZINE	7.76	.012	Reject H_0; the mean ad ratios are not the same for the two magazines

Note that the order of the results here is different from Minitab's display. The test for the interaction effect is listed first in this text because the main effect tests are usually performed only if you do not reject the null hypothesis of the interaction test.

The results indicate a nonsignificant interaction between year and magazine (p-value = 0.338). You conclude that the mean ad ratios are probably the same for the three years (p-value = 0.494). The two magazines have different ad ratios. In addition, you conclude that the mean ad ratios for the two magazines are not the same at a significance level of 0.05.

Now that you have not rejected the null hypothesis that the mean ad ratio remained the same for 1989, 1991, and 1993, and rejected the null hypothesis that the mean ad ratio was the same for the two magazines, you decide to include the mean ad ratios for each of the three years, each of the two magazines, and each of the six combinations in the study as part of a report you are preparing. To obtain these means:

■ Choose **Edit > Edit Last Command Dialog**

■ Click the **Display means for (list of terms)** text box

■ Type **YEAR MAGAZINE YEAR*MAGAZINE** in the **Display means for (list of terms)** text box

The completed Balanced Analysis of Variance dialog box should look like Figure 9-14.

FIGURE 9-14

*The completed Balanced
Analysis of Variance
dialog box*

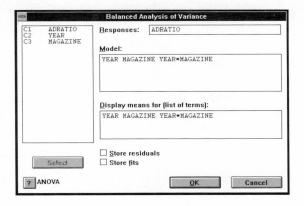

■ Click **OK**

The results appear in the Session window as shown in Figure 9-15.

FIGURE 9-15

*Average ad ratios for the
different years, magazines,
and combination of years
and magazines*

```
         MEANS

       YEAR   N    ADRATIO
         1    8    0.58875
         2    8    0.56125
         3    8    0.51250

       MAGAZINE   N    ADRATIO
              1   12   0.62667
              2   12   0.48167

       YEAR MAGAZINE   N    ADRATIO
         1       1     4    0.71250
         1       2     4    0.46500
         2       1     4    0.62750
         2       2     4    0.49500
         3       1     4    0.54000
         3       2     4    0.48500

       MTB >
```

The sports magazine has the lower mean ad ratio (0.48167) regardless of
year. The news magazine had the sample's highest mean ad ratio in 1989, but
you observe that the mean ad ratio has become smaller in 1991 and 1993.
When you present your report, you plan to recommend advertising in the
sports magazine so that your ads have the greatest impact.

You can see that using Minitab's analysis of variance capability can help
you make decisions in any discipline. As a student in the journalism class, you
used an ANOVA test to affirm that different newspapers produced different
average sizes for nonprint displays. As a data analyst in a marketing department,
you performed ANOVA tests on two factors to determine the magazine in
which to advertise.

Now stop your outfile:

■ Choose **File > Other Files > Stop Recording Session**

If you plan to continue directly to the next tutorial:

■ Choose **File > Restart Minitab**

If you want to take a longer break:

■ Choose **File > Exit**

▼
Minitab Command Summary
▲

This section describes the Minitab menu commands introduced in or related to this tutorial. To find a complete explanation of all menus and commands, refer to the Reference section of this manual.

Minitab Menu Commands

Menu	Command	Description
Stat		
	ANOVA	
	Oneway	Performs a one-way analysis of variance when the response is stored in one column and the sample indicator or subscript is stored in another column
	Oneway [Unstacked]	Performs a one-way analysis of variance when the response is stored in separate columns
	Twoway	Performs a two-way analysis of variance when the response is stored in one column and the two factor level indicators or subscripts are stored in two other columns; the data must be balanced
	Balanced ANOVA	Performs a multiway analysis of variance when the response is stored in one column and the factor level indicators or subscripts are stored in other columns; the data must be balanced

Matching

Match the following terms to their definitions by placing the correct letter next to the term it describes.

_____ Model

_____ Set Patterned Data

_____ Response variable

_____ Balanced Analysis of Variance

_____ Balanced

_____ Comparisons

_____ Factor

_____ *

_____ Hsu

_____ F statistics and p-values

a. The Minitab option that performs multiple comparisons of the means in a one-way ANOVA using the Oneway command

b. The Minitab dialog box that lets you display means for a list of terms

c. The Minitab command you can use to create data that represent factors

d. The character used to denote interaction between effects

e. A term that denotes that there are equal numbers of observations for each factor combination

f. The term used to denote a representation of a relationship between the response variable and the factors

g. The term used in ANOVA to denote a variable that affects a continuous variable

h. The term used in ANOVA to denote the continuous variable whose mean is affected by the factor(s)

i. A multiple comparison procedure

j. Output not produced by the Twoway command

True/False

Mark the following statements with a *T* or an *F*.

_____ 1. Minitab's Twoway command allows unbalanced data, whereas the Balanced ANOVA command must have balanced data.

_____ 2. You can use any of the ANOVA commands to store residuals and fitted values.

_____ 3. Minitab can perform multiple comparisons only for stacked data.

_____ 4. For the Oneway command, the fits can be saved without saving the residuals.

_____ 5. The user specifies the columns in which the ANOVA commands store the residuals and/or fitted values.

_____ 6. Minitab can perform multiway ANOVA by using the Balanced ANOVA command.

_____ 7. 95% confidence intervals for each population mean are part of the default output for the ANOVA command.

_____ 8. Minitab uses the pooled standard deviation in analysis of variance.

_____ 9. Only two multiple comparison procedures are available with the Oneway command.

_____ 10. The NSCORES function is useful in determining if a population is normally distributed.

Practice Problems

1. Open YOGURT.MTW. Determine if the mean cost per ounce and mean calories per serving are different for different nutritional ratings. Since some of the ratings occur only once or twice, you may wish to combine some of them. What would be one logical way of doing this?

2. Open TECHN.MTW. Determine if the average salary is different for the four departments at Technitron. Use fits and residuals to check the assumptions of the ANOVA.

3. Open CRIMEU.MTW. Determine if the crime rates are different for different regions at a significance level of 0.10. If there are differences, provide a Tukey multiple comparison test to determine the pairwise differences.

4. Open AGE.MTW.

   a. Perform a two independent sample mean test for age at death assuming equal variances. What is the test's p-value?

   b. Perform a one-way ANOVA on the same data. What is this test's p-value?

   c. Since the tests are equivalent, your two p-values should be identical. If they are not identical, check your work in steps a and b.

5. Open VPVH.MTW.

   a. Create two new columns: C6 GENDER with men coded as 1, and women coded as 2; and C7 AGE with ages 18 through 34 coded as 1, and ages 55+ coded as 2.

   b. Obtain an ANOVA table from a two-way ANOVA on C1 MOVIES with C6 GENDER and C7 AGE as the factors.

   c. Test the following set of hypotheses:

   H_0: There is no interaction between gender and age group.
   H_1: There is an interaction between gender and age group.

   d. Based upon your answer to part b, should you test for any difference in average movie rating for gender or for age group? Briefly explain your answer.

e. Redo your two-way ANOVA but this time save all of the possible mean movie ratings. What are the mean movie ratings for each gender? What are the mean movie ratings for each age group? What are the mean movie ratings for each gender/age group combination?

f. Construct a plot from the combination mean movie ratings with mean movie rating on the vertical axis and gender on the horizontal axis. Connect the values from the 18-to-34 age group with a line. Do the same with the values from the 55+ age group. If your lines are parallel, you have an indication of no interaction. Are your lines parallel? How does your answer relate to part c?

TUTORIAL 10

Fundamentals of Linear Regression

In this tutorial, you return to the role of the managerial consultant who is analyzing the salary structure of Technitron, Inc. Your preliminary report, which contained graphic displays of the salaries in the Sales Department, was well received. As a result, Technitron now asks you to examine the relationship between salary and the other variables for the entire company. You begin with a simple linear regression problem that relates salary to one other variable — years at the company. Then you use Minitab to perform a multiple regression analysis on the salary structure at Technitron. This problem is much more complex because it relates salary to several predictor variables. Finally, for both simple and multiple linear regression, you obtain three estimates for salary based on one or more predictor variables: a point estimate, a 95% confidence interval, and a 95% prediction interval.

Objectives

In this tutorial, you learn how to:

- use simple linear regression to describe a linear relationship between two variables

- obtain a 95% confidence interval for the expected value of the response variable

- obtain a 95% prediction interval for an individual value of the response variable

- use multiple linear regression to investigate the form of the linear relationship between one variable and several other variables

- transform variables to improve a straightforward simple or multiple linear regression

CASE STUDY: MANAGEMENT — SALARY STRUCTURE (CONTINUED)

After you completed your assignment in Tutorial 4, management provided you with information about the employees in the purchasing, advertising, and engineering departments, which you saved in the file TECHN.MTW. This file contains data on 46 employees: C1 SALARY, C2 YRS EM (years at Technitron), C3 PRIOR YR (prior years of experience), C4 EDUC (number of years of education), C5 ID (company identification number), C6 GENDER (coded 0 = male, 1 = female), C7 DEPT (coded 1 = sales, 2 = purchasing, 3 = advertising, and 4 = engineering), and C8 SUPER (number of employees supervised).

To start Minitab and start an outfile:

■ Start Minitab and maximize the Minitab window and the Data window

■ Start an outfile named **T10** on your Student disk

■ Open **TECHN.MTW**

▼

Finding a Straight Line Fit to Data: Simple Linear Regression

▲

You begin your investigation by analyzing the relationship between salary and the length of time an employee has worked at Technitron. Verify that the relationship between these variables is linear.

■ Choose **Graph > Character Graphs > Scatter Plot**

■ Double-click **C1 SALARY** to enter it in the **Y variable** text box

■ Double-click **C2 YRS EM** to enter it in the **X variable** text box

■ Click **OK**

The scatter plot should resemble Figure 10-1.

FIGURE 10-1

Scatter plot of SALARY versus YRS EM

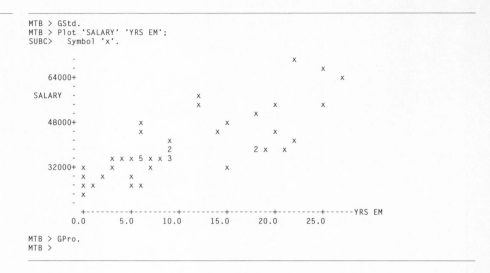

```
MTB > GStd.
MTB > Plot 'SALARY' 'YRS EM';
SUBC>    Symbol 'x'.
              -                                          x
              -                                              x
        64000+                                                   x
              -
   SALARY -                             x
              -                         x          x       x
              -                              x
        48000+        x              x
              -          x         x        x
              -          x      x        x      x
              -            x           2       x   x
              -      x x x 5 x x 3       2 x  x
        32000+ x     x     x              x
              - x   x     x
              - x x       x x
              - x
              -
              +---------+---------+---------+---------+---------+------YRS EM
             0.0       5.0      10.0      15.0      20.0      25.0

MTB > GPro.
MTB >
```

The plot suggests a positive linear trend. Measure the strength of the linear relationship by computing the correlation coefficient:

■ Choose **Stat > Basic Statistics > Correlation**

■ Double-click **C1 SALARY** and **C2 YRS EM** to enter them in the **Variables** text box

■ Click **OK**

The Session window reports a correlation coefficient of 0.765. Since this value is close to 1, it seems there is a strong linear relationship between salary and years employed at Technitron. You are ready to obtain the linear equation that relates salary to years employed:

■ Choose **Stat > Regression > Regression**

■ Double-click **C1 SALARY** to enter it in the **Response** text box

■ Double-click **C2 YRS EM** to enter it in the **Predictors** text box

The completed Regression dialog box should look like Figure 10-2.

FIGURE 10-2

The completed Regression dialog box

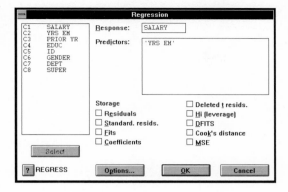

■ Click **OK**

The Session window display resembles Figure 10-3.

FIGURE 10-3

Results of salary regression analysis

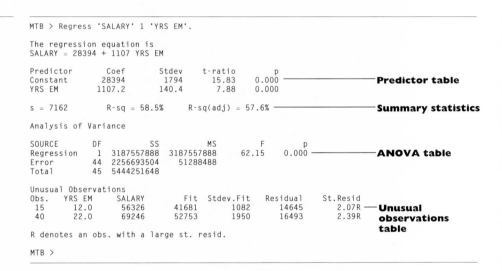

```
MTB > Regress 'SALARY' 1 'YRS EM'.

The regression equation is
SALARY = 28394 + 1107 YRS EM

Predictor        Coef      Stdev    t-ratio        p
Constant        28394       1794      15.83    0.000
YRS EM         1107.2      140.4       7.88    0.000

s = 7162         R-sq = 58.5%     R-sq(adj) = 57.6%

Analysis of Variance

SOURCE        DF          SS          MS         F        p
Regression     1   3187557888   3187557888     62.15    0.000
Error         44   2256693504     51288488
Total         45   5444251648

Unusual Observations
Obs.    YRS EM      SALARY        Fit   Stdev.Fit  Residual   St.Resid
 15      12.0       56326      41681        1082     14645      2.07R
 40      22.0       69246      52753        1950     16493      2.39R

R denotes an obs. with a large st. resid.

MTB >
```

Predictor table

Summary statistics

ANOVA table

Unusual observations table

The regression equation is SALARY = 28394 + 1107 YRS EM.

Using this equation, you would predict a starting salary of $28,394 for an individual who is new to Technitron (YRS EM = 0). The formula adds $1107 (slope) for each year of employment at Technitron; therefore the predicated salary of an employee with five years of experience is $33,929. Later in this tutorial, you use Minitab to obtain this estimate and two related interval estimates.

The predictor table contains the estimate for each of the regression coefficients, their standard deviations, as well as the t-ratios and p-values for testing the hypothesis that a coefficient is zero (the variable has no significant effect on the response variable). The p-value of 0.000 for YRS EM in the prediction table indicates that there is significant evidence of a nonzero population slope.

Minitab does not compute confidence intervals for regression coefficients. You can, however, use an estimated regression coefficient and its standard deviation to compute such an interval. For example, you could compute a 95% confidence interval for the population slope by using the point estimate of 1107.2 and the related standard deviation of 140.4 in the predictor table. You would choose Calc > Probability > T (as you did in Tutorial 6) to obtain the t critical value of 2.0154. The confidence interval is 1107.2 ± 2.0154 (140.4), or (1107.2 ± 282.96), or (824.24, 1390.16). (In order to use hypothesis tests and confidence intervals, certain assumptions must be satisfied. These are discussed in Tutorial 11.)

The display shown in Figure 10-3 also contains information that helps you assess the usefulness of the model, as described in the following paragraphs.

The summary statistics line includes s, the estimated standard deviation around the regression line. This statistic is often called the *standard error of the estimate*; in this case, its value is $7162. *R-sq*, the *coefficient of determination*, indicates that 58.5% of the salary variation can be explained by the linear relationship to the number of years employed at the company. The higher the R^2 value, the better the data fit the estimated regression equation. *R-sq(adj)* is the R^2 value adjusted for degrees of freedom.

Minitab computes an F-ratio to test the hypothesis that all of the predictor coefficients are zero and prints the result in an ANOVA table. In this model, the F-value of 62.15 corresponds to a p-value of 0.000. This finding provides statistically significant evidence that the YRS EM coefficient is not zero. The predictor variable, YRS EM, affects the response variable, SALARY.

In the next table, Minitab lists two types of unusual observations. First, Minitab lists outliers that have a standardized residual of more than 2 or less than –2. Then Minitab lists any X values that are substantially different from the other predictor values in the data. For example, Minitab reports that the employees in row 15 (12 years at Technitron with a salary of $56326) and row 40 (22 years at Technitron with a salary of $69246) as unusual observations. You look into such unusual observations in Tutorial 11.

Minitab can compute (and store for later use) the fitted values and residuals for each observation. You can also use the fitted values and residuals to check assumptions and investigate possible salary inequities. You also explore these matters in Tutorial 11.

To compute and then save the fitted and residual values in the worksheet:

■ Choose **Edit > Edit Last Command Dialog**

Minitab redisplays the Regression dialog box. (If you used the T command to obtain the critical value, that dialog box appears instead, in which case you should choose Stat > Regression > Regression.)

- Click the **Residuals**, **Standard. resids.**, and **Fits** check boxes in the Storage section

- Click **OK**

- Return to the Data window

- Scroll right to display columns C9, C10, and C11, as shown in Figure 10-4

FIGURE 10-4

Data window showing storage statistics

	Student Edition of MINITAB - TECHN.MTW - [Data]						
File	Edit	Manip	Calc	Stat	Window	Graph	Editor	Help

	C5	C6	C7	C8	C9	C10	C11	C1
→	ID	GENDER	DEPT	SUPER	SRES1	FITS1	RESI1	
1	412	0	1	5	-1.33399	48324.1	-9339.1	
2	458	1	1	4	-1.71313	45002.4	-12082.4	
3	604	0	1	0	-0.62215	33930.3	-4382.3	
4	598	1	1	1	-1.45786	35037.5	-10288.5	
5	351	0	1	7	-1.57655	52753.0	-10864.0	
6	674	0	1	6	-0.02680	31715.8	-187.8	
7	356	0	1	9	-1.85685	51645.7	-12854.7	
8	415	1	1	5	-1.21358	48324.1	-8496.1	
9	693	1	1	4	0.08522	28394.2	590.8	
10	694	0	1	0	0.63287	28394.2	4387.8	
11	625	0	2	2	1.22379	35037.5	8636.5	
12	354	1	2	3	0.53526	31715.8	3751.2	
13	268	1	2	5	-0.10486	30608.6	-732.6	
14	984	1	2	2	-0.27230	38359.1	-1928.1	
15	651	0	2	6	2.06870	41680.8	14645.2	
16	359	0	2	2	0.21730	35037.5	1533.5	
17	647	1	2	5	-0.40830	38359.1	-2891.1	
18	845	1	2	2	-0.26195	28394.2	-1816.2	
19	972	0	3	4	0.35923	45002.4	2533.6	

Minitab computes the residuals, standardized residuals, and fitted values for each observation in the data set. In addition, Minitab automatically names the columns.

The new columns contain the following information:

Column Name	Description
C9 SRES1	Records each residual divided by its standard deviation; extreme standardized residuals (with an absolute value greater than 2) determine the unusual observations, which are marked with an R in the Session window display.
C10 FITS1	Lists each employee's salary, as predicted by the regression equation; for example, compare the result on the third line with the earlier result for an employee with five years of experience
C11 RESI1	Records the difference between each employee's actual salary and the predicted (fitted) salary

Before continuing, save your work:

- Save your worksheet with the name **10TECHN** on your Student disk

   To graph the fitted values of the regression equation:

- Choose **Graph > Character Graphs > Scatter Plot**

- Double-click **C10 FITS1** to enter it in the **Y variable** text box

- Double-click **C2 YRS EM** to enter it in the **X variable** text box

- Click **OK**

   The graph of the fits versus the predictor appears (Figure 10-5).

FIGURE 10-5

Scatter plot of fits versus predictor

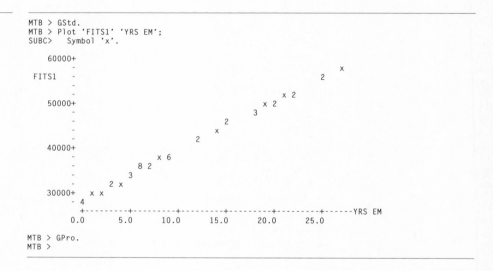

```
MTB > GStd.
MTB > Plot 'FITS1' 'YRS EM';
SUBC>    Symbol 'x'.
    60000+
         -                                                         x
  FITS1  -                                               2
         -
         -                                          x 2
    50000+                                       x 2
         -                                  3
         -                             2
         -                           x
         -                      2
    40000+
         -                 x 6
         -            8 2
         -          3
         -       2 x
    30000+   x x
         - 4
         +---------+---------+---------+---------+---------+------YRS EM
         0.0       5.0      10.0      15.0      20.0      25.0
MTB > GPro.
MTB >
```

Note that a slight staircase effect occurs in the Character graph. Still you observe the appearance of a straight line.

   To see how well the line fits the data, construct a scatter plot that displays SALARY versus YRS EM. Annotate the scatter plot with a line showing the fitted values versus the years employed.

   To plot the data points:

- Choose **Graph > Plot**

- Double-click **C1 SALARY** to enter it in the **Y variable** text box

- Double-click **C2 YRS EM** to enter it in the **X variable** text box

   To add the plot of the fitted points on the regression line:

- Click the **Annotation** drop-down arrow

- Click **Line** in the drop-down list box

- Click the **Points** drop-down arrow

- Click **Use Variables** in the drop-down list box

- Click the **Use columns** text box

- Double-click **C2 YRS EM** to enter it as the first variable

- Double-click **C10 FITS1** to enter it as the second variable

- Click **OK** three times to create the plot

The annotated scatter plot appears (Figure 10-6).

FIGURE 10-6

Scatter plot of SALARY versus YEARS EM, annotated with a fitted regression line

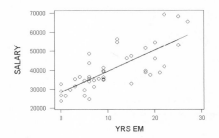

You conclude that there is quite a bit of variation around the regression line. Salary at Technitron is not based solely on time with the company; there are other factors at work. You plan to look into the relationship between salary and additional predictor variables. Before you do, though, use Minitab to obtain point and interval estimates for SALARY for a given value of YRS EM.

Computing Response Variable Estimates

You can use Minitab to compute the value of the response (dependent) variable for a given value of a predictor (independent) variable. Minitab can also construct a 95% confidence interval for the expected value of the response variables and a 95% prediction interval for an individual value of the response variable for a given predictor value (Minitab does not directly compute interval estimates with confidence levels not equal to 95%).

Compute such salary estimates for a Technitron employee with five years of experience:

- Choose **Stat > Regression > Regression**

- Click the Control-menu box to open the Control menu, and then choose **Reset Defaults** to clear all the text boxes and options

- Double-click **C1 SALARY** to enter it in the **Response** text box

- Double-click **C2 YRS EM** to enter it in the **Predictors** text box

- Click the **Options** button

- Click the **Prediction intervals for new observations** text box

- Type **5,** the value of the predictor variable

    The completed Regression Options dialog box should look like Figure 10-7.

FIGURE 10-7

*The completed Regression
Options dialog box*

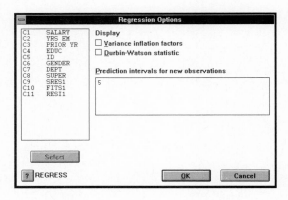

- Click **OK** twice

    When the analysis is complete, the Sessions window display should resemble Figure 10-8.

FIGURE 10-8

*Results of simple linear
regression analysis and
response variable estimates*

```
MTB > Regress 'SALARY' 1 'YRS EM';
SUBC>    Predict 5.

The regression equation is
SALARY = 28394 + 1107 YRS EM

Predictor        Coef       Stdev     t-ratio         p
Constant        28394        1794       15.83     0.000
YRS EM         1107.2       140.4        7.88     0.000

s = 7162        R-sq = 58.5%      R-sq(adj) = 57.6%

Analysis of Variance

SOURCE          DF          SS          MS          F         p
Regression       1  3187557888  3187557888      62.15     0.000
Error           44  2256693504    51288488
Total           45  5444251648

Unusual Observations
Obs.    YRS EM       SALARY         Fit  Stdev.Fit    Residual    St.Resid
 15      12.0        56326       41681       1082       14645        2.07R
 40      22.0        69246       52753       1950       16493        2.39R

R denotes an obs. with a large st. resid.

     Fit   Stdev.Fit        95% C.I.            95% P.I.
   33930        1294   (  31322,   36539) (  19260,   48601)


MTB >
```

The predicted salary of a Technitron employee with five years tenure is $33,930. You are 95% confident that the expected salary will be between $31,322 and $36,539 for all employees who have the same amount of experience. For an individual employee with five years of experience, you can predict with 95% confidence that his or her salary will be between $19,260 and $48,601.

You can display all the possible fitted values, 95% confidence interval values, and 95% prediction interval values on a scatter plot of data for a simple linear regression.

■ Choose **Stat > Regression > Fitted Line Plot**

■ Double-click **C1 SALARY** to enter it in the **Response (Y)** text box

■ Double-click **C2 YRS EM** to enter it in the **Predictor (X)** text box

The completed Fitted Line Plot dialog box should look like Figure 10-9.

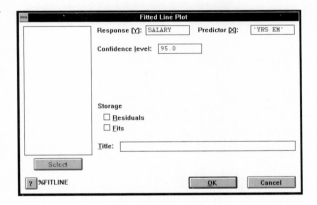

■ Press Enter

The resulting graph should resemble Figure 10-10.

FIGURE 10-10

Fitted line plot of salary versus years employed

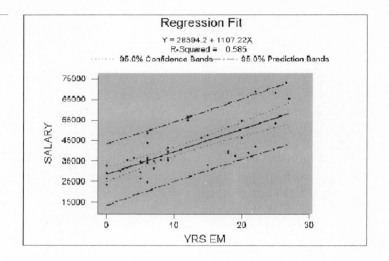

This plot prints the actual values and the fitted values. In addition, it shows the 95% confidence bands and 95% prediction bands for values between the minimum and maximum values of YRS EM. Note that one employee appears on the upper prediction interval band and another is above this band.

▼

Performing Multiple Linear Regression with Polynomial Regression Models

▲

You have just examined the simplest case, in which salary is expressed as a linear function of years employed. Perhaps this relationship can be better described by a curve. Use the Mathematical Expressions command to create a second degree variable, $(YRS EM)^2$. Using this new variable, you can form a quadratic (polynomial) equation for SALARY. With two predictor variables, this becomes a multiple regression model.

- Choose **Calc > Mathematical Expressions**

- Type **'YRS**★★**2'** in the **Variable (new or modified)** text box and press $\boxed{\text{Tab}}$ twice

- Type **C2**★★**2** in the **Expression** text box and press $\boxed{\leftarrow\text{Enter}}$

   Minitab records a new variable, the square of each term in C2, in C12 YRS★★2.
   Now try a regression model for salary, using C2 and C12:

- Choose **Stat > Regression > Regression**

- Click the Control-menu box to open the Control menu, and then choose **Reset Defaults** to clear all the text boxes and options

- Double-click **C1 SALARY** to enter it in the **Response** text box

- Double-click **C2 YRS EM** and **C12 YRS**2** to enter them in the **Predictors** text box

- Click **OK**

Figure 10-11 displays the results of the polynomial regression.

FIGURE 10-11

Results of polynomial regression

```
MTB > Name c12 = 'YRS**2'
MTB > Let 'YRS**2' = C2**2
MTB > Regress 'SALARY' 2 'YRS EM' 'YRS**2'.

The regression equation is
SALARY = 29323 + 863 YRS EM + 9.7 YRS**2

Predictor       Coef      Stdev    t-ratio          p
Constant       29323       2640      11.11      0.000
YRS EM         863.3      523.9       1.65      0.107
YRS**2          9.74      20.14       0.48      0.631

s = 7225       R-sq = 58.8%     R-sq(adj) = 56.9%

Analysis of Variance

SOURCE         DF         SS         MS          F          p
Regression      2 3199762944 1599881472      30.65      0.000
Error          43 2244488448   52197404
Total          45 5444251648

SOURCE         DF     SEQ SS
YRS EM          1 3187557888
YRS**2          1   12205007

Unusual Observations
Obs.   YRS EM     SALARY       Fit  Stdev.Fit   Residual   St.Resid
 15      12.0      56326     41086       1644      15240      2.17R
 40      22.0      69246     53031       2050      16215      2.34R
 41      27.0      65487     59734       3956       5753      0.95 X

R denotes an obs. with a large st. resid.
X denotes an obs. whose X value gives it large influence.

MTB >
```

The second-order equation, which appears at the top of the output, is

$$SALARY = 29323 + 863 \text{ YRS EM} + 9.7 \text{ YRS}**2$$

This model predicts a salary of $29323 + 863(5) + 9.7(25) = \$33880.5$ for an employee with five years of experience.

The predictor table reports a p-value of 0.107 for the YRS EM coefficient; it is not significant in this model. The quadratic term, YRS**2, has a p-value of 0.631; it is also not significant.

The standard error estimate of the quadratic regression equals $7225. This value is greater than the simple linear regression value of $7162. The regression explains 58.8% of the variation, which isn't much better than the simple linear regression model used earlier.

The ANOVA table reports an F-ratio of 30.65. The corresponding p-value of 0.000 indicates that at least one of the coefficients in the model is not zero. The results imply that SALARY depends on YRS EM or the quadratic term, YRS**2. Note that this result appears to contradict the results of the t-tests. In the next tutorial, you explore this contradiction further. Based on these results, you decide not to recommend the quadratic (polynomial) model to management.

Using Transformations

Minitab can include not only higher powers of a predictor variable, but other transformations of the response and predictor variables. Among the most common transformations of the response variables are square roots, logarithms, and negative reciprocals. You often use products of predictor variables in complex multiple regression models. In addition, more advanced transformations are sometimes appropriate. For example, if a variable is cyclic in nature, you may consider including the cosine of that variable.

▼

Performing Multiple Linear Regression with Additional Variables

▲

You suspect that many factors other than years employed influence salary levels at Technitron. To investigate this possibility, you can model salary as a function of the four available quantitative variables (years employed, prior years of experience, years of education, and number of employees supervised.) To fit a multiple regression model:

- Choose **Stat > Regression > Regression**

- Click the **Control menu box** and then click **Reset Defaults**

- Double-click **C1 SALARY** to enter it in the **Response** text box

- Double-click **C2 YRS EM**, **C3 PRIOR YR**, **C4 EDUC**, and **C8 SUPER** to enter them in the **Predictors** text box

- Click **OK**

The Session window shows the results (Figure 10-12).

```
MTB > Regress 'SALARY' 4 'YRS EM' 'PRIOR YR' 'EDUC' 'SUPER'.

The regression equation is
SALARY = 24496 + 655 YRS EM - 161 PRIOR YR + 1636 EDUC + 179 SUPER

Predictor      Coef      Stdev    t-ratio        p
Constant      24496       2049      11.95    0.000
YRS EM        655.3      139.6       4.69    0.000
PRIOR YR     -161.1      231.5      -0.70    0.490
EDUC         1636.4      406.1       4.03    0.000
SUPER        178.80      97.59       1.83    0.074

s = 5643       R-sq = 76.0%     R-sq(adj) = 73.7%

Analysis of Variance

SOURCE        DF          SS          MS        F        p
Regression     4  4138631168  1034657792    32.49    0.000
Error         41  1305620224    31844396
Total         45  5444251648

SOURCE        DF      SEQ SS
YRS EM         1  3187557888
PRIOR YR       1      160191
EDUC           1   844012864
SUPER          1   106900216

Unusual Observations
Obs.   YRS EM     SALARY       Fit  Stdev.Fit   Residual   St.Resid
  1      18.0      38985     50785       1745     -11800      -2.20R
  2      15.0      32920     49285       1700     -16365      -3.04R
 40      22.0      69246     62839       3535       6407       1.46 X
 41      27.0      65487     69693       3779      -4206      -1.00 X
 42       6.0      48695     45610       4249       3085       0.83 X

R denotes an obs. with a large st. resid.
X denotes an obs. whose X value gives it large influence.
MTB >
```

The multiple regression equation is

SALARY = 24496 + 655 YRS EM - 161 PRIOR YR + 1636 EDUC +179 SUPER

Minitab displays the t-ratio for each of the coefficients and the corresponding p-values. The table indicates that given the other variables in the model, there is significant evidence that the coefficients for years employed and education are each different from zero at any reasonable level of significance. In addition, there may be significant evidence that the coefficient for the number of employees supervised is different from zero. On the other hand, there is no significant evidence that the coefficient for prior years is different from zero.

With a standard error of estimate of $5643, this model explains 76.0% of the variation in salary at Technitron. The adjusted percentage of variation is only slightly less at 73.7%. The addition of other variables substantially improved your model over the linear and quadratic models considered earlier.

The ANOVA table (which tests the hypothesis that all predictor coefficients are zero) reports a p-value of 0.000; you can conclude that at least one of the coefficients is different from zero at any reasonable level of significance.

MINITAB AT WORK

ECOLOGY: Ecologists who study the reproductive success of fish that tend their young on river and lake bottoms need efficient ways to count the young that each adult produces. An ecologist in Ontario, Canada, developed just such a technique for one species of fish, the rock bass. He used Minitab to investigate the accuracy of his procedure.

The ecologist used an ordinary plastic kitchen meat baster to suction the newly hatched rock bass young from their nests. The male parent guarded the empty nest while the ecologist placed the young in a pan on the river bank, photographed each brood several times, and then quickly returned it to the parent who resumed caring for its brood with no apparent behavioral changes. The technique resulted in no detectable harm to either parent or progeny.

Back in the lab the ecologist gridded each photograph, counted the number of young in each grid square, and from those numbers determined a total count. He suspected that his counting method became less accurate the more young there were in a brood, so differences in the counts of various photographs for the same brood should have increased with increasing brood size.

To test this prediction, the ecologist used Minitab's regression capabilities to produce an equation relating the average count of young from photographs of the same brood to the variability of those counts: $\ln(\text{variance} + 1) = 0.092 + 0.129(\text{mean count})$. This outcome convinced the ecologist that his initial suspicions were true: with more young, his counts did tend to vary more from photo to photo. By calculating the confidence limits about the regression line, the ecologist could test his subsequent use of the technique. For any new test, if the count variance for a particular mean fell outside the regression confidence limits, the ecologist would quickly know to check for possible counting errors.

Note: The content and interpretation of the SEQ SS table following the ANOVA table is rather involved. See your instructor for details.

Minitab has noted several unusual observations in the data set. There are two outliers (in rows 1 and 2) and three influence points (in rows 40, 41, and 42). You investigate these values in Tutorial 11.

▼
Obtaining
Multiple Linear
Regression
Response
Variable
Estimates
▲

Based on this output, you decide to obtain a regression equation without C3 PRIOR YR. In addition, you want to generate response estimates for this multiple linear regression. You will find salary estimates for an employee with five years of experience, four years of post-secondary education, and supervisory responsibility for two employees.

- Choose **Edit > Edit Last Command Dialog**

- Highlight **'PRIOR YR'** in the **Predictor** text box and press Del

- Click the **Options** button

- Click the **Prediction intervals for new observations** text box

- Type **5 4 2**

- Click **OK** twice

    Now Minitab reports a model of SALARY = 23783 + 659 YRS EM + 1639 EDUC + 165 SUPER (Figure 10-13).

FIGURE 10-13

Results of multiple linear regression with three predictors and response variable estimates

```
MTB > Regress 'SALARY' 3 'YRS EM' 'EDUC' 'SUPER';
SUBC>    Predict 5 4 2.

The regression equation is
SALARY = 23783 + 659 YRS EM + 1639 EDUC + 165 SUPER

Predictor        Coef       Stdev     t-ratio          p
Constant        23783        1765       13.48      0.000
YRS EM          658.7       138.7        4.75      0.000
EDUC           1639.4       403.6        4.06      0.000
SUPER          164.82       94.91        1.74      0.090

s = 5608       R-sq = 75.7%     R-sq(adj) = 74.0%

Analysis of Variance

SOURCE        DF           SS           MS          F          p
Regression     3   4123200768   1374400256      43.70      0.000
Error         42   1321050752     31453590
Total         45   5444251648

SOURCE        DF       SEQ SS
YRS EM         1   3187557888
EDUC           1    840790272
SUPER          1     94852544

Unusual Observations
Obs.    YRS EM      SALARY         Fit   Stdev.Fit    Residual    St.Resid
  1       18.0       38985       51218        1621      -12233       -2.28R
  2       15.0       32920       49077        1663      -16157       -3.02R
 40       22.0       69246       62085        3343        7161        1.59 X
 41       27.0       65487       68492        3341       -3005       -0.67 X
 42        6.0       48695       47443        3313        1252        0.28 X

R denotes an obs. with a large st. resid.
X denotes an obs. whose X value gives it large influence.

   Fit   Stdev.Fit        95% C.I.              95% P.I.
 33964        1024   ( 31896,   36031)   ( 22456,   45472)


MTB >
```

You are pleased with this model. The descriptive measures and test results are similar to the last attempt, but there is one less predictor variable.

You have completed your initial regression analysis of salaries at Technitron and are ready to submit your preliminary recommendations. At this point, you will recommend the model that incorporates years at Technitron, years of education after high school, and number of employees supervised to determine the salary structure. You will also show how the regression can provide salary estimates for different types of employees and thereby assist management in setting future salaries.

Save your worksheet and stop your outfile:

■ Save your worksheet with the name **10TECHN** on your Student disk

■ Choose **File > Other Files > Stop Recording Session**

In the next tutorial, you continue this analysis. If you plan to continue directly to Tutorial 11:

■ Choose **File > Restart Minitab**

If you want to take a longer break:

■ Choose **File > Exit**

▼
Minitab Command Summary
▲

This section describes the Minitab menu commands introduced in or related to this tutorial. To find a complete explanation of all menus and commands, refer to the Reference section of this manual.

Minitab Menu Commands

Menu	Command	Description
Stat		
	Basic Statistics	
	Correlation	Provides the correlation between pairs of variables
	Regression	
	Regression	Performs simple or multiple linear regression
	Fitted Line Plot	Graphs confidence bands and prediction bands around a simple linear regression line; also presents a scatter plot of the regression data

Review and Practice

Matching

Match the following terms to their definitions by placing the correct letter next to the term it describes.

_____ SRES

_____ FITS

_____ X**2

_____ X

_____ R

_____ X1*X2

_____ Predictor

_____ 95%

_____ Response

_____ 99%

a. The Minitab symbol that denotes an influential point

b. An elementary quadratic model variable

c. The name given to the column of standardized residuals

d. The name assigned to the column of predicted values

e. The only confidence level that Minitab generates when it produces a prediction interval for an individual response

f. Minitab's name for an independent variable

g. A complex multiple linear regression variable

h. A confidence level that isn't available when Minitab produces a confidence interval for an expected response

i. Minitab's name for a dependent variable

j. The symbol that Minitab uses to identify an unusual observation with a large standardized residual

True/False

Mark the following statements with a *T* or an *F*.

_____ 1. You use the Regression command to perform simple linear regression and multiple regression.

_____ 2. The Fitted Line Plot command can graph 90% confidence bands and prediction bands for a simple linear regression line.

_____ 3. The number of entries in the Prediction intervals for new observations text box is equal to the number of predictors plus one.

_____ 4. Among the most used transformations of the response variable are cube roots, logarithms, and negative reciprocals.

_____ 5. Minitab regression output includes an ANOVA table.

_____ 6. A quadratic model is an example of a polynomial model.

_____ 7. The Regression command can print a 95% confidence interval for the slope of a simple linear regression.

_____ 8. You can save fitted values to the worksheet only if you also save the residual values.

_____ 9. Even if you don't save the residual and fitted values, Minitab displays these values for unusual observations.

_____ 10. Minitab uses s to denote the estimated standard deviation about the regression line.

Practice Problems

1. Open HOMES.MTW. Perform a simple linear regression with C1 PRICE as the response variable and C2 AREA as the predictor variable, as follows.

   a. Construct a scatter plot with C1 PRICE on the vertical axis and C2 AREA on the horizontal axis. Based on this plot, do you believe there is a linear relationship between these two variables?

   b. Compute the correlation coefficient between these two variables. Does its value surprise you?

   c. What is the regression equation for this simple linear regression?

   d. What are the values of the standard error of estimate and the coefficient of determination?

   e. Test the hypothesis that the population slope is equal to 0 against the alternative hypothesis that it is not equal to 0.

   f. Construct a 95% confidence interval for the population slope.

2. Open HOMES.MTW. Consider C1 PRICE as the response variable and C2 AREA as the predictor variable for a simple linear regression.

   a. Construct a fitted line plot.

   b. Obtain fitted values, 95% confidence intervals for expected price, and 95% prediction intervals for an individual price. (_Hint:_ Enter C2 AREA in the Prediction intervals for new observations text box.)

   c. Verify the accuracy of the fitted line plot based on your findings in part b.

3. Open MNWAGE.MTW.

   a. Perform a simple linear regression to explain the minimum wage based on year.

   b. Attempt to perform a quadratic regression to explain the minimum wage based on YEAR and YEAR**2. What happens? (_Hint:_ Construct a plot of YEAR and YEAR**2 and compute the associated correlation coefficient.)

4. Open MNWAGE.MTW.

   a. Plot minimum wage versus year. Perform a related simple linear regression.

   b. Compute the square root of minimum wage. Plot this new variable versus year. Perform a related simple linear regression.

c. Compute the natural logarithm of minimum wage. Plot this new variable versus year. Perform a related simple linear regression.

d. Compute the negative reciprocal of minimum wage. Plot this new variable versus year. Perform a related simple linear regression.

e. Which is the best model? Explain your answer using the plots and the regression output.

5. Open HOMES.MTW.

a. Perform a multiple linear regression with C1 PRICE as a response variable and the other four variables as predictors.

b. Based on your analysis in part a, do you believe that any predictor(s) should be dropped from the model? Briefly explain your answer. If you believe any predictor(s) should be dropped, perform a multiple or simple linear regression analysis with the appropriate subset of predictors.

TUTORIAL 11

Advanced Linear Regression

You begin this tutorial by looking at a set of data that illustrate the need for more than just examining basic computer output when performing a regression. You then continue in your role as the managerial consultant hired to analyze the Technitron salary structure. In the report you generated in Tutorial 10, you developed a model for salary based on quantitative variables. You saw how you could use this model to estimate salaries for employees with different profiles. Now you consider some techniques that you should apply to any linear regression model: checking for the presence of collinearity, verifying that the assumptions of the model are satisfied, and examining unusual observations. You also use Minitab to include qualitative variables in your model. Finally, you perform a stepwise regression to select the variables that best predict salary.

Objectives

In this tutorial, you learn how to:

- appreciate the importance of graphs in a regression analysis

- identify the presence of collinearity in a multiple linear regression

- perform a residual analysis to check the assumptions of a linear regression

- examine unusual observations (outlying points and points of influence) in a linear regression

- create indicator (dummy) variables so that you can use qualitative variables as predictors in a linear regression

- use stepwise regression to explore the relative importance of predictor variables

Illustrating Regression with the Anscombe Data

▼

▲

Statistician Frank J. Anscombe created a data set to illustrate the importance of doing more than just examining the standard computer regression output. These data are saved in the file FJA.MTW. There are 11 cases for each of the following variables: C1 X, C2 Y1, C3 Y2, C4 Y3, C5 X4, and C6 Y4. (X represents predictors and Y represents response variables.)

To start Minitab and start an outfile:

- Start Minitab and maximize the Minitab window and the Data window

- Start an outfile named **T11** on your Student disk

- Open **FJA.MTW**

Anscombe created this data set so that students could examine the output from four simple linear regressions: Y1 on X, Y2 on X, Y3 on X, and Y4 on X4. Before you start the regressions, enter the BRIEF Session command to limit the amount of output (BRIEF 1 produces minimal output, BRIEF 2 is the default, and BRIEF 3 produces the most output):

- Choose **Window > Session**

- Type **BRIEF 1** and press ⏎Enter

- Choose **Stat > Regression > Regression**

- Select **C2 Y1** to enter it in the **Response** text box

- Select **C1 X** to enter it in the **Predictors** text box

- Click **OK**

Minitab produces the first regression. To perform the next three regressions:

- Choose **Stat > Regression > Regression** three more times, and enter the following pairs:

Response	Predictors
Y2	X
Y3	X
Y4	X4

When you have finished the four regressions, the Session window contains the output shown in Figure 11-1.

FIGURE 11-1

*Results of four BRIEF 1
regression analyses*

```
MTB > BRIEF 1
MTB > Regress 'Y1' 1 'X'.

The regression equation is
Y1 = 3.00 + 0.500 X ───────────────────────────────── First regression
                                                       equation
Predictor      Coef       Stdev      t-ratio        p
Constant      3.000       1.125        2.67      0.026
X            0.5001      0.1179        4.24      0.002

s = 1.237      R-sq = 66.7%     R-sq(adj) = 62.9%

Analysis of Variance

SOURCE         DF           SS          MS        F        p
Regression      1       27.510      27.510    17.99    0.002
Error           9       13.763       1.529
Total          10       41.273


MTB > Regress 'Y2' 1 'X'.

The regression equation is
Y2 = 3.00 + 0.500 X ───────────────────────────────── Second regression
                                                       equation
Predictor      Coef       Stdev      t-ratio        p
Constant      3.001       1.125        2.67      0.026
X            0.5000      0.1180        4.24      0.002

s = 1.237      R-sq = 66.6%     R-sq(adj) = 62.9%

Analysis of Variance

SOURCE         DF           SS          MS        F        p
Regression      1       27.500      27.500    17.97    0.002
Error           9       13.776       1.531
Total          10       41.276


MTB > Regress 'Y3' 1 'X'.

The regression equation is
Y3 = 3.00 + 0.500 X ───────────────────────────────── Third regression
                                                       equation
Predictor      Coef       Stdev      t-ratio        p
Constant      3.002       1.124        2.67      0.026
X            0.4997      0.1179        4.24      0.002

s = 1.236      R-sq = 66.6%     R-sq(adj) = 62.9%

Analysis of Variance

SOURCE         DF           SS          MS        F        p
Regression      1       27.470      27.470    17.97    0.002
Error           9       13.756       1.528
Total          10       41.226
```

FIGURE 11-1 (continued)

```
MTB > Regress 'Y4' 1 'X4'.

The regression equation is
Y4 = 3.00 + 0.500 X4 ──────────────────────────────────────

Predictor       Coef      Stdev    t-ratio        p
Constant       3.002      1.124       2.67    0.026
X4            0.4999     0.1178       4.24    0.002

s = 1.236      R-sq = 66.7%    R-sq(adj) = 63.0%

Analysis of Variance

SOURCE        DF         SS         MS        F        p
Regression     1     27.490     27.490    18.00    0.002
Error          9     13.742      1.527
Total         10     41.232


MTB >
```

Fourth regression equation

Note that the four regression equations are alike. In addition, they all have a t-ratio of 4.24 with a corresponding p-value of 0.002, which Minitab uses to test whether the population slope is zero. Except for rounding, the standard error of estimates and the coefficients of determinations are the same. Many analysts would assume that the response and predictor variables are the same. But, as you can see from the Data window, this is not true.

■ Go to the Data window (Figure 11-2)

FIGURE 11-2

The Data window showing the Anscombe data set

	C1	C2	C3	C4	C5	C6
→	X	Y1	Y2	Y3	X4	Y4
1	10	8.04	9.14	7.46	8	6.58
2	8	6.95	8.14	6.77	8	5.76
3	13	7.58	8.74	12.74	8	7.71
4	9	8.81	8.77	7.11	8	8.84
5	11	8.33	9.26	7.81	8	8.47
6	14	9.96	8.10	8.84	8	7.04
7	6	7.24	6.13	6.08	8	5.25
8	4	4.26	3.10	5.39	19	12.50
9	12	10.84	9.13	8.15	8	5.56
10	7	4.82	7.26	6.42	8	7.91
11	5	5.68	4.74	5.73	8	6.89

Now try producing scatter plots of the data.

■ Choose **Graph > Character Graphs > Scatter Plot**

■ Select **C2 Y1** to enter it in the **Y variable** text box

■ Select **C1 X** to enter it in the **X variable** text box

■ Click **OK**

■ Produce the next three scatter plots (Y2 vs. X, Y3 vs. X, and Y4 vs. X4)

The Session window should look like Figure 11-3.

FIGURE 11-3

*Four Anscombe data set
scatter plots*

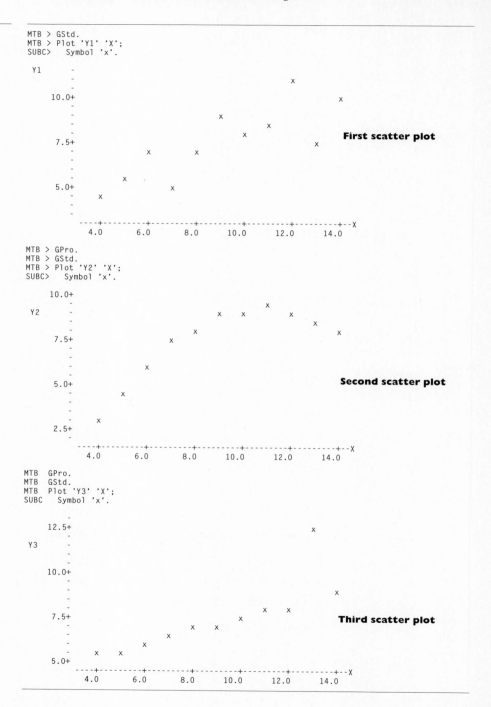

```
MTB > GStd.
MTB > Plot 'Y1' 'X';
SUBC>   Symbol 'x'.

Y1    -
      -
      -                                        x
10.0+ -
      -                                              x
      -                            x
      -                                  x
 7.5+ -                         x
      -      x        x                    x
      -
      -
      -        x
 5.0+ -    x        x
      -  x
      -
      ----+---------+---------+---------+---------+---------+--X
         4.0       6.0       8.0      10.0      12.0      14.0
```

First scatter plot

```
MTB > GPro.
MTB > GStd.
MTB > Plot 'Y2' 'X';
SUBC>   Symbol 'x'.

10.0+ -
      -                         x   x   x
Y2    -                                   x
      -                      x
      -                  x              x
 7.5+ -              x                x
      -
      -
      -          x
 5.0+ -
      -        x
      -
      -      x
 2.5+ -
      -
      ----+---------+---------+---------+---------+---------+--X
         4.0       6.0       8.0      10.0      12.0      14.0
```

Second scatter plot

```
MTB  GPro.
MTB  GStd.
MTB  Plot 'Y3' 'X';
SUBC   Symbol 'x'.

      -
12.5+ -                                      x
      -
Y3    -
      -
10.0+ -
      -                                          x
      -
      -                            x   x
 7.5+ -                      x
      -              x   x
      -          x
      -        x
 5.0+ -  x   x
      ----+---------+---------+---------+---------+---------+--X
         4.0       6.0       8.0      10.0      12.0      14.0
```

Third scatter plot

FIGURE 11-3 (continued)

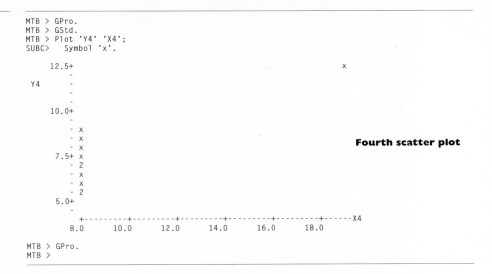

```
MTB > GPro.
MTB > GStd.
MTB > Plot 'Y4' 'X4';
SUBC>   Symbol 'x'.

        12.5+                                                        x
            -
     Y4     -
            -
            -
        10.0+
            -
            - x
            - x
            - x
        7.5+ x
            - 2
            - x
            - x
            - 2
        5.0+
            -
            +---------+---------+---------+---------+---------+------X4
           8.0      10.0      12.0      14.0      16.0      18.0

MTB > GPro.
MTB >
```

Fourth scatter plot

These plots demonstrate why Anscombe constructed this data set. The first scatter plot resembles the type of plot you see in most textbooks. The second plot clearly calls for a quadratic model to describe the relationship. An outlying observation — the third observation with coordinates (13, 12.74) — is apparent in the third scatter plot. Finally, the fourth scatter plot shows an unusual variable: 10 out of the 11 observations have an X4 value of 8 while the other observation is 19. This eighth observation greatly influences the regression analysis.

Reset the regression output to the default level:

■ Type **BRIEF 2** at the Minitab prompt and press ⏎Enter

Repeat the four regressions by copying your previous commands from the History window and pasting them to the Session window. This time, Minitab will produce more output.

■ Choose **Window > History**

■ Highlight the four regression command lines

■ Choose **Edit > Copy**

■ Choose **Window > Session**

■ Click after the MTB > prompt, if necessary, to move the insertion point

■ Choose **Edit > Paste**

The Session window should resemble Figure 11-4.

FIGURE 11-4

*Session window with
pasted Regression
commands*

```
MTB > BRIEF 2
MTB > Regress 'Y1' 1 'X'.
Regress 'Y2' 1 'X'.
Regress 'Y3' 1 'X'.
Regress 'Y4' 1 'X4'.
```

■ Press ⏎Enter to accept the commands

The Session screen displays the output shown in Figure 11-5.

FIGURE 11-5

*Results of four BRIEF 2
regression analyses*

```
MTB > BRIEF 2
MTB > Regress 'Y1' 1 'X'

The regression equation is
Y1 = 3.00 + 0.500 X

Predictor       Coef        Stdev      t-ratio        p
Constant       3.000        1.125        2.67      0.026
X              0.5001      0.1179        4.24      0.002

s = 1.237       R-sq = 66.7%       R-sq(adj) = 62.9%

Analysis of Variance

SOURCE        DF          SS          MS        F         p
Regression     1      27.510      27.510    17.99     0.002
Error          9      13.763       1.529
Total         10      41.273


MTB > Regress 'Y2' 1 'X'.

The regression equation is
Y2 = 3.00 + 0.500 X

Predictor       Coef        Stdev      t-ratio        p
Constant       3.001        1.125        2.67      0.026
X              0.5000      0.1180        4.24      0.002

s = 1.237       R-sq = 66.6%       R-sq(adj) = 62.9%

Analysis of Variance

SOURCE        DF          SS          MS        F         p
Regression     1      27.500      27.500    17.97     0.002
Error          9      13.776       1.531
Total         10      41.276
```

FIGURE 11-5 (continued)

```
MTB > Regress 'Y3' 1 'X'.

The regression equation is
Y3 = 3.00 + 0.500 X
Predictor       Coef       Stdev     t-ratio        p
Constant       3.002       1.124       2.67      0.026
X              0.4997      0.1179      4.24      0.002

s = 1.236      R-sq = 66.6%      R-sq(adj) = 62.9%

Analysis of Variance

SOURCE          DF          SS          MS         F         p
Regression       1       27.470      27.470     17.97     0.002
Error            9       13.756       1.528
Total           10       41.226

Unusual Observations
Obs.        X         Y3       Fit   Stdev.Fit   Residual   St.Resid
  3      13.0     12.740    9.499      0.601      3.241       3.00R

R denotes an obs. with a large st. resid.

MTB > Regress 'Y4' 1 'X4'.

The regression equation is
Y4 = 3.00 + 0.500 X4

Predictor       Coef       Stdev     t-ratio        p
Constant       3.002       1.124       2.67      0.026
X4             0.4999      0.1178      4.24      0.002

s = 1.236      R-sq = 66.7%      R-sq(adj) = 63.0%

Analysis of Variance

SOURCE          DF          SS          MS         F         p
Regression       1       27.490      27.490     18.00     0.002
Error            9       13.742       1.527
Total           10       41.232

Unusual Observations
Obs.       X4         Y4       Fit   Stdev.Fit   Residual   St.Resid
  8      19.0     12.500   12.500      1.236      0.000        * X

X denotes an obs. whose X value gives it large influence.
```

Minitab notes the unusual observations you saw in the last two scatter plots. In the third plot, it flags the third observation with an R; in the fourth plot, it marks the eighth observation with an X. Notice that Minitab doesn't notify you of the need for a quadratic model for the second data set. Although Minitab's unusual observation regression output block is valuable, you should still plot your data whenever you perform a regression.

CASE STUDY: MANAGEMENT — SALARY STRUCTURE (CONTINUED)

Return again to the Technitron salary data. TECHN2.MTW contains the original salary data from all four Technitron departments and the variables created in Tutorial 10. In all, there are 12 variables for the 46 Technitron employees.

Column	Name	Description
C1	SALARY	The salary of an employee
C2	YRS EM	The number of years employed at Technitron
C3	PRIOR YR	The number of years of prior experience
C4	EDUC	Years of education after high school
C5	ID	The company identification number for the employee
C6	GENDER	The coded gender of the employee; 0 = female and 1 = male
C7	DEPT	The employee's department; 1 = sales, 2 = purchasing, 3 = advertising, and 4 = engineering
C8	SUPER	The number of employees supervised by this employee
C9	SRES1	The standardized residuals for the simple linear regression of SALARY versus YRS EM
C10	FITS1	The fitted values for the simple linear regression of SALARY versus YRS EM
C11	RESI1	The residuals for the simple linear regression of SALARY versus YRS EM
C12	YRS**2	The square of YRS EM

- Open **TECHN2.MTW**

- Choose **Window > Data**

Identifying Collinearity

In Tutorial 10, you performed a quadratic regression analysis: a multiple linear regression analysis with C1 SALARY as the response variable with C2 YRS EM and C12 YRS**2 as the predictor variables. If you look back at Figure 10-11, you see the regression equation of SALARY = 29323 + 863 YRS EM + 9.7 YRS**2. According to the predictor table, each coefficient is not significant at reasonable levels of significance in the presence of the other. (The p-value is 0.107 for the YRS EM coefficient and 0.631 for the YRS**2 coefficient.) However, the ANOVA table reports that at least one of the two coefficients is not zero because its p-value is 0.000.

This contradiction is due to the high degree of linear association between the two predictors. The value of their correlation coefficient is 0.963. (You could use Stat > Basic Statistics > Correlation to verify this value.)

This is an example of *collinearity* (or *multicollinearity*) that occurs in multiple linear regression when there is a linear relation connecting the predictors.

Minitab's Variance inflation factors option helps identify collinearity. You decide to redo the quadratic regression analysis from Tutorial 10 using this option.

- Choose **Stat > Regression > Regression**

- Click the **Control menu box**, then click **Reset Defaults**

- Select **C1 SALARY** to enter it in the **Response** text box

- Select **C2 YRS EM** and **C12 YRS**2** to enter them in the **Predictors** text box

- Click the **Options** button

- Click the **Variance inflation factors** check box

- Click **OK** twice

Figure 11-6 displays the results of the quadratic regression with the variance inflation factors.

FIGURE 11-6

Results of quadratic regression with variance inflation factors

```
MTB > Regress 'SALARY' 2 'YRS EM' 'YRS**2';
SUBC>    VIF.

The regression equation is
SALARY = 29323 + 863 YRS EM + 9.7 YRS**2

Predictor        Coef       Stdev     t-ratio         p        VIF
Constant        29323        2640       11.11     0.000
YRS EM          863.3       523.9        1.65     0.107       13.7
YRS**2           9.74       20.14        0.48     0.631       13.7

s = 7225       R-sq = 58.8%      R-sq(adj) = 56.9%

Analysis of Variance

SOURCE          DF          SS           MS          F          p
Regression       2  3199762944   1599881472      30.65      0.000
Error           43  2244488448     52197404
Total           45  5444251648

SOURCE          DF      SEQ SS
YRS EM           1  3187557888
YRS**2           1    12205007

Unusual Observations
Obs.   YRS EM      SALARY         Fit   Stdev.Fit    Residual    St.Resid
  15     12.0       56326       41086        1644       15240        2.17R
  40     22.0       69246       53031        2050       16215        2.34R
  41     27.0       65487       59734        3956        5753        0.95 X

R denotes an obs. with a large st. resid.
X denotes an obs. whose X value gives it large influence.

MTB >
```

Variance inflation factors

The predictor table contains the *variance inflation factors (VIF)*. Each coefficient's VIF is 13.7 — with only two predictors, the VIFs are always the same.

Since these values indicate a high degree of collinearity, there may be statistical and computational difficulties with this model.

Now that you have identified a problem with this quadratic regression, try to remedy it by subtracting the mean of YRS EM from YRS EM and then squaring this new variable.

- Choose **Calc > Standardize**

- Select **C2 YRS EM** to enter it in the **Input Column(s)** text box and press [Tab]

- Type **'YRSSM'** in the **Store results in** text box

- Click the **Subtract mean** option button

The completed Standardize dialog box should look like Figure 11-7.

FIGURE 11-7

Standardize dialog box

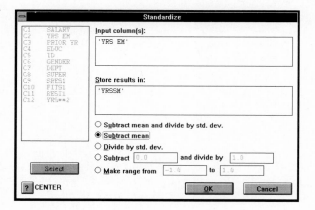

- Click **OK**

- Choose **Calc > Mathematical Expressions**

- Type **'YRSSM**∗∗**2'** in the **Variable (new or modified)** text box and press [Tab] twice

- Type **C13**∗∗**2** in the **Expression** text box and press [←Enter]

Perform a regression for salary using these two new variables as your solution to collinearity in polynomial regression.

- Choose **Stat > Regression > Regression**

- Verify that **C1 SALARY** is the entry in the **Response** text box

- Press [Tab] and select **C13 'YRSSM'** and **C14 'YRSSM**∗∗**2'** to replace the contents of the **Predictors** text box

- Click **OK**

Figure 11-8 displays the results of this new regression.

FIGURE 11-8

Results of quadratic regression with centered predictors

```
MTB > Regress 'SALARY' 2 'YRSSM' 'YRSSM**2';
SUBC>    VIF.

The regression equation is
SALARY = 39277 + 1065 YRSSM + 9.7 YRSSM**2

Predictor       Coef      Stdev     t-ratio       p        VIF
Constant       39277       1559       25.19     0.000
YRSSM         1064.5      167.0        6.38     0.000        1.4
YRSSM**2        9.74      20.14        0.48     0.631        1.4

s = 7225       R-sq = 58.8%      R-sq(adj) = 56.9%

Analysis of Variance

SOURCE         DF         SS          MS         F         p
Regression      2   3199762944   1599881472    30.65     0.000
Error          43   2244488448     52197404
Total          45   5444251648

SOURCE         DF       SEQ SS
YRSSM           1    3187557888
YRSSM**2        1      12205007

Unusual Observations
Obs.    YRSSM     SALARY       Fit   Stdev.Fit   Residual   St.Resid
 15       1.7      56326     41086        1644      15240      2.17R
 40      11.7      69246     53031        2050      16215      2.34R
 41      16.7      65487     59734        3956       5753      0.95 X

R denotes an obs. with a large st. resid.
X denotes an obs. whose X value gives it large influence.

MTB >
```

The VIF column now contains variance inflation factors of 1.4. You no longer have a problem with collinearity. Note that there are many similarities between the output in Figures 11-6 and 11-8. The values of s, R-sq, F, and the p-value for F are identical. In addition, Minitab flags the same unusual observations. However, there is a difference in the predictor table; the first predictor coefficient changed. Minitab indicates that this coefficient is significant by its p-value of 0.000. You no longer have a contradiction between the t- and F-tests. You decide to forgo inclusion of polynomial terms based on YRS EM in developing your salary model for Technitron.

Verifying Linear Regression Assumptions

In order to employ the t-test, F-tests, and interval estimates introduced in Tutorial 10, you assumed that the data met certain conditions. Most of these criteria concern the error component, or unexplained portion, in a model. Here are the three major assumptions of linear regression:

1. Normality: the error component is normally distributed

2. Constant variation (homoscedasity): the error component has a constant standard deviation

3. Independence: the error component is independently distributed

Serious departures from these assumptions affect the results of the inference associated with simple and multiple linear regression.

Storing the Residuals

The difference between the response variable and its fitted values are called *residuals*. Residuals are estimates of the error terms in a linear regression model. Minitab allows you to store many columns of useful information when you perform a linear regression. In Tutorial 10, you stored the standardized residuals, the fitted values, and the residuals for a simple linear regression. Then you used the fits to obtain an understanding of the regression equation.

Now, store this same information, along with two other statistics, for the multiple linear regression model you recommended to the Technitron management at the end of Tutorial 10 (with C1 SALARY as the response and C2 YRS EM, C4 EDUC, and C8 SUPER as the predictors). Use the results to check the three major assumptions of linear regression. (You'll also use this information in the next section when you examine unusual observations.)

- Choose **Edit > Edit Last Command Dialog**

- Verify that **C1 SALARY** is the entry in the **Response** text box

- Press Tab and select **C2 YRS EM**, **C4 EDUC**, and **C8 SUPER** to enter them in the **Predictors** text box

- Click the **Residuals**, **Standard. resids.**, **Fits**, **Hi (leverage)**, and **Cook's distance** check boxes in the Storage section

- Click **OK**

Figure 11-9 shows the results.

FIGURE 11-9

Results of multiple linear regression with storage

```
MTB > Name c15 = 'SRES2' c16 = 'FITS2' c17 = 'RESI2' c18 = 'HI2' &
CONT>        c19 = 'COOK2'
MTB > Regress 'SALARY' 3 'YRS EM' 'EDUC' 'SUPER';
SUBC>    SResiduals 'SRES2';
SUBC>    Fits 'FITS2';
SUBC>    Residuals 'RESI2';
SUBC>    Hi 'HI2';
SUBC>    Cookd 'COOK2';
SUBC>    VIF.

The regression equation is
SALARY = 23783 + 659 YRS EM + 1639 EDUC + 165 SUPER

Predictor      Coef      Stdev    t-ratio        p      VIF
Constant      23783       1765      13.48    0.000
YRS EM        658.7      138.7       4.75    0.000      1.6
EDUC         1639.4      403.6       4.06    0.000      1.9
SUPER        164.82      94.91       1.74    0.090      1.3

s = 5608      R-sq = 75.7%      R-sq(adj) = 74.0%

Analysis of Variance

SOURCE       DF           SS           MS          F        p
Regression    3   4123200768   1374400256      43.70    0.000
Error        42   1321050752     31453590
Total        45   5444251648

SOURCE       DF       SEQ SS
YRS EM        1   3187557888
EDUC          1    840790272
SUPER         1     94852544
```

FIGURE 11-9 (continued)

```
Unusual Observations
Obs.    YRS EM     SALARY        Fit  Stdev.Fit   Residual   St.Resid
   1      18.0      38985      51218       1621     -12233      -2.28R
   2      15.0      32920      49077       1663     -16157      -3.02R
  40      22.0      69246      62085       3343       7161       1.59 X
  41      27.0      65487      68492       3341      -3005      -0.67 X
  42       6.0      48695      47443       3313       1252       0.28 X

R denotes an obs. with a large st. resid.
X denotes an obs. whose X value gives it large influence.

MTB >
```

Notice that Minitab has created five new variables in the Name command line. Also observe that there doesn't appear to be a problem with collinearity based on the three VIF values. The rest of the output is identical to Figure 10-13.

You can use either the residuals or the standardized residuals for a residual analysis. Some statisticians prefer residuals (with a mean of 0); others prefer standardized residuals (with most values between –3 and 3). You decide to use standardized residuals.

- Save your worksheet with the name 11TECHN2 on your Student disk

Checking the Normality Assumption

To check the normality assumption, you decide to let Minitab construct a normal probability plot rather than constructing it yourself, as you did in Tutorial 6. You can choose either of two tests in the Normal Probability Plot dialog box to verify normality.

- Choose **Graph > Normal Plot**

- Select **C15 SRES2** to enter it in the **Variable** text box

The completed Normal Probability Plot dialog box looks like Figure 11-10.

FIGURE 11-10

The completed Normal Probability Plot dialog box

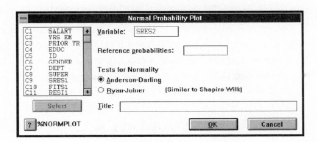

Use the default test for normality (Anderson-Darling).

- Click **OK**

The normal plot appears in its own Graph window (Figure 11-11).

FIGURE 11-11

*Normal plot of
standardized residuals
using the
Anderson-Darling
normality test*

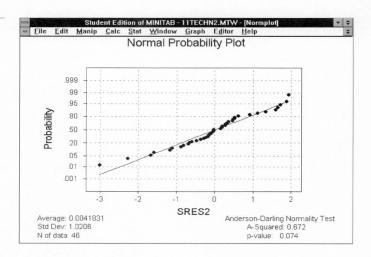

The vertical axis is a probability scale; the horizontal axis is a data scale. Minitab has fitted and drawn a least-squares line for the points that estimate the cumulative distribution function from which the data are drawn. Note that there are a number of points away from the line. The average, standard deviation, and sample size appear in the lower left corner. The results of the Anderson-Darling normality test display in the lower right corner. The plot's p-value is 0.074, so you do not reject the null hypothesis that the standardized residuals are normally distributed at a significance level of 0.05.

Using Scatter Plots to Verify the Constant Variation Assumption

The best single check for constant variance is a scatter plot with the standardized residuals on the vertical axis and the fits on the horizontal axis. In addition, you should construct three scatter plots with the standardized residuals on the vertical axis and each predictor variable on the horizontal axis. There should be the same amount of variation in the standardized residuals for each range of the horizontal variable in each plot; otherwise, the assumption is violated. Begin by plotting the SRES2 versus FITS2.

- Choose **Graph > Plot**

- Select **C15 SRES2** to enter it in the first **Y** text box in the **Graph variables** section

- Select **C16 FITS2** to enter it in the first **X** text box in the **Graph variables** section

- Click **OK**

The scatter plot appears in its own Graph window (Figure 11-12).

FIGURE 11-12

*Scatter plot of
standardized residuals
versus fits*

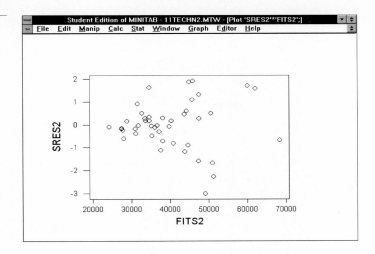

There appears to be more variation for the fitted values between $45,000 and $50,000 than for the other fitted values. You could construct the scatter plots for SRES2 versus YRS EM and for SRES2 versus EDUC to observe similar results for larger values on the horizontal axis. Based on these plots, you decide to perform some transformations to correct this potential problem.

First, construct one more plot: SRES2 versus SUPER (Figure 11-13).

- Choose **Graph > Plot**

- Verify that **C15 SRES2** is in the first **Y** text box in the **Graph variable** section

- Select **C8 SUPER** to enter it in the first **X** text box in the **Graph variable** section

- Click **OK**

FIGURE 11-13

*Scatter plot of
standardized residuals
versus SUPER*

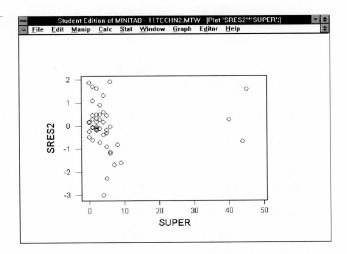

This plot reveals constant SRES2 variation, except for three employees. Looking back at the scatter plot in Figure 11-12, you identify two of these same employees as potential unusual observations. You decide to examine all three in more detail before you construct your final model.

Although you construct scatter plots such as these to check the constant variation assumption, they are also useful in detecting other problems with the model. You should study any unusual pattern in a residual analysis, because it may well indicate an underlying weakness in the model.

Checking the Independence Assumption with a Time Series Plot

Usually, you check only the independence assumption when you know the order in which the data were collected. Even though this isn't the case in this instance, you decide to check this assumption with a time series plot because it may reveal an unusual pattern. In the past, statisticians have discovered "lurking variables" by checking this assumption.

- Choose **Graph > Time Series Plot**

- Select **C15 SRES2** to enter it in the first **Y variable** text box

- Click **OK**

The time series plot appears in its own Graph window (Figure 11-14).

FIGURE 11-14

Time series plot of standardized residuals

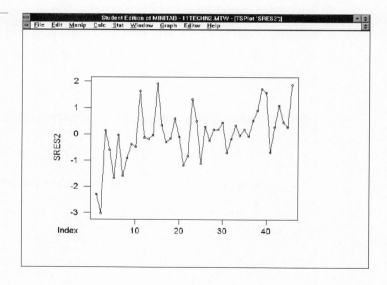

You discover no unusual patterns in this plot. However, you notice that the first two observations have negative standardized residuals with the largest absolute values. You want to examine the data for these two employees in more detail before you submit your final model.

The Residual Plot command on the Stat > Regression submenu presents four residual model diagnostics plots: a normal plot of residuals, a histogram of the residuals to check for normality, a residual versus fits scatter plot to check the constant variation assumption, and a time series plot of the residuals to check the independence assumption. (This final plot type, which is discussed more fully in Tutorial 14, is often called an *I chart of residual*.) An additional way to check the independence assumption is by using the Durbin-Watson statistic, available in the Regression Options dialog box.

▼
Examining Unusual Observations
▲

Now turn your attention to the five unusual observations identified at the bottom of the output in Figure 11-9, and depicted again in Figure 11-15.

FIGURE 11-15

Unusual observations table from Figure 11-9

```
Unusual Observations
Obs.   YRS EM    SALARY      Fit   Stdev.Fit   Residual    St.Resid
  1     18.0     38985     51218      1621      -12233       -2.28R
  2     15.0     32920     49077      1663      -16157       -3.02R
 40     22.0     69246     62085      3343        7161        1.59 X
 41     27.0     65487     68492      3341       -3005       -0.67 X
 42      6.0     48695     47443      3313        1252        0.28 X

R denotes an obs. with a large st. resid.
X denotes an obs. whose X value gives it large influence.
```

The first two unusual observations, each flagged with an R, identify employees whose standardized residuals have absolute values that exceed 2. Employee 1's salary is $38,985, but the regression equation fits a value of $51,218, leaving a residual of $12,233. At $16,157, Employee 2's residual is even greater. If you look at the Data window, you can see that Employee 1 has been with Technitron 18 years, has 9 years of post-secondary education, and supervises 5 employees, while Employee 2 has been with the company for 15 years, has the same amount of education, and supervises 4 other employees. Both of these employees appear to be undercompensated according to your multiple linear regression model. These are the same two employees identified in the time series plot (Figure 11-14).

The last three unusual observations, each flagged with an X, identify employees that have hat matrix diagonal elements greater than 0.99 or 3 times the number of predictor variables plus 1 divided by the sample size $(3 \times (3 + 1)/46 = 0.2609)$, whichever is smaller. To check for X values that have a substantial influence, take a look at the HI2 column.

- Choose **File > Display Data**
- Select **C1 SALARY**, **C2 YRS EM**, **C4 EDUC**, **C8 SUPER**, **C16 FITS2**, and **C18 HI2** to enter them in the **Columns and constants to display** text box
- Click **OK**

The printed data appear in the Session window (Figure 11-16).

FIGURE 11-16

Data display containing hat matrix diagonal elements and five other variables

MTB > Print 'SALARY' 'YRS EM' 'EDUC' 'SUPER' 'FITS2' 'HI2'.

ROW	SALARY	YRS EM	EDUC	SUPER	FITS2	HI2
1	38985	18	9	5	51217.8	0.083494
2	32920	15	9	4	49077.0	0.087899
3	29548	5	1	0	28716.2	0.069012
4	24749	6	0	1	27900.3	0.106784
5	41889	22	7	7	50903.4	0.078817
6	31528	3	3	6	31666.5	0.048594
7	38791	21	5	9	47295.6	0.094417
8	39828	18	5	5	44660.3	0.059073
9	28985	0	4	4	31000.2	0.070142
10	32782	0	7	0	35259.1	0.161452
11	43674	6	4	2	34622.6	0.029652
12	35467	3	6	3	36090.1	0.075685
13	29876	2	3	5	30843.0	0.051978
14	36431	9	4	2	36598.6	0.025890
15	56326	12	8	6	45791.3	0.057845
16	36571	6	4	2	34622.6	0.029652
17	35468	9	4	5	37093.0	0.025383
18	26578	0	2	2	27391.8	0.066559
19	47536	15	6	4	44158.9	0.034035
20	23654	0	0	2	24113.1	0.104344
21	37548	19	4	6	43844.5	0.091417
22	36578	4	8	8	40851.6	0.121836
23	54679	20	6	4	47452.2	0.069414
24	53234	25	6	3	50580.7	0.138223
25	31425	7	5	6	37579.9	0.028207
26	39743	9	5	1	38073.1	0.028396
27	26452	1	2	0	27720.9	0.059139
28	34632	5	4	0	33634.3	0.036174
29	35631	6	4	2	34622.6	0.029652
30	46211	14	6	5	43665.1	0.028869
31	34231	6	6	3	38066.1	0.049357
32	26548	5	0	2	27406.4	0.105553
33	36512	6	4	2	34622.6	0.029652
34	34869	7	4	1	35116.4	0.028394
35	41255	9	6	4	40206.9	0.031941
36	39331	9	6	1	39712.5	0.039944
37	35487	8	2	2	32661.1	0.052726
38	36487	6	2	3	31508.6	0.050173
39	68425	25	12	1	60087.3	0.249751
40	69246	22	10	45	62084.5	0.355404
41	65487	27	12	44	68491.8	0.354810
42	48695	6	8	40	47443.1	0.349048
43	51698	18	6	1	45640.4	0.060878
44	46184	20	4	1	43679.0	0.108105
45	34987	9	2	3	33484.6	0.057685
46	54899	12	8	0	44802.4	0.084544

MTB >

This display verifies that employees 40, 41, and 42 are the only ones with HI2 values greater than 0.2609. You observe that two of the three employees have spent many years at Technitron and have the most education of any of Technitron employees. Employees 40 and 41, identified in the residual analysis, supervise 45 and 44 employees, respectively. In contrast, Employee 42 supervises 40 employees but has only been at Technitron for six years. You are not surprised that these employees are classified as unusual observations. Their predictor values greatly influence your regression equation. If you removed them from the analysis, you might obtain a strikingly different equation.

Observing Cook's Distance

Cook's distance is a function of the standardized residuals and the hat matrix diagonal elements. You are interested in observations with Cook's distances greater than an inverse cumulative F distribution probability of 0.5. These observations usually have standardized residuals with large absolute values or a substantial impact on the regression equation. You can check the Data window to compare the Cook's distance values to 0.8529 (the value that results from an F distribution with 4 numerator degrees of freedom and 42 denominator degrees of freedom). There are no such observations.

Creating Indicator (Dummy) Variables

You are concerned about the results of both your residual analysis and your examination of unusual observations. You need to construct a better model. Thus far, you have considered only quantitative variables in your modeling. But there are also two qualitative variables, C6 GENDER and C7 DEPT, that you could include as predictors in your regression equation. Before you can do so, however, you must convert them to the proper form. (Using quantitative and qualitative predictors together in a regression model is an example of analysis of covariance, as your instructor can tell you.)

Qualitative variables must be "dummied up" in order to use them as predictors. An *indicator* (or *dummy*) *variable* is one that takes on two values — typically 0 and 1.

Recall that C6 GENDER is already coded in this form (0 = male and 1 = female). C7 DEPT is not "dummied up." It currently contains four codes representing employees in the different departments: 1 for the sales department,

2 for purchasing, 3 for advertising, and 4 for engineering. To include this qualitative variable in your regression analysis, you must transform its contents into four dummy variables (or exclude the intercept from the regression model).

- Choose **Calc > Make Indicator Variables**
- Select **C7 DEPT** to enter it in the **Indicator variables for** text box
- Type **DEPT1 DEPT2 DEPT3 DEPT4** in the **Store results in** text box

    The completed Make Indicator Variables dialog box should look like Figure 11-17.

- Press ←Enter

    Print out C7 DEPT and its four indicator (dummy) variables.

- Choose **File > Display Data**
- Select **C7 DEPT, C20 DEPT1, C21 DEPT2, C22 DEPT3,** and **C23 DEPT4** to enter them in the **Columns and constants to display** text box
- Click **OK**

    The printed data appear in the Session window (Figure 11-18).

FIGURE 11-18

Session window displaying qualitative variable DEPT and its four indicator (dummy) variables

```
MTB > Name c20 = 'DEPT1' c21 = 'DEPT2' c22 = 'DEPT3' c23 = 'DEPT4'
MTB > Indicator 'DEPT' 'DEPT1' 'DEPT2' 'DEPT3' 'DEPT4'.
MTB > Print  'DEPT' 'DEPT1'-'DEPT4'.

ROW   DEPT  DEPT1  DEPT2  DEPT3  DEPT4

  1     1     1      0      0      0
  2     1     1      0      0      0
  3     1     1      0      0      0
  4     1     1      0      0      0
  5     1     1      0      0      0
  6     1     1      0      0      0
  7     1     1      0      0      0
  8     1     1      0      0      0
  9     1     1      0      0      0
 10     1     1      0      0      0
 11     2     0      1      0      0
 12     2     0      1      0      0
 13     2     0      1      0      0
 14     2     0      1      0      0
 15     2     0      1      0      0
 16     2     0      1      0      0
 17     2     0      1      0      0
 18     2     0      1      0      0
 19     3     0      0      1      0
 20     3     0      0      1      0
 21     3     0      0      1      0
 22     3     0      0      1      0
 23     3     0      0      1      0
 24     3     0      0      1      0
 25     3     0      0      1      0
 26     4     0      0      0      1
 27     4     0      0      0      1
 28     4     0      0      0      1
 29     4     0      0      0      1
 30     4     0      0      0      1
 31     4     0      0      0      1
 32     4     0      0      0      1
 33     4     0      0      0      1
 34     4     0      0      0      1
 35     4     0      0      0      1
 36     4     0      0      0      1
 37     4     0      0      0      1
 38     4     0      0      0      1
 39     4     0      0      0      1
 40     4     0      0      0      1
 41     4     0      0      0      1
 42     4     0      0      0      1
 43     4     0      0      0      1
 44     4     0      0      0      1
 45     4     0      0      0      1
 46     4     0      0      0      1

MTB >
```

Observe that the employees from the Sales Department (coded 1 in C7 DEPT) have a 1 in C20 DEPT1 and a 0 in DEPT2, DEPT3, and DEPT4. Employees from the other three departments have similar coded columns.

You are ready to include C6 GENDER and C7 DEPT in your regression analysis. You will model salary as a function of the four quantitative variables, gender, and three of the four indicator variables (there is a problem with collinearity if you include all of these variables).

To fit a multiple linear regression:

■ Choose **Stat > Regression > Regression**

■ Verify that **C1 SALARY** is the entry in the **Response** text box

- Press [Tab] and select **C2 YRS EM**, **C3 PRIOR YR**, **C4 EDUC**, **C6 GENDER**, **C8 SUPER**, **C20 DEPT1**, **C21 DEPT2**, and **C22 DEPT3** to enter them in the **Predictors** text box

- Deselect all the check boxes in the **Storage** section

- Click **OK**

The Session window shows the regression output (Figure 11-19).

FIGURE 11-19

FIGURE 11-19

Results of multiple linear regression with the four quantitative and four indicator variables

```
MTB > Regress 'SALARY' 8 'YRS EM'-'EDUC' 'GENDER' 'SUPER' 'DEPT1'-'DEPT3';
SUBC>    VIF.

The regression equation is
SALARY = 27409 + 709 YRS EM - 73 PRIOR YR + 1545 EDUC - 2040 GENDER + 130 SUPER
            - 8096 DEPT1 + 360 DEPT2 - 3047 DEPT3

Predictor       Coef       Stdev    t-ratio          p        VIF
Constant       27409        2202      12.45      0.000
YRS EM         709.5       121.0       5.87      0.000        1.8
PRIOR YR       -72.8       198.4      -0.37      0.716        1.1
EDUC          1544.5       338.2       4.57      0.000        1.9
GENDER         -2040        1449      -1.41      0.167        1.1
SUPER         130.17       81.68       1.59      0.120        1.5
DEPT1          -8096        1831      -4.42      0.000        1.2
DEPT2            360        2004       0.18      0.859        1.2
DEPT3          -3047        2065      -1.48      0.149        1.2

s = 4650       R-sq = 85.3%      R-sq(adj) = 82.1%

Analysis of Variance

SOURCE          DF          SS          MS          F          p
Regression       8  4644236288   580529536      26.85      0.000
Error           37   800015296    21622036
Total           45  5444251648

SOURCE          DF      SEQ SS
YRS EM           1  3187557888
PRIOR YR         1      160191
EDUC             1   844012864
GENDER           1    22447266
SUPER            1   111966256
DEPT1            1   424900960
DEPT2            1     6136690
DEPT3            1    47054040

Unusual Observations
Obs.   YRS EM     SALARY       Fit   Stdev.Fit    Residual    St.Resid
   2     15.0      32920     42118        2147       -9198      -2.23R
  23     20.0      54679     46080        2120        8599       2.08R
  42      6.0      48695     47846        3572         849       0.29 X
  46     12.0      54899     45875        1838        9024       2.11R

R denotes an obs. with a large st. resid.
X denotes an obs. whose X value gives it large influence.

MTB >
```

You are encouraged by the introduction of the indicator variables. There is a smaller s, a higher R^2, a significant F statistic, one less unusual observation, and no collinearity problem. Your only concern is that five coefficients are individually insignificant as indicated by their p-values. You decide to obtain a regression equation without the predictors associated with these insignificant coefficients. You might simplify your model without decreasing its predictive ability by omitting these insignificant variables.

- Choose **Edit > Edit Last Command Dialog**

- Select **C2 YRS EM, C4 EDUC,** and **C20 DEPT1** to enter them in the **Predictors** text box, replacing the current entries

- Click **OK**

The Session window shows the regression results (Figure 11-20).

```
MTB > Regress 'SALARY' 3 'YRS EM' 'EDUC' 'DEPT1';
SUBC>    VIF.

The regression equation is
SALARY = 24868 + 700 YRS EM + 1858 EDUC - 7714 DEPT1

Predictor       Coef       Stdev      t-ratio         p        VIF
Constant       24868        1515        16.42     0.000
YRS EM         699.6        117.7        5.95     0.000        1.6
EDUC          1858.3        314.8        5.90     0.000        1.6
DEPT1          -7714         1704       -4.53     0.000        1.0

s = 4760        R-sq = 82.5%      R-sq(adj) = 81.3%

Analysis of Variance

SOURCE        DF           SS             MS         F         p
Regression     3   4492787200     1497595776     66.11     0.000
Error         42    951464128       22653908
Total         45   5444251136

SOURCE        DF        SEQ SS
YRS EM         1    3187557888
EDUC           1     840790272
DEPT1          1     464439136

Unusual Observations
Obs.   YRS EM     SALARY        Fit   Stdev.Fit   Residual   St.Resid
  2     15.0       32920      44372        1827     -11452      -2.61R
 40     22.0       69246      58842        1529      10404       2.31R

R denotes an obs. with a large st. resid.

MTB >
```

Interpreting the Regression Equation

You are pleased with this output. There is still an improvement in s and R^2 compared to your previous model with three predictors. There are significant results for all three t-tests and the F-tests. In addition, there are now only two unusual observations and no problem with collinearity. (Normally, you would perform a residual analysis as well; in this case, you would find no obvious problems.)

Now take a look at the regression equation:

$$SALARY = 24868 + 700 \text{ YRS EM} + 1858 \text{ EDUC} - 7714 \text{ DEPT1}.$$

The base salary for an employee starting at Technitron with no post-secondary education who is not in the Sales Department is $24,868. However, the same employee in the Sales Department would earn only $17,154.

Only employees 2 and 40 are unusual. According to this model, Employee 2 is underpaid while Employee 40 is overpaid.

▼

Performing Stepwise Regression

▲

You are still concerned that you obtained your model by trial and error. You decide to construct a matrix plot for the nine variables under consideration.

■ Choose **Graph > Matrix Plot**

■ Select **C1 SALARY, C2 YRS EM, C3 PRIOR YR, C4 EDUC, C6 GENDER, C8 SUPER, C20 DEPT1, C21 DEPT2,** and **C22 DEPT3** to enter them in the **Graph variables** text box

■ Click **OK**

The matrix plot appears in its own Graph window (Figure 11-21).

Note: Depending on your computer speed, it may take several minutes to create this plot.

FIGURE 11-21

Matrix plot with response variable and eight possible predictor variables

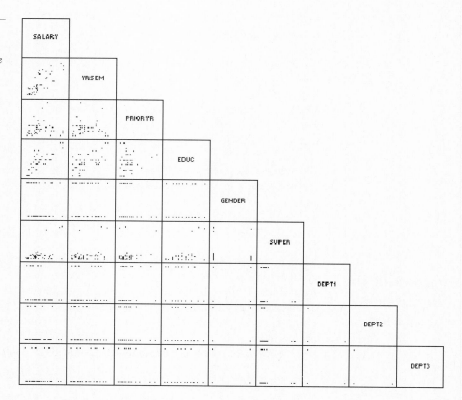

The left column reassures you that YRS EM, EDUC, DEPT1, and possibly SUPER are each linearly related to SALARY. Still another variable may have a strong linear relationship with salary if some other variables are already in the model. So you decide to use a popular variable selection procedure — *stepwise regression*.

This procedure yields a model that contains only those terms with significant F-values at specified levels. To determine which variables are significant predictors of salary at Technitron, you will perform a stepwise regression using SALARY as the response variable and the variables C2 YRS EM, C3 PRIOR YR, C4 EDUC, C6 GENDER, C8 SUPER, C20 DEPT1, C21 DEPT2, and C22 DEPT3 as the potential predictors.

By using different options, you can tell Minitab to select variables in any of three ways:

Stepwise selection At each step Minitab calculates an F-statistic for each predictor in the equation. If the F-value associated with any predictor is less than the specified value of FREMOVE (default = 4), Minitab removes the smallest one from the model. Minitab then calculates a new regression equation, prints the result, and proceeds to the next step. At the next step, Minitab tries to add a variable by calculating an F-statistic for each predictor not in the equation. It then includes the variable with the largest F, provided its F-statistic exceeds a specified value (default = 4). If Minitab neither adds nor deletes a predictor, the stepwise procedure stops.

Forward selection Minitab adds predictor variables one at a time; none are removed. To perform a forward selection, set F to remove at 0. (Since F-statistics are the t-ratios squared, they can never be less than 0.)

Backward elimination Minitab begins with an equation that contains all the predictors. It then removes predictors in the same way as in the stepwise procedure, except that it doesn't re-enter any of them in the equation. To perform a backward elimination, set F to enter at 10000 (a value virtually impossible to attain) and list all the predictors in the Enter option.

Using Stepwise Selection

To conduct a general stepwise regression:

- Choose **Stat > Regression > Stepwise**

- Double-click **C1 SALARY** to enter it in the **Response** text box

- Select **C2 YRS EM, C3 PRIOR YR, C4 EDUC, C6 GENDER, C8 SUPER, C20 DEPT1, C21 DEPT2**, and **C22 DEPT3** to enter them in the **Predictors** text box

- Click **OK**

The Session window displays the results (Figure 11-22).

FIGURE 11-22

Initial results of stepwise regression

```
MTB > Stepwise 'SALARY' 'YRS EM'-'EDUC' 'GENDER' 'SUPER' 'DEPT1'-'DEPT3';
SUBC>    FEnter 4.0;
SUBC>    FRemove 4.0.

Stepwise regression of  SALARY  on  8 predictors, with N =    46

        STEP       1       2       3
    CONSTANT   24582   23177   24868

    EDUC        3010    1916    1858
    T-RATIO     8.19    5.05    5.90

    YRS EM              672     700
    T-RATIO             4.75    5.95

    DEPT1                      -7714
    T-RATIO                    -4.53

    S           7002    5738    4760
    R-SQ       60.37   73.99   82.52
    More? (Yes, No, Subcommand, or Help)
SUBC>
```

The display contains the following information. (For each step, read down the column to obtain information about the variable that Minitab enters or removes, as well as summary information about the regression model.)

Step 1 Minitab enters the EDUC variable because it had the highest F-ratio of all the variables not in the regression equation. The one-variable equation is

$$SALARY = 24582 + 3010 \ EDUC$$

The t-ratio of 8.19 provides the test statistic for the hypothesis that coefficient of EDUC = 0. The estimated standard deviation around the regression line is $7002. This model explains 60.37% of the variation in salary.

Step 2 Of the remaining variables, Minitab determines that YRS EM produced the largest F-ratio that is greater than 4. Consequently, it adds (or enters) the variable into the equation to produce an estimated regression model of

$$SALARY = 23177 + 1916 \ EDUC + 672 \ YRS \ EM$$

The t-ratios are 5.05 and 4.75, respectively. This model explains 73.99% of the variation in salary.

Step 3 Of the remaining variables, Minitab determines that DEPT1 produces the largest F-ratio that is greater than 4; it enters that variable to produce the estimated regression model that you had already obtained.

No other variables meet the criteria for removal or addition, so Minitab asks you if you want to perform another step.

- Type **YES** at the SUBC> prompt and press ⏎Enter

Minitab reports that it neither entered nor removed any variables and ends the stepwise process.

Note: Normally, you would type **NO** at the above prompt, but, in this case, you want to explore another issue before you do so.

In the "real" world, there may be certain variables that you must consider for inclusion in the equation. For example, at Technitron, the number of employees supervised indicates an employee's level of responsibility; management deems this an important variable. To force Minitab to include it in the equation:

- Type **ENTER 'SUPER'.** (be sure to include the period at the end) and press ⏎Enter

The Session window displays the additional results of the stepwise regression (Figure 11-23).

FIGURE 11-23

Additional results of stepwise regression

```
SUBC> ENTER 'SUPER'.

    STEP       4       5
CONSTANT   25297   24868

EDUC        1638    1858
T-RATIO     4.88    5.90

YRS EM       688     700
T-RATIO     5.96    5.95

DEPT1      -7456   -7714
T-RATIO    -4.45   -4.53

SUPER        132
T-RATIO     1.67

S           4662    4760
R-SQ       83.64   82.52
  More? (Yes, No, Subcommand, or Help)
SUBC>
```

Step 4 Minitab adds SUPER to the model along with EDUC and YRS EM. Note that the t-ratio for SUPER is 1.67. This model accounts for 83.64% of the variation in salary.

Step 5 Minitab determines that SUPER is not significant and deletes it from the regression equation, returning you to the regression equation in the second step.

Using the ENTER or REMOVE subcommands, you can add or delete variables and readily determine their impact on the model.

You do not want to enter any other variables into the model and are therefore finished using the stepwise command. At the prompt:

- Type **NO** and press ⟨←Enter⟩

Using Forward Selection

In forward selection, you use the stepwise procedure, but you enter a zero in the F to remove text box. By using this minimum value, you ensure that once entered, a variable can never leave the model. To use the forward selection stepwise regression procedure:

- Choose **Edit > Edit Last Command Dialog**
- Click the **Options** button

The Stepwise Options dialog box (Figure 11-24) appears.

FIGURE 11-24

The Stepwise Options dialog box

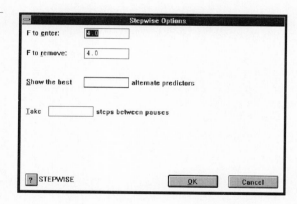

You must enter 0 in the F to remove value (FREMOVE) text box to perform a forward selection stepwise regression.

- Press ⟨Tab⟩ and type **0** in the **F to remove** text box
- Click **OK** twice

The forward selection results are displayed in Figure 11-25.

```
MTB > Stepwise 'SALARY' 'YRS EM'-'EDUC' 'GENDER' 'SUPER' 'DEPT1'-'DEPT3';
SUBC>    FEnter 4.0;
SUBC>    FRemove 0.

 Stepwise regression of  SALARY  on  8 predictors, with N =    46

       STEP        1        2        3
   CONSTANT    24582    23177    24868

   EDUC         3010     1916     1858
   T-RATIO      8.19     5.05     5.90

   YRS EM                 672      700
   T-RATIO               4.75     5.95

   DEPT1                         -7714
   T-RATIO                       -4.53

   S            7002     5738     4760
   R-SQ        60.37    73.99    82.52
   More? (Yes, No, Subcommand, or Help)
SUBC>
```

The results are identical to those of the general stepwise method (Figure 11-22). Your conclusions remain the same. To end the forward selection procedure without entering any other variables:

- Type **NO** and press ⏎Enter

Using Backward Elimination

In backward elimination, you use the stepwise procedure but input a very high number in the F to enter text box. By using an essentially unattainable value, you ensure that, once deleted, a variable can never re-enter the model. To perform the backward elimination stepwise regression:

- Choose **Edit > Edit Last Command Dialog**

- Select **C2 YRS EM, C3 PRIOR YR, C4 EDUC, C6 GENDER, C8 SUPER, C20 DEPT1, C21 DEPT2,** and **C22 DEPT3** to enter them in the **Enter** text box

- Click the **Options** button to open the Stepwise Options dialog box

- Type **10000** in the **F to enter** text box and press Tab

- Type **4** in the **F to remove** text box and click OK twice

The backward elimination stepwise regression begins with all the predictors in the equation and ends when no variable in the model has an F-statistic less than 4. The six steps (Figure 11-26) appear in the Session window.

Results of backward elimination stepwise regression

```
MTB>  Stepwise 'SALARY' 'YRS EM'-'EDUC' 'GENDER' 'SUPER' 'DEPT1'-'DEPT3';
SUBC>    Enter 'YRS EM'-'EDUC' 'GENDER' 'SUPER' 'DEPT1'-'DEPT3';
SUBC>    FEnter 10000;
SUBC>    FRemove 4.
```

Stepwise regression of SALARY on 8 predictors, with N =   46

STEP	1	2	3	4	5	6
CONSTANT	27409	27525	27149	25803	25297	24868
YRS EM	709	705	708	724	688	700
T-RATIO	5.87	6.02	6.12	6.23	5.96	5.95
PRIOR YR	-73	-72				
T-RATIO	-0.37	-0.37				
EDUC	1545	1549	1552	1590	1638	1858
T-RATIO	4.57	4.65	4.71	4.79	4.88	5.90
GENDER	-2040	-2023	-1915			
T-RATIO	-1.41	-1.42	-1.39			
SUPER	130	129	122	123	132	
T-RATIO	1.59	1.60	1.58	1.57	1.67	
DEPT1	-8096	-8191	-8290	-8080	-7456	-7714
T-RATIO	-4.42	-4.74	-4.91	-4.75	-4.45	-4.53
DEPT2	360					
T-RATIO	0.18					
DEPT3	-3047	-3132	-3102	-2981		
T-RATIO	-1.48	-1.58	-1.58	-1.50		
S	4650	4590	4539	4591	4662	4760
R-SQ	85.31	85.29	85.24	84.51	83.64	82.52

```
 More? (Yes, No, Subcommand, or Help)
SUBC>
```

Step	Results
1	Minitab includes all the variables
2	Minitab eliminates DEPT2; all the other variables remain
3	Minitab eliminates PRIOR YR; all the other variables remain
4	Minitab eliminates GENDER; all the other variables remain
5	Minitab eliminates DEPT3; all the other variables remain
6	Minitab eliminates SUPER; all the other variables remain

The backward elimination process is complete. The only variables left have F-statistics that are greater than 4; again, YRS EM, EDUC, and DEPT1 end up in the salary equation. To end the Stepwise command:

■ Type **NO** and press ⎡←Enter⎤

All three stepwise procedures identified the same variables as important: YRS EM, EDUC, and DEPT1. (Frequently the three procedures yield different regression equations.) You decide not to include the variable SUPER even though it was suggested.

You have completed your regression analysis on the salaries at Technitron and are ready to submit your recommendations. Stepwise analysis helped you determine the best variables to use as predictors. You will recommend a model that uses years at Technitron, years of post-secondary education, and whether an employee is in the Sales Department to determine the salary structure. You will review the salaries of those individuals whose standardized residuals fall above 2 and below –2 to determine why their salaries differ significantly from the estimated average. Your results will be valuable to the management as they determine raises during the next year.

Save your file on your Student disk and stop the outfile:

■ Save your worksheet with the name **11TECHN2** on your Student disk

■ Choose **File > Other Files > Stop Recording Session**

If you plan to continue directly to the next tutorial:

■ Choose **File > Restart Minitab**

If you want to take a longer break:

■ Choose **File > Exit**

Minitab Command Summary

▼

This section describes the Minitab menu commands and Session command introduced in or related to this tutorial. To find a complete explanation of all menus and commands, refer to the Reference section of this manual.

Minitab Menu Commands

Menu	Command	Description
Edit		
	Copy	Copies the highlighted text to the Clipboard
	Paste	Inserts the contents of the Clipboard at the insertion point's location
Calc		
	Make Indicator Variables	Creates indicator (dummy) variables that you can use in a regression analysis
	Standardize	Centers and scales columns of data
Stat		
	Fit Intercept	Specifies whether to include or exclude the intercept in a regression model; lets you perform regression through the origin
	Regression	
	Regression	Performs simple or multiple linear regression
	Stepwise	Performs stepwise regression, using backward elimination, forward selection, or both
	Residual Plot	Provides four residual plots: a normal plot, a histogram, a plot of residuals versus fits, and an I chart
Graph		
	Matrix Plot	Produces a scatter plot matrix of 3 to 10 matrices
	Normal Plot	Draws a normal probability plot that resembles the usual form of normal probability paper

Minitab Session Command

BRIEF K   Controls the amount of output from the Regression (and ARIMA) commands displayed in the Session window; K = 1 produces the least output and K = 3 (4 for ARIMA) displays the most

▼

Review and Practice

▲

Matching

Match the following terms to their definitions by placing the correct letter next to the term it describes.

_____ Time Series Plot

_____ SRES versus FITS plot

_____ HI

_____ Remove

_____ Enter

_____ COOK

_____ INDICATOR

_____ BRIEF

_____ 3

_____ 2

a. The number of major linear regression assumptions

b. The display you can use to check the independence assumption

c. The number of dummy variables that Minitab includes in a regression model when a qualitative variable has three levels

d. Minitab notation for a regression diagnostic statistic that considers standardized residuals with large absolute values and points of large influence

e. The Minitab Session command that you use to control the amount of output produced by the Regression command

f. Minitab notation for the hat matrix diagonal elements

g. The Minitab subcommand that adds one or more variables from the regression model in the Stepwise command

h. The Minitab subcommand that deletes one or more variables from the regression model in the Stepwise command

i. The Minitab Session command for creating dummy variables

j. The display you can use to check constant variation assumption

True/False

Mark the following statements with a *T* or an *F*.

_____ 1. High VIF values indicate the presence of collinearity.

_____ 2. Make Indicator Variables is the Minitab command that creates dummy variables you can use in a regression analysis.

_____ 3. The Normal Plot command provides a choice of two tests: the Anderson-Darling normality test and the Ryan-Joiner W test.

_____ 4. Residuals are estimates of the error component in a regression model.

_____ 5. To end the Stepwise command, you type END at the SUBC> prompt.

_____ 6. You create indicator variables so you can use a qualitative variable as a response variable in a linear regression.

_____ 7. The Stepwise command can perform a forward selection by setting the FREMOVE to a large value.

_____ 8. Minitab identifies an observation that has an unusual standardized residual with an R and prints out the value of its standardized residual.

_____ 9. Minitab identifies an observation that has high leverage with an X and prints out its HI value.

_____ 10. A normal probability plot is an excellent way to check one of the major linear regression assumptions.

Practice Problems

1. Open MNWAGE.MTW.

   a. Perform a simple linear regression to explain the minimum wage based on year.

   b. Attempt to perform a quadratic regression to explain the minimum wage based on year and year squared. You cannot perform this analysis due to extreme collinearity. Verify this fact by computing the correlation coefficient between these two variables.

   c. Perform a quadratic regression to explain the minimum wage based on a centered year variable and a centered year squared variable. Is there any problem with collinearity in this model? Briefly explain your answer.

2. Open HOMES.MTW.

   a. Perform a simple linear regression with C1 PRICE as the response variable and C2 AREA as the predictor variable.

   b. Is there collinearity present in this model?

   c. Discuss any unusual observations.

   d. Perform a complete residual analysis using the techniques introduced in this tutorial. Are you comfortable with constructing interval estimates and performing hypotheses based on this model?

   e. Perform a residual analysis using the Residual Plot command. Compare this analysis with the analysis in part d.

3. Open CRIMES.MTW.

   a. Create four indicator variables for the qualitative variable C3 REGION. Name your indicator variables REGION1, REGION2, REGION3, and REGION4.

   b. Perform a multiple linear regression to explain CRIMERTE based on REGION1, REGION2, and REGION3.

   c. What is this model's F-statistic value and corresponding p-value?

   d. Perform a one-way ANOVA with CRIMERTE as the response variable and REGION as the factor. (Choose Stat > ANOVA > Oneway.)

   e. What is this model's F-statistic value and corresponding p-value? They should equal the values you reported in part c because regression and ANOVA are related analyses.

4. Open HOMES.MTW.

   a. Perform a stepwise multiple regression to determine a model to estimate C1 PRICE using stepwise selection.

   b. Repeat step a using forward selection.

   c. Repeat step a using backward elimination.

   d. Did you obtain the same models in parts a, b, and c? Would you expect to obtain the same model? Briefly explain your answer.

5. Open NOTE.MTW. Use stepwise and multiple linear regression to determine which of the variables in the data set affect the price of a computer. Note that many of the variables are not numeric; you need to "dummy them up" (provide numeric equivalents). Be sure to consider the unusual observations and to perform a complete residual analysis.

TUTORIAL
12

Analyzing Categorical Data

Most of the data you worked with in previous tutorials were quantitative. In this tutorial, you use Minitab to make statistical decisions about categorical data. First you perform a goodness-of-fit test for simulated employee-size class data. Then, as an intern in a marketing research firm, you test for independence of variables. In both cases, you use the chi-square distribution.

Objectives

In this tutorial, you learn how to:

- compare an observed distribution to a hypothesized distribution

- test the relationship between two categorical variables using a contingency table in the worksheet

- test the relationship between two categorical variables, using Minitab to construct the contingency table with data in the worksheet

CASE STUDY: MANAGEMENT — ENTREPRENEURIAL STUDIES (CONTINUED)

In Tutorial 7, you learned how to test hypotheses using data from binomial experiments (those with two categorical outcomes for each trial, such as winning or losing an election). You now examine *multinomial experiments*, which have more than two categorical outcomes for each trial. Recall that in your management class (Tutorial 6) you simulated employee-size class data for probabilities generated by information found in the *Statistical Abstract of the United States 1993*. These five probabilities were 0.2607, 0.2933, 0.2453, 0.0701, and 0.1306.

Dr. Michaels asks you to check how well the distribution of your simulated 1000 firms matches the given discrete distribution. You will use a chi-square *goodness-of-fit test* with these hypotheses:

H_0: There is no change in distribution. The simulated firms have 26.07% in class 1, 29.33% in class 2, 24.53% in class 3, 7.01% in class 4, and 13.06% in class 5.

H_1: The distribution changes.

Comparing an Observed Distribution to a Hypothesized Distribution

In Tutorial 6, you saved the worksheet containing your simulated class data as 6FIRM.MTW. The file ECLASS.MTW contains data from the same procedures you performed in Tutorial 6. In this tutorial, you use ECLASS.MTW to ensure that you get the same results as in this manual.

To get started:

- Start Minitab and maximize the Minitab window and the Data window

- Start an outfile named **T12** on your Student disk

- Open **ECLASS.MTW**

The first two columns of the worksheet display the five numeric values of the employee-size classes (C1 CLASS) and the corresponding probabilities (C2 PROB). C3 SAMPLE lists the classes from your random sample of 1000 firms. Minitab does not have a single command to perform the chi-square goodness-of-fit test, but in earlier tutorials you saw the commands necessary to perform the test.

You use Minitab to perform the chi-square goodness-of-fit calculations, using the formula:

$$\chi^2 = \sum \frac{(\text{Obs}-\text{Exp})^2}{\text{Exp}}$$

where Obs and Exp are the observed and expected number of firms from a given class, respectively. You then calculate the p-value by comparing the observed chi-square value to a chi-square distribution with $5 - 1 = 4$ degrees of freedom.

For your sample data, use the Tally command to compute the observed values for each of the five categories:

- Choose **Stat > Tables > Tally**

- Double-click **C3 SAMPLE** to enter it in the **Variables** text box

- Click **OK**

The Session window displays the counts (Figure 12-1).

FIGURE 12-1

Tally of employee-size class

```
MTB > Retrieve  'C:\MTBSEW\STUDENT9\ECLASS.MTW'.
Retrieving worksheet from file: C:\MTBSEW\STUDENT9\ECLASS.MTW
Worksheet was saved on 2/2/1994
MTB > Tally 'SAMPLE';
SUBC>   Counts.

   SAMPLE   COUNT
        1     274
        2     290
        3     243
        4      64
        5     129
       N=    1000

MTB >
```

Store these observed values in C4:

- Return to the Data window and click the data-entry arrow so that it is pointing down

- Type the name **OBSERVED** as the name row entry for column C4 and then click C4 row 1

- Type **274**, **290**, **243**, **64**, and **129** in the first five rows of C4 (be sure to press ⏎Enter or ↓ after entering each number)

Obtain the expected number under H_0 for each class by multiplying its probability (stored in C2 PROB) by the sample size, 1000. To compute the expected frequencies:

- Choose **Calc > Mathematical Expressions**

- Type **EXPECTED** in the **Variable (new or modified)** text box and press Tab twice

- Type **'PROB'*1000** in the **Expression** text box and press ⏎Enter

C5 EXPECTED now lists the expected numbers: 260.7, 293.3, 245.3, 70.1, and 130.6.

To compute the chi-square statistic, first compute the $(\text{Obs} - \text{Exp})^2/\text{Exp}$ value for each employment class:

- Choose **Edit > Edit Last Command Dialog**

- Type **CHISQR** in the **Variable (new or modified)** text box and press Tab twice

- Type **(C4-C5)**2/C5** in the **Expression** text box and press ⏎Enter

The Data window should resemble Figure 12-2.

	C1	C2	C3	C4	C5	C6	C7	C8
	CLASS	PROB	SAMPLE	OBSERVED	EXPECTED	CHISQR		
1	1	0.2607	4	274	260.7	0.678521		
2	2	0.2933	4	290	293.3	0.037129		
3	3	0.2453	3	243	245.3	0.021565		
4	4	0.0701	2	64	70.1	0.530813		
5	5	0.1306	1	129	130.6	0.019602		

To obtain the chi-square statistic, sum the individual chi-square values in C6 CHISQR and store the total in constant location K1 for later use (refer to Tutorial 2, "Summarizing Columns," if necessary, to review constants):

- Choose **Calc > Column Statistics** and select **Sum** if necessary
- Click the **Input variable** text box and then double-click **C6 CHISQR**
- Click **Store result in** and press ⎋Tab
- Type **CHISQRST** and press ⏎Enter
- Go to the Session window

The chi-square statistic is 1.2876, the sum of C6 CHISQR (Figure 12-3).

```
MTB > Name c5 = 'EXPECTED'
MTB > Let 'EXPECTED' = 'PROB'*1000
MTB > Name c6 = 'CHISQR'
MTB > Let 'CHISQR' = (C4-C5)**2/C5
MTB > Name k1 = 'CHISQRST'
MTB > Sum 'CHISQR' 'CHISQRST'.
   SUM    =       1.2876
MTB >
```

To determine whether there is significant evidence that the simulated frequencies differ from the given frequencies, name the two constants and then compute the p-value of the observed statistic:

- Type **NAME K2 '1-PVAL'** at the MTB > prompt and press ⏎Enter
- Type **NAME K3 'PVAL'** and press ⏎Enter
- Choose **Calc > Probability Distributions > Chisquare**
- Click **Cumulative probability**
- Press ⎋Tab and type **4** in the **Degrees of freedom** text box (the degrees of freedom in this case study are obtained by subtracting one from the number of categories: 5–1)

- Click **Input constant** and press Tab

- Double-click **K1 CHISQRST**

- Type **K2** in the **Optional storage** text box and press ↵Enter

    The cumulative probability function computes the probability of a value being less than or equal to the input value. To compute the p-value:

- Type **LET K3=1-K2** after the Minitab prompt (MTB >) in the Session window and press ↵Enter

- Type **PRINT K3** and press ↵Enter

    The bottom of the Session window should resemble Figure 12-4.

FIGURE 12-4

The Session window with p-value of 0.863471

```
MTB > NAME K2 '1-PVAL'
MTB > NAME K3 'PVAL'
MTB > CDF 'CHISQRST' K2;
SUBC>    Chisquare 4.
MTB > LET K3 = 1-K2
MTB > PRINT K3

PVAL      0.863471
MTB >
```

Since the p-value of the chi-square statistic is 0.863471, fail to reject the null hypothesis at any reasonable significance level and conclude that the distribution has not changed. In your class report, note that you can use these 1000 cases to simulate the employee-size class of United States firms in 1993.

Save your file on your Student disk and clear the worksheet:

- Save your worksheet with the name **12ECLASS** on your Student disk

- Choose **File > Other Files > Stop Recording Session**

- Choose **File > Restart Minitab**

CASE STUDY: MARKETING — MARKET RESEARCH

As an intern in a market research firm, your supervisor presents you with a 4×5 contingency table based on a well-conducted survey that contains the number of individuals who last bought jeans from four major stores, classified according to their approximate yearly total household income before taxes. Your supervisor asks you to determine if the stores are independent of the salary category (salary is often placed in categories to avoid nonresponse). If the two variables are dependent on each other, differently priced jeans might be heavily marketed at different stores. For example, a store that seemed to attract wealthier shoppers might display higher-priced jeans.

Testing the Relationship Between Two Categorical Variables in a Contingency Table

Display the data stored in the file STORES.MTW:

- Maximize the Minitab window and the Data window

- Start the T12 outfile again on your Student disk; Minitab appends the subsequent session record to your previous outfile

- Open **STORES.MTW**

The Data window displays the contingency table. The first column lists the number of each store. The next five columns list the number of individuals who last bought jeans at each store by income category. The lowest and highest categories have been combined to ensure that there are not too many cells with small expected frequencies.

To test for the independence of variables, first formulate the hypotheses:

H_0: Store and income are independent.

H_1: Store and income are dependent.

To run the test:

- Choose **Stat > Tables > Chisquare Test**

- Highlight **C2 UNDER25K, C3 25KTO35K, C4 35KTO50K, C5 50KTO75K,** and **C6 75K&OVER** and then click **Select**

The completed Chisquare Test dialog box should resemble Figure 12-5.

FIGURE 12-5

The completed Chisquare Test dialog box

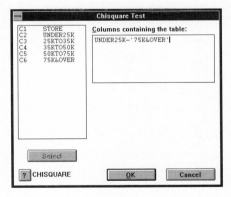

- Click **OK**

- Go to the Session window

The Session window (Figure 12-6) displays the results of the chi-square test.

```
MTB > Retrieve 'C:\MTBSEW\STUDENT9\STORES.MTW'.
Retrieving worksheet from file: C:\MTBSEW\STUDENT9\STORES.MTW
Worksheet was saved on  2/ 1/1994
MTB > ChiSquare 'UNDER25K'-'75K&OVER'.

Expected counts are printed below observed counts

        UNDER25K 25KTO35K 35KTO50K 50KTO75K 75K&OVER   Total
    1        14       10       24       12        3       63
          12.77    10.82    19.48    12.77     7.14

    2        21       22       29       15        3       90
          18.25    15.46    27.84    18.25    10.21

    3        11        8       14       17       14       64
          12.98    11.00    19.79    12.98     7.26

    4        13       10       23       15       13       74
          15.00    12.71    22.89    15.00     8.39

Total        59       50       90       59       33      291

ChiSq =  0.118 +  0.063 +  1.046 +  0.047 +  2.404 +
         0.415 +  2.763 +  0.049 +  0.578 +  5.088 +
         0.301 +  0.817 +  1.696 +  1.248 +  6.263 +
         0.268 +  0.580 +  0.001 +  0.000 +  2.531 = 26.273
df = 12

MTB >
```

Minitab prints the expected counts below the observed counts for each cell. It then lists the individual chi-square contributions from each cell and sums them to obtain the chi-square statistic, 26.273. From this, you can see which cells contribute the most to the chi-square total. Note that fewer than expected individuals with incomes of $75,000 and over bought their last pair of jeans at stores 4 and 5 (rows 1 and 2); on the other hand, more people in this income bracket than expected made purchases at stores 6 and 10 (rows 3 and 4). The degrees of freedom of the chi-square statistic (D.F. = 12) appears last.

To determine the p-value for this test:

- Choose **Calc > Probability Distributions > Chisquare**

- Click **Cumulative probability**

- Click the **Degrees of freedom** text box and type **12**

- Click **Input constant** and press (Tab)

- Type **26.273** in the **Input constant** text box and press (Tab)

- Type **K1** and press (←Enter)

After the MTB > prompt in the Session window:

- Type **LET K2=1-K1** and press (←Enter)

- Type **PRINT K2** and press (←Enter)

Minitab prints a value of 0.00981158 for K2 (the p-value), so reject H_0 at levels of 0.01 and 0.05. you inform your supervisor that store and income are dependent, as stated in H_1. You also mention that a major contribution of the chi-square statistic comes from the individuals whose income is $75,000 and over.

- Save your worksheet with the name **12STORES** on your Student disk

- Choose **File > Other Files > Stop Recording Session**

- Choose **File > Restart Minitab**

Testing the Relationship Between Two Categorical Variables Using Raw Data

You ask your supervisor if you can examine the actual raw data from which the table was constructed. If so, you can perform additional analyses, such as calculating contingency table percentages. You can also compute the chi-square statistic from these data. She tells you that the data are stored in the file JEANSB.MTW.

Note: Because of the large quantity of data, the JEANS data have been divided into three files: JEANSA, JEANSB, and JEANSC. You'll work with just JEANSB in this tutorial, which contains the data in C5-C8.

- Maximize the Minitab window and the Data window

- Start the T12 outfile again on your Sudent disk; Minitab appends the subsequent session record to your previous outfile

- Open **JEANSB.MTW** and scroll right if necessary

To continue your assignment, you want to ascertain whether there is a relationship between store and income. First, set up the two hypotheses:

H_0: Store and income are independent.

H_1: Store and income are dependent.

Now you must modify the data in JEANSB.MTW. First, you change its missing value codes of 999 to *. Second, you transform the column identifying the stores into a new column so that only the observations with codes of the four stores you want to work with are not missing. Third, you collapse the income data into five categories. You use the Code Data Values command to make all of these modifications.

Caution: When you use the Chisquare command from the previous section, Minitab warns you if you have expected cell counts below 5 or expected cell counts below 1. However, the Tables command you use here does not issue this warning; keep this in mind when defining your categories.

To change the missing values code 999 to *:

- Choose **Manip > Code Data Values**

- Select **C5 EMPLOY** through **C8 JEANSHOP** and click **Select** to enter them in the **Code data from columns** text box and press Ⓣab

- Select **C5 EMPLOY** through **C8 JEANSHOP** and click **Select** to enter them in the **Into columns** text box and press Ⓣab

- Type **999** in the **Original values** text box, press Ⓣab, type *, and then press ⏎Enter

Now all of the values of 999 have been replaced by the Minitab missing value code of *. Now code the data in JEANSHOP so that only the codes for stores 4, 5, 6, and 10 are present; all the other entries are missing (you'll store the transformed data in C14 so that if you ever do want to merge the three JEANS files back together again, you won't have to move columns):

- Choose **Edit > Edit Last Command Dialog**

- Select **C8 JEANSHOP** to enter it in the **Code data from columns** text box and press Ⓣab

- Type **C14** in the **Into columns** text box and press Ⓣab

- Type **1:3 7:9 11:12** in the **Original values** text box and press ⏎Enter

- Name C14 **'JEANSHOP'** and press ⏎Enter

Minitab codes the data for only stores 4, 5, 6, and 10 in C14 JEANSHP2; the other stores are missing.

Finally, collapse the income data into five categories:

■ Choose **Edit > Edit Last Command Dialog**

■ Select **C7 INCOME** to enter it in the **Code data from columns** text box and press Ⓣ Tab

■ Type **C15** in the **Into columns** text box and press ⓉTab

■ Type **1:2** in the first **Original values** text box, press ⓉTab, type **1**, and then press ⓉTab

■ Type **6:7**, press ⓉTab, type **7**, and then press ↵Enter

■ Name C15 **'INCOME2'** and press ↵Enter

C15 INCOME2 now contains values that correspond to the five categories present in the original contingency table.

Create the contingency table from the data in C14 JEANSHP2 and C15 INCOME2:

■ Choose **Stat > Tables > Cross Tabulation**

■ Double-click **C14 JEANSHP2** and **C15 INCOME2** to enter them in the **Classification Variables** text box

■ Click the **Chisquare analysis** check box

The completed Cross Tabulation dialog box should look like Figure 12-7.

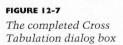

FIGURE 12-7

The completed Cross Tabulation dialog box

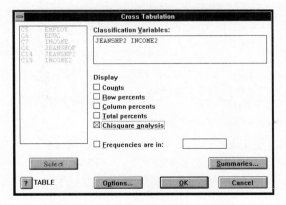

■ Click **OK**

Minitab displays the contingency table and chi-square test results in the Session window (Figure 12-8).

```
MTB > Code (999) '*' 'EMPLOY'-'JEANSHOP' 'EMPLOY'-'JEANSHOP'
MTB > Code (1:3 7:9 11:12) '*' 'JEANSHOP' C14
MTB > Code (1:2) 1 (6:7) 7 'INCOME' C15
MTB > Table 'JEANSHP2' 'INCOME2';
SUBC>   ChiSquare.


     ROWS: JEANSHP2    COLUMNS: INCOME2

                1        3        4        5        7      ALL

         4     14       10       24       12        3       63
         5     21       22       29       15        3       90
         6     11        8       14       17       14       64
        10     13       10       23       15       13       74
       ALL     59       50       90       59       33      291

    CHI-SQUARE =    26.273   WITH D.F. =    12

      CELL CONTENTS --
                    COUNT

MTB >
```

Minitab displays the four stores (4, 5, 6, and 10) in the first column. The next five columns contain the counts of the coded income ranges. Each cell contains a count. The chi-square statistic (26.273) and the degrees of freedom for this table (12) appear last, with a note that the contents of each cell represent a count.

Compute the p-value to determine whether the chi-square statistic of 26.273 with 12 degrees of freedom is significant:

- Choose **Calc > Probability Distributions > Chisquare**

- Click **Cumulative probability**

- Click the **Degrees of freedom** text box and type **12**

- Click **Input constant** and press (Tab)

- Type **26.273** in the **Input constant** text box and press (Tab)

- Type **K1** in the **Optional storage** text box and press (←Enter)

- Type **LET K2=1-K1** after the MTB > prompt and press (←Enter)

- Type **PRINT K2** and press (←Enter)

The Session window (Figure 12-9) shows that the p-value, represented by K2 for this test, is 0.00981158.

FIGURE 12-9

The p-value for the chi-square statistic

```
MTB > CDF 26.273 K1;
SUBC>   Chisquare 12.
MTB > LET K2 = 1-K1
MTB > PRINT K2

K2      0.00981158
MTB >
```

On the basis of the p-value, you reject H$_0$. Your data indicate that store and income are dependent.

You would like more detail on the income distribution. In particular, you want to determine the percentage of individuals in each income category. The Tables command offers subcommand options that display more information:

- Choose **Stat > Tables > Cross Tabulation**

- Click the **Counts**, **Row percents**, **Column percents**, and **Total percents** options to select them

- Click the **Chisquare analysis** check box to deselect it

- Click **OK**

Each cell shown in Figure 12-10 contains the count, the row percent, the column percent, and the total percent, as described by Minitab at the bottom of the output.

FIGURE 12-10

The Session window, with percentages of individuals in various categories

```
MTB > Table 'JEANSHP2' 'INCOME2';
SUBC>    Counts;
SUBC>    RowPercents;
SUBC>    ColPercents;
SUBC>    TotPercents.


     ROWS: JEANSHP2     COLUMNS: INCOME2

               1         3         4         5         7       ALL

      4        14        10        24        12         3        63
             22.22     15.87     38.10     19.05      4.76    100.00
             23.73     20.00     26.67     20.34      9.09     21.65
              4.81      3.44      8.25      4.12      1.03     21.65

      5        21        22        29        15         3        90
             23.33     24.44     32.22     16.67      3.33    100.00
             35.59     44.00     32.22     25.42      9.09     30.93
              7.22      7.56      9.97      5.15      1.03     30.93

      6        11         8        14        17        14        64
             17.19     12.50     21.87     26.56     21.87    100.00
             18.64     16.00     15.56     28.81     42.42     21.99
              3.78      2.75      4.81      5.84      4.81     21.99

     10        13        10        23        15        13        74
             17.57     13.51     31.08     20.27     17.57    100.00
             22.03     20.00     25.56     25.42     39.39     25.43
              4.47      3.44      7.90      5.15      4.47     25.43

    ALL        59        50        90        59        33       291
             20.27     17.18     30.93     20.27     11.34    100.00
            100.00    100.00    100.00    100.00    100.00    100.00
             20.27     17.18     30.93     20.27     11.34    100.00

     CELL CONTENTS --
                     COUNT
                     % OF ROW
                     % OF COL
                     % OF TBL

MTB >
```

Store 10, household income of less than $25,000 — (points to row 10)

Look at the cell describing individuals who last purchased jeans from store 10 and whose households earn less than $25,000. There are 13 individuals in this category, representing 17.57% of the store 10 shoppers and 22.03% of all the individuals with incomes in this category. The individuals in this cell represent 4.47% of the individuals currently in the study.

Note that the chi-square test is an option available with the Cross Tabulation command. Typically you request the summary information and the test with the same command.

Save your file on your Student disk.

■ Choose **File > Other Files > Stop Recording Session**

■ Save your worksheet with the name **12JEANSB** on your Student disk

In this tutorial, you used the chi-square statistic to perform a goodness-of-fit test and tests for independence of variables on categorical data. In the next tutorial, you use Minitab to perform nonparametric analyses in which you make fewer assumptions about the distribution of the data than you did in the analyses considered in earlier tutorials.

If you plan to continue directly to the next tutorial:

■ Choose **File > Restart Minitab**

If you want to take a longer break:

■ Choose **File > Exit**

▼
Minitab Command Summary
▲

This section describes the Minitab menu commands introduced in or related to this tutorial. To find a complete explanation of all menus and commands, refer to the Reference section of this manual.

Minitab Menu Commands

Menu	Command	Description
Stat		
	Tables	
	Cross Tabulation	Performs a contingency table analysis using numeric raw data comprised of integers, from which Minitab computes the contingency table
	Tally	Calculates a count (or frequency) of each value of an integer variable
	Chisquare Test	Performs contingency table analysis using a table in the worksheet

Review and Practice

▼

Review and Practice

▲

Matching

Match the following terms to their definitions by placing the correct letter next to the term it describes.

_____ D.F.

_____ expected frequency

_____ observed frequency

_____ Chisquare Test

_____ K

_____ total percents

_____ Cross Tabulation

_____ C

_____ number of categories less 1

_____ (number of rows less 1) × (number of columns less 1)

a. A Minitab command on the Tables submenu that generates the chi-square test of independence from two categorical variables

b. The number of sample items with a given characteristic

c. A statistic presented by default in the Minitab Chisquare Test output

d. Ratios of observed counts to sum of counts in a contingency table multiplied by 100

e. A Minitab command on the Tables submenu that generates the chi-square test of independence from a table of observed counts

f. A Minitab notation for the degrees of freedom of a chi-square statistic

g. Minitab notation for a stored constant

h. Minitab notation for a stored column

i. Degrees of freedom for a chi-square test for independence

j. Degrees of freedom for a chi-square goodness-of-fit test

True/False

Mark the following statements with a *T* or an *F*.

_____ 1. You use the Fit command to perform chi-square goodness-of-fit tests in Minitab.

_____ 2. When computing p-values for the chi-square test, you must always store intermediate results as constants.

_____ 3. To combine columns prior to using the chi-square test, use the Minitab Code command.

_____ 4. Percent rows, Percent cols, and Percent tols are Minitab options available on the Tables dialog boxes that produce percentage summaries.

_____ 5. You can use alpha data columns with the Cross Tabulation command but not the Tally command.

_____ 6. When you are using the Tally command, you can obtain both the cell's chi-square value and its standardized value by clicking the appropriate options.

_____ 7. Minitab provides the chi-square's p-value when you perform a chi-square test of independence.

_____ 8. The Sum function is the default for the Column Statistics command.

_____ 9. In addition to the chi-square statistic, Minitab also prints the contribution of each cell when you choose the Chisquare Test command.

_____ 10. The Cross Tabulation command automatically shows marginal totals.

Practice Problems

1. Many states have lotto games. In a certain state, you pay $1 and choose six numbers between 1 and 47. If your numbers match those selected, you win. Each Friday, the state publishes a summary of how many times each number has been drawn in all of the drawings. If the drawings are random, then you would expect to see each number the same number of times.

   The file LOTTO.MTW contains the state lotto information. Rows 1 through 47 contain the frequency with which that number has been drawn over the past three years of a particular state's biweekly lotto drawing. Determine if there is any indication that the drawings are not random.

2. Analyze the PROF.MTW data to determine whether the level of the class and the instructor's rating are independent. First, code the instructor's rating variable with these intervals: 1 up to 2, 2 up to 2.5, 2.5 up to 3, 3 up to 3.5, and 3.5 to 4. You might code the ratings in the following order: (3.5:4) code to 5, (3:3.5) code to 4, (2.5:3) code to 3, (2:2.5) code to 2, and (1:2) code to 1. The order is important because Minitab codes sequentially, and this ensures that the boundary points are coded to the higher value.

3. Use the NOTE.MTW data to determine whether the type of monitor and the type of pointing device are independent. You need to convert each of these variables from an alpha variable to a numeric variable.

4. To combine categories when using the Cross Tabulation command on the Tables submenu, you usually code the variables. To combine categories when using the Chisquare Test command on the Tables submenu, you usually sum variables. Use the STORES.MTW data to determine whether store and salary are independent when there are three income categories: UNDER35K, 35KTO50K, and 50K&OVER. Compare your resulting p-value with the one obtained in the tutorial.

5. Open NOTE.MTW.

   a. Construct a contingency table from the CHIP and SPEED variables. You need to convert the CHIP variable from an alpha variable to a numeric variable. How many SX-chip machines have a speed of 25?

   b. Construct a related contingency table with counts, row percents, column percents, and total percents. Explain the meaning of all the numbers in the cell for SX-chip machines with a speed of 25.

   c. Construct another related contingency table that performs a chi-square analysis. What is the value of the test statistic? What is the associated degrees of freedom?

   d. Verify that it is inappropriate to use the chi-square statistic found in part c by entering the counts of the contingency table into two columns and using the Chisquare Test command.

TUTORIAL 13

Analyzing Data with Nonparametric Methods

Until now, the techniques you have used to make inferences about parameters have required random samples and populations that were approximately normally distributed. In this tutorial, you check data for randomness and analyze data from populations that are not necessarily normally distributed. Techniques that require less stringent assumptions about the nature of the population probability distributions are called *nonparametric* statistical methods.

Objectives

In this tutorial, you learn how to:

- check a sampling process for randomness
- compare the median of a population to a constant
- compare the medians of two populations
- compare the medians of more than two populations

CASE STUDY: METEOROLOGY — SNOWFALL

Since the late 1880s, the United States government has collected snowfall measurements. In your meteorology class, Professor Russell asks you to determine whether the yearly amount of snowfall between 1962 and 1993 for a major United States city followed a random pattern. The presence of a nonrandom pattern would be of interest to many people, like municipal authorities who allocate money for snow removal. The data are stored in SNOW.MTW.

To get started:

- Start Minitab and maximize the Minitab window and the Data window

- Start an outfile named **T13** on your Student disk

- Open **SNOW.MTW**

    C1 YEAR lists the year for each measurement and C2 SNOWFALL shows the amount of snowfall in inches. (C3 RAIN is the corresponding amount of rainfall in inches for the actual amount of snowfall.)

Plotting a Sequence

It is hard to determine by looking at the data whether this sequence of 32 snowfall measurements is random. You decide to construct Character and Professional time series plots to get a better picture of the snowfall data over time. (You constructed a time series plot in Tutorial 3.)

Character Time Series Plot

To create the Character time series plot:

- Choose **Graph > Character Graphs > Time Series Plot**

- Double-click **C2 SNOWFALL** to enter it in the first **Series** text box

- Type **1962** in the first **Origin** text box

- Click the **Period** option and press (Tab)

- Type **10** in the **Period** text box

    The completed Time Series Plot dialog box should look like Figure 13-1.

FIGURE 13-1

The completed Time Series Plot dialog box

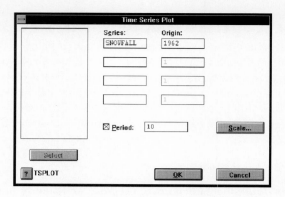

- Press (←Enter)

The time series plot appears in the Session window (Figure 13-2).

FIGURE 13-2

Character time series plot

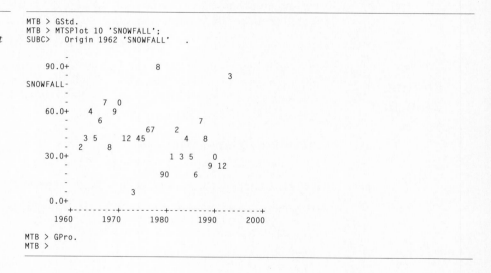

Minitab plots snowfall on the vertical axis and the year on the horizontal axis. It assigns a digit to the unit portion of each year. The plot indicates a slight downward trend in the amount of snowfall over the 32 years with outlying values in 1973, 1978, and 1993. There seems to be a random pattern of snowfall amounts, but it is difficult to see in this plot.

Professional Time Series Plot

Now construct the Professional time series plot:

- Choose **Graph > Time Series Plot**

- Select **C2 SNOWFALL** to enter it in the first **Y** text box in the **Graph variables** section

- Click **Options**

- Verify that **Index** is selected

- Click the **Start time** text box and type **1962**

- Click **OK** twice

  The time series plot appears in the Graph window (Figure 13-3).

FIGURE 13-3

Professional time series plot

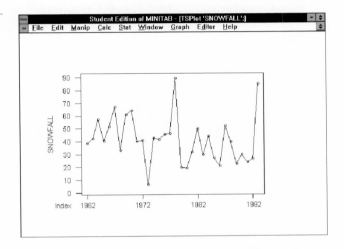

Notice that each snowfall value connects to the next one with a straight line. The irregular pattern of high and low snowfalls evidenced by these connected line segments seem to indicate a random pattern (a pattern in which what happens in one year does not affect what happens in another year).

▼

Checking a Sampling Process for Randomness with the Runs Test

▲

To determine whether you have statistical evidence to conclude nonrandomness, you perform a runs test. A *runs test* is a procedure that helps you determine if the order of the data is random. In some of the tests considered in previous tutorials, you had to assume that the data were randomly ordered. Now, you use the runs test to verify that assumption.

A *run* is a series of consecutive observations that either fall above a specified constant (the default is the sample mean), or fall on or below the specified constant. You use Minitab to determine whether your data have too few or too many runs.

First set up the hypotheses:

H_0: The values of the sampling process are random.

H_1: The values of the sampling process are not random.

Use Minitab to test the null hypothesis:

- Choose **Stat** > **Nonparametrics** > **Runs Test**
- Double-click **C2 SNOWFALL** to enter it in the **Variables** text box

The completed Runs Test dialog box looks like Figure 13-4.

FIGURE 13-4

The completed Runs Test dialog box

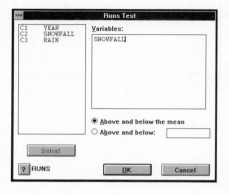

- Click **OK**

The Session window (Figure 13-5) appears.

FIGURE 13-5

The Session window, showing the results of the runs test

```
MTB > Runs 'SNOWFALL'.

    SNOWFALL

    K =     41.5344


    The observed no. of runs =   18
    The expected no. of runs =   16.7500
    14 Observations above K    18 below
            The test is significant at   0.6480
            Cannot reject at alpha = 0.05

MTB >
```

Minitab used the sample mean, K = 41.5344, as the constant. In all, there were 18 observed runs. (You can verify this from the raw data.) When there are too many or too few runs, the sample is in nonrandom order.

Minitab calculates that the expected number of runs is 16.75, assuming a random process, and displays the number of observations above and below the constant. The p-value for this test is 0.6480, so do not reject H_0 at the 0.05 level of significance. You report to your meteorology class that you cannot reject the hypothesis that the pattern of the amount of yearly snowfall is random. Hence city planners do not have any evidence to request more or less money for snow removal in future years. (Note that Tutorial 15 discusses additional ways to analyze a time series.)

- Choose **File** > **Other Files** > **Stop Recording Session**

- Choose **File** > **Restart Minitab**

Testing the Population Median with the Wilcoxon Test

In Tutorial 7, you constructed a confidence interval and used a t-test to make inferences about the value of a population mean, under the assumption that the populations were nearly normal. In Tutorial 8, you used a t-test and constructed a confidence interval to make inferences about the value of a population mean of the difference between two dependent populations, again assuming nearly normal populations.

In this tutorial, you could use two of Minitab's nonparametric techniques — the Sign and Wilcoxon tests — to determine the central tendency of a population that is not necessarily normal. The Sign test requires only an ordinal measurement scale, while the Wilcoxon test requires at least an interval measurement scale.

CASE STUDY: FINANCE — MORTGAGE INTEREST RATES (CONTINUED)

In Tutorial 8, your finance professor asked you to investigate the perception that 30-year mortgage interest rates decreased in the last year. You concluded that mean rates had decreased at a 1% level of significance. You also constructed a 98% confidence interval for the mean difference in the rates. For both of these analyses you assumed that the difference between the rates was normally distributed. Now Professor Ruiz informs you that this assumption is false (you can use a normal probability plot to verify this statement) and asks you to perform related nonparametric inferences.

You decide to perform the Wilcoxon test on the data in MORT.MTW because the rates are measured on an interval scale.

- Start the T13 outfile again; Minitab appends the subsequent session record to your previous outfile

- Open **MORT.MTW**

C1 30YR1992 and C2 30YR1993 contain the mortgage interest rates (in percentages) in 1992 and 1993, respectively, for each of the six lenders in the study. Compute the differences between the interest rates in these two years and place the results in C3:

- Choose **Calc** > **Mathematical Expressions**

- Type **'D=92-93'** in the **Variable (new or modified)** text box and press Tab twice

- Type **C1-C2** in the **Expressions** text box

- Press ⏎Enter

Minitab stores each difference in C3. Now, form the hypotheses:

H_0: Median = 0.

H_1: Median > 0.

The alternative hypothesis is upper-tailed, since your difference is the 1992 rates minus the 1993 rates. If mortgage rates had dropped over time, the 1993 values would be smaller than the 1992 ones, and the median difference would be greater than 0.

To perform the Wilcoxon test:

- Choose **Stat > Nonparametrics > 1-Sample Wilcoxon**

- Double-click **C3 D=92-93** to enter it in the **Variables** text box

- Click **Test median**

Since you are testing a median difference of 0, use the default of 0.0.

- Choose **greater than** in the **Alternative** drop-down list box

The completed 1-Sample Wilcoxon dialog box should look like Figure 13-6.

FIGURE 13-6

The completed 1-Sample Wilcoxon dialog box

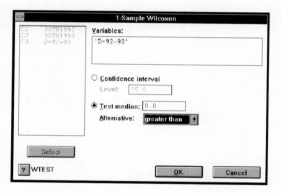

- Click **OK**

The Session window appears (Figure 13-7).

FIGURE 13-7

The Session window, showing results of the Wilcoxon test

```
MTB > WTest 0.0 'D=92-93';
SUBC>   Alternative 1.

TEST OF MEDIAN = 0.000000 VERSUS MEDIAN G.T. 0.000000

                      N FOR   WILCOXON            ESTIMATED
               N      TEST    STATISTIC  P-VALUE  MEDIAN
D=92-93        6      6       21.0       0.018    1.118
MTB >
```

The p-value for this test is 0.018, so you would reject the null hypothesis at the 0.05 level (but fail to reject it at the 0.01 level). The estimated median of 1.118% suggests that 1993 mortgage rates have indeed decreased from 1992. Note that the median of the six differences is 1.1185; 1.118% is the median of the Walsh averages (pairwise averages of all pairs of data points).

▼ Estimating the Population Median with the Wilcoxon Interval Estimate ▲

Minitab can form a confidence interval for the median just as it did for the mean.

- Choose **Edit > Edit Last Command Dialog**
- Click **Confidence interval** and press [Tab]
- Type **98** in the **Level** text box
- Press [←Enter]

Minitab displays the 96.4% confidence interval for the median as (0.866, 1.142), as shown in Figure 13-8.

FIGURE 13-8

The nonparametric confidence interval

```
MTB > WInterval 98 'D=92-93'.

              ESTIMATED   ACHIEVED
          N    MEDIAN    CONFIDENCE   CONFIDENCE INTERVAL
D=92-93   6    1.118       96.4     (  0.866,   1.142)
MTB >
```

In many nonparametric procedures, the degree of confidence that Minitab generates won't exactly match your request. For example, in this case, Minitab achieves a 96.4% level confidence interval. It would appear that the median rate difference from 1992 to 1993 is between 0.866 and 1.142%. Is it time to start looking for a new home?

Now save your file on your Student disk.

- Save your worksheet with the name **13MORT** on your Student disk
- Choose **File > Other Files> Stop Recording Session**
- Choose **File > Restart Minitab**

▼ Comparing the Medians of Two Independent Populations with the Mann-Whitney Procedure ▲

In Tutorial 8, you performed t-tests for the equality of two population means, assuming near normality. The Mann-Whitney (Wilcoxon) procedure is the nonparametric counterpart of the independent 2-sample t-test. It uses a 2-sample rank test to compare two population medians. It then computes the corresponding point and confidence interval estimates of the difference between these medians.

CASE STUDY: SOCIOLOGY — DEATH AGE (CONTINUED)

In Tutorial 8, you investigated whether there was a difference in the mean age at death between men and women, as reported in a newspaper. You concluded that there was no significant difference based on the sample. Now you investigate whether there is a difference in the median age at death between men and women, based on the same data.

You decide to explore this possibility even though the assumptions are reasonable. Some statisticians maintain that if parametric and nonparametric procedures yield the same results, then these results are more credible and the conclusions strengthened.

The file AGE.MTW contains data from the study. C1 DAGEF displays the age at death of 19 females; C2 DAGEM shows the age at death of 18 males.

■ Start the T13 outfile again on your Student disk; Minitab appends the subsequent session record to your previous outfile

■ Open **AGE.MTW**

You will use the Mann-Whitney nonparametric procedure. Formulate the hypotheses:

H_0: The median ages at death for females and for males are equal.

H_1: The median ages at death for females and for males are not equal.

Leave the significance level equal 0.05. To perform the test:

■ Choose **Stat > Nonparametrics > Mann-Whitney**

■ Double-click **C1 DAGEF** to enter it in the **First Sample** text box

■ Double-click **C2 DAGEM** to enter it in the **Second Sample** text box

The completed Mann-Whitney dialog box looks like Figure 13-9.

FIGURE 13-9

The completed Mann-Whitney dialog box

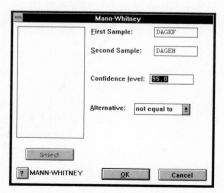

MINITAB AT WORK

MEDICAL DIAGNOSTICS: Although most of us associate heart failure with older people, it can affect children and infants when the main artery of the heart, the aorta, becomes obstructed and blood cannot flow freely. Doctors treat these blockages by inserting small balloons into the constricted aorta and inflating them to clear the obstruction.

A pediatrician at a midwestern university hospital used the balloon treatment on 30 children, ages 14 days to 13 years, who had obstructed aortas. He monitored their recovery carefully to see what factors would predict whether the operation was a success. One factor the pediatrician used was the measurement of aorta diameter at five points. In a normal aortic valve, the diameters at all five locations would be approximately the same, and hence the variance in diameter measurements would be close to zero.

The pediatrician used Minitab's Mann-Whitney test to compare diameter variances before and after treatment of two groups of patients: those who eventually required a second balloon treatment and those who did not. The results indicated that the children who would completely recover showed a greater decline in diameter variance from pretreatment levels than those who would require more surgery. This result gave the pediatrician another diagnostic tool to predict whether more treatment would be needed at a later date for a particular patient. Being able to predict patients' future needs enables doctors to better treat them in the present.

■ Click **OK**

The results of the test appear in the Session window (Figure 13-10).

FIGURE 13-10

Results of the Mann-Whitney test

```
MTB > Mann-Whitney 95.0 'DAGEF' 'DAGEM';
SUBC>   Alternative 0.

Mann-Whitney Confidence Interval and Test

DAGEF     N =  19    Median =       75.00
DAGEM     N =  18    Median =       72.50
Point estimate for ETA1-ETA2 is       2.00
95.3 Percent C.I. for ETA1-ETA2 is (-8.00,13.00)
W = 375.0
Test of ETA1 = ETA2  vs.  ETA1 = ETA2 is significant at 0.6816
The test is significant at 0.6812 (adjusted for ties)

Cannot reject at alpha = 0.05

MTB >
```

Minitab first lists medians for each gender and then displays the point estimate for the difference (ETA1 − ETA2 = 2 years). The 95.3% confidence interval for the difference in population medians ranges from −8.00 to 13.00. Minitab reports a test result of 375.0 and a p-value of 0.6816, so you cannot reject H_0 at the 0.05 level. You have no evidence to reject the equality of the median ages at death for the two genders. Note that this p-value is different from the one produced by the independent 2-sample t-test, which isn't surprising given that the two tests are not equivalent. There doesn't seem to be any difference in median age at death between the two genders. These results are similar to the ones you obtained in Tutorial 8.

■ Choose **File > Other Files > Stop Recording Session**

■ Choose **File > Restart Minitab**

Computing the Medians of K Independent Populations with the Kruskal-Wallis Test

In Tutorial 9, you used analysis of variance to compare the means of more than two populations. To perform ANOVA, you had to make the parametric assumption of normality of each population. The Kruskal-Wallis H-test is the nonparametric counterpart of one-way ANOVA. It is a generalization of the Mann-Whitney (Wilcoxon) test.

CASE STUDY: JOURNALISM — PAGE LAYOUT (CONTINUED)

In Tutorial 9, you analyzed the average size of nonprint displays present on easily seen pages in three different types of newspapers. Now you analyze the maximum size of nonprint displays present on these same pages of the same three different types of newspapers. You run a Kruskal-Wallis test on the data in NONPRT2.MTW to test whether there is a difference among the median maximum sizes of nonprint displays in the three newspapers. You decide to use this test since maximum values usually are not normally distributed.

■ Start the T13 outfile again; Minitab appends the subsequent session record to your previous outfile on your Student disk

■ Open **NONPRT2.MTW**

To use the Kruskal-Wallis procedure, the samples must be random and independent, with five or more measurements in each (or at least six measurements in one). You must list the data in one column, called the *Response*, and the subscripts in a second column, called the *Factor*.

To perform the Kruskal-Wallis test:

■ Choose **Stat > Nonparametrics > Kruskal-Wallis**

■ Double-click **C3 MAXSIZE** to enter it in the **Response** text box

■ Double-click **C2 PAPER** to enter it in the **Factor** text box

The completed Kruskal-Wallis dialog box should look like Figure 13-11.

FIGURE 13-11

*The completed
Kruskal-Wallis dialog box*

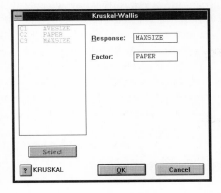

■ Click **OK**

The results of the test appear in the Session window (Figure 13-12).

FIGURE 13-12

*Results of the
Kruskal-Wallis test*

```
MTB > Kruskal-Wallis 'MAXSIZE' 'PAPER'.

LEVEL    NOBS    MEDIAN   AVE. RANK    Z VALUE
  1        6      36.47      5.8        0.43
  2        2      50.01      7.5        1.04
  3        2      30.89      2.5       -1.57
OVERALL   10                 5.5

H = 2.91  d.f. = 2   p = 0.234

* NOTE  * One or more small samples
MTB >
```

Minitab first reports summary statistics for each paper. Paper 2 has the largest median maximum size (50.01 square inches); paper 3 has the smallest (30.89 square inches). The Kruskal-Wallis H-value is 2.91. The p-value corresponding to 2.91 is 0.234. Since Minitab warns you that the size of one or more samples is small (one has six maximums and two have two), you decide to examine the standard small sample table for the Kruskal-Wallis test. This situation is not covered in the tables; you decide to use the p-value since in practice it is a reasonable approximation. Based on its value of 0.234, you do not reject the null hypothesis that median maximum sizes of nonprint displays in the three newspapers are the same. (If there are ties when you perform this test, Minitab provides another Kruskal-Wallis H-value adjusted for ties, as well as the corresponding p-value.)

■ Choose **File > Other Files > Stop Recording Session**

In this tutorial, you used the runs test to determine whether a process was random. Then you performed nonparametric procedures that correspond to the parametric procedures introduced in Tutorials 7, 8, and 9. Nonparametric techniques test hypotheses on the median of a single population or compare medians of more than one population; they are useful when the underlying assumption of normality is not justified. Minitab can also perform numerous nonparametric tests that are not listed on any menu. For example, with the Friedman command, you can compare medians of more than two related populations. Or, by using ranked and sorted data; pairwise averages, differences, and slopes; and other Minitab commands, you can perform many other nonparametric inference procedures, like the Spearman's rank correlation statistic.

In Tutorial 14, you use Minitab in a quality-control setting to verify the output of a production process.

If you plan to continue directly to the next tutorial:

- Choose **File > Restart Minitab**

    If you want to take a longer break:

- Choose **File > Exit**

▼ Minitab Command Summary ▲

This section describes the Minitab menu commands introduced in or related to this tutorial. To find a complete explanation of all menus and commands, refer to the Reference section of this manual.

Minitab Menu Commands

Menu	Command	Description
Stat		
	Nonparametrics	
	1-Sample Sign	Performs a nonparametric one-sample sign inference (test or confidence level) on a median
	1-Sample Wilcoxon	Performs a nonparametric Wilcoxon one-sample inference (test or confidence level) on a median
	Mann-Whitney	Performs two-sample nonparametric inference (test and confidence interval) on two medians
	Kruskal-Wallis	Performs a nonparametric comparison of more than two medians
	Friedman	Performs a nonparametric analysis of a randomized block experiment

Menu	Command	Description
	Runs Test	Performs a test to evaluate random order of data
	Pairwise Averages	Computes Walsh averages (the averages of each pair of data points in a column, including of each value with itself)
	Pairwise Differences	Computes the difference between all possible pairs of data values in two columns
	Pairwise Slopes	Computes the slopes using each pair of data values in two columns

▼
Review and Practice
▲

Matching

Match the following terms to their definitions by placing the correct letter next to the term it describes.

_____ H

_____ ETA1-ETA2

_____ Nonparametric

_____ K

_____ Estimated median

_____ Run

_____ Factor

_____ Response

_____ Friedman

_____ Mann-Whitney

a. A series of Minitab statistical techniques that do not assume the population(s) possess any particular distribution

b. Minitab notation for the difference between two population medians

c. A sequence of observations that share a similar characteristic

d. Minitab notation for the column in which the data are stored for the Kruskal-Wallis command

e. Minitab notation for the test statistic from the Kruskal-Wallis test

f. Minitab notation for the constant used in the runs test to identify a run

g. Minitab name for the statistic equal to the middle value of all pairwise averages of data values

h. Minitab dialog box notation for the subscript column used in the Kruskal-Wallis command

i. Minitab command that performs a nonparametric analysis of a randomized block experiment

j. Minitab command that is the nonparametric counterpart of the 2-sample t-test with independent samples

True/False

Mark the following statements with a *T* or an *F*.

_____ 1. The Runs Test command requires numeric data since a run is determined by comparing a data value to a number.

_____ 2. You can always use Minitab's nonparametric commands to obtain confidence intervals that correspond to exact levels of confidence.

_____ 3. You can only perform two-tailed tests with the Minitab nonparametric tests.

_____ 4. For extremely small samples, you should ignore the p-value produced by the Kruskal-Wallis command.

_____ 5. By default, the Wilcoxon command provides confidence intervals as part of the output.

_____ 6. The Kruskal-Wallis command requires the data to be in one column with a subscript identifier in another.

_____ 7. The default null hypothesis value for the median in the Wilcoxon command is zero.

_____ 8. The Runs Test command uses the sample median as the default value to identify runs.

_____ 9. The Mann-Whitney command assumes that the two samples of data are stored in different columns.

_____ 10. The Friedman command compares medians of more than two related populations.

Practice Problems

1. Open SNOW.MTW. Recall that the data were presented in chronological order and that there are three outliers. Perform a runs test on the snowfall data with K equal to the median, which is less sensitive to outliers. Based on your results, are the snowfall amounts random?

2. Open PAY.MTW. The industry median salary is approximately $29,000.

   a. Use a Wilcoxon 1-sample test to determine if this company's median salary is comparable to the industry's, with a significance level of 0.05.

   b. Use a Wilcoxon 1-sample "95%" confidence interval to determine if this company's median salary is comparable to the industry's.

3. Open the RIVERS.MTW data set. Determine if the median temperature of the river is different at site 2, which is directly up river from the power plant, than at site 3, which is directly down river from the power plant's discharge from its cooling towers. You need to create a new column that contains 1 for site 2, 2 for site 3, and the missing symbol for all the others. Use the Code Data Values command.

4. Open HOMES.MTW.

   a. Create a new variable with 3 categories: homes with 1 bath, homes with 1.5 or 2 baths, and homes with more than 2 baths.

   b. Is the mean acreage the same for these three types of homes?

   c. Is the median acreage the same for these three types of homes?

   d. Should you report the results of part b or c? Briefly explain your answer.

5. Open MARKS.MTW.

   a. Use a parametric test to determine if the class performed the same on exams 1 and 2.

   b. Use a nonparametric test to determine if the class performed the same on exams 1 and 2.

   c. Comment on the similarities and differences between the results of parts a and b.

   d. Use a parametric test to determine if the class performed the same on exams 1, 2, and 3. (*Hint:* You need to stack the exam data in one column, store the subscripts in another column, and use the Balanced ANOVA test.)

   e. Use a nonparametric test to determine if the class performed the same on exams 1, 2, and 3. (*Hint:* Structure your data according to the hint in part d and use the Friedman test.)

   f. Comment on the similarities and differences between the results of parts d and e.

TUTORIAL 14

Total Quality Management Tools

Total quality management (TQM) is a philosophy used by many businesses and individuals to improve their processes. The foundation of TQM is making decisions based on data. This is often accomplished by using *quality tools*. In this tutorial, you first learn about the quality tools available in Minitab. You then construct and interpret various types of control charts in Minitab.

Objectives

In this tutorial you learn how to:

- describe the quality tools available, including Pareto charts and cause-and-effect diagrams

- construct an $\overline{X}$ chart to monitor the mean value of a process

- create a range chart to monitor variability in a process

- produce an individuals chart to monitor individual observations from a process

- construct a moving range chart to monitor variability in a process from individual observations

- create a proportion chart to monitor the proportion from a process

Examining Two Quality Tools (Pareto Chart and Cause-and-Effect Diagram)

▼

▲

Today many managers employ total quality management (TQM) techniques to strengthen their businesses. TQM is also used by individuals for self-improvement. Data-driven decisions are a fundamental premise of TQM. In order to make such decisions, you can use a number of quality tools, many of which are available in Minitab.

To start Minitab and start an outfile:

- Start Minitab and maximize the Minitab window and the Data window

- Start an outfile named **T14**

You can use Minitab for quality planning by constructing a Pareto chart or a cause-and-effect (fishbone) diagram. *Pareto charts* are bar charts with the bars ordered from largest to smallest, often with defects plotted. You use Pareto charts to determine the "vital few" from the "trivial many."

You can see what a Pareto chart looks like in Chapter 2 of the Reference Section. You will construct a Pareto chart in one of the practice problems at the end of this tutorial.

Cause-and-effect diagrams let you graphically represent the factors that influence a problem. The graph is arranged with the problem on the right side and a list of causes on the left side, in a structure resembling the skeleton of a fish. Minitab has six default main causes (Men, Machines, Materials, Methods, Measures, and the Environment).

CASE STUDY: EDUCATION — FACULTY SURVEY (CONTINUED)

In Chapter 5 of Getting Started you did a preliminary analysis of the results of a faculty survey taken by the student government. The process connected with such surveys is often flawed. You record some of the reasons for this flawed process for another article for the student government newsletter. You classify each of these reasons into one of Minitab's six default main causes. For example, the in-class instructions, which may be unclear, are placed under the Methods cause. Then you enter these reasons into a Minitab file called PROCES.MTW.

- Open **PROCES.MTW**

- Go to the Data window to examine these data (you may have to scroll to see them all)

You observe that there are six alpha variables, C1 MEN, C2 MACHINES, C3 MATERIAL, C4 METHODS, C5 MEASURES, and C6 ENVIRON, each giving possible reasons for a flawed survey process. You decide to represent these reasons in a more informative graphical display.

To construct this cause-and-effect diagram:

- Choose **Stat > SPC > Cause-and-Effect**
- Select **C1-C6** for the six **Cause** text boxes by double-clicking one at a time
- Type **Flawed Process** in the **Effect** text box and press ⌑Tab⌑
- Type **Cause and Effect Diagram for Faculty Surveys** in the Title text box

The completed Cause-and-Effect Diagram dialog box should resemble Figure 14-1.

FIGURE 14-1

The completed Cause-and-Effect Diagram dialog box

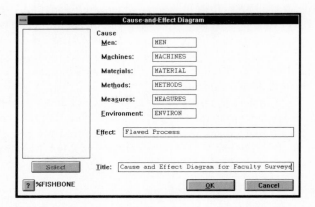

- Press ⌑←Enter⌑

Minitab produces a cause-and-effect diagram (Figure 14-2).

FIGURE 14-2

Cause-and-effect diagram

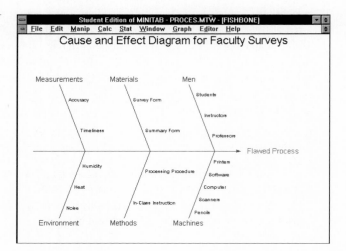

You are pleased with this graphical display. It presents the numerous factors that can affect a flawed survey process.

Using Control Charts

You have already used some quality tools in earlier tutorials: the histogram, scatter plot, and time series plot. Another frequently used tool is the *control chart*. Minitab offers 11 control chart types. Quality control technicians use them to monitor processes because they may show when a process is getting out of control. Control charts help manufacturers achieve a high level of quality by meeting certain specifications. In addition, you can use these charts to discover interesting features in a process. In this tutorial, you construct and interpret five Minitab control charts.

CASE STUDY: PRODUCTION — QUALITY CONTROL CHARTS

The instructor of your production course wants to illustrate the use of control charts. He has brought three bags of candy to class. Each bag contains 19 "fun packs" of these candies. He identifies each pack and asks the class to imagine that the 57 packs come from a production line. He informs the class that the weight of each candy is 2.32 grams, based on product information. He then divides the class into three groups and asks each group to measure different characteristics of these candies from all 57 packs.

Group A measures the weight of five candies randomly selected from each pack. They enter these 285 weights into CANDYA.MTW, along with the bag and pack identification numbers.

Group B measures the total weight of each pack. They then measure the weight of the pack paper and compute the weight of the candies in each pack. CANDYB.MTW contains these three variables along with the bag and pack numbers and the number of candies in each pack.

Group C also records the number of each bag and pack ID, as well as the number of candies in each pack. In addition they count the number of red, brown, green, orange, and yellow candies in each pack. They enter their data in CANDYC.MTW.

The instructor then asks each student to determine whether the production line process is "in control" by constructing control charts relevant to their data sets. A process is *in control* when the mean and variability of the process is stable, and any variation in the process is due to random causes.

<table>
<tr><td>

▼

**Constructing an
Xbar Chart**

▲

</td><td>

Group A sampled five random candies (subgroups of size 5) for 57 packs, weighed each candy in grams, and placed the results in C3 WEIGHT of CANDYA.MTW.

■ Open **CANDYA.MTW**

    To determine whether the mean of the candy-making process is in control, produce an $\overline{X}$ chart to look at the 57 sample means. You want to place this control chart in your outfile, so you can submit it to your instructor along with the other charts you create. Minitab's Professional control charts are available on the menus, but Character control charts that appear in outfiles are not. You must type the Session commands instead. (The Quick Reference Card contains all the Session commands and their syntax.)

■ Choose **Window > Session**

■ Type **GSTD** to disable the Professional graphics and press (←Enter)

    Now tell Minitab to construct an $\overline{X}$ chart for the WEIGHTS variables and that they are in subgroups of size 5. The semicolon indicates that a subcommand follows. The MU subcommand indicates the historical mean is 2.32 grams.

■ Type **XBARCHART 'WEIGHTS' 5;** and press (←Enter) (be sure to include the semicolon)

■ Type **MU 2.32;** and press (←Enter) (be sure to include the semicolon)

    Minitab can perform eight different tests to determine if there are any extreme observations, or any unusual sequences or runs in the data. These tests refer to three zones: Zone A represents the area up to one standard deviation from the center line; Zone B, the area between one and two standard deviations from the center line; and Zone C, the area between two and three standard deviations from the center line. These tests require equal sample sizes. To perform all eight tests:

■ Type **TEST 1:8.** and press (←Enter) (be sure to include the period)

    Minitab computes the 57 sample means (using subgroups of size 5) and plots them on the $\overline{X}$ chart that appears in the Session window (Figure 14-3).

</td></tr>
</table>

FIGURE 14-3

Character XBARCHART

```
MTB > GSTD
* NOTE  * Standard Graphics are enabled.
          Professional Graphics are disabled.
          Use the GPRO command to enable Professional Graphics.
MTB > XBARCHART 'WEIGHTS' 5;
SUBC> MU 2.32;
SUBC> TEST 1:8.
                         X-bar Chart for WEIGHTS
       2.750+
            -
            -------------------------------------------------UCL=2.659
     S      -                                            +
     a      -      +                    +                      +
     m 2.500+
     p      -         +    +      +
     l      -  +            +              +    +
     e      -      +                  +    +         +
            ---++---------++--++-+--+------+----+-+-----+-----MU=2.320
     M 2.250+         +         +         + +    +    +    + +
     e      -              +         +              ++
     a      -+    +    +              + *
     n      -         +              +    +6*
            -              +              2       +
       2.000+-------------------------------------------------LCL=1.981
            -
            -
            +---------+---------+---------+---------+---------+
            0        10        20        30        40        50
                              Sample Number
```

```
       2.750+
            -
            --------UCL=2.659
     S      -
     a      -
     m 2.500+
     p      -
     l      -   ++
     e      -
            -+-----+MU=2.320
     M 2.250+
     e      - +
     a      -      +
     n      -   +
            -
       2.000+-------LCL=1.981
            -
            -
            +---------+
            50        60
              Sample Number
```

TEST 2. Nine points in a row in Zone C or beyond (on one side of CL).
Test Failed at points: 29

TEST 6. Four of 5 points in a row in zone B or beyond (on one side of CL).
Test Failed at points: 28 29

MTB >

Minitab marks the center line at 2.32. It also places an upper-control-limit line at 2.659 and a lower-control-limit line at 1.981; each of these limits is three estimated standard deviations from the mean. (You can also enter known values for the control limits.) Note that Minitab uses a pooled estimate for sigma by default; it doesn't use the more traditional $\overline{X}$ estimate. The $\overline{X}$ chart shows that the process is out of control, because there are nine points that have failed Test 2 and four that have failed Test 6.

Minitab reports that Test 2 failed at point 29; the nine sample averages before this average were in Zone C, all on one side of the center line. Test 6 failed at points 28 and 29, where Minitab found that four of the five previous sample averages were in Zone B or beyond. Unusual patterns might indicate that the process is drifting away from the target value of 2.32 grams.

Even though you learned something about the process, you are dissatisfied with this control chart. It is split into two blocks. The sample averages are not connected to their neighboring values. You decide to construct a Professional $\overline{X}$ chart even though it won't be included in your outfile.

- Choose **Stat > Control Charts > Xbar** (the fourth command, not the first)

- Select **C3 WEIGHTS** to enter it in the **Variable** text box and press [Tab]

- Type **5** in the **Subgroup size** text box and press [Tab]

- Type **2.32** in the **Historical mu** text box

- Click the **All eight** option button to select all eight tests for special causes

    The completed Xbar Chart dialog box should resemble Figure 14-4.

FIGURE 14-4

The completed Xbar Chart dialog box

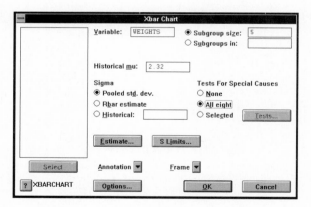

- Click **OK**

Note: On slow computers this plot may take a few minutes.

Minitab displays the Xbar chart for WEIGHTS in its own Graph window (Figure 14-5).

FIGURE 14-5

Professional Xbar chart for WEIGHTS

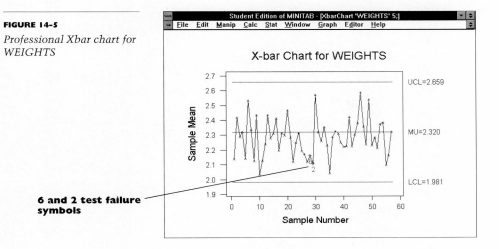

6 and 2 test failure symbols

You are more satisfied with this plot. Minitab eliminated both of the problems you noted with the Character control chart. To interpret the 6 and 2 test failure symbols, however, you need to take a look at the Session window.

■ Go to the Session window (Figure 14-6)

FIGURE 14-6

The Session window, showing the test failures for the Professional Xbar chart

```
MTB > XbarChart 'WEIGHTS' 5;
SUBC>    Mu 2.32;
SUBC>    Test 1:8;
SUBC>    Symbol;
SUBC>    Connect.
TEST 2. Nine points in a row in Zone C or beyond (on one side of CL).
Test Failed at points: 29

TEST 6. Four of 5 points in a row in zone B or beyond (on one side of CL).
Test Failed at points: 28 29
```

These test results are, of course, the same as the ones produced for the Character control chart. Based on this chart, you decide to construct Professional control charts for the rest of this assignment.

Note: Another way to construct a Character control chart is to construct a Professional control chart, type the GSTD Session command, copy and paste the Character control chart commands generated by the Professional chart into the Session window, and then press ⌨Enter. This may be the quickest way to ensure that the control charts end up in your outfile, if desired.

MINITAB AT WORK

QUALITY CONTROL: The hockey puck that slides across the ice of a skating arena must withstand incredible levels of stress. Plastics manufacturers continually monitor the process that creates the pucks so they won't shatter when first whacked on the ice. Unipar, Inc., based in Pennsylvania, produces a wide variety of plastics, from medical products to fuel tank parts to children's toys. Unipar hockey pucks are manufactured by filling puck molds with plastic, mounting the molds, 80 at a time, on rotating arms, and cooking them in a very hot oven for about 10 minutes. When the molds are ready, the arms release the pucks, which are then cooled in a cooling chamber and packaged.

The most important part of quality assurance in this process is careful temperature monitoring. If the pucks are overcooked beyond the cure point, they become brittle and are prone to shattering like glass on impact. When undercooked, they are susceptible to tearing. Quality assurance specialists at Unipar determined that to produce high-quality pucks, the oven temperatures must range no more than ±5° from the base temperature of 450° F.

To ensure that the ovens stay within this range, Unipar employees measure oven temperature every hour. A quality assistant regularly enters the temperature readings into Minitab and produces Xbar and R charts that show the distribution of temperature readings over time. When control limits are exceeded, Unipar inspectors search for causes, such as machine malfunctions or incorrect manual temperature settings.

Unipar quality assurance employees who monitor the Minitab SPC charts recently noticed that some of the temperature measurements were ranging outside the control limits. They saw a definite change from shift to shift and operator to operator, and realized that one of the three operators was more successful at manually setting oven temperature than the other two. By meeting with the first operator, the other two learned new techniques that enabled them to improve their manual setting of the oven temperature and control the temperature readings so they stayed within the control limits.

▼ Constructing a Range Chart ▲

You should investigate the variability of any process because it determines the control limits for the process mean. To ascertain whether the variance of the process is stable and random, you examine the spread in your samples. You can use either the sample range (R) or the sample standard deviation (S) in Minitab to create R and S charts, respectively. For small samples such as this, the R chart is appropriate.

To obtain the R chart for your data:

- Choose **Stat > Control Charts > R**
- Double-click **C3 WEIGHTS** to enter it in the **Variable** text box and press $\boxed{\text{Tab}}$
- Type **5** in the **Subgroup size** text box

The completed R Chart dialog box should resemble Figure 14-7.

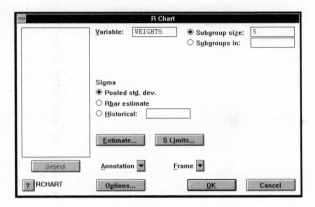

- Click **OK**

Minitab computes the range of each of the 57 groups of five samples and then plots them on the R chart, as shown in Figure 14-8.

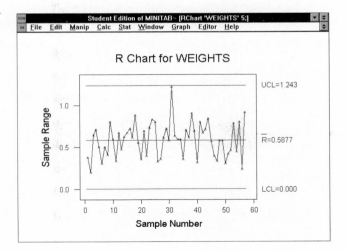

Minitab draws the center line at 0.5877 (the average of the sample ranges), and the lower and upper control limits at 0.000 and 1.243, respectively. The R chart indicates that process variability is not out of control. The observed variation in the range of the candy weights appears to be random.

You decide to place both charts together to better present the data. Use the Xbar-R control chart:

- Choose **Stat > Control Charts > Xbar-R**

- Select **C3 WEIGHTS** to enter it in the **Variable** text box and press ⌈Tab⌉

- Type **5** in the **Subgroup size** text box and press ⌈Tab⌉

- Type **2.32** in the **Historical mu** text box and press ⌈←Enter⌉

The Xbar-R chart appears in its own Graph window (Figure 14-9).

FIGURE 14-9

Xbar-R chart for WEIGHTS

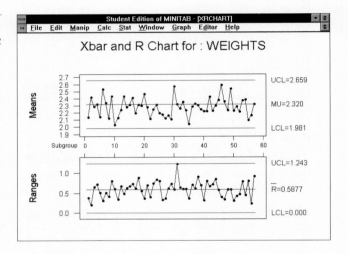

You are pleased with this chart even though it doesn't display any tests.

You conclude that the candy-making process is prone to some substantial changes in the mean or center, but that it produces consistent weights. You tell your instructor that you would recommend that management meet with the process personnel to determine the sources of the process mean being out of control. Perhaps together they can identify the causes and avoid the problems in the future.

Constructing an Individuals Chart

Now turn your attention to the second group's data. Group B obtained the weights of the 57 fun packs. These values are stored in C6 NETWGT of CANDYB.MTW.

■ Open **CANDYB.MTW**

You decide to investigate each pack individually using an *individuals* chart. Specify the historical mu of 20.89 grams for the pack weight to center the chart, and the historical sigma of 1.41 grams to determine what fraction of the production process is within the specification limits of 20.89 ± 3 (1.41) (16.66 and 25.12) grams. Note that for individual values, the control limits are determined by the center line ± 3σ.

To obtain the individuals chart:

■ Choose **Stat > Control Charts > Individuals**

■ Double-click **C6 NETWGT** to enter it in the **Variable** text box

■ Type **20.89** in the **Historical mu** text box

■ Click **Historical** under **Sigma** and press (Tab)

■ Type **1.41** in the **Historical** text box

■ Click **All eight** to produce all eight tests for special causes

The completed Individuals Chart dialog box should resemble Figure 14-10.

FIGURE 14-10

The completed Individuals Chart dialog box

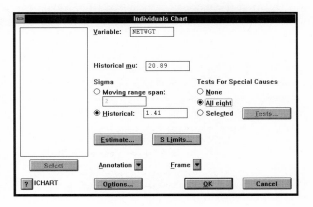

■ Click **OK**

The I (individuals) chart appears in its own window (Figure 14-11).

FIGURE 14-11

I chart for NETWGT

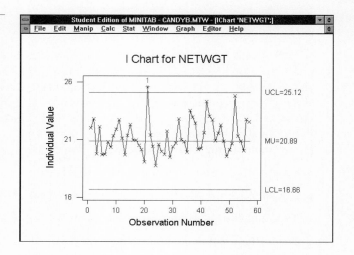

Analysis of the resulting graphs is revealing. The Session window shows that point 21 failed Test 1. There appears to be a problem with the twenty-first observation. It has a net weight of 25.62 grams. You contact a member of Group B. She informs you that this pack had a number of crushed candies. You suspect that the damage caused this pack to be outside the specification limits: a most interesting discovery found by analyzing the control chart.

▼

Constructing a Moving Range Chart

▲

You decide to analyze the variability of the second group's data. In your first investigation, you selected five randomly selected candies. Now you have selected only one pack; you cannot estimate process variability using only one sample. Instead, you use the *moving range* — the range of two or more consecutive observations — to investigate the variability of the process:

■ Choose **Stat > Control Charts > Moving Range**

■ Double-click **C6 NETWGT** to enter it in the **Variable** text box

■ Click **Historical** under **Sigma** and press Tab

■ Type **1.41** in the **Historical** text box

The completed Moving Range Chart dialog box looks like Figure 14-12.

FIGURE 14-12

The completed Moving
Range Chart dialog box

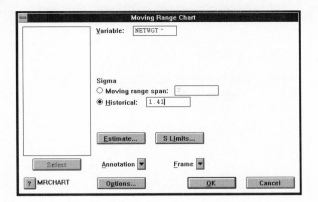

- Press ⏎Enter

The moving range chart appears in its own window (Figure 14-13).

FIGURE 14-13

The moving range chart
for NETWGT

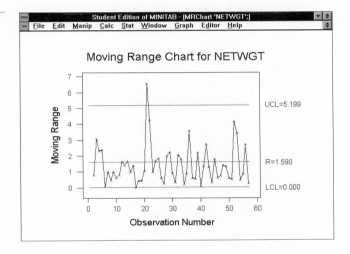

Process variability is not in control, due to the twenty-first pack. Again, your control chart identifies a problem. While this finding agrees with the problem identified by the individuals chart, this is not always the case. It's a good idea to construct both plots. Minitab lets you do that with a single command, the I-MR command.

- Choose **Stat > Control Charts > I-MR**
- Double-click **C6 NETWGT** to enter it in the **Variable** text box
- Type **20.89** in the **Historical mu** text box
- Click **Historical** under **Sigma** and press Tab

■ Type **1.41** in the **Historical** text box and press ⎵Enter⏎

The I-MR chart appears in its own Graph window (Figure 14-14).

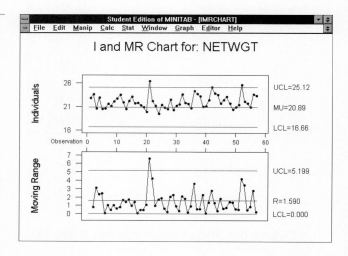

You plan to include this combination chart in your final report. It clearly reveals a problem with the twenty-first pack.

Constructing a Proportion Chart

Now you turn to CANDYC.MTW. You decide to investigate product quality by studying the proportion of defects in each of the 57 packs (like crushed candies). You hope it is in control.

■ Open **CANDYC.MTW**

Group C entered the number of candies in each pack in C3 NUMBER, and the number of defects in each pack in C9 DEFECTS. You can conceptualize this as an *attribute data* problem since each candy is classified as defective or not defective. Contrast this type of data to the weight data, which is called *variables data*.

To analyze attribute data, use P (proportion) charts:

■ Choose **Stat > Control Charts > P**

■ Double-click **C9 DEFECTS** to enter it in the **Variable** text box

■ Click the **Subgroups in** option button and then click the corresponding text box

■ Double-click **C3 NUMBER** to enter it in the **Subgroups in** text box

The completed P Chart dialog box should resemble Figure 14-15.

FIGURE 14-15

*The completed P Chart
dialog box*

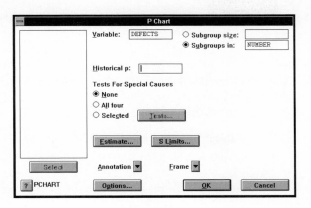

■ Click **OK**

The P chart appears (Figure 14-16).

FIGURE 14-16

P chart for DEFECTS

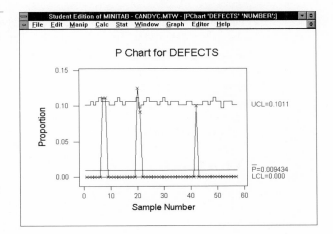

Minitab draws the center line at 0.009434 (the average of the sample proportions). It draws a *lower control limit (LCL)* of 0.000, which is often called
a *zero-valued control limit* because an LCL of 0 is as low as possible. Minitab
displays a *staircased upper control limit (UCL)* at approximately 0.1011,
which is a nonconstant control limit that is not a horizontal straight line.
The upper control limit is staircased because there are a different number of
candies in each pack. Even though tests cannot be performed since the UCL
is not constant, you identify a problem with three packs (seventh, eighth, and
twentieth) based on points that exceed the upper control limit.

You conclude that this process is not in control. There are too many
defective candies among the 57 packs. The charts tell you to recommend that

the company determine the cause of the crushed candies immediately so that fewer defects will be produced in the future.

You have seen only a small part of what Minitab can do in SPC. Minitab can also chart standard deviations, moving averages, numbers (instead of proportions), and numbers per unit — all methods that are used routinely in the monitoring and analysis of a process.

Stop your outfile:

■ Choose **File > Other Files > Stop Recording Session**

In Tutorial 15, you use Minitab to analyze and forecast trends in time series data.

If you plan to continue directly to the next tutorial:

■ Choose **File > Restart Minitab**

If you want to take a longer break:

■ Choose **File > Exit**

▼
Minitab Command Summary
▲

This section describes the Minitab menu commands and Session commands introduced in or related to this tutorial. To find a complete explanation of all menus and commands, refer to the Reference section of this manual.

Minitab Menu Commands

Menu	Command	Description
Stat		
	Control Charts	
	Xbar-R	Produces a control chart for subgroup means and a control chart for subgroup ranges
	Xbar-S	Produces a control chart for subgroup means and a control chart for subgroup standard deviations
	I-MR	Produces a chart of individual observations and a moving range chart
	Xbar	Constructs an $\overline{X}$ chart for variables data stored in a column
	R	Constructs a range chart using the variables data stored in a column
	S	Constructs a standard deviation chart using the variables data stored in a column

Menu	Command	Description
	Individuals	Constructs an individuals chart using the variables data stored in a column
	Moving Range	Constructs a moving range chart using the variables data stored in a column
	EWMA	Constructs an exponentially weighted moving average chart
	Moving Average	Constructs a moving average chart
	P	Constructs a proportions defective chart using attribute data stored in a column
	NP	Constructs a number defective chart using attribute data stored in a column
	C	Constructs a number of defects per unit chart using attribute data stored in a column for constant sample size
	U	Constructs a chart of the number of defects per unit sampled
SPC		
	Pareto Chart	Generates a Pareto chart, a bar chart with the bars ordered from largest to smallest
	Cause-and-Effect	Generates a cause-and-effect (fishbone) diagram that depicts the potential causes of a problem

Minitab Session Commands

XBARCHART	Constructs an $\overline{X}$ chart for variables data stored in a column
RCHART	Constructs a range chart using the variables data stored in a column
SCHART	Constructs a standard deviation chart using the variables data stored in a column
ICHART	Constructs an individuals chart using the variables data stored in a column
MRCHART	Constructs a moving range chart using the variables data stored in a column

EWMACHART	Constructs an exponentially weighted moving average chart
MACHART	Constructs a moving average chart
PCHART	Constructs a proportions defective chart using attribute data stored in a column
NPCHART	Constructs a number defective chart using attribute data stored in a column
CCHART	Constructs a number of defects per unit chart using attribute data stored in a column for constant sample size
UCHART	Constructs a chart of the number of defects per unit sampled

▼

Review and Practice

▲

Matching

Match the following terms to their definitions by placing the correct letter next to the term it describes.

_____ Professional control chart

_____ Individuals

_____ Sigma historical

_____ Historical mu

_____ Character control chart

_____ Tests for Special Causes

_____ Pareto chart

_____ Cause-and-effect diagram

_____ Non-constant control limit

_____ Zero-valued control limit

a. A Minitab dialog box option that fixes the center line at a specified value in a control chart

b. A Minitab dialog box option that fixes the variability value in a control chart at a specified value

c. A control chart in which neighboring points are connected

d. A control chart in which neighboring points are not connected

e. Output in which zones are an important component

f. Minitab notation that refers to variables data consisting of samples of size 1

g. A staircased limit that is possible in a P chart

h. A lower control limit that is possible in a MR chart

i. A chart that depicts potential causes of a problem

j. A bar chart with the bars ordered from largest to smallest

True/False

Mark the following statements with a *T* or an *F*.

_____ 1. You can directly specify the control limits and center line in Minitab's control charts.

_____ 2. Control charts can be either Professional or Character displays.

_____ 3. Minitab has an Xbar-MR command.

_____ 4. The Xbar command lets you perform nine special-cause tests.

_____ 5. There are four Tests For Special Causes available with the P chart command.

_____ 6. You can specify multiple columns using the Xbar chart command.

_____ 7. Minitab uses a default of two values to compute the moving range.

_____ 8. The Graph window displays details of the special-cause tests along with the chart.

_____ 9. All of Minitab's control chart commands require you to specify the subgroup size.

_____ 10. You can request special-cause tests with the Moving Range command.

Practice Problems

1. Open PUBS.MTW.

   a. Investigate the process mean weight by constructing an $\overline{X}$ control chart. Is the process "in control"? Briefly explain your answer.

   b. Investigate the variability of the process weight by constructing an R control chart. Is the process "in control"? Briefly explain your answer.

   c. Construct an Xbar-R control chart for the weights. What are the advantages of using this chart instead of separate control charts? What are the disadvantages?

2. Open SNOW.MTW. Investigate the yearly snowfall by constructing an I chart and an MR chart. Is the snowfall process "in control"? Note that there was a major blizzard in 1978, one of the years for which snowfall was measured.

3. In the illustration of proportions charts in this tutorial, you used the sample proportion to determine the center line and control limits. Redo the analysis letting Minitab use the specified values of 0.01 and 2 to compute the center line and control limits. Are your results similar? If not, can you explain why?

4. Redo the Xbar and R control charts in this tutorial but use the Rbar estimate for sigma. Does the use of this more traditional estimate of variability affect the charts? Briefly explain your answer.

5. There are many reasons why you might be late for class.

   a. List reasons why you might be late in six columns in a Minitab worksheet, one column for each of Minitab's Cause-and-Effect default categories (Men, Machines, Materials, Methods, Measures, and Environ).

   b. Construct a cause-and-effect diagram using the six columns you just created.

6. An inspector examines a newly repainted automobile for defects. She observes eight defects on the car, in the following order: Scratch, Scratch, Bend, Chip, Dent, Scratch, Chip, and Scratch. Create two Pareto charts for these defects by performing the following steps.

   a. Enter these alpha data in the first eight rows of C1.

   b. Choose **Stat > SPC > Pareto Chart**.

   c. Select **C1** for the **Defects** text box.

   d. Click **OK**.

   e. Choose **Edit > Edit Last Command Dialog**.

   f. Type **70** into the **Combine all defects after the first [ ]% into one bar** text box.

   g. Click **OK.**

   h. Which of these two Pareto charts do you prefer? Briefly explain your choice.

TUTORIAL 15

Time Series Analysis

In Tutorials 10 and 11, you used regression analysis to determine a suitable model. In addition, you predicted a response variable from one or more predictor variables. When your data come from observations over equally spaced intervals of time, Minitab can help you determine an appropriate model and then predict or forecast future values of the series.

Objectives

In this tutorial you learn how to:

- perform a classical decomposition to model and forecast a time series
- identify a model using autocorrelation and partial autocorrelation plots
- transform a time series
- use Box-Jenkins autoregressive integrated moving average (ARIMA) techniques to model and forecast a time series
- compare the classical decomposition and ARIMA models
- realize that there are other time series modeling and forecasting techniques available in Minitab

CASE STUDY: ENVIRONMENT — TEMPERATURE VARIATION

During the summer of 1988, which was one of the hottest on record in the Midwest, the state Environmental Protection Agency wanted to study the impact of an electric generating plant along a river. The EPA worried that the plant's use of river water for cooling was raising its temperature and thereby endangering the aquatic life. The EPA established a site directly downstream from the cooling discharge outlets of the plant at which they measured the water temperature on an hourly basis for 95 consecutive hours.

In this case study, you are an Environmental Science graduate student working for the EPA on this project. You use time series methods to analyze the problem. You perform the time series analysis in eight phases:

Phase I	Plot the time series
Phase II	Perform a classical decomposition on the time series using a multiplicative model
Phase III	Apply the model to forecast future values
Phase IV	Investigate the autocorrelation and partial autocorrelation structure of the time series to determine an appropriate Box-Jenkins ARIMA model
Phase V	Transform the data (if necessary) using lags and differences to obtain a stationary time series
Phase VI	Fit an adequate Box-Jenkins ARIMA model
Phase VII	Apply this model to forecast future values
Phase VIII	Examine the strengths and weaknesses of the two models

To get started:

- Start Minitab and maximize the Minitab window and the Data window

- Start an outfile named **T15**

- Open **RIVERC.MTW**

C1 HOUR lists the time of day (in military format) of each measurement; C2 TEMP gives the temperature measurement in °C. The other columns in RIVERC.MTW contain additional measurements taken at the same time as the temperature. Refer to the data set descriptions for this file in Part III, Exploring Data, for more information about these other measurements.

▼
Plotting a Time Series
▲

To obtain an initial picture of the temperature data over time, construct Character and Professional time series plots. (You first constructed a time series plot in Tutorial 3.)

Creating a Character Time Series Plot

Start with the Character plot:

- Choose **Graph > Character Graphs > Time Series Plot**

- Double-click **C2 TEMP** to enter it in the **Series** text box

- Click the **Period** check box and press ⟨Tab⟩

- Type **24** in the **Period** text box

    The completed Time Series Plot dialog box should look like Figure 15-1.

FIGURE 15-1

The completed Character Time Series Plot dialog box

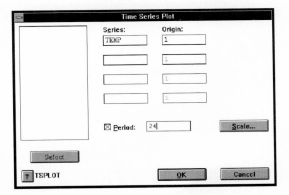

- Click **OK**

The time series plot appears in the Session window (Figure 15-2).

■ Scroll up in the Session window to see the beginning of the plot

The Session window, showing the time series plot of temperature

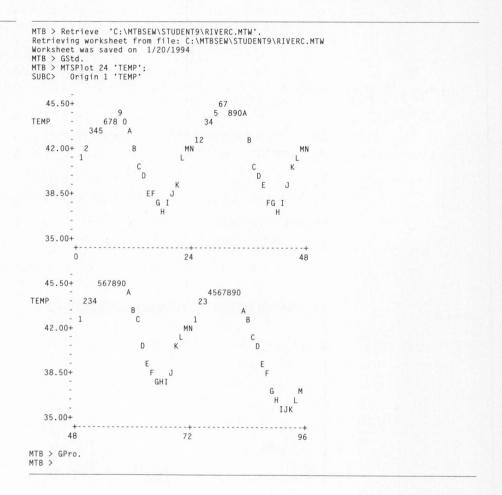

```
MTB > Retrieve  'C:\MTBSEW\STUDENT9\RIVERC.MTW'.
Retrieving worksheet from file: C:\MTBSEW\STUDENT9\RIVERC.MTW
Worksheet was saved on  1/20/1994
MTB > GStd.
MTB > MTSPlot 24 'TEMP';
SUBC>   Origin 1 'TEMP'
```

Minitab plots the temperature on the vertical axis and the hour on the horizontal axis. It assigns a symbol (a digit or a letter) to each hour of the day and uses these symbols as the plot character for that hour. Minitab begins with the digits 1 (for 1400 = 2 p.m.), 2 (1500 = 3 p.m.), and 3 (1600 = 4 p.m.). Since the period you specified in the plot (24 hours) is more than 9, Minitab uses 0 for 2300 = 11 p.m., then A for 2400 = 12 p.m., B for 0100 = 1 a.m., and so on, up to N for 1300 = 1 p.m. After N, the series starts again with 1, 2, 3, and so on. You can plot a time series with any period up to 36 units (Minitab can use 10 digits and 26 letters).

The plot indicates a cyclical pattern beginning with temperatures at 2 p.m. (represented by the digit 1) around 42 degrees, which rise for the next 8 hours and then fall until they reach a low of about 37 degrees at 7 a.m. (represented by the letter H). This cycle repeats through the next 24-hour period but with some variation. The peaks and valleys occur roughly 24 hours apart; this suggests that your time series model might include a periodic component. In time series terminology, this is more commonly referred to as a *seasonal component*, even though the cycle might be over hours or days.

Producing a High-Resolution Time Series Plot

Now construct the high-resolution time series plot:

■ Choose **Graph > Time Series Plot**

Note: You can also choose Stat > Time Series > Time Series Plot; the Time Series Plot command is available on both menus.

■ Select **C2 TEMP** to enter it in the first **Y** text box in the **Graph variables** section

The completed Time Series dialog box looks like Figure 15-3.

FIGURE 15-3

The completed Professional Time Series Plot dialog box

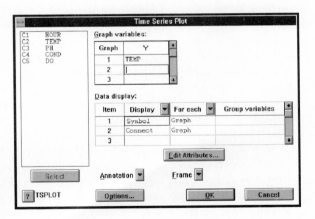

■ Click **OK**

The time series plot appears in the Graph window (Figure 15-4).

FIGURE 15-4

*Professional time
series plot*

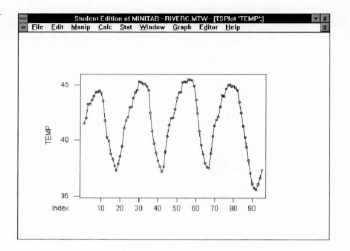

Note that this plot indicates the same cyclical pattern as the Character plot. There are two major differences between the two plots, however. First, the high-resolution plot is not broken into two blocks. Second, it connects all of the time series points with a straight line.

▼
Performing a Classical Decomposition of a Time Series
▲

In Tutorials 10 and 11, you used a linear regression to model and forecast a response variable based on one or more predictor variables. When the variables are time series variables, Minitab provides a number of other techniques especially designed to accomplish the same goals. They appear on the Time Series submenu of the Stat menu.

Trend analysis is closely related to simple linear regression. You choose from among four models to fit a particular type of trend line to a time series. This command provides three measures of the accuracy of the fitted values: Mean Squared Deviation (MSD), Mean Absolute Deviation (MAD), and Mean Absolute Percentage Error (MAPE). You can also detrend the time series. In addition, you can generate forecasts of future values of the series.

The Moving Average command uses moving averages to smooth out the "noise" in a time series. It also forecasts future values.

Decomposition performs a classical decomposition on a time series. You can select either a multiplicative or an additive model. *Classical decomposition* separates the time series into trend, seasonal, and error components by using least-squares analysis, trend analysis, and moving averages. You can also generate forecasts.

Based on your examination of the time series plot, you decide to use the Decomposition command to obtain the trend, seasonal, and error components of the default multiplicative model. In addition, you want to generate forecasts for the next two days (48 hours).

- Choose **Stat > Time Series > Decomposition**

- Select **C2 TEMP** to enter it in the **Variable** text box

- Type **24** in the **Seasonal length** text box

- Click **Generate forecasts**, press (Tab), and type **48** in the **Number of forecasts** text box

- Click the **Storage** button and then click **Forecasts** in the Decomposition-Storage dialog box, then press (←Enter)

The completed Decomposition dialog box should resemble Figure 15-5.

FIGURE 15-5

The completed Decomposition dialog box

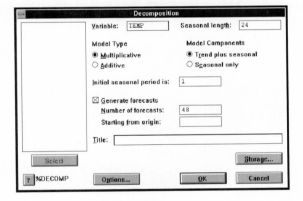

- Click **OK**

Minitab displays the results of the decomposition in the Session window and three Graph windows, and it adds a column, C6 FORE1, that contains the forecasts.

- Go to the Session window

■ Scroll up in the Session window to view the initial results of the decomposition analysis (Figure 15-6).

FIGURE 15-6

Decomposition results

```
Data      TEMP
Length    95.0000
NMissing  0

Trend Line Equation

Yt = 42.6710 - 2.11E-02*t


Seasonal Indices

Period    Index

   1      1.02167
   2      1.03768
   3      1.04624
   4      1.05749
   5      1.06885
   6      1.07383
   7      1.07158
   8      1.07528
   9      1.07626
  10      1.07279
  11      1.06180
  12      1.02159
  13      0.972796
  14      0.961675
  15      0.932260
  16      0.914849
  17      0.895907
  18      0.887141
  19      0.894304
  20      0.922715
  21      0.954326
  22      0.982208
  23      0.997388
  24      0.999377


Accuracy of Model

MAPE:     2.03659
MAD:      0.83921
MSD:      1.15545
```

Minitab provides the trend line equation $Yt = 42.6710 - 2.11E\text{-}02*t$ and the seasonal indices, which you can combine to obtain predicted and forecasted values. It also indicates the three measures you can use to determine the accuracy of the fitted values: MAPE (2.03659), MAD (0.83921), and MSD (1.15545). Minitab repeats these values in the Graph window (Figure 15-7), which displays a plot of the actual, predicted, and forecasted values along with the trend line.

■ Choose **Window > DECOMP1** to open the Graph window

FIGURE 15-7

Decomposition Fit for TEMP window

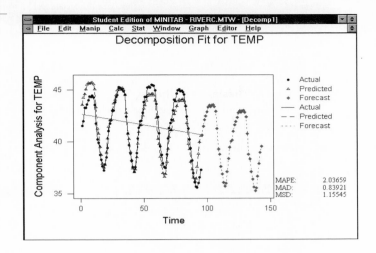

The graph depicts a slight downward trend, with a 24-hour seasonal component. It also reflects the divergence of the predicted values from the actual values at the top of peaks 1, 3, and 4, and at valley 4 (the last of the 95 observations).

Open the next Graph window (Figure 15-8), which provides a component analysis for TEMP.

■ Choose **Window > DECOMP2**

FIGURE 15-8

Component Analysis for TEMP

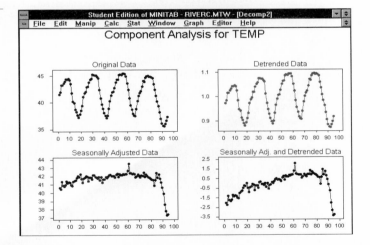

This window includes plots of the original data, detrended data, seasonally adjusted data, and the seasonally adjusted and detrended data. Note the unusual pattern at the end of the last two time series plots.

The third Graph window (Figure 15-9) provides a seasonal analysis for TEMP. It contains a plot of the seasonal indices. In addition, by seasonal period, it contains plots of the original data, present variation, and residuals. Note the large number of negative residuals present in four of the five last periods in the Residuals plot.

■ Choose **Window > DECOMP3**

FIGURE 15-9

Seasonal Analysis for TEMP

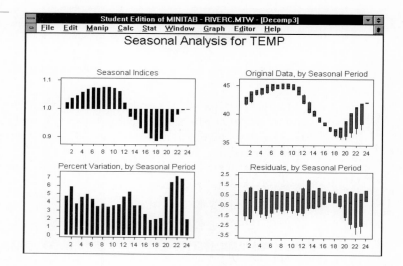

Scroll down in the Session window to view the rest of the results from the decomposition analysis, shown in Figure 15-10.

■ Choose **Window > Session**

FIGURE 15-10

*Session window showing
the forecasts*

Forecasts

ROW	Period	Forecast
1	96	40.6248
2	97	41.5096
3	98	42.1381
4	99	42.4635
5	100	42.8982
6	101	43.3363
7	102	43.5157
8	103	43.4021
9	104	43.5290
10	105	43.5461
11	106	43.3831
12	107	42.9165
13	108	41.2696
14	109	39.2780
15	110	38.8088
16	111	37.6021
17	112	36.8806
18	113	36.0981
19	114	35.7262
20	115	35.9959
21	116	37.1200
22	117	38.3716
23	118	39.4720
24	119	40.0610
25	120	40.1199
26	121	40.9934
27	122	41.6139
28	123	41.9350
29	124	42.3640
30	125	42.7963
31	126	42.9732
32	127	42.8607
33	128	42.9858
34	129	43.0024
35	130	42.8411
36	131	42.3801
37	132	40.7534
38	133	38.7866
39	134	38.3229
40	135	37.1311
41	136	36.4184
42	137	35.6455
43	138	35.2780
44	139	35.5440
45	140	36.6538
46	141	37.8894
47	142	38.9757
48	143	39.5571

MTB >

Your forecasts display the same pattern as your data. They peak between periods 102 and 105. Period 104 corresponds to 9:00 p.m. (the same time you saw a peak in your data). Still, the initial forecasting overestimates what you would expect, indicating that a problem may exist.

You decide to obtain another model and set of forecasts for the same time series. To do so, you plan to examine autocorrelation and partial autocorrelation plots and then construct the suggested ARIMA model.

▼ Checking the Autocorrelation and Partial Autocorrelation Plots ▲

For time series data, *autocorrelation* and *partial autocorrelation* measure the degree of relationship between observations k time periods, or *lags*, apart. These plots provide valuable information to help you identify an appropriate ARIMA model:

- Choose **Stat > Time Series > Autocorrelation**
- Double-click **C2 TEMP** to enter it in the **Series** text box
- Click the **Number of lags** option and press Tab
- Type **24** in the **Number of lags** text box to tell Minitab to compute and plot 24 autocorrelations

The completed Autocorrelation Function dialog box should look like Figure 15-11.

FIGURE 15-11

The completed Autocorrelation Function dialog box

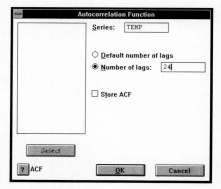

- Click **OK**

The autocorrelation plot appears in the Session window, as shown in Figure 15-12.

FIGURE 15-12

*The complete
autocorrelation plot in the
Session window*

```
MTB > ACF 24 'TEMP'.

ACF of TEMP

        -1.0 -0.8 -0.6 -0.4 -0.2  0.0  0.2  0.4  0.6  0.8  1.0
        +----+----+----+----+----+----+----+----+----+----+
    1    0.949                          XXXXXXXXXXXXXXXXXXXXXXXXX
    2    0.836                          XXXXXXXXXXXXXXXXXXXXXX
    3    0.675                          XXXXXXXXXXXXXXXXX
    4    0.477                          XXXXXXXXXXXXX
    5    0.261                          XXXXXXX
    6    0.039                          XX
    7   -0.172                     XXXXX
    8   -0.355                 XXXXXXXXX
    9   -0.504              XXXXXXXXXXXXX
   10   -0.611            XXXXXXXXXXXXXXX
   11   -0.673          XXXXXXXXXXXXXXXXX
   12   -0.696          XXXXXXXXXXXXXXXXX
   13   -0.679          XXXXXXXXXXXXXXXXX
   14   -0.623           XXXXXXXXXXXXXXX
   15   -0.532             XXXXXXXXXXXXX
   16   -0.409                XXXXXXXXXX
   17   -0.263                 XXXXXXX
   18   -0.097                    XXX
   19    0.076                         XXX
   20    0.243                         XXXXXX
   21    0.394                         XXXXXXXXXX
   22    0.524                         XXXXXXXXXXXXX
   23    0.617                         XXXXXXXXXXXXXXX
   24    0.662                         XXXXXXXXXXXXXXXX

MTB >
```

The autocorrelation plot resembles a sine pattern. This suggests that temperatures close in time are strongly and positively correlated, while temperatures about 12 hours apart are highly negatively correlated. (The large positive autocorrelation at lag 24 is indicative of the 24-hour seasonal component.) The pattern in the autocorrelation plot suggests that your ARIMA model may have an *autoregressive (AR)* component. The two positive, large autocorrelations at lags 1 and 2 call for an AR component of degree 2.

Now construct a plot of the partial autocorrelation function to gather additional information about an appropriate ARIMA model:

■ Choose **Stat > Time Series > Partial Autocorrelation**

■ Double-click **C2 TEMP** to enter it in the **Series** text box

■ Click **Number of lags** and press Tab

■ Type **24** in the **Number of lags** text box

The completed Partial Autocorrelation Function dialog box should look like Figure 15-13.

FIGURE 15-13

The completed Partial Autocorrelation Function dialog box

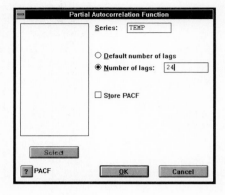

■ Click **OK**

The partial autocorrelation plot (Figure 15-14) appears in the Session window.

FIGURE 15-14

The partial autocorrelation plot in the Session window

```
MTB > PACF 24 'TEMP'.

PACF of TEMP

            -1.0 -0.8 -0.6 -0.4 -0.2  0.0  0.2  0.4  0.6  0.8  1.0
            +----+----+----+----+----+----+----+----+----+----+
    1  0.949                             XXXXXXXXXXXXXXXXXXXXXXXXX
    2 -0.660          XXXXXXXXXXXXXXXXXX
    3 -0.287                   XXXXXXX
    4 -0.234                   XXXXXX
    5 -0.086                      XXX
    6 -0.164                     XXXX
    7 -0.011                      X
    8  0.025                      XX
    9 -0.079                     XXX
   10 -0.031                      XX
   11 -0.079                     XXX
   12 -0.140                    XXXXX
   13 -0.072                     XXX
   14  0.036                      XX
   15  0.041                      XX
   16  0.098                      XXX
   17  0.074                      XXX
   18  0.160                      XXXXX
   19  0.007                      X
   20 -0.017                      X
   21  0.020                      X
   22  0.139                      XXXX
   23 -0.095                     XXX
   24 -0.128                    XXXX

MTB >
```

The partial autocorrelation plot shows two large partial autocorrelations (spikes) at lags 1 and 2, which also suggests an AR component of degree 2. Later in this tutorial, you fit an ARIMA model based on your findings thus far.

▼ Transforming a Time Series ▲

Luckily, the river data are fairly well-behaved, as evidenced by the time series plots in Figures 15-2 and 15-4. If you were to draw a horizontal line at the mean of the series, you would see that the data oscillate with the same cyclical pattern. A time series like this, whose mean and variance do not change with time, is called *stationary*.

Conversely, a time series that appears to wander and does not systematically fluctuate around a single value is called *nonstationary*. By lagging and differencing a nonstationary time series, you can usually make it stationary. To practice using these components, you obtain lags and differences for the river data, even though they are already stationary.

Lagging Data

You can think of *lagging* as "time shifting"; it shifts each element in a time series plot to a later point so that it lags behind by the number of time units you specify. When you lag a column in Minitab and store the lagged data, the new column is identical to the former one, except that the entries are shifted down or lagged by a specified number of rows. The empty rows at the beginning of the resulting column are filled with *s to indicate missing values. Minitab uses a default lag of 1.

- Choose **Stat > Time Series > Lag**

- Double-click **C2 TEMP** to enter it in the **Series** text box

- Type **LAGS** in the **Store lags in** text box

The completed Lag dialog box should look like Figure 15-15.

FIGURE 15-15

The completed Lag dialog box

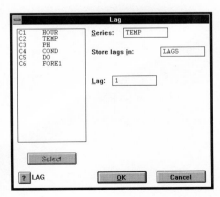

- Click **OK**

- Return to the Data window

Compare the temperature data in C2 with the data in column C7 LAGS in Figure 15-16.

FIGURE 15-16

The Data window, showing lagged temperature data in C7

	C1	C2	C3	C4	C5	C6	C7	C
→	HOUR	TEMP	PH	COND	DO	FORE1	LAGS	
1	1400	41.52	8.67	0.92	2.92	40.6248	*	
2	1500	41.99	8.65	0.94	2.34	41.5096	41.52	
3	1600	43.29	8.64	0.95	2.78	42.1381	41.99	
4	1700	43.29	8.67	0.95	2.39	42.4635	43.29	
5	1800	43.63	8.74	0.96	2.54	42.8982	43.29	
6	1900	44.01	8.82	0.96	3.31	43.3363	43.63	
7	2000	44.39	8.85	0.96	3.43	43.5157	44.01	
8	2100	44.35	8.83	0.97	3.98	43.4021	44.39	
9	2200	44.48	8.88	0.96	4.85	43.5290	44.35	
10	2300	44.27	8.84	0.97	4.74	43.5461	44.48	
11	2400	43.55	8.84	0.95	5.09	43.3831	44.27	
12	100	41.77	8.81	0.93	5.36	42.9165	43.55	
13	200	40.25	8.80	0.97	5.57	41.2696	41.77	
14	300	39.92	8.76	1.11	5.12	39.2780	40.25	
15	400	38.73	8.73	0.99	5.07	38.8088	39.92	
16	500	38.27	8.69	0.99	4.64	37.6021	38.73	
17	600	37.68	8.66	1.01	4.55	36.8806	38.27	
18	700	37.25	8.62	1.01	4.15	36.0981	37.68	
19	800	37.85	8.61	1.00	3.89	35.7262	37.25	

Student Edition of MINITAB - RIVERC.MTW - [Data]

File   Edit   Manip   Calc   Stat   Window   Graph   Editor   Help

Note that a value in C7 LAGS is one row lower but one number higher than the corresponding value in C2 TEMP. The first entry in C7 LAGS is missing.

Computing Differences

The Differences command computes differences of observations that are a specified lag apart. For example, if you specify a lag of 1, Minitab computes differences between adjacent values in the time series and stores them in a column. To apply the Differences command to the temperature data with differences of lag 1:

- Choose **Stat > Time Series > Differences**

- Double-click **C2 TEMP** to enter it in the **Series** text box

- Type **DIFF** in the **Store differences in** text box

The completed Differences dialog box should look like Figure 15-17.

FIGURE 15-17

The completed Differences dialog box

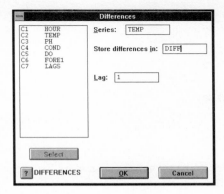

■ Click OK

C8 DIFF contains the differences between adjacent values in the time series for C2 TEMP (Figure 15-18). In other words, C8 DIFF is the difference between columns C2 TEMP and C7 LAGS.

FIGURE 15-18

The Data window, showing LAGS and DIFF columns

Student Edition of MINITAB - RIVERC.MTW - [Data]

File   Edit   Manip   Calc   Stat   Window   Graph   Editor   Help

	C2	C3	C4	C5	C6	C7	C8	C9
→	TEMP	PH	COND	DO	FORE1	LAGS	DIFF	
1	41.52	8.67	0.92	2.92	40.6248	*	*	
2	41.99	8.65	0.94	2.34	41.5096	41.52	0.47000	
3	43.29	8.64	0.95	2.78	42.1381	41.99	1.30000	
4	43.29	8.67	0.95	2.39	42.4635	43.29	0.00000	
5	43.63	8.74	0.96	2.54	42.8982	43.29	0.34000	
6	44.01	8.82	0.96	3.31	43.3363	43.63	0.38000	
7	44.39	8.85	0.96	3.43	43.5157	44.01	0.38000	
8	44.35	8.83	0.97	3.98	43.4021	44.39	-0.04000	
9	44.48	8.88	0.96	4.85	43.5290	44.35	0.13000	
10	44.27	8.84	0.97	4.74	43.5461	44.48	-0.21000	
11	43.55	8.84	0.95	5.09	43.3831	44.27	-0.72000	
12	41.77	8.81	0.93	5.36	42.9165	43.55	-1.78000	
13	40.25	8.80	0.97	5.57	41.2696	41.77	-1.52000	
14	39.92	8.76	1.11	5.12	39.2780	40.25	-0.33000	
15	38.73	8.73	0.99	5.07	38.8088	39.92	-1.19000	
16	38.27	8.69	0.99	4.64	37.6021	38.73	-0.46000	
17	37.68	8.66	1.01	4.55	36.8806	38.27	-0.59000	
18	37.25	8.62	1.01	4.15	36.0981	37.68	-0.43000	
19	37.85	8.61	1.00	3.89	35.7262	37.25	0.60000	

Recall that the shape of your time series plot indicates whether the time series is stationary or nonstationary. Consider taking differences when the time series plot indicates a nonstationary time series. You can then use the resulting differenced data as your time series, plotting the differenced time series to determine if it is stationary.

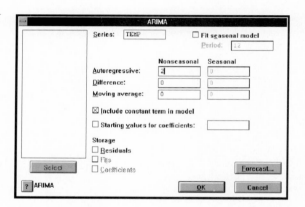

Performing a Box-Jenkins ARIMA Analysis of a Time Series

▼

▲

Your investigation of the autocorrelation and partial autocorrelation plots suggested that you should consider an ARIMA model with an AR component of degree 2, called AR 2, and a 24-hour seasonal AR component of degree 1, called SAR 1. Hoping to keep the model as simple as possible, you first try a model with AR 2.

Use the ARIMA command to estimate the parameters for this model and investigate its fit:

- Choose **Stat > Time Series > ARIMA**
- Double-click **C2 TEMP** to enter it in the **Series** text box and press (Tab)
- Type **2** in the **Nonseasonal Autoregressive** text box

The completed ARIMA dialog box should resemble Figure 15-19.

FIGURE 15-19

The completed ARIMA dialog box

Note: The columns next to Autoregressive, Difference, and Moving average correspond to the nonseasonal and seasonal components of the ARIMA model, respectively.

- Click **OK**
- Scroll up in the Session window to view the results of the ARIMA analysis (Figure 15-20)

FIGURE 15-20

*Iteration estimates from
the ARIMA analysis*

```
MTB > ARIMA 2 0 0 'TEMP';
SUBC>   Constant.

Estimates at each iteration
Iteration      SSE      Parameters
     0      556.993   0.100    0.100   33.408
     1      460.739   0.250    0.020   30.500
     2      376.654   0.400   -0.064   27.719
     3      301.680   0.550   -0.147   24.946
     4      235.673   0.700   -0.231   22.176
     5      178.602   0.850   -0.315   19.408
     6      130.452   1.000   -0.399   16.643
     7       91.073   1.150   -0.482   13.865
     8       60.786   1.300   -0.566   11.110
     9       39.320   1.450   -0.650    8.351
    10       26.746   1.600   -0.734    5.611
    11       22.933   1.733   -0.810    3.202
    12       22.919   1.742   -0.815    3.069
    13       22.919   1.742   -0.816    3.060
Relative change in each estimate less than  0.0010
```

Minitab provides a history of this iterative process, with the sum of squared errors (SSE) and the parameter estimates for each iteration. In Figure 15-20 the parameter estimates correspond to the two AR 2 components and the constant parameters, respectively. If the estimates do not converge after 25 iterations, Minitab stops the process.

Next Minitab displays the final parameter estimates in detail, as shown in Figure 15-21.

FIGURE 15-21

*Final parameter estimates
from the ARIMA analysis*

```
Final Estimates of Parameters
Type      Estimate    St. Dev.   t-ratio
AR   1      1.7421     0.0629     27.70
AR   2     -0.8156     0.0639    -12.76
Constant   3.05969    0.05129     59.66
Mean      41.6201     0.6977

No. of obs.:  95
Residuals:    SS = 22.8843  (backforecasts excluded)
              MS =  0.2487  DF = 92

Modified Box-Pierce (Ljung-Box) chisquare statistic
Lag                12           24           36            48
Chisquare    25.2(DF=10)  48.7(DF=22)  58.4(DF=34)  76.7(DF=46)

MTB >
```

Minitab estimates the first autoregressive coefficient (AR 1) as 1.7421, with a standard deviation of 0.0629 and a t-ratio of 27.70. The second autoregressive coefficient (AR 2) is estimated at –0.8156, with a standard deviation of 0.0639 and a t-ratio of –12.76. The estimated constant term is 3.05969.

STOCK MARKET: Stock market analysts must be able to model and predict prices accurately to make wise decisions about futures trade contracts. A mathematician in South Carolina used Minitab's ARIMA capability to model the Chicago Board of Trade's wheat contract.

The mathematician assumed that the current wheat contract price is a function of price trends; it is this statistical dependence that time series analysts study. He used 1054 previous wheat contract prices over a period of four years and entered that data into Minitab. Testing several different configurations led him to a successful model that used an autoregressive component of 1, a differencing component of 1, and a moving average of 2.

Once Minitab helps identify a statistically correct model, a stock market or commodities analyst can use Minitab's forecasting capability to predict future wheat contract prices and maybe even catch a short-term profit.

You conclude that both the AR 1 and AR 2 parameters are significantly different from zero since the t-ratios are so large. You could compute the estimated temperature at time T as follows:

$$\text{TEMP at time } T = 3.05969 + 1.7421 * \text{TEMP (at time } T-1)$$
$$- 0.8156 * \text{TEMP (at time } T-2)$$

The modified Box-Pierce (Ljung-Box) chi-square statistic, which measures how well the model fits the data, appears last in Figure 15-21. For the following hypotheses, chi-square statistics are computed at lags of 12, 24, 36, and 48:

H_0: The specified ARIMA model fits the data.

H_1: The specified ARIMA model does not fit the data.

To check the significance of the value for the lag of 12:

- Choose **Calc > Probability Distributions > Chisquare**

- Click the **Cumulative probability** option

- Click the **Degrees of freedom** text box and type **10**

- Click **Input constant** and press Tab

- Type **25.2** in the **Input constant** text box and press Tab

- Type **K1** in the **Optional storage** text box and press ↵Enter

After the MTB > prompt in the Session window:

- Type **LET K2=1-K1** and press ⏎Enter
- Type **PRINT K2** and press ⏎Enter

The p-value for the test is 0.00497365, indicating that the chi-square statistic is significant. If you check the p-values for the other chi-square statistics, you find that they are also small. You conclude that your specified ARIMA model does not fit the data at most standard levels of significance.

Constructing a Seasonal Model

Based on this lack of fit, you decide to specify a new ARIMA model (0,0,0) (1,0,0) (24) that is seasonal.

- Choose **Stat > Time Series > ARIMA**
- Verify that **C2 TEMP** appears in the **Series** text box
- Click the **Fit seasonal model** check box and press Tab
- Type **24** in the **Period** text box and press Tab
- Type **0** in the **Nonseasonal Autoregressive** text box and press Tab three times
- Type **1** in the **Seasonal Autoregressive** text box

The modified ARIMA dialog box should look like Figure 15-22.

FIGURE 15-22

The ARIMA dialog box with the seasonal model

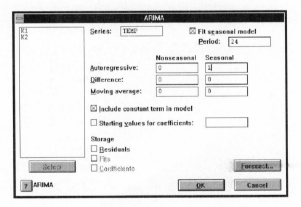

■ Click **OK**

Minitab alerts you that it is unable to estimate this model (Figure 15-23).

```
MTB > ARIMA 0 0 0 1 0 0 24 'TEMP';
SUBC>   Constant.

Estimates at each iteration
Iteration        SSE    Parameters
        0    715.281    0.100   37.584
        1    570.425    0.250   31.278
        2    443.907    0.400   25.001
        3    333.375    0.550   18.729
        4    237.159    0.700   12.468
        5    154.825    0.850    6.222
        6    106.324    1.000    0.000
Unable to reduce sum of squares any further
* ERROR * Model cannot be estimated with these data

MTB >
```

Now you consult with an EPA statistician. After examining some additional plots, the statistician suggests that you try ARIMA (2,0,0) (1,1,0) (24).

■ Choose **Edit > Edit Last Command Dialog**

■ Press [Tab] three times, type **2** in the **Nonseasonal Autoregressive** text box, and then press [Tab] four times

■ Type **1** in the **Seasonal Difference** text box

The modified ARIMA dialog box should resemble Figure 15-24.

FIGURE 15-24

The completed ARIMA dialog box with new model

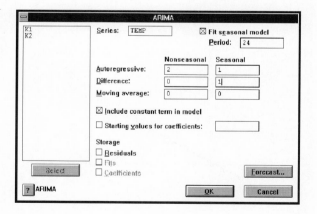

■ Click **OK**

The Session window shows the results of your new model (Figure 15-25).

```
Final Estimates of Parameters
Type      Estimate    St. Dev.   t-ratio
AR   1      1.0065      0.1242      8.10
AR   2      0.0467      0.1418      0.33
SAR 24     -0.3164      0.1534     -2.06
Constant-0.0737137  -0.0750197      0.98

Differencing: 0 regular, 1 seasonal of order 24
No. of obs.:  Original series 95, after differencing 71
Residuals:    SS = 12.6416  (backforecasts excluded)
              MS =  0.1887  DF = 67

Modified Box-Pierce (Ljung-Box) chisquare statistic
Lag              12          24          36          48
Chisquare   13.2(DF= 9)  24.9(DF=21)  37.3(DF=33)  46.6(DF=45)

MTB >
```

The modified Box-Pierce (Ljung-Box) chi-square statistics seem much better for this model. Again, check the significance of the value for the lag of 12 for the following hypotheses:

H_0: The specified ARIMA model fits the data.

H_1: The specified ARIMA model does not fit the data.

■ Choose **Calc > Probability Distributions > Chisquare**

■ Verify that the **Cumulative probability** option button is selected

■ Double-click the **Degrees of freedom** text box and type **9**

■ Double-click the **Input constant** text box, type **13.2**, and then press ⌨Tab

■ Type **K3** in the **Optional storage** text box and press ⌨←Enter

After the MTB > prompt in the Session window:

■ Type **LET K4=1-K3** and press ⌨←Enter

■ Type **PRINT K4** and press ⌨←Enter

The p-value for the test is 0.153697, so the chi-square statistic is not significant at the usual levels. If you computed the other p-values, you would reach the same conclusion. Consequently, you do not reject the hypothesis that this model fits the data.

Forecasting Using ARIMA

Once you determine the model, the final step is to forecast future values. Predict the temperatures for the next 48 hours and then store the forecasts and prediction limits:

- Choose **Stat > Time Series > ARIMA**

- Verify that the dialog box entries still appear as shown in Figure 15-24

- Click the **Forecast** button

    In the ARIMA-Forecasts dialog box:

- Type **48** in the **Lead** text box and press Tab twice

- Type **AFORECST** in the **Forecasts** text box and press Tab

- Type **LAFORCST** in the **Lower limits** text box and press Tab

- Type **UAFORCST** in the **Upper limits** text box

    The completed ARIMA-Forecasts dialog box should resemble Figure 15-26.

FIGURE 15-26

The completed ARIMA-Forecasts dialog box

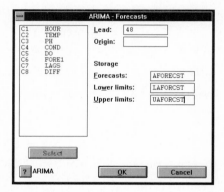

- Click **OK** twice

    Minitab displays forecasts with 95% confidence limits in the Session window (Figure 15-27).

FIGURE 15-27

Forecasts in the Session window

```
Forecasts from period 95
                            95 Percent Limits
 Period    Forecast        Lower        Upper        Actual
   96      37.1863       36.3347      38.0378
   97      37.7163       36.5081      38.9244
   98      38.4370       36.9291      39.9450
   99      38.1437       36.3624      39.9250
  100      38.2775       36.2364      40.3185
  101      38.3947       36.1007      40.6886
  102      38.0443       35.5001      40.5886
  103      37.4721       34.6774      40.2668
  104      37.1260       34.0784      40.1735
  105      36.5488       33.2445      39.8531
  106      35.8928       32.3264      39.4592
  107      34.4395       30.6043      38.2746
  108      32.8131       28.7015      36.9247
  109      31.0372       26.6405      35.4339
  110      29.2210       24.5295      33.9124
  111      27.5802       22.5834      32.5770
  112      25.8372       20.5235      31.1509
  113      24.0700       18.4270      29.7130
  114      22.5706       16.5849      28.5562
  115      21.5042       15.1616      27.8468
  116      21.0156       14.3008      27.7304
  117      20.9608       13.8577      28.0640
  118      20.7370       13.2283      28.2458
  119      20.4378       12.5051      28.3704
  120      19.4505       10.8700      28.0309
  121      19.0421        9.8085      28.2758
  122      18.7644        8.8589      28.6700
  123      17.3607        6.7626      27.9588
  124      16.4588        5.1450      27.7726
  125      15.3600        3.3051      27.4149
  126      13.7878        0.9641      26.6114
  127      11.9256       -1.6968      25.5479
  128      10.2123       -4.2409      24.6654
  129       8.2115       -7.1069      23.5299
  130       6.0519      -10.1685      22.2722
  131       2.9693      -14.1922      20.1308
  132      -0.2658      -18.4100      17.8784
  133      -3.7619      -22.9329      15.4091
  134      -7.3321      -27.5766      12.9123
  135     -10.8402      -32.2076      10.5272
  136     -14.6234      -37.1661       7.9192
  137     -18.5328      -42.3059       5.2403
  138     -22.2984      -47.3603       2.7635
  139     -25.7184      -52.1306       0.6937
  140     -28.7921      -56.6193      -0.9648
  141     -31.5231      -60.8338      -2.2123
  142     -34.4856      -65.3520      -3.6192
  143     -37.5977      -70.0956      -5.0999

MTB >
```

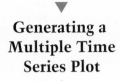

Generating a Multiple Time Series Plot

A graph might provide a clearer picture of the same forecasts with 95% confidence intervals. You decide to construct a multiple time series plot:

- Choose **Graph > Time Series Plot**

- Select **C9 AFORECST** to enter it in the first **Y** text box in the **Graph variables** section

- Select **C10 LAFORECST** to enter it in the second **Y** text box in the **Graph variables** section

- Select **C11 UAFORECST** to enter it in the third **Y** text box in the **Graph variables** section

- Scroll up the Graph variables text box to verify that the three columns are listed

- Click the **Frame** button and click **Multiple Graphs**

- Click the **Overlay graphs on the same page** option button

- Click **OK** twice

The graph appears in a Graph window (Figure 15-28).

FIGURE 15-28

Multiple time series plot graph

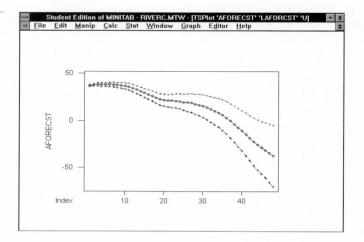

Your forecasts indicate a limited amount of seasonality. Your initial 95% forecast intervals are fairly narrow, with lengths of roughly 2 degrees. Later the lengths increase to approximately 70 degrees. As you recall from your statistics course, forecast intervals increase as you forecast further into the future.

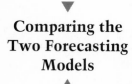

Comparing the Two Forecasting Models

The forecasts from the classical decomposition and the ARIMA (2,0,0) (1,1,0) (24) models are different. First, you observe that the initial values of the forecasts for the ARIMA model are much closer to what you would expect based on the last few observations. Second, each set of forecasts produces a distinct pattern, which you can examine by constructing another multiple time series plot with both the FORE1 and AFORECST forecast variables:

- Choose **Edit > Edit Last Command Dialog**

- Replace the entry in the second **Y** text box in the **Graph variables** section with **C6 FORE1**

- Delete the entry in the third **Y** text box in the **Graph variables** section

- Press (←Enter)

The graph appears in a Graph window (Figure 15-29).

FIGURE 15-29

Time series plot comparing models

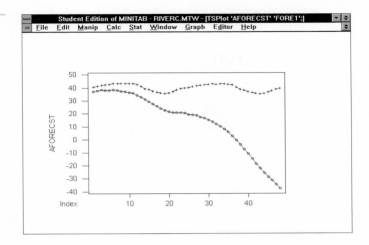

Note that the classical decomposition preserves the seasonality over the 48 forecasts much better than the ARIMA model. It also produces forecast values similar in value and magnitude to the observed data.

You wonder if there might be an even better model for this time series. Your EPA statistician suggests you might try an ARIMA (2,1,0) (1,0,0) (24) model. Other possibilities might include models using single exponential smoothing, double exponential smoothing, or seasonal exponential smoothing. You can implement these three procedures by using the Single Exp Smoothing, Double Exp Smoothing, and Winters' Method commands on the Time Series submenu, respectively. See online Help for more information about time series procedures.

For now, save your worksheet because you may want to use it for additional modeling.

■ Save your worksheet with the name **15RIVERC** on your Student disk

■ Choose **File > Other Files > Stop Recording Session**

In this tutorial, you analyzed a time series with classical decomposition and Box-Jenkins ARIMA techniques. You used autocorrelation and partial autocorrelation plots, together with lagging and differencing transformations, to help you identify an appropriate model. The interactive nature of Minitab makes it possible to try as many preliminary models as your patience allows before you settle on a final model and begin to make forecasts. The techniques you have seen in this tutorial provide a powerful and flexible forecasting tool that can fit virtually any such model.

If you plan to continue directly to the next tutorial:

■ Choose **File > Restart Minitab**

If you want to take a longer break:

■ Choose **File > Exit**

This section describes the Minitab menu commands introduced in or related to this tutorial. To find a complete explanation of all menus and commands, refer to the Reference section of this manual.

Minitab Menu Commands

Menu	Command	Description
Stat		
	Time Series	
	Time Series Plot	Produces a Professional time series plot for one or more columns of data against time on the same axes
	Trend Analysis	Uses trend analysis to fit a particular type of trend line to a time series or to detrend a time series
	Decomposition	Performs classical decomposition on a time series
	Moving Average	Uses moving averages to smooth out the noise in a time series and forecast future values of the series
	Single Exp Smoothing	Uses single exponential smoothing to smooth out the noise in a time series
	Double Exp Smoothing	Performs Holt or Brown double exponential smoothing for a time series
	Winters' Method	Performs Holt-Winters seasonal exponential smoothing for a time series
	Differences	Computes and saves the differences of a time series
	Lag	Forms the lag of a time series
	Autocorrelation	Computes and produces a Character graph of the autocorrelations of a time series
	Partial Autocorrelation	Computes and produces a Character graph of the partial autocorrelations of a time series

Menu	Command	Description
	Cross Correlation	Computes and produces a Character graph of the cross correlations between two time series
	ARIMA	Fits a specified autoregressive integrated moving average model to time series data, stored in a constant; can provide forecasts

Review and Practice

Matching

Match the following terms to their definitions by placing the correct letter next to the term it describes.

_____ Multiplicative

_____ Box-Jenkins

_____ Time Series Plot

_____ Lag

_____ Number of lags

_____ AR1

_____ Winter's Method

_____ Ljung-Box

_____ Stationary

_____ Trend Analysis

a. The option that specifies the number of autocorrelations and partial autocorrelations to compute and display in the autocorrelation and partial autocorrelation plots

b. The default decomposition model

c. The command that shifts a particular column of data down a specified number of rows and saves the results in another column

d. (1,0,0) (0,0,0) (0)

e. A command found on both the Graph menu and Time Series submenu

f. Another name for ARIMA

g. The command that detrends a time series

h. A time series whose mean and variance do not change with time

i. The name of the chi-square statistic you use to test the fit of an ARIMA model

j. The command that performs seasonal exponential smoothing

True/False

Mark the following statements with a *T* or an *F*.

_____ 1. When you use the Differences command, storing the results in a column is optional.

_____ 2. You always produce forecasts of future events when you use the ARIMA command.

_____ 3. A Character time series plot connects sequential points with lines.

_____ 4. Before Minitab can compute differences, you must issue the Lag command.

_____ 5. The ARIMA output contains p-values that determine the significance of the ARIMA model's fit.

_____ 6. You can request interval forecasts of any specified confidence level when you use the ARIMA command.

_____ 7. The Decomposition command produces three Graph windows.

_____ 8. Autocorrelation and partial autocorrelation plots always output a test of significance.

_____ 9. MADE, MAP, and MSD are three measures you use to determine the accuracy of the fitted values in classical decomposition.

_____ 10. There are two menu or submenu commands you can use to create Professional time series plots.

Practice Problems

1. Open the SP500.MTW data.

   a. Plot the CLOSE variable.

   b. Perform a classical decomposition.

   c. Is there a trend component? Is there a seasonal component? Explain your answers.

2. Open RIVERC.MTW. Reanalyze the time series in this tutorial using an ARIMA (2,1,0) (1,0,0) (24) model. How does it compare to the two models considered in the tutorial?

3. Open the RIVERC.MTW data set. In addition to the river's temperature, the EPA measured three other river characteristics: pH, conductivity, and dissolved oxygen content. The pH (PH) variable indicates the acidity or alkalinity of the water. Perform a time series analysis of pH. Your analysis should follow the approach used in the tutorial. That is, for each characteristic, plot the series, fit and forecast a classical decomposition model, obtain the autocorrelation and partial autocorrelation plots, and, finally, fit and forecast an appropriate ARIMA model.

4. The EPA monitored several sites in the river study. Site B was directly upriver from the plant's intake pipes. Redo the analysis described in this tutorial using the Site B's data, which are stored in the file RIVERB.MTW.

5. Open the RIVERC2.MTW data set, which contains the results of the work you performed in this tutorial. Stack the actual values of the studied time series on top of the fitted values from the classical decomposition and the fitted values from the final ARIMA model. Produce a multiple time series plot of both variables. What does this plot show you?

TUTORIAL 16

Exec Macros

In addition to using Minitab's menu and Session commands, you can also write and store your own sets of commands in files called *macros*. In this tutorial, you work with *Exec macros*, one of the types of macros available in Minitab (the other type, *%Macros*, is more powerful, but it is available only in the full commercial version). You can use Execs to perform repetitive analyses and statistical analyses that are not available as commands on Minitab's menus. This macro feature of Minitab essentially gives you the power to "program" in Minitab. (Refer to Chapter 5 in the Reference section for more information about Execs.)

Objectives

In this tutorial you learn how to:

- create an Exec in Minitab by copying and pasting commands from the History window to the Session window

- execute an Exec more than once

- create an Exec using a word processor

- modify Execs to make them more flexible

Comparing Menu Commands and the Minitab Command Language

An Exec is a series of Minitab commands stored in a file. Exec files must be in text (ASCII) format. When you store an Exec, Minitab automatically saves the file in ASCII format and adds the .MTB extension to the file name.

To practice writing an Exec, you will investigate statistical confidence intervals. Recall that the level of confidence (for example, 90%) of a confidence interval is the percentage of all such confidence intervals that are expected to include the true population mean. You "simulate" what would happen if you were to repeat the experiment a large number of times.

In this tutorial, you generate random samples of data from a normal population with a mean of 10 and a sigma of 4, and store them in columns. You then obtain confidence intervals for the mean and, finally, determine how many of them actually include the population mean, 10.

So far in the tutorials, you have executed Minitab commands primarily through menu choices. With few exceptions, you can also issue these commands by typing them in the Session window. To use Minitab's Exec feature to its fullest, you must "know" the commands and subcommands by name. However, the History window (introduced in Tutorial 5) can be a great help in this matter, because it allows you to see the Minitab command that corresponds to any menu command.

Note: To find the Session command equivalent for any menu command, you can consult the Quick Reference Card. To find the menu command equivalent for any Session command, you can consult Appendix A, "Session Command/Menu Command Equivalents."

To investigate the relationship between menu commands and Session commands, you issue commands from menus and view them in the History window.

- Start Minitab

- Choose **Window > History**

The History window appears (Figure 16-1). Your window may be a different size or may be maximized.

FIGURE 16-1

The History window

Now generate the simulation data, which consist of 30 observations stored in each of 25 columns (C1 through C25):

- Maximize the History window

- Choose **Calc > Random Data > Normal**

- Type **30** in the **Generate rows of data** text box and press Tab

- Type **C1-C25** in the **Store in column(s)** text box and press Tab

- Type **10** in the **Mean** text box and press Tab

- Type **4** in the **Standard deviation** text box and press ←Enter

It takes Minitab a while to generate the simulation data. As you wait, note the Minitab commands in the History window (Figure 16-2). Figure 16-2 shows the Set Base command, indicating a base from which Minitab starts generating the random numbers. This book uses a base so that your instructor can replicate this example; you, however, don't set a base, so the command won't appear in your History window.

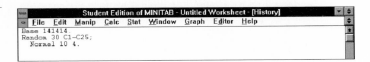

Compare what you typed in the dialog box to the contents of the History window. The first Minitab command, Random, generates the random data. The 30 after "Random" in the History window corresponds to the number of rows of random values for each sample generated. The C1-C25 tells Minitab to store the results in columns 1 through 25, inclusive. The semicolon at the end of the command indicates that a subcommand follows it.

The subcommand is automatically indented in the History window, which makes it easier to differentiate between commands and subcommands. The subcommand Normal 10 4 tells Minitab the distribution from which to sample (in this case, a normal distribution with a mean of 10 and a sigma of 4). The period at the end of the subcommand indicates that no other subcommands follow.

The random data are displayed in the Data window (you can switch windows to see the data, if desired). Next, compute the 90% confidence intervals for the population mean, using the 25 samples stored in columns C1 through C25. Since you assume the population standard deviation is 4, use the 1-Sample Z command:

- Choose **Stat > Basic Statistics > 1-Sample Z**

- Type **C1-C25** in the **Variables** text box and press Tab twice

- Type **90** in the **Level** text box and press Tab

- Type **4** in the **Sigma** text box and press ←Enter

The Session window becomes active and displays the 25 confidence intervals. You will come back to these intervals soon; first, however, return to the History window to see the Minitab command used to obtain confidence intervals:

■ Choose **Window > History**

The *ZInterval* command obtains confidence intervals for a population mean when the population standard deviation is known. The desired degree of confidence (90) comes next, then the population sigma (4), and, finally, the columns containing the data (C1 through C25). Return to the Session window to investigate the confidence intervals:

■ Choose **Window > Session**

The Session window displays the 25 90% confidence intervals (Figure 16-3).

FIGURE 16-3

The 90% confidence intervals

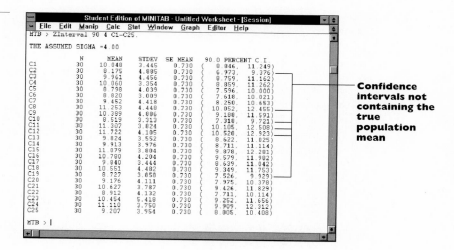

Your data will probably be different because Figure 16-3 shows data generated using a base of 141414, which you didn't use. Of the 25 90% confidence intervals generated for this tutorial, six (C2, C8, C10, C11, C12, and C19) do not contain the true population mean of 10. You can expect that approximately 10% of your confidence intervals won't contain the true population mean.

Creating an Exec File Using Commands

▼

▲

Take this idea one step further. Generate 100 samples and see how many confidence intervals fail to trap the true population mean. You could simply repeat the steps above three more times, but it is simpler to store these commands in an Exec and then execute it.

Rather than switching back and forth between the Session and History windows, you can tile them to see both at the same time:

■ Choose **Window > Minimize All**

■ Double-click the **Session** icon and then the **History icon**

■ Choose **Window > Tile**

The History and Session windows are both open and visible; your screen looks similar to Figure 16-4 (except that your History window won't show the Base command because you didn't issue it).

FIGURE 16-4

Tiled Session and History windows

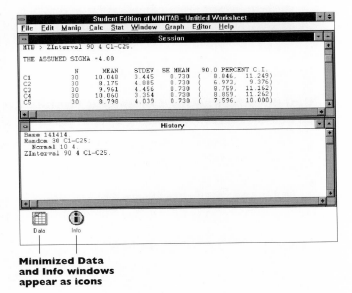

Minimized Data and Info windows appear as icons

Examining the Options for Storing Commands in an Exec

To store commands in an Exec:

■ Choose **File > Other Files > Start Recording Exec**

■ Insert your Student disk in drive A (or a different drive, if appropriate)

■ Click the **Drives** drop-down list arrow and then click **a:**

■ Double-click the **File Name** text box, type **CONFINTS**, and then press ⏎Enter

Both windows show the corresponding Minitab command (Store 'A:\CONFINTS.MTB'). Note that the prompt in the Session window changes from MTB > to STOR>, to indicate that Minitab is storing commands for an Exec. In this mode, Minitab simply stores the commands you issue — it doesn't execute them.

At this point you have several options. You could type the Exec commands in the Session window. This requires that you have a very good knowledge of the command language. Also, when typing commands into an Exec, you must be careful. If you make a typing mistake and happen to notice it before you press ⎵Enter⎵, you can go back and fix it. But once you've pressed ⎵Enter⎵, Minitab accepts your command and moves to the next prompt.

Your second alternative is to use the menus. Minitab translates the menu command into its own language equivalent and stores it in the Exec. A word of caution is due, though: some commands might not work because Minitab won't execute a command that includes columns that don't currently contain data.

The third and easiest alternative is to copy and paste the commands from the History window to the Session window. This method has the advantage of letting you try the commands in a given sequence beforehand, verifying that the Exec will perform as you intend. Also, because you are copying and pasting commands that have worked correctly, there should be no typos.

Copying and Pasting Commands to the Exec File

To have Minitab copy and paste the commands from the History window:

- Highlight the **Random, Normal, and ZInterval** commands in the History window (be sure to include the period after C25)

- Release the mouse button

  The History window should look like Figure 16-5.

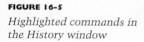

FIGURE 16-5

Highlighted commands in the History window

- Choose **Edit > Copy**

At this point, the commands you want to include in your Exec are on the Clipboard. You can now paste them into the Session window:

- Place the I-beam to the right of the bottom STOR> prompt in the Session window and click the mouse

- Choose **Edit** > **Paste** and press ⏎Enter

Minitab automatically enters the commands after the STOR> prompt, repeating them in the History window. To end the Exec:

- Choose **File** > **Other Files** > **Stop Recording Exec**

The Minitab command language equivalent of the Stop Recording Exec menu command is End. Your Session window should look like Figure 16-6.

FIGURE 16-6

The completed Exec

```
MTB > Store  'A:\CONFINTS.MTB';
SUBC>    Replace.
Storing in file: A:\CONFINTS.MTB
STOR> Random 30 C1-C25;
STOR>    Normal 10 4.
STOR> ZInterval 90 4 C1-C25.
STOR> End.
```

Running an Exec

You are ready to run your Exec. In Tutorial 7, you executed the PINF.MTB Exec. You can execute the confidence interval simulation Exec you just created in the same way:

- Choose **File** > **Other Files** > **Run an Exec**

- Click **Select File** to execute the Exec once

- Select **a:** in the **Drives** drop-down list box

- Double-click **CONFINTS.MTB** in the **Files** list box

Watch the results in the Session window as Minitab executes the Exec. In the History window, Minitab displays only the Execute command and none of the results.

If you inspect the Session window and the 25 confidence intervals in Figure 16-7, you find that three (C12, C16, and C18) do not include the true population mean of 10. Because your output will differ from that shown in Figure 16-7, you may find fewer or more intervals that do not include 10.

FIGURE 16-7

Additional confidence intervals

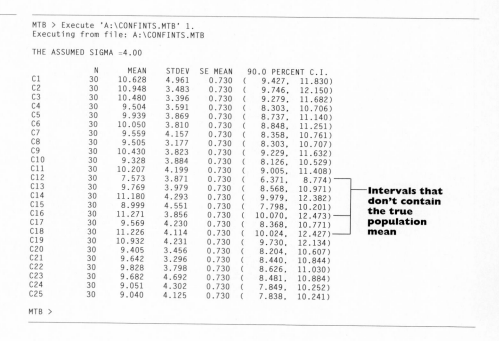

```
MTB > Execute 'A:\CONFINTS.MTB' 1.
Executing from file: A:\CONFINTS.MTB

THE ASSUMED SIGMA =4.00

             N      MEAN    STDEV   SE MEAN    90.0 PERCENT C.I.
C1          30    10.628    4.961    0.730   (  9.427,   11.830)
C2          30    10.948    3.483    0.730   (  9.746,   12.150)
C3          30    10.480    3.396    0.730   (  9.279,   11.682)
C4          30     9.504    3.591    0.730   (  8.303,   10.706)
C5          30     9.939    3.869    0.730   (  8.737,   11.140)
C6          30    10.050    3.810    0.730   (  8.848,   11.251)
C7          30     9.559    4.157    0.730   (  8.358,   10.761)
C8          30     9.505    3.177    0.730   (  8.303,   10.707)
C9          30    10.430    3.823    0.730   (  9.229,   11.632)
C10         30     9.328    3.884    0.730   (  8.126,   10.529)
C11         30    10.207    4.199    0.730   (  9.005,   11.408)
C12         30     7.573    3.871    0.730   (  6.371,    8.774)
C13         30     9.769    3.979    0.730   (  8.568,   10.971)
C14         30    11.180    4.293    0.730   (  9.979,   12.382)
C15         30     8.999    4.551    0.730   (  7.798,   10.201)
C16         30    11.271    3.856    0.730   ( 10.070,   12.473)
C17         30     9.569    4.230    0.730   (  8.368,   10.771)
C18         30    11.226    4.114    0.730   ( 10.024,   12.427)
C19         30    10.932    4.231    0.730   (  9.730,   12.134)
C20         30     9.405    3.456    0.730   (  8.204,   10.607)
C21         30     9.642    3.296    0.730   (  8.440,   10.844)
C22         30     9.828    3.798    0.730   (  8.626,   11.030)
C23         30     9.682    4.692    0.730   (  8.481,   10.884)
C24         30     9.051    4.302    0.730   (  7.849,   10.252)
C25         30     9.040    4.125    0.730   (  7.838,   10.241)

MTB >
```

Intervals that don't contain the true population mean

So far, 9 out of 50 intervals do not contain the mean. In the next section, you generate 50 more intervals to see how many of the 100 do not contain the mean. You expect approximately 90% of confidence intervals with a confidence level of 90% to include the true population mean.

Running an Exec Twice

To obtain 50 more confidence intervals, tell Minitab to run the Exec two more times (or as many times as you want):

- Choose **File > Other Files > Run an Exec**
- Type **2** in the **Number of times to execute** text box and press [←Enter]
- Make sure **a:** is selected in the **Drives** drop-down list box and then double-click **CONFINTS.MTB** in the **Files** list box

Note: To run or execute an Exec from the Session window, you enter the Execute command, the Exec's file name enclosed in single quotes, and the number of times you want the Exec to execute, all separated by one or more blank spaces. For example, to execute CONFINTS.MTB three times from the Session window, you would type:

EXECUTE 'A:\CONFINTS.MTB' 3.

The 50 additional confidence intervals appear in Figure 16-8; again, your results will be different.

FIGURE 16-8

Additional 50 confidence intervals

```
MTB > Execute 'A:\CONFINTS.MTB' 2.
Executing from file: A:\CONFINTS.MTB

THE ASSUMED SIGMA =4.00

          N      MEAN    STDEV   SE MEAN    90.0 PERCENT C.I.
C1        30     9.421   3.577    0.730   (   8.219,  10.622)
C2        30     9.666   3.954    0.730   (   8.464,  10.868)
C3        30    10.549   4.300    0.730   (   9.347,  11.750)
C4        30     9.165   3.515    0.730   (   7.963,  10.366)
C5        30    10.903   2.737    0.730   (   9.702,  12.105)
C6        30    10.766   4.250    0.730   (   9.564,  11.967)
C7        30     9.758   3.717    0.730   (   8.556,  10.960)
C8        30     9.660   3.552    0.730   (   8.458,  10.862)
C9        30    10.340   3.427    0.730   (   9.138,  11.541)
C10       30     9.594   3.902    0.730   (   8.392,  10.795)
C11       30    10.013   4.095    0.730   (   8.811,  11.215)
C12       30    11.130   4.192    0.730   (   9.928,  12.331)
C13       30     8.868   4.596    0.730   (   7.666,  10.069)
C14       30    10.256   4.238    0.730   (   9.054,  11.457)
C15       30    10.582   3.537    0.730   (   9.380,  11.783)
C16       30     8.642   3.564    0.730   (   7.440,   9.843)
C17       30    10.683   3.758    0.730   (   9.481,  11.884)
C18       30    10.967   3.436    0.730   (   9.765,  12.169)
C19       30     9.923   3.888    0.730   (   8.721,  11.125)
C20       30     9.553   3.024    0.730   (   8.351,  10.755)
C21       30    11.632   4.354    0.730   (  10.430,  12.833)
C22       30    10.061   4.195    0.730   (   8.859,  11.262)
C23       30     9.072   3.450    0.730   (   7.871,  10.274)
C24       30     9.565   5.203    0.730   (   8.363,  10.767)
C25       30    11.668   4.380    0.730   (  10.466,  12.869)
```

Intervals that don't contain the true population mean

```
THE ASSUMED SIGMA =4.00

          N      MEAN    STDEV   SE MEAN    90.0 PERCENT C.I.
C1        30    10.369   4.139    0.730   (   9.167,  11.571)
C2        30    10.511   4.087    0.730   (   9.309,  11.712)
C3        30     9.908   4.061    0.730   (   8.706,  11.109)
C4        30    10.795   4.611    0.730   (   9.594,  11.997)
C5        30     8.652   4.905    0.730   (   7.451,   9.854)
C6        30    11.740   2.625    0.730   (  10.539,  12.942)
C7        30     9.065   3.575    0.730   (   7.863,  10.266)
C8        30     9.756   4.436    0.730   (   8.554,  10.957)
C9        30     9.795   3.938    0.730   (   8.593,  10.996)
C10       30    10.082   4.250    0.730   (   8.881,  11.284)
C11       30     9.161   3.932    0.730   (   7.960,  10.363)
C12       30    10.471   3.619    0.730   (   9.269,  11.673)
C13       30     8.915   3.239    0.730   (   7.713,  10.116)
C14       30     9.854   4.265    0.730   (   8.653,  11.056)
C15       30     9.874   4.717    0.730   (   8.673,  11.076)
C16       30    10.414   4.368    0.730   (   9.213,  11.616)
C17       30     9.358   4.214    0.730   (   8.156,  10.559)
C18       30    10.409   4.400    0.730   (   9.208,  11.611)
C19       30     9.054   3.479    0.730   (   7.852,  10.256)
C20       30    10.414   4.387    0.730   (   9.212,  11.615)
C21       30    10.927   4.131    0.730   (   9.726,  12.129)
C22       30    10.535   4.766    0.730   (   9.334,  11.737)
C23       30     9.559   4.182    0.730   (   8.358,  10.761)
C24       30     9.498   4.449    0.730   (   8.296,  10.699)
C25       30    10.091   4.894    0.730   (   8.890,  11.293)

MTB >
```

Of the 50 additional confidence intervals, five do not contain the true population mean (C16, C21, and C25 in the first set of 25 confidence intervals, and C5 and C6 in the second).

Consider the results of the 100 confidence intervals shown in the Session window. Fourteen did not contain the value 10; you expected only 10 not to include the mean. Your results, in conjunction with the results presented here, represent 200 samples. In total, you should observe approximately 20 confidence intervals that do not contain the mean.

To get an accurate picture, many statisticians argue that simulations should include more than 1000 replications; some even advocate 10,000. If you were to continue generating confidence intervals, you would see that the percentage that include the mean would approach 90%. By using Execs that take advantage of Minitab's ability to generate random data from almost any distribution, you can perform simulations to investigate many other statistical properties.

In the next section, you explore another major use of Execs — creating a set of commands to perform an analysis or special function that does not exist in Minitab.

▼ Creating an Exec with a Text Editor ▲

In this section, you create an Exec to perform a chi-square goodness-of-fit (GOF) test for a set of data. You use the employment class data from Tutorial 12 to verify your Exec.

To create this Exec, you use the Notepad text editor that comes with Microsoft Windows. You can find this application in the Accessories window in Program Manager. To close Minitab and open Notepad:

- Choose **File > Exit**

- Click **No** (do not save the confidence intervals worksheet)

- Double-click the **Accessories** group icon in Program Manager to open it, if necessary

- Double-click the **Notepad** program-item icon in the Accessories window

    Notepad displays a blank page (Figure 16-9).

FIGURE 16-9

The Notepad window

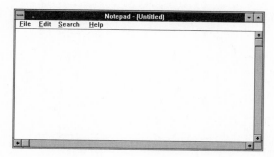

You can use any word processor to create an Exec file and then save it as a text file. Notepad is ideal for this purpose because it always creates text files.

Now review the data and commands you used in Tutorial 12 that you must include in your Exec. In the employment class example in Tutorial 12, you used five employment class categories, stored in C1 CLASS. The hypothesized probabilities for the number of firms falling in a given employment class are in C2 PROB. C3 SAMPLE contains the class categories. You recreate C4, which contains the observed frequency of each category (274, 290, 243, 64, and 129).

When you performed the chi-square GOF test in Tutorial 12, you used the Minitab menus to accomplish four tasks:

- You computed the expected frequency of each class by multiplying each expected probability in C2 by 1000 (the total number of firms sampled); you stored those frequencies in C5.

- You then computed the chi-square values for each class — (C4-C5)**2/C5 — and stored them in C6.

- You computed the chi-square GOF statistic by summing C6.

- You computed the p-value using the Probability Distributions command and the General Expressions command in the Session window.

The Minitab commands to perform these four steps are:

```
LET C5=C2*1000
LET C6=(C4-C5)**2/C5
LET K1=SUM(C6)
CDF K1 K2;
CHISQUARE 4.
LET K3=1-K2
PRINT K1 K3
```

You could verify these commands by repeating the steps from Tutorial 12. To create your Exec, type these commands in Notepad:

- Type **LET C5=C2*1000** and press (←Enter)

- Type **LET C6=(C4-C5)**2/C5** and press (←Enter)

- Type **LET K1=SUM(C6)** and press (←Enter)

- Type **CDF K1 K2;** (do not forget the semicolon) and press (←Enter)

- Type **CHISQUARE 4.** (do not forget the period) and press (←Enter)

- Type **LET K3=1-K2** and press (←Enter)

- Type **PRINT K1 K3** and press (←Enter)

- Type **END** (to end the Exec) and press (←Enter)

The Notepad window should look like Figure 16-10.

FIGURE 16-10

The Notepad window with GOF commands

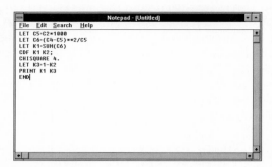

```
                              Notepad - [Untitled]
 File  Edit  Search  Help
LET C5=C2*1000
LET C6=(C4-C5)**2/C5
LET K1=SUM(C6)
CDF K1 K2;
CHISQUARE 4.
LET K3=1-K2
PRINT K1 K3
END
```

After you finish typing, verify that each line is correct and then save the Exec in a file:

■ Choose **File > Save as** from the Notepad menu bar

■ Insert your Student disk in drive A (or a different drive, if appropriate)

■ Click the **Drives** drop-down list arrow and then click **a:**

■ Double-click the **File Name** text box, type **GOF.MTB**, and then press ⌐Enter

Note: When you create an Exec with a word processor, you don't need to save it with the .MTB file extension, but you must save the file in text or ASCII format. You must then include the extension in the EXEC command.

You are ready to execute the Exec from Minitab. Close Notepad, start the Minitab application, and open ECLASS.MTW:

■ Choose **File > Exit**

■ Double-click the **Accessories Control menu box** to close the Accessories group window

■ Start Minitab and maximize the Minitab window and the Data window

■ Open **ECLASS.MTW**

Tally the samples in C3:

■ Choose **Stat > Tables > Tally**

■ Double-click **C3 SAMPLE** to enter it in the **Variables** text box

■ Click **OK**

The Session window displays the counts. Store these observed values in C4:

■ Return to the Data window and click the data-entry arrow so it is pointing down

- Type the name **OBSERVED** in the name row as the label for column C4

- Type **274**, **290**, **243**, **64**, and **129** in the first five rows of C4 (be sure to press ⏎Enter after entering each number)

The data described earlier should be stored in the appropriate columns. Now run the Exec you just created:

- Choose **File > Other Files > Run an Exec**

- Click **Select File**

- Select **a:** in the **Drives** drop-down list box and then double-click **GOF.MTB** in the **Files** list box

The Session window appears, as shown in Figure 16-11.

FIGURE 16-11

GOF.MTB results from the Session window

```
MTB > Execute 'A:\GOF.MTB' 1.
Executing from file: A:\GOF.MTB

K1      1.28763
K3      0.863471
MTB >
```

Minitab executed each command you typed in your Exec. Minitab reports the chi-square statistic and its corresponding p-value: 1.28763 and 0.863471, respectively. Compare the results in Figure 16-11 to those in Tutorial 12.

Your results should be the same. If they aren't, reenter the commands in Notepad, verifying each line as you type it, and then save the file again. When Notepad asks whether you want to replace the existing GOF.MTB, click Yes. Notepad erases your previous version and saves the new version using this name. Run the Exec and make sure that it works properly before continuing to the next section.

You now have a GOF test Exec; it is essentially a new Minitab command. Anytime you need to perform a chi-square GOF test, you can use this Exec. However, in its present form, the Exec works only with certain data sets. In the next section, you modify this Exec to make it more flexible.

Generalizing an Exec

The GOF.MTB Exec you created in the previous section performs a chi-square GOF test on a data set, but only if the expected probabilities and observed frequencies are stored in columns C2 and C4, respectively. The Exec also assumes that there are exactly five categories (because you used a chi-square with 4 degrees of freedom to compute the p-value) and that the sample size is 1000.

You will generalize your Exec so that it automatically determines the appropriate sample size and number of categories. You also annotate it for future reference.

The Exec will still require the user to enter the hypothesized probabilities in C2 and observed frequencies in C4.

Exit Minitab and open Notepad to edit the Exec:

- Save ECLASS.MTW with the name **16ECLASS**

- Choose **File > Exit**

- Open Notepad as you did before

- Choose **File > Open**

- Click the **Drives** drop-down arrow and click **a:**

- Click the **List Files of Type** drop-down arrow and click **All Files**

- Double-click **GOF.MTB** in the **Files** list box (you may have to scroll to see it)

The GOF.MTB Exec should appear as in Figure 16-10.

You can tell Minitab to compute the sample size by summing the observed frequencies in C4. To do so, replace the 1000 in the first line of your Exec with SUM(C4):

- Highlight **1000** in the first line of the Exec

- Type **SUM(C4)**

Next, you need to determine the degrees of freedom of the chi-square statistic. The degrees of freedom is the number of categories minus one. Since the p-value computations depend on this value, Minitab must calculate and store it before the Exec executes the CDF command.

Insert a blank line above the CDF command:

- Position the I-beam at the beginning of the LET K1 = SUM(C6) line (just before the L in "LET") and click the mouse

- Press (←Enter) to insert a row above the LET K1 = SUM(C6) line

- Press (↑) to move the cursor to the beginning of the blank line

Instruct Minitab to count the number of rows in C4 (you could also use C2) using the Count command; use LET (the corresponding Session command to General Expressions) to store this value in a constant location and subtract one to yield the degrees of freedom. You can accomplish all this with a single command and then use this value to compute the p-value.

- Type **LET K4 = COUNT(C4)-1** on the blank line

- Highlight the **4** in the CHISQUARE line (be careful not to highlight the period at the end of the line)

- Type **K4**

Annotating an Exec

Finally, you want to annotate the Exec so that the user knows its restrictions and exactly what the Exec expects to find in various columns. To add an annotation to an Exec, use the NOTE command. Minitab ignores any information following the word *NOTE*.

The Exec expects that C2 and C4 contain the hypothesized probabilities and the observed counts, respectively. You want to add this information at the beginning of the Exec, so add a blank line at the top:

■ Position the I-beam in front of the first line, LET C5 = C2*SUM(C4), and click the mouse

■ Press ⌨Enter

■ Press ↑ to position the I-beam on the new blank line

You are ready to insert notes to inform the user that this is a chi-square goodness-of-fit test, the hypothesized probabilities must be stored in C2, and the observed frequencies must be stored in C4.

You also decide to name K1 and K3 to identify them as the chi-square GOF test statistic and p-value, respectively.

To add these notes:

■ Type **NOTE CHISQUARE GOODNESS-OF-FIT PROCEDURE** and press ⌨Enter

■ Type **NOTE HYPOTHESIZED PROBABILITIES MUST BE IN C2** and press ⌨Enter

■ Type **NOTE OBSERVED FREQUENCIES MUST BE IN C4**

■ Click at the right end of the Exec line that reads LET K3 = 1-K2 and press ⌨Enter

■ Type **NAME K1 'TESTSTAT' K3 'PVALUE'** and press ⌨Enter

■ Type **NOTE TESTSTAT IS THE STATISTIC AND PVALUE IS THE P-VALUE**

FIGURE 16-12

The generalized GOF.MTB Exec in Notepad

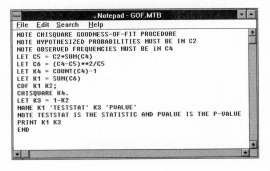

Verify that your Exec is identical to the one in Figure 16-12, save the Exec, and close Notepad. Then open Minitab and the 16ECLASS.MTW file that you just saved, which contains the values you entered into C4:

■ Choose **File > Save**

- Choose **File > Exit**

- Start Minitab and maximize the Minitab window and the Data window

- Open **16ECLASS.MTW** from your Student disk

    Now run your generalized Exec:

- Choose **File > Other Files > Run an Exec**

- Click **Select File**

- Select **a:** in the **Drives** drop-down list box and double-click **GOF.MTB** in the **Files** list box

    Minitab displays the Session window as it executes the Exec. When it finishes (assuming your changes are correct), your screen should look like Figure 16-13.

FIGURE 16-13

Session window, showing results of the GOF.MTB Exec

```
MTB > Execute 'A:\GOF.MTB' 1.
Executing from file: A:\GOF.MTB
CHISQUARE GOODNESS-OF-FIT PROCEDURE
HYPOTHESIZED PROBABILITIES MUST BE IN C2
OBSERVED FREQUENCIES MUST BE IN C4
TESTSTAT IS THE STATISTIC AND PVALUE IS THE P-VALUE

TESTSTAT 1.28763
PVALUE   0.863471
MTB >
```

The test statistic and p-value are identical to those you produced earlier. Always check your Exec using results that you have previously verified. You know that the statistic and the p-value should be 1.28763 and 0.863471, respectively. If your Exec yields different results, you need to correct an error.

The Session window displays the notes that you added; whenever you return to this Exec in the future, they will remind you what the Exec does and what you need to store in the worksheet before executing the macro. In the future, when you need to perform a GOF test, you can simply run the Exec GOF.MTB.

Notes can also help you identify output. For example, the values of K1 TESTSTAT and K3 PVALUE are identified as the test statistic and p-value. Both notes and labels, therefore, serve two purposes: to describe the Exec and to describe the output.

Viewing Other Enhancements to Execs

In this section, you examine the PINF.MTB Exec from Tutorial 7 to see other Exec functions you can use. This Exec, written by Minitab Inc., features several tricks and techniques that make it very flexible. You execute the Exec and then follow along to observe the function of the Exec steps.

Start with empty Session and Data windows:

- Choose **File > Restart Minitab**

- Click **No** (do not save the changes to 16ECLASS.MTW)

Figure 16-14 lists the entire PINF.MTB Exec. You could also view this file in Notepad.

FIGURE 16-14

PINF.MTB

Nonechoed #s

Echoed notes

SET command

Direction of test

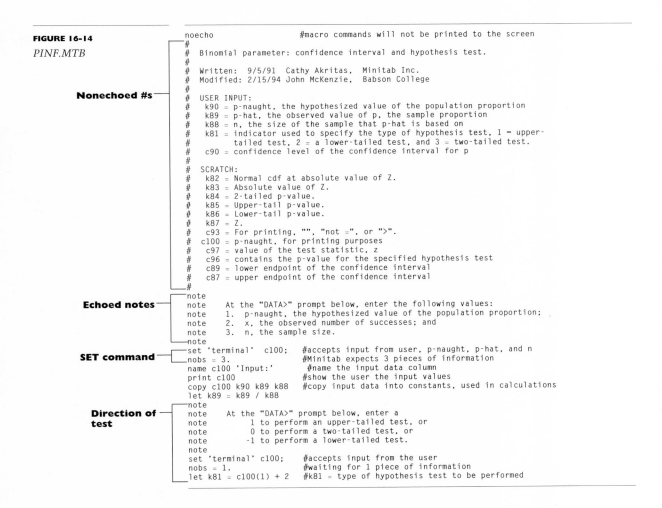

```
noecho                    #macro commands will not be printed to the screen
#
#  Binomial parameter: confidence interval and hypothesis test.
#
#  Written:  9/5/91  Cathy Akritas,  Minitab Inc.
#  Modified: 2/15/94 John McKenzie,  Babson College
#
#  USER INPUT:
#    k90 = p-naught, the hypothesized value of the population proportion
#    k89 = p-hat, the observed value of p, the sample proportion
#    k88 = n, the size of the sample that p-hat is based on
#    k81 = indicator used to specify the type of hypothesis test, 1 = upper-
#          tailed test, 2 = a lower-tailed test, and 3 = two-tailed test.
#    c90 = confidence level of the confidence interval for p
#
#  SCRATCH:
#    k82 = Normal cdf at absolute value of Z.
#    k83 = Absolute value of Z.
#    k84 = 2-tailed p-value.
#    k85 = Upper-tail p-value.
#    k86 = Lower-tail p-value.
#    k87 = Z.
#    c93 = For printing, "", "not =", or ">".
#   c100 = p-naught, for printing purposes
#    c97 = value of the test statistic, z
#    c96 = contains the p-value for the specified hypothesis test
#    c89 = lower endpoint of the confidence interval
#    c87 = upper endpoint of the confidence interval
#
note
note     At the "DATA>" prompt below, enter the following values:
note     1.  p-naught, the hypothesized value of the population proportion;
note     2.  x, the observed number of successes; and
note     3.  n, the sample size.
note
set 'terminal' c100;    #accepts input from user, p-naught, p-hat, and n
nobs = 3.               #Minitab expects 3 pieces of information
name c100 'Input:'      #name the input data column
print c100              #show the user the input values
copy c100 k90 k89 k88   #copy input data into constants, used in calculations
let k89 = k89 / k88
note
note     At the "DATA>" prompt below, enter a
note         1 to perform an upper-tailed test, or
note         0 to perform a two-tailed test, or
note        -1 to perform a lower-tailed test.
note
set 'terminal' c100;    #accepts input from the user
nobs = 1.               #waiting for 1 piece of information
let k81 = c100(1) + 2   #k81 = type of hypothesis test to be performed
```

FIGURE 16-14 (continued)

```
# The z-test statistic = (phat - pnaught)/sqrt(pnaught(1-pnaught)/n)

let k87 = (k89 - k90) / sqrt (k90*(1-k90)/k88)
```

p-values computed
```
# Calculate p-value from z for all 3 alternatives

cdf k87 k86              # cdf(z) = p-value for the lower-tailed test
let k85 = 1- k86         #(1-cdf(z)) = p-value for upper-tailed test
let k83 = absolute(k87)  #k83 = absolute value of z.
cdf k83 k82              #2*(1-cdf(absolute(z)) = p-value for two-tailed test
let k84 = 2*(1-k82)
```

```
erase c100 c97 c96      #empty out future storage columns
copy k90 c100           #copy p-naught into c100, use later in output
copy k87 c97            #copy z into c97, use later in reporting reults
copy k86 k84 k85 c96    #copy the p-values into c96
set c93;                #c93 used in reporting the type of test selected
format (a6).

not =
  >
end
```

Output of appropriate p-value
```
copy  c93 c96 c93 c96;   #copy the p-value column and the type of test column,
use k81.                 #but only use row that corresponds to specified test
print c100 c93 c100 c97 c96; #print the results
format ('     Ho: p = ',f6.4,'  vs.  Ha: p ',a6,f6.4,//,&
',                      z =',f8.5,'        p-value =', f8.5).
```

```
note
note    A confidence interval for the true population proportion will be
note    produced below.  At the "DATA>" prompt below, enter the confidence
note    level (95 for a 95% confidence interval) for the confidence interval.
note
```

Input of confidence level
```
set 'terminal' c90;      #c90 = confidence level, specified by the user
nobs = 1.                #waiting for one piece of information
name c90 'CI Level'
print c90                #show the user the confidence level
# k90 is used in finding the critical value, Z(alpha/2) used in the confidence interval
let k90 =  (c90(1)/100) + (1-c90(1)/100)/2
invcdf k90 k91           #k91 = critical value used in confidence interval
let c89 = k89 - k91*sqrt(k89*(1-k89)/k88) #c89 is the lower endpoint
let c87 = k89 + k91*sqrt(k89*(1-k89)/k88) #c87 is the upper endpoint
```

Formatted output of confidence interval
```
print c90 c89 c87;       #report the results
format ('     The ',i2,'% confidence interval is (', f7.4,'  to  ',f6.4,')').
```

```
erase k81-k90 c90 c93 c100
echo                     #restore the screen echo feature
```

Quickly browse the PINF.MTB Exec in Figure 16-14. The programmer who created this Exec annotated it extensively. Almost every line is either a note or uses the comment symbol, #. This makes it easy to understand the details of the Exec and make any changes necessary.

Now, execute the PINF.MTB Exec:

- Choose **File > Other Files > Run an Exec**

- Click **Select File**

- Double-click **PINF.MTB**

The Session window appears (Figure 16-15). At this point the Exec is waiting for you to enter the test null hypothesized value of p and the sample results. Before you enter these values, note the commands that Minitab has executed from the Exec.

FIGURE 16-15

*The first prompt of
PINF.MTB Exec in the
Session window*

```
MTB > Execute 'C:\MTBSEW\STUDENT9\PINF.MTB' 1.
Executing from file: C:\MTBSEW\STUDENT9\PINF.MTB

   At the "DATA>" prompt below, enter the following values:
   1.  p-naught, the hypothesized value of the population proportion;
   2.  x, the observed number of successes; and
   3.  n, the sample size.

DATA>
```

In Figure 16-14, the first command in the PINF.MTB Exec is NOECHO. In Figure 16-15, you can see that Minitab didn't "echo" the commands it executed in the Exec. The ECHO and NOECHO commands let you determine whether and when you want Exec commands to appear on the screen. Minitab's default is NOECHO to prevent the Session window from becoming cluttered with Exec commands. The NOECHO command also suppresses the display of the MTB > prompt in the Session window.

NOECHO is usually the first command in the Exec to suppress the display, if perchance ECHO is in effect when the Exec begins. The PINF.MTB Exec turns the echo function back on by including ECHO just before END, as shown in Figure 16-14.

Next, notice the difference between comments using NOTE and #. When the NOECHO command is in effect, Minitab echoes NOTE lines in the Session window, but not # lines. In this case, Minitab doesn't echo any of the lines in the USER INPUT section in the Session window because they start with #. However, it displays each line that begins with NOTE. By using NOTE and # selectively, you can tailor your output.

The programmer tells you, up front, what constants the Exec uses and to what they relate. For example, Minitab will store the hypothesized value of *p* in K90, the sample size in K88, and so on. By storing results and values in constant locations near K100 and column values near C100, you are less likely to write over information in your worksheet. This is a wise practice.

The PINF.MTB Exec is interactive. In other words, the program stops and asks you for a response. You, the user, supply it with information, namely, *p-naught*, *x*, and *n*. In Figure 16-15, PINF.MTB stops at the SET 'TERMINAL' C100 command from Figure 16-14 and waits for you to type the three requested values, which it will store in C100.

To make an Exec interactive, the programmer used the SET command to store the values the user inputs from the *terminal*, or keyboard, in column C100. The NOBS = 3 (number of observations) subcommand tells Minitab to proceed with the Exec after you enter the three values.

Enter the sample information to continue the Exec:

■ Type **.5 62 100** and press ⏎Enter

After recording the values (Figure 16-16), Minitab prompts you for the direction of your test and waits for your response.

FIGURE 16-16

The second prompt of the PINF.MTB Exec in the Session window

```
DATA> .5 62 100

Input:
     0.5     62.0    100.0

   At the "DATA>" prompt below, enter a
         1 to perform an upper-tailed test, or
         0 to perform a two-tailed test, or
        -1 to perform a lower-tailed test.

DATA>
```

You want to perform a two-tailed test:

■ Type **0** and press ⏎Enter

The Exec computes all three p-values, corresponding to upper-tailed, lower-tailed, and two-tailed tests. Using an innovative technique, the Exec outputs the appropriate p-value for the alternative you specify. Notice the USE subcommand in Figure 16-14, which allows you to select the appropriate alternative hypothesis and p-value by specifying the appropriate row of columns.

Finally, enter the desired level of confidence for the confidence interval for *p*:

■ Type **95** and press ⏎Enter

Continue reading through the Exec. Note the use of the FORMAT subcommand when printing results. The result is the informative output you see in the Session window (Figure 16-17).

FIGURE 16-17

Output from the PINF.MTB Exec

```
DATA> 0
                     Ho: p = 0.5000   vs.   Ha: p not = 0.5000

                     z = 2.40000      p-value = 0.01640


   A confidence interval for the true population proportion will be
   produced below.  At the "DATA>" prompt below, enter the confidence
   level (95 for a 95% confidence interval) for the confidence interval.

DATA> 95

CI Level
    95

   The 95% confidence interval is ( 0.5249  to  0.7151)

MTB >
```

The FORMAT subcommand uses FORTRAN notation. You can include words as part of the output to make the results more impressive. (See the online Minitab Help topic "Format Statements" for information about formatting codes.)

You might want to take some additional time now to work your way through this Exec command by command to see exactly where the programmer stored the various quantities. When you are finished, exit Minitab:

■ Choose **File > Exit**

■ Click **No** to exit without saving the changes to the worksheet

Given Minitab's many functions, it is easy to build your own set of unique programs. The only limits are your imagination. If you are interested in learning more about Execs, or %Macros, ask your instructor for more information. If you want to pursue it yourself, refer to Chapter 5, Execs, in the Reference section (Part IV) of this manual.

Congratulations! You have explored some of Minitab's capabilities — but this is only the beginning. If you use Minitab in your school or on the job, you will undoubtedly find many new and interesting features that show you just how powerful it is.

▼ Minitab Command Summary ▲

This section describes the Minitab menu commands and Session commands introduced in or related to this tutorial. To find a complete explanation of all menus and commands, refer to the Reference section of this manual.

Minitab Menu Commands

Menu	Command	Description
File		
	Other Files	
	Start Recording Exec	Stores commands in a file, called an Exec, that you can execute any number of times
	Stop Recording Exec	Stops entering Minitab commands into the Exec file
	Run an Exec	Executes the commands in an Exec file a user-specified number of times

Minitab Session Commands

ECHO	Restores the echo printing of Minitab commands
END	Ends storage of Minitab commands in an Exec
NOECHO	Suppresses the echo printing of Minitab commands
NOTE	Displays messages to the user on the screen during the execution of an Exec
YESNO	Prompts the user of an Exec to execute or skip a block of commands
#	Provides internal documentation to an Exec

▼
Review and Practice
▲

Matching

Match the following terms to their definitions by placing the correct letter next to the term it describes.

_____ NOECHO

_____ NOBS

_____ END

_____ ASCII

_____ STOR>

_____ NOTE

_____ Paste

_____ STORE

_____ Run an Exec

_____ Notepad

a. The Edit command that inserts Session commands after the STOR> prompt

b. The Minitab command to stop entering commands in an Exec file

c. The Minitab command to store commands in an Exec file

d. A Windows text editor available for creating Execs

e. The Minitab prompt that appears when you are creating an Exec

f. The Minitab SET subcommand that determines the number of values to be typed

g. The Minitab Session command that allows the user to document an Exec by including comments in the Exec that annotate the function of the Exec

h. An acronym that means the same thing as text format

i. The default option for printing Minitab commands during the execution of an Exec

j. The command that executes the commands in an Exec file a user-specified number of times

True/False

Mark the following statements with a *T* or an *F*.

_____ 1. Exec macros and %Macros are the two types of macros available in Minitab.

_____ 2. Minitab allows you to label variables, but not constants.

_____ 3. Minitab can execute an Exec created in a word processor if the Exec filename has an MTB extension.

_____ 4. The maximum number of times you can execute an Exec is three.

_____ 5. Once a command is entered in an Exec in Minitab, you cannot change it using Minitab.

_____ 6. * is the Minitab comment symbol that provides internal documentation to an Exec.

_____ 7. The Stop Recording Exec submenu command is equivalent to the END command in the Session window.

_____ 8. You must enclose file names in single quotes when you refer to them in elementary Minitab Session commands.

_____ 9. When you store commands in a Minitab Exec, the commands simultaneously execute in the Session window.

_____ 10. When you use Notepad to create files, it saves them in ASCII or text format.

Practice Problems

1. Display the CONFINTS.MTB Exec in a word processor or text editor.

    a. Change the sample size in each column of the CONFINTS.MTB Exec from 30 to 5 and save the Exec as P16CONF.MTB.

    b. Execute the Exec four times. How has the smaller sample size affected your results? How many of the confidence intervals do not contain the mean? Should the smaller sample size affect this? What can you say about the widths of your confidence intervals? Would you expect this to happen?

2. Create a new Exec that performs the same computations as CONFINTS.MTB but assume that you do not know sigma and must use the t distribution to obtain the confidence intervals. Create the Exec by copying and pasting commands within the Session window. Call this Exec P16CONF2.MTB.

3. Many states have daily "numbers" games or lotteries. Most have three-number games and some also have four-number games. You bet on a certain number; if that number is chosen, you win.

    In some states, the four-digit number is selected as follows (the three-digit number is similar): there are four bins labeled 1, 2, 3, and 4. Each bin contains

10 identical ping pong balls, each labeled with a digit from 0 to 9. One ball is selected randomly from each bin and the resulting four-digit number is the winning number.

After monitoring the outcomes for a month (after 30 numbers have been drawn), you decide to check if the numbers are being chosen randomly. One way to check would be to determine if the digits 0 to 9 are uniformly distributed. Use the information below and the GOF Exec to determine if the digits are uniformly distributed.

Digit	0	1	2	3	4	5	6	7	8	9
Frequency	16	17	10	11	5	13	8	12	13	15

4. Using a word processor or text editor, create an Exec similar to your CONFINTS.MTB Exec, but generate data from a chi-square distribution with 8 degrees of freedom. The variance of a chi-square (8 d.f.) is $2 \times 8 = 16$, so sigma is 4. Generate 100 95% confidence intervals using normal theory results (use ZInterval) and decide whether it is wise to use normal theory results (based on samples of n = 30) when the population is clearly not normal. Call this Exec P16CONF3.MTB.

5. Create an Exec that prints out the mean, sample standard deviation, sample variance, and mean absolute deviation (MAD) for data in C1. Document the Exec commands and output by using NOTE and #, and by naming the variable (call it DATA) and constants.

PART III

EXPLORING DATA

This part summarizes all the data sets provided in the STUDENT9 directory of *The Student Edition of MINITAB for Windows*. Some of these data sets are not used in the tutorials, so you can explore them to get additional practice.

All descriptions inlude:

- a discusson of the source of the data and its contents

- a listing of each variable name, its column number, a count of nonmissing values, and a description

ADS.MTW and ADS2.MTW

This data set contains information about full-page ads in two magazines in 1989, 1991, and 1993. ADS.MTW contains only C1-C4, while ADS2.MTW adds C5 ADRATIO.

Column	Name	Count	Description
C1	MAGAZINE	24	Magazine
C2	YEAR	24	Year
C3	PAGES	24	Number of pages
C4	FULLADS	24	Number of full-page ads
C5	ADRATIO	24	Ratio of pages to the number of pages with full-page ads

This file is used in Tutorial 3 (Practice Problems), Tutorial 4 (Practice Problems), Tutorial 5 (Practice Problems), and Tutorial 8 (Practice Problems).

AGE.MTW

To determine the death age reported in a major metropolitan U.S. city, a sociology class randomly selected 37 obituaries from the city's largest newspaper. The sample consists of 18 males and 19 females.

Column	Name	Count	Description
C1	DAGEF	19	Death age for females
C2	DAGEM	18	Death age for males

This file is used in Tutorial 7, Tutorial 8, Tutorial 9 (Practice Problems), and Tutorial 13.

ASSESS.MTW

Assessors base their home assessments on many different variables. This data set includes a number of those variables, plus the final value of the home and land.

Column	Name	Count	Missing	Description
C1	LAND$	81	2	Assessed value of the land
C2	TOTAL$	81	2	Assessed value of the home and the land
C3	ACREAGE	81	0	Number of acres
C4	HEIGHT	81	0	Story height (number and type of floors); 1 = 1 story; 2 = 1 story plus attic; 3 = 1.5 stories; 4 = 2 stories; 5 = 2 stories plus attic; 6 = 3 stories; 7 = attic; 8 = split level; 9 = bi-level; 10 = not available
C5	1STFAREA	81	0	Area of first floor, in square feet
C6	EXTERIOR	81	0	Exterior condition; 1 = excellent, 2 = good, 3 = average
C7	FUEL	81	0	Type of fuel; 1 = natural gas, 2 = electric, 3 = oil, 4 = solar, 5 = wood, 6 = coal, 7 = other, and 8 = none
C8	ROOMS	81	0	Number of rooms
C9	BEDROOMS	81	0	Number of bedrooms
C10	FULLBATH	81	0	Number of full baths
C11	HALFBATH	81	0	Number of half baths
C12	FIREPLCE	81	0	Number of fireplaces
C13	GARAGE?	81	0	Presence of a garage; 1 = garage present and 0 = garage not present

CANDYA.MTW — CANDYC.MTW

Students in a statistics class opened three bags of candy containing individually wrapped snack packs of candies. They determined the average size of each individual candy (CANDYA.MTW), the weight of the packs (CANDYB.MTW), and the proportion of candies of one color to the others in the pack and the number of defects (CANDYC.MTW).

CANDYA.MTW

Column	Name	Count	Description
C1	BAG	285	Bag number from which the individually wrapped packs came
C2	PACK	285	Pack identification number
C3	WEIGHTS	285	Weight of the individual candies

CANDYB.MTW

Column	Name	Count	Description
C1	BAG	57	Bag number from which the individually wrapped packs came
C2	PACK	57	Pack identification number
C3	NUMBER	57	Number of candies in each pack
C4	TOTWGT	57	Total weight of the pack
C5	PCKWGT	57	Weight of the packaging for each pack
C6	NETWGT	57	Total weight minus the package weight

CANDYC.MTW

Column	Name	Count	Description
C1	BAG	57	Bag number from which the individually wrapped packs came
C2	PACK	57	Pack identification number
C3	NUMBER	57	Number of candies in each pack
C4	RED	57	Number of red candies
C5	BROWN	57	Number of brown candies
C6	GREEN	57	Number of green candies
C7	ORANGE	57	Number of orange candies
C8	YELLOW	57	Number of yellow candies
C9	DEFECTS	57	Number of defects

These files are used in Tutorial 6 (Practice Problems), Tutorial 7 (Practice Problems), Tutorial 14, and Tutorial 14 (Practice Problems).

▼

CPI.MTW

▲

This data set records recent percent changes in the Consumer Price Index (CPI).

Column	Name	Count	Description
C1	YEAR	33	Year
C2	CPICHNGE	33	Percent change in the Consumer Price Index (CPI)

This file is used in Tutorial 3.

▼

CRIMES.MTW and CRIMEU.MTW

▲

This data set contains 1991 violent crime rates for the 50 states and the District of Columbia by U.S. Census division and region. CRIMES.MTW is stacked. CRIMEU.MTW contains the same data, unstacked by region (northeast, north central, south, and west).

CRIMES.MTW

Column	Name	Count	Description
C1-A	STATE	51	State
C2	DIVISION	51	Division (a subdivision of region)
C3	REGION	51	Region (the country is divided into 4 regions)
C4	CRIMERTE	51	Violent crime rate per 100,000 people

CRIMEU.MTW

Column	Name	Count	Description
C1-A	NESTATE	9	Northeastern state
C2	NECRIME	9	Northeastern crime rate
C3-A	NCSTATE	12	North central state
C4	NCCRIME	12	North central crime rate
C5-A	SSTATE	17	Southern state
C6	SCRIME	17	Southern crime rate
C7-A	WSTATE	13	Western state
C8	WCRIME	13	Western crime rate

These files are used in Tutorial 5 (Practice Problems), Tutorial 6 (Practice Problems), Tutorial 9 (Practice Problems), and Tutorial 11.

This data set contains information about a driver education class.

▼
DRIVE.MTW
▲

Column	Name	Count	Missing	Description
C1	MAX	85	2	Maximum number of students in a class
C2	INIT	85	2	Initial number of students who signed up
C3	DROPPED	85	2	Number of students who dropped
C4	REPLACED	85	2	Number of students who were replaced
C5	FINISHED	85	2	Number of students who finished the course
C6	TYPE	85	0	Type of class; 1 = automobile and 2 = motorcycle
C7	ORDER	85	0	Order in which classes were held

ECLASS.MTW

The 1993 Statistical Abstract of the United States contains information about how many U.S. employees worked in firms with fewer than 20 employees, 20 to 99 employees, 100 to 499 employees, 500 to 999 employees, and 1000 or more employees in 1990:

Class	Size	Number of Employees
1	Under 20 employees	24,373,000
2	20 to 99 employees	27,414,000
3	100 to 499 employees	22,926,000
4	500 to 999 employees	6,551,000
5	1000 or more employees	12,212,000

ECLASS.MTW is a randomly simulated sample of employee-size class data for five probabilities generated by the information found in the Statistical Abstract of the United States 1993: 0.2607, 0.2933, 0.2453, 0.0701, and 0.1306.

Column	Name	Count	Description
C1	CLASS	5	Employee class
C2	PROB	5	Probability
C3	SAMPLE	1000	Random sampling of employee-class sizes for each probability

This file is used in Tutorial 6 (the data are used, but not the file), Tutorial 12, and Tutorial 16.

FBALL.MTW

The data in FBALL.MTW came from a newspaper article listing the salaries of all players on a professional football team prior to the start of the 1991 season.

Column	Name	Count	Missing	Description
C1-A	POSITION	50	0	The position of the player
C2	EXPERNCE	50	0	The years experience of the player
C3	1990 SAL	50	3	The 1990 salary of the player
C4	1991 SAL	50	11	The 1991 salary of the player
C5	1992 SAL	50	31	The 1992 salary of the player
C6	BONUS	50	33	The signing bonus the player received

FJA.MTW

A statistician named Frank Anscombe used this data to illustrate the need for regression diagnostics. When you regress combinations of some of these columns, you get the same regression line. However, if you plot the data, each plot is strikingly different. These results show why you can't depend upon traditional measures for regression.

Column	Name	Count	Description
C1	X	11	Predictor variable
C2	Y1	11	Response variable
C3	Y2	11	Response variable
C4	Y3	11	Response variable
C5	X4	11	Predictor variable
C6	Y4	11	Response variable

This file is used in Tutorial 11.

GAS.MTW

This data set contains a driver's record of gas usage for maintenance records.

Column	Name	Count	Description
C1	GASDAY	180	Day on which driver purchased gas (the first is coded as 0)
C2	MILEAGE	180	Mileage at the time of gas purchase
C3	GALLONS	180	Number of gallons purchased
C4	COST	180	Cost in dollars of gas purchased
C5	MPG	180	Miles per gallon
C6	LOCAL	180	Gas station locale; 1 = local and 0 = nonlocal

GOLF.MTW

A college student, who is also an avid golfer, kept track of his golf scores in the fall of 1991. Based on playing nine holes, he recorded his score, how many greens he hit in regulation, and how many pars or better he made for the nine holes.

Column	Name	Count	Description
C1	SCORE	22	The score for nine holes of golf
C2	REGLTN	22	The number of greens made in the regulation number of strokes
C3	PARS	22	The number of pars or better (birdies, eagles, and so on) made in the nine holes

HEIGHT.MTW

A professor in the physiology department of a medical school collects data on the self-reported height of 60 females in an introductory physiology class. Students were asked to provide their height (in inches) on the first day of class.

Column	Name	Count	Description
C1	ID	60	The student's ID number
C2	HEIGHTS	60	The self-reported heights, in inches

This file is used in Tutorial 6.

HOMES.MTW

This data set contains real estate data on 150 randomly selected homes.

Column	Name	Count	Description
C1	PRICE	150	Price
C2	AREA	150	Area, in square feet
C3	ACRES	150	Acres
C4	ROOMS	150	Number of rooms
C5	BATHS	150	Number of baths

This file is used in Tutorial 4 (Practice Problems), Tutorial 7, Tutorial 8, Tutorial 10 (Practice Problems), Tutorial 11 (Practice Problems), and Tutorial 13.

JEANSA.MTW — JEANSC.MTW

A marketing research firm collected data on individuals who last bought jeans from four major stores. The data are divided into three files.

JEANSA.MTW

Column	Name	Count	Description
C1	SIZE	394	Jean size; 1 = petite, 2 = junior, 3 = misses, and 4 = half sizes or larger sizes
C2	AGE	394	Age; 1 = 10 to 24, 2 = 24 to 34, 3 = 35 to 44, 4 = 45 to 54, 5 = 55 to 64, and 6 = 65 or over
C3	MARITAL	394	Marital status; 1 = single, 2 = divorced or separated, 3 = widowed, 4 = married, 5 = living as married
C4	EARNERS	394	Number of full-time earners

JEANSB.MTW

Column	Name	Count	Description
C5	EMPLOY	394	Employment status; 1 = full-time (30 or more hours a week), 2 = part-time (less than 30 hours a week), and 3 = not employed
C6	EDUC	394	Education completed; 1 = grade school or less, 2 = some high school, 3 = high school graduate, 4 = business, nursing, or technical school, 5 = some college, 6 = college graduate, 7 = graduate degree
C7	INCOME	394	Total yearly pretax income; 1 = under $15,000, 2 = $15,000 to $24,999, 3 = $25,000 to $34,999, 4 = $35,000 to $49,999, 5 = $50,000 to $74,999, 6 = $75,000 to $99,999, and 7 = $100,000 or more
C8	JEANSHOP	394	Identification number of store where last pair of jeans purchased

JEANSC.MTW

Column	Name	Count	Description
C9	PAY_JEAN	394	Price in dollars of last pair of jeans purchased
C10	FASHION	394	*I consider myself to be fashion/style conscious*; response on scale of 1 to 6, with 1 = definitely disagree and 6 = definitely agree
C11	COST	394	*I'm very cost conscious when it comes to clothes*; response on scale of 1 to 6, with 1 = definitely disagree and 6 = definitely agree
C12	INTERST	394	*I take more interest in my wardrobe than most women I know*; response on scale of 1 to 6, with 1 = definitely disagree and 6 = definitely agree
C13	SPEND	394	*I spend a lot of money on clothes and accessories*; response on scale of 1 to 6, with 1 = definitely disagree and 6 = definitely agree

These files are used in Tutorial 12.

LAKES.MTW

▼

▲

An extensive study was conducted to determine if the characteristics of lakes in Wisconsin had changed over the last 60 years. Historical data were obtained on 149 lakes between 1925 and 1931. Similar data were obtained on these same lakes between 1979 and 1983.

The collected information included the physical characteristics of the lake, such as maximum depth and surface area, as well as the type of lake. Other variables reported the total area of the lake's watershed and the percentage of the lake that was bog. The data also indicated the amount of development as represented by the number of permanent dwellings within 100 meters of the shore.

In addition, several water quality variables were measured. These included the pH, alkalinity, conductivity, and calcium. Since measurement techniques changed from 1925 to 1979, the data were adjusted to be comparable (the stored data represent the adjusted values).

Column	Name	Count	Missing	Description
C1	LAKE ID	149	0	An identification number assigned to the lake
C2	TYPE	149	0	The type of lake; 1 = seepage, 2 = drained, 3 = drainage, and 4 = spring
C3	DEPTH	149	0	Maximum lake depth in meters
C4	AREA	149	0	Lake surface area in hectares
C5	WS AREA	149	0	Watershed area in hectares
C6	% BOG	149	1	Percentage of lake that is bog
C7	DW HIST	149	1	Number of lake shore dwellings, circa 1930
C8	DW CURNT	149	0	Number of lake shore dwellings, circa 1980
C9	PH HIST	149	0	Historical pH reading
C10	PH CURNT	149	0	Current pH reading
C11	COND HST	149	0	Historical conductivity reading
C12	COND CUR	149	0	Current conductivity reading
C13	ALK HIST	149	0	Historical alkalinity reading
C14	ALK CURN	149	0	Current alkalinity reading
C15	CA HIST	149	33	Historical calcium reading
C16	CA CURNT	149	0	Current calcium reading

LANG.MTW

▼
▲

One way of measuring people's attitudes toward others is to ask them to evaluate speakers of other languages. However, if the speakers they rate are different, one does not know whether to attribute variability in ratings to the speaker or to the language. To control this factor, Wallace Lambert at McGill University pioneered the *matched guise technique.* Subjects listen to a number of language segments and then rate certain qualities of the speaker, such as friendliness, honesty, and trustworthiness. However, three of the segments they hear are actually the same speaker, using different language "guises." Differences in ratings of that speaker, then, can be attributed to attitudes toward the particular languages and those who speak them.

In the LANG.MTW data set, students at an American high school rated five language segments for various qualities, on a 1-to-5 bipolar rating scale. (A prior survey asked students which qualities they considered most important for friendship.)

Segment A was the language of a recently arrived immigrant group, Segment C was English, Segment E was French, and Segments B and D were "distracter" languages, which were not included in the data set. Students also filled out questionnaires with background information about their experience with other languages, the length of time they lived in the area, and gender.

The immigrant language used was the language of a rather large, recently arrived immigrant population. This study attempted to determine if high school–age students held significantly negative attitudes toward speakers of the immigrants' language. It was predicted that they would have positive attitudes toward English and French.

All questions answered on a 1-to-5 bipolar rating scale, with 1 the most negative rating (inconsiderate, unfriendly, and so on) and 5 the most positive (considerate, friendly, and so on).

Column	Name	Count	Missing	Description
C1	IMM CONS	59	0	Immigrant language: *Is the person considerate?* (1 = inconsiderate, 2 = somewhat inconsiderate, 3 = neutral, 4 = somewhat considerate, 5 = considerate)
C2	IMM FRND	59	0	Immigrant language: *Is the person friendly?*
C3	IMM TRST	59	0	Immigrant language: *Is the person trustworthy?*
C4	IMM HON	59	0	Immigrant language: *Is the person honest?*
C5	IMM HLP	59	2	Immigrant language: *Is the person helpful?*
C6	IMM UND	59	1	Immigrant language: *Is the person understanding?*
C7	IMM RESP	59	0	Immigrant language: *Is the person responsible?*
C8	IMM ?	59	0	*Can you identify this language?* 1 = yes and 2 = no

continued

Column	Name	Count	Missing	Description
C9	ENG CONS	59	0	English language: *Is the person considerate?*
C10	ENG FRND	59	0	English language: *Is the person friendly?*
C11	ENG TRST	59	0	English language: *Is the person trustworthy?*
C12	ENG HON	59	0	English language: *Is the person honest?*
C13	ENG HLP	59	0	English language: *Is the person helpful?*
C14	ENG UND	59	1	English language: *Is the person understanding?*
C15	ENG RESP	59	0	English language: *Is the person responsible?*
C16	ENG ?	59	0	*Can you identify this language?* 0 = no and 1 = yes
C17	FRN CONS	59	1	French language: *Is the person considerate?*
C18	FRN FRND	59	1	French language: *Is the person friendly?*
C19	FRN TRST	59	1	French language: *Is the person trustworthy?*
C20	FRN HON	59	1	French language: *Is the person honest?*
C21	FRN HLP	59	1	French language: *Is the person helpful?*
C22	FRN UND	59	2	French language: *Is the person understanding?*
C23	FRN RESP	59	1	French language: *Is the person responsible?*
C24	FRN ?	59	0	*Can you identify this language?* 1 = yes and 2 = no
C25	ENGLISH?	59	0	*Is English your native language?* 1 = yes and 2 = no
C26	STATE?	59	0	*Have you lived in this state all your life?* 1 = yes and 2 = no
C27	LANGTIME	59	14	*For how many years have you studied a language at school?* 0 = none, 1 = 0 to 1 years, 2 = 1 to 2 years, and 3 = 2+ years
C28	2ND LANG	59	14	*How, if at all, are you exposed to a language other than English in your home?* 0 = not exposed at all, 1 = speak one, 2 = hear one but do not understand, and 3 = hear one and do understand
C29	TIME 2 L	59	22	*How long have you been exposed to a language other than English in your home?* 0 = 0 years, 1 = 1 to 7 years, and 2 = 8 to 15 years
C30	GENDER	59	17	The student's gender; 1 = male and 2 = female

LOTTO.MTW

A state lotto randomly selects six numbers from the numbers 1 through 47. There are two drawings per week. To check whether the drawings are random, a student monitored the game for several years. Based on information provided by the local newspaper, the student determined the number of times each of the numbers 1 through 47 had been drawn over the course of the past three years, for a total of 156 drawings.

Column	Name	Count	Description
C1	OBSERVED	47	The observed number of times each number has been drawn

This file is used in Tutorial 12 (Practice Problems).

MARKS.MTW

This data set is the grade summary for a social studies class in a secondary school. Three test scores have been recorded for the 24 students in the class.

Column	Name	Count	Description
C1	LAST NAM	24	Student's last name
C2	FIRST	24	Student's first name
C3	TEST1	24	The score (out of 100) on the first test
C4	TEST2	24	The score (out of 100) on the second test
C5	TEST3	24	The score (out of 100) on the third test

This file is used in Tutorial 2, Tutorial 3 (Practice Problems), and Tutorial 13 (Practice Problems).

MNWAGE.MTW

This data set contains information about the minimum wage from 1950 to 1994.

Column	Name	Count	Description
C1	YEAR	45	Year
C2	MINWAGE	45	Minimum wage, in dollars

This file is used in Tutorial 3 (Practice Problems), Tutorial 4 (Practice Problems), Tutorial 5 (Practice Problems), Tutorial 10 (Practice Problems), and Tutorial 11 (Practice Problems).

▼
MORT.MTW
▲

This data set contains the mortgage interest rates of six lenders in December 1992 and December 1993.

Column	Name	Count	Description
C1	30YR1992	6	Interest rate of a 30-year mortgage in 1992
C2	30YR1993	6	Interest rate of a 30-year mortgage in 1993

This file is used in Tutorial 8 and Tutorial 13.

▼
NIEL.MTW
▲

Each year the Nielsen company does an extensive survey of TV-viewing habits of the U.S. population. Many of the surveys are conducted by age and gender because sponsors are interested in how these variables relate to the programs people watch. (For example, see the VPVH data set.)

Column	Name	Count	Missing	Description
C1	YEAR	25	0	Year
C2	TV STNS	25	8	The number of TV stations, both VHF and UHF
C3	NUM TVS	25	8	The number of households in the U.S. with TVs, in thousands
C4	CABLE	25	11	The number of operating cable stations
C5	SUBSCBRS	25	9	The number of cable subscribers, in thousands
C6	TIME	25	5	The average number of hours of viewing per TV household per week

NONPRT.MTW and NONPRT2.MTW

This data set contains information about the average number of nonprint displays present on easily seen pages of three different types of newspapers. The easily seen pages are the top half of a full-sized paper's sections, and the front and back pages of a tabloid. (The section sizes are all the same.) NONPRT contains just C1 and C2, while NONPRT2 contains an additional column, C3 MAXSIZE.

Column	Name	Count	Description
C1	AVESIZE	10	The average size of nonprint displays, in square inches
C2	PAPER	10	The paper from which the displays come; 1 = regional newspaper, 2 = local tabloid, and 3 = national newspaper
C3	MAXSIZE	10	Maximum ad size

These files are used in Tutorial 9 and Tutorial 13.

NOTE.MTW

This data set contains information about a selection of notebook (portable) computers on the market.

Column	Name	Count	Missing	Description
C1-A	CHIP	24	0	Chip type
C2	SPEED	24	0	Speed, in megahertz
C3	RECHARGE	24	0	Minutes before battery needs recharging
C4	RAM	24	2	Maximum RAM, in megabytes
C5-A	MONITOR	24	0	Monochrome or color monitor
C6-A	PDEVICE	24	0	Pointing device
C7-A	800NUM	24	0	Availability of an 800 telephone number
C8	PRICE	24	0	Price

This file is used in Tutorial 1 (Practice Problems), Tutorial 2 (Practice Problems), Tutorial 11 (Practice Problems), and Tutorial 12 (Practice Problems).

PAY.MTW and PAY2.MTW

This data set contains the salary information of the 11 salaried employees in the sales department of the Technitron company. This data set is part of the larger data set TECHN, which contains the salary information of all employees in four departments at Technitron. PAY.MTW contains the first eight variables; PAY2.MTW contains these variables (except for C5 AGE), plus two more — C9 SAL MALE (the six male salaries) and C10 SAL FEM (the five female salaries) — in addition to incorporating the changes made to these data in Tutorial 1.

Column	Name	Count	Description
C1	SALARY	10	The salary of an employee in the sales department
C2	YRS EM	10	The number of years employed at Technitron
C3	PRIOR YR	10	The number of prior years' experience
C4	EDUC	10	Years of education after high school
C5	AGE	10	Current age
C6	ID	10	The company identification number for the employee
C7-A	GENDER	10	The gender of the employee
C8	GENDER N	10	The coded gender of the employee; 0 = female and 1 = male

These files are used in Tutorial 1, Tutorial 3, Tutorial 4, Tutorial 7 (Practice Problems), and Tutorial 13.

PIZZA.MTW

This data set contains campus newspaper ratings for 13 pizza shops for two fall semesters.

Column	Name	Count	Missing	Description
C1-A	PIZZERIA	13	0	Pizza shop
C2-A	TYPE	13	0	Local or chain
C3	FALLRANK	13	0	Ranking (first is best)
C4	FALLSCOR	13	0	Score (highest is best)
C5	LSPRING	13	3	Scores from previous spring
C6	LFALL	13	3	Ranking from previous fall

This file is used in Tutorial 1 (the data are used in Practice Problems, but not the file) and Tutorial 2 (Practice Problems).

PROCES.MTW

The process of creating, administering, and tallying the student government surveys whose results are in the file PROF.MTW involves a number of causes that could contribute to process problems. This file contains six columns corresponding to the six variables used to create a Minitab Cause-and-Effect diagram.

Column	Name	Count	Description
C1-A	MEN	3	Potential process problems caused by people
C2-A	MACHINES	5	Potential process problems caused by machines
C3-A	MATERIAL	2	Potential process problems caused by materials
C4-A	METHODS	2	Potential process problems caused by methods
C5-A	MEASURES	2	Potential process problems caused by the measuring process
C6-A	ENVIRON	3	Potential process problems caused by the environment

This file is used in Tutorial 14.

PROF.MTW

▼

▲

The student government randomly distributed surveys to 15 students in each of 146 sections in a variety of disciplines. The survey asked students to evaluate the course and the instructor. Each participating section received 15 surveys. Some sections returned all 15 surveys, whereas others returned fewer. The results for each section were averaged for use in this worksheet. There are nine columns and 146 rows. Each row presents a summary of the information taken from the 1 to 15 surveys returned by a particular class.

Column	Name	Count	Missing	Description
C1-A	DEPT	146	0	The academic department of the course to which the 15 surveys were distributed
C2	NUMBER	146	0	The course number
C3	INTEREST	146	0	The section average of the surveyed students' responses to *The course stimulated your interest in this area*; 0 = strongly disagree, 1 = disagree, 2 = neutral, 3 = agree, and 4 = strongly agree
C4	MANNER	146	0	The section average of the surveyed students' responses to *The instructor presented course material in an effective manner*; 0 = strongly disagree, 1 = disagree, 2 = neutral, 3 = agree, and 4 = strongly agree
C5	COURSE	146	0	The section average of the surveyed students' responses to *Overall, I would rate this course as...*; 0 = poor, 1 = below average, 2 = average, 3 = above average, and 4 = excellent
C6	INSTRUCR	146	0	The section average of the surveyed students' responses to the statement: *Overall, I would rate this instructor as...*; 0 = poor, 1 = below average, 2 = average, 3 = above average, and 4 = excellent
C7	RESPONDS	146	0	The number of completed surveys returned out of the 15 surveys distributed
C8	SIZE	146	16	The number of students in the section
C9	YEAR	146	0	The level of the course; 1 = freshman, 2 = sophomore, 3 = junior, and 4 = senior

This file is used in Getting Started Chapter 5, Tutorial 5 (Practice Problems), Tutorial 7 (Practice Problems), Tutorial 8 (Practice Problems), and Tutorial 12 (Practice Problems).

This data set includes information about a series of publications over time.

Column	Name	Count	Description
C1	VOLUME	84	Volume of publication
C2	NUMBER	84	Number of publication within the volume
C3	PAGES	84	Number of pages
C4	WEIGHT	84	Weight, in grams
C5	COVER	84	Cover type; 1 = plain brown, 2 = glossy green, 3 = plain green, and 4 = glossy brown
C6	BINDER	84	Binding status; 1 = binder and 0 = no binder

This file is used in Tutorial 14 (Practice Problems).

A television station in southwestern Ohio did a survey to determine the radon levels in homes in its viewing area. Questionnaires and radon detection kits were sent to all viewers who requested one. This file includes the results of only certain questions from the full questionnaire.

Column	Name	Count	Missing	Description
C1	RADON	543	30	Radon measurement, in pico curies
C2	AGE	543	60	Age of the house, in years
C3	DAYS	543	65	Number of days the kit was exposed
C4	INSULATE	543	9	Amount of insulation in the house; 0 = poor, 1 = average, 2 = excellent, and 9 = don't know
C5	SUMP?	543	17	*Was the sample taken near a sump pump?* 0 = yes, 1 = no

This file is used in Tutorial 2 (Practice Problems).

▼ RATIO.MTW ▲

This data set contains ratios of full-page ads to the number of pages in a magazine (using the data from ADS.MTW) from 1989, 1991, and 1993. The first 12 values in C1 ADRATIO correspond to a news magazine; the last 12 to a sports magazine. Likewise, the first through fourth values and the thirteenth through the sixteenth values correspond to 1989. The other values in C1 ADRATIO correspond to the other years.

Column	Name	Count	Description
C1	ADRATIO	24	Ratio of full-page ads to the total number of pages in a magazine

This file is used in Tutorial 9.

▼ RIVERA.MTW — RIVERE.MTW and RIVERS.MTW ▲

During the summer of 1988, one of the hottest on record in the midwest, a graduate student in environmental science conducted a study for a state Environmental Protection Agency. She studied the impact of an electric generating plant along a river by observing several water characteristics at five sites along the river. Site 1 was approximately four miles upriver from the electrical plant, about six miles down river from a moderately large midwestern city, and directly down river from a large suburb of this city. Site 2 was directly upriver from the cooling inlets of the plant. Site 3 was directly down river from the cooling discharge outlets of the plant. Site 4 was approximately ¾ of a mile down river from site 3, and site 5 was approximately six miles down river from site 3.

The EPA was most concerned with the plant's use of river water for cooling. The scientists feared that the plant was raising the temperature of the water and hence endangering the aquatic species that lived in the river.

The student anchored data sounds (battery-operated and self-contained canisters that float in the river) at five sites and took hourly measurements of the temperature, pH, conductivity, and dissolved oxygen content. She left them there for five consecutive days.

RIVERA.MTW, RIVERB.MTW, RIVERC.MTW, RIVERD.MTW, and RIVERE.MTW

The data sets RIVERA through RIVERE contain the recordings for each separate site; they therefore do not include columns C6 SITE and C7 HOUR1 described below. RIVERS.MTW contains the recordings from all five sites and includes all of the columns described below (it also contains the three missing values from RIVERB).

Column	Name	Count	Description
C1	HOUR	†	The hour of the measurement, in military time
C2	TEMP	†	The temperature, in °C, of the river at the given hour
C3	PH	†	The pH of the river at the given hour
C4	COND	†	The conductivity, in electrical potential, of the river at the given hour
C5	DO	†	The dissolved oxygen content of the river at the given hour
C6	SITE	478	Site
C7	HOUR1	478	The hour recorded as a number from 1 through 100

†The counts for the different data sets are: RIVERA = 95; RIVERB = 95; RIVERC = 95; RIVERD = 96; RIVERE = 97; RIVERS = 478. Note that RIVERB and RIVERS have three missing values.

RIVERC2.MTW

RIVERC2 contains six additional variables and four constants. The four constants are K1 = 0.995026, cumulative probability up to 25.2 for a chi-square distribution with 10 degrees of freedom; K2 = 0.004974 (= 1–K1); K3 = 0.846303, cumulative probability up to 13.2 for a chi-square distribution with 9 degrees of freedom; K4 = 0.153697 (= 1–K3).

Column	Name	Count	Missing	Description
C1	HOUR	95	0	The hour of the measurement, in military time
C2	TEMP	95	0	The temperature, in °C, of the river at the given hour
C3	PH	95	0	The pH of the river at the given hour
C4	COND	95	0	The conductivity, in electrical potential, of the river at the given hour
C5	DO	95	0	The dissolved oxygen content of the river at the given hour
C6	FORE1	48	0	Forecasts for the next two days (48 hours)
C7	LAGS	95	1	Lags
C8	DIFF	95	1	Differences
C9	AFORECST	48	0	ARIMA forecasts
C10	LAFORCST	48	0	Lower limits
C11	UAFORCST	48	0	Upper limits

These files are used in Tutorial 8 (Practice Problems), Tutorial 13, Tutorial 15, Tutorial 15 (Practice Problems).

SALARY.MTW

A small private college conducts a yearly study of its faculty's salaries. Information on gender, department, years at the school, beginning salary, current salary, and an "experience" variable are recorded. Many other variables are combined to yield an "experience" score. The higher the score, the more experience the person had when he or she first started. The faculty member's current rank is also measured.

Column	Name	Count	Description
C1	ID	171	The college's identification number for the faculty
C2-A	GENDER	171	The gender of the faculty member, coded F and M
C3	GENDER N	171	The gender of the faculty member; 0 = female and 1 = male
C4	START YR	171	The starting year of the faculty member
C5	DEPTCODE	171	The department of the faculty member coded as a number
C6	BEGIN $	171	The starting salary of the faculty member
C7	1991 $	171	The current salary (1991) of the faculty member
C8	EXPERNC	171	The "experience variable" value when the person started at the college
C9	RANKCODE	171	The current rank of the faculty member; 1 = instructor, 2 = assistant professor, 3 = associate professor, and 4 = professor

SALMAN.MTW

Zoologists housed 14 salamanders in individual cages. During the period of study, they exposed the salamanders to normal conditions and monitored each cage separately. They recorded the activity level in each cage hourly over the course of six days, for a total of 144 hourly assessments. These results were subsequently used to compare other experimental conditions (not included in this data set).

Column	Name	Count	Description
C1	ACTIVITY	144	The daily activity level for 14 salamanders

SNOW.MTW

This data set contains the total snowfall amounts (in inches) for a large city on the East Coast recorded for the 32 years between 1962 and 1993.

Column	Name	Count	Description
C1	YEAR	32	Year
C2	SNOWFALL	32	Snowfall, in inches
C3	RAIN	32	The equivalent rainfall, in inches

This file is used in Tutorial 1 (the data are used in Practice Problems, but not the file), Tutorial 2 (Practice Problems), Tutorial 13, Tutorial 13 (Practice Problems), and Tutorial 14.

SP500.MTW

A professor in a business school at a southern university monitored the stock market over several years. This data set contains 500 consecutive daily high, low, and closing values for the Standard and Poor's 500 Cash (Spot) Index.

Column	Name	Count	Description
C1	HIGH	506	The high value of Standard and Poor's 500 Cash (Spot) Index on a given day
C2	LOW	506	The low value of Standard and Poor's 500 Cash (Spot) Index on a given day
C3	CLOSE	506	The closing value of Standard and Poor's 500 Cash (Spot) Index on a given day

This file is used in Tutorial 15 (Practice Problems).

▼

SPCAR.MTW

▲

Fuel economy ratings for 1994 vehicles constitute this data set.

Column	Name	Count	Missing	Description
C1-A	VEHICLE	19	0	Manufacturer and model
C2	CT	19	0	Miles per gallon in city driving
C3	HW	19	0	Miles per gallon in highway driving
C4	CM	19	0	Miles per gallon in combination of city and highway driving (EPA assumes that 55% of the miles are under city conditions)
C5	COST	19	0	Estimate of the cost of one year's fuel for the vehicle
C6	ENGDISPL	19	0	Engine displacement in liters
C7	ENGCYLIN	19	0	Number of cylinders
C8	TRNTYPE	19	0	Type of transmission; 1 = automatic, 2 = creeper gear, 3 = automatic with fuel-saving device that eliminates slippage, 4 = manual, and 5 = semi-automatic
C9	TRNGEARS	19	0	Number of gears
C10	FL	19	7	Fuel information; 1 = diesel engine, 2 = gas guzzler tax, 3 = vehicle requires premium fuel and is subject to gas guzzler tax, 4 = vehicle requires premium fuel

STEALS.MTW

Early in the 1991 major league baseball season, Rickey Henderson of the Oakland Athletics baseball team became the stolen base leader, passing Lou Brock. Newspapers reported the number of bases Mr. Henderson stole for each day of the week.

Column	Name	Count	Description
C1-A	DAY	7	The day of the week
C2	BASES	7	The total number of bases that Mr. Henderson stole on the given day of the week

STORES.MTW

A marketing research firm collected data on the number of individuals who last bought jeans from four major stores, classified according to their approximate yearly total household income before taxes.

Column	Name	Count	Description
C1	STORE	4	Store identification
C2	UNDER25K	4	The number of individuals earning less than $25,000 who purchased jeans at each store
C3	25KTO35K	4	The number of individuals earning from $25,000 to $35,000 who purchased jeans at each store
C4	35KTO50K	4	The number of individuals earning from $35,000 to $50,000 who purchased jeans at each store
C5	50KTO75K	4	The number of individuals earning from $50,000 to $75,000 who purchased jeans at each store
C6	75K&OVER	4	The number of individuals earning more than $75,000 who purchased jeans at each store

This file is used in Tutorial 12 and Tutorial 12 (Practice Problems).

▼
TBILL.MTW
▲

This data set lists the Treasury Bill values for 1991 and 1992.

Column	Name	Count	Description
C1	HIGH	104	High value for a day
C2	LOW	104	Low value for a day
C3	CLOSE	104	Closing value

▼
TECHN.MTW and TECHN2.MTW
▲

This data set contains the salary information for all salaried employees in four departments at the Technitron company. TECHN.MTW contains C1–C8, while TECHN2.MTW adds four columns that store the standardized residuals, fits and residuals calculated from regression YRS EM on SALARY, and the square of YRS EM. The data set PAY is a subset of this larger data set.

Column	Name	Count	Description
C1	SALARY	46	The salary of an employee
C2	YRS EM	46	The number of years employed at Technitron
C3	PRIOR YR	46	The number of prior years' experience
C4	EDUC	46	Years of education after high school
C5	ID	46	The company identification number for the employee
C6	GENDER	46	The gender of the employee; 0 = female and 1 = male
C7	DEPT	46	The employee's department; 1 = sales, 2 = purchasing, 3 = advertising, and 4 = engineering
C8	SUPER	46	The number of employees supervised by this employee
C9	SRES1	46	Standardized residuals
C10	FITS1	46	Fits
C11	RESI1	46	Residuals
C12	YRS**2	46	Square of YRS EM

These files are used in Tutorial 9 (Practice Problems), Tutorial 10, and Tutorial 11.

TEXTS.MTW

These data were collected to facilitate analysis of the emphasis on quality control in introductory business and economics statistics texts published between 1989 and 1994.

Column	Name	Count	Missing	Description
C1	YEAR	52	0	Year of publication
C2	ED	52	0	Edition
C3	PAGES	52	0	Number of pages in text
C4	CHAPTERS	52	0	Number of chapters
C5	QCHAPTER	52	0	Number of quality chapter
C6	QCPAGES	52	0	Number of pages in quality chapter
C7	QPRATIO	52	0	Number of quality pages/number of pages
C8	QCRATIO	52	19	Number of quality chapter/total number of chapters in text

TVHRS.MTW

This file includes the results of a study of TV-viewing patterns.

Column	Name	Count	Description
C1-A	ID	120	Subject identification number
C2	AGEGRP	120	Age group; 1 = grade school; 2 = college students; and 3 = 50+
C3	AGE	120	Ages
C4	GENDER	120	Gender; 1 = male and 2 = female
C5	SESAME	120	Whether or not they watched Sesame Street; 1 = no and 2 = yes
C6	HRSTV	120	Hours spent watching TV in a week
C7	HRSMTV	120	Hours spent watching MTV
C8	HRSNEWS	120	Hours spent watching news
C9	EDUCA	120	Educational background; 1 = some grade school, 2 = some high school, 3 = high school diploma, 4 = some college, 5 = college degree, 6 = 2 or less years of graduate school, 7 = more than 2 years of graduate school

TVVIEW.MTW

Ten married couples were randomly selected and asked the average amount of time (in hours) each spent watching TV per week.

Column	Name	Count	Description
C1	HUSBAND	10	The average number of hours that the husband spent watching TV per week
C2	WIFE	10	The average number of hours that the wife spent watching TV per week
C3	TOTAL	10	The average number of hours that the husband and wife spent watching TV per week
C4	DIFF	10	The difference between the average number of hours spent watching TV per week by the husband and wife

This file is used in Tutorial 1 (the data are used in Practice Problems, but not the file), Tutorial 2 (Practice Problems), Tutorial 5 (Practice Problems), and Tutorial 8 (Practice Problems).

USDEM.MTW

This data set displays census values for the U.S., including the estimated population and population density.

Column	Name	Count	Description
C1	YEAR	21	Year
C2	US POPLN	21	Population of the U.S., in millions
C3	POP DENS	21	Population density of the U.S., in people per square mile

VPVH.MTW

Each year the Nielsen company conducts extensive surveys of TV-viewing habits of the U.S. population. Many of the surveys are coded by age and gender groups, because sponsors are interested in how these variables affect which programs people watch.

This data set contains the VPVH estimates for several different categories of television programming. The *VPVH estimate* is the estimated number of viewers per 1000 viewing households tuned to a station or program. This data set includes the 10 VPVH estimates for each of four commonly surveyed gender/age groups (men aged 18 to 34, women aged 18 to 34, men aged 55+, and women aged 55+) for the following types of programs: network movies, situation comedy, and sports. For the sports program, only data for the two male age groups were given.

Column	Name	Count	Missing	Description
C1	MOVIES	40	0	The VPVH data for the top 10 network movies
C2	COMEDY	40	0	The VPVH data for the top 10 situation comedies
C3	SPORTS	40	20	The VPVH data for the top 10 sporting events
C4-A	GROUP	40	0	The gender/age group
C5	GROUP N	40	0	The gender age/group coded numerically

This file is used in Tutorial 9 (Practice Problems).

WASTES.MTW

New and abandoned hazardous waste sites are being discovered across the U.S. This data set lists the number of hazardous waste sites found in each region of the country.

Column	Name	Count	Description
C1	NENGLAND	6	The number of hazardous waste sites in each New England state
C2	MATLANTC	3	The number of hazardous waste sites found in each mid-Atlantic state
C3	ENCENTRL	5	The number of hazardous waste sites found in each east-north central state
C4	WNCENTRL	7	The number of hazardous waste sites found in each west-north central state
C5	SATLANTC	9	The number of hazardous waste sites found in each southern Atlantic state
C6	ESCENTRL	4	The number of hazardous waste sites found in each east-south central state
C7	WSCENTRL	4	The number of hazardous waste sites found in each west-south central state
C8	MOUNTAIN	8	The number of hazardous waste sites found in each mountain state
C9	PACIFIC	5	The number of hazardous waste sites found in each Pacific state

This file is used in Tutorial 7 (Practice Problems) and Tutorial 8 (Practice Problems).

▼
WHEAT.MTW
▲

A professor in a business school at a southern university studied wheat futures. This data set contains the daily high, low, and closing values for wheat futures for 500 consecutive days, representing approximately 1½ years' worth of data. In addition, the number of wheat future contracts traded on the day is recorded.

Column	Name	Count	Description
C1	HIGH	500	The high value of wheat futures traded on that day
C2	LOW	500	The low value of wheat futures traded on that day
C3	CLOSE	500	The closing value of wheat futures traded on that day
C4	VOLUME	500	The total number of contracts traded on that day

▼
YOGURT.MTW
▲

These data, collected by a research company, show the results of testing 14 brands of plain yogurt. The tests evaluated overall nutritional value, cost per ounce, and the number of calories per serving.

Column	Name	Count	Description
C1-A	RATING	14	Nutritional rating of excellent, very good, good, fair, or poor
C2	CENTS	14	Cost per ounce, in cents
C3	CALS	14	Calories per 8-oz. serving, in cents

This file is used in Tutorial 1 (the data are used, but not the file), Tutorial 5, and Tutorial 9 (Practice Problems).

PART IV

REFERENCE

CHAPTER 1

Special Topics

This chapter summarizes the basics of working with Minitab and its menu interface, including using the Data window. It also covers some special topics, such as time-saving hints, alpha data, and file types. Some of these topics are described in a variety of places in the tutorials; others are described only indirectly.

The Worksheet

Minitab places the data that you enter or retrieve in a temporary storage area called the *worksheet*. The worksheet consists of columns and stored constants. Columns generally represent variables; rows generally represent individual cases. Each cell contains one piece of data. The worksheet can handle 3500 data pieces. The Info window displays an updated summary of your current worksheet.

Columns. Most operations use columns. You can refer to columns by column number (for example, C1 or C22) or by name (for example, *Sales* or *Year*). You name a column either by typing the name in the Data window underneath the column header, or by using the Session command NAME.

Stored constants. A constant contains a single number. You can refer to a constant by number (such as K5) or by name (such as *First*). To view a stored constant, choose File > Display Data; stored constants do not appear in the Data window. Minitab automatically assigns the values of missing, e, and π to these three stored constants: K998 = *; K999 = 2.71828; K1000 = 3.14159. You can change these values, if you wish.

Size of Worksheets. When you start Minitab, the Session window displays the current worksheet size, which is the maximum number of cells (individual data values) that can store data. *The Student Edition of MINITAB for Windows* allows worksheets of up to 3500 cells, if your computer has enough memory to support a worksheet of that size. All cells can contain data; Minitab will not use any of these cells for worksheet space when it executes commands.

If you try to open a worksheet containing more than 3500 cells, Minitab disables all functions except those that let you reduce worksheet size.

Windows

When you first start Minitab, the main Minitab window opens. The main Minitab window includes six different window types:

Data window: Displays your data.

Graph window: Displays Professional graphs created by Minitab's Graph commands (opens when you create a graph).

Help window: Contains information about using Minitab (opens when you choose Help).

History window: Contains a record of all commands issued in a given session.

Info window: Contains summary information about the current worksheet.

Session window: Contains a record of all the commands you issued in the current session and the resulting output.

Minitab's windows are fully compatible with Microsoft conventions: you can minimize and maximize windows, reduce them to icons, and move among them using the Window menu commands. To change the size of a window, point to any of the window borders with your mouse. When the mouse pointer turns into a two-sided arrow ⌖, drag the border accordingly to size the window.

Moving among Windows

You can switch to a window using any of these techniques: you can click anywhere in the window, you can choose Window > *window name*, you can press Ctrl+Tab, or you can use one of the following keyboard shortcuts:

Session Window	Ctrl+**M**
Data Window	Ctrl+**D**
History Window	Ctrl+**H**
Info Window	Ctrl+**I**

commands (Minimize, Maximize, or Restore), and then press ←Enter.

To move a window or a dialog box: First, open the Control menu by pressing Alt+ – in a window, or Alt+Spacebar in a dialog box. Next, move the cursor to Move and press ←Enter. Use the arrow keys to move the box or window, and then press ←Enter.

To change the size of a window: First, press Alt+ – to display the Control menu. Move the cursor to Size and press ←Enter. Next, press an arrow key to select the window border that you want to adjust. Finally, use the arrow keys to move the border, and then press ←Enter.

Working with Menus

The menu bar contains the nine main Minitab menus: File, Edit, Manip, Calc, Stat, Window, Graph, Editor, and Help. These menus list the Minitab commands.

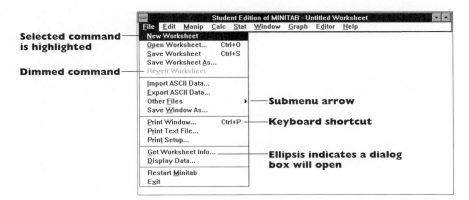

Working with Windows Using the Keyboard

To switch among applications: Hold down Alt and press Tab as many times as necessary to cycle through the names of all the open applications. Release Alt when the name of the application to which you want to switch appears.

Alternatively, press Ctrl+Esc to display the Task List, use the arrow keys to highlight the task you want, and then press ←Enter.

To minimize, maximize, or restore a window: Press Alt+ – to display the Control menu, highlight the appropriate

Commands followed by an ellipsis (...): A dialog box opens when you select the command.

Arrow: A submenu with more commands appears when you select the command.

Dimmed commands: The command is currently unavailable (certain Editor commands, for example, are dimmed if you haven't activated the Data window).

Keyboard shortcuts: If available, they are displayed to the right of the command name on the menu. You can choose those commands directly from the keyboard to bypass the menu.

Check mark: A check mark indicates that a command is currently active. For example, when Stat > Fit Intercept is checked, Minitab always fits an intercept; when the command isn't checked, Minitab omits an intercept.

To select a menu command using the mouse: Click the menu name and then click the command (followed by the command on the submenu if necessary). If the command requires information from you, Minitab opens a dialog box; otherwise, Minitab executes the command immediately.

To select a menu command using the keyboard: Press [Alt] plus the underlined letter in the menu name (such as F for File or E for Edit) to open the menu, then press the underlined letter of the command you want. Alternatively, you can use the arrow keys to move through the menus on the menu bar or to move down through the commands on an open menu. When the appropriate menu or command is highlighted, press [←Enter]. Note that you may not always be able to use [Alt] plus a letter as a shortcut if other software uses the same key combination as Minitab.

To close a menu without making a choice: Press [Esc] or click anywhere outside the menu.

The next sections summarize the commands available on the Minitab menus. Chapter 2 documents each command.

File Menu

New Worksheet: Opens a new, blank worksheet.

Open Worksheet: Opens a saved worksheet (MTW) file, a portable saved worksheet (MTP) file, or a Lotus file.

Save Worksheet: Saves the current worksheet as an existing MTW, MTP, or Lotus file.

Save Worksheet As: Saves the current worksheet as a new MTW, MTP, or Lotus file to which you assign a name.

Revert Worksheet: Returns the current worksheet to its original state when you first opened it.

Import ASCII Data: Enters data into the worksheet from the keyboard, the Windows Clipboard, or a text file.

Export ASCII Data: Saves the worksheet columns in a text file.

Other Files: Displays commands for viewing a saved Minitab graph (MGF) file, recording all or part of your session in a file, and recording and running an Exec macro.

Save Window As: Saves the active window in a file.

Print Window: Prints the active window.

Print Text File: Prints the text file that you specify.

Print Setup: Displays information about your printer that you can modify.

Get Worksheet Info: Summarizes the current worksheet.

Display Data: Displays any combination of columns stored constants in the Session window.

Restart Minitab: Starts a new Minitab session and clears the worksheet.

Exit: Exits Minitab.

Edit Menu

These commands change, depending on the active window.

Undo: Reverses, or undoes, your most recent editing operation.

Delete: Deletes the highlighted text or data.

Copy: Copies the highlighted text or data to the Clipboard.

Cut: Removes the highlighted text or data and copies it to the Clipboard.

Paste/Insert: Inserts the contents of the Clipboard in the cursor's current position.

Paste/Replace: Replaces the highlighted area of the Data window with the contents of the Clipboard.

Select All: Highlights all the contents of the active window.

Edit Last Command Dialog: Redisplays the most recently used dialog box, with the previous selections still specified.

Save Preferences: Saves any changes you make to the window arrangement, printer setup, and default Lotus file format.

Manip Menu

Sort: Sorts one or more columns of data.

Rank: Assigns rank scores to the values in a column.

Delete Rows: Deletes the specified rows from the columns in the worksheet.

Erase Variables: Erases any combination of columns and stored constants.

Copy Columns: Copies columns from one position in the worksheet to another; it can copy entire columns or just a portion of them.

Code Data Values: Recodes numbers in columns.

Stack: Stacks blocks of columns or constants on top of one another.

Unstack: Separates blocks of columns into multiple, smaller blocks.

Convert: Converts alpha data to numbers and vice versa.

Concatenate: Combines two or more alpha columns that are next to each other into a single new column.

Calc Menu

Set Base: Fixes a starting point for Minitab's random number generator.

Random Data: Displays commands for generating a random sample of numbers, sampled either from columns of the worksheet or from a variety of distributions.

Probability Distributions: Displays commands that allow you to compute probabilities, probability densities, cumulative probabilities, and inverse cumulative probabilities for continuous and discrete distributions.

Mathematical Expressions: Performs arithmetic using an algebraic expression, which may contain arithmetic operators, comparison operators, logical operators, and functions.

Functions: Performs a variety of mathematical functions on a number, stored constant, or a column.

Column Statistics: Calculates various statistics based on a column you select.

Row Statistics: Calculates various statistics for each row of the columns you select.

Set Patterned Data: Provides a quick way to enter data that follow a pattern, such as the numbers one through ten, in a column of the worksheet.

Make Indicator Variables: Creates indicator (dummy) variables that you can use in regression analysis.

Standardize: Centers and scales columns of data.

Stat Menu

Fit Intercept: Fits regression models with or without an intercept term.

Basic Statistics: Calculates basic statistics, including descriptive statistics, Z- and t-tests, correlation, and covariance.

Regression: Performs simple, polynomial, multiple, or stepwise regression, forward selection, and backward elimination, and produces fitted line plots and residual plots.

ANOVA (Analysis of Variance): Performs one-way and two-way analysis of variance, balanced analysis of variance for balanced models, and residual plots.

Control Charts: Produces a variety of control charts to facilitate the study of variation in a process.

SPC (Statistical Process Control): Produces Pareto and Cause-and-Effect charts.

Time Series: Produces plots to facilitate investigation of the behavior of data collected over time.

Tables: Produces one-way and multi-way contingency tables, statistics for associated variables, and performs Chi-square analysis.

Nonparametrics: Performs a variety of nonparametric tests.

Window Menu

Cascade: Arranges all the open Minitab windows so that they overlap with each title bar visible (if possible).

Tile: Arranges all the open Minitab windows so that they fit next to each other on the desktop without overlapping (if possible).

Minimize All: Reduces all the open windows to icons at the bottom of the screen.

Restore Icons: Reopens all the minimized windows to their most recent size during the current session.

Arrange Icons: Arranges any icons along the bottom of the Minitab window.

Discard Graph: Deletes the active Graph window or all Graph windows.

Set Graph Size/Location: Determines how Minitab displays Graph windows.

Session: Switches to the Session window, in which you enter Session commands and/or view analysis results.

Data: Switches to the Data window, in which you view and edit your worksheet.

History: Switches to the History window, in which you view and copy commands previously executed during the current session.

Info: Switches to the Info window, which contains a concise summary of your worksheet.

Graph Menu

Plot: Produces a scatter plot that shows the relationship between pairs of variables.

Chart: Produces several types of charts, including bar charts, line charts, symbol charts, and area charts.

Histogram: Produces histograms, which are useful for showing the distribution of data.

Boxplot: Produces a box-and-whisker plot.

Time Series Plot: Produces a time series plot.

Matrix Plot: Produces a scatter plot matrix of 3 to 10 variables.

Normal Plot: Produces a normal probability plot to help determine whether or not your data follow a normal distribution.

Character Graphs: Displays commands that produce a variety of Character (not Professional) graphs.

Editor Menu

Next Column: Moves the cursor to the top of the next column.

Next Row: Moves the cursor to the beginning of the next row.

Go To: Moves the cursor to the cell you specify.

Go To Active Cell: Displays the part of the worksheet that contains the active cell.

Format Column: Allows you to specify how a column displays in the Data window.

Set Column Widths: Sets the width of the selected columns in the Data window.

Compress Display: Hides empty, unnamed columns from view, or reveals previously hidden columns.

Change Entry Direction: Changes the direction of the data-entry arrow, which determines whether the cell to the right of the active cell or the one below it becomes active when you press ⏎Enter.

Insert Cell: Inserts a cell above the active cell.

Insert Row: Inserts a row above the active cell.

Cell Edit Mode: Turns cell Edit mode on or off for the active cell.

Clipboard Settings: Allows you to specify a character other than an asterisk (*) to represent a missing value in the Clipboard.

Help Menu

Contents: Displays the Help system's table of contents.

Getting Started: Provides the introductory and overview information you need to begin using Minitab.

How do I: Displays step-by-step instructions for performing a specific task.

Search for Help on: Opens the Windows Search dialog box, which lets you look up information in Help just like you would in a book's index.

How to Use Help: Explains how to use the Help system, including how to print, copy, and paste Help text.

About Minitab: Displays the Minitab serial number, product name, release number, and other information.

Working with Dialog Boxes

Most menu commands display a dialog box that lets you specify variables and options. Many dialog boxes access other dialog boxes that contain less frequently used options. For the most part, you use Minitab's dialog boxes just as you do those in other Windows applications.

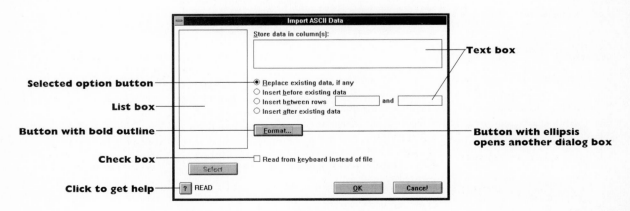

Text boxes: you enter information, like columns or values, in text boxes. You separate columns and constants with spaces, not commas. You can move the insertion point from one box to another by pressing Tab. You can also move directly to a text box by clicking it.

Option buttons and check boxes: Option buttons are mutually exclusive choices. Check boxes, on the other hand, are additive; you can select as many as you want. You can click the label next to a button or check box to select it, which is often easier than clicking the item itself.

Keyboard Shortcuts: You can press ←Enter instead of clicking the button with the bold outline (usually the OK button).

Keyboard Operations in Dialog Boxes

- To move forward, press Tab.

- To move backward, press Shift+Tab.

- To move among items within a section, press arrow keys.

- To choose OK, press Alt+**O**.

- To choose Cancel, press Esc.

- To choose the Help button, press F1.

- To recall the last dialog box, press Ctrl+**E**.

- To reset all the dialog box settings to their defaults, press F3.

Pressing ←Enter is the same as choosing the button in the dialog box with the bold outline, which is usually the OK button.

Selecting Columns from a List Box

To select columns from a list box, first place the insertion point in the text box to activate it. Next, highlight the column or columns you want to select. Finally, click the Select button. The method of highlighting the columns in the list box depends on whether the text box can contain only one or more than one column.

If the text box can contain only one column, you can highlight only a single column in the list box. Clicking a column highlights it; double-clicking a column selects it.

If the text box can contain multiple columns, you can drag to highlight several columns at once. You can also press Ctrl and click the individual columns or select a group of columns by clicking the first, then pressing Shift and clicking the last.

The following three examples show you some of the ways you use dialog boxes in Minitab. More information about dialog boxes appears after these examples.

Example 1: The Normal Distribution Dialog Box

1. Choose **Calc > Random Data > Normal** (short for choosing the Normal command from the Random Data submenu in the Calc menu). The Normal Distribution dialog box appears:

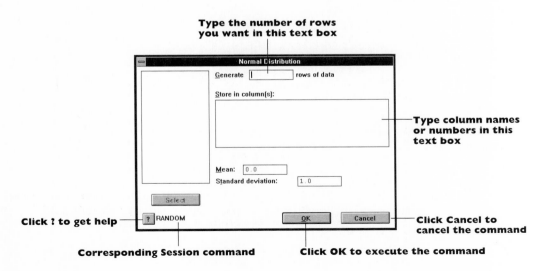

Type the number of rows you want in this text box

Type column names or numbers in this text box

Click ? to get help

Corresponding Session command

Click OK to execute the command

Click Cancel to cancel the command

To indicate the number of rows of data:

2. Type the number of rows of data you want in the **Generate [ ] rows of data** text box.

1. Choose **Stat > Regression > Regression**.

This text box requires a single column

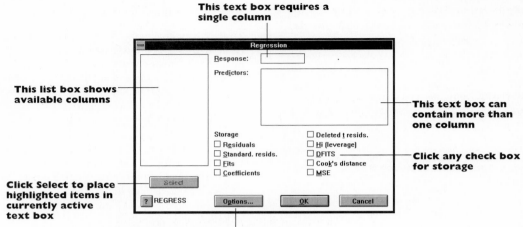

This list box shows available columns

This text box can contain more than one column

Click any check box for storage

Click Select to place highlighted items in currently active text box

Click Options to display a dialog box containing less frequently used options

To move the insertion point (indicated by the blinking vertical bar) to the text box:

3. Click anywhere in the text box or press Tab.

To tell Minitab where to store the random data:

4. Type column names or numbers in the **Store in column(s)** text box, separated by spaces, not commas.

If you type a name that has not already been assigned to a column, Minitab automatically chooses the next unused column and assigns the name to it.

The text boxes labeled Mean and Standard deviation contain default values. If you prefer another value, simply type the value in the appropriate box.

To display context-sensitive Help for this dialog box:

5. Click the **?** button. (Tutorial 1 provides more information about Minitab's Help system.)

To cancel the command:

6. Click **Cancel**.

To begin processing the command:

7. Click **OK** or press ←Enter.

With a file open, to specify the column C1 as the response variable and C2–C5 as predictors, make sure the insertion point is in the text box labeled Response and:

2. Click **C1** in the list box to highlight it, then click the **Select** button.

3. Move the insertion point to the **Predictors** text box.

4. Click **C2**, **C3**, **C4**, and **C5** in the list box to highlight them.

You can also drag through several columns to highlight them in one step.

5. Click **Select** to specify columns C2 through C5 as the predictors.

The insertion point remains in the text box, allowing you to add more columns. Note that Minitab abbreviates a set of consecutive columns with a dash (-). You can also type column names or numbers (for example, C1) in the text boxes, if you prefer, separated by spaces.

If you click any of the check boxes for optional storage, Minitab automatically chooses the next unused column or stored constant. If the storage is in a column, Minitab assigns it an appropriate name.

To display a dialog box containing less frequently used options:

6. Click the **Options** button, select your choices, then click **OK** to return to the main dialog box.

7. Click **OK** in the **Regression** dialog box to execute the command.

If you decide that you don't want to change anything in the dialog box, click **Cancel** instead.

Whenever the label of a button ends with an ellipsis (...), clicking the button displays an additional dialog box. Because you can always click Cancel in the dialog box, there is no danger in exploring these additional options.

Example 3: The 1-Sample t Dialog Box

1. Choose **Stat > Basic Statistics > 1-Sample t**.

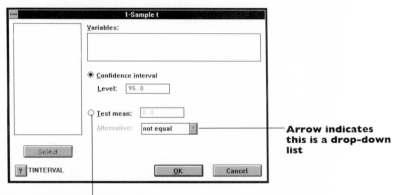

Click this option button to select a hypothesis test rather than a confidence interval

Arrow indicates this is a drop-down list

Specify the variable or variables to analyze:

2. Type column names or numbers in the **Variables** text box or copy them from the list box.

To choose the hypothesis test rather than the confidence interval:

3. Click the **Test mean** option button.

To choose an alternative hypothesis:

4. Click the **Alternative** drop-down arrow and then click an alternative hypothesis from the list that appears.

5. Click **OK** or **Cancel.**

Abbreviating a Range in a Text Box

You can abbreviate a range of columns or stored constants with a dash. For example, C3-C7 is short for C3, C4, C5, C6, and C7. If C3 and C7 are named *First* and *Last*, respectively, you can type them as First-Last, First-C7, or C3-Last.

Column Names in Text Boxes

A name consists of one to eight characters, with no leading or trailing spaces, single quotation marks ('), or octothorpes (#). Also, a name cannot consist of a single *. You cannot use special characters in names. Names are not case-sensitive.

With certain exceptions, you can type names that start with a letter and consist of only letters and digits without quotation marks. The exceptions are names that might be mistaken for column numbers or stored constant

numbers, for example, C2 or K3. In particular, if a name consists of the character > or K followed by one or more digits, it must be enclosed in single quotation marks, such as 'K3'. In any case, try to avoid such names because they are likely to produce confusion.

Any other name must be enclosed in single quotation marks. Thus, a name starting with anything other than a letter, or containing any character other than a letter or a digit, must be enclosed in single quotation marks.

Missing Value Code

You can type Minitab's missing value code, *, in text boxes without enclosing it in quotation marks.

What Happens When You Click OK?

When you click OK, Minitab enters commands in the Session window that correspond to the menu commands, variables, and options you selected in the dialog box. Minitab then executes the Session commands, just as if you had typed them.

Using the Data Window

Minitab provides many different ways to enter and edit data. If you want to enter data from the keyboard, edit individual values, or view your data, you work in the Data window and use the features described in this section.

Note: There are also some other ways of entering and manipulating data. If you want to enter patterned data, use Calc > Set Patterned Data. If you want to edit and manipulate more than one value at a time, or if you want to erase columns, use the commands in the Manip menu.

Column containing alpha data has A-suffix　　　　**Columns**

	C1-A	C2	C3	C4	C5	C6	C7
	DEPT	NUMBER	INTEREST	MANNER	COURSE	INSTRUCR	RESPONDS
1	ACC	221	2.07	2.67	2.27	2.73	15
2	ACC	221	2.40	3.07	2.75	3.38	15
3	ACC	321	2.64	3.36	3.00	3.45	11
4	ACC	344	3.42	3.67	3.42	3.67	12
5	AER	101	3.25	3.50	3.13	3.13	8
6	ARC	426	3.29	3.12	3.35	3.41	15
7	ART	111	2.47	1.73	2.33	2.00	15

Data entry arrow — pointing to row 1
Active cell — the ACC cell in row 1
Rows — the numbered rows

A command may display its results in the Session window or in one or more Graph windows. Some commands do not display any results, but the Info and Data windows display their effect on the worksheet.

What about Mistakes?

Minitab catches most mistakes before it places the Session commands in the Session window. It reports any mistake in an alert box, and indicates how to correct the problem. When you click OK in the alert box, Minitab places the insertion point in the text box that contains the error; if appropriate, it highlights the portion of the text that is causing the problem.

　Minitab does not discover errors involving the data values in a column until it attempts to execute the Session commands. In this case, the Session window moves to the front and displays a message about the error. To return to the last dialog box to correct the mistake, choose Edit Last Command Dialog from the Edit menu, or use the keyboard shortcut, Ctrl+**E**.

Data Window Techniques

　To enter a new value into the active cell: Type the value, and then accept it either by pressing Tab, ←Enter, or an arrow key or by clicking another cell. It overwrites any previous contents of the cell.

　To edit the active cell: Double-click the active cell to enter Edit mode, and then press either Alt+←Enter, Alt+→ or Alt+← to move the insertion point. Remove text by using either Del or Bksp.

　To enter or edit a column name: Follow the same steps as for entering or editing an active cell.

　To delete the active cell: Choose Edit > Delete Cells; the remaining cells move up in the column.

　To delete the active row: Click the row header to select the entire row, then choose Edit > Delete Cells. Use Manip > Delete Rows to specify the rows you want to delete.

　To insert one cell above the active cell: Choose Editor > Insert Cell; the remaining cells in the column move down.

Extension	File Type	Description
MTW	Minitab worksheet	A binary file that stores worksheet data — rows and columns of data, variable names, constants, and Data window settings. Can be used only by Minitab on the same computer operating system that saved it. Opened with File > Open Worksheet > Minitab worksheet; saved with either File > Save Worksheet > Minitab worksheet or File > Save Worksheet As > Minitab worksheet.
MTP	Portable worksheet	Used to transfer data saved by Minitab running under one operating system to Minitab running under another. Used with the same commands as .MTW files, but you select Minitab portable worksheet instead.
DAT	Exported or imported ASCII text file	Contains raw ASCII data. Can be used with other software. Generated by File > Export ASCII Data.
LIS	ASCII file	Contains Session window output produced by File > Other Files > Start Recording Session.
MGF	Minitab Graphics Format file containing Minitab-produced graph	Generated by File > Save Window As when graphics window is open. Opened by File > Other Files > Open Graph.
MTJ	ASCII file containing the commands entered during a Minitab session	Produced by File > Other Files > Start Recording History. Use this file type to assemble an Exec or re-execute previously executed commands. History window also shows commands used during a session, so you can create a command file by pasting commands from the History window into a text editor.
MAC	ASCII file containing %Macro commands	In *The Student Edition of MINITAB for Windows*, MAC files are limited to the %Macros that come with the software.
MTB	ASCII file containing Exec macro commands	You can execute this type of macro with File > Other Files > Run an Exec.

Files That Store Data

There are three types of files that store data.

Saved worksheet: A saved worksheet (the default file type when you save a Minitab worksheet) contains all the information in the current worksheet — columns, column names, constants, and Data window settings. Use saved worksheets when you are using Minitab on only one type of computer. Saved worksheets are a very efficient way to store data and are retrieved quickly. You cannot edit or print saved worksheets outside of Minitab, nor can you import them into other applications.

Portable worksheet: Except for Data window settings, portable worksheets contain the same information as a saved worksheet. Use portable worksheets to transfer your worksheet data from Minitab on one type of computer to Minitab on another type of computer: for example, from Minitab on a mainframe to Minitab on the Macintosh. Portable worksheets are not as fast to retrieve as saved worksheets.

Data file: Data files contain columns of data in a text (ASCII) file; they do not include stored constants. By default, data files do not include column names; however, Minitab can read column names if the data file is tab-delimited. Use data files to transfer worksheet data between Minitab and another application, such as a spreadsheet or a database application.

Files That Store Minitab Output

Outfile: When you choose the Start Recording Session command from the File menu, Minitab stores a record of your Minitab session (all commands and output except for Professional graphs) in a text (ASCII) file. Use outfiles to keep a permanent record of your session and to produce reports. You can print and edit an outfile with a text editor or word processor.

Graphics file: You use the Save Window As command from the File menu to store a Professional graph in a graph file. You can copy a graph file to the Clipboard and paste it into word processing applications. You can also save graphics files as bitmaps by using the Print Screen key to copy the bitmap to the Clipboard, and then open it in a graphics editor such as Paintbrush. Use graphics files to store your graphs and charts so you can print them and/or include them in reports.

Files That Store Minitab Commands

Exec file: An Exec file is a text (ASCII) file that consists of Session commands that you can execute in a batch. Use Exec files to automate frequently used Minitab procedures or to extend Minitab's functionality. You can create an Exec file using the File > Other Files > Start Recording Exec command. You can also create and edit an Exec file with a word processor or a text editor such as Notepad.

Journal file: A journal file is a text (ASCII) file that records the Session commands you execute during your Minitab session. You can print and edit a journal file with a word processor or a text editor; you can also execute a journal file as an Exec.

Printing Data and Output from within Minitab

To print your worksheet data, you can:

- Make the Data window active, and then choose File > Print Window. Select options in the Data Window Print Options dialog box, and then click OK twice.

- List the worksheet data in the Session window by choosing File > Display Data. Select the data in the Session window, and then choose File > Print Window. The Windows Print dialog box appears; leave the Selection option button selected and click OK.

To print a copy of your Minitab Session commands and output: Choose File > Other Files > Start Recording Session and then give your outfile a name. From this point on, Minitab stores all the commands and output displayed in the Session window in an outfile. After you choose File > Other Files > Stop Recording Session, you can choose File > Print Text File to select and then print the outfile. You can also highlight only the portion of the Session window that you want to print, choose File > Print Window, and then click OK in the Print dialog box.

To print Professional graphs and charts, while the Graph window is active: Choose File > Print Window.

To print a window or to print selected text: Choose File > Print Window.

Combining Worksheet Files

You may want to combine data stored in separate saved worksheet files. To combine only selected data, open the first worksheet, highlight the cells you want to combine, and choose Edit > Copy Cells. Alternatively, if you want to copy the entire worksheet, choose Edit > Select All Cells first to highlight all the cells. (Names of columns are not be copied.) Next, open the second worksheet, click the cell that you want to be the upper left corner of the block, and choose Edit > Paste Cells to complete the copy.

CHAPTER 2

Menu Reference

The File Menu

```
File
New Worksheet
Open Worksheet...      Ctrl+O
Save Worksheet         Ctrl+S
Save Worksheet As...
Revert Worksheet

Import ASCII Data...
Export ASCII Data...
Other Files                      ►
Save Window As...

Print Window...        Ctrl+P
Print Text File...
Print Setup...

Get Worksheet Info...
Display Data...

Restart Minitab
Exit
```

The File menu contains all the commands necessary to create, maintain, and use Minitab files; to access non-Minitab files; and to produce printed copies of information in Minitab files and windows.

File > New Worksheet

The New Worksheet command creates a new worksheet by erasing all columns and constants. It also redefines the values of the constants K998, K999, and K1000, which are set by default to missing ($*$), e, and π, respectively. If you modified the current worksheet, Minitab prompts you to save the changes before closing the file.

File > Open Worksheet

Keyboard: Ctrl+O

Open Worksheet copies data from a saved worksheet file and places it in the current worksheet. Retrieving a saved worksheet always replaces the existing worksheet with the new one. To copy data from a file to your current worksheet without overwriting existing data, see "Combining Worksheet Files" in Chapter 1 of the Reference section.

Dialog Box Options

Type of Worksheet: Choose what kind of worksheet you want to open, and then click **Select File.**
Minitab worksheet: Choose to open a saved Minitab worksheet file.
Minitab portable worksheet: Choose to open a Minitab worksheet saved in a portable format.
Lotus 1-2-3 worksheet: Choose to open a Lotus 1-2-3 worksheet. See Chapter 4 of the Reference section for information about conversion methods.
Select File: Choose to open the next Open Worksheet dialog box.

File > Open Worksheet > Select File

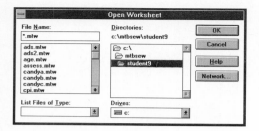

Tell Minitab which worksheet file you want to open. Choose the appropriate drive and directory, and then enter or select the name of the file. Double-clicking the file's name opens it.

File Name: The mask in this box determines which files are displayed below. For example, the mask *.MTW displays all the files in the selected directory with the extension MTW.

Directories: This option displays the current drive and directory. Double-click the drive folder to see all the directories on that drive; to see all the files in a directory, double-click that directory.

Drives: Choose to list available drives; click one to display the drive and its directories.

Corresponding Session Command
RETRIEVE
    See also Tutorial 1.

File > Save Worksheet

Keyboard: [Ctrl]+S
    To copy data from the current open worksheet to a file, you use the Save Worksheet command. If there is a saved worksheet with the same name, this command overwrites it. Use File > Save Worksheet As to rename your worksheet or save it to a new location.
    If your current worksheet is untitled (*Untitled Worksheet* appears in the title bar of the Minitab window), this command opens the Save Worksheet As dialog box, where you specify a name for your saved worksheet file.
    See "File > Open Worksheet > Select File" for more information about the dialog box options.

Corresponding Session Command
SAVE
    See also Tutorial 1.

File > Save Worksheet As

This command copies data from the current open worksheet to a file. Use this command if you want to rename your worksheet or save it to a new location.
    If your current worksheet is untitled (*Untitled Worksheet* appears in the title bar of the Minitab window), choosing File > Save Worksheet also opens this dialog box in which you specify a name for your saved worksheet file.
    See "File > Open Worksheet > Select File" for more information about the dialog box options.

Corresponding Session Command
SAVE
    See also Tutorials 1 and 2.

File > Revert Worksheet

Revert Worksheet returns a worksheet file to the state it was in when it was last saved. If you modified the current worksheet, Minitab prompts you to save the changes before reverting to the file's original state.

File > Import ASCII Data

This command enters data into one or more worksheet columns. You can skip over the first several lines of header information, if any, in your data file by choosing the Format button and then specifying the number of lines to skip in the Import ASCII Data-Format dialog box. See Chapter 4 of Reference for more information about importing and exporting data.

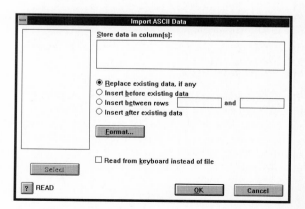

Dialog Box Options

Store data in column(s): Enter the columns in which Minitab should place the data (for example, C1-C3).

Replace existing data, if any: Choose to replace existing values in the specified columns with the new data.

Insert before existing data: Choose to insert the imported data at the top of the indicated columns.

Insert between rows [ ] and [ ]: Choose to insert the imported data between the two rows you specify.

Insert after existing data: Choose to insert the imported data at the bottom of the indicated columns.

Format: See "Format Dialog Box Options."

Read from keyboard instead of file: Select if you intend to type the data from the keyboard or paste it in from the Clipboard rather than read it from a data file. When you choose OK, Minitab opens the Session window and displays the DATA> prompt.

If you are pasting data from the Clipboard:

■ Choose **Paste** from the **Edit** menu.

■ Press (←Enter) to read the data.

■ Type **END**.

■ Press (←Enter).

If you are typing the data from the keyboard, enter the first row of the data. When you press (←Enter), a new DATA> prompt appears for the next row. When you are finished entering data, type END on a line by itself and press (←Enter). Unless you specify a different format by choosing the Format button, separate each value in a row with one or more spaces.

OK: When you click OK, Minitab opens the Import ASCII Data from File dialog box, unless you checked the Read from keyboard instead of file option.

Format Dialog Box Options

Format dialog box options let you import data from a text file that includes alpha data or data not separated by spaces or commas. See Chapter 4 in Reference for more information about importing and exporting data.

Data Selection: This option lets you read a portion of the data file. You can read the first part of a file or skip over a specified number of lines in your data file. This is useful if the data file contains header information that cannot be used by Minitab. The following options may be used in combination to import a block of rows from the middle of the data file.

Use first [ ] rows of data: Enter the number of rows you want to import. Minitab imports only the specified portion of the file.

Skip first [ ] lines of a file: Enter the number of lines of the data file you want to skip. Minitab imports only the specified portion of the file.

Data Format:

Blank delimited (numeric data only): Choose to import data separated by at least one space or comma.

Tab delimited: Choose to import data separated by tabs.

Column names in first row: Select to read the first row as column names in tab-delimited files.

User-specified alpha columns: Override Minitab's automatic checking for alpha columns by specifying the columns to be designated as alpha columns.

User-specified format: To import data using a format with or without delimiters, enter a format statement (see Chapter 4 in Reference for more information about format statements). You must use a format statement to input data files that contain alpha data without tab delimiters, designate missing values with spaces, or are wider than 160 characters.

Corresponding Session Commands

READ
INSERT

File > Export ASCII Data

You use this command to export data in the specified columns to an ASCII (text) file or display them in the Session window. If you want to export stored constants, you must copy them to columns and then export the columns. You copy constants to columns by using the COPY Session command.

[Import ASCII Data - Format dialog box]

Import ASCII Data - Format

Data Selection
Use first [   ] rows of data   Skip first [   ] lines of a file

Data Format
◉ Blank delimited (numeric data only)

○ Tab delimited   ☒ Column names in first row
   User-specified alpha columns:
   [   ]

○ User-specified format:
   [   ]

[?] READ   [OK]   [Cancel]

Use File > Export ASCII Data if you want to import your worksheet data into another application, such as a word processor or database application.

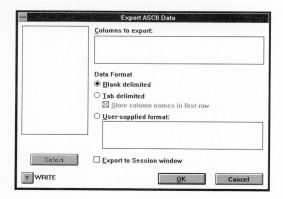

Dialog Box Options

Columns to export: Select the columns to be written to a data file. When exporting columns of unequal length, Minitab adds missing value symbols (*) to the shorter numeric columns.

Data Format:

Blank delimited: Choose to have spaces separate the columns in the new data file. If the data from all the columns do not fit on a single line, Minitab adds the continuation symbol (&) at the end of it and then continues the data on the next line.

Tab delimited: Choose to have tabs separate the columns in the new data file. It is easier to import data into certain applications, such as spreadsheet applications, if the data are tab-delimited.

Store column names in first row: Select to have your worksheet's column names appear as the first row of data in the new data file. This option is available only when you use tabs as delimiters.

User-supplied format: Choose to export data using a fixed format (for example, columns not separated by spaces), then enter a format statement in the text box (see Chapter 4 in Reference for information about format statements).

Export to Session window: Select to display the data in the Session window instead of storing it in a file.

OK: When you click OK, Minitab opens the Export Data To File dialog box, as long as the Export to Session window option isn't selected. See "File > Open Worksheet > Select File" for information about the dialog box that appears.

Corresponding Session Command
WRITE

File > Other Files

Choosing Other Files opens a submenu that lets you open files and, depending on the file type, view graphs, record commands or output, or store and execute commands.

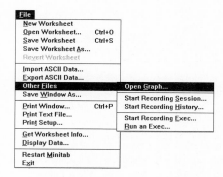

File > Other Files > Open Graph

This command opens a Minitab graph file. You save a graph by selecting the Save Window As command from the File menu when a Graph window is active. See "File > Open Worksheet > Select File" for information about the dialog box that appears.

Corresponding Session Command
GVIEW

See also Tutorial 4.

File > Other Files > Start Recording Session

You choose Start Recording Session to store a record of subsequent commands and output, except Professional graphs, in a text or ASCII file until you end the session or close the file by choosing File > Other Files > Stop Recording Session. Files containing commands and output are called *outfiles*.

An outfile serves as a permanent record of your session that you can edit to produce a final report, if you wish. You can view, edit, or print an outfile using any text editor or word processor.

Dialog Box Options

Record output in file and display in Session window: Choose to send the commands and resulting output to the file you specify as well as display it in the Session window.

Record output in file only: Choose to send your commands and the resulting output to the file, and not the Session window.

Set output width to: Select to specify an output width other than the default. Enter the number of characters you want on each line in the text box. The default width is 78 characters, corresponding to the width of most screens. To change the line width, enter any number from 30 to 132. Some commands cannot produce output narrower than 70 spaces.

Set output height to: Select to change the number of lines per page of your output to a value other than the default value of zero. Enter the desired number of lines per page in the text box. Because Minitab tries not to insert a page break in a logical block of output, some pages may have fewer lines than you specify.

Select File: Click to name your outfile and indicate the location in which Minitab should save it. See "File >

Open Worksheet > Select File" for more information about the dialog box that appears.

Corresponding Session Commands

OUTFILE
NOOUTFILE
OW
OH

See also Tutorial 2.

File > Other Files > Start Recording History

Start Recording History places a copy of the commands you have used in your Minitab session in a journal file until you end the session or close the file by choosing File > Other Files > Stop Recording History. Unlike an outfile, a journal file does not include Minitab output. See "File > Open Worksheet > Select File" for information about the dialog box that appears.

Corresponding Session Commands

JOURNAL
NOJOURNAL

See also Tutorial 5.

File > Other Files > Start Recording Exec

You use this command to store a set of commands in a macro file called an Exec.

After you select this command, the Session window displays the STOR> prompt. Type the commands you want to include in the Exec, each on its own line. When you are finished entering the commands to save in the file, type **END.** Minitab stores the commands in an Exec file but does not execute them (unlike the Start Recording History command). To run the Exec, choose the File > Other Files > Run an Exec command. See Chapter 5 for more information about Execs.

See "File > Open Worksheet > Select File" for information about the dialog box that appears.

Corresponding Session Commands

STORE
END

See also Tutorial 16.

File > Other Files > Run an Exec

This command runs an Exec that was defined with the File > Other Files > Start Recording Exec command, or created using a word processor or text editor. Execs may be nested; that is, you can write one Exec that invokes another. You can nest a maximum of five Execs. See Chapter 5 of Reference for more information about Execs.

Dialog Box Options

Number of times to execute: Specify the number of times you want to run the Exec. This ability to execute a macro several times is useful for simulations and looping operations.

Select File: See "File > Open Worksheet > Select File" for information about the dialog box that appears.

Corresponding Session Command
EXECUTE

See also Tutorials 7 and 16.

File > Save Window As

You use this command to save the entire contents — not just the visible section — of the active Session, Info, Graph, or History window to a file. See "File > Open Worksheet > Select File" for information about the dialog box that appears.

Corresponding Session Command (for Graph Window)
GSAVE

File > Print Window

Keyboard: Ctrl+P

This command prints the contents of the active Session, Data, Info, Graph, or History window. Depending on which window is active, and whether or not you have highlighted a section of a window, Minitab offers different printing options.

When you print from the Data window, Minitab opens the Data Window Print Options dialog box, which lets you select what Data window elements to print, and how to format the data. In the other windows, Minitab opens the standard Microsoft Print dialog box, shown here.

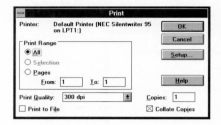

Dialog Box Options

Printer: This displays the name of the default printer. If your computer is connected to more than one printer, you can change the default by clicking Setup and choosing a different printer.

Print Range: Lets you specify which part of the window you want to print.

All: Prints the entire document.

Selection: Prints only the highlighted section.

Pages From [ ] to [ ]: Prints the range of pages you specify.

Print Quality: If your printer lets you select the print quality, click the drop-down arrow and choose the appropriate dpi value from the drop-down list.

Print to File: Select to print to a file rather than a printer. Minitab prompts you to name the file. If you want to store the file in a directory other than the current one, type the path information as well.

Copies: Enter the number of copies you want to print.

Collate Copies: Select to collate multiple page output. If you would rather print all the copies of the first page and then all the copies of the second page, do not check this box.

Setup: Opens the standard Microsoft Windows Print Setup dialog box. See your Microsoft Windows *User's Guide* for more information.

See also Tutorial 2.

File > Print Text File

The Print Text File command lets you specify which text file you want to print. See "File > Open Worksheet > Select File" for information about the dialog box that appears. When you click OK, Windows opens the standard Print dialog box. Your options may differ depending on your printer setup.

File > Print Setup

This command opens the standard Microsoft Windows Print Setup dialog box. See your Microsoft Windows *User's Guide* for information. To save your printer setup for subsequent Minitab sessions, use Edit > Save Preferences.

File > Get Worksheet Info

Get Worksheet Info displays information about the current worksheet in the Session window, including column names, counts, and the number of missing values. An A appears before the column numbers of alpha columns. Minitab displays stored constants and names along with their values.

Dialog Box Options

Include all columns and constants: Choose to display all worksheet information.
Include only: Choose to display information about only a portion of the worksheet, and then enter any combination of columns or constants for which you want information.

Corresponding Session Command
INFO

Example: Using Get Worksheet Info

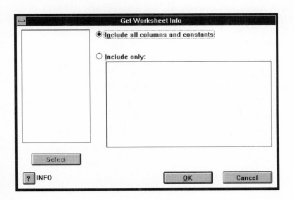

When you use this command to request information about the PROF.MTW data set, Minitab displays the following information in the Session window:

```
MTB > Info.

   Column  Name       Count  Missing
A  C1      DEPT         146        0
   C2      NUMBER       146        0
   C3      INTEREST     146        0
   C4      MANNER       146        0
   C5      COURSE       146        0
   C6      INSTRUCR     146        0
   C7      RESPONDS     146        0
   C8      SIZE         146       16
   C9      YEAR         146        0
```

See also Tutorial 2.

File > Display Data

You can use this command to display data you select from the current worksheet in the Session window, including any combination of columns or stored constants.

Dialog Box Options

Columns and constants to display: Select the variables you want Minitab to print in the Session window. If you select only one column, Minitab prints it across the Session window; if you select multiple columns, they display vertically.

Corresponding Session Command
PRINT

Example: Using Display Data

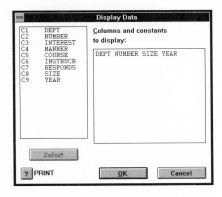

This command produces the following display in the Session window when PROF.MTW is the current worksheet (only the first portion is shown in the illustration):

```
MTB > Print 'DEPT' 'NUMBER' 'SIZE' 'YEAR'.

ROW    DEPT   NUMBER   SIZE   YEAR
  1    ACC      221      41     2
  2    ACC      221      41     2
  3    ACC      321      31     3
  4    ACC      344      36     3
  5    AER      101      52     1
  6    ARC      426      15     4
  7    ART      111      22     1
  8    ART      111      21     1
  9    ART      211      15     2
 10    ART      485      15     4
 11    ATH      155      49     1
 12    ATH      212      46     2
 13    CHM      111      68     1
 14    CHM      141     114     1
 15    CHM      142      64     1
```

See also Tutorial 2.

File > Restart Minitab

Restart Minitab not only starts Minitab again, but erases the worksheet and clears the Session window. It cancels any controls in effect, such as BRIEF, IW, and NOCONSTANT. It also closes all open files, such as OUTFILE and JOURNAL. Restart Minitab resets all parameters and commands to their defaults. It redefines the values of constants K998, K999, and K1000 (set by default to missing ($*$), e, and π).

If you modified the open worksheet, you can save it by using the Save Worksheet or Save Worksheet As command. Minitab prompts you to save the changes before restarting the application.

Corresponding Session Command
RESTART
See also Tutorial 2.

File > Exit

Choose this command to exit Minitab. If you modified the open worksheet, you can save it by using the Save Worksheet or Save Worksheet As command. Minitab prompts you to save the changes before closing the application.

Corresponding Session Command:
STOP
See also Tutorial 1.

The Edit Menu

The Edit menu lets you undo some operations; delete, copy, cut, paste, or select cells in a window; return to the last dialog box used; and save preferences for window size, location, visibility, and operation. The appearance of the menu varies depending on which window is active.

Edit > Undo or Can't Undo

You use this command to undo your most recent editing operation and return the worksheet to its previous state.

When Can't Undo appears on the menu instead, it indicates either that you haven't performed an action yet or that Minitab can't reverse the most recent operation.

The Undo command is dynamic — it changes depending on the circumstances. For example, if you just pasted some data from the Clipboard to the Data window, the command that appears is Undo Paste. However, if you last edited data in a cell, the command becomes Undo Change Within Cell.

Edit > Delete or Delete Cells

Keyboard: Del

This command is dynamic and changes depending on the circumstances. It deletes highlighted text in the Session window. In the Data window, this command deletes highlighted cells from the worksheet and moves up all the cells below them. To delete the contents of a Data window cell without moving the cells up:

- Double-click the cell so that the cursor appears.

- Backspace over the contents you want to delete.

- Type in the new cell contents.

Corresponding Session Command

DELETE

See also Tutorial 1.

Edit > Copy, Copy Cells, or Copy Graph

Keyboard: Ctrl+**C**

In the Session, History, or Info window, choosing this command copies a highlighted selection to the Clipboard, leaving the selection in its current location. Alternatively, you choose Edit > Cut to remove text from its current location and copy it to the Clipboard.

- Highlight the text you want to copy to the Clipboard.

- Choose **Edit > Copy**.

- Click the new location for the text.

- Select **Edit > Paste** to copy the Clipboard text to its new location.

In the Data window, this command copies cells from the worksheet to the Clipboard, leaving them in their current location. (Alternatively, choose Edit > Cut Cells to delete worksheet cells from their current location and copy them to the Clipboard.) If the column is numeric and any empty cells appear above the copied cells, Minitab marks them as missing values when you select them.

- Highlight the worksheet cells you want to copy.

- Choose **Edit > Copy Cells**.

- Click the upper left corner of the area to which you want to paste the data.

- Select either **Edit > Paste/Insert Cells** or **Edit > Paste/Replace Cells**, depending on whether you want to insert cells with the copied data without overwriting any existing data or replace the cells' current contents with the copied data.

In the Graph window, this command copies the graph in the current window to the Clipboard.

- Choose **Edit > Copy Graph**.

- Click the new location for the graph, like a word processor document.

- Select **Edit > Paste** from the application into which you are copying, in order to copy the Clipboard graph to its new location.

See also Tutorial 11.

Edit > Cut or Cut Cells

Keyboard: Ctrl+**X**

In the Data window, the command cuts cells from the worksheet and copies them to the Clipboard, shifting up the cells below it. Use Edit > Copy Cells to copy data to the Clipboard while leaving them in their current location, and Edit > Delete Cells to remove cells without placing their contents on the Clipboard.

- Highlight the worksheet cells you want to copy.

- Choose **Edit > Cut Cells**.

- Click the upper left corner of the area to which you want to paste the data.

- Select either **Edit > Paste/Insert Cells** or **Edit > Paste/Replace Cells**, depending on whether you want to insert cells with the copied data without overwriting any existing data or replace the cells' current contents with the copied data.

Edit > Paste or Paste/Insert Cells

Keyboard: Ctrl+**V**

In the Session window, you use these commands to paste data that you copied to the Clipboard with Edit > Cut or Edit > Copy to the cursor's current location.

In the Data window, these commands paste data that you copied to the Clipboard with Edit > Cut or Edit > Copy to the cursor's current location. Click the upper left corner of the new location for the worksheet cells. Minitab inserts the Clipboard data above any existing worksheet data. To overwrite existing data, use Edit > Paste/Replace.

See also Tutorial 11.

Edit > Paste/Replace Cells

You use this command, which is only available in the Data window, to paste cells stored on the Clipboard with Edit > Cut Cells or Edit > Copy Cells to a new location. Highlight the destination area. This command replaces any existing data in the specified area.

To paste Clipboard data without overwriting the cells's existing contents, use Edit > Paste/Insert Cells.

Edit > Select All or Select All Cells

Keyboard: Ctrl+A

In the Session window, choosing either of these commands highlights all the contents, which is useful for cutting, copying, and pasting data.

In the Data window, this command highlights all the cells that contain data.

This command is not available in the Graph window.

Edit > Edit Last Command Dialog

Keyboard: Ctrl+E

Edit Last Command Dialog opens the most recently used dialog box, which displays the selections from the last time you used it. This command is useful for issuing the same command a second time, or for repeating a procedure with only minor changes.

See also Tutorial 1.

Edit > Save Preferences

This command saves changes you make to the size, location, and state of any Minitab window during your session, as well as the Minitab printer setup and default Lotus worksheet type. The next time you start Minitab, the windows open with the same configuration. You check or clear the check box that corresponds with each configuration option to indicate whether you want to save its current status or revert to its default.

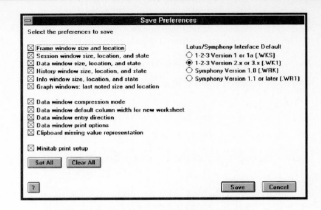

Dialog Box Options

Frame window size and location: Select to save changes to the main Minitab window.

Session window size, location, and state: Select to save changes to the Session window.

Data window size, location, and state: Select to save changes to the Data window.

History window size, location, and state: Select to save changes to the History window.

Info window size, location, and state: Select to save changes to the Info window.

Graph windows: last noted size and location: Select to display the next high-resolution graph you create in the Graph window that is the same size and in the same location as the current one. See "Window > Set Graph Size/Location."

Data window compression mode: Select to have the Data window in subsequent sessions start in the same data compression mode. See "Editor > Compress Display."

Data window default column width for new worksheet: Select to set the column widths of new worksheets to those in the current worksheet. The default width is eight characters. See "Editor > Set Column Widths" and "Editor > Format Column."

Data window entry direction: Select to save the current direction of the data-entry arrow. See "Editor > Change Entry Direction."

Data window print options: Select to save any changes made to the print options using File > Print Window.

Clipboard missing value representation: Select to save a new representation for missing values in the Clipboard. See "Editor > Clipboard Settings."

Minitab print setup: Select to save any changes made using File > Print Setup.

Lotus/Symphony Interface Default: Choose the version of Lotus 1-2-3 or Symphony from which you import or to which you export worksheet files. This option tells Minitab how to exchange worksheet information between Minitab and Lotus applications. See "File > Open Worksheet" and "File > Save Worksheet."

1-2-3 Version 1 or 1a (WKS): Choose if you are retrieving a spreadsheet created by or exporting a worksheet to version 1 or 1a of Lotus 1-2-3. To be retrieved by Minitab, the spreadsheet must have a WKS extension.

1-2-3 Version 2.x or 3.x (WK1): Choose if you are retrieving a spreadsheet created by or exporting a worksheet to version 2.x or 3.x of Lotus. The spreadsheet created with version 2.x or 3.x of Lotus must have a WK1 extension.

Symphony Version 1.0 (WRK): Choose if you are retrieving a spreadsheet created by or exporting a worksheet to version 1.0 of Symphony. To be retrieved by Minitab, the spreadsheet created with version 1.0 of Symphony must have a WRK extension.

Symphony Version 1.1 or later (WR1): Choose if you are retrieving a spreadsheet created by or exporting a worksheet to version 1.1 or later of Symphony. To be retrieved by Minitab, the spreadsheet created with version 1.1 or later of Symphony must have a WR1 extension.

Set All: Click to select all the check boxes.

Clear All: Click to clear all the check boxes.

The Manip Menu

The Manip menu lets you manipulate data. You can sort and rank rows; delete cases; erase variables; copy columns; code data values; and stack, unstack, convert, or concatenate columns.

Manip > Sort

You use this command to sort one or more columns of data, according to the values in the column(s) you indicate. You can sort both alpha and numeric data. See "Alpha Data" in Reference Chapter 1 for the rules Minitab observes when sorting alpha data.

Dialog Box Options

Sort column(s): Select the column(s) you want to sort.

Store sorted column(s) in: Indicate the column(s) in which you want to store the sorted data. You may specify the same columns you enter in the Sort column(s) text box to replace the original data with the sorted version.

Sort by column: Select up to four columns to use as sorting criteria. You can sort on either alpha or numeric columns. To sort by more than four columns, use the Session command SORT with the BY subcommand. When two or more values are equal for all sorting variables, Minitab retains their original order in the column. Minitab sorts missing values in alpha columns (blanks) first, and missing values in numeric columns (*) last.

Descending: Select to sort from highest to lowest value; otherwise, Minitab sorts from lowest to highest.

Corresponding Session Command

SORT

Example: Using Sort

The following dialog box and equivalent Session commands illustrate how to sort students by their test grades, from best score to worst score, using MARKS.MTW from Tutorial 2.

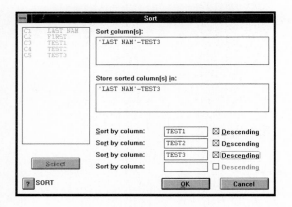

```
MTB > Sort 'LAST NAM'-'TEST3' 'LAST NAM'-'TEST3';
SUBC>   By 'TEST1' 'TEST2' 'TEST3';
SUBC>   Descending 'TEST1' 'TEST2' 'TEST3'.
```

These commands reorder the rows in the Data window, using the first test as the first sort criterion:

	C1-A	C2-A	C3	C4	C5	C6	C7
→	LAST NAM	FIRST	TEST1	TEST2	TEST3		
1	PIERSON,	RICHARD	100	77	100		
2	NORMAN,	BARBARA	99	95	84		
3	BENSON,	MELISSA	99	86	83		
4	GOLDBERG,	JONATHAN	98	98	94		
5	SHEPPARD,	KATHLEEN	94	97	100		
6	MESSINA,	STEVEN	94	93	95		
7	GREEN,	JENNIFER	92	91	99		
8	NOWICKI,	AMY	91	81	79		
9	PATEL,	HIMA	90	100	62		
10	WATSON,	KEISHA	88	93	41		
11	SCHMIDT,	NANCY	83	79	52		
12	SMITH,	HOLLY	82	51	25		
13	SCOTT,	MICHAEL	81	75	100		
14	DOUGHERTY,	MEGAN	79	69	60		
15	GIGLIOTTI,	ANDREW	78	94	50		
16	RYAN,	MATT	77	79	85		
17	ROJAS,	LUIS	73	79	83		
18	ADAMS,	JAMES	72	93	93		
19	KENNEDY,	KEVIN	71	78	62		

See also Tutorial 2.

Manip > Rank

The Rank command assigns rank scores to values in a column: 1 to the smallest value in the column, 2 to the next smallest, and so on. Ties are assigned the average rank for that value.

Dialog Box Options

Rank data in: Enter the column you want to rank.
Store ranks in: Indicate the column in which you want to store the ranked data.

Corresponding Session Command

RANK

Example: Using Rank

The following dialog box and equivalent Session commands illustrate how to obtain a student's rank based on his or her first test scores, using MARKS.MTW.

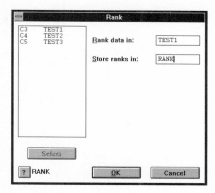

```
MTB > Name c6 = 'RANK'
MTB > Rank 'TEST1' 'RANK'.
```

These commands produce a column called C6 RANK that displays the rank of each student in the class. The first portion of the data appears in the following illustration:

Manip > Delete Rows

You can use this command to delete specified rows from columns in the worksheet and move up the remaining rows.

Dialog Box Options

Delete rows: Specify the rows or range of rows you want to delete, using a colon (:) to indicate an inclusive range. For example, if you enter 1:4 7 8, Minitab deletes rows 1, 2, 3, 4, 7, and 8.

From columns: Enter or select the column(s) from which you want to delete the specified rows.

Corresponding Session Command

DELETE

Example: Using Delete Rows

Suppose you have the following data set:

	C1	C2	C3	C4	C5
→					
1	1	6	11	16	21
2	2	7	12	17	22
3	3	8	13	18	23
4	4	9	14	19	24
5	5	10	15	20	25

Student Edition of MINITAB - MARKS.MTW - [Data]

File Edit Manip Calc Stat Window Graph Editor Help

	C1-A	C2-A	C3	C4	C5	C6	C7
→	LAST NAM	FIRST	TEST1	TEST2	TEST3	RANK	
1	ADAMS,	JAMES	72	93	93	7.0	
2	BENSON,	MELISSA	99	86	83	22.5	
3	BROWN,	LAMAR	59	59	90	3.5	
4	DOUGHERTY,	MEGAN	79	69	60	11.0	
5	DOUGLAS,	JASON	48	77	25	1.0	
6	GIGLIOTTI,	ANDREW	78	94	50	10.0	
7	GOLDBERG,	JONATHAN	98	98	94	21.0	
8	GREEN,	JENNIFER	92	91	99	18.0	
9	KENNEDY,	KEVIN	71	78	62	6.0	
10	LEE,	SANG	64	68	97	5.0	
11	MCCLURE,	MARK	49	79	43	2.0	
12	MESSINA,	STEVEN	94	93	95	19.5	
13	NORMAN,	BARBARA	99	95	84	22.5	
14	NOWICKI,	AMY	91	81	79	17.0	
15	PATEL,	HIMA	90	100	62	16.0	
16	PIERSON,	RICHARD	100	77	100	24.0	
17	ROJAS,	LUIS	73	79	83	8.0	
18	RYAN,	MATT	77	79	85	9.0	
19	SCHMIDT,	NANCY	83	79	52	14.0	

See also Tutorial 2.

You can complete the Delete Rows dialog box or use the equivalent Session commands, as shown, to delete rows 3 and 4:

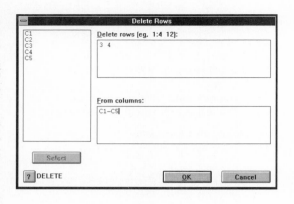

```
MTB > Delete 3 4 C1-C5
```

This command deletes the third and fourth rows, and moves up all the others so that the Data window looks like this:

	C1	C2	C3	C4	C5
→					
1	1	6	11	16	21
2	2	7	12	17	22
3	5	10	15	20	25
4					
5					

See also Tutorial 1.

Manip > Erase Variables

Choosing this command erases any combination of columns or constants, including their names. It's a good idea regularly to erase variables you no longer need to help you keep track of the worksheet's contents.

Dialog Box Options

Columns or constants to erase: Select the columns (C) or constants (K) that you want to remove from the worksheet.

Corresponding Session Command

ERASE

Example: Using Erase Variables

Suppose you have this data set:

	C1	C2	C3	C4	C5
→					
1	1	6	11	16	21
2	2	7	12	17	22
3	5	10	15	20	25
4					
5					

Use the following dialog box and equivalent Session commands to erase C2 and C3:

```
MTB > Erase C2 C3.
```

This command erases the second and third column, which are now blank. Unlike Delete Rows, the remaining columns do not move — the deleted, now empty, columns remain in the Data window. The Data window looks like this:

	C1	C2	C3	C4	C5
→					
1	1			16	21
2	2			17	22
3	5			20	25
4					
5					

See also Tutorial 1.

Manip > Copy Columns

This command copies data from existing worksheet columns to new columns, including all the rows or a specified subset. To copy data to the Clipboard, see "Edit > Copy Cells." To copy constants, you must use the Session command COPY.

Dialog Box Options

Copy from columns: Enter the column(s) you want to copy.

To columns: Specify the target columns to store the copied data.

Use Rows or Omit Rows Dialog Box Options

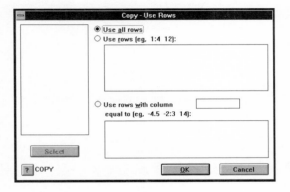

You can specify a subset of data for Minitab to copy by designating the rows to copy or those to omit. This illustration shows the Copy-Use Rows dialog box; the Copy-Omit Rows dialog box looks similar, except the options begin with the word *Omit,* not *Use.*

Use all rows: Choose to copy all rows in the column(s).

Use rows: Choose to copy only certain rows of the column. Enter the rows and/or a range of rows to copy, using a colon (:) to indicate an inclusive range. For example, if you enter 1:4 7 8, Minitab copies rows 1, 2, 3, 4, 7, and 8.

Use rows with column [ ] equal to: Choose to use certain column values as criteria to select which rows to copy. Enter the column whose contents Minitab should evaluate; the specified column does not need to be one of the columns you want to copy. Then input the value and/or a range of values to use as the selection criteria. Use a colon (:) to indicate an inclusive range. For example, if you enter 3 7:10, Minitab copies the rows with values equal to those in rows 3, 7, 8, 9, and 10 of the specified column.

Corresponding Session Command

COPY

Example: Using Copy Columns

For this data set, assume you want to copy C2 to C4:

	C1	C2	C3	C4	C5
↓					
1	1	6	11		
2	2	7	12		
3	3	8	13		
4	4	9	14		
5	5	10	15		

You can use the following dialog box or the equivalent Session command to perform the copy operation:

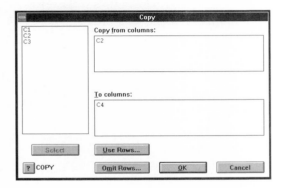

```
MTB > Copy C2 C4.
```

This command produces a new column, C4, which contains the same values as C2:

	C1	C2	C3	C4	C5
↓					
1	1	6	11	6	
2	2	7	12	7	
3	3	8	13	8	
4	4	9	14	9	
5	5	10	15	10	

See also Tutorial 1.

Manip > Code Data Values

You use the Code Data Values command to recode one or more columns. The command searches the specified columns for one or more values and then replaces them with a new value. You can only recode numeric columns. To convert numeric values to alpha values and vice versa, see "Manip > Convert."

You can also use Code Data Values to replace a value with the missing value symbol. For example, to change –99 to *, use –99 as the original value and * as the new one.

Dialog Box Options

Code data from columns: Enter the column(s) you want to recode.

Into columns: Specify the column(s) in which you want to store the recoded values.

Original values: Specify the values or range of values to recode.

New: Specify the new value with which to replace the corresponding original value(s).

Corresponding Session Command

CODE

Example: Using Code Data Values

The following dialog box and equivalent Session commands code each student's test average (generated, rounded, and stored in C6 AVERAGE) to a number that represents his or her final grade, using the MARKS.MTW data set from Tutorial 2. Any score in the range 90 through 100 is coded as a 4 (a grade of A), any score from 80 through 89 is coded as a 3 (a grade of B), and so on. In order to complete this example, you need to use the column AVERAGE that you created in Tutorial 2.

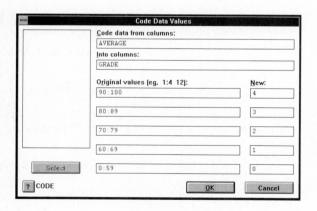

These commands produce a new column, GRADE, that shows each student's numeric grade. Use the Convert command (see "Manip > Convert") to translate the numeric grade into an alphabetic grade.

	C2-A	C3	C4	C5	C6	C7
→	FIRST	TEST1	TEST2	TEST3	AVERAGE	GRADE
1	JAMES	72	93	93	86	3
2	MELISSA	99	86	83	89	3
3	LAMAR	59	59	90	69	1
4	MEGAN	79	69	60	69	1
5	JASON	48	77	25	50	0

See also Tutorial 2.

Manip > Stack

This command stacks (or appends) blocks of columns and/or constants on top of each other in a new column. Minitab always places the first block on top of the second block, and so on.

You can stack constants on top of constants to form one or more or columns. You can also stack columns on top of columns to make longer columns.

Dialog Box Options

Stack the following blocks: Specify the blocks you want to stack. A block can consist of one or more columns or constants. Each block is stacked on top of the next block. When you specify more than one item in a block, each block must have the same number of items. When you specify more than one item in a block, the first item in the first block is stacked on top of the first item in the second block, which is stacked on top of the first item in the third block, and so on.

Store results in: Specify a column or columns in which Minitab stores the stacked variables in the blocks.

Store subscripts in: Select to create a new column of subscripts that indicates the block from which each numbers came, (1 for the first block, 2 for the second block, and so on), and then specify a column to store the subscripts. These subscripts may be used for factor levels in analysis of variance procedures or as a By variable for use in other descriptive and investigative procedures. You can also use subscripts to unstack a column at a later time.

```
MTB > Name C7 = 'GRADE'
MTB > Code (90:100) 4 (80:89) 3 (70:79) 2 (60:69) 1 (0:59) 0 'AVERAGE' &
CONT>    'GRADE'
```

Corresponding Session Command

STACK

Example: Using Stack

The following dialog box and equivalent Session commands illustrate how to stack the three test scores in C3 through C5 in a single column named STACK, with subscripts which identify each cell's original location. These data come from the MARKS.MTW data set.

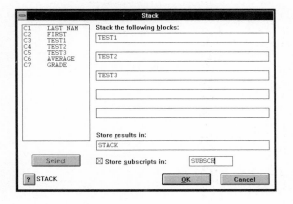

```
MTB > Name c8 = 'STACK' c9 = 'SUBSCR'
MTB > Stack ('TEST1') ('TEST2') ('TEST3') ('STACK');
SUBC>    Subscripts 'SUBSCR'.
```

This command produces a column of stacked data in the Data window, with TEST1 on top, TEST2 next, and then TEST3, and the SUBSCR column to the right:

	C4	C5	C6	C7	C8	C9
→	TEST2	TEST3	AVERAGE	GRADE	STACK	SUBSCR
1	93	93	86	3	72	1
2	86	83	89	3	99	1
3	59	90	69	1	59	1
4	69	60	69	1	79	1
5	77	25	50	0	48	1

See also Tutorial 2.

Manip > Unstack

Unstack separates one or more columns into several blocks of columns or stored constants, according to subscript values stored in a column.

Dialog Box Options

Unstack: Enter one or more column(s) to unstack. The first column in this field is unstacked into the first column or constant in each block that you specify in the first Store Results in Blocks text box. The second column in this field is unstacked into the second column or constant in each block that you specify in the second Store Results in Blocks text box, and so on.

Using subscripts in: Enter the column that contains the subscripts. Subscripts must be integers from –10000 to +10000 or missing values; they need not be consecutive or in any special order. Minitab stores rows with the smallest subscript in the first block, those with the next smallest subscript in the second block, and so on.

Store results in blocks: Specify the columns or constants that will store the unstacked blocks. In each block, you must specify the same number of columns or constants as you specified in the Unstack text box.

Corresponding Session Command

UNSTACK

Example: Using Unstack

The following dialog box and equivalent Session commands illustrate how to unstack all the test scores into three columns (UNS1, UNS2, and UNS3), using the MARKS.MTW data with columns created as in the previous examples.

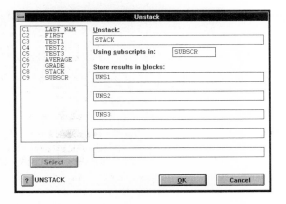

```
MTB > Name c10 = 'UNS1' c11 = 'UNS2' c12 = 'UNS3'
MTB > Unstack ('STACK') ('UNS1') ('UNS2') ('UNS3');
SUBC>    Subscripts 'SUBSCR'.
```

This command produces the following columns in the Data window:

	C7	C8	C9	C10	C11	C12
→	GRADE	STACK	SUBSCR	UNS1	UNS2	UNS3
1	3	72	1	72	93	93
2	3	99	1	99	86	83
3	1	59	1	59	59	90
4	1	79	1	79	69	60
5	0	48	1	48	77	25

See also Tutorial 2.

Manip > Convert

You use this command to convert alpha data to numeric data and vice versa, using codes you specify.

To recode numeric values, use Manip > Code Data Values.

Dialog Box Options

Input data: Select the column that contains the data you want to convert.

Output data: Specify the column to store the converted data.

Conversion Table: Prior to using this command to convert your data, you must set up two worksheet columns to serve as a conversion table: one listing the alpha expressions and one listing the corresponding numeric values. The alpha expressions must use the same case as the alpha data to be converted. For example, if the column to be converted contains the entry *Yellow* and the conversion table contains *yellow*, Minitab converts Yellow to the missing symbol. In addition, the conversion table's spacing must coincide with the alpha data column's.

Original: Enter the column that contains the first part of the conversion table, that is, the values you want to convert.

Converted: Enter the column that contains the second part of the conversion table, that is, the codes Minitab will use to represent the original data.

Corresponding Session Command

CONVERT

Example: Using Convert

The following dialog box and equivalent Session commands illustrate how to convert the alpha yogurt ratings stored in C1 RATING to numeric data, using the YOGURT.MTW data. First, set up the conversion table in columns C4 and C5 in the Data window:

	C1-A	C2	C3	C4-A	C5
↓	RATING	CENTS	CALS	CONVA	CONVN
1	EXCELLENT	11	120	EXCELLENT	1
2	EXCELLENT	11	120	VERY GOOD	2
3	VERY GOOD	9	100	GOOD	3
4	GOOD	9	90	FAIR	4
5	POOR	12	253	POOR	5
6	GOOD	8	250		

Then, complete the dialog box, as shown:

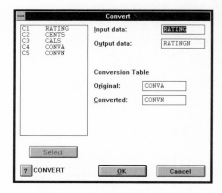

```
MTB > Name c6 = 'RATINGN'
MTB > Convert 'CONVA' 'CONVN' 'RATING' 'RATINGN'.
```

This command produces a new column, RATINGN, in the Data window:

	C1-A	C2	C3	C4-A	C5	C6
↓	RATING	CENTS	CALS	CONVA	CONVN	RATINGN
1	EXCELLENT	11	120	EXCELLENT	1	1
2	EXCELLENT	11	120	VERY GOOD	2	1
3	VERY GOOD	9	100	GOOD	3	2
4	GOOD	9	90	FAIR	4	3
5	POOR	12	253	POOR	5	5
6	GOOD	8	250			3

See also Tutorial 5.

Manip > Concatenate

The Concatenate command combines two or more alpha columns side-by-side and stores them in one new column.

Dialog Box Options

Concatenate alpha columns: Enter the columns in the order in which you want to combine them from left to right (total up to 80 characters wide). Each column must contain alpha data; Minitab designates the new column as an alpha column.

Store result in: Specify a storage column for the concatenated data.

Corresponding Session Command

CONCATENATE

Example: Using Concatenate

The following dialog box and equivalent Session commands combine the first and last names of the students currently stored in C1 and C2 in MARKS.MTW, into a single column.

```
MTB > Name c6 = 'FULLNAME'
MTB > Concatenate 'LAST NAM' 'FIRST' 'FULLNAME'.
```

This command produces a column containing the full name of each student, which appears in the Data window:

	C2-A	C3	C4	C5	C6-A
→	FIRST	TEST1	TEST2	TEST3	FULLNAME
1	JAMES	72	93	93	ADAMS, JAMES
2	MELISSA	99	86	83	BENSON, MELISSA
3	LAMAR	59	59	90	BROWN, LAMAR
4	MEGAN	79	69	60	DOUGHERTY, MEGAN
5	JASON	48	77	25	DOUGLAS, JASON

The Calc Menu

The Calc menu lets you generate and work with random data and probability distributions; apply various functions to data; obtain basic column and row statistics; place repetitive data in a column; create indicator (dummy) variables; and standardize data.

Calc > Set Base

The Set Base command fixes a starting point for Minitab's random number generator. Minitab normally chooses its own starting point for this process so that you don't see the same random data each time you generate random data. If you need to generate the same random data, use the Set Base command. The generator uses this base until you set a new one or exit Minitab.

Dialog Box Options

Set base of random data generator to: Enter the integer you want to begin the random number sequence.

Corresponding Session Command

BASE

See also Tutorial 6.

Calc > Random Data

This command lets you generate a random sample of numbers, either from columns in the open worksheet or from one of the given distributions listed. Generates up to 99 columns of random data.

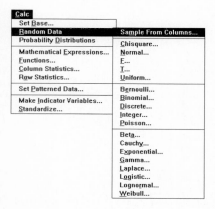

Calc > Random Data > Sample From Columns

You can use this command to sample rows randomly from one or more columns.

Dialog Box Options

Sample [ ] rows from column(s): Specify the number of rows to select randomly, then enter the column(s) from which you want Minitab to sample the data. The number of rows to sample cannot exceed the number of rows in the columns being sampled.

Store samples in: Specify the column(s) to store the sampled values. If you sample data from several columns at once, they must all have the same length. Minitab selects the same rows from each column.

Sample with replacement: Select to sample with replacement. Otherwise, Minitab samples without replacement and therefore does not select the same row more than once.

Corresponding Session Command

SAMPLE

Example: Using Sample From Columns

The following dialog box and equivalent Session command illustrate how to sample four student ID numbers, stored in C1 ID, in the HEIGHT.MTW data set into a new column called CHICAGO, as in Tutorial 6

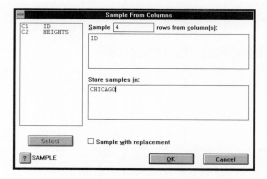

```
MTB > Name c3 = 'CHICAGO'
MTB > Sample 4 'ID' 'CHICAGO'.
```

Minitab randomly selects four ID numbers and stores them in C3 'CHICAGO' in the Data window:

	C1	C2	C3
	ID	HEIGHTS	CHICAGO
1	441	65.0	648
2	805	71.3	413
3	555	69.5	599
4	390	62.8	184
5	49	67.1	

Your numbers will vary because the numbers are randomly generated.

See also Tutorial 6.

Options on the Random Data Submenu

The dialog boxes that open when you select a distribution from the Random Data submenu all function in the same way. The Chisquare Distribution dialog box illustrates the main elements.

center of the normal distribution. Enter the standard deviation value you want to define the normal distribution.

Calc > Random Data > F: Generates an F distribution. Enter the number of degrees of freedom for the effect (numerator) and the number of degrees of freedom for the error (denominator) to define the F distribution.

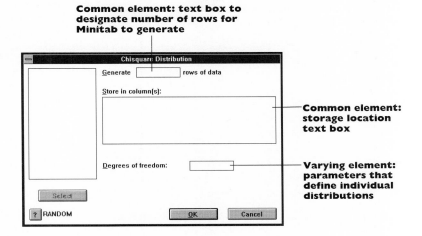

Common element: text box to designate number of rows for Minitab to generate

Common element: storage location text box

Varying element: parameters that define individual distributions

Common Elements

All the Random Data dialog boxes have two common elements:

Generate [ ] rows of data: Indicate the number of rows of random data you want to generate.

Store in column(s): Specify storage column(s) for the generated values.

Varying Elements

Each of the Random Data dialog boxes contains parameters that define individual distributions; Minitab defines default parameter values for some distributions. For example, you define a chi-square distribution by Degrees of freedom. Other options are listed below.

Calc > Random Data > Chisquare: Generates a chi-square distribution. Enter the number of degrees of freedom you want to define the chi-square distribution.

Calc > Random Data > Normal: Generates a normal distribution. Enter the mean value you want to use as the

Calc > Random Data > T: Generates a Student's t distribution. Enter the number of degrees of freedom you want to define the t distribution.

Calc > Random Data > Uniform: Generates a continuous uniform distribution between two points that you designate. Enter numbers to define the minimum and maximum values for the continuous uniform distribution.

Calc > Random Data > Bernoulli: Generates a Bernoulli distribution. Enter a number between 0 and 1 for the probability of success used to define the Bernoulli distribution.

Calc > Random Data > Binomial: Generates a binomial distribution. Enter the number of trials you want to define the binomial distribution. Enter a number between 0 and 1 for the probability of success used to define the binomial distribution.

Calc > Random Data > Discrete: Generates a discrete distribution. Select the column containing the values you want to include in the distribution. Select the column containing the probabilities that correspond to the discrete numbers in the Values in text box.

Calc > Random Data > Integer: Generates a discrete uniform distribution. Enter numbers to define the lower and upper endpoints of the discrete uniform distribution.

Calc > Random Data > Poisson: Generate a Poisson distribution. Enter a mean value greater than 0 and less than 51 to define the Poisson distribution.

Calc > Random Data > Beta: Generates a beta distribution. Enter numbers for the first and second shape parameters you want to define the beta distribution.

Calc > Random Data > Cauchy: Generates a Cauchy distribution. Enter numbers for the location and scale you want to define the Cauchy distribution.

Calc > Random Data > Exponential: Generates an exponential distribution. Enter the mean value you want to define the exponential distribution. Note that Minitab uses b (b = mean) in the defining function whereas some books use $1/b$.

Calc > Random Data > Gamma: Generates a gamma distribution. Enter numbers for the first and second shape parameters you want to define the gamma distribution. Note that Minitab uses b (b = second shape parameter) in the defining function whereas some books use $1/b$.

Calc > Random Data > Laplace: Generates a Laplace or double exponential distribution. Enter numbers for the location and scale you want to define the Laplace distribution.

Calc > Random Data > Logistic: Generates a logistic distribution. Enter numbers for the location and scale you want to define the logistic distribution.

Calc > Random Data > Lognormal: Generates a lognormal distribution. Enter numbers for the location and scale you want to define the lognormal distribution.

Calc > Random data > Weibull: Generates a Weibull distribution. Enter numbers for the first and second shape parameters you want to define the Weibull distribution.

Corresponding Session Command

RANDOM

Example: Using Random Data

The following dialog box and equivalent Session command illustrate how to generate a sample of ten observations of female heights from a normal population with a mean of 64 inches and a standard deviation of 3.1.

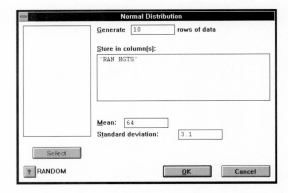

```
MTB > Name c1 = 'RAN HGTS'
MTB > Random 10 'RAN HGTS';
SUBC>    Normal 64 3.1.
```

This command produces a new RAN HGTS column that contains 10 rows of randomly generated data, distributed normally. The first portion appears in the Data window:

	C1
→	RAN HGTS
1	67.2402
2	61.7589
3	67.0188
4	66.8305
5	63.2119

Your numbers will vary because the numbers are randomly generated.

See also Tutorial 6.

Calc > Probability Distributions

When you choose Probability Distributions on the Calc menu, a submenu opens that lets you compute probabilities, probability densities, cumulative probabilities, and inverse cumulative probabilities for continuous and discrete distributions.

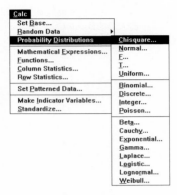

Options on the Probability Distributions Submenu

All the dialog boxes on the Probability Distributions submenu function the same way. The first one on the submenu, Chisquare, illustrates the main components.

Inverse cumulative probability: Choose to compute the inverse of the cumulative probabilities. If this value is not defined, Minitab returns a missing value. This option provides a convenient way to look up percentage points or critical values.

Input column and **Input constant:** Enter the column or constant you want to evaluate.

Optional storage: Specify a storage location for the generated value(s). Minitab displays the stored values in the specified column in the Data window, not the Session window. If you choose the Inverse cumulative probability option, Minitab stores the larger of the two values, if two are printed.

Varying Elements

Each of the Probability Distributions dialog boxes contains parameters that define individual distributions; Minitab defines default parameter values for some distributions. For example, the chi-square distribution is defined by Degrees of freedom. Other options are listed next.

Calc > Probability Distributions > Chisquare: Lets you calculate the probability densities, cumulative probabilities, and inverse cumulative probabilities for a chi-square distribution. Enter the number of degrees of freedom you want to define the chi-square distribution.

Calc > Probability Distributions > Normal: Lets you calculate the probability densities, cumulative probabilities, and inverse cumulative probabilities for a

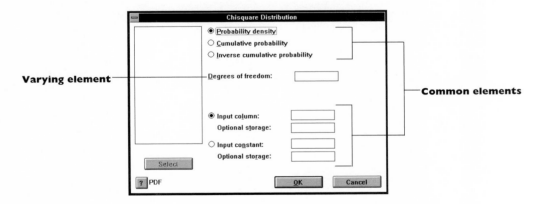

Common Elements

Probability density: Choose to calculate the probability densities.

Cumulative probability: Choose to compute the cumulative probabilities. This option provides a convenient way to compute p-values.

normal distribution. Enter the mean value you want to use as the center point for the normal distribution. Enter the standard deviation you want to define the normal distribution.

Calc > Probability Distributions > F: Lets you calculate the probability densities, cumulative probabilities, and inverse cumulative probabilities for an F distribution. Specify the degrees of freedom for the effect (numerator) and for the error (denominator) to define the F distribution.

Calc > Probability Distributions > T: Lets you calculate the probability densities, cumulative probabilities, and inverse cumulative probabilities for a t distribution. Enter the number of degrees of freedom you want to define the t distribution.

Calc > Probability Distributions > Uniform: Lets you calculate the probability densities, cumulative probabilities, and inverse cumulative probabilities for a continuous uniform distribution. Enter numbers to define the minimum and maximum values for the continuous uniform distribution.

Calc > Probability Distributions > Binomial: Lets you calculate probabilities, cumulative probabilities, and inverse cumulative probabilities for a binomial distribution. Enter the number of trials you want to define the binomial distribution. Enter number between 0 and 1 for the probability of success used to define the binomial distribution.

Calc > Probability Distributions > Discrete: Lets you calculate probabilities, cumulative probabilities, and inverse cumulative probabilities for a discrete distribution. Select the column containing the values you want to be included in the distribution. Select the column containing the probabilities that correspond to the discrete numbers in the Values in text box.

Calc > Probability Distributions > Integer: Lets you calculate probabilities, cumulative probabilities, and inverse cumulative probabilities for a discrete uniform distribution. Enter numbers to define the lower and upper endpoints of the discrete uniform distribution.

Calc > Probability Distributions > Poisson: Lets you calculate probabilities, cumulative probabilities, and inverse cumulative probabilities for a Poisson distribution. Enter a mean value greater than 0 and less than 51 to define the Poisson distribution.

Calc > Probability Distributions > Beta: Lets you calculate the probability densities, cumulative probabilities, and inverse cumulative probabilities for a beta distribution. Enter numbers for the first and second shape parameters you want to define the beta distribution.

Calc > Probability Distributions > Cauchy: Lets you calculate the probability densities, cumulative probabilities, and inverse cumulative probabilities for a Cauchy distribution. Enter numbers for the location and scale you want to define the Cauchy distribution.

Calc > Probability Distributions > Exponential: Lets you calculate the probability densities, cumulative probabilities, and inverse cumulative probabilities for an exponential distribution. Enter the mean value you want to define the exponential distribution. Note that Minitab uses b (b = mean) in the defining function, whereas some books use $1/b$.

Calc > Probability Distributions > Gamma: Lets you calculate the probability densities, cumulative probabilities, and inverse cumulative probabilities for a gamma distribution. Enter numbers for the first and second shape parameters you want to define the gamma distribution.

Calc > Probability Distributions > Laplace: Lets you calculate the probability densities, cumulative probabilities, and inverse cumulative probabilities for a Laplace distribution. Enter numbers for the location and scale you want to define the Laplace distribution.

Calc > Probability Distributions > Logistic: Lets you calculate the probability densities, cumulative probabilities, and inverse cumulative probabilities for a gamma distribution. Enter numbers for the location and scale you want to define the logistic distribution. Note that Minitab uses b (b = second shape parameter) in the defining function whereas some books use $1/b$.

Calc > Probability Distributions > Lognormal: Lets you calculate the probability densities, cumulative probabilities, and inverse cumulative probabilities for a lognormal distribution. Enter numbers for the location and scale you want to define the lognormal distribution.

Calc > Probability Distributions > Weibull: Lets you calculate the probability densities, cumulative probabilities, and inverse cumulative probabilities for a Weibull distribution. Enter numbers for the first and second shape parameters you want to define the Weibull distribution.

Corresponding Session Commands

PDF
CDF
INVCDF

Calc > Mathematical Expressions

The Mathematical Expressions command performs arithmetic using an algebraic expression, which may contain arithmetic operations, comparison operators, logical operators, and functions. Arguments may be columns, stored constants, or numbers.

Dialog Box Options

Variable (new or modified): Enter the column or constant you want to compute or manipulate.

Row number (optional): Enter a row number if you want to compute or manipulate a single row. The expression then operates only on the row you specify.

Expression: Enter the mathematical operation you want Minitab to perform, for example, SIN(C3) + 10. Use the list of operations in the dialog box and observe the following rules.

Expression Rules

1. You can nest parentheses up to nine deep.

2. The maximum length of the expression is 78 characters. If you have a longer expression, break it into separate expressions.

3. Minitab evaluates expressions within parentheses first.

4. Minitab performs exponentiation first, followed by multiplication and division, and finally addition and subtraction.

5. Operations of "equal order" are performed from left to right.

6. Extra text is only allowed following a #.

Operations that you can use in the Mathematical Expressions dialog box include:

With comparison and logical operators, Minitab sets the result to 1 if the expression is true and 0 if it is false. For example, if you perform the operation (C1 EQ C2) and specify C3 as the new variable, Minitab returns these results:

C1	C2	C3
3	7	0
4	4	1
4	5	0
1	1	1

You may use the missing value symbol (*) with the comparison operators = and ~=. For example, the expression C1 ~= '*' places a 1 in all the rows in which C1 has a nonmissing value, and a 0 in the rows in which C1 has a missing value.

In addition to the operations, there are additional arithmetic, comparison, and logical functions that you can use.

Arithmetic Operations		Comparison Operators		Logical Operators	
+	addition	=	EQ (equal to)	&	AND
−	subtraction	<>	NE (not equal to)	|	OR
*	multiplication	<	LT (less than)	~	NOT
/	division	>	GT (greater than)		
**	exponentiation	<=	LE (less than or equal to)		
		>=	GE (greater than or equal to)		

Functions that operate on column values or on a single value include:

Sqrt	Calculates square roots. When applied to negative numbers, the result is * (missing value).
Absolute	Calculates absolute values.
Round	Rounds numbers to the nearest integer. Numbers halfway between two integers are rounded up in magnitude.
Signs	Converts negative numbers, zero, and positive numbers to –1, 0, and +1, respectively, and prints a summary table. You may optionally store the new values in a column.
Loge	Calculates logarithms to the base e (natural logarithms). Loge of 0 or of a negative number results in * (missing value).
Logten	Calculates logarithms to the base 10. Logten of 0 or of a negative number results in * (missing value).
Expo	Calculates the power of e to the argument value.
Antilog	Calculates the power of 10 to the argument value.
Sin	Calculates the trigonometric function sine; the argument must be in radians.
Cos	Calculates the trigonometric function cosine; the argument must be in radians.
Tan	Calculates the trigonometric function tangent; the argument must be in radians.
Asin	Calculates the inverse sine, and displays the results in radians.
Acos	Calculates the inverse cosine, and displays the results in radians.
Atan	Calculates the inverse tangent, and displays the results in radians.
Nscores	Computes normal scores for use in probability plots.

Parsums	Calculates partial sums. The sum of the first i rows of the input column appears in the ith row of the storage column.
Parproducts	Calculates partial products. The product of the first i rows of the input column appears in the ith row of the storage column.

Functions that operate on columns only include:

Count	Displays the total number of values, including missing values.
N	Indicates the number of values in the arguments.
Nmiss	Indicates the number of missing values in the arguments.
Sum	Sums the values of the arguments.
Mean	Determines the mean of a column.
Stdev	Computes the standard deviation of a column.
Median	Calculates the median of a column.
Min	Shows the minimum value in a column.
Max	Shows the maximum value in a column.
SSQ	Calculates the uncorrected sum of squares of the column.
Sort	Sorts one or more columns.
Rank	Computes ranks of the values in a column.
Lag	Lags data.

You can issue many of these functions as direct commands using either Calc > Column Statistics or Calc > Row Statistics.

Corresponding Session Commands

LET
ADD
SUBTRACT
MULTIPLY
DIVIDE
RAISE

Example: Using Mathematical Expressions

The following example shows how to compute individual chi-square values for the observed and expected number of firms from a given class size, as described in Tutorial 12, using 12ECLASS.MTW. The observed values for each class size (1, 2, 3, 4, or 5) are in C4 OBSERVED: 274, 290, 243, 64, and 129. The expected values are in C5 EXPECTED: 260.7, 293.3, 245.3, 70.1, and 130.6.

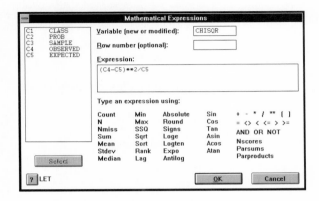

```
MTB > Name c6 = 'CHISQR'
MTB > Let 'CHISQR' = (C4-C5)**2/C5
```

This command produces the following chi-square values in C6 CHISQR:

C4	C5	C6
OBSERVED	EXPECTED	CHISQR
274	260.7	0.678521
290	293.3	0.037129
243	245.3	0.021565
64	70.1	0.530813
129	130.6	0.019602

See also Tutorials 1 and 2.

Calc > Functions

The command lets you perform various functions on a column, constant, or number in a row-wise manner. It includes a useful subset of commands available to the Mathematical Expressions command. For information

about these commands, refer to "Calc > Mathematical Expressions."

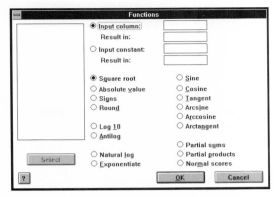

See also Tutorials 1 and 2.

Calc > Column Statistics

You use this command to calculate various statistics on the column you select, displaying the results and optionally storing them in a constant. It includes a useful subset of commands available to the Mathematical Expressions command. For information about these commands, refer to "Calc > Mathematical Expressions."

Range, which computes the extent of the data, is not included there, and Sum of squares corresponds to SSQ, whereas N total corresponds to Count. See also Tutorials 1 and 2 and "Arithmetic" on the Quick Reference Card.

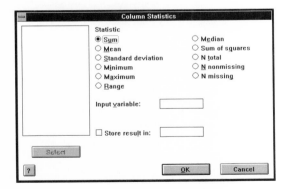

Calc > Row Statistics

This command computes one value for each row in a set of columns. Minitab calculates the statistic across the rows of the specified column(s) and stores the answers in the corresponding rows of a new column. This command includes a useful subset of commands available to the Mathematical Expressions command. For information about these commands, refer to "Calc > Mathematical Expressions" and "Calc > Column Statistics."

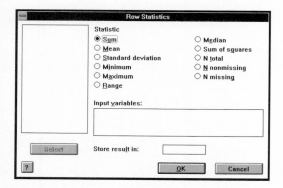

See also Tutorials 1 and 2 and "Arithmetic" on the Quick Reference Card.

Calc > Set Patterned Data

You can use Set Patterned Data to enter repetitive data into a column according to your specifications. This command is particularly useful for entering factor levels for analysis of variance designs.

Dialog Box Options

Store result in column: Specify a column to store the repetitive data.

Patterned sequence: Choose to enter a sequential set of numbers with a beginning and an end point. Minitab repeats each value, the whole list, or both as many times as you specify in the Repeat text boxes.

Start at: Enter the starting point of the sequence. You may enter a number or a stored constant.

End at: Enter the end point of the sequence. You may enter a number or a stored constant.

Increment: Enter a number if you want Minitab to increment the starting value by a specified amount until it reaches the end value.

Arbitrary list of constants: Choose to enter a set of numbers that isn't sequential. Enter the numbers separated by spaces in the text box. Minitab repeats each value, the whole list, or both as many times as you specify in the Repeat text boxes.

Repeat each value: Enter the number of times you want each value in the list repeated.

Repeat the whole list: Enter the number of times you want the entire list repeated.

Corresponding Session Command
SET

Example: Using Set Patterned Data

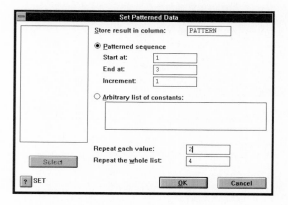

```
MTB > Name c1 = 'PATTERN'
MTB > Set 'PATTERN'
DATA>    4( 1 : 3 / 1 )2
DATA>    End.
```

This command produces these data in the Session window (use PRINT to display the column):

```
MTB > PRINT C1

PATTERN
    1    1    2    2    3    3    1    1    2    2    3    3    1    1    2
    2    3    3    1    1    2    2    3    3
```

See also Tutorial 6.

Calc > Make Indicator Variables

To create indicator (dummy) variables that you can use in regression analysis, you use the Make Indicator Variables command. You can create up to 100 indicator variables.

Dialog Box Options

Indicator variables for: Select the column for which you want to create an indicator variable. This column must contain integers from –10000 to +10000, or missing values.

Store results in: Specify as many columns as there are levels. If there are K distinct possible levels, then you must enter K storage locations. The first storage column displays a 1 in every row that has the smallest number in the levels column, and a 0 in all other rows. The second storage column displays a 1 in every row that has the second smallest level number, a 0 in all other rows, and so on. For example, if the range of the data in the levels column is between 2 and 6, you need five storage columns, regardless of whether the levels column contains all the values between 2 and 6.

Corresponding Session Command
INDICATOR

Example: Using Make Indicator Variables

The following dialog box and equivalent Session command show how to create indicator variables for the C3 REGION variable in the CRIMES data set. Once you produce these indicator variables, you can use them in a regression analysis to determine the effect of region on crime rate.

```
MTB > Indicator 'REGION' C5-C8.
```

This command produces four new columns that indicate whether a given crime rate (C4) is from a given region. Only the first portion is shown in the illustration.

	C3 REGION	C4 CRIMERTE	C5	C6	C7	C8
1	1	132	1	0	0	0
2	1	119	1	0	0	0
3	1	117	1	0	0	0
4	1	736	1	0	0	0
5	1	462	1	0	0	0

See also Tutorial 11.

Calc > Standardize

You use this command to center and scale columns of data.

Dialog Box Options

Input column(s): Enter the column(s) you want to standardize.

Store results in: Specify storage column(s) for the standardized scores.

Subtract mean and divide by std. dev.: Choose to transform each input column by subtracting its mean and then dividing the result by its standard deviation.

Subtract mean: Choose to transform each Input column by subtracting its mean.

Divide by std. dev.: Choose to transform each input column by dividing by its standard deviation.

Subtract [ ] and divide by [ ]: Choose to specify values other than the mean and standard deviation to use to transform the column(s). Minitab transforms each input column by subtracting the first value and then dividing the result by the second value.

Make range from [ ] to [ ]: Choose to specify the range of the transformed variable. Specify the minimum and maximum values. Minitab transforms each input column by performing a linear transformation within the range you specify.

Corresponding Session Command
CENTER

Example: Using Standardize

The following example standardizes test grades in the MARKS.MTW data set:

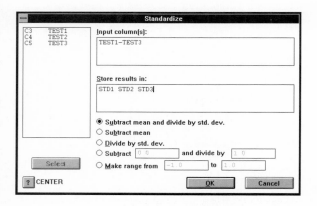

```
MTB > Name c6 = 'STD1' c7 = 'STD2' c8 = 'STD3'
MTB > Center 'TEST1'-'TEST3' 'STD1' 'STD2' 'STD3'.
```

This command produces the following display (only the first portion is shown):

	C3	C4	C5	C6	C7	C8
→	TEST1	TEST2	TEST3	STD1	STD2	STD3
1	72	93	93	−0.51215	0.88157	0.76592
2	99	86	83	1.21635	0.35451	0.35376
3	59	59	90	−1.34439	−1.67844	0.64227
4	79	69	60	−0.06402	−0.92550	−0.59419
5	48	77	25	−2.04859	−0.32314	−2.03672

See also Tutorials 2 and 11.

The Stat Menu

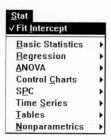

The Stat menu lets you fit with and without an intercept; obtain basic descriptive and inferential statistics; perform linear regression; perform ANOVA; display statistical process control charts and Pareto and cause-and-effect charts; and perform time series analyses, cross-tabulation, chi-square analysis, and various nonparametric tests.

Stat > Fit Intercept

This command fits regression equations with or without an intercept term. By default, Minitab fits a constant term (the y-intercept of the regression line) to all regression and time series models.

When you choose this command and remove the checkmark, Minitab omits the constant term from regression and time series models until you choose the command again or end the session. Minitab does not display the R-squared value if it fits the model without a constant, since interpretation is difficult.

Corresponding Session Commands

CONSTANT
NOCONSTANT

Stat > Basic Statistics

This command opens a submenu that lets you calculate basic statistics, including descriptive statistics, Z- and t-tests, correlation, and covariance.

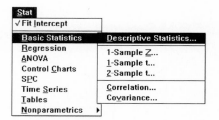

Stat > Basic Statistics > Descriptive Statistics

The Descriptive Statistics subcommand calculates summary statistics for each column you specify.

Statistic	Description
N	Number of nonmissing observations
N*	Number of missing observations
MEAN	Average value
MEDIAN	Median value
TRMEAN	A 5% trimmed mean; Minitab removes the top and bottom 5%, and then computes the mean of the remaining values
STDEV	Standard deviation
SEMEAN	Standard error of the mean
MIN	Smallest number
MAX	Largest number
Q1	First quartile (25th percentile)
Q3	Third quartile (75th percentile)

To calculate most of the descriptive statistics individually and store them as constants, see "Calc > Column Statistics."

Dialog Box Options

Variables: Enter the columns you want to describe.

By variable: Select the box to display descriptive statistics separately for each value of the specified variable, and then select the column that contains the By variable in the text box. The By variable must contain integers from –9999 to +9999, or *, the missing value code.

Corresponding Session Command

DESCRIBE

Example: Using Descriptive Statistics

Use the following dialog box and equivalent Session command to calculate descriptive statistics for the variable C3 INTEREST (the students's level of interest in their classes) by the variable C9 YEAR (year in college), using the PROF.MTW data set.

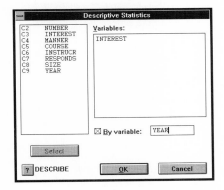

```
MTB > Describe 'INTEREST';
SUBC>   By 'YEAR'.
```

This command displays the following in the Session window:

	YEAR	N	MEAN	MEDIAN	TRMEAN	STDEV	SEMEAN
INTEREST	1	46	2.4937	2.5000	2.4964	0.6046	0.0891
	2	45	2.6818	2.7300	2.6751	0.6174	0.0920
	3	34	2.636	2.615	2.638	0.602	0.103
	4	21	2.786	3.000	2.834	0.685	0.149

	YEAR	MIN	MAX	Q1	Q3
INTEREST	1	1.1000	3.7100	2.1600	2.8725
	2	1.4600	4.0000	2.0700	3.0950
	3	1.560	3.930	2.287	3.145
	4	1.000	3.670	2.295	3.290

See also Tutorial 5.

Stat > Basic Statistics > 1-Sample Z

You use this command to perform a one-sample Z-test or to determine a Z-confidence interval for the mean.

Dialog Box Options

Variables: Enter the column(s) that contain the variable(s) you want to analyze.

Confidence interval: Choose to calculate a separate one-sample confidence interval for the mean of one or more variables.

Level: Specify the desired level of confidence. (If you specify a decimal, Minitab automatically multiplies it by 100 and converts it to a percent. For example, 0.80 becomes 80%.)

Test mean: Choose to perform a one-sample Z-test and then enter the null hypothesis test mean value in the text box.

Alternative: Specify less than (lower-tailed), not equal (two-tailed), or greater than (upper-tailed), depending on the type of test you want to perform.

Sigma: You must enter the value for the population standard deviation; the test assumes it is known.

Corresponding Session Commands

ZINTERVAL
ZTEST

Example: Using 1-Sample Z

The following dialog box and equivalent Session command tests whether, based on the results of previous studies stored in the AGE.MTW data set, there is significant evidence that the mean death age for women is less than 75 years.

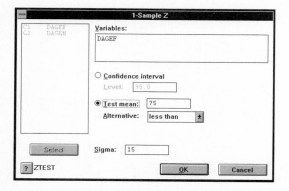

```
MTB > ZTest 75 15 'DAGEF';
SUBC>   Alternative -1.
```

This command produces the following display in the Session window:

```
TEST OF MU = 75.00 VS MU L.T. 75.00
The assumed sigma = 15.0

            N     MEAN    STDEV   SE MEAN      Z   P VALUE
DAGEF      19    75.53    13.15      3.44    0.15      0.56
```

See also Tutorial 7.

Stat > Basic Statistics > 1-Sample t

You use this command to perform a one sample t-test or to determine a t-confidence interval for the mean.

Dialog Box Options

Variables: Enter the column(s) that contain the variable(s) you want to analyze.

Confidence interval: Choose to calculate a separate one-sample t-confidence interval for the mean of one or more variables.

Level: Specify the desired level of confidence. (If you specify a decimal, Minitab automatically multiplies it by 100 and converts it to a percent. For example, 0.80 becomes 80%.)

Test mean: Choose to perform a one sample t-test and then specify the null hypothesis test mean value in the text box.

Alternative: Specify less than (lower-tailed), not equal (two-tailed), or greater than (upper-tailed), depending on the type of test you want to perform.

Corresponding Session Commands

TINTERVAL
TTEST

Example: Using 1-Sample t

The following dialog box and equivalent Session command illustrate how to test whether mean housing prices have changed from $165,000, using the data in HOMES.MTW.

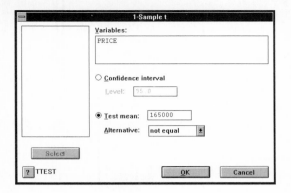

```
MTB > TTest 165000 'PRICE';
SUBC>   Alternative 0.
```

This command produces the following display in the Session window:

```
TEST OF MU = 165000 VS MU N.E. 165000

              N       MEAN      STDEV    SE MEAN         T      P VALUE
PRICE       150     153775      41611       3398     -3.30       0.0012
```

See also Tutorial 8.

Stat > Basic Statistics > 2-Sample t

This command performs a two-independent-sample t-test and generates a confidence interval for the difference of population means.

Dialog Box Options

Samples in one column: Choose this option if the groups are stacked in the same column, differentiated by subscript values in a second column.

Samples: Enter the column that contains the data.

Subscripts: Enter the column that contains the subscripts. The subscript indicates to which group each value belongs. Subscripts may be integers from –9999 to +9999, or the missing value symbol (*). The subscript column must contain two different integers.

Samples in different columns: Choose this option if the groups are stored in two separate columns.

First: Enter the column that contains the first group.

Second: Enter the column that contains the second group.

Alternative: Specify less than (lower-tailed), not equal (two-tailed), or greater than (upper-tailed) depending on the type of test you want to perform.

Confidence level: Specify the level of confidence desired. (If you specify a fraction, Minitab automatically multiplies it by 100 and converts it to a percent. For example, 0.80 becomes 80%.)

Assume equal variances: Select to assume that the populations have equal variances. Although the method that assumes equal variances (uses a pooled variance estimate) is slightly more powerful than the method that doesn't, serious error can result if the variances are not equal. Therefore, in most cases, you should not use a pooled variance estimate.

Corresponding Session Commands

TWOT
TWOSAMPLE

Example: Using 2-Sample t

The following dialog box and equivalent Session command illustrate how to test whether there is a difference between the male and female mean death ages, with the assumption of equal variances, using AGE.MTW.

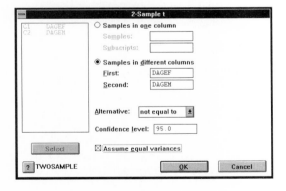

```
MTB > TwoSample 95.0 'DAGEF' 'DAGEM';
SUBC>   Alternative 0;
SUBC>   Pooled.
```

This command produces the following display in the Session window:

```
TWOSAMPLE T FOR DAGEF VS DAGEM
          N      MEAN    STDEV   SE MEAN
DAGEF    19      75.5     13.2      3.0
DAGEM    18      74.2     13.2      3.1

95 PCT CI FOR MU DAGEF - MU DAGEM: ( -7.5,  10.1)

TTEST MU DAGEF = MU DAGEM (VS NE): T= 0.30  P=0.77  DF=  35

POOLED STDEV =        13.2
```

See also Tutorial 8.

Stat > Basic Statistics > Correlation

Correlation calculates the Pearson product moment correlation coefficient between each pair of variables you list.

Minitab does not use the pairs of column values when one or both values are missing. This method is the best for each individual correlation, but the correlation matrix as a whole may not be "well behaved."

Dialog Box Options

Variables: Enter the column that contains the variables you want to correlate. If you list two columns, Minitab calculates the correlation coefficient for the pair. If you list more than two columns, Minitab calculates the correlation for every possible pair, printing the lower triangle of the correlation matrix.

Corresponding Session Command
CORRELATION

Example: Using Correlation

The following dialog box and equivalent Session command illustrate how to determine the correlation to provide numeric information about the direction and strength of the linear relationship between cents per ounce (C2 CENTS), calories per serving (C3 CALS), and nutritional rating (C7 RATING N) using the 5YOGURT.MTW data set that you worked with in Tutorial 5.

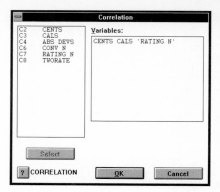

```
MTB > Correlation 'CENTS' 'CALS' 'RATING N'.
```

This command produces the following display in the Session window:

```
                 CENTS      CALS
CALS             0.136
RATING N        -0.054    0.766
```

See also Tutorials 5 and 10.

Stat > Basic Statistics > Covariance

You can use this command to calculate the covariance between each pair of columns. Minitab does not use the pairs of column values when one or both values are missing.

Dialog Box Options

Variables: Enter the columns that contain the variables for which you want to calculate the covariance. Minitab prints the lower triangle of the covariance matrix.

Corresponding Session Command
COVARIANCE

Example: Using Covariance

The following dialog box and equivalent Session command illustrate how to determine the covariance between cents per ounce (C2 CENTS) and calories per serving (C3 CALS), using the 5YOGURT.MTW data set that you worked with in Tutorial 5.

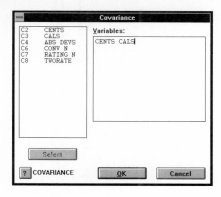

```
MTB > Covariance 'CENTS' 'CALS'.
```

This command produces the following display in the Session window:

```
              CENTS        CALS
CENTS        2.8626
CALS        14.9505   4228.9946
```

See also Tutorial 5.

Stat > Regression

The Regression command lets you perform simple, polynomial, multiple, or stepwise regression; and forward selection and backward selection.

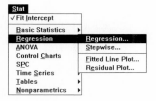

Stat > Regression > Regression

This subcommand performs simple, polynomial, and multiple regression using the least squares method. You can predict future observations, and store the residuals, fitted values, and many other diagnostics for further analysis.

Minitab prints the linear regression equation, a table of coefficients, an estimate of standard deviation about the regression line, the coefficient of determination (R-squared), R-squared adjusted for degrees of freedom, the analysis of variance table, and unusual observations. Minitab marks an unusual observation with an X if the predictor is unusual, and an R if the response is unusual. If you enter the Session command BRIEF 3 before the Regression command, Minitab prints a full table of fits and residuals for all the observations. If you choose any of the storage options, the new data appear in the Data window.

To fit a model without a constant (intercept), see "Stat > Fit Intercept."

Dialog Box Options

Response: Enter the column that contains the Y, or response, variable. Minitab does not use observations that contain missing values in the analysis.

Predictors: Enter the column(s) that contain the X, or independent, variable(s). Minitab does not use observations that contain missing values in the analysis.

Storage: You can store additional regression information, depending on which check boxes you select. Minitab stores these values in the next available columns and assigns column names.

Residuals: Select to store the residuals.

Standard resids.: Select to store the standardized residuals.

Fits: Select to store the fitted values.

Coefficients: Select to store the coefficients of the regression equation.

Deleted t resids.: Select to store the Studentized residuals.

Hi (leverage): Select to store the leverages.

DFITS: Select to store the DFITS.

Cook's distance: Select to store Cook's distance.

MSE: Select to store the mean square error. (This is also printed in the Analysis of Variance output, in the Error row under MS).

Regression Options Dialog Box Options

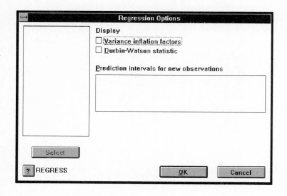

You can calculate prediction intervals for new observations.

Display:

Variance inflation factors: Select to calculate the variance inflation factor associated with each predictor.

Durbin-Watson statistic: Select to perform the Durbin-Watson test of autocorrelation in the data. Minitab omits missing observations from the calculations, using all the non-missing observations. To reach a conclusion from the test, you need to compare the printed statistic with the one that appears in a table of critical values.

Prediction intervals for new observations: Enter new values for predictors (one column or constant for each predictor) to compute the fitted Ys for those values. The output includes the fitted values, standard deviation of the fit, a 95% confidence interval, and a 95% prediction interval. If you want to list multiple rows of new predictor values without storing them in a column, you can use the Session command REGRESS followed by multiple PREDICT subcommands.

Corresponding Session Command

REGRESS

Example: Using Regression

The following dialog box and equivalent Session command illustrate how to produce a regression model for the current pH level of lakes based on the lake area, % bog, and depth, using LAKES.MTW.

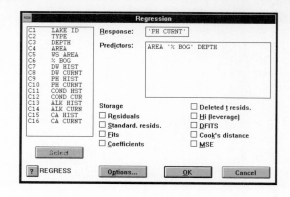

```
MTB > Regress 'PH CURNT' 3 'AREA' '% BOG' 'DEPTH'.
```

This command produces the following display in the Session window, a section of which is shown:

```
The regression equation is
PH CURNT = 7.16 + 0.00278 AREA - 0.0100 % BOG - 0.0287 DEPTH

148 cases used 1 cases contain missing values

Predictor       Coef        Stdev     t-ratio        p
Constant      7.1590       0.1574       45.49    0.000
AREA        0.0027799    0.0005656        4.91    0.000
% BOG      -0.010021     0.004144       -2.42    0.017
DEPTH      -0.02869      0.01277        -2.25    0.026

s = 0.7668      R-sq = 16.8%      R-sq(adj) = 15.0%
```

See also Tutorials 10 and 11.

Stat > Regression > Stepwise

You use Stepwise to identify a useful subset of up to 100 predictors for regression. To fit a model without a constant (intercept), see "Stat > Fit Intercept."

This command offers three commonly used procedures:

1. Stepwise: In step 1, Minitab calculates an F-statistic for each predictor already in the model. If that value is less than the value specified in the F to remove text box under Options for any predictor, Minitab removes the predictor with the lowest F-statistic and prints output from the resulting model. In step 2, Minitab

calculates an F-statistic for each predictor not in the current model. If any value is greater than the value specified in the F to enter text box under Options for any predictor, Minitab enters the predictor with the highest F-statistic and prints the output from the resulting model. These steps are repeated until no variables meet the criteria for addition or removal.

2. Forward selection: Minitab adds predictors to the model as in Stepwise, but never removes any. Set F to remove to 0. These steps are repeated until no additional variables have an F-value greater than the value in the F to enter text box.

3. Backward elimination: This begins with a model containing all the possible predictors and removes them one at a time without reentering any. Enter 10000 (a value virtually impossible to obtain) in the F to enter text box and list all the predictors in the Enter text box in the Stepwise Regression dialog box. These steps are repeated until no variable in the model has an F-value less than the one specified in the F to remove text box.

Minitab alternates between stages of adding and removing variables until no more predictors can enter or leave the model. During each pause in the procedure, Minitab displays the prompt *MORE?* You can answer **YES** to continue, **NO** to quit, or add a subcommand. See the Session command STEPWISE on the Quick Reference Card or in online Help for the available subcommands.

Dialog Box Options

Response: Enter the Y, or response variable, you want to regress. Minitab does not use observations containing missing values.

Predictors: Enter the column that contains the X, or predictor, variable(s) to include in the model. Minitab does not use observations containing missing values.

Enter: Enter the columns that contain the variables you want Minitab to start with in the initial stepwise model. If their F-statistic falls below the value in the F to remove text box under Options, Minitab removes them.

Force: Enter the columns that contain the variables you do not want to remove from the regression model. You can change their status at the *MORE?* prompt by using the Session subcommand REMOVE.

Stepwise Options Dialog Box Options

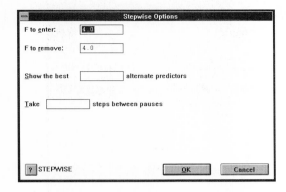

F to enter: Specify the minimum F-value required to enter a predictor variable in a model; this value must be greater than or equal to the one that appears in the F to remove text box. The procedure looks for variables not yet in the equation whose F-statistics are greater than the value specified in this text box. If Minitab finds one or more such variables, it enters the variable with the largest F in the equation.

F to remove: Specify the F-value required to remove a predictor variable from the model. If any F is less than the specified value, the one with the smallest F is removed from the equation.

Show the best [ ] alternate predictors: For each step in which Minitab adds a variable to the model, it prints the next K best alternatives in terms of the F-value, along with their t-statistics. Minitab obtains each t-ratio shown by replacing the variable actually chosen with the alternative variable.

Take [ ] steps between pauses: Specify the number of steps to perform between pauses. You can enter any number from 1 to the maximum allowed by the width of your screen (or by the Session command OW). Use smaller values when you want to intervene in the variable selection procedure more often. During each pause in the procedure, Minitab displays the *MORE?* prompt. You can answer YES to continue, NO to quit, or add a subcommand. See the Session command STEPWISE on the Quick Reference Card or in online Help for available subcommands.

Corresponding Session Command

STEPWISE

Example: Using Stepwise

The following dialog box and equivalent Session command illustrate how to use Stepwise to fit a model that predicts lake pH based on the depth, lake area, % bog, and watershed area, with watershed area initially entered into the regression using LAKES.MTW.

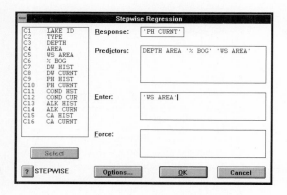

```
MTB > Stepwise 'PH CURNT' 'DEPTH' 'AREA' '% BOG' 'WS AREA':
SUBC>    Enter 'WS AREA':
SUBC>    FEnter 4.0:
SUBC>    FRemove 4.0.
```

This command produces the following display in the Session window, which shows Minitab's first pass on this model:

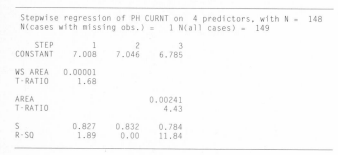

```
Stepwise regression of PH CURNT on  4 predictors, with N =  148
N(cases with missing obs.) =   1 N(all cases) =  149

    STEP        1         2         3
CONSTANT    7.008     7.046     6.785

WS AREA    0.00001
T-RATIO      1.68

AREA                            0.00241
T-RATIO                            4.43

S           0.827     0.832     0.784
R-SQ         1.89      0.00     11.84
```

See also Tutorial 11.

Stat > Regression > Fitted Line Plot

Minitab plots a fitted regression line. This plot shows how close the actual data lie to the fitted regression line. It also includes confidence bands and prediction bands about the regression line.

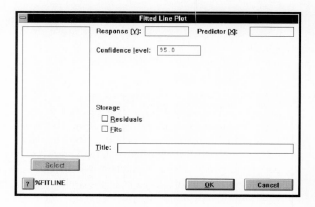

Dialog Box Items

Response [Y]: Select the column containing the Y, or response variable.

Predictor [X]: Select the column(s) containing the X, or independent variable(s).

Confidence level: Enter the level of confidence desired for computation of confidence and prediction bands.

Storage: You can store the residuals and fits from the regression analysis. These values are stored in the next available columns, and are assigned column names.

Residuals: Check to store the residuals.

Fits: Check to store the fitted values.

Title: Enter a title. If you leave this space blank, Minitab displays a default title.

Corresponding Session Command

%FITLINE

See also Tutorial 10.

Stat > Regression > Residual Plot

This command produces four residual plots: a normal plot, an I chart, a histogram, and a scatter plot of the residuals versus the fits. You must have stored the residuals and fits from a previous command. This command can be used to check models from Regression, Oneway, Twoway, Balanced ANOVA, and ARIMA.

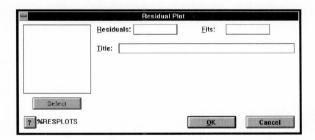

Dialog Box Items

Residuals: Select the column containing the residuals.
Fits: Select the column containing the fitted values.
Title: Enter a title. If you leave this field blank, a default title is displayed.

Corresponding Session Command

%RESPLOTS

See also Tutorial 11.

Stat > ANOVA

The ANOVA command opens a submenu that lets you perform one-way analysis of variance, two-way analysis of variance, and balanced analysis of variance, and obtain residual plots.

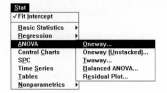

Stat > ANOVA > Oneway

The Oneway command on the ANOVA submenu performs a one-way analysis of variance, with the response variable in one column and subscripts in another.

Dialog Box Options

Response: Enter the column that contains the response variable.
Factor: Enter the column that contains the subscripts that identify the factor level or group. Subscripts may be any integers from –10000 to +10000, or missing values (*); they need not be consecutive. The Set Patterned Data command is useful for entering subscripts.
Store Residuals: Select to store residuals in the next available column.
Store fits: Select to store the fitted values in the next available column. For a one-way analysis of variance, the fits are the level means.

Oneway Multiple Comparisons Dialog Box Options

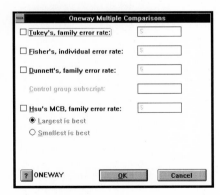

This command provides confidence intervals for the differences between means, using four different methods: Tukey's, Fisher's, Dunnett's, and Hsu's MCB. Tukey, Dunnett, and Hsu's MCB tests use a family error rate, whereas Fisher's LSD procedure uses an individual error rate.

Minitab presents the multiple comparisons as a set of confidence intervals, rather than as a set of hypothesis tests. You can then assess the practical significance of differences among means, in addition to statistical significance. If the confidence interval does not contain zero, Minitab rejects the null hypothesis of no difference between means.

Tukey's, family error rate: Select to obtain confidence intervals for all pairwise differences between level means using Tukey's method. Specify the family error rate desired. The error rate must be between 0.5 and 0.001; Minitab treats a value greater than 1.0 as a percentage.

Fisher's, individual error rate: Select to obtain confidence intervals for all pairwise differences between level means using Fisher's LSD procedure. Specify the individual error rate desired. The error rate must be between 0.5 and 0.01; Minitab treats a value greater than 1.0 as a percentage.

Dunnett's, family error rate: Select to obtain a two-sided confidence interval for the difference between each treatment mean and a control mean. Specify the family error rate desired. The error rate must be between 0.5 and 0.001; Minitab treats a value greater than or equal to 1.0 as a percentage.

Control group subscript: Enter the numerical value that corresponds to the control group factor level.

Hsu's MCB, family error rate: Select to obtain a confidence interval for the difference between each level mean and the best of the other level means.

Largest is best: Choose to have the largest mean considered the best.

Smallest is best: Choose to have the smallest mean considered the best.

Corresponding Session Command
ONEWAY

Example: Using Oneway

The following dialog box and equivalent Session command illustrate how to perform an analysis of variance to test whether the mean average ad size is different depending on whether a paper is regional, local, or national, using NONPRT.MTW.

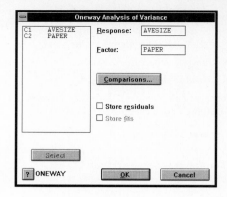

```
MTB > Oneway 'AVESIZE' 'PAPER'.
```

This command produces the following display in the Session window:

```
ANALYSIS OF VARIANCE ON AVESIZE
SOURCE     DF      SS       MS       F       p
PAPER       2   1222.6    611.3    9.03   0.012
ERROR       7    474.1     67.7
TOTAL       9   1696.7
                                 INDIVIDUAL 95% CI'S FOR MEAN
                                 BASED ON POOLED STDEV
LEVEL       N    MEAN     STDEV   ----------+---------+---------+------
    1       6  30.582     9.091              (---*---)
    2       2  50.015     7.050                           (------*------
    3       2  15.190     3.338   (------*-----)
                                 ----------+---------+---------+------
POOLED STDEV =    8.230                    20        40        60
```

See also Tutorial 9.

Stat > ANOVA > Oneway (Unstacked)

To perform a one-way analysis of variance, with each group in a separate column, use the Oneway [Unstacked] subcommand.

Dialog Box Options

Responses [in separate columns]: Enter the columns that contain the response variable. Minitab does not require that each column have the same number of observations.

Corresponding Session Command
AOVONEWAY

Example: Using Oneway (Unstacked)

The following dialog box and equivalent Session command illustrate how to perform an analysis of variance to test whether the average test scores are equal, using MARKS.MTW.

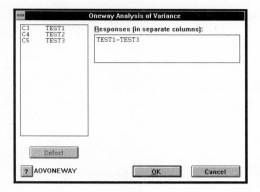

```
MTB > AOVOneway 'TEST1'-'TEST3'.
```

This command produces the following display in the Session window:

```
ANALYSIS OF VARIANCE
SOURCE     DF        SS       MS       F       p
FACTOR      2       641      320    0.95   0.391
ERROR      69     23209      336
TOTAL      71     23850
                               INDIVIDUAL 95% CI'S FOR MEAN
                               BASED ON POOLED STDEV
LEVEL       N      MEAN     STDEV   -------+---------+---------+-------
TEST1      24     80.00     15.62            (-----------*-----------)
TEST2      24     81.29     13.28              (-----------*-----------)
TEST3      24     74.42     24.26   (-----------*-----------)
                                   -------+---------+---------+-------
POOLED STDEV =     18.34           72.0      78.0      84.0
```

See also Tutorial 9.

Stat > ANOVA > Twoway

This command performs a two-way analysis of variance for balanced data. Each cell must contain an equal number of observations.

Dialog Box Options

Response: Enter the column that contains the response variable.

Row Factor: Enter the column that contains the first factor. This column may include any integers between –10000 and +10000, or missing values (*); the numbers need not be consecutive.

Display means: Select to compute marginal means and 95% confidence intervals for each level of the row factor.

Column factor: Enter the column that contains the second factor. This column must contain integers between –10000 and +10000, or missing values (*); they need not be consecutive.

Display means: Select to compute marginal means and 95% confidence intervals for each level of the column factor.

Store residuals: Select to store the residuals in the next available column.

Store fits: Select to store the fitted value for each group. If you do not fit an additive model, the fitted value is the cell mean.

Fit additive model: Select to fit a model without an interaction term.

Corresponding Session Command

TWOWAY

Example: Using Twoway

The following dialog box and equivalent Session command compute a two-way analysis of variance that examines the mean ad ratio (ratio of full page ads to the number of pages) as a factor of year and magazine type, using ADS2.MTW.

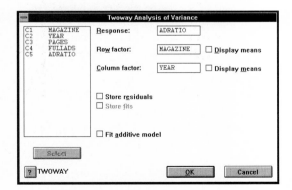

```
MTB > Twoway 'ADRATIO' 'MAGAZINE' 'YEAR'.
```

This command produces the following display in the Session window:

```
ANALYSIS OF VARIANCE   ADRATIO

SOURCE         DF        SS        MS
MAGAZINE        1    0.1247    0.1247
YEAR            2    0.0231    0.0115
INTERACTION     2    0.0394    0.0197
ERROR          18    0.2997    0.0166
TOTAL          23    0.4869
```

See also Tutorial 9.

Stat > ANOVA > Balanced ANOVA

You can perform univariate analysis of variance by using the Balanced ANOVA subcommand. Factors may be crossed or nested, fixed or random. Nesting must be balanced and the subscripts used to indicate levels of B within each level of A must be the same.

For one-way analysis of variance you may have unbalanced designs, but you must balance data (all cells have the same number of observations) for multiway designs.

Dialog Box Options

Responses: Enter the column that contains the response variable. You can analyze up to 50 columns.

Model: Specify the terms to be use in the model. The factor levels must be integers from –9999 to +9999, or missing values (*). They need not be consecutive or in any special order. The Set Patterned Data command can be helpful in entering the level numbers of a factor.

Display means for (list of terms): Minitab displays a table of means corresponding to each term. Specify the list of terms, both main effects and interactions, as you did in the Model text box. For example, the list of terms A, B, D, A*B*D displays four tables: one table for each main effect and one for the three-way interaction.

Store Residuals: Select to store the residuals using one column for each dependent variable.

Store Fits: Select to store the fitted values for each observation in the data set in the next available columns, using one column for each response.

Specifying a Model

Specify a model in the Model text box using the syntax Y = *expression*. Do not enter Y in the text box, only the expression. The Set Patterned Data command can be helpful in entering the level numbers of a factor.

Expression Rules:

1. * indicates an interaction term.

2. ( ) indicate nesting. When B is nested within A, type **B(A)**. When C is nested within both A and B, type **C(AB)**.

3. Terms in parentheses are always factors in the model and are listed with blank spaces between them.

4. Abbreviate a model using a | or ! to indicate crossed factors, and a - to remove terms.

Models with many terms take a long time to compute.

The following are examples of what to type in the Model text box:

Two factors crossed: A B A*B

Three factors crossed: A B C A*B A*C B*C A*B*C

Three factors nested: A B(A) C(AB)

Crossed and nested (B nested within A, and both crossed with C): A B(A) C A*C B(A)*C

Corresponding Session Command

ANOVA

Example: Using Balanced ANOVA

The following dialog box and equivalent Session command compute a two-way analysis of variance between year and magazine type to determine whether there is a significant effect of these two factors and their interaction on the mean ad ratio, using ADS2.MTW.

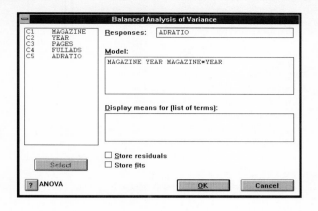

MTB > ANOVA 'ADRATIO' = MAGAZINE YEAR MAGAZINE*YEAR.

This command produces the following display in the Session window:

```
Factor     Type Levels Values
MAGAZINE   fixed     2    1     2
YEAR       fixed     3 1989  1991  1993

Analysis of Variance for ADRATIO

Source        DF        SS        MS       F      P
MAGAZINE       1   0.12471   0.12471    7.49  0.014
YEAR           2   0.02309   0.01155    0.69  0.513
MAGAZINE*YEAR  2   0.03941   0.01971    1.18  0.329
Error         18   0.29969   0.01665
Total         23   0.48691
```

See also Tutorial 9.

Stat > ANOVA > Residual Plot

See "Stat > Regression > Residual Plot" for information.

Stat > Control Charts

You use the commands on this submenu to produce a wide variety of Variables control charts (for data that measure, not count) and Attributes control charts (for data with counts of defects or nonconformities in a sample, or the presence or absence of characteristics or attributes). See Tutorial 14.

Most of these control charts are actual Minitab commands, but others are %*Macros*, or a series of com-

mands. You can use many of the Professional Graphics features with the command charts; the %Macro charts are less flexible. Command charts have the standard Professional Graphics buttons; %Macro charts don't. Minitab indicates a chart by displaying % before the Session name in the lower left corner of each dialog box. You must use Session commands to create Character control charts instead of Professional charts. At the end of the Control Charts section is a summary of the Character control chart Session command syntax.

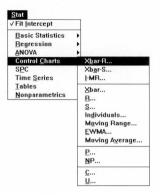

For all charts the data consist of samples taken, usually over time. Minitab calculates a summary statistic (such as a sample mean or sample proportion) and plots it against the sample number. This plot is the control chart. Minitab draws three lines on the chart:

1. The center line, which is an estimate of the average value of the summary statistic.

2. An upper control limit (UCL), which appears at 3 σ limits (standard deviations) above the center line.

3. A lower control limit (LCL), which appears at 3 σ limits (standard deviations) below the center line.

If the process is "in control," or stable, it is very unlikely that a point (a value of the summary statistic) will fall outside the control limits. If one does, you should investigate it.

Minitab omits missing observations (*) from the calculations.

Control Charts for Data in Subgroups

The Xbar, R, S, Xbar-R, and Xbar-S commands produce control charts for data in subgroups with subgroup indicators in another column (unless the subgroup sizes are all equal). Xbar produces a chart of subgroup means, R creates a chart of subgroup ranges, and S displays a chart of subgroup standard deviations. Xbar-R plots an Xbar chart and an R chart on one screen, while Xbar-S plots an Xbar chart and an S chart. These commands must have two or more observations in at least one subgroup. Subgroups do not need to be the same size. Minitab plots summary statistics for each subgroup on the charts for estimating process parameters.

If a single observation is missing, Minitab omits it from the calculations of the summary statistics for its subgroup and adjusts the formulas accordingly. This modification may yield different control chart limits and a different center line for that subgroup. If an entire subgroup is missing, a gap appears in the chart where the summary statistic for that subgroup would have been plotted.

Since the control limits are functions of the subgroup size, unequal-sized subgroups affect them. In general, the limits are closer to the center line for larger subgroups, and further away for smaller ones. In charts for subgroup ranges and standard deviations, the center line also changes when the subgroup size changes.

Control Charts for Individual Observations

The Individuals, Moving Range, and I-MR commands produce control charts for individual observations. You must store all the data from a process in a single column to use these commands. Since there are no subgroups, you do not need a subgroup indicator column or a subgroup size.

If an observation is missing, a gap appears in the Individuals chart where that observation would have been plotted. When calculating moving ranges, each value is the range of K consecutive observations, where K is the length of the moving ranges. If any of the observations for a particular moving range are missing, Minitab does not calculate them, leaving a gap corresponding to each moving range that includes the missing observation.

Other Control Charts

The EWMA and Moving Average commands produce control charts either for data in subgroups or for individual observations. EWMA produces an exponentially weighted moving average; whereas Moving Average plots an unweighted moving average.

When you enter the data column, use an indicator to tell Minitab the size of the subgroups or the column containing subscripts to indicate the subgroups. Whenever the subscript changes, Minitab begins a new subgroup.

To use these commands with individual observations, enter a subgroup size of 1.

If a single observation is missing and you have data in subgroups, Minitab omits it from the calculations of the summary statistics for its subgroup and adjusts all the formulas accordingly. This may cause the control chart limits to have different values. If an entire subgroup is missing, EWMA cannot calculate any more values, because it plots an exponentially weighted moving average of all past subgroup means. Starting with the missing subgroup, the chart is empty. The Moving Averages chart leaves a gap corresponding to all the moving averages that would have used that subgroup mean.

Attributes Control Charts

The P, NP, U, and C commands produce control charts for attributes data. P produces a chart of the proportion of defectives in each subgroup, whereas NP produces a chart of the number of defectives in each subgroup, the raw data. C produces a chart of the number of defects in each sample, whereas U produces a chart of the number of defects per unit sampled in each subgroup (for example, number of defects per square inch).

If an observation is missing, Minitab leaves a gap in the chart where it would have plotted the summary statistic for that subgroup.

P, NP, and U handle unequal-size subgroups. With P and U, the control limits are a function of the subgroup size, while the center line is always constant. With NP, differing subgroup sizes affect both the control limits and the center line. In general, the control limits are further from the center line for smaller subgroups than for larger ones.

Control Charts Commands

Note that the dialog boxes for all the control charts are similar, with some variation based on the individual requirements of each command. For each Control Chart command, this section lists the corresponding Session command in parentheses, provides a brief description, and displays the particular Control Chart dialog box associated with the command. The following section discusses all the possible options that appear in the various Control Charts dialog boxes.

Stat > Control Charts > Xbar-R (%XRCHART): Produces a control chart for subgroup means (in the upper half of the screen) and a control chart for subgroup ranges (in the lower half of the screen) so you can examine both process level and process variation at the same time.

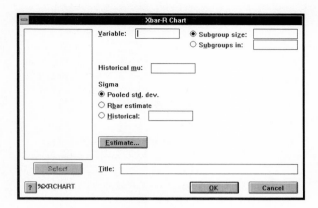

Stat > Control Charts > Xbar-S (%XSCHART): Produces a control chart for subgroup means (in the upper half of the screen) and a control chart for subgroup standard deviation (in the lower half of the screen) so you can examine both process level and process variation at the same time.

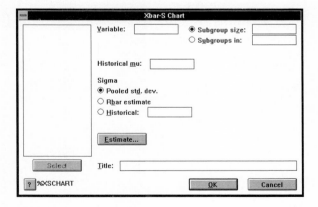

Stat > Control Charts > I-MR (%IMRCHART): Produces a chart of individual observations (in the upper half of the screen) and a moving range chart (in the lower half of the screen).

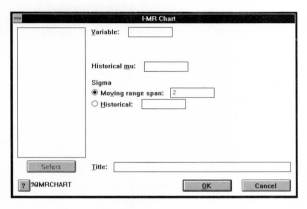

Stat > Control Charts > Xbar (XBARCHART): Produces a control chart for subgroup means.

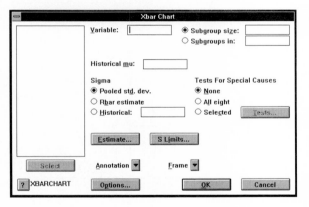

Stat > Control Charts > R (RCHART): Produces a control chart for subgroup ranges.

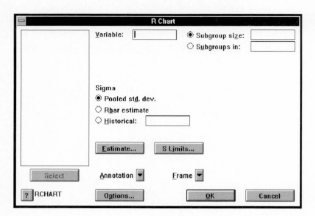

Stat > Control Charts > Individuals (ICHART): Produces a control chart for individual observations.

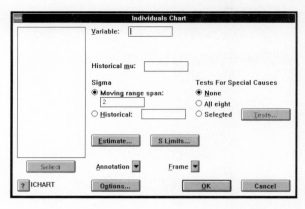

Stat > Control Charts > S (SCHART): Produces a control chart for subgroup standard deviations.

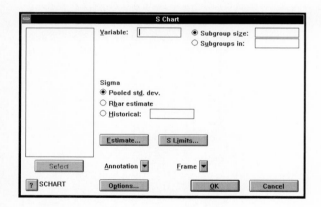

Stat > Control Charts > Moving Range (MRCHART): Produces an MR (Moving Range) chart.

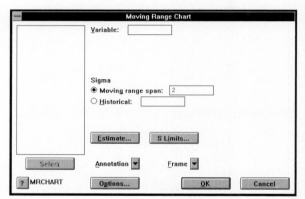

Stat > Control Charts > EWMA (EWMACHART):
Produces an exponentially weighted moving average control chart.

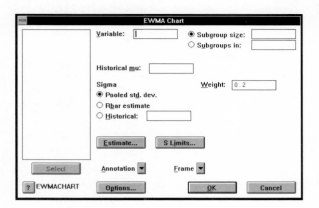

Stat > Control Charts > Moving Average (MACHART): Produces an MA (Moving Average) chart based on either subgroup means or individual observations.

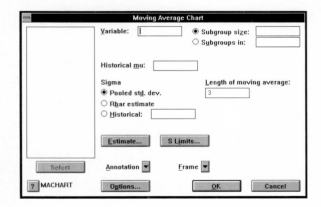

Stat > Control Charts > P (PCHART): Draws a chart of the proportion of defectives.

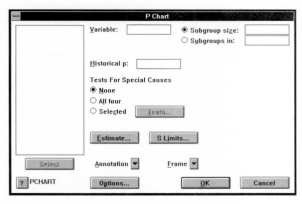

Stat > Control Charts > NP (NPCHART): Draws a chart for the number of defectives.

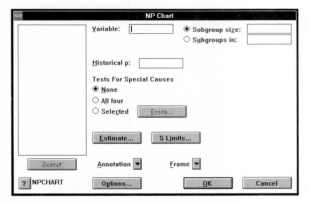

Stat > Control Charts > C (CCHART): Draws a chart of the number of defects.

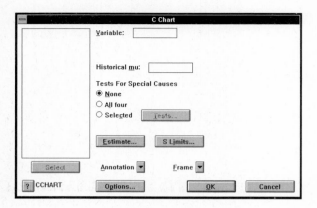

Stat > Control Charts > U (UCHART): Draws a chart of the number of defects per unit sampled.

Control Charts Dialog Box Options

This section describes all the possible options that appear in the various Control Chart dialog boxes. No single dialog box displays all these options. You can simply refer to the options that appear in the dialog box for which you need help, as shown in the illustrations in the "Control Charts Commands" section.

Variable: Enter the column that contains the outcome measure.

Subgroup size: Choose if subgroups are equal and then enter the subgroup size. If you enter 5, for example, Minitab uses the first five rows as the

first sample, the second five rows as the second sample, and so on, and then plots the mean and range of each subgroup.

Subgroups in: Choose if the subgroup sizes are unequal and then indicate the column containing the subscripts that indicate group membership. Minitab forms a new subgroup every time the value in the specified column changes, and then plots the mean and range for each subgroup. If the subgroups are not equal, the control limits are not straight lines, but vary with the subgroup size. If the subgroup sizes do not vary much, you may want to force the control limits into straight lines by specifying a fixed subgroup size using Estimate.

Historical mu: Specify a value for μ (mean of the population distribution), if you have a known process parameter or an estimate obtained from past data. If you do not specify a value for μ, Minitab estimates it from the data.

Historical p: Specify a value for p (the process proportion defective), if you have a known process parameter or an estimate obtained from past data. Minitab uses this value to calculate the control limits and as the center line on the chart. If you do not specify a value for p, Minitab estimates it from the data. You can select certain samples to estimate p using Estimate.

Sigma: Minitab estimates σ (standard deviation of the population distribution) using a number of different methods for the various control charts:

Pooled std. dev.: Choose to use a pooled standard deviation.

Rbar estimate: Choose to base the estimate on the average of the subgroup ranges.

Historical: Choose to specify a known process parameter or an estimate obtained from past data. Enter the value for sigma in the text box.

Moving range span: Choose to base the estimate on a moving range span, and then enter the span you want to use to compute sigma. By default, Minitab uses a span of 2 because consecutive values have the best chance of being alike.

Tests For Special Causes: Minitab controls whether you perform one or more of the eight tests for special causes. Each test detects a specific pattern in the data plotted on the chart. The occurrence of a pattern suggests a special cause for the variation that should be investigated.

None: Choose to omit all tests.

All four: Choose to perform all four tests. See "Tests Dialog Box Options" for a list of the tests for special causes.

All eight: Choose to perform all eight tests. See "Tests Dialog Box Options" for a list of the tests for special causes.

Selected: Choose to select a subset of the eight tests for special causes, then click the Tests button.

Weight: Specify the weight to use in the exponentially weighted moving average. The specified value must be a number between 0 and 1. By changing the weight used and the number of sigmas for the control limits, you can construct a chart with very specific properties.

Length of moving average: Specify the length of the moving averages. The value you enter determines the number of subgroup means that Minitab includes in each average. If you have individual observations (that is, you specified a subgroup size of 1), Minitab uses these instead of the subgroup means in all calculations.

Title: Type a subtitle in this text box, if desired.

Estimate: Minitab lets you force the control limits to be straight lines.

Tests: Minitab lets you select a subset of the four or eight tests for special causes that detect specific patterns in the data plotted on the chart. The subgroup sizes must be equal to perform the tests. The occurrence of a pattern suggests a special cause for the variation that you should investigate. When a point fails a test, Minitab marks it with the test number on the plot. If a point fails more than one test, Minitab prints the number of the first test you select in the list and prints a summary table in the Session window with complete information.

S Limits: Specify where the control limits are drawn. By default, Minitab draws control limits at three standard deviations above and below the center line.

Options: Minitab controls the attributes of the control chart symbols and connection lines. See "Graph Menu" for information about customizing line and symbol options.

Annotation: See "Graph Menu" for information about annotating graphs.

Frame: See "Graph Menu" for information about graph frames.

Xbar-Estimation of Mu and Sigma

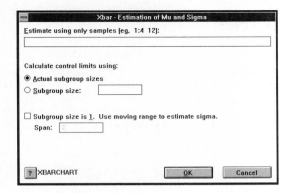

Note that this dialog box shows only some of the options listed here, because the options vary depending on which control chart you are producing.

Estimate using only samples: List the individual sample numbers or a range of samples to specify the subgroups of data to use in the computations for mu and sigma. Note that this option refers only to entire samples, not individual observations. If you want to omit one observation from a sample, change that value to missing.

Estimate using only individuals: Specify individual observations to include in the computations for mu and sigma by listing rows or a range of rows.

Calculate control limits using: This tells Minitab how to calculate control limits. If the subgroup sizes are unequal, the control limits vary with the size and are not straight lines. The center line of charts for ranges and standard deviations also varies with the subgroup size. If the sizes do not vary much, you may want to force the control limits to be straight lines.

Actual subgroup sizes: Choose to use the subgroups defined in the parent dialog box to estimate mu and sigma.

Subgroup size: Choose to force straight control limits, and then enter a sample size if sample sizes are unequal. This option only affects the control limits; the data that Minitab actually plots do not change.

Subgroup size is 1. Use moving range to estimate sigma: Select if the subgroup size is 1 and you want to specify the number of observations to use in calculating the moving range.

Span: Specify the number of observations to calculate the moving range. Minitab estimates the process variation using the sample standard deviations of each subgroup. If the subgroup size is 1, you cannot calculate sample standard deviations; Minitab estimates the process variation using moving ranges instead. By default, a span of 2 is used because consecutive values have the best chance of being alike.

S Limits Dialog Box Options

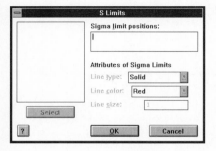

The options for this dialog box vary depending on which type of control chart you are producing.

Sigma limit positions: Specify the position(s) at which Minitab draws the upper and lower control limits in relation to the center line. The values you enter represent the number of standard deviations above and below the center line at which Minitab places the control limits. If you specify more than one value, a set of control limits is drawn for each number in the list.

Attributes of Sigma Limits: See "Graph Menu" for information about graphical attributes of lines.

Tests Dialog Box Options

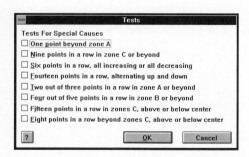

The options for this dialog box vary depending on which control chart you are producing.

Tests For Special Causes: Select any combination of the tests listed in the dialog box. Zone A represents the area up to one standard deviation from the center line, Zone B is the area between one and two standard deviations from the center line, and Zone C is the area between two and three standard deviations from the center line.

Character Control Charts

The Character control charts are not available through the menus, but you can enter their corresponding Session commands to produce them. The following subcommands are available for all Character control charts:

SLIMITS	at **E...E**
ESTIMATE	using just samples **K...K**
HLINES	at **E...E**
TITLE	= 'text'
FOOTNOTE	= 'text'
YLABEL	= 'text'
XLABEL	= 'text'
YINCREMENT	= **K**
YSTART	at **K** [end at **K**]
XSTART	at **K** [end at **K**]

Each Character control chart command is listed below, with its subcommands indented immediately after it.

XBARCHART	for **C...C**, subgroups are in **E**

Produces a control chart for subgroup means.

MU	= **K**
SIGMA	= **K**
RBAR	use R-bar to estimate sigma
RSPAN	= **K**
TEST	**K...K**
SUBGROUP	size is **K**

RCHART	for **C...C**, subgroups are in **E**

Produces a separate R chart (a chart of sample ranges).

SIGMA	= **K**
RBAR	use R-bar to estimate sigma
SUBGROUP	size is **K**

SCHART	for **C...C**, subgroups are in **E**

Produces a control chart for subgroup standard deviations.

SIGMA	= **K**
RBAR	use R-bar to estimate sigma
SUBGROUP	size is **K**

ICHART	for **C...C**

Produces a control chart for individual observations.

MU	= **K**
SIGMA	= **K**
RSPAN	= **K**
TEST	**K...K**

Has all subcommands but ESTIMATE

MACHART	for **C...C**, subgroups are in **E**

Produces a moving average control chart.

MU	= **K**
SIGMA	= **K**
RBAR	use R-bar to estimate sigma
SPAN	= **K**
RSPAN	= **K**
SUBGROUP	size is **K**

EWMACHART	for **C...C**, subgroups are in **E**

Produces an exponentially weighted moving average control chart.

MU	= **K**
SIGMA	= **K**

RBAR	use R-bar to estimate sigma
WEIGHT	= **K**
RSPAN	= **K**
SUBGROUP	size is **K**

MRCHART	for **C...C**

Produces a moving range control chart.

SIGMA	= **K**
RSPAN	= **K**

PCHART	**C E**

Draws a chart for the proportion of defectives.

P	= **K**
TEST	**K...K**
SUBGROUP	size is **K**

NPCHART	number of defectives are in **C**, sample size is **E**

Produces a control chart for the number of defectives.

P	= **K**
TEST	**C...C**
SUBGROUP	size is **K**

CCHART	number of defects are in **C**

Produces a control chart for the number of defects.

MU	= **K**
TEST	**K...K**

UCHART	number of defects per unit are in **C**, sample size = **E**

Produces a control chart for the number of defects per unit sampled.

MU	= **K**
TEST	**K...K**
SUBGROUP	size is **K**

Example: Using Control Charts

The following dialog box and equivalent Session command produces an Xbar chart for a sampling of the weights of individually wrapped packets of candy, one pack per sample, using CANDYB.MTW.

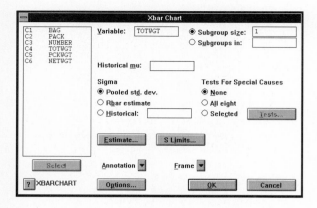

```
MTB > XbarChart 'TOTWGT' 1:
SUBC>   Symbol:
SUBC>   Connect.
```

This command produces the following chart in a separate Graph window:

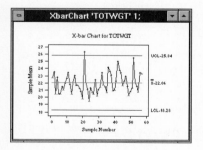

See also Tutorial 14.

Stat > SPC

The Statistical Process Control (SPC) commands help you produce quality planning charts.

Pareto charts order the bars from largest to smallest to focus improvement efforts on areas where the largest gains can be made. Cause-and-effect, or *fishbone*,

diagrams let you graphically map out the factors that influence your process.

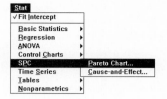

Stat > SPC > Pareto Chart

This command generates a Pareto chart, with the bars ordered from largest to smallest. Often, the data that are plotted are defects. A Pareto chart provides a visual representation of the contribution that each defect makes to the total. By ranking them from largest to smallest, you can focus on the defects that have the greatest impact.

Dialog Box Options

Defects: Enter the column that contains the raw data or a list of the defect names. There are two ways to generate a Pareto chart. You can enter a column of raw data, in which each observation is an occurrence of a type of defect. Alternatively, you can enter a list of defect names or codes in a column, list the frequencies in a separate column, and enter this column in the Frequencies text box. The defects can be either alpha or numeric data, so you can use the defect names or numeric codes representing the defects. If you use alpha data, each defect name can have up to 72 characters; however, the first 15 characters must be distinct for each one. Minitab also creates a bar for missing data.

Frequencies: Choose this option if column listed in Defects contains defect names or codes rather than raw data. Then select the column containing the frequency of occurrence corresponding to the names or codes.

Combine all defects after the first [ ] % into one bar: Specify the cumulative percentage for which you want to generate bars. Minitab generates bars for defects until the cumulative percentage surpasses the % specified, at which point, it lumps the rest into a bar labeled *Others*.

Title: To display a subtitle below the default title, type it in this text box.

Corresponding Session Command

%PARETO

Example: Using Pareto

This dialog box and the equivalent Session command show you how to produce a Pareto chart for the defects in a process. The Session command illustration also lists the defects in C1 DEFECTS if you want to enter them in a column to reproduce this Pareto chart.

```
MTB > NAME C1 'DEFECTS'
MTB > READ C1;
SUBC> FORMAT (A15).
DATA> Scratch
DATA> Scratch
DATA> Bend
DATA> Chip
DATA> Dent
DATA> Scratch
DATA> Chip
DATA> Scratch
DATA> END
         8 rows read.
MTB > %Pareto 'DEFECTS';
SUBC>    Others 95.
Executing from file: C:\MTBSEW\MACROS\Pareto.MAC
Macro is running ... please wait
```

This command produces the following Pareto chart:

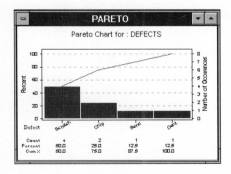

See also Tutorial 14.

Stat > SPC > Cause-and-Effect

You use this command to generate a cause-and-effect (fishbone) diagram that depicts the potential causes of a problem. The problem (effect) appears on the right side of the graph; the list of causes appears on the left in a tree structure. The main branches represent the major categories of causes and lists specific causes in that category. Minitab can display a blank fishbone diagram, with just the labels on the main branches. If, on the other hand, you supply a list of causes for each branch, Minitab includes them in the diagram.

Dialog Box Options

Cause: The columns you enter here should contain the lists of causes that you want Minitab to display on the corresponding branches of the diagram. Entries in the column can contain up to 72 characters; Minitab displays only the first 15. If you enter no columns, Minitab generates a diagram with the main branches but no causes.

Men: Enter the column that contains the personnel causes.

Machines: Enter the column that contains the machine causes.

Materials: Enter the column that contains the materials causes.

Methods: Enter the column that contains the methods causes.

Measures: Enter the column that contains the measures causes.

Environment: Enter the column that contains the environment causes.

Effect: To display a label for the effect or problem that you are trying to solve, enter the desired text in this text box. You may use up to 72 characters.

Title: To display a title in lieu of the default title, type the desired text in this box.

Corresponding Session Command

%FISHBONE

Example: Using Fishbone

This dialog box and corresponding Session command illustrate how to produce a Fishbone with blank branches:

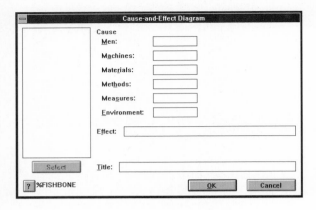

```
MTB > %Fishbone.
Executing form file: C:\MTBSEW\MACROS\Fishbone.MAC
Macro is running ... please wait
```

This command produces the following Fishbone chart:

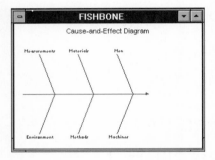

See also Tutorial 14.

Stat > Time Series

Minitab lets you investigate the behavior of data collected over time; to lag, difference, and plot a series; determine an appropriate model that describes the observed time series; and then use the model to predict or forecast future values of the series.

Stat > Time Series > Time Series Plot

This command is available on both the Stat > Time Series submenu and the Graph menu. See "Graph > Time Series Plot" for information.

Stat > Time Series > Trend Analysis

Use trend analysis to fit a particular type of trend line to a time series, or to detrend a time series. You may fit one of four models.

The Trend Analysis command generates a time series plot that shows the original data, the fitted trend line, and forecasts. It also displays the fitted trend equation and three measures to help you determine the accuracy of the fitted values: MAPE, MAD, and MSD.

Dialog Box Options

Variable: Enter the column containing the time series.

Model Type: Select the model you want to use. Be careful when interpreting the coefficients from the different models, as they have different meanings.

Linear: Tells Minitab to fit the linear trend model.

Quadratic: Tells Minitab to fit the quadratic trend model.

Exponential growth: Tells Minitab to fit the exponential growth trend model.

S-Curve (Pearl-Reed logistic): Tells Minitab to fit the Pearl-Reed logistic S-curve trend model.

Generate forecasts: Select if you want to generate forecasts. Forecasts appear in red on the time series plot.

Number of forecasts: Enter an integer to indicate how many forecasts you want.

Starting from origin: Enter a positive integer to specify a starting point for the forecasts. For example, if you specify 4 forecasts and 48 as the origin, Minitab computes forecasts for periods 49, 50, 51, and 52. If you leave this space blank, Minitab generates forecasts from the end of the data.

Title: Enter a title for the time series plot. (If you leave this blank, Minitab displays a default title.)

Trend Analysis Storage Dialog Box Options

Fits (trend line): Select to store the fitted values in the worksheet; Minitab uses these values to plot the trend line.

Residuals (detrended data): If you store the residuals you can generate diagnostic plots, or *detrended data*, which you can use to perform further analysis.

Forecasts: Select to store the forecasts. This option is available only if you generated forecasts in the initial Trend Analysis dialog box.

Trend Analysis Options Dialog Box Options

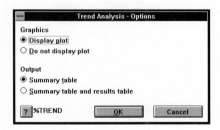

Graphics:

Display plot: Generate a time series plot that shows the original data, the fitted trend line, and forecasts.

Do not display plot: Suppress the time series plot.

Output:

Summary table: Display the default output — fitted trend equation, accuracy measures, and forecasts.

Summary table and results table: Display the default output plus a table of the original series, the fitted values, and the residuals (detrended data).

Corresponding Session Command
%TREND

Example: Using Trend Analysis

The following dialog box and equivalent Session command plot a linear trend of snowfall against time, using SNOW.MTW.

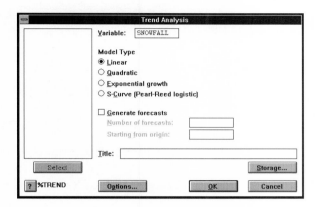

```
MTB > %Trend 'SNOWFALL'.
Executing from file: C:\MTBSEW\MACROS\Trend.MAC
```

This command produces output in both the Session window and the Graph window. The Graph window output is shown here:

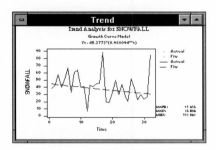

See also Tutorial 15.

Stat > Time Series > Decomposition

This subcommand performs classical decomposition on a time series, using either a multiplicative or an additive model. Classical decomposition decomposes a time series into trend, seasonal, and error components.

Decomposition displays a summary table and a set of plots. The summary table includes the trend equation, the seasonal indices, and three measures to help you determine the accuracy of the fitted values: MAPE , MAD , and MSD.

Dialog Box Options

Variable: Select the column containing the time series.

Seasonal length: Enter a positive integer greater than or equal to 2.

Model Type:

Multiplicative: Use the multiplicative model when the size of the seasonal pattern in the data depends on the level of the data. This model assumes that as the data increase, so does the seasonal pattern. Most time series exhibit such a pattern. The multiplicative model is

$$yt = Trend * Seasonal * Error$$

Additive: The additive model is

$$yt = Trend + Seasonal + Error$$

Model Components:

Trend plus seasonal: Select to include the trend component in the decomposition.

Seasonal only: Select to omit the trend component from the decomposition.

Initial seasonal period is: By default this value is 1 because Minitab assumes that the first data value in the series corresponds to the first seasonal period. Enter a different number to specify a different starting value. For example, if you have monthly data and the first observation is in June, then enter 6 to set the seasonal periods correctly.

Note: If the data contain a trend component but you omit it from the decomposition by selecting **Seasonal only**, it can adversely influence the estimates of the seasonal indices.

Generate forecasts: See "Time Series > Trend Analysis."

Title: Enter a custom title to each set of default plots. Minitab uses this title for all three sets of plots. (If you leave this blank, Minitab displays a default title.)

Options: See "Time Series > Trend Analysis" for information on Options.

Decomposition Storage Dialog Box Options

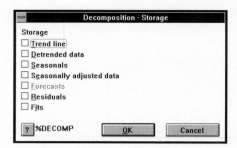

Trend line: Select to store the trend component data in the worksheet. This option includes only the trend component; it does not contain the error or seasonal component.

Detrended data: Select to store the detrended data. This option includes only the error and seasonal components; it does not contain the trend data.

Seasonals: Select to store the seasonal component data. This option includes only the seasonal component; it does not contain the error component or the trend data.

Seasonally adjusted data: Select to store the data which has had the seasonal component removed. This option includes only the trend and error components; it does not contain the seasonal component.

Forecasts: Select to store the forecasts. This option is available only if you generated forecasts in the main Decomposition dialog box.

Residuals: Select to store the residuals. If you store the residuals, you can generate diagnostic plots.

Fits: Select to store the fitted values. These values represent the combination of the trend and seasonal components, without the error component.

Corresponding Session Command

%DECOMP

Example: Using Decomposition

The following dialog box and equivalent Session command fit a linear trend and a six-year seasonal factor to the SNOW.MTW data.

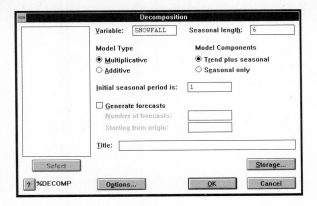

```
MTB > %Decomp 'SNOWFALL' 6;
SUBC>   Start 1.
Executing from file: C:\MTBSEW\MACROS\Decomp.MAC
```

This command produces output in the Session window and in three separate Graph windows. The following illustration shows the Graph arranged as tiles.

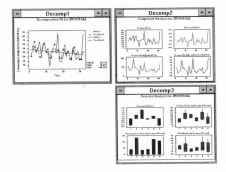

See also Tutorial 15.

Stat > Time Series > Moving Average

You can use moving averages to smooth out the noise in a time series and forecast future values of the series.

Minitab calculates a moving average by averaging consecutive groups of observations in a series. For example, suppose a series begins with the numbers 4, 5, 8, 9, and 10. The first two values of the moving average are missing. The third value of the moving average is the average of 4, 5, and 8; the fourth value is the average of 5, 8, and 9; the fifth value is the average of 8, 9, and 10; and so on.

Dialog Box Options

Variable: Select the column that contains the time series.

MA Length: Enter a positive whole number to indicate the desired length for the moving average. With non-seasonal time series, it is common to use short moving averages to smooth the series, although the length you select may depend on the amount of noise in the series. A longer moving average filters out more noise, but is also less sensitive to changes in the series. With seasonal series, it is common to use a moving average with a length equal to that of an annual cycle.

Center the moving averages: If you select this option, Minitab places the moving average values at the period in the center of the range rather than at the end of it. This feature is called *centering the moving average,* and positions the moving average values at their central positions in time.

Generate forecasts: See "Time Series > Trend Analysis."

Title: Enter a title for the time series plot. (If you leave this blank, Minitab enters a default title.)

Options: See "Time Series > Trend Analysis" for information on Options. You can also choose to plot one-period-ahead forecasts (predicted vs. actual) or smoothed values (smoothed vs. actual.)

Moving Average Storage Dialog Box Options

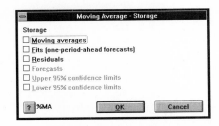

Moving averages: Select to store the moving averages, which are averages of consecutive groups of data in a time series, in the worksheet.

Fits (one-period-ahead forecasts): Select to store the fitted values. The uncentered moving average at time T is the fitted value for time $T + 1$.

Residuals: Select to store the residuals (the difference at time T between the actual data at time T and the fitted value at time T.

Forecasts: Select to store the forecasts. This option is available only if you generated forecasts in the initial Moving Average dialog box.

Upper 95% confidence limits: Select to store the upper 95% prediction limits for the forecasts.

Lower 95% confidence limits: Select to store the lower 95% prediction limits for the forecasts.

Corresponding Session Command

%MA

Example: Using Moving Average

The following dialog box and equivalent Session command average the first set of data values. They then average the next set, starting with the second value in the first set, and so on, using SNOW.MTW.

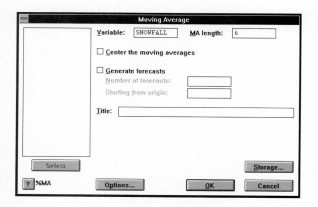

```
MTB > %MA 'SNOWFALL' 6.
Executing from file: C:\MTBSEW\MACROS\MA.MAC
```

This command produces the following graph in its own Graph window:

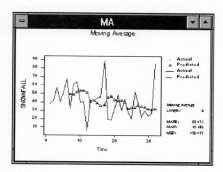

See also Tutorial 15.

Stat > Time Series > Single Exp Smoothing

This subcommand smooths out the noise in a time series and forecasts future values of the series.

This method uses an exponentially weighted average of all the past values of the series to calculate the smoothed value at each period. Minitab computes the initial smoothed value either by backcasting (if you choose Optimize), or by using the average of the first six observations (if you choose Use).

Dialog Box Options

Variable: Select the column that contains the time series. The time series cannot contain any missing values.

Weight to Use in Smoothing: Single exponential smoothing uses an exponentially weighted average of all the past values of the series to calculate the smoothed value at each period. This weight is usually between 0 and 1, although a range of 0 to 2 is theoretically acceptable.

Optimize: Uses the default weight, which Minitab computes by minimizing the sum of squared errors using the equivalent ARIMA (0,1,1) model. With this option, Minitab finds the initial smoothed value by backcasting.

Use: Select to enter a specific weight and enter a number between 0 and 2 (although it is unusual to use a number greater than 1). With this option, the initial smoothed value is the average of the first six observations.

Generate forecasts: See "Time Series > Trend Analysis."

Title: Enter a title for the time series plot. (If you leave this blank, Minitab enters a default title.)

Options: See "Time Series > Trend Analysis" for information about Options. You can also choose to plot one-period-ahead forecasts (predicted vs. actual) or smoothed values (smoothed vs. actual.)

Single Exponential Smoothing Storage Dialog Box Options

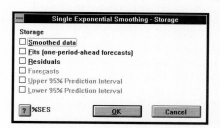

Smoothed data: Select to store the smoothed data in the worksheet. The smoothed value at time T is the fitted value for time $T + 1$.

See "Time Series > Moving Averages" for information about the remaining dialog box options.

Corresponding Session Command

%SES

Example: Using Single Exponential Smoothing

This dialog box and the equivalent Session command smooth out the noise in the yearly snowfall data stored in SNOW.MTW.

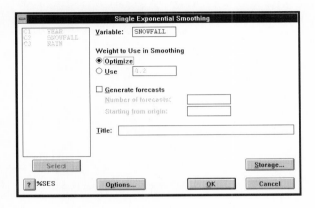

```
MTB > %SES 'SNOWFALL'.
Executing from file: C:\MTBSEW\MACROS\SES.MAC
```

This command produces the following graph in its own Graph window:

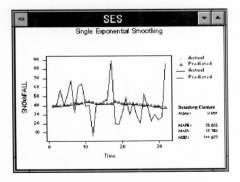

See also Tutorial 15.

Stat > Time Series > Double Exp Smoothing

You can use this command to perform Holt or Brown double exponential smoothing for a time series.

Use double exponential smoothing to smooth out noise and to forecast data that exhibit a trend. Both the Holt and Brown methods calculate a level component and a trend component at each period. Holt's method uses two smoothing parameters for updating these components, while Brown's method uses only one. Double exponential smoothing uses the level and trend components to generate forecasts. Initial values for these components are obtained either by backcasting (if you choose Optimize), or from a linear regression on time (if you choose Use).

Dialog Box Options

Variable: Select the column that contains the time series. The time series cannot contain any missing values.

Weight to Use in Smoothing:

Optimize: Select to use the default weights, or smoothing parameters, which Minitab computes by minimizing the sum of squared errors using the equivalent ARIMA (0,2,2) model. Using this option results in the Holt method. (Since Brown's method is equivalent to an equal-root ARIMA model, this option rarely corresponds to Brown's method.) To use Brown's method, choose the Use option instead. With Optimize, Minitab initializes the trend and level components by backcasting.

Use: select to enter specific values for the smoothing parameters. The first weight updates the level component, the second weight updates the trend component. Each weight must be a number from 0 to 1. To use Brown's method, enter two equal weights. With Use, Minitab initializes the trend and level components using a linear regression on time.

Generate forecasts: See "Time Series > Trend Analysis."

Title: Enter a title for the time series plot. (If you leave this blank, Minitab displays a default title.)

Options: See "Time Series > Trend Analysis" for information about Options. You can also choose to plot one-period-ahead forecasts (predicted vs. actual) or smoothed values (smoothed vs. actual.)

Double Exponential Smoothing Storage Dialog Box Options

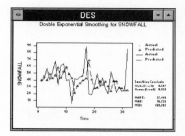

Smoothed data: Select to store the smoothed data in the worksheet.

Level estimates: Select to store the level components. Note that the level component at time T equals the smoothed value at time T, while adding the level and trend components at time T equals the one-period-ahead forecast for time $T + 1$.

Trend estimates: Select to store the trend components in the worksheet.

Fits (one-period-ahead-forecasts): Select to store the fitted values in the worksheet.

See "Time Series > Moving Averages" for information about the remaining dialog box options.

Corresponding Session Command

%DES

Example: Using Double Exponential Smoothing

The following dialog box and equivalent Session command use double exponential smoothing to smooth out the noise in the yearly snowfall data given in SNOW.MTW.

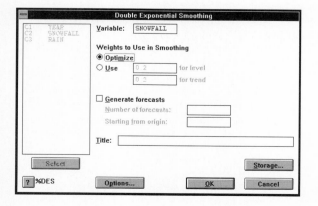

```
MTB > %DES 'SNOWFALL'.
Executing from file: C:\MTBSEW\MACROS\DES.MAC
```

This command produces the following graph in its own Graph window:

See also Tutorial 15.

Stat > Time Series > Winters' Method

This command performs Holt-Winters seasonal exponential smoothing, using either a multiplicative or an additive model, to smooth and forecast data that exhibit both a trend and a seasonal pattern.

This method employs a level component, a trend component, and a seasonal component at each period. It uses three weights, or smoothing parameters, to update the components at each period. Minitab obtains initial values for the level and trend components from a linear regression on time; it obtains initial values for the seasonal component from a dummy-variable regression using detrended data.

Dialog Box Options

Variable: Select the column containing the time series. The time series cannot contain any missing values.

Seasonal Length: Enter the length of the seasonal pattern. This must be a positive integer greater than or equal to 2.

Model Type:

Multiplicative: Choose the multiplicative model when the seasonal pattern in the data depends on the size of the data. In other words, the magnitude of the seasonal pattern increases as the series goes up, and decreases as the series goes down.

Additive: Choose the additive model when the seasonal pattern in the data does not depend on the size of the data. In other words, the magnitude of the seasonal pattern does not change as the series goes up or down.

Weights to Use in Smoothing: By default, all three weights, or smoothing parameters, are set to 0.2. Since an equivalent ARIMA model exists only for a very restricted form of the Holt-Winters model, optimal parameters are not found for Winters' Method as they are for Single Exponential Smoothing and Double Exponential Smoothing.

Level: Specify the level component weight; must be a number from 0 to 1.

Trend: Specify the trend component weight; must be a number from 0 to 1.

Seasonal: Specify the seasonal component weight; must be a number from 0 to 1.

Generate forecasts: See "Time Series > Trend Analysis."

Title: Enter a title for the time series plot. (If you leave this blank, Minitab displays a default title.)

Options: See "Time Series > Moving Averages" for information on Options.

Winters' Method Storage Dialog Box Options

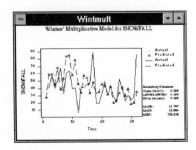

Check each item that you want to store in the worksheet.

Smoothed data: Select to store the smoothed data.

Level estimates: Select to store the level components. Note that multiplying (or adding for an additive model) the level and seasonal components for the same period results in the smoothed value for that period. Also, adding the level and trend components at time T and multiplying (or adding for an additive model) by the seasonal component for the same period from the previous year gives the one-period-ahead forecast for time $T + 1$.

Trend estimates: Select to store the trend components.

Seasonal estimates: Select to store the seasonal components.

Fits (one-period-ahead forecasts): Check to store the fitted values.

See "Time Series > Moving Averages" for the remaining dialog box options.

Corresponding Session Commands

%WINTMULT
%WINTADD

Example: Using Winters' Method

This dialog box and equivalent Session command perform Holt-Winters seasonal exponential smoothing using a multiplicative model to smooth snowfall data from SNOW.MTW.

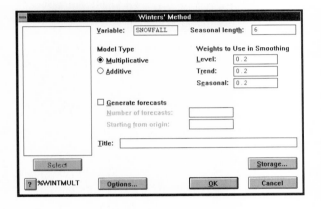

```
MTB > %Wintmult 'SNOWFALL' 6;
SUBC>    Weight 0.2 0.2 0.2.
Executing from file: C:\MTBSEW\MACROS\Wintmult.MAC
```

This command produces the following graph:

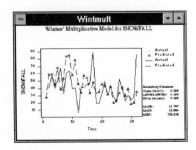

See also Tutorial 15.

Stat > Time Series > Differences

Choose the Differences subcommand to compute the differences between the elements of a column.

Dialog Box Options

Series: Select the column that contains the variable for which you want to compute differences.

Store differences in: Specify a storage column for the differences.

Lag: Specify the value for the lag. Minitab subtracts from each row the element K rows above, where K is the lag specified, and stores the differences in a new column. Minitab places asterisks in the first K rows of the new column.

Corresponding Session Command

DIFFERENCES

Example: Using Differences

The following dialog box and equivalent Session command compute differences in lag 2 for C1 SAMPLE, which contains the numbers 1, 3, 8, 12, and 7.

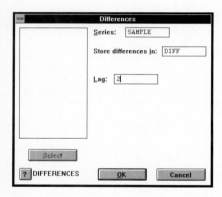

```
MTB > Name c2 = 'DIFF'
MTB > Difference 2 'SAMPLE' 'DIFF'.
```

This command produces a new column, C2 DIFF, in the Data window. Since the lag is 2, Minitab places *s in the first two rows of box C2. Row 3 of C2 contains 7 (= 8 – 1), row 4 contains 9 (= 12 – 3), and row 5 contains –1 (= 7 – 8).

C1	C2
SAMPLE	DIFF
1	*
3	*
8	7
12	9
7	−1

See also Tutorial 15.

Stat > Time Series > Lag

The Lag command moves numbers in a column down a specified number of rows, storing the result in a new column of the same length.

Dialog Box Options

Series: Select the column that contains the variable you want to lag.

Store lags in: Select the storage column for the lags.

Lag: Specify the value for the lag. Minitab moves the row elements of a column down K rows, where K is the lag specified, storing the result in a new column of the same length. Minitab places K missing value symbols (*) at the top of the output column. The output column has the same number of rows as the input column, so Minitab doesn't lag the last K values from the input column.

Corresponding Session Command

LAG

Example: Using Lag

The following dialog box and equivalent Session command compute the lags of the following observations in C1 SAMPLE: 1, 3, 8, 12, and 7, using a lag of 3, and stores the results in the next available column, naming the column LAGS.

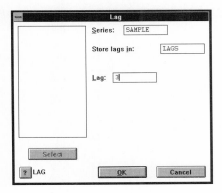

```
MTB > Name c2 = 'LAGS'
MTB > Lag 3 'SAMPLE' 'LAGS'.
```

This command produces a new column, C2 LAG, shown in the Data window. Since the lag is 3, the first value of 1 in C1 SAMPLE becomes the fourth value in C2 LAGS.

C1	C2
SAMPLE	LAGS
1	*
3	*
8	*
12	1
7	3

See also Tutorial 15.

Stat > Time Series > Autocorrelation

Use this command to compute and plot the autocorrelation of a time series.

Dialog Box Options

Series: Select the column that contains the response variable from the time series.

Default number of lags: Choose to have Minitab set $K = \sqrt{n} + 10$, where K is the number of lags and n is the number of observations in the series.

Number of lags: Choose to specify the number of lags desired and then enter the number in the text box.

Store ACF: Select to store the autocorrelation values. Minitab stores the values in the next available column.

Corresponding Session Command

ACF

Example: Using Autocorrelation

The following dialog box and equivalent Session command compute the autocorrelations for observations of river temperatures (stored in C2 TEMP) taken upstream from a power plant over a period of time with a 24-hour lag, using RIVERB.MTW.

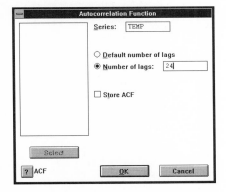

```
MTB > ACF 24 'TEMP'.
```

This command produces the following autocorrelation plot:

```
ACF of TEMP

             -1.0 -0.8 -0.6 -0.4 -0.2  0.0  0.2  0.4  0.6  0.8  1.0
             +----+----+----+----+----+----+----+----+----+----+
  1   0.843                            XXXXXXXXXXXXXXXXXXXXXXX
  2   0.703                            XXXXXXXXXXXXXXXXXXX
  3   0.550                            XXXXXXXXXXXXXXX
  4   0.380                            XXXXXXXXXX
  5   0.231                            XXXXXXX
  6   0.079                            XXX
  7  -0.067                         XXX
  8  -0.187                       XXXXX
  9  -0.265                     XXXXXXXX
 10  -0.352                   XXXXXXXXXX
 11  -0.379                   XXXXXXXXXX
 12  -0.380                   XXXXXXXXXX
 13  -0.361                   XXXXXXXXXX
 14  -0.292                     XXXXXXX
 15  -0.212                       XXXXXX
 16  -0.126                         XXXX
 17  -0.013                           X
 18   0.056                            XX
 19   0.112                            XXXX
 20   0.205                            XXXXXX
 21   0.289                            XXXXXXXX
 22   0.341                            XXXXXXXXX
 23   0.363                            XXXXXXXXXX
 24   0.321                            XXXXXXXXX
```

See also Tutorial 15.

Stat > Time Series > Partial Autocorrelation

You can compute and plot the partial autocorrelation of a time series by choosing this subcommand.

Dialog Box Options

Series: Select the column that contains the response variable of the time series.

Default number of lags: Choose to have Minitab set $K = \sqrt{n} + 10$, where K is the number of lags and n is the number of observations in the series.

Number of lags: Choose to indicate the number of lags desired and then specify the number in the text box.

Store PACF: Select to store the partial autocorrelation values. They will be stored in the next available column.

Corresponding Session Command

PACF

Example: Using Partial Autocorrelation

The following dialog box and equivalent Session command compute the partial autocorrelations for observations of river temperatures (stored in C2 TEMP) taken upstream from a power plant over a period of time with a 24-hour lag, using RIVERB.MTW.

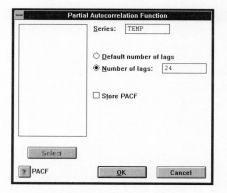

```
MTB > PACF 24 'TEMP'.
```

This command produces the following partial autocorrelation plot:

```
PACF of TEMP

             -1.0 -0.8 -0.6 -0.4 -0.2  0.0  0.2  0.4  0.6  0.8  1.0
             +----+----+----+----+----+----+----+----+----+----+
  1   0.843                            XXXXXXXXXXXXXXXXXXXXXXX
  2  -0.023                           XX
  3  -0.128                         XXXX
  4  -0.161                       XXXXX
  5  -0.052                          XX
  6  -0.123                         XXXX
  7  -0.118                         XXXX
  8  -0.068                          XXX
  9   0.018                            X
 10  -0.157                       XXXXX
 11   0.049                            XX
 12   0.004                            X
 13  -0.009                           X
 14   0.079                            XXX
 15   0.042                            XX
 16   0.010                            X
 17   0.102                            XXXX
 18  -0.102                         XXXX
 19  -0.009                           X
 20   0.166                            XXXXX
 21   0.123                            XXXX
 22  -0.007                           X
 23  -0.038                          XX
 24  -0.122                         XXXX
```

See also Tutorial 15.

Stat > Time Series > Cross Correlation

This command computes and plots the cross correlation between two time series.

Dialog Box Options

First Series: Select the column that contains the response variable of first time series.

Second Series: Select the column that contains the response variable of the second time series.

Default number of lags: Choose to have Minitab set $K = -(\sqrt{n} + 10)$ to $K = +(\sqrt{n} + 10)$, where K is the number of lags and n is the number of observations in the series.

Number of lags: Choose to specify the number of lags desired and then enter the number in the text box.

Corresponding Session Command

CCF

Example: Using Cross Correlation

The following dialog box and equivalent Session command cross correlate river temperatures (stored in C2 TEMP) taken hourly upstream from a power plant with the pH value of the water (stored in C3 pH) using the data in RIVERB.MTW.

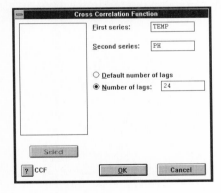

```
MTB > CCF 24 'TEMP' 'PH'
```

This command produces the following display:

```
CCF - correlates TEMP(t) and PH(t+k)

       -1.0 -0.8 -0.6 -0.4 -0.2  0.0  0.2  0.4  0.6  0.8  1.0
       +----+----+----+----+----+----+----+----+----+----+
 -24   0.381                        XXXXXXXXXX
 -23   0.331                        XXXXXXXXX
 -22   0.231                        XXXXXXX
 -21   0.093                        XXX
 -20  -0.053                     XX
 -19  -0.201                  XXXXXX
 -18  -0.303                XXXXXXXX
 -17  -0.392              XXXXXXXXXX
 -16  -0.489            XXXXXXXXXXXXX
 -15  -0.555           XXXXXXXXXXXXXX
 -14  -0.590          XXXXXXXXXXXXXXX
 -13  -0.585          XXXXXXXXXXXXXXX
 -12  -0.539           XXXXXXXXXXXXXX
 -11  -0.473            XXXXXXXXXXXX
 -10  -0.377              XXXXXXXXXX
  -9  -0.229                 XXXXXXX
  -8  -0.076                     XXX
  -7   0.071                        XXX
  -6   0.242                        XXXXXXX
  -5   0.374                        XXXXXXXXXX
  -4   0.491                        XXXXXXXXXXXXX
  -3   0.572                        XXXXXXXXXXXXXXX
  -2   0.625                        XXXXXXXXXXXXXXXXX
  -1   0.653                        XXXXXXXXXXXXXXXXX
   0   0.700                        XXXXXXXXXXXXXXXXXXX
   1   0.575                        XXXXXXXXXXXXXXX
   2   0.455                        XXXXXXXXXXXX
   3   0.340                        XXXXXXXXX
   4   0.209                        XXXXXX
   5   0.098                        XXX
   6  -0.019                     X
   7  -0.121                  XXXX
   8  -0.213                 XXXXXX
   9  -0.257                XXXXXXX
  10  -0.288               XXXXXXXX
  11  -0.283               XXXXXXXX
  12  -0.259                XXXXXXX
  13  -0.210                 XXXXXX
  14  -0.123                  XXXX
  15  -0.030                     XX
  16   0.069                        XXX
  17   0.172                        XXXX
  18   0.234                        XXXXXX
  19   0.287                        XXXXXXX
  20   0.339                        XXXXXXXXX
  21   0.373                        XXXXXXXXXX
  22   0.371                        XXXXXXXXXX
  23   0.363                        XXXXXXXXXX
  24   0.305                        XXXXXXXXX
```

See also Tutorial 15.

Stat > Time Series > ARIMA

The ARIMA command computes an autoregressive integrated moving average: it fits seasonal or nonseasonal models to a time series and lets you predict values.

Dialog Box Options

Series: Select the column that contains the response variable of the time series you want to fit.

Fit seasonal model: Select to fit a seasonal model.

Period: Specify the number of units in a complete cycle.

Nonseasonal and **Seasonal:** The ARIMA model uses three parameters designated: Autoregressive, Difference, and Moving average.

Autoregressive: Specify the order of the autoregressive (AR) component (p). Specify the order of the seasonal component (P) in the second box.

Difference: Specify the number of differences (d) used to discount trends over time. There must be at least three data points left after differencing. Specify the number of differences for the seasonal component (D) in the second box.

Moving average: Specify the order of the moving average (MA) component (q). Specify the order of the seasonal component (Q) in the second box.

Include constant term in model: Select to include a constant term (the y-intercept) in the ARIMA model.

Starting values for coefficients: Select to specify the initial parameter values, and then specify the column that contains the values. You must enter the values in the order that the parameters appear in the output: p (AR values), P (seasonal AR values), q (MA values), Q (seasonal MA values), and then (optionally) the constant. If you do not specify the initial parameter values, the default is 0.1 for the parameters, except for the constant.

Storage: You can store certain diagnostics for further analysis.

Residuals: Select to store the residuals.

Fits: Select to store the fitted values.

Coefficients: Select to store estimated coefficients.

There are a number of specifications you must observe:

1. At least one of the p/P or q/Q parameters must be non-zero, and none may exceed five.

2. The maximum number of parameters that Minitab can estimate is ten.

3. There must be at least three data points left after differencing. That is, $S*D + d + 2$ must be less than the number of points, where S is the length of a season.

4. The maximum "back order" for the model is 100. In practice, this condition is always satisfied if $S*D + d + p + P + q + Q$ is at most 100.

5. The ARIMA model normally includes a constant term only if there is no differencing (that is, $d = D = 0$).

6. Minitab allows missing observations only at the beginning or the end of a series, not in the middle.

7. The seasonal component of this model is multiplicative, and thus is appropriate when the amount of cyclical variation is proportional to the mean.

ARIMA Forecast Dialog Box Options

Lead: Specify the number of forecasts you want Minitab to generate.

Origin: Specify the origin at which the forecasts should begin. If the origin is not specified, Minitab sets it to the end of the series and the forecasts are for the future.

Storage: Control the storage of ARIMA results.

Forecasts: Specify a storage column for the forecasted values (possibly for later plotting).

Lower limits: Specify a storage column for the lower confidence limits for the forecasts.

Upper limits: Specify a storage column for the upper confidence limits for the forecasts.

Corresponding Session Command
ARIMA

The BRIEF Session command can be used to control the amount of output that Minitab produces, although it is not available as a menu command. K is an integer from 0 to 4. BRIEF 2 is the default output. The levels of output are as follows:

K = 0	Minitab doesn't print anything but it stores all requested output.
K = 1	Minitab prints the table of final estimates, differencing information, residual sum of squares, and number of observations
K = 2	Minitab prints the table of estimates at each iteration. If back forecasts are not dying out rapidly, Minitab also prints them.
K = 3	Minitab prints the same information as for K = 2 plus the correlation matrix of the estimated parameters.
K = 4	Minitab prints the back forecasts, regardless of status.

Example: Using ARIMA

These dialog boxes and equivalent Session commands use ARIMA to forecast river temperatures, based on the temperature data in RIVERB.MTW.

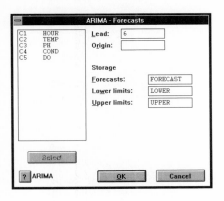

```
MTB > Name c6 = 'FORECAST' c7 = 'LOWER' c8 = 'UPPER'
MTB > ARIMA 2 0 0 0 0 0 12 'TEMP';
SUBC>    Constant;
SUBC>    Forecast 6 'FORECAST' 'LOWER' 'UPPER'.
```

This command produces the following display in the Session window (only the forecast portion of the output is shown). See also Tutorial 15.

```
Forecasts from period 95
                         95 Percent Limits
Period    Forecast      Lower      Upper      Actual
  96      30.0795      28.6768    31.4823
  97      30.2830      28.3902    32.1758
  98      30.4596      28.2692    32.6500
  99      30.6126      28.2233    33.0018
 100      30.7449      28.2169    33.2729
 101      30.8595      28.2324    33.4867
```

Stat > Tables

The commands on the Tables submenu let you print one-way and multiway contingency tables, print statistics for counts and percents of associated variables, and perform a chi-square analysis.

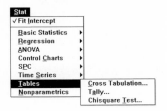

Stat > Tables > Cross Tabulation

The Cross Tabulation command produces one-way or multiway contingency tables and tables of statistics for associated variables, and displays the output in an easy-to-read format in the Session window. To compute and store these statistics plus additional statistics, such as skewness and kurtosis, see the Session command STATS in online Help (this is an experimental command).

Dialog Box Options

Classification Variables: Select the columns that contain the classification variables. The first column determines the row headings of the table; the second column determines the column headings (list up to 10). Minitab produces a separate table for every possible combination of values from the remaining columns. All columns must contain integers between –10000 and +10000, or the missing value symbol (*).

Display: You can obtain summary statistics only for a set of associated variables. For summary statistics of a specific classification variable, use Stat > Tables > Tally.

Counts: Select to display the total number of non-missing values for each cell and for the margins.

Row percents: Select to display the percentage each cell represents of the total observations in the row.

Column percents: Select to display the percentage each cell represents of the total observations in the column.

Total percents: Select to display the percentage each cell represents of all the observations in the table.

Chisquare analysis: Select to display the chi-square statistic.

Frequencies are in: Select if the data have been input as partial- or full-frequency counts rather than raw data values. Minitab normally assumes that each row in the columns you list in the Classification Variables text box refers to one case. Select the column(s) that contain the frequencies (or weights) for each column of the table.

Cross Tabulation Summaries Dialog Box Options

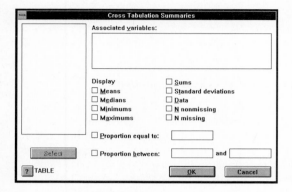

Associated variables: Select the columns that contain the variable(s) to be summarized.

Display: You can obtain summary statistics for a set of associated variables. For summary statistics on a specific column, use Stat > Basic Statistics > Descriptive Statistics.

Means: Select to display cell means.

Medians: Select to display cell medians.

Minimums: Select to display cell minimums.

Maximums: Select to display cell maximums.

Sums: Select to display cell sums.

Standard deviations: Select to display cell standard deviations.

Data: Select to list all of the data in each cell.

N nonmissing: Select to display the number of non-missing values.

N missing: Select to display the number of missing values.

Proportion equal to: Select to print the proportion of observations with the specified value for each cell in

the table. Specify the desired value in the text box. You cannot use tables that contain missing values.

Proportion between [ ] and [ ]: Select to print the proportion of observations that fall in the specified range for each cell in the table. Specify the low and high values in the boxes. Minitab cannot use tables that contain missing values.

Cross Tabulation Options Dialog Box Options

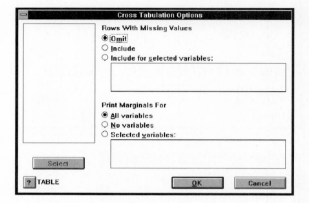

Rows with Missing Values: Minitab provides options for the inclusion of missing data in the classification table.

Omit: Choose to omit rows with missing values.

Include: Choose to include rows with missing values. Minitab adds a row or column labeled *missing* that contains counts of the missing observations in each cell for any variables with missing values.

Include for selected variables: Choose to include rows with missing values for specific classification variables, and then specify the column(s) to include. Minitab adds a row or column labeled *missing* to the display that contains counts of the missing observations in each cell for variables with missing values.

Print Marginals For: Minitab provides options for displaying row and column marginal statistics for the designated classification variable.

All variables: Choose to display marginal statistics for all classification variables.

No variables: Choose to exclude marginal statistics from the display.

Selected variables: Choose to include marginal statistics for specific classification variables, and then specify the column(s) for which to display marginals.

Corresponding Session Command
TABLE

Example: Using Cross Tabulation

The following dialog box and equivalent Session command produce a contingency table of income and stores, using the 12 JEANSB.MTW file you produced in Tutorial 12.

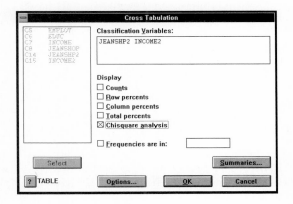

```
MTB > Table 'JEANSHP2' 'INCOME2';
SUBC>   ChiSquare.
```

This command produces the following display:

```
ROWS: JEANSHP2    COLUMNS: INCOME2

             1      3      4      5      7     ALL

   4        14     10     24     12      3      63
   5        21     22     29     15      3      90
   6        11      8     14     17     14      64
  10        13     10     23     15     13      74
 ALL        59     50     90     59     33     291

CHI-SQUARE =   26.273   WITH D.F. =    12
```

See also Tutorial 12.

Stat > Tables > Tally

To print a one-way table of counts and percents for the specified variables, choose the Tally subcommand.

Dialog Box Options

Variables: Select the columns for tallying. The columns must contain integers between –9999 and +9999, or the missing value symbol (*).

Display: Minitab can display summary information for each distinct value in the column.

Counts: Select to display the number of times each distinct value occurs.

Percents: Select to display the relative frequency of each nonmissing value.

Cumulative counts: Select to display cumulative counts of the nonmissing values.

Cumulative percents: Select to display cumulative relative frequencies of the nonmissing values.

Corresponding Session Command
TALLY

Example: Using Tally

The following dialog box and equivalent Session command illustrate how to tally a column of firms by employment class size, using ECLASS.MTW.

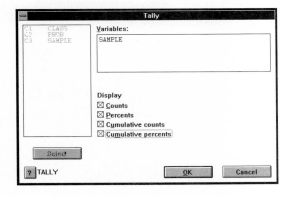

```
MTB > Tally 'SAMPLE';
SUBC>   Counts;
SUBC>   Percents;
SUBC>   CumCounts;
SUBC>   CumPercents.
```

This command produces the following display:

```
SAMPLE   COUNT  PERCENT  CUMCNT  CUMPCT
    1     274    27.40    274    27.40
    2     290    29.00    564    56.40
    3     243    24.30    807    80.70
    4      64     6.40    871    87.10
    5     129    12.90   1000   100.00
   N=    1000
```

See also Tutorials 5 and 12.

Stat > Tables > Chisquare Test

This command performs a chi-square test for the table of counts in the specified columns. If you have raw data and first need to form the contingency table, use Stat > Tables > Cross Tabulation and select the Chisquare analysis check box.

Minitab prints a table of observed values and expected values, the total chi-square statistic as the sum of its components from each cell of the table, and the number of degrees of freedom. Minitab also lists the number of cells with small expected frequencies (less than five), if any.

Dialog Box Options

Columns containing the table: Select the columns that contain the frequency table. You may select up to seven columns and they must contain integer values.

Corresponding Session Command

CHISQUARE

Example: Using Chisquare Test

The following Session command and equivalent dialog box perform a chi-square test of income categories using STORES.MTW.

```
MTB > ChiSquare 'UNDER25K' '25KTO35K' '35KTO50K' '50KTO75K' '75K&OVER'.
```

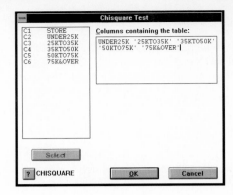

This dialog box and command produce the following display:

```
Expected counts are printed below observed counts

         UNDER25K 25KTO35K 35KTO50K 50KTO75K 75K&OVER    Total
    1        14       10       24       12        3        63
          12.77    10.82    19.48    12.77     7.14

    2        21       22       29       15        3        90
          18.25    15.46    27.84    18.25    10.21

    3        11        8       14       17       14        64
          12.98    11.00    19.79    12.98     7.26

    4        13       10       23       15       13        74
          15.00    12.71    22.89    15.00     8.39

Total        59       50       90       59       33       291

ChiSq =  0.118 +  0.063 +  1.046 +  0.047 +  2.404 +
         0.415 +  2.763 +  0.049 +  0.578 +  5.088 +
         0.301 +  0.817 +  1.696 +  1.248 +  6.263 +
         0.268 +  0.580 +  0.001 +  0.000 +  2.531 = 26.273
df = 12
```

See also Tutorial 12.

Stat > Nonparametrics

The commands on the Nonparametrics submenu let you perform a one-sample sign test and confidence interval, one-sample Wilcoxon signed rank test and confidence interval, Mann-Whitney test, Kruskal-Wallis test, Friedman test, or runs test. You can also compute pairwise (Walsh) averages, pairwise differences, and pairwise slopes.

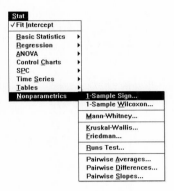

Stat > Nonparametrics > 1-Sample Sign

The 1-Sample Sign subcommand computes a nonparametric sign test for the median for one or more columns, or a sign confidence interval for the median.

Dialog Box Options

Variables: Select the column(s) that contain the variable(s) you want to analyze.

Confidence interval: Choose to calculate a sign confidence interval. Minitab calculates three confidence intervals for the median for each column listed. The first interval shows the achievable confidence just below the level specified, the middle interval approximates the level specified using nonlinear interpolation, and the third shows the achievable confidence just below the level specified.

Level: Specify the desired level of confidence.

Test median: Choose to perform a sign-test, and then specify the null hypothesis test median value.

Alternative: Click the drop-down arrow to choose the type of test that Minitab performs by selecting less than (lower-tailed), not equal (two-tailed), or greater than (upper-tailed) from the drop-down list box.

Corresponding Session Commands

SINTERVAL
STEST

Example: Using 1-Sample Sign

The following dialog box and equivalent Session command give confidence intervals for the median TV-viewing times of husbands, using the data in TVVIEW.MTW.

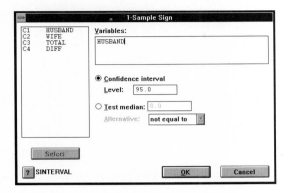

```
MTB > SInterval 95.0 'HUSBAND'.
```

This command produces the following display:

```
Sign confidence interval for median

                              ACHIEVED
              N   MEDIAN    CONFIDENCE    CONFIDENCE INTERVAL
POSITION
HUSBAND      10    32.00      0.8906      (  27.00,    38.00)
3
                             0.9500      (  24.95,    39.71)
NLI
```

See also Tutorial 13.

Stat > Nonparametrics > 1-Sample Wilcoxon

You can perform either a one-sample Wilcoxon signed-rank test of the median or a one-sample Wilcoxon confidence interval for the median by choosing this command.

The test assumes that the data are a random sample from a symmetric continuous population. This test is slightly less powerful than the t-test if the population is normal, but it may be considerably more powerful for other populations.

Dialog Box Options

Variables: Select the column(s) that contain the variable(s) you want to analyze. Each column must be a random sample from a continuous, symmetric distribution.

Confidence interval: Choose to calculate a one-sample Wilcoxon confidence interval for the median for each column listed.

Level: Specify the desired level of confidence.

Test median: Choose to perform a Wilcoxon signed-rank test, and then specify the null hypothesis test median value. The Wilcoxon statistic is the sum of the ranks corresponding to positive differences, and the point estimate of the population median is the center of the Walsh averages.

Alternative: Click the drop-down arrow to choose the type of test that Minitab performs by selecting less than (lower-tailed), not equal (two-tailed), or greater than (upper-tailed) from the drop-down list box.

Corresponding Session Commands

WINTERVAL
WTEST

Example: 1-Sample Wilcoxon

The following dialog box and equivalent Session command give an approximate 95% confidence interval for the median TV-viewing times of husbands, using the data in TVVIEW.MTW.

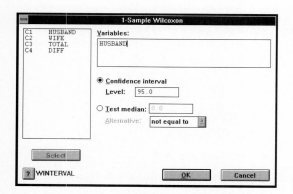

```
MTB > WInterval 95.0 'HUSBAND'.
```

This command produces the following display:

	N	ESTIMATED MEDIAN	ACHIEVED CONFIDENCE	CONFIDENCE INTERVAL
HUSBAND	10	32.5	94.7	(25.5, 41.5)

See also Tutorial 13.

Stat > Nonparametrics > Mann-Whitney

The Mann-Whitney command performs a two-sample rank test for the difference between two population medians; it also calculates the corresponding point estimate and confidence interval. The Mann-Whitney test is sometimes called the two-sample Wilcoxon rank sum test.

Dialog Box Options

First sample: Select the column that contains the response variable of the first group.

Second sample: Select the column that contains the response variable of the second group.

Confidence level: Specify the desired level of confidence; Minitab attains the closest level possible.

Alternative: Click the drop-down arrow to choose the type of text that Minitab performs by selecting less than (lower-tailed), not equal (two-tailed), or greater than (upper-tailed) from the drop-down list box.

Corresponding Session Command

MANN-WHITNEY

Example: Using Mann-Whitney

The following dialog box and corresponding Session command use the data in AGE.MTW to test whether there is a difference between the median death age for males and females.

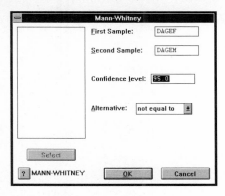

```
MTB > Mann-Whitney 95.0 'DAGEF' 'DAGEM';
SUBC>   Alternative 0.
```

This command produces the following display:

```
DAGEF     N =  19    Median =      75.00
DAGEM     N =  18    Median =      72.50
Point estimate for ETA1-ETA2 is      2.00
95.3 Percent C.I. for ETA1-ETA2 is (-8.00,13.00)
W = 375.0
Test of ETA1 = ETA2  vs.  ETA1 ~= ETA2 is significant at 0.6816
The test is significant at 0.6812 (adjusted for ties)

Cannot reject at alpha = 0.05
```

See also Tutorial 13.

Stat > Nonparametrics > Kruskal-Wallis

Use the Kruskal-Wallis command to perform a nonparametric test for differences among several population medians. This command extends the Mann-Whitney test to any number of groups.

Dialog Box Options

Response: Select the column that contains the response variable from all the samples.

Factor: Select the column that contains the subscripts to identify each group. The factor levels must be integers from –9999 to +9999, or missing values (*). They need not be consecutive nor in any special order. The Set Patterned Data command can be helpful in entering the level numbers of a factor.

Corresponding Session Command

KRUSKAL

Example: Using Kruskal-Wallis

The following dialog box and equivalent Session command test whether there is a difference among the crime rates reported in C4 CRIMERTE in different regions (C3 REGION), using CRIMES.MTW.

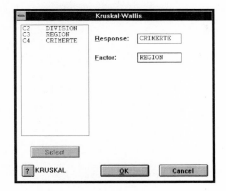

```
MTB > Kruskal-Wallis 'CRIMERTE' 'REGION'.
```

This command produces the following display:

```
LEVEL    NOBS    MEDIAN   AVE. RANK   Z VALUE
   1       9      462.0      21.1      -1.09
   2      12      417.5      21.1      -1.31
   3      17      726.0      33.9       2.70
   4      13      523.0      23.5      -0.69
OVERALL  51                  26.0

H = 7.49  d.f. = 3  p = 0.058
```

See also Tutorial 13.

Stat > Nonparametrics > Friedman

This subcommand performs a nonparametric analysis of a randomized block experiment, and thus provides an alternative to the Twoway command.

Randomized block experiments are a generalization of paired experiments, and Friedman is a generalization of the paired sign test. Friedman tests the null hypothesis that treatment has no effect. Additivity is not required for the test, but is necessary for the estimate of treatment effects.

This command requires exactly one observation per cell; missing data are not allowed for the response variable.

Dialog Box Options

Response: Select the column that contains the response variable.

Treatment: Select the column that contains the subscripts to identify each treatment. The factor levels must be integers from –9999 to +9999, or missing values (*). They need not be consecutive nor in any special order. The Set Patterned Data command can be helpful in entering the level numbers of a factor.

Blocks: Select the column that contains the subscripts to identify the blocks. The subscripts must be integers from –9999 to +9999, or missing values (*). They need not be consecutive nor in any special order. The Set Patterned Data command can be helpful in entering the level numbers of a factor.

Store residuals: Select to store the residuals. Minitab calculates the residuals by subtracting the adjusted block median from the observation adjusted for treatment effect.

Store fits: Select to store the fitted values. The fits are the sum of the treatment effect plus the adjusted block median.

Corresponding Session Command

FRIEDMAN

Example: Using Friedman

The following dialog box and equivalent Session command test whether there is a differences in student grades from test to test, using MARKS.MTW. The Session commands show how to create the necessary columns. (Be sure you type TREATMNT with just eight characters.)

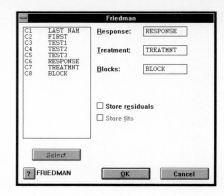

```
MTB > Name c6 = 'RESPONSE' c7 = 'TREATMNT'
MTB > Stack ('TEST1') ('TEST2') ('TEST3') ('RESPONSE');
SUBC>   Subscripts 'TREATMNT'.
MTB > Name c8 = 'BLOCK'
MTB > Set 'BLOCK'
DATA>   3( 1 : 24 / 1 )1
DATA>   End.
MTB > Friedman 'RESPONSE' 'TREATMNT' 'BLOCK'.
```

This command produces the following display:

```
Friedman test of RESPONSE by TREATMNT blocked by BLOCK

S = 0.65  d.f. = 2  p = 0.724
S = 0.67  d.f. = 2  p = 0.714 (adjusted for ties)

                     Est.    Sum of
TREATMNT    N      Median    RANKS
      1    24       80.25     48.5
      2    24       79.75     50.5
      3    24       76.25     45.0

Grand median  =    78.75
```

See also Tutorial 13.

Stat > Nonparametrics > Runs Test

You can perform a two-sided runs test to determine if the order of the data is random by choosing the Runs Test command. A *run* is a series of one or more observations in a row that are greater than a given number, or one or more observations in a row that are less than or equal to that number.

Dialog Box Options

Variables: Select the column(s) that contain the variable(s) whose order you want to test for randomness.

Above and below the mean: Choose to use the mean as the baseline to determine the number of runs.

Above and below: Choose to use a value other than the mean as the baseline to determine the number of runs; specify the desired value in the text box.

Corresponding Session Command

RUNS

Example: Using Runs Test

The following dialog box and equivalent Session command determine whether heights data were collected in random order, using HEIGHT.MTW.

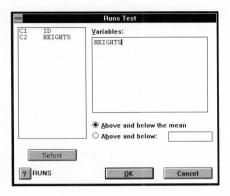

```
MTB > Runs 'HEIGHTS'.
```

This command produces the following display:

```
HEIGHTS

K =    65.3567

The observed no. of runs =   35
The expected no. of runs =   30.8667
32 Observations above K   28 below
        The test is significant at  0.2798
        Cannot reject at alpha = 0.05
```

See also Tutorial 13.

Stat > Nonparametrics > Pairwise Averages

The Pairwise Averages command calculates the averages of all possible pairs of values in a column, including each value with itself.

For n data values, Minitab stores $n \times (n + 1) / 2$ pairwise (or Walsh) averages.

Dialog Box Options

Variable: Select the column for which you want to obtain averages.

Store averages in: Specify the storage column for the Walsh averages.

Store indices in: Select to store the indices for each average in the two columns you specify in the text boxes. The Walsh average, $(x_i + y_j) / 2$, has indices i and j. Minitab places the values of i and j in the first and second columns, respectively.

Corresponding Session Command

WALSH

Example: Using Pairwise Averages

The following dialog box and equivalent Session command obtain Walsh averages for C1 SAMPLE, which contains the values 1, 2, and 3.

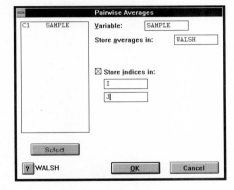

```
MTB > Name c2 = 'WALSH' c3 = 'I' c4 = 'J'
MTB > Walsh 'SAMPLE' 'WALSH' 'I' 'J'.
```

This command produces the following display:

C1	C2	C3	C4
SAMPLE	WALSH	I	J
1	1.0	1	1
2	1.5	1	2
3	2.0	2	2
	2.0	1	3
	2.5	2	3
	3.0	3	3

See also Tutorial 13.

Stat > Nonparametrics > Pairwise Differences

This command computes all the possible differences between pairs of elements from two columns by subtracting a value in the second column from the corresponding value in the first column.

Dialog Box Options

First variable: Select the first column. Minitab subtracts the values in the second column from the values in this column.

Second variable: Select the second column. Minitab subtracts the values in this column from the first column specified.

Store differences in: Specify the storage column for the differences.

Store indices in: Select to store the indices for each difference, and then specify two columns to contain them. The difference, $(x_i - y_j)$, has indices i and j. Minitab places the values of i and j in the first and second columns, respectively.

Corresponding Session Command

WDIFF

Example: Using Pairwise Differences

The following dialog box and equivalent Session command obtain pairwise differences for C1 SAMPLE1, which contains the values 1, 2, and 3; and for C2 SAMPLE2, which contains the values 10, 12, and 13.

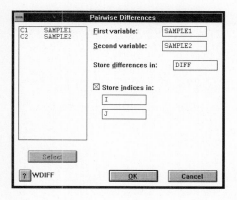

```
MTB > Name c3 = 'DIFF' c4 = 'I' c5 = 'J'
MTB > WDifferences 'SAMPLE1' 'SAMPLE2' 'DIFF' 'I' 'J'.
```

This command produces the following display:

C1	C2	C3	C4	C5
SAMPLE1	SAMPLE2	DIFF	I	J
1	10	−9	1	1
2	12	−11	1	2
3	13	−12	1	3
		−8	2	1
		−10	2	2

See also Tutorial 13.

Stat > Nonparametrics > Pairwise Slopes

You can compute the slope between every pair of data from two columns of equal length by choosing Pairwise Slopes.

You can use slopes to find robust estimates of the slope of a line through the data from two columns. There will be $n \times (n - 1) / 2$ slopes. If any observations are missing or the slope is undefined, Minitab computes the slope as missing.

Dialog Box Options

Y variable: Select the column that contains the y-variable.

X variable: Select the column that contains the x-variable.

Store slopes in: Specify the storage column for the slopes.

Store indices in: Select to store the indices for each slope, then specify two columns to contain them.

Corresponding Session Command

WSLOPE

Example: Using Pairwise Slopes

The following dialog box and equivalent Session command obtain pairwise slopes for C2 SAMPLE2, which contains values 3, 5, 2, and 6; and for C1 SAMPLE1, which contains values 1.1, 2.0, 1.1, and 3.0.

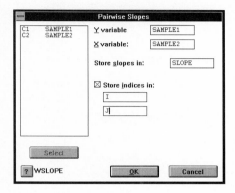

```
MTB > Name c3 = 'SLOPE' c4 = 'I' c5 = 'J'
MTB > WSlopes 'SAMPLE1' 'SAMPLE2' 'SLOPE' 'I' 'J'.
```

This command produces the following display:

C1	C2	C3	C4	C5
SAMPLE1	SAMPLE2	SLOPE	I	J
1.1	3	0.45000	2	1
2.0	5	0.00000	3	1
1.1	2	0.30000	3	2
3.0	6	0.63333	4	1
		1.00000	4	2

See also Tutorial 13.

The Window Menu

The Window menu lets you control the placement of windows that appear on your screen, work with Graph windows, and move among windows.

At the bottom of the Window menu, Minitab displays a list of all the available windows, including Session, Data, History, Info, and any open Graph windows. To move to any of these windows, you either select it from the Window menu, use the corresponding keyboard shortcuts, or press Ctrl+Tab to cycle through the Minitab windows.

See also Tutorials 1, 2, and 5.

Window > Cascade

The Cascade command arranges all the open Minitab windows so that they overlap with each title bar visible (if possible).

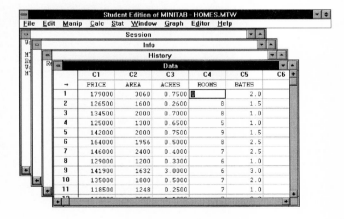

Window > Tile

If you choose Tile, Minitab arranges all the open Minitab windows so that they fit next to each other without overlapping, like a checkerboard (if possible).

Occasionally, some Minitab windows overlap due to a minimum size requirement.

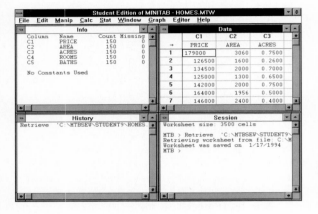

Window > Minimize All

This command reduces all the open windows to icons and places them at the bottom of the screen; it functions like the minimize button found to the right of the title bar.

Window > Restore Icons

Restore Icons opens any icons into windows the same size they were before you minimized them during the session.

Window > Arrange Icons

This command automatically arranges any icons along the bottom of the Minitab window.

Window > Discard Graph

You can delete Professional graphs by choosing Discard Graph. You may elect to delete a single graph or delete all the graphs with one command. Minitab can retain at most 15 Graph windows at a time. Ordinarily, Minitab discards older Graph windows as necessary to avoid exceeding this limit.

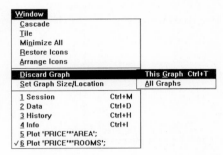

Click This Graph to delete the active Professional graph. Minitab opens a new Graph window for each Professional graph you produce and leaves it open until you exit Minitab or choose to discard one or all the open Graph windows. Click All Graphs to delete all the open Professional Graph windows.

See also Tutorial 4.

Window > Set Graph Size/Location

This command lets you save the size and arrangement of Graph windows.

Minitab generates all subsequent graphs at the new size, and places them in the location you specify. When you have multiple graphs, Minitab displays them in a cascade starting at the location you specify. Once your Graph windows are satisfactorily arranged, use Edit > Save Preferences to display them in the same way each session.

Session Window

Keyboard: [Ctrl]+**M**

The Session window contains commands, Character-based graphs, and statistical analyses. See Reference Chapter 1 for information on using the Session window and Reference Chapter 3 for information about using Session commands.

Data Window

Keyboard: [Ctrl]+**D**

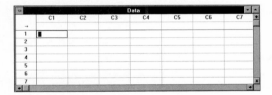

The Data window contains a spreadsheet-like view of your worksheet, providing a convenient way to enter and edit data. See Chapter 1 of Reference for information about using the Data window.

History Window

Keyboard: [Ctrl]+**H**

The History window displays all the Session commands from the Session window, but not the output. You cannot edit the contents of this window, but you can copy the commands to the Clipboard. You can then paste them into the Session window to execute them again, or into a text editor to create an Exec macro. See Reference Chapter 5 for information about creating and using Exec files.

Info Window

Keyboard: [Ctrl]+**I**

The Info window displays an automatically updated summary of the columns and constants stored in the current worksheet. It displays the numbers of all the columns that contain data and their names, any stored constants and their names, the number of values in the column, and the number of missing values in the column. See also "File > Get Worksheet Info."

Graph Window

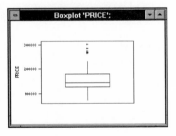

The Graph window option on the Window menu appears only if you have created a Professional graph in the current Minitab session.

To save a graph, choose File > Save Window As while the Graph window is active. To print a graph, choose File > Print Window while the Graph window is active. To delete an active Graph window, double-click its Control menu box, press [Ctrl]+**T**, or choose Window > Discard Graph.

If you use a Session command to produce a graph, you can specify a title for the Graph window. On the main graph command line, add a # symbol followed by a comment; Minitab uses the first 31 characters of the comment as the window title.

Minitab can retain up to 15 Graph windows at a time. Minitab discards older Graph windows as necessary to make room for new Graph windows.

The Graph Menu

You use the Graph menu to display various graphs, including plots, charts, histograms, boxplots, and time series plots in high-resolution, customized form (Professional) or as Character graphs. You can also create matrix plots and normal plots with limited Professional graph capabilities. Each Professional graph you create displays in its own Graph window. The Reference section first documents Professional graphs and then Character graphs.

The Professional graphs on the Graph menu share many common attributes, which are documented first. Then, each Graph menu command is covered, with cross references to the common attributes.

Common Elements in Professional Graphs

The Professional graph dialog boxes all have the same layout, shown here:

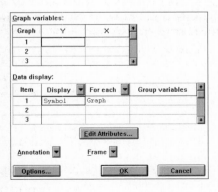

The following tables and buttons appear in the Professional graph dialog boxes (these are covered in more detail after this summary):

Graph variables: The Graph variables table defines the variables to be used in each graph. If you want a simple graph, just fill in row 1 and click OK. To produce multiple graphs, or when overlaying graphs on the same page (click Frame, then Multiple Graphs, then Overlay graphs), fill in more than one row of the table.

Data display: The Data display table defines the way data points look on the graph. You can display points in the following ways by clicking the drop-down arrow and then clicking the option you want (some are not available for all graph types). Then click the Edit Attributes button to open a dialog box that gives specific options.

Area: Controls attributes (fill type, colors, edges, connections) for the area between the line connecting points on a graph and the x-axis.

Connect: Controls attributes (line type, color, size, connections) for lines connecting points on a graph.

Project: Controls attributes (line type, color, size, connections) for lines that project to a base from points on a graph.

Symbol: Displays symbols for each point on the graph.

Bar: Controls attributes (fill type, color, size, base position) for bars for Charts and Histograms.

Box: Controls attributes (fill, color, size) for boxes used in a boxplot.

The **For Each** column tells whether to give different attributes to each graph, to different groups, or to each point in a graph. For example, specifying Symbol for each Graph in row 1 and Connect for each Graph in row 2 displays each point as a symbol and connects all of the points on a graph. You use the **Group variables** column to specify 1 to 3 grouping variables only when you specify Group in For Each.

Edit Attributes: You can define properties such as color, size, etc. for the elements in the Data display table. When you click Edit Attributes, you go to the attributes subdialog box for the active row in the Data display table (that is, the row that currently has the darkened box). Moving to a new row, then clicking Edit Attributes, gives you the attributes subdialog for the active row in the Data display table. For example, if Symbol is in the active row of the Data display table and you click Edit Attributes, you get a subdialog box that allows you to change the type of symbols, the color of symbols, and the size of symbols.

Options: Click this button to go to another dialog box with options specific to each graph type and to transpose the axes on the graph.

Annotation: Choose to open a menu of choices for the following customizable elements: titles, footnotes, text, and line.

Frame: Choose to open a menu of choices for axis options, minimum and maximum scaling, and multiple graph scaling.

Using the Tables in Professional Graphics Dialog Boxes

When you create a graph using Professional graphs, you enter data into tables like the Display Data table or Graph variables table that let you define attributes and features for different parts of your graph. To enter data quickly into cells:

- In columns with menu buttons, you can click the button or press F4 to bring up a list of choices for the active cell in that column. When the menu is displayed, you can click the choice you want.

- In an Edit Attributes table column that takes a data (worksheet) column as an argument, click the column header to highlight all cells in the column, then choose **Use Variables** from the drop-down list, click **Use columns**, and specify a column in the text box. When you click **OK,** the values from the column appear in the table.

    To change multiple cell values:

- You can change all values in a column by (1) clicking the column header or pressing F5, then (2) pressing F4 or clicking the pop-up menu button, and (3) clicking the value you want from the menu.

- You can select a range of values in a table and change them in the following ways:

1. Drag from the first cell in the range to the last cell, then select the value you want from the drop-down list. Do not click an active cell first to do this. Clicking an active cell puts you into edit mode.

2. Use Shift + click; that is, click the first value in the range to make it active, then scroll to the last cell and press Shift and click the last value, then click the pop-up menu and select the value you want.

3. From the keyboard, you can press Shift+↑ or Shift+↓ to select the range, then click the pop-up up menu button and select the value you want.

4. In the Group variables column of the Data display table, you can highlight a range of cells and use the variables list to choose a column or constant for every cell in the highlighted range at once.

    Moving between cells in a table:

- to move between cells within a table, use arrow keys or click on the cell you want

- to move to the first cell in a column, press Home

- to move to the last occupied cell in a column, press End

- to move to the first cell in the visible range of the current column, press Ctrl+↑

- to move to the last cell in the visible range of the current column, press Ctrl+↓

- to move to the first cell in the visible range of the current row, press Ctrl+←

- to move to the last cell in the visible range of the current row, press Ctrl+→

- to move a page to the left or right, press Ctrl+Pg Up or Ctrl+Pg Dn

    Moving within a cell:

- to move left and right, press Alt+← and Alt+→

- to move to the beginning or end of cell contents, press Alt+Home and Alt+End

- to move a word to the left or right, press Ctrl+Alt+← or Ctrl+Alt+→

Edit Attributes

Depending on the Display option selected in the Data Display table, the Edit Attributes button opens a dialog box that lets you customize the attributes of your graphs. A typical Edit Attributes dialog box looks like this:

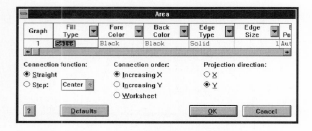

The following list contains all the dialog box items you might find in one of the Edit Attributes dialog boxes. Which ones appear depends on which Display option is selected.

Area (these may apply to other Edit Attributes dialog boxes, too)

Fill Type: Enter a number or click the arrow to select a fill type.

Fore Color: Enter a number or click the arrow to select a color for the fill type pattern you have selected (if dots, for example, this will color the dots) and for the edge line.

Back Color: Enter a number or click the arrow to select a color for the background of the fill type pattern you have selected (if dots, for example, this will color the surface the dots are on). For a solid fill, click Solid for Fill type and choose a Back color.

Edge Type: Enter a number or click the arrow to select a line type for the edge of the area (the line that connects the points).

Edge Size: Enter a number or click the arrow to select a line thickness (base unit is 1 pixel; other units are in relation to that).

Base Position: Enter a number or click the arrow to select a base position or positions. The default base is the data minimum or 0. You can specify a different base, in which case areas connected by points less than the base line coordinate will extend up, while areas connected by points greater than the base line coordinate will extend down.

Connection function: Specify how points are connected.

Straight: Connects points with straight lines, then fills the area underneath.

Step: Connects points using a step pattern. Choose Left to make steps with each point at the left of a step level, Center to put each point in the middle of the step level (the default), or Right to put each point to the right of the step level.

Connection order: Specify the order in which points are connected (use only with Plot).

Increasing X: Connects points from least to greatest horizontally.

Increasing Y: Connects points from least to greatest vertically.

Worksheet: Connects points as they occur on the worksheet.

Projection direction: Change the way areas extend from the data points on the graph.

X: Extends areas vertically towards the x axis minimum or specified base value.

Y: Extends areas horizontally towards the y axis minimum or specified base value.

Bar (in addition to attributes listed in "Area")

Bar Width: Enter a number to specify width of the boxes. It can be any real number from 0 to 1, with 0 a line and 1 the largest possible, enclosing the full extent of the data. The default is 0.5, which makes each box take half the maximum width.

Box (in addition to attributes listed in "Area")

Box Width: Enter a number or use List to specify the proportional width of the boxes. It can be any real number from 0 to 1, with 0 a line and 1 the largest possible, enclosing the full extent of the data. The default for IQRange boxes is 0.5, which makes each box take half the maximum width. The default for CI Boxes is 0.25, and the default for Range boxes is 0.75.

Box width proportional to sample size: Click to make the width of each box proportional to the square root of the number of observations in the box.

Maximum width: Enter a number as in Box Width to specify the maximum width.

Confidence level (CI Boxes only): Enter a number (either as a percentage or a decimal) to determine the confidence interval above and below the median.

Hide whiskers: Click to suppress the display of whiskers (lines showing the extent of the data beyond the part enclosed by the box).

Project (in addition to attributes listed in "Area")

Line Type: Enter a number or click the arrow to select a line type for the line that connects the points.

Line Color: Enter a number or click the arrow to select a color for the line.

Line Size: Enter a number or click the arrow to select a line thickness (the base unit is 1 pixel; other units are in relation to that).

Projection direction: Change the way lines extend from the data points on the graph.

X: Extends projections vertically to the x-axis minimum or base value.

Y: Extends projections horizontally to the y-axis minimum or base value.

Defaults: Click to return all attributes in the dialog box to their default values.

Symbol (in addition to attributes listed in "Area")

Type: Enter a number or click the arrow to select a symbol type for the symbols representing the points. Circle, symbol number 1, is the default.

Color: Enter a number or click the arrow to select a color for the symbol you have selected (if dots, for example, this will color the dots). Black, color number 1, is the default.

Size: Enter a number or click the arrow to select a symbol size. A size of 1 is the default.

Defaults: Click to return all Symbol attributes in the dialog box to their default values.

Annotation

Choose to annotate graphs or entire pages, including titles, footnotes, text, and lines. You can specify colors, fonts, sizes, justification, offset, placement, and other attributes of the labels you create. These options are also available for control chart commands.

Title

Create titles for a graph.

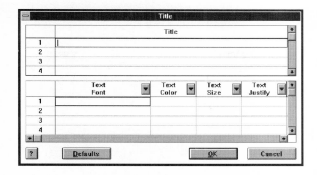

Title: Enter a title of up to 80 characters in the first row. Once you enter a title and move from this field, attributes fields for the title in the lower table assume their default values. You can enter multiple titles by using rows 2 and up. Each row generates a title on a new line in the graph and can be customized separately.

Text Font: Enter a number or click the arrow to select a font type for the text. Arial, font number 2, is the default.

Text Color: Enter a number or click the arrow to select a color for the text. The default color is black, color number 1.

Text Size: Enter a number or click the arrow to select a size. 1.5 is the default title size.

Text Justify: Enter L, C, or R to put the title at the Left, Center, or Right of the graph. The default is Center.

Text Angle: Enter a number or click the arrow to select an angle for rotating text. The default is 0 degrees.

Horizontal Offset: Enter a number or click the arrow to move the title to a new location; this number moves the title away from the reference point to the left or right on the figure region coordinate grid. When you specify Left in Text Justify, the default horizontal reference position is 0.01, for Center 0.5, for Right 0.99. The default offsets changes automatically with the Auto setting depending on the value in the Text Justify field.

Vertical Offset: Enter a number or click the arrow to move the title to a new location; this number moves the title away from the reference point up (positive numbers) or down (negative numbers) in figure units. The vertical reference position for all titles is 0.99. When you use more than one title, the vertical offset for subsequent reference points continues to get larger in the negative direction. These offsets change automatically with the Auto setting.

Horizontal Placement: Enter a number (–1, 0, or 1) or click the arrow to select where the title text attaches to the reference point (left, centered, or right). The default varies with the Text Justify setting: for Left it is to the right of the reference point (1); for Center it is centered on the reference point (0); for Right it is to attach the text to the left of the reference point (–1). The placement changes automatically with the Auto setting.

Vertical Placement: Enter a number (–1, 0, or 1) or click the arrow to specify where the title text attaches to the reference point (below, centered, or above). The default is to attach the text below the reference point (–1). The placement changes automatically with the Auto setting.

Defaults: Click to set any highlighted row of attributes back to their default values. If no row is highlighted, clicking this button resets the current row. Clicking this button does not erase values in the Title column. If you highlight a column by clicking the column header, pressing this button resets all attribute values in the dialog box.

Footnote

Minitab creates footnotes for a graph, placed in the lower left corner of the figure region. You can create as many footnotes as you want, specifying different attributes for each footnote in the corresponding attribute rows (font, color, size, and so on).

This dialog box is also used for footnotes in control chart commands.

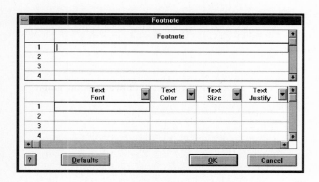

Footnote: Enter a footnote of up to 80 characters in the first row. Once you move from this field, other fields in the current row assume their default values. You can enter multiple footnotes by using rows 2 and up. Each row generates a new footnote that is put on a new line in the graph and can be customized separately. Row 1 of the lower table contains attributes for the footnote in row 1 of the upper table. Each additional footnote goes beneath the preceding footnote. All footnotes apply to every graph in the Graph variables table.

See "Title" for more information on the other dialog box options.

Text

Minitab creates text strings anywhere on a graph. Indicate the location by giving x,y coordinates using data units. You can enter and customize up to 100 different text strings using this dialog box. Row 1 in the lower table contains attributes for the text in row 1 in the upper table.

This dialog box is also used for text in control chart commands.

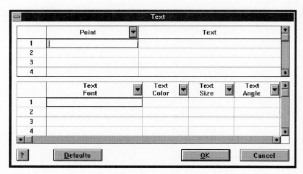

Point: Enter an x,y coordinate pair in data units to specify which point should mark the starting point of the text. Once you make an entry in Point or in Text, other fields in the same row assume their default values.

Text: Enter up to 80 characters of text. Once you make an entry in Point or in Text and move to another field, other fields in the same row assume their default values.

See "Title" for more information on the other dialog box options.

Line

You can creates a line on a graph or page and control attributes of the line. Each row contains a separate line, which can connect as many points as you specify.

This dialog box is also used for control chart commands.

Points: Enter a minimum of two data points (x1,y1) and (x2,y2) in each row separated by spaces to indicate x,y coordinates (using data units) of the starting point and ending point for each line you want to draw. To make a line connect to another point, enter a third pair of coordinates in the same row. You can create as many connected segments as you want by listing additional x,y pairs in the same row. If you want to start a new line, enter the points on a new row. If you specify coordinates greater or less than the scale minimum or maximum, the line may extend off the page, either partly or completely. For lines with many points, you can put the x-arguments in one worksheet column, and the y-arguments in another and specify both columns instead of using a long sequence of arguments.

Type: Enter a number or click the arrow to select a line type. The default is Solid, type number 1.

Color: Enter a number or click the arrow to select a line color. The default is Black, color number 1.

Size: Enter a number or click the arrow to select a line width in pixels. The default is 1, which makes a line that is 1 pixel wide.

Defaults: Click to set the current row of attributes back to their default values. Clicking this button does not erase values in the Points column. If you highlight a column by clicking the column header, pressing this button resets all attribute values in the dialog box.

Frame

Each graph is surrounded by a frame that includes different elements that you can customize. You can control axis lines and labels, tick lines and labels, grid lines, and reference lines and labels. You can also specify the maxi-

mums and minimums of the graph scales. For multiple graphs, you can overlay graphs on top of each other, or keep the scale the same on one or both scales across all graphs.

These dialog boxes (except for the Multiple Graph dialog box) are also used by the control chart commands.

Axes

This dialog box lets you control axis labels, tick marks, reference lines, and grid lines.

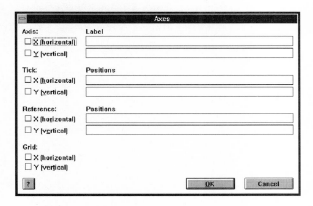

Axis: Click the axis you want to modify.

Tick: Click the axis you want to modify. While you cannot change positions of category ticks, you can specify which ticks on a category axis to display, and you can change their line and label attributes. For a category axis, the tick positions are always referred to by the integer values 1, 2, ..., c, where c is the number of categories.

Reference: Click the axis you want to modify. Indicate the position where you want to start the reference line by category number. You can generate reference lines for the third and fifth categories by specifying 3 and 5, or midway between categories 4 and 5 by specifying 4.5.

Grid: Click the axis you want to modify. Generates horizontal or vertical lines that extend across the graph from the tick positions.

Label: Enter a label for the selected axis.

Positions: Enter a number or numbers to give the location(s) of the tick, reference, or grid.

Min and Max

This dialog box lets you define the minimum and maximum values for the scales in the data region.

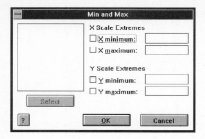

This dialog box is also used by control chart commands.

X Scale Extremes

X minimum: Click and enter a number for the minimum data value of the horizontal axis.

X maximum: Click and enter a number for the maximum data value of the horizontal axis.

Y Scale Extremes

Y minimum: Click and enter a number for the minimum data value of the vertical axis.

Y maximum: Click and enter a number for the maximum data value of the vertical axis.

Multiple Graphs

This dialog box lets you arrange multiple graphs created using the same dialog box.

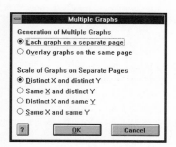

Generation of Multiple Graphs: When you specify more than one graph in a dialog box, you can either produce each on a separate page or window or you can overlay them, one on top of the other.

Each graph on a separate page: Click to display each graph on its own page (in its own window).

Overlay graphs on the same page: Click to overlay graphs on the same page (in the same window).

Scale of Graphs on Separate Pages: You can keep one or both scales of a graph the same for all graphs generated.

Distinct X and distinct Y: Click to keep the scales of both axes distinct.

Same X and distinct Y: Click to keep the horizontal axis the same and the vertical axis distinct.

Distinct X and same Y: Click to keep the horizontal axis distinct and the vertical axis the same.

Same X and same Y: Click to keep both the scales of both axes the same.

Use Variables

This dialog box is used in many locations throughout the Professional Graphics dialogs. It allows you to select columns or constants for use in the currently active cell(s) of the dialog box and to view available constants and columns.

You can also fill an Edit Attributes dialog box column with values from a Minitab worksheet column by clicking the column header in the dialog box, selecting Use variables by using the pop-up menu button, selecting Use columns and selecting a column, then clicking OK.

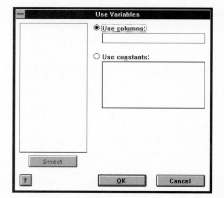

Use columns: Click the option button and enter a column or columns in the text box. Column may not always be a valid option.

Use constants: Click the option button and enter a constant or constants in the text box.

Example: Using Professional Graphs

The following dialog boxes and equivalent Session commands illustrate how to create a boxplot of lake depth using LAKES.MTW. The other Professional graph commands operate the same way.

First, you indicate the variable you want in the first Y cell on the Graph variables table (in this example, accept the default Display options, which specify displaying the quartile range box and outliers for each graph):

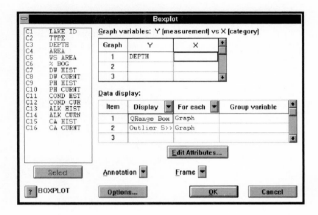

Now, create a title for your boxplot that is colored blue and is twice as large as the default by clicking Annotation, then clicking Title, and filling out the Title dialog box:

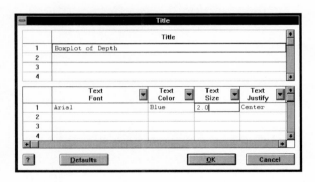

Now, create a footnote for your boxplot that is colored blue and is also twice as large as the default by click-

ing Annotation, then clicking Footnote, and filling out the Footnote dialog box:

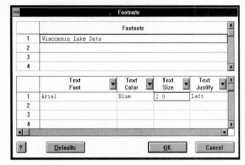

Now, select a different symbol for the outliers (the default is an asterisk, and you want a red circle) by clicking the Outlier Symbol Display option in the Data display table(row 2 in the Display column), clicking Edit Attributes, and then filling out the Outlier Symbol dialog box:

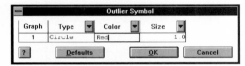

Now, click OK in the Boxplot dialog box, and Minitab produces this boxplot (though you can't see the colors, you can see the different shades they create):

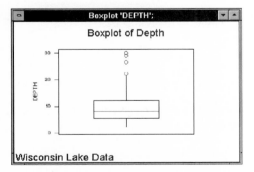

The equivalent Session commands and sub-commands to create this boxplot are:

```
MTB > Boxplot 'DEPTH';
SUBC> Box;
SUBC> Symbol;
SUBC> Outlier
SUBC> Type 1;
SUBC> Color 2
SUBC> Title "Boxplot of Depth";
SUBC> TColor 4;
SUBC> TSize 2.0;
SUBC> Footnote "Wisconsin Lake Data";
SUBC> TColor 4;
SUBC> TSize 2.0.
```

The next sections document each Professional graph command on the Graph menu, discussing only the features that are unique to each graph type.

Graph > Plot

This command produces a scatter plot that shows the relationship between two columns. See "Common Elements in Professional Graphs" at the beginning of this section for more information.

Dialog Box Items

Graph variables:

Y: Enter a column for the vertical axis on the graph.

X: Enter a column for the horizontal axis on the graph.

This command contains options specific to Plot and allows you to transpose axes.

Plot Options Dialog Box Items

Add Jitter to Direction: Click to randomly offset points so you can see overlapping points. You can change the average offset distance by specifying a range of from 0 to 1 that determines how far the points can be offset. The smaller the numbers are, the less offset there will be. Since jittering relies on a random function, jittered plots do not look the same each time you generate them. To produce identical graphs repeatedly, use Set Base to set the base of the Minitab random number generator.

X: Enter a number between 0 and 1 that specifies a horizontal range for points to be randomly offset. The default is 0.025.

Y: Enter a number between 0 and 1 that specifies a vertical range for points to be offset. The default is 0.025.

Transpose X and Y: Click to interchange the variables defining the vertical and horizontal axes.

Corresponding Session Command

PLOT (after GPRO)

See also Tutorial 4.

Graph > Chart

Minitab produces many kinds of charts, including bar charts, line charts, symbol charts, and area charts. See "Common Elements in Professional Graphs" at the beginning of this section for more information.

Chart has two forms. If you enter values in both Y and X, the X column functions as a category or grouping variable: One bar displays each group in X, using whatever function you specify. If you do not specify a function, the height of each bar is the sum of the observations in the corresponding group by default.

If you enter only a variable in X, Chart displays bars showing the count of each unique observation in the column.

To emphasize variation in the data, Minitab often does not place the y-scale minimum at 0. If you want to set it to 0, use Frame > Min and Max > Y minimum. Click Y-minimum and set at 0.

Dialog Box Items

Graph variables:

Function: When you use two columns, the default height of the bar is the sum of the observations in the bar if you don't fill this in. You can, however, choose from among any of the following functions for the y-variable: Count (total number of values), N (number of nonmissing values), NMissing (number of missing values), Sum (sum of values), Mean, StDev (standard deviation), Median, Minimum, Maximum, or SSQ (sum of squares of values). Leave this blank if you only put a variable in X.

Y: Enter a column containing data for the vertical axis on the graph.

X: Enter a column containing the categories or groups for the horizontal axis on the graph.

Chart Options Dialog Box Items

Groups Within X: You can cluster or show subgroups of data based on a specified column.

Cluster: Click and enter a column that provides subgroups.

Offset: Enter a number greater than or equal to 0 and less than 1 to adjust the offset between bars in a cluster. The default offset is 1/(the number of bars in each cluster + 1).

Stack: Enter a column that provides subgroups to show bars as blocks stacked on top of each other.

Order X Groups Based on: You can present the groups in the chart in increasing or decreasing order based on the y-axis values. Your choice does not affect the order within clusters, stacks, or cluster/stack combinations, but moves entire clusters, stacks, or cluster/stack combinations into order by the sum of the values in each category specified by the x-axis variable.

Default: X-values (categories) are in numeric order in a numeric column or, for alpha columns in the order they first occur in the worksheet.

Increasing Y: Click to present groups from smallest to largest based on y-axis values.

Decreasing Y: Click to present groups from largest to smallest based on y-axis values.

Accumulate Y across X: Click to use a cumulative scale. The height of the third bar, for example, is the sum of the observations in the first three categories. All possible combinations of cluster and stack groups must have at least one nonmissing (or zero) observation.

Total Y to 100% within X: Click to use a percent scale on the y-axis. You would usually use this with Cluster or Stack, so that the parts of each cluster or stack (each category) add up to 100%.

Transpose X and Y: Click to interchange the variables defining the vertical and horizontal axes.

Corresponding Session Command

CHART

See also Tutorial 4.

Graph > Histogram

This command produces a histogram. It separates the data into intervals on the x-axis and draws a bar for each interval whose height, by default, is the number of observations (or frequency) in the interval. Minitab places observations that fall on interval boundaries into the interval to the right (except those in the interval farthest to the right, which are placed in the left interval). See "Common Elements in Professional Graphs" at the beginning of this section for more information.

Dialog Box Items

Graph variables:

X: Enter the column you want to graph.

Histogram Options Dialog Box Items

Type of Histogram: Click to select which function of x the y-axis should display.

Frequency: (Default) uses a frequency scale on the y-axis. The height of the bar is the number of observations in the corresponding interval on the x-axis.

Percent: Uses a percent scale on the y-axis. The height of the bar is the percentage of the total number of observations that fall in the corresponding interval on the x-axis.

Density: Uses a density scale on the y-axis, and is most useful for histograms with unequal width intervals. The total area under the histogram is one. The area of one bar is the proportion of the observations in that bar.

Cumulative Frequency: Uses a cumulative frequency scale on the y-axis. The height of the third bar, for example, is the sum of the number of observations in the first three intervals.

Cumulative Percent: Uses a cumulative percent scale on the y-axis. The height of the third bar, for example, is the sum of the percents in the first three intervals.

Cumulative Density: Uses a cumulative density scale on the y-axis. The height of the third bar, for example, is the sum of the densities in the first three intervals.

Type of Intervals: Click to select where the tick marks appear.

MidPoint: Ticks appear at the midpoints of the intervals.

CutPoint: Ticks appear at the end points of the intervals.

Define intervals using values: Enter constants or a column to specify your own midpoints or end points (or cutpoints). Specify arguments in order, from smallest to largest. Midpoints require equally spaced intervals; cutpoints do not. You can specify a column that contains all the cutpoint or midpoint values, or use shorthand notation (for example, 5:40/5 means intervals from 5 to 40 by 5).

Transpose X and Y: Click to interchange the variables defining the vertical and horizontal axes.

Corresponding Session Command
HISTOGRAM (after GPRO)

See also Tutorial 4.

Graph > Boxplot

This command produces a boxplot (also called box-and-whisker plot). A default boxplot consists of a box, whiskers, and outliers. Minitab draws a line across the box at the median. By default, the bottom of the box is at the first quartile (Q1) and the top is at the third quartile (Q3). The whiskers are the lines that extend from the top and bottom of the box to the adjacent values, the lowest and highest observations still inside the region defined by the lower limit $Q1 - 1.5 \times (Q3 - Q1)$ and the upper limit $Q1 + 1.5 \times (Q3 - Q1)$. Outliers are points outside the lower and upper limits, plotted with asterisks (*s).

Boxplot has two forms. If you enter values in both Y and X, a box displays for each group in X. If you do not specify a variable in X, a single box is drawn for all values in the column. See "Common Elements in Professional Graphs" at the beginning of this section for more information.

Dialog Box Items

Graph variables:

Y: Enter a column containing the measurements for the vertical axis.

X: Enter a column containing the categories for the horizontal axis; Minitab will produce a boxplot for each category.

Boxplot Options Dialog Box Items

Transpose X and Y: Click to interchange the variables defining the vertical and horizontal axes.

Corresponding Session Command
BOXPLOT (after GPRO)

Graph > Time Series Plot

Minitab produces a time series plot, with time on the x-axis and the specified column on the y-axis. By default, it displays symbols for each point and joins the points with a line. See "Common Elements in Professional Graphs" at the beginning of this section for more information. This command is also available on the Time Series submenu.

Dialog Box Items

Graph variables:

Y: Enter a column containing the observations on the graph. Minitab assumes that the values in the column are entered in the order they occurred, with equally spaced time intervals between each observation. The x-axis is automatically the time axis.

Time Series Options Dialog Box Items

Time Scale: Click the time scale you want.
Start time: Enter a number or constant to specify the time of the first observation. The defaults and permissible values are as follows (regardless of what combination you specify):

Time Unit	Range	Default Start Value
Index	All integers	1
Month	1 to 12	1
Quarter	1 to 4	1
Year	Positive integers	1900

Transpose X and Y: Click to interchange the vertical and horizontal axes.

Corresponding Session Command
TSPLOT (after GPRO)

See also Tutorial 15.

Graph > Matrix Plot

Minitab produces a scatter plot matrix of 3 to 10 variables. A separate plot is displayed for each pair of variables. These plots are then arranged in a matrix. Scatter plot matrices help you see the relationships between several pairs of variables at once. If you use groups, each group is given a separate color. This command is written using the Minitab %Macro language, so it may execute more slowly than regular Minitab commands. The speed depends on the number of variables, the number of observations, and whether you ask for a half or a full matrix. See "Common Elements in Professional Graphs" at the beginning of this section for more information.

Dialog Box Items

Graph variables: Select from 3 to 10 column variables.

Group variable: The symbols, connection lines, and/or projection lines specified in the graphs are given different colors based on this variable.

Data display: There are three ways to represent the points on the graph. You may use any one, two, or all three of these.

Symbol: Check to display points with symbols.

Connect: Check to connect points with a line.

Project: Check to project points to the y-axis minimum.

Matrix Display:

Lower half of matrix: Click to display the lower half of the matrix.

Full matrix: Click to display the full matrix.

Title: Enter text as the title for the graph.

See also Tutorial 11.

Graph > Normal Plot

Minitab draws a normal probability plot that resembles the usual form of normal probability paper. The vertical axis has a probability scale; the horizontal axis, a data scale. Minitab fits and draws a least-squares line for the points that estimates the cumulative distribution function for the population from which data are drawn. Minitab displays estimates of the population parameters at the top of the plot. See "Common Elements in Professional Graphs" at the beginning of this section for more information.

Dialog Box Items

Variable: Enter a column.

Reference probabilities: Enter a column to specify a set of probabilities to mark on the plot. The values in this column must be between 0 and 1. Minitab marks each probability in the column with a horizontal reference line on the plot, and marks each line with the value of the

probability. Minitab draws a vertical reference line where the horizontal reference line intersects the least-squares line fit to the data, and marks this line with the estimated data value.

Tests for Normality:

Anderson-Darling: Click to perform an Anderson-Darling test for normality.

Ryan-Joiner: Click to perform a Ryan-Joiner test, similar to the Shapiro-Wilk test.

Title: Enter text for an additional title line below the default title.

Corresponding Session Command

%NORMPLOT

See also Tutorial 11.

Graph > Character Graphs

Minitab displays Character graphs in the Session window. Character graphs consist of keyboard characters; they are not high-resolution. If you want to include a graph in an ASCII outfile along with a record of your session, create a Character graph. All printers can print Character graphs.

Graph > Character Graphs > Set Options

Use the Set Options command to specify the height and width of all subsequent graphs.

Use the Session command OW (output width) to control the width of time series plots. Scales tend to be better if you use odd numbers (especially the numbers 1, 5, 9, and so on).

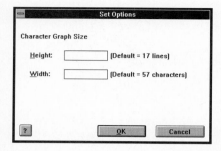

Dialog Box Options

Height: Enter a number from 5 to 400 lines.
Width: Enter a number from 10 to 150 spaces.

Corresponding Session Commands

HEIGHT
WIDTH

Graph > Character Graphs > Histogram

You use this command to produce a character-based histogram in the Session window, using a horizontal line of *s to represent data points. If there are more than 50 observations in an interval, Minitab indicates how many observations each * represents. Minitab places any observations falling on an interval boundary in the interval with the largest midpoint. Minitab can display up to 100 intervals in a single histogram.

Dialog Box Options

Variables: Enter one or more columns; Minitab produces a separate histogram for each one.
By variable: Select this option to produce a separate histogram for each value of the By variable. In the text box, enter the column that contains the By variables, which must be integers from –9999 to +9999, or the missing value symbol. The column may include up to 20 distinct groups.

Same scale for all variables: Select to draw all displays on axes with the same scale (based on the extremes of all the data).
First midpoint: Enter a number to specify the midpoint for the first plotting interval; Minitab omits any observations beyond this interval from the display.
Last midpoint: Enter a number to specify the midpoint for the last plotting interval; Minitab omits any observations beyond this interval from the display.
Interval width: Enter a number to specify the distance between midpoints.

Corresponding Session Command

HISTOGRAM (after GSTD)

Example: Using Histogram

The following dialog box and equivalent Session command illustrate how to produce a Character histogram of the salary data in PAY2.MTW.

```
MTB > GStd.
MTB > Histogram 'SALARY'.
```

This command produces the following graph in the Session window:

```
Histogram of SALARY   N = 11

Midpoint   Count
   24000      1    *
   26000      0
   28000      2    **
   30000      1    *
   32000      3    ***
   34000      0
   36000      0
   38000      2    **
   40000      1    *
   42000      1    *
```

See also Tutorial 3.

Graph > Character Graphs > Boxplot

As its name indicates, this command produces a character-based boxplot in the Session window.

Dialog Box Options

Variable: Enter the column that contains the observations you want to display graphically.

By variable: Select and enter a grouping column. Minitab produces a separate boxplot for each distinct value in the column. This option lets you compare several groups of data. Levels must be integers between –10000 and +10000 or the missing value symbol; they need not be consecutive. Minitab allows up to 100 separate group values (or levels) in the column.

Use levels: Enter one or more numbers to display boxplots only for those values in the By variable. Use this option to omit displays for some subgroups. Minitab draws a boxplot for each of the By variable subscript values you list here, in the order in which you enter them.

Notch, confidence level: Select to change the default confidence level (90%) that Minitab uses in the boxplots. Minitab uses parentheses (notches) to indicate the confidence interval limits for the population median (calculated using the 1-Sample Sign command). Minitab uses a priority system to determine the symbols to display in the boxplot. If the median falls on the same space as a notch (CI parentheses), Minitab doesn't display the notch. Similarly, if the median and a box edge fall on the same space, the box edge is not displayed.

Axis: Minimum or Maximum: Enter a number to specify the first and, optionally, the last tick mark (+) on the horizontal axis to customize the boxplot display.

Tick increment: Specify the distance between tick marks (+).

Condensed display: Select to display each boxplot with only one line instead of three (the default).

Corresponding Session Command

BOXPLOT (after GSTD)

Example: Using Boxplot

The following dialog box and equivalent Session command illustrate how to produce a Character boxplot of the salary data in PAY2.MTW.

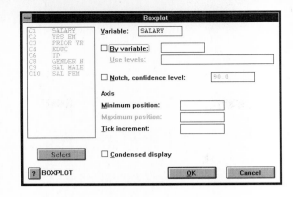

```
MTB > GStd.
MTB > BoxPlot 'SALARY'.
```

This command produces the following graph in the Session window:

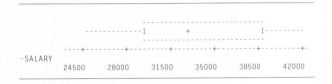

See also Tutorial 3.

Graph > Character Graph > Dotplot

You choose this command to produce a character-based dotplot in the Session window.

Dialog Box Options

Variables: Enter one or more columns. Minitab generates a separate dotplot for each column specified.

By variable: Select and enter the column that contains the By variable values. Minitab produces a separate dotplot for each value, which must be an integer between –10000 and +10000, or the missing value symbol.

Same scale for all variables: Select to use the same scale in drawing the dotplots for all the columns listed (based on the extremes of the data).

First midpoint and **Last midpoint:** Enter two numbers to specify the first and, optionally, the last plotting position of the data.

Tick increment: Specify the distance between tick marks (+).

Corresponding Session Command

DOTPLOT (after GSTD)

Example: Using Dotplot

The following dialog box and equivalent Session command illustrate how to produce a Character dotplot of the salary data in PAY2.MTW.

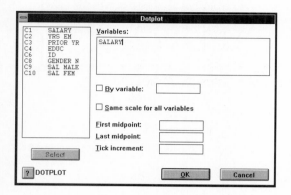

```
MTB > DotPlot 'SALARY'.
```

This command produces the following graph in the Session window:

See also Tutorial 3.

Graph > Character Graphs > Stem-and-Leaf

You can produce a character-based stem-and-leaf plot in the Session window by choosing this command.

Dialog Box Options

Variables: Enter the column(s) you want to display. Each column generates a separate stem-and-leaf diagram.

By variable: Select and enter a column to produce stem-and-leaf displays for the subsets defined by distinct values in the By variable, which must be integers from −10000 to +10000, or the missing value symbol (*). You cannot use this option with Trim outliers.

Trim outliers: Select to trim all outliers and show them on special lines labeled LO and HI. You cannot use this option with By variable.

Increment: Enter a number to control vertical scaling by setting the increment between display lines (the difference between the smallest possible values on adjacent lines).

Corresponding Session Command

STEM

Example: Using Stem-and-Leaf

The following dialog box and equivalent Session command illustrate how to produce a Character stem-and-leaf plot of the salary data in PAY2.MTW.

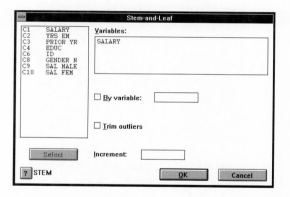

```
MTB > Stem-and-Leaf 'SALARY'.
```

This command produces the following graph in the Session window:

```
Stem-and-leaf of SALARY    N  = 11
Leaf Unit = 1000

    1     2 5
    1     2
    3     2 99
    4     3 0
   (3)    3 233
    4     3
    4     3
    4     3 99
    2     4 0

       HI  42,
```

See also Tutorial 3.

Graph > Character Graphs > Scatter Plot

To display a character-based scatter plot in the Session window, choose this command.

Dialog Box Options

Y variable: Enter a column.

X variable: Enter a column.

Use symbol: Enter a symbol from the keyboard to mark each point: Minitab accepts any number, letter, or symbol.

Use labels: Enter a column; Minitab marks each data point with a letter coded to its tag variable value. A = 1, B = 2, and so on.

Character Graphs Annotate Dialog Box Options

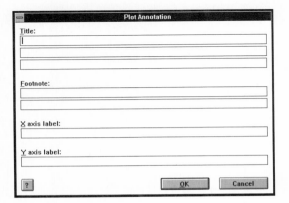

The options in this dialog box allow you to add titles, footnotes, and axis labels to Character graphs that appear in the Session window.

Title: Enter up to three lines of text to display at the top of the graph.

Footnote: Enter up to two lines of text to display at the bottom of the graph, below the horizontal axis label.

X axis label and **Y axis label:** Minitab automatically labels axes with column names, but you can replace those labels with your own.

Character Graphs Scale Dialog Box Options

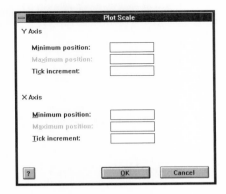

Y Axis

Minimum position: Enter a number for the minimum value on the y, or vertical, axis.

Maximum position: Enter a number for the maximum value on the y, or vertical, axis.

Tick increment: Specify the increment that marks the distance between tick marks (+) on the y, or vertical, axis.

X Axis

Minimum position: Enter a number for the minimum value on the x, or horizontal, axis.

Maximum position: Enter a number for the maximum value on the x, or horizontal, axis.

Tick increment: Specify the increment that marks the distance between tick marks (+) on the x, or horizontal, axis.

Corresponding Session Commands

PLOT (after GSTD)

LPLOT

Example: Using Scatter Plot

The following dialog box and equivalent Session command illustrate how to produce a Character scatter plot of the salary versus years employed data in PAY2.MTW.

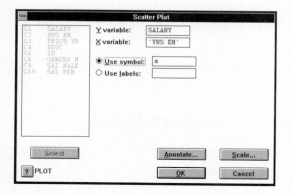

```
MTB > GStd.
MTB > Plot 'SALARY' 'YRS EM';
SUBC>   Symbol 'x'.
```

This command produces the following graph in the Session window:

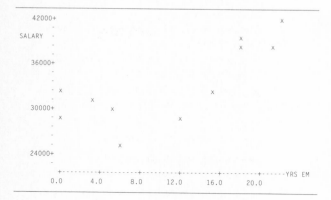

See also Tutorial 3.

Graph > Character Graphs > Multiple Scatter Plot

The Multiple Scatter Plot command displays several character-based scatter plots on a single set of axes in the Session window. Minitab plots the first pair of columns with the symbol A, the second with the symbol B, and so on. If several points fall on the same spot, Minitab provides a count. If the count is more than 9, a + symbol is used.

Dialog Box Options

Y Variables and **X Variables::** Enter up to four pairs of columns that you want to plot against one another. If you want to plot more than four pairs, use the Session command MPLOT.

Annotate: See "Graph > Character Graphs > Scatter Plot" for information.

Scale: See "Graph > Character Graphs > Scatter Plot" for information.

Corresponding Session Command

MPLOT

Example: Using Multiple Scatter Plot

The following dialog box and equivalent Session command illustrate how to produce a Character multiple scatter plot of salary versus education level and years employed data in PAY2.MTW.

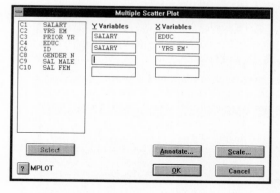

```
MTB > GStd.
MTB > MPlot 'SALARY' 'EDUC' 'SALARY' 'YRS EM'.
```

This command produces the following graph in the Session window:

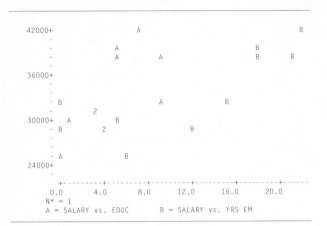

```
42000+               A                              B
     -
     -         A                          B
     -         A        A                 B      B
36000+
     -
     -   B                     A          B
     -        2                           B
30000+ A            B
     - B          2                   B
     -
     - A          B
24000+
       +---------+---------+---------+---------+---------+------
      0.0       4.0       8.0      12.0      16.0      20.0
    N* = 1
    A = SALARY vs. EDUC      B = SALARY vs. YRS EM
```

See also Tutorial 3.

Graph > Character Graphs > Time Series Plot

You choose this command to produce a character-based time series plot in the Session window, with one or more series plotted on the vertical axis versus the integers 1, 2, 3, ... on the horizontal axis. Often the data are a series of observations made at equally spaced intervals of time, such as monthly sales figures or yearly growth increments.

Dialog Box Options

Series: Enter a column for the vertical axis that you want to plot against time. If you specify more than one column, Minitab plots them on the same graph. In this case, Minitab uses special symbols that it explains at the bottom of the graph.

Origin: Enter a number for a starting point.

Period: Enter a positive integer up to 36 to set the distance between tick marks. Minitab uses periodic numbers as plotting symbols. If you specify a period of 5, each group of five observations is plotted with the numbers 1, 2, 3, 4, and 5. For a period length greater than 9, data are plotted with a 0 for 10, A for 11, B for 12, and so on.

Time Series Plot Scale Dialog Box Options

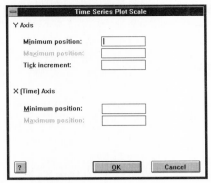

Y Axis: You can control the range and scale of the vertical axis.

Minimum position and Maximum position: Enter numbers for the minimum and maximum positions to control the range.

Tick increment: Enter a number to indicate the time range. This number specifies the increment that marks the distance between tick marks (+) on the axis.

X (Time) Axis: Enter numbers to control the subset of the time series that Minitab plots. These entries work with the Origin specified in the Time Series Plot dialog box. For example, with Origin set to 1921, First time set to 1930, and Last time set to 1950, Minitab plots only those observations from 1930 to 1950.

Minimum position: Enter a number. If you enter 15, Minitab plots the 15th observation as the first point.

Maximum position: Enter a number.

Equivalent Session Commands

TSPLOT (after GSTD)
MTSPLOT

Example: Using Time Series Plot

The following dialog box and equivalent Session command illustrate how to produce a Character time series plot of the data showing the percent change in the Consumer Price Index, which is stored in C2 CPICHNGE in CPI.MTW.

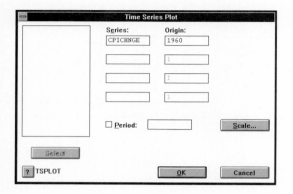

```
MTB > GStd.
MTB > MTSPlot 'CPICHNGE';
SUBC>   Origin 1960 'CPICHNGE'   .
```

This command produces the following graph in the Session window:

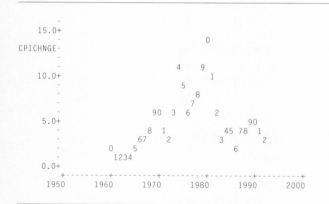

See also Tutorial 3.

The Editor Menu

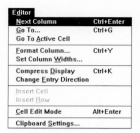

The commands on the Editor menu let you move around the Data window, format columns and column widths, compress the display, change the data entry direction, insert cells and rows, move to cell edit mode and change the Clipboard settings.

Editor > Next Column

Keyboard: Ctrl + ←Enter

Next Column moves the cursor to the first cell at the top of the column to the right of the current active cell in the Data window. This command is functional only when the Data window is active and the data-entry arrow points down.

Editor > Next Row

Keyboard: Ctrl + ←Enter

Next Row moves the cursor to the first cell of the row below the current active cell in the Data window. This command is functional only when the Data window is active and the data-entry arrow points right.

Editor > Go To

Keyboard: Ctrl + G

To move to a specific cell in the Data window, choose the Go To command on the Editor menu. This command is functional only when the Data window is active.

Dialog Box Options

Column: Specify the number or name of the column to which you want to move.

Row: Specify the number of the row to which you want to move.

See also Tutorial 1.

Editor > Go To Active Cell

This command moves to the active cell in the Data window; it's useful when you are scrolling through a large worksheet and you need to return to the cell with which you most recently worked. This command is functional only when the Data window is active and the cell is still highlighted.

Editor > Format Columns

Keyboard: Ctrl+**Y**

Choose Format Column to specify how an individual column of data displays in the Data window. This command is functional only when the Data window is active. To set the width of all columns, use Editor > Set Column Widths. These two commands can be used in combination to customize your Data window display.

Dialog Box Options

Format for: Minitab displays the number and name of the column you are formatting.

Column Width:

Automatic Widening: Choose to have Minitab determine the format depending on the width and type of the data in the column.

Fixed Width: Choose to specify a fixed column width, and then enter a number corresponding to the width of the field you want to display.

Format:

Automatic Format: Choose to have Minitab determine the format depending on the width and type of data in the column.

Fixed decimal with [ ] decimal places: Choose to specify a fixed format with decimal places, and then enter the number of decimal places you want to display in the text box.

Exponential with [ ] decimal places: Choose to specify an exponential format with decimal places, and then enter the number of decimal places you want to display in the text box.

Alpha: Minitab automatically formats a column depending on the first entry in that column. If the entry is numeric data, the format alpha option is unavailable. If the first entry is alpha data, Minitab automatically formats it as an alpha column.

Editor > Set Column Widths

This command sets all the column widths in the Data window. This command is functional only when the Data window is active.

Dialog Box Options

Set Column Widths to: Enter a number corresponding to the width of the field you want to display. Minitab sets column widths to the specified value, except for those you have changed individually using Editor > Format Column.

Change widths that were set individually: Select to change the widths for columns that you set individually by using Editor > Format Column.

Editor > Compress Display

Keyboard: Ctrl+**K**

To hide empty, unnamed columns from the Data window, use the Compress command. Choose this command again to return the display to its original, uncompressed format. The Data window is in a compressed format when a check mark appears to the left of this menu command. This command is functional only when the Data window is active. See "Edit > Save Preferences" if you want to retain compression settings.

Editor > Change Entry Direction

This command changes the direction of the data-entry arrow in the Data window. You can also change the direction of the data-entry arrow by clicking it. Select this command again to change the direction back again. This command is only functional when the Data window is active.

Editor > Insert Cell

As the name implies, this command inserts one empty cell above the active cell in the Data window and moves the remaining cells in the column down. This command is functional only when the Data window is active.

Corresponding Session Command
INSERT

See also Tutorial 1.

Editor > Insert Row

Similar to Insert Cell, the Insert Row command adds one empty row above the active row in the Data window and moves the remaining rows down. This command is only functional when the Data window is active.

Corresponding Session Command
INSERT

See also Tutorial 1.

Editor > Cell Edit Mode

Keyboard: Alt+←Enter

You can edit the contents of an existing cell by using this command. Edit the text by typing the new text, using Del and Backspace. To exit cell Edit mode, choose this command again or click another cell. Cell Edit mode is active when a check mark appears to the left of this menu command. This command is functional only when the Data window is active.

Editor > Clipboard Settings

To specify a value other than an asterisk (*) to represent missing values in the Clipboard when you copy data from a worksheet, choose Clipboard Settings from the Editor menu. This command allows you to control how Minitab exports missing values to and imports them from the Clipboard.

Dialog Box Options

String for Missing Value: Enter the symbol or value you want to represent missing values in the Clipboard. When data are copied to the Clipboard, missing values are represented by the symbol or value you specify rather than an asterisk (*). When pasting data that contain this string from the Clipboard to the worksheet, Minitab replaces the string with an asterisk (*).

The Help Menu

The Help menu provides access to Minitab's online Help system. You can open Help directly to the Contents screen, to Getting Started, to a list of common "How do I" questions, to the Index, to Microsoft's How to Use Help window. Help also gives basic information about your release of Minitab. The quickest way to get help on individual commands is by clicking the question mark in the lower-left corner of the dialog boxes.

Corresponding Session Command
HELP

See also Tutorial 1.

Help Window

The Help window displays information about how to use Minitab. You can print, copy, paste, and annotate Help text using commands on the Help window's File and Edit menus. For complete information about how to use Help, choose Help > How to Use Help.

You can also view the Help window and the Minitab windows side by side. To do so, resize and position your main Minitab window and the Help window so they do not overlap.

Contents

This command opens the Help window to the main Minitab Contents screen. From the Contents screen you can access basic information about Minitab or you can look through the menu structure or Session commands to find the command you want.

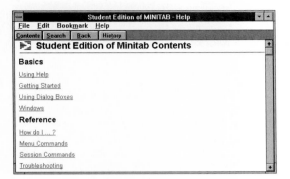

Getting Started

This command opens the Help window to the Getting Started screen, which lets you select from a number of options that describe how to start using Minitab.

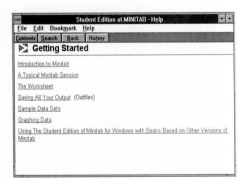

How do I

This command opens the Help window to the How do I screen, which lists commonly asked questions. Click any question to jump to the screen that provides an answer.

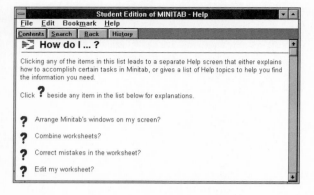

Search for Help on

This command opens the Search window, which contains an alphabetized list of all the Minitab procedures, commands, and topics. Type or scroll to the name of the procedure for which you need help, click Show Topics, click the topic you want to see, and then click Go To. Help finds the information for you.

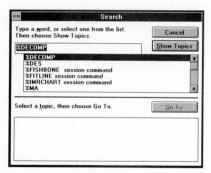

How to Use Help

For general information about using Microsoft Windows Help, select How to Use Help from the main Help menu. Help shows you how to navigate through the help tree, search for a particular topic, and use handy Help functions.

Ways to get help in Minitab:

1. Press F1 or choose **Help > Contents**.

2. Click ? in the lower-left corner of the dialog box to open Help directly to the command with which you are working.

3. From the Session window, type **HELP** after the MTB > or SUBC> prompt and then enter the name of the command about which you want information (for example, HELP REGRESS).

About Minitab

This command opens the About Minitab window, which displays the serial number, product name, release number, and other information about your copy of Minitab.

CHAPTER

3

Session Commands

Entering Session Commands

There are two ways to issue commands in Minitab: choosing commands from the menu bar, or directly typing Session commands. When you execute a command by choosing it from a menu, Minitab displays the corresponding Session command in the Session window. You can also execute a command by typing or pasting it directly into the Session window. Session commands start with a command word such as READ, ERASE, REGRESS, or PLOT. You usually follow this command word with a simple list of arguments, which consist of columns, constants, numbers, file names, or text strings. A few commands (LET and ANOVA, for example) allow more complex expressions. You type each command on a new line in either upper- or lower-case letters.

Subcommands

Many Session commands have subcommands that provide Minitab with more information. To signal Minitab that you want to use a subcommand:

- Type the main command after the MTB > prompt and enter a semicolon (;) at the end of the line.

- Press Enter.

- At the SUBC> prompt that appears, type as many subcommands as you need; enter a semicolon (;) and press Enter after each one.

- Enter a period (.) after the last subcommand to tell Minitab you are done with the command. If you forget

to end the last subcommand with a period, you can type the period all by itself on the next SUBC> line.

- To cancel the entire command, type **ABORT** as the next subcommand.

Here is a simple example of a Session command with three subcommands:

```
TABLE C1 C2;
MEANS C10;
MEDIANS C10;
COUNTS.
```

If you are entering a Session command with no subcommands, punctuation is unnecessary.

Syntax Rules for Session Commands

When you issue a command after the MTB > prompt in the Session window, you use Minitab's command language. You enter a special word for each command, with the correct syntax and the appropriate arguments.

Syntax Conventions

1. You need to type only the first four letters of any command.

2. Commands are not case-sensitive; you can type them in upper or lower case.

3. Many commands have optional subcommands that can be entered on one or more lines following the main command.

4. Start each command or subcommand on a new line and press (Enter) at the end of it.

5. When entering data, indicate missing values with the missing value symbol (*).

6. You can continue a command or a row of data on the next line with the continuation symbol (&).

7. Insert comments in your commands by entering the comment symbol (#).

8. You can abbreviate lists of consecutive columns or stored constants by using a dash (for example, HISTOGRAM C2-C5).

9. Enclose file names and column names with single quotation marks or use the column number instead (for example, HISTOGRAM 'Height' or HISTOGRAM C2).

  Professional Graphics commands have a few additional syntax rules:

10. You do not need to enclose column names or constants in quotes, except when the names contain special characters like underscores (_) and ampersands (&).

11. Do not enter additional text in the command line.

12. Always enclose text strings and file names in single quotes (').

13. To use the name of an existing column as a string or label, enclose it in double quotes (").

  The Session commands below are all equivalent. In this example, columns C1 through C4 are named A, B, C, and D.

    HISTOGRAM C1 C2 'C' 'D'

    HISTOGRAM C1 - C4

    HISTOGRAM of the data for males in 'A'-'B' & and females in 'C'-'D'

    HISTOGRAM C1 - C4 # data from June 24, 1994

    HISTC1-C4

    HISTOGRAM C1 C2 C3 C4

    hist c1-c4

Typographical Conventions

The Quick Reference Card and on-line Help list each Minitab Session command, its subcommands, and its syntax. It also shows menu commands and their corresponding Session commands. The menu command documentation in Chapter 2 also shows each corresponding Session command. Minitab uses the following conventions to describe the syntax of individual commands:

C	denotes a column, such as C12 or Height.
K	denotes a constant, such as 8.3 or K14.
E	denotes either a constant or a column.
[ ]	encloses an optional argument.
(Alt)	denotes a key,, in this case,, the (Alt) key.
CAPS	denotes a Minitab command or subcommand.

Prompts

The prompts that appear in the Session window (like MTB >) indicate the type of input Minitab expects. There are five prompts:

  MTB > Command prompt; type the Session command and press (Enter).

  SUBC> Subcommand prompt; type the subcommand, or type **ABORT** to cancel the entire command.

  DATA> Data prompt; enter data and then type **END** and press (Enter) to return to the MTB > prompt.

  CONT> Continuation prompt; continue entering the command or data started on the previous line (the line before must end with the continuation symbol, &).

  Continue? Output prompt; enter **Y** or press (Enter) to continue displaying output, or **N** to stop the display. Your response to this prompt does not affect the execution of a command, only the screen display. By default, the output height (OH) is set to 0, which tells Minitab to scroll the output without pausing. (You can always scroll backwards through the window to browse through the output.) If you set OH to another value, such as 17, Minitab pauses and displays *Continue?* after every 17 lines.

Using Symbols

Missing Values

Minitab uses an * in numeric columns and a blank space in alpha columns to represent missing values in a column. Most commands exclude any case with a missing value in any input variable from analysis. For example, scatter plots exclude points where one or both x, y coordinates are missing and Minitab displays the number of excluded points, accordingly. Regression commands use only those cases that have the response variable and all the predictor variables present. When an arithmetic command operates on a missing value, Minitab sets the result equal to *. For example, if you add columns C1 and C2, Minitab stores the sum in C3 as shown here:

C1	C2	C3
5	7	12
2	*	*
4	*	10

You can enter an * just as you would use a number in many commands. For example, when you copy columns you can include or omit rows equal to *. The time series commands LAG and DIFFERENCE produce output columns with asterisks at the top. To code numbers as the missing value symbol *, choose Code Data Values from the Manip menu, or use the Session command CODE. When you use an * in a Session command, you must enclose it in single quotation marks. For example:

CODE (2:4) '*' C1 C3

The # Comment Symbol

Minitab ignores everything you type between a # symbol and the end of a line. You can use this symbol to include comments on command lines, subcommand lines, data lines, or on lines by themselves. The Session command syntax is:

text

The & Continuation Symbol

You can type an & at the end of any line to indicate that the command, subcommand, or data row continues on to the next line. Minitab displays a CONT> prompt, after which you enter the remaining information.

Additional Session Command Functionality

There are a number of additional Session commands available to you that don't have specific menu counterparts:

BATCH	GPRO	NOECHO
BRIEF	GSTD	NOTE
ECHO	IW	OW
END	NAME	TSHARE
GPAUSE	NEWPAGE	YESNO

Character control charts also don't have specific menu counterparts. The CK capability (looping) cannot be used with menu commands. See Minitab Help for more information about these commands. Reference Chapter 5, Execs, explains the CK feature.

The following table shows restrictions put on Session commands when you use them through the menus. If you use the Session commands, the restrictions do not apply:

Command	Menu Restrictions
CDF	CDF with no argument for discrete distributions is not available.
CENTER	Only 0 or 1 values are allowed for LOCATION and SCALE.
CODE	Only five sets of old/new values are allowed.
COPY	Copying from or to constants is not allowed.
INVCDF	INVCDF with no argument for discrete distributions is not available.
LET	A subscript of a column on the left side cannot be an expression; it can only be a positive integer constant (stored or stated).
LPLOT	Only six LINE subcommands are allowed.
MPLOT	Only four (y,x) pairs are allowed. Only six LINE subcommands are allowed.
MTSPLOT	Only four series are allowed.
NAME	Not directly available; you can name columns in the Data window or in a dialog box when they are created.
PDF	PDF with no argument for discrete distributions is not available.
PLOT	Only six LINE subcommands are allowed.
PRINT	FORMAT subcommand is not available.
REGRESS	Only one PREDICT subcommand is allowed; the NOCONSTANT subcommand is not available.
Row Statistics	(RCOUNT, RMAXIMUM, RMEAN, RMEDIAN, RMINIMUM, RN, RNMISS, RRANGE, RSSQ, RSTDEV, RSUM,) Empty columns are not allowed.
SET	Only patterned data options are allowed.
SORT	Only four BY variables are allowed.
SPC charts	The HLINES subcommand can only be specified using constants, not columns.
STACK	Only five blocks are allowed.
STEPWISE	No dialog box is provided for the interactive part of STEPWISE.
TABLE	The same set of associated variables must be used for all of the summary statistics (MEANS, MEDIANS, and so forth). No control over the level of output from the CHISQUARE subcommand is available; the default level is used.
UNSTACK	Only five blocks are allowed.

CHAPTER 4

Importing and Exporting Data

Minitab offers many options for transferring data between Minitab and other applications. This section describes these options, discusses when to use which one, and includes some examples of transferring data.

Data Formats

You can use the Clipboard or files to move data into and out of Minitab. The Clipboard is most useful for small to medium-sized blocks of data that you don't plan to import or export again. Files are the preferred option for large data sets and for data that you expect to transfer between applications multiple times.

Portable Worksheet

Save your data as a portable worksheet when you want to transfer it from Minitab on one type of computer, such as a mainframe or a PC, or to Minitab on another type of computer, such as a Macintosh. A portable worksheet is a text file that contains all the data in a worksheet, including constants and column names, but not window settings. To save a file as a portable worksheet, choose File > Save Worksheet As, click Portable, click Select File, and then enter a file name.

Tab-Delimited Text

Many applications, including Minitab, recognize text files that contain a tab character between values in a row, and a return character between rows. The following table illustrates the format of tab-delimited text by showing Tab in place of the tab characters:

> Row 1, Col. 1 [Tab] Row 1, Col. 2
>
> Row 2, Col. 1 [Tab] Row 2, Col. 2
>
> Row 3, Col. 1 [Tab] Row 3, Col. 2

You can use the same format when importing or exporting data to and from other programs. Minitab uses only the tab-delimited format for the contents and names of columns. Usually the easiest way to transfer column data between Minitab and other applications is to use the tab-delimited format. Column names are neither recognized nor saved in tab-delimited text files.

Blank-Delimited Text

Blank-delimited text contains numeric data separated by spaces or a comma. Minitab uses only blank-delimited text for numeric columns. Column names are neither recognized nor saved. The blank-delimited format is a convenient way to enter a small data set manually. However, if you are importing a single column, use the SET Session command.

Formatted Text

In a formatted text file, each column of data appears in a fixed character position on each line. For example, characters 1 through 8 in each line of a formatted text file might represent the values in the first column of data; characters

9 through 12 might represent the data on the second column. Usually, but not always, columns are separated by one or more spaces. Column names are neither recognized nor saved in formatted text files. Formatted text is useful for combinations of numeric and alpha data.

Missing Data

Minitab uses an asterisk (*) to indicate a missing value in a numeric column. Other applications use different conventions. For example, suppose you are using an application that represents a missing value with a period. Because Minitab doesn't recognize a period as a number, it displays an error if you try to import data that contains one or more periods. There are two solutions to this problem:

1. If you are importing a file, replace all the periods with an asterisk (*) or a special number, such as (-99). After you've imported the data into Minitab, you can use Manip > Code Data Values to recode occurrences of -99 (or whatever value you chose) as the missing value symbol (*).

2. If you are using the Clipboard, activate the Data window. Choose Editor > Clipboard Settings and type a period (or whatever string is used for missing data in the other application) in the String for Missing Value text box. Click OK. When you paste the data into Minitab, the periods automatically change to asterisks.

Examples of Importing Data

Clipboard

You can use this method to import data into Minitab from any Windows application that lets you copy data to the Clipboard as columns separated by tab characters, including Excel, Lotus 1-2-3 for Windows, and Quattro Pro for Windows.

To copy data from one of these or a similar application in a tab-delimited format, select the block of cells that contains the column names and the data and then choose Edit > Copy. Omit rows that are blank or contain information that is not part of the data you want to copy to Minitab.

Start Minitab and move to the Data window, if necessary. Click the cell that you want to become the upper left corner of the pasted block of data and then choose Edit > Paste Cells. Adjust the column widths in the Data window, if necessary, to better display the data.

Excel

To transfer Excel data to Minitab, save the information in a text file. From the Excel menu, choose File > Save As, click the Save File as Type drop-down arrow, and select Text from the list. Click OK to create a tab-delimited file with a TXT extension.

Now start Minitab. Choose File > Import ASCII Data. Specify which columns should hold the data. The number of columns you specify must match the number of columns in the file. Click Format. Type the number of rows containing titles and blank lines in the Skip first text box to instruct Minitab to skip those rows at the top of the file, and then click Tab delimited.

Click OK twice to close the dialog boxes, and then open the file that contains the tab-delimited data. You may want to adjust the column widths in the Data window to show all the data.

Blank- or Comma-Delimited Data Via a File

You can use this method if the data file consists of columns with only numbers, not alphabetic characters; separated by at least one space or a comma; and without any blank cells. Each row can contain up to but no more than 512 characters of data.

Choose File > Import ASCII Data and complete the Import ASCII Data dialog box, specifying into which columns to import the data. The number of columns you list must match the number of columns in the file.

If the file contains one or more lines of alphabetic text at the top, such as titles or column names, tell Minitab to skip those lines. From the File > Import ASCII Data dialog box, choose the Format button and enter the correct number of lines to skip.

If the data file is very wide (more than 160 characters per row), move to the Session window and type the command:

IW 512

Then choose File > Import ASCII Data, complete the dialog box, and click OK.

If the data file includes blank cells, Minitab usually converts the entire row that contains a blank cell to missing values (*) since Minitab has no way to determine which cell is missing. Minitab then indicates the affected rows so you can edit them as necessary.

Fixed Format Data

Presuming your data follow a fixed format with the values in each column aligned and no tab characters, you should note the position and width of each segment of the data before you import it.

For example, a mainframe computer might produce class records in the following format:

```
Rose, A.       123456789  8  7 20 23 58
Fischer, W.    234567890  9 10 23 21 63
Peters, B.     345678901  5  4 15 18 42
Grayson, M.    456789012  7  8 21 19 55
Harris, L.     567890123  4  6 13 18 41
```

The name contains sixteen characters, the ID contains nine characters, and the scores contain three characters each (including one or more leading spaces).

To import the data into Minitab, download the data to a file on your PC and then start Minitab. Choose File > Import Text. Specify the columns in which you want to import the data and then click Format. Click Formatted and enter the *format statement* A16,A9,5F3 in the associated text box to specify the location of the data in the text files. F designates numbers, A indicates alpha data, X says to skip spaces, and / tells Minitab to go to the next line. (For additional information about and examples of format statements, see online Help.) Click OK twice to close the dialog boxes. Now open the file that contains the data.

If the mainframe data contain column names, you must remove them before you import since the formatted option does not recognize them. If the data contain only numbers, you could use the default Blank delimited option in the Import Text-Format dialog box to read the data instead. In this case, you wouldn't need to determine the position of each column in the file.

Lotus 1-2-3 and Symphony

There are two methods that you can use to import files from Lotus 1-2-3 and Symphony. If your file consists of only numbers (for example, no alpha data, named ranges, or header information) and you want to read the entire file, the easiest way to import the data is by using the Open Worksheet command from the File menu. If you want to import a noncontiguous portion of the file, you can use named range conversion with the Open Worksheet command. However, if you are using Lotus for Windows and you have alpha data or column names that you would like

to retain, you may want to import your spreadsheet files using the method described in the "Clipboard" section.

To use the Open Worksheet command method, first choose File > Save As in Lotus 1-2-3 or Symphony. Enter a filename with the extension WK1 and click OK. Start Minitab, choose File > Open Worksheet > Lotus 1-2-3 worksheet, click Select File, and then open the file.

Note: You can import other Lotus file formats by choosing Edit > Save Preferences and selecting the worksheet version of your choice. Click Save. The next time you start Minitab, the new default takes effect.

If your Lotus file contains column names and alpha columns, you need to insert the symbol & in front of each column name to indicate that it is not data. (Minitab needs a way to distinguish the column name from other alpha columns in the spreadsheet.) Use Range > Name > Create to assign a range name to each column, such as ACOL1, which tells Minitab to include this column as an alpha column in C1. Then follow the same procedure described for files that contain only numbers to save the file and open it in Minitab. The ampersands do not appear in the column names.

Examples of Exporting Data

Word Processor

Tab-delimited data can be used by word processors that allow you to adjust the positions of tab stops. To transfer the data via the Clipboard, choose File > Export ASCII Data, select all of the columns to transfer, click Tab delimited, click Export to Session window, and then click OK. Minitab displays the tab-delimited text in the Session window. Select the text and then choose Edit > Copy. Start the word processor and choose Edit > Paste to import the data. Adjust the tab settings, if necessary, to align the data.

Excel

To export data from Minitab to Excel, open the file and choose File > Export ASCII data. Select the columns you want to export, click Tab delimited, and then click OK. Type a name for the file and click OK; Minitab automatically adds a DAT extension. Start Excel and choose File > Open. Click the List Files of Type drop-down arrow and select Text Files. Enter a file name with the DAT file extension in the File Name box to display DAT files. Select the file and then click OK to open it in Excel.

Lotus 1-2-3 and Symphony

To transfer data from Minitab to Lotus, open the worksheet and choose File > Save Worksheet As > Lotus 1-2-3 worksheet. Click Select File, type a file name, and then click OK. Minitab adds the extension WK1.

Note: You can save your worksheet to other Lotus file formats by choosing Edit > Save Preferences, selecting a different worksheet type, and then clicking Save. The next time you start Minitab, the new default takes effect.

Start Lotus 1-2-3 and open the spreadsheet.

Exporting Graphs

Often, you may want to export Minitab graphs to include them in a report or presentation prepared in another application. There are three ways to export a graph:

1. Copy it to the Clipboard
2. Print it to a file
3. Copy a bitmap to the Clipboard

Copying a Graph to the Clipboard

Using the Clipboard is generally the easiest way to bring a Minitab graph into another Windows application. With the Graph window active, choose Copy Graph from the Minitab Edit menu to copy the graph to the Clipboard. Switch to the other application, such as Microsoft Word, and paste the graph using the appropriate command (usually Edit > Paste). Different applications have different methods of pasting in graphs; they usually include an explanation under "Graphics" or "Importing Graphics" in the documentation or Help.

Print a Graph to a File

You may want to save a graph as a file so that you can send it directly to your printer or plotter or import it into

a word-processing application, such as Microsoft Word. For example, many applications can import a graph saved as an EPS file (Encapsulated PostScript), which generally results in higher-quality output than a graph copied and pasted using the Clipboard.

To save a Minitab graph as an EPS file, make sure the Graph window that contains the graph you want to save is active. Choose File > Print Window, click Print to File, and click the Setup button. Click the Specific Printer drop-down arrow to display the available printers. Double-click a PostScript printer. Next, click the Options button, click Encapsulated PostScript File, and type a filename including the EPS file extension. Click OK to close all the dialog boxes.

Once you have saved a graph in an EPS file, you can import it into another application. You can also send it directly to your PostScript printer from the DOS prompt by typing this command: COPY *filename* PRN:

You can save graphs in other printer file formats in a similar fashion — just make sure that you select the correct printer before you print to a file.

Importing EPS Graphs into Microsoft Word

Importing a EPS file into Microsoft Word for Windows 2.0 or 6.0 is a one-step process. Simply open a Microsoft Word document, choose Insert > Picture, select Encapsulated PostScript File from the List Files of Type drop-down list, choose the correct filename, and click OK.

You can then crop and scale the graph as necessary to remove any additional space or size it to fit the desired space. To do so, click the graph, choose Format > Picture, and complete the dialog box. Scaling and cropping are related. Suppose at full size you want to crop 1 inch from the top and bottom. If you scale down the graph by 50%, you need to first double the crop amount to 2 inches top and bottom to achieve the same effect.

Exporting Session Output

When you copy Session output to the Clipboard and paste it into a word processor, be sure to use a non-proportional font, such as Courier or Helvetica.

CHAPTER
5

Execs

Using Execs

You usually use Minitab interactively, which means it carries out each command as soon as you enter it. You can also use a *Minitab Exec* (an executable macro file), a set of Minitab commands stored in a file, to automate repetitive tasks, such as generating a monthly report, or to extend Minitab's functionality, such as computing a special test statistic. In other words, you can use Minitab commands to write programs tailored to your needs.

In the full commercial package, Minitab's macro facility includes *%Macros*, some of which appear as commands on the menus (for example, Trend Analysis on the Time Series submenu). Their corresponding Session commands include a % sign as a prefix, which you may see on the dialog boxes.

The Student Edition of MINITAB for Windows only provides support for Minitab Execs, which are a simpler macro files with limited programming capability. An Exec is a set of commands stored in a file. You execute an Exec by choosing File > Other Files > Run an Exec or by typing the following in the Session window:

    EXECUTE *'filename'* K

The optional argument, K, specifies the number of times Minitab executes the macro. K can be any integer; by default, Minitab executes an Exec once. The default file extension for Execs is MTB.

    Execs allow you to:

- store commands that you use repeatedly, so you don't have to retype them.

- repeat a block of commands many times; this is useful for simulations.

- loop through columns of the worksheet, performing the same analysis on each block of columns.

- loop through rows of the worksheet, performing the same analysis on each block of rows.

- use Minitab as a programming language to perform operations not provided as stand-alone commands, as you did in Tutorial 16 with the goodness-of-fit test.

You can even write an interactive Exec that pauses during execution, prompts the user for information, and then continues. To interrupt the execution of an Exec, press Ctrl+Break. Minitab completes the command in progress before it stops the Exec.

A Simple Example

Each month, a laboratory sends you data on three chemical measurements: YIELD, CHEM1, and CHEM2. You always perform the same analysis: descriptive statistics, plots of YIELD versus the two other measures, a regression, and a residual plot. Suppose you enter the following commands in a text editor (such as Notepad) to create an Exec:

    NAME C1='YIELD' C2='CHEM1' C3='CHEM2'
    DESCRIBE C1-C3
    PLOT C1 C2
    PLOT C1 C3
    NAME C10 = 'SRESIDS' C11 = 'FITS'

```
REGRESS C1 2 C2 C3;
    SRES C10;
    FITS C11.
PLOT C10 C11
```

Save the file with the name ANALYSIS.MTB. Now, if you place the data for January in the file JAN.DAT with the yield data in C1, the chemical 1 data in C2, and the chemical 2 data in C3, you can perform the analysis by executing the ANALYSIS Exec from the Run an Exec dialog box. You can repeat this analysis each month simply by executing the Exec.

Creating an Exec

There are three ways to create command files:

- With a text editor, as in the previous example and in Tutorial 16. If you use an editor such as Notepad, store the file in a standard format (usually ASCII). If you create an Exec with a word processor, save the file as text only. You can also cut and paste commands from the History window into a text editor rather than type them in.

- With the command JOURNAL (File > Other Files > Start Recording History). This command stores a copy of all the commands issued in the current Minitab session in a file with the extension MTJ. When you execute this file, you must provide the MTJ extension.

- With the command STORE (File > Other Files > Start Recording Exec). This command lets you create a command file during your Minitab session.

Looping through Commands and Rows of Data

Suppose you want to train your eye to judge normal probability plots. You decide to generate 20 plots of data from a normal distribution. First, store the following commands in a macro called NPLOT.MTB:

```
RAND 50 C1
NSCORES C2 C1
NAME C1='DATA' C2='NSCORES'
PLOT C2 C1
```

To execute this file 20 times to generate 20 different normal probability plots, either use the Run an Exec dialog box or type:

```
EXECUTE 'NPLOT' 20
```

You can also loop through rows of data. Suppose you have a full year — one month stacked on top of another — of the laboratory data from the previous example stored in a file called LAB.DAT. There are now four variables: YIELD, CHEM1, CHEM2, and MONTH. To perform the same analysis as described in "A Simple Example" for each month (in C4) individually, enter these commands in the file YEAR.MTB:

```
NAME C11='YIELD' C12='CHEM1' C13='CHEM2'
& C20='SRESIDS' C21='FITS'
COPY C1-C3 C11-C13;
    USE C4 = K1.
PRINT K1
DESCRIBE C11-C13
PLOT C11 C12
PLOT C11 C13
REGRESS C11 2 C12 C13;
    SRES C20;
    FITS C21.
PLOT C20 C21
LET K1 = K1 + 1
```

Then, to analyze the file LAB.DAT, type:

```
LET K1 = 1
READ 'LAB' C1-C4
EXECUTE 'YEAR' 12
```

Looping through Columns and Rows

A special Minitab feature, called the *CK capability*, lets you loop through the columns of the worksheet. Suppose you have a file, MYDATA.DAT, that contains 21 variables, and you want to plot the last variable versus each of the first 20 variables in 20 separate Character plots. First store the following commands in a file called PLOTS.MTB:

```
GSTD
PLOT C21 CK1
LET K1 = K1 + 1
```

Then type:

```
READ 'MYDATA' C1-C21
LET K1 = 1
EXECUTE 'PLOTS' 20
```

The first time through the loop, K1 = 1. Minitab substitutes this value for K1 in the PLOT command, which becomes PLOT C21 C1. The next time through the loop, K1 = 2, which yields PLOT C21 C2, and so on.

The next example shows how to accumulate column statistics in one column. Suppose you have data in

C1 through C30. To compute the mean of each column and store it in C40, create a file called MEAN.MTB:

```
LET C40(K1) = MEAN(CK1)
LET K1 = K1 + 1
```

To execute the file, type:

```
LET K1 = 1
EXECUTE 'MEAN' 30
```

The first time through the loop, K1 = 1, so row 1 of C40 equals the mean of C1. The next time through the loop, K1 = 2, so row 2 of C40 equals the mean of C2, and so on.

Another example of how the CK capability is used would be the case of a researcher who collects data from tomato plants each month. Some months she has 20 plants, other months as few as 5. The data for one month consist of one variable for each plant. This PLANTS.MTB Exec, containing the following two commands, lets the researcher analyze a different number of plants each month:

```
HISTOGRAM C1-CK50
DESCRIBE C1-CK50
```

If the researcher has data on 12 plants stored in JAN.DAT, she types:

```
READ 'JAN.DAT' C1-C12
LET K50 = 12
EXECUTE 'PLANTS'
```

Each time she runs the Exec, she simply defines K50 as the correct number of plants.

Conditional Execution and Nesting Execs

If the argument K equals zero or a negative value at the point that a macro reaches the EXECUTE command, Minitab doesn't execute the Exec. This feature lets you set up a conditional execution. As an example, modify the Exec MEAN.MTB so that it accumulates means for only those columns that have more than nine observations. You need two macro files. MEAN10.MTB contains:

```
LET K3 = (COUNT(CK1) > 9)
EXECUTE 'OVER9' K3
LET K1 = K1 + 1
```

and OVER9.MTB contains:

```
LET C40(K2) = MEAN(CK1)
LET K2 = K2 + 1
```

To use this Exec, type:

```
LET K1 = 1
LET K2 = 1
EXECUTE 'MEAN10' 30
```

Notice that you have nested two Execs, that is, MEAN10.MTB *calls* (or executes) OVER9.MTB. Nesting helps you write more sophisticated Execs. You can nest Execs up to five deep on most computers.

To see how this Exec works, consider a worksheet with three columns. Suppose C2 contains 23 observations, C2 has 7, and C3 stores 35. When you first execute MEAN10.MTB, K1 = K2 = 1. Then K3 = 1 since COUNT (C1) > 9. Since K3 = 1, OVER9 is executed once, MEAN (C1) is stored in C40 (1), and K2 = 2. The second time through the loop, K2 = 2 and K1 = 2. This time K3 = 0 since COUNT (C2) < 9, and OVER9.MTB is not executed. The third time through the loop, K1 = 3 and K2 = 2. Then K3 = 1 since COUNT (C3) > 9, OVER9.MTB is executed, and MEAN (C3) is stored in C40 (2).

Interactive Execs

You can write a Minitab Exec that begins to execute, pauses for user input, and then continues to execute. You create such an *interactive Exec* by using the READ, SET, and INSERT commands and a special file name, TERMINAL.

Suppose you have two command files. The first, PLANTS.MTB, is the same as before. The second, TOMATO.MTB, contains:

```
NOECHO
NOTE Number of tomato plants?
SET 'TERMINAL' C50;
    NOBS = 1.
COPY C50 K50
EXEC 'PLANTS'
ECHO
```

When you type EXECUTE 'TOMATO', Minitab displays the note, "How many tomato plants do you have this month?" The terminal then waits for you to respond. You enter a number and press [Enter]. Because the subcommand NOBS = 1 tells SET to expect only one number, you don't need to type END to signal that you've finished entering data; the Exec TOMATO.MTB continues to execute with the correct number of plants.

The PINF.MTB Exec in Tutorial 16 is an interactive Exec.

Using YESNO

The YESNO command, with the syntax

YESNO K

also takes input from the terminal. It prompts the user to decide whether Minitab should execute or skip a block of commands. You enter either YES or NO at the terminal and YESNO changes the value of the K argument accordingly. K = 1 when the user responds YES; K = 0 when the user responds NO. YESNO takes only one argument, which must be a stored constant. Any response that begins with a y or Y is interpreted as YES; any answer that starts with n or N is translated as NO. All other responses are invalid; the user receives the message *Please answer Yes or No* and is given another opportunity. If Minitab does not obtain a valid response after five tries, it assumes a NO answer.

YESNO does not issue a prompt; it only reads a response. When you write the Exec, you must use the NOTE command to prompt the user.

Using NOECHO and ECHO

The NOECHO command suppresses the echo printing of commands, whereas ECHO enables it. The default is NOECHO, so when you run an Exec you won't see the commands on the screen. Normally NOECHO is the first line in a command file and ECHO is the last. If the NOECHO command is used, then Minitab only prints the output and the comments on NOTE commands. Minitab does not print any comments that appear after the # symbol. The PINF.MTB Exec in Tutorial 16 uses these commands.

Exec Session Commands

The following commands are available to you for using Minitab Exec macros:

EXECUTE	'filename' K times
STORE	in 'filename' the following commands
END	the storing of commands
NOTE	displays messages to user
#	provides internal documentation
NOECHO	the commands that follow
ECHO	the commands that follow
YESNO	K

APPENDIX A

Session Command/Menu Command Equivalents

This appendix is intended for those who are familiar with Minitab and who want to find the menu equivalent for Session commands. The Session commands are listed on the left, and the menu equivalents of those commands are on the right. GPRO in parentheses after a Session command means that the equivalent command produces a Professional graph; GSTD in parentheses, a Character graph.

The symbol > indicates submenus; for example, Calc > Set Base means "Choose Set Base from the Calc menu." The sequence Stat > Time Series > Autocorrelation means "Choose Time Series and then Autocorrelation from the Stat menu."

Not available means that there is no menu equivalent for the given Session command. *Not available in the Student Edition* means that that command is available from the menus in Minitab, Release 10 for Windows, but is not available (either from the menus or from the Session window) in the Student Edition.

%ACF	*Not available in the Student Edition*
%ANOM	*Not available in the Student Edition*
%BANOM	*Not available in the Student Edition*
%CAPA	*Not available in the Student Edition*
%CONTOUR	*Not available in the Student Edition*
%CUSUM	*Not available in the Student Edition*
%DECOMP	Stat > Time Series > Decomposition...
%DES	Stat > Time Series > Double Exp Smoothing...
%FISHBONE	Stat > SPC > Cause-and-Effect...
%FITLINE	Stat > Regression > Fitted Line Plot...
%FORM	*Not available in the Student Edition*
%IMRCHART	Stat > Control Charts > I-MR...

%INTERACT	*Not available in the Student Edition*
%INTPLOT	*Not available in the Student Edition*
%MA	Stat > Time Series > Moving Average...
%MAIN	*Not available in the Student Edition*
%MARGPLOT	*Not available in the Student Edition*
%MESH	*Not available in the Student Edition*
%NORMPLOT	Graph > Normal Plot...
%PACF	*Not available in the Student Edition*
%PANOM	*Not available in the Student Edition*
%PARETO	Stat > SPC > Pareto Chart...
%PIE	*Not available in the Student Edition*
%RESPLOTS	Stat > Regression > Residual Plot...
	Stat > ANOVA > Residual Plot...
%SES	Stat > Time Series > Single Exp Smoothing...
%SIXPACK	*Not available in the Student Edition*
%TREND	Stat > Time Series > Trend Analysis...
%WEIBPLOT	*Not available in the Student Edition*
%WINTADD	Stat > Time Series > Winters' Method...
%WINTMULT	Stat > Time Series > Winters' Method...
%XRCHART	Stat > Control Charts > Xbar-R...
%XSCHART	Stat > Control Charts > Xbar-S...

ABORT	*Session Command*
ABSOLUTE	Calc > Mathematical Expressions...
	Calc > Functions...
ACF	Stat > Time Series > Autocorrelation...
ACOS	Calc > Mathematical Expressions...
	Calc > Functions...
ADD	Calc > Mathematical Expressions...
ALPHA	*Not available*
ANCOVA	*Not available in the Student Edition*
ANOVA	Stat > ANOVA > Balanced ANOVA...
ANTILOG	Calc > Mathematical Expressions...
	Calc > Functions...
AOVONEWAY	Stat > ANOVA > Oneway (Unstacked)...
ARIMA	Stat > Time Series > ARIMA...
ASIN	Calc > Mathematical Expressions...
	Calc > Functions ...
ATAN	Calc > Mathematical Expressions...
	Calc > Functions...

BASE	Calc > Set Base...
BATCH	*Session Command*
BBDESIGN	*Not available in the Student Edition*
BOXPLOT (GPRO)	Graph > Boxplot...
BOXPLOT (GSTD)	Graph > Character Graphs > Boxplot...
BREG	*Not available in the Student Edition*
BRIEF	*Session Command*

CCDESIGN	*Not available in the Student Edition*
CCF	Stat > Time Series > Cross Correlation...
CCHART (GPRO)	Stat > Control Charts > C...
CCHART (GSTD)	*Session Command*
CD	*Session Command*
CDF	Calc > Probability Distributions > distribution
CENTER	Calc > Standardize...
CHART	Graph > Chart...
CHISQUARE	Stat > Tables > Chisquare Test...
CLUOBS	*Not available in the Student Edition*
CLUVARS	*Not available in the Student Edition*
CODE	Manip > Code Data Values...
CONCATENATE	Manip > Concatenate...
CONSTANT	Stat > Fit Intercept
CONTOUR	*Not available in the Student Edition*
CONTOURPLOT	*Not available in the Student Edition*
CONVERT	Manip > Convert...
COPY	Manip > Copy Columns...
CORRELATION	Stat > Basic Statistics > Correlation...
COS	Calc > Mathematical Expressions...
	Calc > Functions ...
COUNT	Calc > Mathematical Expressions ...
	Calc > Column Statistics...
COVARIANCE	Stat > Basic Statistics > Covariance...
CPLOT	*Not available in the Student Edition*
CTABLE	*Not available in the Student Edition*

DEFINE	*Not available in the Student Edition*
DELETE	Manip > Delete Rows
DESCRIBE	Stat > Basic Statistics > Descriptive Statistics...
DIAGONAL	*Not available in the Student Edition*
DIFFERENCES	Stat > Time Series > Differences...
DIR	*Session Command*
DISCRIMINANT	*Not available in the Student Edition*
DIVIDE	Calc > Mathematical Expressions...
DOTPLOT	Graph > Character Graphs > Dotplot...

ECHO	*Session Command*
EIGEN	*Not available in the Student Edition*
END	File > Other Files > Stop Recording Exec... and Session command for data entry
ERASE	Manip > Erase Variables...
EWMACHART (GPRO)	Stat > Control Charts > EWMA...
EWMACHART (GSTD)	*Session Command*
EXECUTE	File > Other Files > Run an Exec...
EXPONENTIATE	Calc > Mathematical Expressions...
	Calc > Functions...

FACTOR	*Not available in the Student Edition*
FFACTORIAL	*Not available in the Student Edition*
FFDESIGN	*Not available in the Student Edition*
FRIEDMAN	Stat > Nonparametrics > Friedman...

GBOXPLOT	*Not available*
GCCHART	*Not available*
GEWMACHART	*Not available*
GHISTOGRAM	*Not available*
GICHART	*Not available*
GLM	*Not available in the Student Edition*
GLPLOT	*Not available*
GMACHART	*Not available*
GMPLOT	*Not available*
GMRCHART	*Not available*
GNPCHART	*Not available*
GOPTIONS	*Not available*
GPAUSE	*Session Command*
GPCHART	*Not available*
GPLOT	*Not available*
GPRO	*Session Command*
GRCHART	*Not available*
GRID	*Not available in the Student Edition*
GSAVE	File > Save Window As...
GSCHART	*Not available*
GSTD	*Session Command*
GTPLOT	*Not available*
GUCHART	*Not available*
GVIEW	File > Other Files > Open Graph...
GXBARCHART	*Not available*

HEIGHT	Graph > Character Graphs > Set Options...
HELP	Help > ...
HISTOGRAM (GPRO)	Graph > Histogram...
HISTOGRAM (GSTD)	Graph > Character Graphs > Histogram...

ICHART (GPRO)	Stat > Control Charts > Individuals...
ICHART (GSTD)	*Session Command*
INDICATOR	Calc > Make Indicator Variables...
INFO	File > Get Worksheet Info
	Window > Info
INSERT	File > Import ASCII Data...
INVCDF	Calc > Probability Distributions > Distribution
INVERT	*Not available in the Student Edition*
IW	*Session Command*

JOURNAL	File > Other Files > Start Recording History
	Window > History
KRUSKAL	Stat > Nonparametrics > Kruskal-Wallis...
LAG	Calc > Mathematical Expressions...
	Stat > Time Series > Lag...
LC	*Not available*
LET	Calc > Mathematical Expressions...
LOGE	Calc > Mathematical Expressions...
	Calc > Functions...
LOGTEN	Calc > Mathematical Expressions...
	Calc > Functions...
LPLOT	Graph > Character Graphs > Scatter Plot...
LVALS	*Not available in the Student Edition*
MACHART (GPRO)	Stat > Control Charts > Moving Average...
MACHART (GSTD)	*Session Command*
MANN-WHITNEY	Stat > Nonparametrics > Mann-Whitney...
MATRIXPLOT	*Not available in the Student Edition*
MAXIMUM	Calc > Mathematical Expressions...
	Calc > Column Statistics...
MEAN	Calc > Mathematical Expressions...
	Calc > Column Statistics...
MEDIAN	Calc > Mathematical Expressions...
	Calc > Column Statistics...
MINIMUM	Calc > Mathematical Expressions...
	Calc > Column Statistics...
MIXREG	*Not available in the Student Edition*
MOOD	*Not available in the Student Edition*
MPLOT	Graph > Character Graphs > Multiple Scatter Plot...
MPOLISH	*Not available in the Student Edition*
MRCHART (GPRO)	Stat > Control Charts > Moving Range...
MRCHART (GSTD)	*Session Command*
MTSPLOT	Graph > Character Graphs > Time Series Plot...
MULTIPLY	Calc > Mathematical Expressions...
N	Calc > Mathematical Expressions...
	Calc > Column Statistics...
NAME	*Session Command*
NEWPAGE	*Session Command*
NMISS	Calc > Mathematical Expressions...
	Calc > Column Statistics...
NOCONSTANT	Stat > Fit Intercept
NOECHO	*Session Command*

NOJOURNAL	File > Other Files > Stop Recording History
NOOUTFILE	File > Other Files > Stop Recording Session
NOPAPER	*Not available*
NOTE	*Session Command*
NPCHART (GPRO)	Stat > Control Charts > NP...
NPCHART (GSTD)	*Session Command*
NSCORES	Calc > Mathematical Expressions..
	Calc > Functions...
OH	File > Other Files > Start Recording Session
ONEWAY	Stat > ANOVA > Oneway...
OUTFILE	File > Other Files > Start Recording Session...
OW	File > Other Files > Start Recording Session
OW	*Session command (for controlling width of Character plots)*
PACF	Stat > Time Series > Partial Autocorrelation...
PAPER	*Not available*
PARPRODUCTS	Calc > Mathematical Expressions...
	Calc > Functions...
PARSUMS	Calc > Mathematical Expressions...
	Calc > Functions...
PBDESIGN	*Not available in the Student Edition*
PCA	*Not available in the Student Edition*
PCHART (GPRO)	Stat > Control Charts > P...
PCHART (GSTD)	*Session Command*
PDF	Calc > Probability Distributions > Distribution
PLOT (GPRO)	Graph > Plot...
PLOT (GSTD)	Graph > Character Graphs >Scatter Plot...
PLTX	*Not available in the Student Edition*
PRINT	File > Display Data...
RAISE	Calc > Mathematical Expressions...
RANDOM	Calc > Random Data > Distribution
RANGE	Calc > Column Statistics...
RANK	Manip > Rank...
	Calc > Mathematical Expressions...
RCHART (GPRO)	Stat > Control Charts > R...
RCHART (GSTD)	*Session Command*
RCOUNT	Calc > Row Statistics...
READ	File > Import ASCII Data...
REGRESS	Stat > Regression > Regression...
RESTART	File > Restart Minitab
RETRIEVE	File > Open Worksheet...
RLINE	*Not available in the Student Edition*
RMAXIMUM	Calc > Row Statistics...
RMEAN	Calc > Row Statistics...
RMEDIAN	Calc > Row Statistics...

RMINIMUM	Calc > Row Statistics...
RN	Calc > Row Statistics...
RNMISS	Calc > Row Statistics...
ROOTOGRAM	*Not available in the Student Edition*
ROUND	Calc > Mathematical Expressions...
	Calc > Functions...
RRANGE	Calc > Row Statistics...
RSCONTOUR	*Not available in the Student Edition*
RSMOOTH	*Not available in the Student Edition*
RSREG	*Not available in the Student Edition*
RSSURFACE	*Not available in the Student Edition*
RSSQ	Calc > Row Statistics...
RSTDEV	Calc > Row Statistics...
RSUM	Calc > Row Statistics...
RUNS	Stat > Nonparametrics > Runs Test...
SAMPLE	Calc > Random Data > Sample from Columns...
SAVE	File > Save Worksheet...
	File > Save Worksheet As...
SCDESIGN	*Not available in the Student Edition*
SCHART (GPRO)	Stat > Control Charts > S...
SCHART (GSTD)	*Session Command*
SET	Calc > Set Patterned Data...
SIGNS	Calc > Mathematical Expressions...
	Calc > Functions...
SIN	Calc > Mathematical Expressions...
	Calc > Functions...
SINTERVAL	Stat > Nonparametrics > 1-Sample Sign...
SLDESIGN	*Not available in the Student Edition*
SORT	Manip > Sort...
	Calc > Mathematical Expressions...
SQRT	Calc > Mathematical Expressions...
	Calc > Functions...
SSQ	Calc > Mathematical Expressions...
	Calc > Column Statistics...
STACK	Manip > Stack...
STATS	*Not available in the Student Edition*
STDEV	Calc > Mathematical Expressions...
	Calc > Column Statistics...
STEM	Graph > Character Graphs > Stem-and-Leaf...
STEPWISE	Stat > Regression > Stepwise...
STEST	Stat > Nonparametrics > 1-Sample Sign...
STOP	File > Exit
STORE	File > Other Files > Start Recording Exec...
SUBTRACT	Calc > Mathematical Expressions...
SUM	Calc > Mathematical Expressions...
	Calc > Column Statistics...
SURFACEPLOT	*Not available in the Student Edition*
SYSTEM	*Not available in the Student Edition*

TABLE	Stat > Tables > Cross Tabulation...
TALLY	Stat > Tables > Tally...
TAN	Calc > Mathematical Expressions...
	Calc > Functions...
TINTERVAL	Stat > Basic Statistics > 1-Sample t...
TPLOT	*Not available in the Student Edition*
TRANSPOSE	*Not available in the Student Edition*
TSHARE	*Session Command*
TSPLOT (GPRO)	Stat > Time Series > Time Series Plot...
	Graph > Time Series Plot...
TSPLOT (GSTD)	Graph > Character Graphs > Time Series Plot...
TTEST	Stat > Basic Statistics > 1-Sample t...
TWOSAMPLE	Stat > Basic Statistics > 2-Sample t...
TWOT	Stat > Basic Statistics > 2-Sample t...
TWOWAY	Stat > ANOVA > Twoway...
TYPE	*Session Command*
UC	*Not available*
UCHART (GPRO)	Stat > Control Charts > U...
UCHART (GSTD)	*Session Command*
UNSTACK	Manip > Unstack...
VARTEST	*Not available in the Student Edition*
WALSH	Stat > Nonparametrics > Pairwise Averages...
WDIFF	Stat > Nonparametrics > Pairwise Differences...
WIDTH	Graph > Character Graphs > Set Options...
WINTERVAL	Stat > Nonparametrics > 1-Sample Wilcoxon...
WRITE	File > Export ASCII Data...
WSLOPE	Stat > Nonparametrics > Pairwise Slopes...
WTEST	Stat > Nonparametrics > 1-Sample Wilcoxon...
XBARCHART (GPRO)	Stat > Control Charts > Xbar...
XBARCHART (GSTD)	*Session Command*
XDACTIVATE	*Not available in the Student Edition*
XDADD	*Not available in the Student Edition*
XDDEACTIVATE	*Not available in the Student Edition*
XDEXEC	*Not available in the Student Edition*
XDGET	*Not available in the Student Edition*
XDREMOVE	*Not available in the Student Edition*
YESNO	*Session Command*
ZINTERVAL	Stat > Basic Statistics > 1-Sample Z...
ZTEST	Stat > Basic Statistics > 1-Sample Z...

APPENDIX B

Student Edition Limits

This appendix contains lists of the software features that are contained in Minitab, Release 10 for Windows, but are not included or fully supported in this Student Edition package. It is arranged in functional blocks of menu and Session commands.

Data Management
File > Open Worksheet...
        Microsoft Excel spreadsheet files
        Borland Quattro Pro spreadsheet files
        Ashton Tate dBase database files
File > Merge Worksheet...
Edit > Paste Link
Edit > Links > Manage Links...
Edit > Links > Get External Data...
Edit > Links > Execute External Command...
SYSTEM Session Command

Command Editing
Edit > Command Line Editor

Data Manipulation
Calc > Make Mesh Data...

Matrices
Calc > Matrices > Read...
Calc > Matrices > Transpose...
Calc > Matrices > Invert...
Calc > Matrices > Define Constant...
Calc > Matrices > Diagonal...
Calc > Matrices > Copy...
Calc > Matrices > Eigen Analysis...
Calc > Matrices > Arithmetic...
        Add
        Subtract
        Multiply

Basic Statistics   Stat > Basic Statistics > Homogeneity of Variance...

Regression   Stat > Regression > Regression...
                                    X'X inverse
                                    R matrix
                                    Weights
                                    Pure error
                                    Experimental
                            REGRESS TOLERANCE Session subcommand
                            Stat > Regression > Best Subsets...

Analysis of Variance   Stat > ANOVA > Analysis of Means...
                            Stat > ANOVA > Balanced ANOVA...
                                    Random Factors
                                    Use the restricted form of the mixed model
                                    Include multivariate ANOVA
                                    Hypothesis matrices
                                    Partial correlation matrix
                                    Eigen values and vectors
                                    Univariate F-Tests
                                    Display expected mean squares
                            Stat > ANOVA > Analysis of Covariance...
                            Stat > ANOVA > General Linear Model...
                            Stat > ANOVA > Main Effects Plot...
                            Stat > ANOVA > Interactions Plot...
                            %BANOM Session command
                            %PANOM Session command

Design of Experiments   Stat > DOE > Fractional Factorial...
                            Stat > DOE > Plackett - Burman...
                            Stat > DOE > Fit Factorial Model...
                            Stat > DOE > Box - Behnken...
                            Stat > DOE > Central Composite...
                            Stat > DOE > Fit RSM...
                            Stat > DOE > RS Contour...
                            Stat > DOE > RS Wireframe Plot...
                            Stat > DOE > RS Surface Plot...
                            Stat > DOE > Simplex Centroid...
                            Stat > DOE > Simplex Lattice...
                            Stat > DOE > Fit Mixture Model...
                            Stat > DOE > Main Effects Plot...
                            Stat > DOE > Interactions Plot...
                            Stat > DOE > Residual Plots...
                            %FORM Session command

Control Charts   Stat > Control Charts > CUSUM...

Statistical Process   Stat > SPC > Capability Analysis...
Control   Stat > SPC > Capability Sixpack...

Multivariate Statistics	Stat > Multivariate > Principal Components...
	Stat > Multivariate > Factor Analysis...
	Stat > Multivariate > Discriminant Analysis...
	Stat > Multivariate > Balanced MANOVA...
	Stat > Multivariate > General MANOVA...
	Stat > Multivariate > Cluster Observations...
	Stat > Multivariate > Cluster Variables...
	Stat > Multivariate > Cluster K-Means...
Nonparametric Statistics	Stat > Nonparametrics > Mood's Median Test...
Exploratory Data Analysis	Stat > EDA > Letter Values...
	Stat > EDA > Median Polish...
	Stat > EDA > Resistant Line...
	Stat > EDA > Resistant Smooth...
	Stat > EDA > Condensed Plot...
	Stat > EDA > Coded Table...
	Stat > EDA > Rootogram...
	Stat > EDA > Stem-and-Leaf...
	Stat > EDA > Boxplot...

Professional Graphs

Graph > Plot, Chart, Histogram, Boxplot, or Time Series Plot...
    Data Display
        Type Font
        Label
    Annotation
        Data Labels
        Marker
        Polygon
    Frame
        Axis (specialized options)
        Tick (specialized options)
        Reference (specialized options)
        Grid (specialized options)
    Region
        Figure
        Data
        Legend
Graph > Plot, Histogram, or Time Series Plot...
    Data Display
        Lowess
Graph > Matrix Plot...
    Data Display (specialized options)
    Annotation
    Frame
    Region
Graph > Layout...
Graph > 3-D Plot...
Graph > Draftsman Plot...

Graph > Contour Plot...
Graph > 3D Plot...
Graph > 3D Wireframe Plot...
Graph > 3D Surface Plot...
Graph > Pie Chart...
Graph > Interval Chart...
Graph > Marginal Plot...
Graph > Weibull Plot...

Character Graphs

Graph > Character Graphs > Grid...
Graph > Character Graphs > Contour...
Graph > Character Graphs > Pseudo 3-D Plot...

Session Window Editing

Editor > Next Command
Editor > Previous Command
Editor > Disable Command Language
Editor > Make Output Editable
Editor > Find...
Editor > Replace...
Editor > Select Fonts
Editor > Apply I/O Font
Editor > Apply Title Font
Editor > Apply Comment Font

Graphics Editing

Editor > Edit
Editor > View
Editor > Duplicate
Editor > Bring to Front
Editor > Send to Back
Editor > Rotate Left
Editor > Rotate Right
Editor > Align...
Editor > Flip Horizontal
Editor > Flip Vertical
Editor > Show Tool Palette
Editor > Show Attribute Palette
Editor > Retain Tool
Editor > Lock Data Display

Graphics Brushing

Editor > Brush
Editor > Show Brushing Palette
Editor > Set ID Variables...
Editor > Set Brushing Color

%Macros

APPENDIX C

Statistical Reference Texts and Companion Textbooks

Archaeology

Introductory

Fletcher, Mike, and Gary Lock. *Digging Numbers: Elementary Statistics for Archaeologists.* Oxford University Committee for Archaeology, 1991.

Behavioral/Social Sciences

Introductory

Couch, James V. *Fundamentals of Statistics for the Behavioral Sciences*, 2nd ed. West Educational Publishing, 1987.

Gravetter, Frederick J., and Larry B. Wallnau. *Essentials of Statistics for the Behavioral Sciences.* West Educational Publishing, 1991.

Gravetter, Frederick J., and Larry B. Wallnau. *Statistics for the Behavioral Sciences*, 3rd ed. West Educational Publishing, 1992.

> Gravetter, Frederick J., and Larry B. Wallnau. *Instructor's Manual with Test Bank and Solutions* to accompany *Statistics for the Behavioral Sciences*, 3rd ed. West Educational Publishing, 1992.

> Gravetter, Frederick J., and Larry B. Wallnau. *Study Guide* to accompany *Statistics for the Behavioral Sciences*, 3rd ed. West Educational Publishing, 1992.

Howell, David. *Fundamental Statistics for the Behavioral Sciences*, 3rd ed. Duxbury Press, 1992.

Marchal, William, and Douglas Lind. *Statistics: An Introduction*, 3rd ed. Harcourt Brace Jovanovich, 1991.

McCall, Robert B. *Fundamental Statistics for the Behavioral Sciences, Text and Student Guide*, 6th ed. Harcourt Brace Jovanovich, 1994.

> McCall, Robert B., and Richard Sass. *Study Guide* to accompany *Fundamental Statistics for the Behavioral Sciences, Text and Student Guide*, 6th ed. Harcourt Brace Jovanovich, 1994.

Monk, Andrew. *Exploring Statistics with Minitab.* John Wiley & Sons, 1991.

Ott, Lyman, Richard Larson, Cynthia Rexroat, and William Mendenhall. *Statistics: A Tool for the Social Sciences,* 5th ed. Duxbury Press, 1992.

Pagano, Robert. *Understanding Statistics in the Behavioral Sciences,* 4th ed. West Educational Publishing, 1994.

Po, A. Li Wan. *Experimental Design by Example.* Chapman and Hall–UK, 1991.

West, Robert. *Computing for Psychologists: Statistical Analysis Using SPSS and MINITAB.* Harwood Academic Publishers, 1991.

Intermediate

Erickson, B., and T. Nosanchuk. *Understanding Data,* 2nd ed. University of Toronto Press, 1992.

Freed, Joseph, Joseph Ryan, and Robert Hess. *Handbook for Statistical Procedures and Their Computer Applications to Education and the Behavioral Sciences.* Macmillan Publishing Company, 1991.

Howell, David. *Statistical Methods for Psychology,* 3rd ed. Duxbury Press, 1992.

Pedhazur, Elazar, and Liora Pedhazur Schmelkin. *Measurement, Design, and Analysis: An Integrated Approach.* Lawrence Erlbaum Associates, 1991.

Advanced

Marascuilo, Leonard A., and Ronald Serlin. *Statistical Methods for the Social and Behavioral Sciences.* W. H. Freeman, 1988.

Serlin, Ronald. *Minitab Manual* to accompany *Statistical Methods for the Social and Behavioral Sciences.* W. H. Freeman, 1989.

Biological Sciences

Introductory

Dawson-Saunders, Beth, and Robert Trapp. *Basic and Clinical Biostatistics,* 2nd ed. Appleton & Lange Publishing Company, 1993.

Hampton, Raymond. *Introductory Biological Statistics.* Wm. C. Brown Publishers, 1994.

Watt, Trudy A. *Introductory Statistics for Biology Students.* Chapman and Hall–UK, 1993.

Intermediate

Ludbrook, John, and Hugh Dudley. *Guide to Statistics for Biomedical and Clinical Scientists.* Cambridge University Press, 1991.

Salgado-Ugarte, Isaias. *El Analisis Exploratorio de Datos Biologicos: Fundamentos y Aplicaciones.* F. E. S. Zaragoza, U. N. A. M., 1992. (Spanish Text)

Advanced

Festing, Michael, and J. M. Blackwell. *Genetics of Resistance to Bacterial and Parasitic Infection.* Taylor and Francis, 1988.

Business

Introductory

Aczel, Amir D. *Complete Business Statistics.* Richard D. Irwin, 1993.

Anderson, David R., Dennis J. Sweeney, and Thomas A. Williams. *Statistics for Business and Economics,* 5th ed. West Educational Publishing, 1993.

Berenson, Mark L., and David M. Levine. *Basic Business Statistics: Concepts and Applications*, 5th ed. Prentice-Hall, 1992.

Berenson, Mark L., David M. Levine, and David Stephan. *Using Minitab for Business Statistics*. Prentice-Hall, 1990.

Berenson, Mark L., and David M. Levine. *Statistics for Business and Economics*, 2nd ed. Prentice-Hall, 1993.

Black, Ken. *Business Statistics, An Introductory Course*. West Educational Publishing, 1992.

Black, Ken. *Business Statistics: Contemporary Decision Making*. West Educational Publishing, 1994.

Bridge, John. *Managerial Decisions with the Microcomputer*. Paramount Publishing International, 1989.

Canavos, George C., and Don M. Miller. *An Introduction to Modern Business Statistics*. Duxbury Press, 1993.

Croucher, John S. *Introductory Mathematics and Statistics for Business*, 2nd ed. McGraw-Hill Publishing Company, 1993.

Cryer, Jonathan D., and Robert B. Miller. *Statistics for Business: Data Analysis and Modelling*, 2nd ed. Duxbury Press, 1994.

Cryer, Jonathan D., Darin R. Lovelace, and George C. Woodworth. *Minitab Handbook* to accompany *Statistics for Business: Data Analysis and Modelling*, 2nd ed. Duxbury Press, 1994.

Cryer, Jonathan D., and Robert B. Miller. *Instructor's Manual* for *Statistics for Business: Data Analysis and Modelling*, 2nd ed. Duxbury Press, 1994.

Daniel, Wayne W., and James C. Terrell. *Business Statistics for Management and Economics*, 6th ed. Houghton Mifflin Company, 1992.

Farnum, Nicholas R. *Modern Statistical Quality Control and Improvement*. Duxbury Press, 1994.

Farnum, Nicholas R., and LaVerne W. Stanton. *Quantitative Forecasting Methods*. Duxbury Press, 1989.

Freund, John, Frank Williams, and Benjamin Perles. *Elementary Business Statistics: The Modern Approach*, 6th ed. Prentice-Hall, 1993.

Groebner, David F., and Patrick W. Shannon. *Business Statistics: A Decision-Making Approach*, 4th ed. Macmillan Publishing Company, 1993.

Hackl, Peter, and Walter Katzenbeisser. *Statistik: Lehrbuch mit Ubungsaufgaben*, 8th ed. Oldenbourg Verlag GmbH., 1992. (German Text)

Hackl, Peter, and Walter Katzenbeisser. *Statistik fur Sozial und Wirtschaftswissenschaften*. Oldenbourg Verlag GmbH., 1994. (German Text)

Hamburg, Morris, and Peg Young. *Statistical Analysis for Decision Making*, 6th ed. Dryden Press, 1994.

Hanke, John, and Arthur Reitsch. *Understanding Business Statistics*, 2nd ed. Richard D. Irwin, 1994.

Hildebrand, David K., and Lyman Ott. *Statistical Thinking for Managers*, 3rd ed. Duxbury Press, 1991.

Hummelbrunner, Sieg, John Gray, and Len J. Rak. *Contemporary Business Statistics with Canadian Applications.* Prentice-Hall Canada, 1993.

Ingram, John A., and Joseph G. Monks. *Statistics for Business and Economics,* 2nd ed. Harcourt Brace Jovanovich, 1992.

Johnson, Aaron, Marvin B. Johnson, and Rueben C. Buse. *Econometrics: Basic and Applied.* Macmillan Publishing Company, 1987.

Kazmier, Leonard J. *Business Statistics (Schaums Outline Series),* 2nd ed. McGraw-Hill Publishing Company, 1988.

Keller, Gerald, Brian Warrack, and Henry Bartel. *Essentials of Business Statistics,* 2nd ed. Duxbury Press, 1994.

Keller, Gerald, Brian Warrack, and Henry Bartel. *Statistics for Management and Economics,* 3rd ed. Duxbury Press, 1994.

Keller, Gerald, Brian Warrack, and Henry Bartel. *Statistics for Management and Economics* (abbreviated ed.). Duxbury Press, 1994.

Kenkel, James L. *Introductory Statistics for Management and Economics,* 3rd ed. Duxbury Press, 1989.

Kvanli, Alan, C., Stephen Guynes, and Robert Pavur. *Introduction to Business Statistics: A Computer Integrated Approach,* 4th ed. West Educational Publishing, 1995.

Lapin, Lawrence L. *Statistics for Modern Business Decisions,* 6th ed. Harcourt Brace Jovanovich, 1993.

Lee, Cheng-few. *Statistics for Business and Financial Economics.* D. C. Heath, 1993.

> Lee, John. *Introduction to MINITAB* to accompany *Statistics for Business and Financial Economics.* D. C. Heath, 1993.

Lind, Douglas, and Robert D. Mason. *Basic Statistics for Business and Economics.* Richard D. Irwin, 1994.

Mansfield, Edwin. *Statistics for Business and Economics,* 5th ed. W. W. Norton & Company, 1994.

> Soskin, Mark D. *Using Minitab with Statistics for Business and Economics,* 5th ed. W. W. Norton & Company, 1994.

Mason, Robert D., and Douglas Lind. *Statistical Techniques in Business and Economics,* 8th ed. Richard D. Irwin, 1993.

McClave, James T., and P. George Benson. *A First Course in Business Statistics,* 5th ed. Dellen Publishing Company, 1992.

> Meyer, Ruth K., and David D. Krueger. *Minitab Computer Supplement* to accompany *A First Course in Business Statistics,* 5th ed. Dellen Publishing Company, 1992.

McClave, James T., and P. George Benson. *Statistics for Business and Economics,* 6th ed. Dellen Publishing Company, 1994.

Mendenhall, William, and Robert J. Beaver. *A Course in Business Statistics,* 3rd ed. Duxbury Press, 1992.

> Lefkowitz, Jerry M. *Minitab Primer* to accompany *A Course in Business Statistics,* 3rd ed. Duxbury Press, 1992.

Mendenhall, William, James Reinmuth, and Robert J. Beaver. *Statistics for Management and Economics*, 7th ed. Duxbury Press, 1993.

> Lefkowitz, Jerry M. *Minitab Primer* to accompany *Statistics for Management and Economics*, 7th ed. Duxbury Press, 1993.

Mendenhall, William, and Terry Sincich. *A Second Course in Business Statistics: Regression Analysis*, 4th ed. Dellen Publishing Company, 1993.

Miller, Robert B. *Minitab Handbook for Business and Economics*. Duxbury Press, 1988.

Monks, Joseph G., and Byron L. Newton. *Statistics for Business*, 2nd ed. Macmillan Publishing Company, 1988.

Morris, Clare. *Quantitative Approaches in Business Studies*, 2nd ed. Pitman, 1989.

Neter, John, William Wasserman, and G. A. Whitmore. *Applied Statistics*, 4th ed. Allyn and Bacon, 1993.

> Dixon, Warren. *Minitab Workbook for Applied Statistics*. Allyn and Bacon, 1993.

Picconi, Mario, Albert Romano, and Charles L. Olson. *Business Statistics: Elements and Applications*. HarperCollins College Publishers, 1993.

> Yandell, Dirk S. *Study Guide and Student Solution Manual* to accompany *Business Statistics: Elements and Applications*. HarperCollins College Publishers, 1992.

Roberts, Dennis M. *MINITAB: An Introduction for Business*. Kendall/Hunt Publishing Company, 1992.

Sandy, Robert. *Statistics for Business and Economics*. McGraw-Hill Publishing Company, 1990.

> Trower, Jonathan K. *Introduction to Statistics on Minitab*. Macmillan Publishing Company, 1988.

Sincich, Terry. *A Course in Modern Business Statistics*, 2nd ed. Dellen Publishing Company, 1994.

> Meyer, Ruth K., and David D. Krueger. *Minitab Computer Supplement* to accompany *A Course in Modern Business Statistics*. Dellen Publishing Company, 1991.

Sincich, Terry. *Business Statistics by Example*, 4th ed. Dellen Publishing Company, 1992.

> Meyer, Ruth K., and David D. Krueger. *Minitab Computer Supplement* to accompany *Business Statistics by Example*, 4th ed. Dellen Publishing Company, 1992.

Taylor, Bernard W. III. *Introduction to Management Science*, 4th ed. Allyn and Bacon, 1993.

Toh, Rex S., and Michael Y. Hu. *Basic Business Statistics: An Intuitive Approach*. West Educational Publishing, 1991.

Triola, Mario F., and LeRoy A. Franklin. *Business Statistics*. Addison-Wesley Publishing Co., 1994.

> Triola, Mario. *Minitab Student Laboratory Workbook*. Addison-Wesley Publishing Co., 1994.

Trower, Jonathan K. *Using Minitab for Introductory Statistical Analysis*. Macmillan Publishing Company, 1989.

Watson, Collin J., Patrick Billingsley, D. James Croft, and David V. Huntsberger. *Statistics for Management and Economics*, 5th ed. Allyn and Bacon, 1993.

Presby, Leonard. *Minitab Workbook for Statistics for Management and Economics.* Allyn and Bacon, 1993.

Webster, Allen. *Applied Statistics for Business and Economics.* Richard D. Irwin, 1992.

Shin, Kilman. *MINITAB Guide* for use with *Applied Statistics for Business and Economics.* Richard D. Irwin, 1992.

Weiers, Ronald M. *Introduction to Business Statistics,* 2nd ed. Dryden Press, 1994.

Wonnacott, Thomas H., and Ronald J. Wonnacott. *Introductory Statistics for Business and Economics,* 4th ed. John Wiley & Sons, 1990.

Intermediate

Bowers, David. *Statistics for Economics and Business,* 2nd ed. Macmillan Publishing Company, 1991.

Brown, William. *Introducing Econometrics.* West Educational Publishing, 1991.

Dielman, Terry. *Applied Regression Analysis for Business and Economics.* Duxbury Press, 1991.

Doran, Howard Edwin. *Applied Regression Analysis in Econometrics.* Marcel Dekker, 1989.

Evans, Martin, and Luiz Moutinho. *Applied Marketing Research.* Addison-Wesley–UK, 1992.

Evans, Martin, and Nigel Piercy. *Marketing Information System.* Routledge Publishers, 1983.

Frigon, Normand L., and Harry K. Jackson. *Management 2000, A Practical Guide to World Class Competition.* Van Nostrand Reinhold, 1993.

Kohler, Heinz. *Statistics for Business and Economics,* 3rd ed. HarperCollins College Publishers, 1994.

Kohler, Heinz. *Instructor's Resource Manual* to accompany *Statistics for Business and Economics,* 3rd ed. HarperCollins College Publishers, 1994.

Kohler, Heinz. *Student Workbook* to accompany *Statistics for Business and Economics,* 3rd ed. HarperCollins College Publishers, 1994.

Kohler, Heinz. *Test Bank* to accompany *Statistics for Business and Economics,* 3rd ed. HarperCollins College Publishers, 1994.

Pfaffenberger, Roger C., and James H. Patterson. *Statistical Methods for Business and Economics,* 3rd ed. Richard D. Irwin, 1987.

Ryan, Thomas P. *Statistical Methods for Quality Improvement.* John Wiley & Sons, 1989.

Siegel, Andrew F. *Practical Business Statistics,* 2nd ed. Richard D. Irwin, 1994.

Siegel, Andrew F. *The Minitab Guide* for use with *Practical Business Statistics,* 2nd ed. Richard D. Irwin, 1994.

Wilson, J. Holton, and Barry Keating. *Business Forecasting,* 2nd ed. Richard D. Irwin, 1994.

Advanced

Gaynor, Patricia E., and Rickey C. Kirkpatrick. *Introduction to Time Series Modeling and Forecasting in Business and Economics.* McGraw-Hill Publishing Company, 1993.

Hanke, John, and Arthur Reitsch. *Business Forecasting,* 4th ed. Allyn and Bacon, 1992.

Mockler, Robert. *Computer Software to Support Management Decision Making.* Macmillan Publishing Company, 1992.

Pappas, James, and Mark Hirschey. *Managerial Economics*, 7th ed. Dryden Press, 1993.

    Hirschey, Mark, and James Pappas. *Fundamentals of Managerial Economics*, 5th ed. Dryden Press, 1995.

Roberts, Harry. *Data Analysis for Managers with MINITAB*, 2nd ed. Boyd & Fraser Publishing Company, 1991.

Earth Sciences

Intermediate

Jones, Kelvyn. *Minitab for Geographical Analysis*. Environmental Publications, 1993.

Engineering

Introductory

Albert, Lars. *Technical Quality Control with Statistical Methods*. Gamla Vaivege Sweden, 1989. (Swedish Text)

Berger, Roger W. *Statistical Process Control—A Guide for Implementation*. ASQC Quality Press, 1986.

Devore, Jay. *Probability and Statistics for Engineering and the Sciences*, 3rd ed. Duxbury Press, 1991.

Mendenhall, William, and Terry Sincich. *Statistics for the Engineering and Computer Sciences*, 3rd ed. Dellen Publishing Company, 1991.

Miller, Irwin, John Freund, and Richard Johnson. *Probability and Statistics for Engineers*, 5th ed. Prentice-Hall, 1994.

Rauwendaal, Chris. *SPC in Extrusion*. Hanser Publishers, 1993.

Scheaffer, Richard. *Probability and Statistics for Engineers*. 4th ed. Duxbury Press, 1994.

Intermediate

Dougherty, Edward R. *Probability and Statistics for Engineers and Computer Scientists*. Prentice-Hall, 1990.

Lochner, Robert, and Joseph Matar. *Designing for Quality: An Introduction to the Best of Taguchi and Western Methods of Statistical Experimental Design*. Quality Resources, 1990.

Vardeman, Stephen. *Statistics for Engineering Problem Solving*. PWS-KENT, 1993.

General Statistics

Introductory

Anderson, David R., Dennis J. Sweeney, and Thomas A. Williams. *Introduction to Statistics: Concepts and Applications*, 3rd ed. West Educational Publishing, 1994.

Andersen, Espen. *Minitab for Skrekkslagne*, 2nd ed. Norwegian School of Management, 1990. (Norwegian Text)

Blaisdell, Ernest A. *Statistics in Practice*. Saunders College Publishing, 1993.

    Shubert, Ronald. *Instructor's Manual* to accompany *Statistics in Practice*. Saunders College Publishing, 1993.

    Shubert, Ronald. *Student Solutions Manual* to accompany *Statistics in Practice*. Saunders College Publishing, 1993.

Bluman, Allan G. *Elementary Statistics—A Step by Step Approach*. Wm. C. Brown Publishers, 1992.

Brase, Charles, and Corrine Brase. *Understandable Statistics: Concepts and Methods*, 4th ed. D. C. Heath, 1991.

Brase, Charles, and Corrine Brase. *MINITAB Resource Guide for Understandable Statistics: Concepts and Methods*. D. C. Heath, 1991.

Chase, Warren, and Fred Bown. *General Statistics*, 2nd ed. John Wiley & Sons, 1992.

Sevin, Anne. *Minitab Supplement* to accompany *General Statistics*, 2nd ed. John Wiley & Sons, 1992.

Dahmstrom, Karin. *Introducktion Till Det Statistiska Standard programmet MINITAB Version 8.2 for Persondatorer*. Stockholms Universitet, 1993. (Swedish Text)

Devore, Jay, and Roxy Peck. *Introductory Statistics*, 2nd ed. West Educational Publishing, 1994.

Groves, John E. *Instructor Solution Manual* to accompany *Introductory Statistics*, 2nd ed. West Educational Publishing, 1994.

Groves, John E. *Student Solution Manual* to accompany *Introductory Statistics*, 2nd ed. West Educational Publishing, 1994.

Devore, Jay, and Roxy Peck. *Statistics: The Exploration and Analysis of Data*, 2nd ed. Duxbury Press, 1993.

Groves, John E. *Instructor Solution Manual* to accompany *Statistics: The Exploration and Analysis of Data*, 2nd ed. Duxbury Press, 1993.

Groves, John E. *Student Solution Manual* to accompany *Statistics: The Exploration and Analysis of Data*, 2nd ed. Duxbury Press, 1993.

Dietrich, Frank, and Thomas Kearns. *Basic Statistics: An Inferential Approach*, 3rd ed. Dellen Publishing Company, 1989.

Meyer, Ruth K., and David D. Krueger. *Minitab Computer Supplement* to accompany *Basic Statistics: An Inferential Approach*, 3rd ed. Dellen Publishing Company, 1989.

Freund, John, and Gary Simon. *Modern Elementary Statistics*, 8th ed. Prentice-Hall, 1992.

Freund, John, and Gary Simon. *Statistics: A First Course*, 5th ed. Prentice-Hall, 1991.

Goethals, Yves, and Juan Timana. *Estadistica Aplicada a los Negocios*. Escuela de Administracion de Negocios, 1990. (Spanish Text)

Goldman, Robert, and Joel Weinberg. *Statistics: An Introduction*. Prentice-Hall, 1985.

Gonick, Larry, and Woollcott Smith. *The Cartoon Guide to Statistics*. HarperCollins College Publishers, 1993.

Hoaglin, David C., Frederick Mosteller, and John W. Tukey. *Exploring Data Tables, Trends, and Shapes*. John Wiley & Sons, 1985.

Iman, Ronald. *A Data-Based Approach to Statistics*. Duxbury Press, 1994.

Jarrell, Stephen. *Basic Statistics*. Wm. C. Brown Publishers, 1994.

Johnson, Richard, and Gouri Bhattacharyya. *Statistics: Principles and Methods*, 2nd ed. John Wiley & Sons, 1992.

Johnson, Robert. *Elementary Statistics*, 6th ed. Duxbury Press, 1992.

Lefkowitz, Jerry M. *MINITAB Primer* to accompany *Elementary Statistics*, 6th ed. Duxbury Press, 1992.

Judd, Charles, and Gary McClelland. *Data Analysis: A Model-Comparison Approach.* Harcourt Brace Jovanovich, 1989.

Khazanie, Ramakant. *Elementary Statistics in a World of Applications,* 3rd ed. HarperCollins College Publishers, 1990.

Kitchens, Larry. *Exploring Statistics: A Modern Introduction to Data Analysis and Inference.* West Educational Publishing, 1987.

Knudsen, Jon. *Innforing I Minitab.* Scandanavian University Press, 1990. (Norwegian Text)

Knudsen, Jon. *Statistikk og Data.* Scandanavian University Press, 1992. (Norwegian Text)

Koopmans, Lambert. *Introduction to Contemporary Statistical Methods,* 2nd ed. Duxbury Press, 1987.

Kvanli, Alan. *Statistics: A Computer Integrated Approach.* West Educational Publishing, 1988.

Lillestol, Jostein. *Sannsynlighetsregning og Statistikk,* 4th ed. Bedriftsokonomens Forlag, 1991. (Norwegian Text)

> Lillestol, Jostein, and Lars J. Ytrehus. *Statistisk Dataanalyse Med PC: Allmenn innforing med Minitab,* 5th ed. Fagbokforlaget, 1993. (Norwegian Text)

MacFarland, Thomas W., and Cheng Hou. *A Tutorial for the Student Edition of MINITAB.* Nova University, 1989.

Mann, Prem. *Introductory Statistics.* John Wiley & Sons, 1992.

> Peck, Roxy. *MINITAB Supplement* to accompany *Introductory Statistics,* 2nd ed. West Educational Publishing, 1994.

Mansfield, Edwin. *Basic Statistics with Applications.* W. W. Norton & Company, 1986.

Massaro, Jon F. *Essentials of Elementary Statistics Using MINITAB.* RonJon Publishers, 1993.

McClave, James, and Frank Dietrich. *A First Course in Statistics,* 4th ed. Dellen Publishing Company, 1992.

> Meyer, Ruth K., and David D. Krueger. *Minitab Computer Supplement* to accompany *A First Course in Statistics,* 4th ed. Dellen Publishing Company, 1992.

McClave, James, and Frank Dietrich. *Statistics,* 6th ed. Dellen Publishing Company, 1994.

Mendenhall, William, and Robert J. Beaver. *Introduction to Probability and Statistics,* 9th ed. Duxbury Press, 1994.

Moore, David S., and George P. McCabe. *Introduction to the Practice of Statistics,* 2nd ed. W. H. Freeman, 1993.

> McCabe, George, and Linda Doyle McCabe. *Instructor's Guide with Solutions for Introduction to the Practice of Statistics,* 2nd ed. W. H. Freeman, 1993.

> Greenberg, Betsy, and Mark Serva. *MINITAB Handbook* to accompany *Introduction to the Practice of Statistics,* 2nd ed. W. H. Freeman, 1993.

Noether, Gottfried, and Marilynn S. Dueker. *Introduction to Statistics.* Springer-Verlag/New York, 1991.

Ott, Lyman, and William Mendenhall. *Understanding Statistics,* 6th ed. Duxbury Press, 1994.

Owen, William, and W. F. Cutlip. *Finite Mathematics.* Harcourt Brace Jovanovich, 1991.

Rasmussen, Shelley. *An Introduction to Statistics with Data Analysis.* Duxbury Press, 1992.

Roberts, Dennis M. *Data Analysis for the Social Sciences*. Kendall/Hunt Publishing Company, 1992.

Roberts, Dennis M. *Minitab: An Introduction*. Kendall/Hunt Publishing Company, 1992.

Salvia, Anthony A. *Introduction to Statistics*. Saunders College Publishing, 1990.

> Blaisdell, Ernest A. *Minitab Supplement for Introduction to Statistics*. Saunders College Publishing, 1992.

Sanders, Donald H. *Statistics: A Fresh Approach*, 4th ed. McGraw-Hill Publishing Company, 1990.

Scheaffer, Richard L., William Mendenhall, and Lyman Ott. *Elementary Survey Sampling*, 4th ed. Duxbury Press, 1990.

Sellers, Gene, Stephen Vardeman, and Adelbert Hackert. *A First Course in Statistics*, 3rd ed. HarperCollins College Publishers, 1992.

> Sellers, Gene, Stephen Vardeman, and Adelbert Hackert. *Study Guide and Student's Solutions Manual* to accompany *A First Course in Statistics*, 3rd ed. HarperCollins College Publishers, 1992.

Sincich, Terry. *Statistics by Example*, 5th ed. Dellen Publishing Company, 1993.

> Meyer, Ruth K., and David D. Krueger. *Minitab Computer Supplement* to accompany *Statistics by Example*, 5th ed. Dellen Publishing Company, 1993.

Smith, Barbran, and Faith Ripps. *Exploring Statistics with Minitab*, 2nd ed. West Educational Publishing, 1993.

Triola, Mario. *Elementary Statistics*, 6th ed. Addison-Wesley Publishing Co., 1995.

> Triola, Mario. *Minitab Student Laboratory Manual and Workbook*, 3rd ed. Addison-Wesley Publishing Co., 1995.

Weimer, Richard. *Statistics*, 2nd ed. Wm. C. Brown Publishers, 1993.

> Patch, Steve, and Pat McClellan. *Student Study Guide* to accompany *Statistics*, 2nd ed. Wm. C. Brown Publishers, 1993.

Weiss, Neil A. *Elementary Statistics*, 2nd ed. Addison-Wesley Publishing Co., 1993.

> Zehna, Peter W. *MINITAB Supplement* to accompany *Elementary Statistics*, 2nd ed. Addison-Wesley Publishing Co., 1993.

Weiss, Neil A., and Matthew J. Hassett. *Introductory Statistics*, 4th ed. Addison-Wesley Publishing Co., 1995.

> Zehna, Peter W. *MINITAB Supplement* to accompany *Introductory Statistics*, 4th ed. Addison-Wesley Publishing Co., 1995.

Intermediate

Arce, John Franklin. *Herramientas Estadisticas Para La Calidad*. Pontifica Universidad Catolica–Chile, 1991. (Spanish Text)

Fugleberg, Ole, and Olav R. Jenssen. *Regression Analysis and Other Multivariate Methods*, 7th ed. Scandanavian University Press, 1991.

Hoaglin, David C., Frederick Mosteller, and John W. Tukey. *Understanding Robust and Exploratory Data Analysis*. John Wiley & Sons, 1983.

Jarrett, Jeffrey. *Business Forecasting Methods*, 2nd ed. Basil Blackwell, Ltd–UK, 1991.

Kleinbaum, David G., Lawrence L. Kupper, and Keith E. Muller. *Applied Regression Analysis and Other Multivariable Methods*, 2nd ed. Duxbury Press, 1988.

Neter, John, William Wasserman, and Michael H. Kutner. *Applied Linear Regression Models*, 2nd ed. Richard D. Irwin, 1989.

Neter, John, William Wasserman, and Michael H. Kutner. *Applied Linear Statistical Models*, 3rd ed. Richard D. Irwin, 1990.

Ott, Lyman. *An Introduction to Statistical Methods and Data Analysis*, 4th ed. Duxbury Press, 1993.

Saville, Dave J., and Graham R. Wood. *Statistical Methods: The Geometric Approach.* Springer-Verlag/New York, 1991.

Schulman, Robert S. *Reference Book: Statistics in Plain English.* Chapman and Hall–UK, 1992.

Zehna, Peter W. *A Minitab Companion with Macros.* Addison-Wesley Publishing Co., 1992.

Advanced

Allen, Arnold O. *Probability, Statistics and Queueing Theory with Computer Science Applications*, 2nd ed. Academic Press, 1990.

Christensen, Ronald. *Linear Models for Multivariate, Time Series, and Spatial Data.* Springer-Verlag/New York, 1990.

Cryer, Jonathan D. *Time Series Analysis.* Duxbury Press, 1986.

Freund, Rudolf J., and William J. Wilson. *Statistical Methods.* Academic Press, 1992.

Staudte, Robert G., and Simon Sheather. *Robust Estimation and Testing.* John Wiley & Sons, 1990.

Health Sciences

Introductory

Daniel, Wayne W. *Biostatistics: A Foundation for Analysis in the Health Sciences*, 5th ed. John Wiley & Sons, 1991.

Reid, N., and J. Boore. *Research Methods and Statistics in Health Care.* Edward Arnold Publishers, 1991.

Intermediate

Reid, N. *Health Care Research by Degrees.* Blackwell Scientific Publications, 1993.

Library Sciences

Introductory

Hernon, Peter. *Statistics for Library Decision Making.* Ablex Publishing Corporation, 1989.

Hernon, Peter, and John Richardson. *Microcomputer Software for Performing Statistical Analysis: A Handbook for Supporting Library Decision Making.* Ablex Publishing Corporation, 1988.

Mathematics

Introductory

Astruc, J., N. Cracknell, R. Diver, M. Evans, E. Gauld, N. Taylor, and B. Woolacott. *Mathematics with the Macintosh.* Scotch College Publishing, 1993.

Brown, Tim, and Ken Harrison. *Applicable Mathematics.* McGraw-Hill Publishing Company, 1992.

Newmark, Joseph. *Statistics and Probability in Modern Life*, 5th ed. Saunders College Publishing, 1991.

    Blaisdell, Ernest A. *Minitab Supplement for Statistics and Probability in Modern Life*, 5th ed. Saunders College Publishing, 1992.

Piascik, Chester. *Applied Finite Mathematics for Business and the Social and Natural Sciences*. West Educational Publishing, 1992.

Piascik, Chester. *Applied Mathematics for Business and the Social and Natural Sciences*. West Educational Publishing, 1992.

Piascik, Chester. *Calculus for Business and the Social and Natural Sciences*. West Educational Publishing, 1992.

Prichett, Gordon D., and John C. Saber. *Mathematics with Applications in Management and Economics*, 7th ed. Richard D. Irwin, 1994.

Intermediate

Freund, John. *Mathematical Statistics*, 5th ed. Prentice-Hall, 1992.

Meerschaert, Mark. *Mathematical Modeling*. Academic Press, 1993.

Speech Pathology

Introductory

Silverman, Franklin H. *Research Design and Evaluation in Speech-Language Pathology and Audiology*, 3rd ed. Prentice-Hall, 1993.

General Supplements

Introductory

Kaplon, Howard S. *MINITAB Lab Workbook*, 4th ed. McGraw-Hill Publishing Company, 1993.

Meyer, Ruth K., and David D. Krueger. *A Minitab Guide to Statistics: Business and Economics*. Dellen Publishing Company, 1991.

Ryan, Barbara F., and Brian L. Joiner. *MINITAB Handbook*, 3rd ed. Duxbury Press, 1994.

Schaefer, Robert L., and Elizabeth Farber. *The Student Edition of Minitab, Release 8*. Addison-Wesley Publishing Co., 1992.

Shin, Kilman. *Minitab: Irwin Statistical Software Guide*. Richard D. Irwin, 1992.

Intermediate

Keller, Gerald. *Statistics Laboratory Manual: Experiments Using Minitab*. Duxbury Press, 1994.

Videos

Introductory

Statistics: Decisions Through Data (five-tape series on statistics). COMAP, Inc., 1992.

Against All Odds: Inside Statistics (13-tape series on statistics). The Annenberg/CPB Project, 1989.

Smith, J. Wixon. *Introduction to MINITAB: A Videotape Series* (five-tape series on MINITAB using command line version). Rochester Institute of Technology, 1993.

INDEX

Credits

Minitab at Work photographs:
"Forestry" (Tutorial 3): Courtesy of George Bellerose/Stock Boston Inc.
"Public Safety" (Tutorial 6): Courtesy of Virginia L. Blaisdell/Stock Boston Inc.
"Retailing" (Tutorial 7): Courtesy of Kristen Duerr, 1994.
"Scientific Research" (Tutorial 8): Courtesy of Elizabeth Hamlin/Stock Boston Inc.
"Ecology" (Tutorial 10): Courtesy of Dr. Douglas B. Noltie.
"Education" (Tutorial 12): Courtesy of Tim Barnwell/Stock Boston Inc.
"Medical Diagnostics" (Tutorial 13): Courtesy of Norman R. Rowan/Stock Boston Inc.
"Quality Control" (Tutorial 14): Courtesy of Peter Southwick/Stock Boston Inc.
"Stock Market" (Tutorial 15): Courtesy of Jeff Albertson/Stock Boston Inc.

Data Sets:
ADS.MTW and ADS2.MTW; AGE.MTW; ASSESS.MTW; CANDYA.MTW–CANDYC.MTW; DRIVE.MTW; GAS.MTW; NONPRT.MTW and NONPRT2.MTW; PROCES.MTW; PUBS.MTW; RATIO.MTW; TEXTS.MTW; YOGURT.MTW: John D. McKenzie, Jr., Babson College. Reprinted with permission.
CPI.MTW: U.S. Bureau of Labor Statistics, *Monthly Labor Review* and *Handbook of Labor Statistics.*
CRIMES.MTW and CRIMESU.MTW: U.S. Federal Bureau of Investigation.
ECLASS.MTW: U.S. Bureau of the Census, Department of Commerce, County Business Patterns.
FBALL.MTW; GOLF.MTW; RIVERA.MTW–RIVERE.MTW and RIVERS.MTW; SALMAN.MTW; STEALS.MTW: Schaefer and Farber, *The Student Edition of MINITAB, Release 8.* User's Manual © 1992 Addison-Wesley Publishing Co., Reading, MA. Software © 1991 Minitab Inc. Reprinted with permission of Addison-Wesley.
FJA.MTW: Frank Anscombe, Yale University. Reprinted with permission.
HOMES.MTW: Triola and Franklin, Business Statistics, © 1994 Addison-Wesley Publishing Co., Reading, MA, pp. 772–775. Reprinted with permission.
JEANSA.MTW–JEANSC.MTW; STORES.MTW: D. J. Tigert, Babson College. Reprinted with permission.
MNWAGE.MTW: U.S. Department of Labor.
MORT.MTW: Data from Massachusetts Division of Banks.
NIEL.MTW; TVVIEW.MTW; VPVH.MTW: A. C. Nielsen Co. Reprinted with permission.
NOTE.MTW: Data from *Byte,* March 1994.
PIZZA.MTW: Reprinted with permission from *The Rensselaer Polytechnic,* student newspaper, Rensselaer Polytechnic Institute.
SNOW.MTW: National Weather Service Office.
SP500.MTW: Used by permission of Standard & Poor's, a division of McGraw-Hill, Inc.
SPCAR.MTW: Environmental Protection Agency.
TBILL.MTW: Data from Dow Jones *Tradeline.*
TVHRS.MTW: Richard Frost, Babson College. Reprinted with permission.
USDEM.MTW: U.S. Bureau of the Census, Department of Commerce.
WASTES.MTW: *Federal Register,* October 14, 1992.

Sources

Minitab at Work:

"Forestry" (Tutorial 3): Allegheny National Forest.

"Public Safety" (Tutorial 6): From testimony presented to the Atomic Energy Commission, 1971.

"Retailing" (Tutorial 7): "Survival of Selected Indicator and Pathogenic Bacteria in Refrigerated Pizzas," *Journal of Food Protection*, Vol. 50, No. 10, October 1987, pp. 859–861.

"Scientific Research" (Tutorial 8): Roger Johnson, David Spenny, and Tony Forest, "The Distribution of Supernova Remnants in the Large Magellanic Cloud," *Publications of the Astronomical Society of the Pacific*, 100:683–686, June 1988.

"Ecology" (Tutorial 10): Douglas Noltie, "A Method for Measuring Reproductive Success in the Rock Bass (*Amplobites rupestris*), with Applicability to Other Substrate Brooding Fishes," *Journal of Freshwater Ecology*, Vol. 3, No. 3, June 1986.

"Education" (Tutorial 12): Allen Shaughnessy and Ronald O. Nickel, "Prescription-Writing Patterns and Errors in a Family Medicine Residency Program," *The Journal of Family Practice*, Vol. 29, No. 3, 1989, pp. 290–295.

"Medical Diagnostics" (Tutorial 13): Patrick Carey and P. Syamasundar Rao, "Remodeling of the Aorta After Successful Balloon Coarctation Angioplasty," *Journal of American College of Cardiology*, Vol. 14, No. 5, Nov. 1, 1989, pp. 1312–1317.

"Stock Market" (Tutorial 15): Albert Parish, "Market Forecasting Models: ARIMA," *Technical Analysis of Stocks & Commodities*, October 1990, pp. 88–96.